THEORIES OF LEARNING

A Historical Approach

JOHN C. MALONE
University of Tennessee, Knoxville

Wadsworth Publishing Company • Belmont, California • A Division of Wadsworth, Inc.

Psychology Editor: Ken King
Editorial Assistant: Cynthia Campbell
Production Editor: Gary Mcdonald
Designer: Kaelin Chappell
Print Buyer: Karen Hunt
Art Editor: Donna Kalal
Copy Editor: Robin Kelly
Technical Illustrator: Marilyn Krieger/Sid Graphics
Compositor: Omegatype Typography
Cover: Kaelin Chappell
Signing Representative: Mike Dew

Acknowledgments
Excerpts on p. 2 © 1966 by Harper & Row, Publisher, Inc. Reprinted by permission of the publisher.
Excerpts on pp. 9–10 are reprinted by permission of the Optical Society of America.
Photos on pp. 10, 11, 23, 95, 120, 223 are reprinted by permission of The Bettmann Archive.
Photos on pp. 19, 21, 22, 30, 142, 168 appear courtesy of The Archives of the History of American Psychology.
Photos on pp. 94, 146, 190 are reprinted by permission of Clark University Press.
Excerpts on pp. 101, 103, 107, 110–111 are reprinted by permission of W. W. Norton & Co., Inc.
Photo on p. 146 is reprinted by permission of H. M. Hanson.
Excerpts on pp. 146, 147, 166, 176 are reprinted by permission of Richard H. Hull, D.V.M.
Photo on p. 222 (left) is reprinted by permission of Alfred A. Knopf and B. F. Skinner.
Excerpt on pp. 263–264 is reprinted by permission of B. F. Skinner.

Printed in the United States of America 85

2345678910—94 93 92 91

Library of Congress Cataloging-in-Publication Data

Malone, John C.
   Theories of learning : a historical approach / John C. Malone.
     p. cm.
   Includes bibliographical references and index.
   ISBN 0-534-05760-8
   1. Learning. 2. Learning, Psychology of. I. Title.
LB1060.M325 1990
370.15'23–dc20   90-42635

To the memory of my mother, Marjorie, and to my father, John.
Both taught me to value scholarship.

CONTENTS

PREFACE

Learning is the most important and interesting area in psychology and the classic learning theories remain of great value. They provide the best guides for practical applications *and* the best answers to questions about the nature of mind.

I wrote this book because I wanted to provide a text that presented the *best ideas* of the major learning theories. I wanted to show that these theories are *interesting:* They are the culmination of a historical progression in thought and they are the best key we have to understanding how we work.

When I say that I wanted to include the *best ideas* of the theorists, I mean the best, not the standard stuff that is handed down from secondary source to tertiary, and so on. The best ideas are often not the easiest to understand and there is certainly precedent for omitting them. But I strongly believe that a presentation that leaves out the best is not likely to be of much value. How can anyone really understand Hull's theory without exposure to his explanation of knowledge,

foresight, and purpose? Does Pavlov make much sense without consideration of his view of the body as an integrated and living machine? Can one understand Skinner in any but the most superficial way without knowing something of his early writings on the concept of the reflex or his later writings on radical behaviorism? I could not find a text that presented these and other essential aspects of the classic learning theories.

I hope that this book presents the theories clearly and completely, so that apparent conflicts are properly interpreted. They are not as serious as they may seem. A case in point is the classic conflict between behavioral and cognitive theories.

The distinction between behavioral, cognitive, and (sometimes) phenomenological viewpoints has become almost standard during the twentieth century. It has been used as an organizing aid in textbooks in many areas of psychology, from learning theories to social psychology, child development, sensation/perception, and psychopathology. I do not find the behavioral/cognitive distinction useful; it is at best a misleading simplification. Hence, I mention it only in the first chapter, where I present the (not original) argument that the distinction merely turns on the immediacy or remoteness of causes in time (cf. Branch, 1987; Hineline & Wanchisen, 1989; Morris, Higgens, & Bickel, 1982).

When I began writing this book I wanted to offer a textbook that presented such material in a clear and interesting way and that showed how learning theories apply to all areas of psychology, including motivation, sensation/perception, and so on. That turned out to be far too long a book and it was pared down to its present size through a long series of reviews and painful revisions.

The first chapter presents what must be the minimum coverage of historical background; though it is brief, I believe that it is still useful. The subsequent seven chapters cover the major theorists, from Thorndike through Skinner. In each case I have tried to communicate the significance of the theory *for us today*. Each has practical applications and each helps us better understand the nature of "mind." I tried to include relevant and interesting research within those chapters, but much could not be included since, as Mook (1987) put it, "a chapter is only a chapter long." Hence, Chapter 9 is composed of that research that is important and interesting but which could not be included in previous chapters. Much more was originally included in that chapter, but did not survive the review and editing process.

Many anonymous reviewers contributed to this final product and I wish that I could acknowledge their individual contributions. I can thank several whose identities I know, especially Peter Holland at Duke and Charles Brewer at Furman, who reviewed more chapters more often than did other reviewers. Other helpful and nonanonymous reviews came from Edwin Brainerd, Charlie Catania, and Peter Killeen. It was comments by Brainerd and by Brewer that convinced me that I had to drastically reduce the length of the book.

Ken King at Wadsworth helped long ago, when I began writing, and I appreciate his renewed assistance during the last few months preceding completion of the book. I must also acknowledge the help I received from Steve Helba, then at Holt, Rinehart & Winston, who oversaw the scaling down of the book. Gary Mcdonald did a great job as production editor and even Robin Kelley's copyediting helped—more than she thinks I appreciate.

Dean C. W. Minkel and Bill Calhoun both supported me when I needed it, as did the pillars of our office staff: Peggy English, Karen Fawver, and Polly Johnson. And I have been fortunate to have the best secretary on the planet, Kim Axley. I am grateful for encouragement from former students, especially John Hinson and John Horner.

My wife, Carlene, shares my opinions on many matters, especially important ones. Her support has always been very important to me.

Finally, I thank the best teachers I have known over the years. Their methods differ greatly, but whatever good is in this book owes to Al Zimmerman, Shirley Brown, Norm Guttman, Greg Lockhead, John Staddon, Bill Verplanck, and Howard Pollio.

Chapter 1

THE PSYCHOLOGY
OF LEARNING

The psychology of learning really *is* psychology. It includes the study of all the ways in which our life experiences affect our subsequent behavior and experience. That includes our thinking and imagining, our seeing, hearing, and hoping, and our remembering and forgetting, since all of these things are influenced by learning. Learning also affects our pleasures and pains and all of the other aspects of feeling that give life its color. Needless to say, the field of learning also includes the study of how we acquire skills, the education that we gain in school, and how society instills its values in us.

Learning determines to a great extent what we will become in life, who we will consider friends, where we will call home, what we will consider worth doing, and what we will call right and wrong. It even determines what we will call real and unreal. Heredity plays a part in all of these things, of course, but heredity notwithstanding, learning is largely responsible for creating our world.

THE GOAL OF
LEARNING THEORIES:
EXPLAINING THE MIND

What is the mind? That is quite a question, and libraries full of answers have been proposed. There is even a branch of philosophy called "the philosophy of mind." Many people assume that the mind has something to do with awareness. We also tend to assume that the mind includes faculties such as memory, perception, attention, and imagination as well as cognitive skills such as problem solving, planning, and reading.

Skinner (e.g., 1974) noted that we use the word *mind* to refer to all of these things and more; he contended that when we say mind, we really mean person. For that reason he advised that we say what we mean and substitute *person* for *mind*. Other theorists, in trying to pin down what we mean by "the mind," have treated the term as synonymous with "brain." Such a definition would be helpful, however, only if our understanding of the brain were more complete—and, of course, only if the definition were accurate.

Given that "the mind" seems to refer to many things, can we arrive at a practical working definition upon which we might all agree? Edwin Guthrie (1952), one of the theorists discussed in this book, answered this question sensibly. He pointed out that it seems obvious to us that we have minds and that bricks do not. It is easy to believe that some animals (such as dogs) have minds, since they behave in ways that suggest the presence of a mind. Is that true of lower animals, he asked?

> But do angleworms have minds? Are growth and reproduction and defensive reaction enough to qualify the worm for that distinction? Plants also grow and multiply and defend themselves not only by their structures but in many cases by movement. Common sense is inclined to deny that plants have minds, for this is an opinion shared only by a very few detached sentimentalists.
>
> What is it then that plants lack that is to be found in creatures which common sense endows with minds? Strangely enough, common sense will be found to offer a very good answer to this question. Growth and reproduction and defense reactions are life, but they are not mind. Mind is these and something more; it is growth and reproduction and reactions serving these ends plus something that common sense might call *profiting* by experience. The answer to the question of the angleworm's status will be determined by the answer to this question: Does the worm always respond in the same way to the same combination of circumstances, or does the worm alter its response as a result of past experience? . . .
>
> These changes in behavior which follow behavior we shall call learning. The ability to learn, that is, to respond differently to a situation because of past response to the situation, is what distinguishes those living creatures which common sense endows with minds. This is the practical descriptive use of the term "mind." (pp. 1–3)

Is the ability to profit from experience really what we mean by "the mind"? That would mean that the study of learning is the study of the mind.

This book explores such a possibility, examining the ways in which learning theories explain what common sense calls "the mind." Here are some of the general questions we will consider:

- Since learning means that we change, what is the nature of that change? Is it a change in specific behaviors, in general tendencies, in our cognitive representations of the world, or some combination of these things?
- Is learning usually a change for the better?
- How important is awareness?
- How important are the consequences of our actions?
- How do we learn abstract concepts such as "red," "humanity," or "justice"?
- Is language important in learning?
- Do motivation and emotion depend upon learning?

Answers to such questions go a long way toward explaining why we do what we do. When we have enough good answers we no longer need to talk about the mind.

THE CLASSIC LEARNING THEORIES: MORE RELEVANT THAN EVER

There are many theories of learning, often attempting to explain the same phenomena. They are not necessarily conflicting theories, however. How do learning theories evolve? It is not true that older theories are superseded by newer, improved models. Rather, new applications for some older theories are discovered almost daily, applications that were not foreseen by the original theorist. This text explores some of the classic theories of learning and subsequent applications.

Pavlov's theory of learning (classical conditioning) has been widely known for more than half a century. Turkkan (1989) reviewed discoveries in medicine, animal learning, pharmacology, and brain function and concluded that classical conditioning is now the most influential theory of learning, especially for medical purposes. We will examine some of these discoveries in Chapters 3 and 9.

Thorndike first published his views in 1898 and extended them until 1949. Could his theories still be current? We will see that the methods customarily used in behavior therapy are in many ways simplified versions of his methods. Since behavior analysis (and therapy) methods are widely used in education, business, and in the treatment of "mental illness," Thorndike must have had something useful to say. Even in cognitive psychology, theorists still attend to Thorndike (cf. Bower & Hilgard, 1981; Estes, 1969). In Chapter 2, we will explore the reasons why Thorndike has worn so well.

What happens when a college professor, who has spent his life in pure research investigating the behavior of animals and children, is thrown into the "real world" of business? This happened to John B. Watson, who left the academic world at age 42 and entered the most commercial and competitive of businesses—advertising. His skillful application of his theory of learning made him a rich man and the vice president of a large and famous advertising agency within four years! Chapter 4 examines his controversial point of view and the methods that led to his commercial success.

Suppose a likable mathematician became a psychologist and proposed the simplest theory of learning imaginable. Originally a mathematician, Edwin Guthrie presented countless examples of applications of his learning theory, wrote in a charming way, and attracted the attention of both casual readers and mathematical psychologists. His theory applies to many situations and appeals to many modern readers, including Gardner and Gardner (1988) and Malone (1978). Chapter 5 discusses his work.

The dominant learning theory from the 1940s to the 1960s was that of Clark Hull and his associates. Many current theories follow in Hull's tradition as well. Hull was an engineer who believed that the best way to understand the way

we work is to build real or hypothetical machines that mimic our activities. You have probably heard of computer programs that solve problems, play chess, and compose music; the information processing approach cast in computer programs is similar to Hull's point of view. Information processing was displaced by connectionist theories that postulate large networks of elements that mimic the activity of the nervous system. They also represent a continuation of Hull's thinking (Malone, 1990). Chapter 6 presents Hull's theory and its derivatives.

Edward Tolman's cognitive theory stressed the *capacities* of animals and humans, especially the capacity to form accurate and useful representations of the environment. This has always been the focus of cognitive psychologists. Since the 1960s, researchers have been concerned especially with cognition in animals, ranging from concept learning in pigeons to language use in chimpanzees. Tolman's theory is enjoying a revival, as we will see in Chapter 7.

Finally, one learning theorist has promoted a unique point of view for half a century; his ideas have attracted a great number of followers and critics. Skinner has become one of the most famous scientists in history, and his views have had a great impact on animal trainers, social psychologists, mental health workers, and philosophers, as well as psychologists interested in learning theory. The basic terms of his theory are easily understood, but a real understanding eludes many, since his theory is unlike the commonsense interpretations that have been standard for centuries. His "theory" is so comprehensive (although he denies having a theory), that it is discussed and disputed by psychologists and philosophers alike. In Chapter 8 we will examine his theory and see what makes him appealing to some and an anathema to others.

What topics are covered by learning theories? As a preview of practical topics, consider the following questions:

- Can the use of punishment remedy a child's misbehavior? If the misbehavior at school is eliminated, why does misbehavior increase greatly at home? The answers to these questions came from animal research and are discussed in Chapters 8 and 9.

- What is insight and creativity, and how may we teach people to be insightful and creative? Chapters 2, 8, and 9 most directly deal with this question.

- What is the best way to prepare for an important examination or for an important speech that we must make? How can we learn to study in the midst of noise and distraction? Answers to these questions may be found in Chapter 5.

- What is personality? Why is it that some people can dominate a social gathering automatically while others slip into the background? Chapter 4 explores the topic of personality.

- How do our bodies affect our moods? Can Pavlov's methods be used to control the activity of the kidneys, lungs, cardiovascular system, and other organs and systems of the human body? Can we influence the immune system to better fight disease? How do "sugar pills" exert placebo effects that can cure illness? Why is addiction to heroin and other opiates so difficult to treat? Why do some people enjoy dangerous or highly exciting activities such as skydiving? How can electric shock be used to help people relax? Answers to these questions appear in Chapters 3 and 9.

- Are animals capable of cognitive activity? Can birds learn abstract concepts, show insight, and communicate with symbols? Some answers to these questions appear in Chapters 7 and 8.

- Can a machine show real knowledge, purpose, and foresight? What is awareness? These matters are discussed in Chapters 6 and 8.

- Under what conditions can people enjoy work for its own sake, rather than for some kind of payoff? Why does being forbidden to do something often make us more eager to do it? How can we explain self-control? How is drug addiction "normal"? Chapters 5, 6, and 9 deal with these questions.

Learning theories deal with these and many other topics. They are mentioned because they are of interest to most people and because we often see newspaper articles announcing some alleged scientific breakthrough related to them: "Scientists Discover That People Will Work Just for the Sake of It," "Research Shows That Our Bodies Affect Our Moods and Our Minds," and so on. Such announcements of scientific breakthroughs are misleading. Learning theories have explained these phenomena for years. One purpose of this book is to communicate just what learning researchers have discovered and what theories of learning can now explain.

PSYCHOLOGY AS SCIENCE

Researchers in physics and chemistry seldom concern themselves with doubts about whether they are practicing science. However, this question often arises in psychology. That is because much of psychology is obviously *not* science. This statement does not mean that nonscientific psychology is bad or of no value but that it is not science—not any more than law, history, or literature is science. (Properly speaking computer science and library science are not really sciences either.)

From the standpoint of this book, science is "natural science" and it is one of the methods people have used to explain nature; nature covers all "natural" phenomena, including our behavior and experience. There are other methods, such as religion, that also propose explanations for natural phenomena. Some of these other methods even bear resemblance to science, since they make observations of natural phenomena, propose laws based on these observations, and make predictions based on these laws. Astrology is an example of a method that resembles science in some respects. Yet, there is no question that astrology is not a science.

Science (or natural science) is unique in its insistence on the objectivity of its statements. Now, *objectivity* is a difficult term to define, but it has become almost synonymous with *testability*, *verifiability*, and especially *refutability* (cf. Popper, 1968). That is, scientific statements such as "the earth rotates on its axis," "all living things require oxygen," or "all behavior is influenced by the consequences produced" are all testable; in particular, they are capable of refutation. This being the case, we can show that the second two statements are false, since exceptions are not difficult to find.

Other statements are not capable of being tested; there is no conceivable way to refute them, to show them false. The statements "humans are basically good" and "all things are in the process of self-actualization" are not refutable. *Good* is an undefined (or vaguely defined) attribute, and *self-actualization* is a name for the fact that things change over time. Conceivably, both statements could be restated as scientific statements. First, though, both *good* and *self-actualization* would need to be defined in such a way that the statements could be tested.

What about astrology, an ancient discipline that for centuries has made statements about the influence of the stars and planets on people's lives? Are those statements testable? Can we tell when an astrological prediction is wrong? Examine the predictions in several newspapers for a given day and you will find two things: First, the predictions will differ a little or a lot; secondly, they are sufficiently vague that a believer can always find confirmation in them. Believers may also overzealously seek confirmation for predictions made in chemistry and physics, which seems to have been the case in the purported demonstrations of cold fusion in the late 1980s. However, the accepted criteria for testability and falsifiability convinced most researchers that cold fusion did not occur. In astrology, such an issue would never be settled. That is why astrology is not science.

WHAT CONSTITUTES A SCIENTIFIC EXPLANATION?

Science seeks to explain natural phenomena through the phrasing of laws; once we have established a set of laws, we can explain events by showing that they are instances of one of our laws. Ideally, a law is a relation between independent and dependent variables, roughly corresponding to what we usually call causes and effects. An independent variable is an antecedent condition, such as falling water; a dependent variable is a consequent, such as the erosion of rock beneath the falling water. In psychology, independent variables take the form of methods of instruction or therapy, the number of hours deprived of food, the intensity of electric shock, and so on. Dependent variables are always reflected ultimately in behavior; even if we are referring to the gaining of knowledge, we must assess it through observing what the subject does.

Often, we find that explanations seem to explain the same phenomena more or less well and we are left with the problem of choosing an explanation. For example, how may one explain aggression among humans? Without troubling to define the dependent variable (aggression), but accepting the word as it is used, we would consider what independent variables may produce it. Here is a partial list of possible independent variables:

activity in the aggression centers in the brain
imitation (modeling) of others' aggression
pain
consequences (e.g., respect or attention)
instinct
intrapsychic forces (id, ego, etc.)
cognitive processing mechanisms

(Some of these possible causes are actually intervening variables. Since the issue is of no consequence here, we will postpone discussion of intervening variables to Chapter 6, where the issue is of consequence.)

Even without a concrete example of aggression, it is easy to see how several (or all) of these causes could be invoked as an explanation. How do we choose? What makes one explanation better than another? First, a good explanation should be simple. In other words, it should refer to no mysterious or vaguely described agents. For example, if we understood the brain mechanisms controlling aggression, then we might explain aggression by referring to them. But we do not understand this agent well; thus, reference to brain mechanisms is a poor explanation. The same might be said of instinct, intrapsychic forces, and cognitive processing mechanisms.

A second criterion for evaluating an explanation is generality. Does our explanation apply only to this one case or to a variety of other cases? We find that all of these explanations are general and that some are too general; if they can be interpreted to account for every conceivable event, they are not falsifiable. For example, is there any phenomenon that cannot be accounted for by Freud's ego/superego/id theory?

A third criterion for evaluating an explanation is whether the theory fits well with already established facts. For example, social psychologists have recently found that much of what we do in daily life is done without awareness; according to these psychologists, we follow "scripts" that we have learned over our lifetimes, and it is not difficult to show this when we place people in situations in which the standard script does not work (e.g., Nisbett & Wilson, 1977; Langer, 1989). This information fits well with existing data, ranging from the seminal observations of Freud to the current behavioral theories that hold that awareness is not the guide of conduct (see Chapter 2).

A fourth criterion is practical usefulness. The American pragmatic philosophers, such as Dewey and James, stressed the "cash value" of ideas over their purely theoretical significance. This "prediction and control" attitude is now attributed to Skinner and Watson, but it was James (1892) who coined the expression and the American philosophers of the turn of the century who pressed such a goal.

Consider the causes of aggression listed above, and ask yourself which cause provides the greatest practical benefit. Which allows the greatest opportunity to predict and control future aggression? Many of the possible causes offer no such opportunity. For example, to say that aggression is the product of intrapsychic forces, instinct, or aggression centers in the brain does little more than name the behavior, and naming is not explaining. Suppose that a child regularly shows unacceptable aggressive behavior toward other children. When you ask why the behavior occurs, you are told that the child has overly active aggression circuits in his or her brain. What do you then do? You may be able to predict that future aggression will occur, assuming there is no change in the brain mechanisms producing the aggression, but you are no further ahead than if you had been told the child is "bad." The same holds for an explanation referring to instinct, cognitive processing, and intrapsychic forces.

In such a case, it is prudent to ask what conditions set off the brain circuits, cognitive processes, instinct, or intrapsychic forces to produce aggressive behavior. Chances are that when you look into it you will find events in the child's history, aspects of past and present home and school environments, and dealings with other adults and children that may be shown to produce aggressive behavior. Understanding these causes leads to practical prediction and control of behavior.

A BRIEF HISTORY OF PSYCHOLOGY

Much of this text deals with the history of the psychology of learning. To understand some of these issues—and to understand why psychologists consider them important—we must consider some of the general issues that have concerned psychologists throughout the history of the field.

The history of psychology is really the history

of *epistemology*, which is the study of the nature and origin of knowledge. Concern with epistemology began more than 24 centuries ago in the speculations of Democritus, Protagoras, Plato, and Aristotle. Space does not allow consideration of these ancient thinkers nor of the developments that occurred over the 22 centuries that followed them. We must begin more recently, in the nineteenth century, treating the thinkers that lived at that time as the epistemological descendents of all who went before. The first matter to consider is the distinction between empiricism and rationalism.

Empiricism and Rationalism

Empiricism is the doctrine that we gain knowledge only through our senses and that we arrive with no innate knowledge of the world. For example, we are not born with knowledge of right and wrong or knowledge of geometry. This does not mean that we arrive with absolutely nothing, of course, since most empiricists assume that people have basic mental powers present at birth. *Rationalism* is the belief that we are born with innate knowledge or powers of reason that allow us to recognize truth.

When we say basic mental powers, we mean *rational* powers, so most empiricists were also rationalists to a degree. A real empiricist would not take for granted mental powers such as attending, comparing, judging, and so on. Rationalists, beginning with Socrates and Plato, also believe that the senses provide knowledge; however, they emphasize the role of reason and innate ideas, or mental powers and knowledge with which people are born. When we understand a principle of geometry, we experience an "aha" feeling that shows that we already knew the principle and that we merely had to be "reminded" of it. (The Gestalt psychologists are one example of twentieth-century rationalists.)

The English thinkers of the sixteenth and seventeenth centuries were not the first empiricists, but they began the movement known as British empiricism. Among these movement leaders were Francis Bacon and Thomas Hobbes, Bacon's secretary, both of whom were guided by political concerns. The seventeenth-century philosopher John Locke, who really developed the movement, was also politically motivated. George Berkeley and David Hume greatly modified Locke's ideas, but it was Locke's simpler view that lived on in the writings of James Mill during the nineteenth century.

James Mill

Mill was an employee of the British East India Company and an amateur philosopher/psychologist. He is of interest to us because he was the first to show clearly how empiricism and associationism explain what people think, what they feel, what they remember, how they plan, and so on. *Associationism* is the theory that all experience can be reduced to elements such as ideas and sensations. Aspects of our experience can then be explained by showing how they are the product of association.

Mill's thesis was presented in 1829 in his book *Analysis of the Phenomena of the Human Mind*, written during a series of summer vacations. Mill wrote:

> Thought succeeds thought; idea follows idea, incessantly. If our senses are awake, we are continually receiving sensations, of the eye, the ear, the touch, and so forth; but not sensations alone. After sensations, ideas are perpetually excited of sensations formerly received; after those ideas, other ideas; and during the whole of our lives, a series of those two states of consciousness, called sensations, and ideas, is constantly going on. (p. 70)

That is our experience, a sequence of sensations and ideas that just pass by through our lives; in fact, they are our lives! But what is the difference between a sensation and an idea?

> I see a horse: that is a sensation. Immediately I think of his master: that is an idea. The idea of his master makes me think of his office; he is a minister of state:

that is another idea. The idea of a minister of state makes me think of public affairs; and I am led into a train of political ideas; when I am summoned to dinner. This is a new sensation, followed by the idea of dinner, and of the company with whom I am to partake it. The sight of the company and of the food are other sensations; these suggest ideas without end; other sensations perpetually intervene, suggesting other ideas: and so the process goes on. (pp. 70–71)

Experience is thus a succession of sensations and ideas; sensations are produced by present objects and they call up associated memories, or "ideas." Mill then distinguished between what he called *synchronous associations* and *successive associations* of sensations and ideas.

According to this order, in the objects of sense, there is a synchronous, and a successive, order of our sensations. I have SYNCHRONICALLY, or at the same instant, the sight of a great variety of objects; touch of all the objects with which my body is in contact; hearing of all the sounds which are reaching my ears; smelling of all the smells which are reaching my nostrils; taste of the apple which I am eating; the sensation of resistance both from the apple which is in my mouth, and the ground on which I stand; with the sensation of motion from the act of walking. I have SUCCESSIVELY the sight of the flash from the mortar fired at a distance, the hearing of the report, the sight of the bomb, and of its motion in the air, the sight of its fall, the sight and hearing of its explosion, and lastly, the sight of the effects of that explosion. (pp. 71–72)

So our experience is really simple; it is composed solely of successions of sensations and ideas and of synchronous sensations and ideas. Sensations occur either simultaneously or in sequences; ideas are copies of those sensations, and they also appear together or in sequence. This is all there is. What we call "objects" are simply synchronous associations:

From a stone I have had, synchronically, the sensation of colour, the sensation of hardness, the sensations of shape, and size, the sensation of weight. When the idea of one of these sensations occurs, the ideas of all of them occur. They exist in my mind

synchronically; and their synchronical existence is called the idea of the stone; which, it is thus plain, is not a single idea, but a number of ideas in a particular state of combination. (p. 79)

Can everything that we know be reduced to associations formed among simple elements? James Mill believed that everything could be, and that the necessary and sufficient condition for associations to form was the principle of contiguity: Sensations (and ideas) that occur close together in time and space, like the flash of the mortar and the sound of its report, become associated. This extreme and simple view has survived vigorous attack by critics over the past 200 years, but it survives nevertheless. Mill wrote:

Brick is one complex idea, mortar is another complex idea; these ideas, with ideas of position and quantity, compose my idea of a wall. My idea of a plank is a complex idea, my idea of a rafter is a complex idea, my idea of a nail is a complex idea. These, united with the same ideas of position and quantity, compose my duplex ideas of a floor. In the same manner my complex idea of glass, and wood, and others, compose my duplex idea of a window; and these duplex ideas, united together, compose my idea of a house, which is made up of various duplex ideas. How many complex, or duplex ideas, are all united in the idea of furniture? How many more in the idea of merchandize [sic]? How many more in the idea called Every Thing? (pp. 115–116)

Mill called the idea of a brick a complex idea because it was a compound of all of the sensations (simple ideas) of color, texture, weight, and so on that form the complex idea "brick." According to Mill, all of mental life, including the idea of "Every Thing," can be analyzed into simple ideas (elementary sensations).

Sensations that occur together frequently become more strongly associated than those that rarely occur together:

But if the word mama is frequently pronounced, in conjunction with the sight of a particular woman, the sound will by degrees become associated with the sight; and as the pronouncing of the name will call up the idea of the woman, so the sight of the woman will call up the idea of the name. (p. 88)

Thus, Mill describes how a child learns to refer to his or her mother, as well as how we all learn the names of things around us. Every sensation and every idea is capable of calling up a host of other ideas; Mill anticipated today's health psychology when he proposed that some ideas come from our internal organs, producing emotional states:

A friend arrives from a distant country, and brings me the first intelligence of the last illness, the last words, the last acts, and death of my son. The sound of the voice, the articulation of every word, makes its sensation in my ear; but it is to the ideas that my attention flies. It is my son that is before me, suffering, acting, speaking, dying. The words which have introduced the ideas, and kindled the affections, have been as little heeded, as the respiration which has been accelerated, while the ideas were received. (p. 100)

All of these excerpts were published in 1829, and they are included to show just what popular associationism was, because that is still what "pop" associationism is today. It is extremely plausible: What we know of the world comes through our senses. Therefore, the basic element of experience must be the *sensation*. Sensory nerves produce color; feelings of muscular resistance; smells; feelings from the stomach, intestines, and other organs of the body; sounds; tastes; and feelings of warmth, cold, pressure, and pain from the skin surface. The objects of our world are therefore combinations of these sensations.

Associationism is also useful in practical affairs. How might we teach patriotism? We should pair frequently ideas of "good" and "noble" with tales of the history of the country, with the sight of the flag, and with the pledge of allegiance. We can instill morals in children by frequently pairing "good" with the idea of certain deeds and "evil" with the ideas of other deeds, so that proper associations are formed. A supply of proper associations, presumably, helps people succeed in

life. Likewise, people react to temptation by associating the idea of the tempting act with the idea of terrible consequences, produced by the act itself or by the penalties imposed by society.

This simple view of associationism was improved considerably by John Stuart Mill, the son of James Mill, but it is the father's version that has been more influential. The popular connectionist theories that are threatening to dominate psychology as we enter the twenty-first century (e.g., Rumelhart & McClelland, 1986) are essentially formalizations of simple associationism (cf. Smolensky, 1988).

Hermann von Helmholtz

Hermann von Helmholtz was a physicist and one of the great physiologists of the nineteenth century (see Figure 1.1). Along the way, he contributed to psychology in his treatment of vision (1866). In this classic work, which formed the basis for most current theories of sensation and perception, Helmholtz adopted the concept of association from John Stuart Mill to explain visual perception.

Helmholtz proposed that perception includes a great deal of *unconscious inference* (or conclusion). By this he meant that much of our experience depends upon inferences drawn on the basis of a little present stimulation and a lot of past experience. Here are two examples illustrating Helmholtz's proposal (from Helmholtz, 1866). This too is associationism, albeit more sophisticated than James Mill's version:

For example, the spectacle of a person in the act of walking is a familiar sight. We think of this motion as a connected whole, possibly taking note of some of its most conspicuous singularities. But it requires minute attention and a special choice of the point of view to distinguish the upward and lateral movements of the body in a person's gait. We have to pick out points or lines of reference in the background with which we can compare the position of his head. But look through an astronomical telescope at a crowd of people in motion far away. Their images are upside down, but what a curious

FIGURE 1.1 Hermann von Helmholtz, 1821–1894. This German physiologist first measured the speed of the neural impulse, proposed the theory of unconscious inference, coauthored a theory of color vision, and proposed the place-resonance theory of audition. *Photo courtesy of Bettmann Archive*

jerking and swaying of the body is produced by those who are walking about! Then there is no trouble whatsoever in noticing the peculiar motions of the body and many other singularities of gait; and especially differences between individuals and the reasons for them, simply because this is not the everyday sight to which we are accustomed. (section 26, pp. 570–571)

Expectations based on very little present stimulation also are important in the theater, according to Helmholtz:

An actor who cleverly portrays an old man is for us an old man there on the stage, so long as we let the immediate impression sway us, and do not forcibly recall that the programme states that the person moving there is the young actor with whom we are acquainted. We consider him as being angry or in pain according as he shows us one or the other mode of countenance and demeanor. He arouses fright or sympathy in us, we tremble for the moment, which we see approaching, when he will perform or suffer something dreadful; and the deep-seated conviction that all this is only show and play does not hinder our emotions at all, provided the actor does not cease to play his part. (section 26, p. 587)

What Helmholtz was stressing is the fact that what our senses bring before us from moment to moment is a small part of what we see, hear, and feel. Our experience is made up of associations, but the bulk of it comes from ourselves, or rather from our past experiences, which produce our expectancies. When Helmholtz called these expectancies unconscious inferences, he stressed the fact that we need not be aware of the elements that make up the current content of our experience. These concepts of expectancies and inferences are similar to the concept of schemata proposed by cognitive psychologists such as Piaget and Neisser.

THE BEGINNINGS OF MODERN PSYCHOLOGY

In general, the more scientists know about the predecessors of current theories, the more likely it is that they will improve those theories or consider alternatives to them. Unfortunately, scientists are typically ignorant of the history of their disciplines and the brief history just presented can be considered only the barest sketch. Knowing something about associationism and natural science, for example, makes it easier to understand the work of Wilhelm Wundt, a man who was a scientist but who was not really an associationist.

Wilhelm Wundt

Wundt was a physiologist at the University of Leipzig and is credited with founding the first psychological laboratory (see Figure 1.2). The

FIGURE 1.2   Wilhelm Wundt, 1832–1920. This German physiologist founded the first psychology laboratory. Wundt trained many of the early psychologists in America and greatly influenced Edward Titchener. *Photo courtesy of Bettman Archive*

laboratory had existed for some time, but the first published research was produced by a student in 1879. Wundt directed 186 Ph.D. dissertations during his career and published some 54,000 pages of text.

Wundt believed that the subject matter of psychology should be divided into two parts, one requiring laboratory study and the other requiring other methods. Wundt is best known for his laboratory research and the influence it had on others, such as Edward Titchener. But let us briefly mention what could not be studied in his laboratory.

Such topics as thinking and language, learning, problem solving, child development, social psychology, and psycholinguistics cannot easily be studied in the laboratory. Most of the interesting areas of psychology, Wundt believed, could

be studied only through *Volkerpsychologie*, the study of societies, peoples, ethnic groups, and so on. This requires the cooperation of anthropology, history, the arts, philosophy, religion, and all of the other humanities.

What could be studied in the laboratory were relatively simple things. Sensation and perception, memory, attention, and similar simple processes were at least somewhat appropriate for laboratory study. And such study was largely dependent upon self-observation (*Selbstbeobachtung*) by trained subjects, mostly adult and mostly male. This method later came to be called *introspection*, or the examination of one's mental processes by "looking in," as if our experience occurs within us. Wundt did not believe that experience was inside us or outside us; he believed that it was just there. Hence, introspection hardly describes Wundt's view of the method.

To be a proper subject for Wundt required a lot of training; it was important that the subject avoid being influenced by unconscious inferences. The goal was to report actual appearances (or *Vorstellungen*), each consisting of three parts: an image (the sensory part), a feeling (such as pleasant or not), and an impulse (a tendency to approach or withdraw). For example, suppose I watched a blue book being dropped onto a table. I would report seeing blue, an image of motion downward, and a sudden sharp sound. Also, I probably would report feeling an unpleasant tension and a tendency to withdraw. If I merely said that I saw a book fall and heard it hit the table, I would be reprimanded for failing to give an accurate report.

Wundt was not an associationist, in the sense that Mill and Helmholtz were; he did not believe that all experience was the sum of sensations and ideas joined by the law of contiguity, or *similarity*. For Wundt, consciousness was not a container that holds ideas, which otherwise would lapse into the unconscious. (For Wundt [e.g., 1907], there was no unconscious.) Rather, he believed that consciousness flows like a river, constantly changing, and that any attempt to analyze it to static elements would be misguided.

Nonetheless, some analysis is essential and Wundt proposed several laws describing the associations that occur in the river of experience. The most important laws fall under the heading of the laws of *psychic resultants*, or the laws of *mental chemistry*. (The term *mental chemistry* was coined by John Stuart Mill to refer to associations in which the compound is not reducible to its elements.) There are four types of psychic resultants, each expressed in its own law. The first, Wundt's law of *fusion*, refers to compounds such as the clang of a bell, which is not analyzable to the individual tones that combine to produce it.

A second type of psychic resultant is the law of *assimilation*, a term used by many associationists before Wundt and also by modern psychologists. This law sometimes is called the principle of redintegration (see McClelland, Clark, Roby, & Atkinson, 1949). Assimilation occurs when one element of a compound calls up the rest of the compound; for example, the word *Washington* calls up a number of compound ideas, such as specific buildings, government officials, and cherry blossoms. The ideas assimilated depend on the experience of the subject. For some, the word may bring to mind a history of experience, such as ideas of the American Revolution.

Assimilation also occurs when a word calls up its meaning—for example, when black looks blacker because it is contrasted with white. In all of these cases, one element influences others. Assimilation, you may notice, is another word for inferences, which Helmholtz devised, and we will see that assimilation constitutes virtually the whole theory of Edwin Guthrie. Wundt's description of assimilation suggests that he viewed consciousness as a kaleidoscope, with contents constantly changing.

A third form of psychic resultant is the law of *complication*, which refers to compounds that include elements from different senses. For example, the sight of apple pie, its fragrance, and the softness, warmth, and taste as we eat it is an instance of complication. Finally, the last form of psychic resultant is the law of memorial associations. This refers to association by contiguity and similarity, which are important when we attempt to recall past ideas. For example, suppose you want to recall the name of a woman you met. You might try to imagine when you last saw her, who she was with, what she was wearing, and other retrieval cues. These are conditions that were present when you last knew her name, and they should remind you of the name. Most of our experience, however, is not of elements hooked together by closeness in space and time. This view of experience is what James Mill and others had proposed, and it is what psychologists such as the Gestaltists attacked. Wundt is often mentioned as a proponent of such a simple view, but he certainly was not one. In his view, such simple trains of association are typical only in the insane (Wundt, 1896).

Wundt's second major law is the *law of psychic relations*, which refers to the effect of context, as exemplified in Gustav Fechner's work. A candle seems bright if viewed in an otherwise dark room, but less so if viewed outdoors in the noonday sunlight. It is the same candle, but other sensations modify its appearance.

The last major law is the *law of psychic contrast*. This applies mainly to emotional experience in which opposite or dissimilar emotions reinforce each other. Under some circumstances, for example, we may experience a range of emotions from grief to ecstasy; the deeper our grief, the greater will be our ecstasy. The concept that emotions exist in opposite pairs was around long before Wundt and has persisted as a significant notion. In Chapter 9, we will see that the more contemporary work of Solomon and Corbit seems to provide strong support for this concept.

Wundt was an amazing man. He trained many of the early American psychologists. Before the turn of the century, Europe was the only place to get a real education. (Prior to 1900, even the chemistry and physics textbooks used in American colleges were translations of French and German texts!) Wundt trained Edward Titchener, one of the most important American psychologists of the early twentieth century, who oversimplified the ideas of his teacher. Wundt also trained

Oswald Külpe, whose work at Würzburg seemed to show the limitations of Wundt's methods.

Oswald Külpe

Recall that Wundt believed that laboratory methods were useful only for studying the simplest psychological phenomena. He used Gustav Fechner's psychophysical methods, the reaction time method of studying simple mental activities (mental chronometry) and verbal reports given by trained observers instructed to report conscious experience (introspection). All of these methods were useful in studying sensation and perception, simple discriminative judgments, and simple recall activities. The use of introspective reports was perhaps the most important, and the rigorous way in which it was done was called *Beschreibung*. This simply means "description" in German, but at the time it had a technical meaning, referring to the reports of properly trained and experienced subjects. *Beschreibung* was as limited as other laboratory methods, and anyone who wished to study thinking and more complex areas was expected to use different methods, those of *Völkerpsychologie*.

Külpe left Wundt's laboratory at Leipzig and set up his own in Würzburg. Against Wundt's advice, he attempted to study higher mental processes, using the method of *Beschreibung*. This annoyed Wundt greatly, who called Külpe's studies "mock experiments." But Külpe persisted, showing that the use of trained introspectionists was of limited benefit (as Wundt had maintained), and providing difficulties for Edward Titchener, who was using this method at Cornell University.

Külpe and his students, who became known as the Würzburg School, published their work around the turn of the century. One such report, by Meyer and Orth, was an analysis of the course of associative thought, using the method of *Beschreibung*. Subjects had been highly trained to give accurate reports, and they tried to be as accurate as possible. But they could only say that the course of their thoughts was chaos. There seemed to be no rhyme or reason for the direc-

tions that their thoughts took from moment to moment. Experience did not seem to follow the simple course that James Mill had so confidently proposed. (Remember that Wundt had said that such a course of thought was common only in the insane; only in such minds do ideas sometimes pass in a rigid sequence, in which one idea calls up another that has appeared close in time or space to the first or where the second is related by similarity to the first.) Nonetheless, this result was a surprise to the Würzburgers and suggested to them that a large part of our experience is not reportable. We cannot report it because it does not occur as images; there are imageless thoughts that we are unable to report.

A second study by Karl Marbe used the method of introspective report (*Beschreibung*) with subjects making simple judgments of weights held in the hands. A subject was given a weight to hold in one hand and, when another weight was placed in the other hand for comparison, the subject was asked to give an honest introspective account of the feelings involved in making a judgment of heavier or lighter. This seems like a simple task. But Marbe found that the subjects could not describe even so simple an experience as making this judgment! On receiving the second weight, subjects reported that they instantly felt the weight was heavier or lighter.

The expected sequence of feelings, which believers in mental chronometry expected, was not there; this is one reason that mental chronometry fell from favor until more recently. One could expect that a subject would report (1) weight in the right hand, (2) weight in the left hand, and (3) a comparison of the weights. One would expect the subject to describe the feelings corresponding to the three stages. But the third stage was not describable; the judgment occurred, but there was no reportable experience accompanying it. It was as if the placing of the first weight prepared the subject for the second weight, so that the judgment was immediate.

The notion that a person develops a "set" to respond became known as the *Einstellung* effect. Watt, another of Külpe's assistants, explored this notion in his work. He gave subjects a very simple task and instructed them to carefully report all conscious content accompanying its solution. Subjects then were plagued with imageless elements. For example, a subject was presented two numbers, such as six and two, and asked to perform some arithmetic operation with the numbers. It was assumed that four stages of thought were reportable. First, the subject would report feelings that accompanied the initial instructions. Next, the subject would report the experience of the two numbers being presented. Then the subject would report the experience of carrying out the math operation. Finally, the subject would report the experience of giving a response.

Watt found that subjects could give good accounts for all phases of the experiment, except for the final two stages. It was as if the answers were already there, as soon as the initial instructions were given and the numbers shown. When we know that we are to be asked to do something with a six and a three, we immediately think of eighteen, nine, three, and perhaps other numbers. When we are told to multiply, add, or subtract, the answers are already there; they were produced by the initial instructions. This is the *Aufgabe* effect, which means "lesson" in German, and which refers to the effect of the initial instructions on later performance. The *Aufgabe* (instructions) produces an *Einstellung* (preparatory set) and leaves us unable to describe the supposed sequence of events that we thought was required to solve such problems. Our past experience leads to such sets, which are not very different from the expectancies of John Stuart Mill and the unconscious inferences of Helmholtz.

However, a great many psychologists, including Külpe, relied too heavily on the power of introspective analysis by trained observers. As a result, the finding that such simple mental processes were not amenable to introspective report came as a severe blow. We will see that such findings were troublesome to Titchener, who nonetheless proposed a way to deal with them. And they were consistent with findings by Sigmund Freud, who showed that what we are

aware of is virtually unrelated to what we do; he emphasized the importance of unconscious motivation, important mental processes of which we are utterly unaware. This theory is consistent with the results of the Würzburg School. It may seem reasonable for psychologists to study what people think, gathering their data by asking subjects for their thoughts. But the results found by Külpe and his students, as well as Freud's reports, show that we usually cannot report all that much (cf. Nisbett & Wilson, 1977).

Of course, Wundt knew that introspection was limited. But along with the Würzburg School he had other critics, who questioned the value of the analysis of consciousness at all. Chief among these was Franz Brentano, who saw the analysis of consciousness as an emphasis on "things" in experience and urged a shift from such a concentration on statics back to the dynamics of Aristotle.

Franz Brentano

Brentano was a philosopher and a priest who aimed his attacks at Wundt, but who really opposed the whole empiricist tradition, which assumed that our experience is analyzable into ideas, sensations, or other static things. While Külpe's group suggested that consciousness was more than simply a collection of reportable elements, Brentano argued that there were no elements, only unreportable acts. His view, which stressed mental activity, is usually called *act psychology*. Among his pupils were Carl Stumpf (teacher of two of the original Gestaltists), Edmund Husserl (founder of *phenomenology*), and, briefly, Sigmund Freud. The philosophical movement called phenomenology is based on the study of the nature of human experience, especially of one's own experience.

Brentano agreed with John Locke and John Stuart Mill that psychology is more basic than philosophy. This means that we begin with our experience and not with the logical analysis of what must be necessary for us to have experience. But, unlike these and other empiricists, Brentano believed that experience has no content. Experience, he claimed, is by no means a series of ideas or other things that can be described by a trained observer.

What then *is* our experience? Influenced by Aristotle, Brentano saw experience as activity. The psyche, he believed, is not a thing observing some kind of mental content; it, too, is activity. The core of Brentano's psychology lies in his denial of the subject/object distinction; this is the same issue that separated Plato's views from those of Aristotle. We generally are raised to interpret our experience in terms of a subject (ourselves) and separate objects (our thoughts and experiences), as held by the representative theory of perception. Therefore, Brentano's terms may seem as strange as those of Aristotle (perhaps stranger). What was Brentano's point? Why is his emphasis on dynamics rather than statics worth mentioning here?

If we begin with our experience, we see that it is a constantly changing, active thing. We are seeing, hearing, imagining, hurting, remembering, hoping, trying, and so on. What Aristotle suggested and what Brentano agreed with is this emphasis on the psyche as action. Later psychologists were to share this emphasis, though not many of them would have said that they were following in the footsteps of Aristotle and Brentano. Some behaviorists, whom we will consider later, were essentially in agreement with them. But concerns were too narrow to allow them to conceive of any relation between their work and Brentano's. Today, this emphasis on activity is even characteristic of cognitive theories, such as Neisser's (1976). Because Brentano stressed activities instead of mental elements, it was difficult for him to express his views. Our language is arranged to allow communication about things and their movements and conditions, but we have no easy way to talk about activity per se.

This difficulty with language is what made Brentano's views seem so obscure when he tried to explain what he meant by act psychology. Trying to put his view in the terms of the traditional subject/object dichotomy so that he would be understood, he coined the awful terms *immanent objectivity* and (worse) *intentional inexistence!* What he was trying to say is that experience is continual activity and that activity, such as seeing and hearing, is always done with reference to some object. We see things; the things are immanently in the seeing. But the issue is not that we see and that there is something different from us to be seen. Like Aristotle, Brentano viewed the process as a unitary thing. "Seeing" and "things" constitute the act. If we awkwardly look at the process from the point of view of the object, we may see that it seems to be part of the act; it almost exists *in* the act. The act refers to it and it is inexistent in the act. *Intentional* means "refers to" and was borrowed from the medieval churchmen.

Bear in mind that Brentano, like Aristotle, argued against the simple commonsense theory of subject and object, which has been held by virtually every philosopher and psychologist before and since. The commonsense view, which is easy to understand, stresses *statics*—me/you/it, ideas, memories, images, copies, emotions, and so on. The dynamic view, shared by Aristotle, Brentano, and a scattering of other psychologists, including a few behaviorists and some Freudians, stresses *dynamics*, not statics. It speaks of thinking, remembering, imagining, emoting, and other activities.

Darwinism

One of the strongest influences on the psychology at the turn of the century, as well as on modern psychology, came from Darwin's work. Although the theory that evolution comes about through the effects of variation in characteristics, natural selection, and heredity was not new at the time he wrote, Darwin provided a mass of evidence that established the theory beyond a reasonable doubt. In his books *On the Origin of Species* (1859), *The Descent of Man* (1871), and *The Expression of the Emotions in Man and Animals* (1872) Darwin not only drew attention to the continuity among species, including humans, but to the possibility of reason in beasts and instinct in humans.

FIGURE 1.3 Herbert Spencer, 1820–1903. This English writer applied principles of evolution to psychology. He is known for espousing evolutionary associationism, which holds that reflex activities may be passed on as instincts and that instincts may develop into cognition and reason—all of this occurring over many generations. *From Spenser (1904)*

Perhaps most important, he caused psychologists to view behavior and mental activity in terms of their adaptive functions.

Herbert Spencer The Englishman Herbert Spencer was a largely self-taught thinker and writer who was promoting theories of evolution even before Darwin's work was known (see Figure 1.3). Spencer applied principles of variation and selection to economics, politics, biology, and the universe itself. His *Principles of Psychology* (1855) is most often remembered for his theory of evolutionary associationism. According to this view, frequently repeated reflex actions may, through inheritance of acquired characteristics, be passed on as instincts. Thus, an animal that frequently feeds on a specific prey because it is easy to catch may pass on (after many generations) an instinctive preference for that prey. Similarly, instincts may give rise to memory and cognition in succeeding generations. In the course of evolution, simpler behaviors thus give rise to more complex ones.

Perhaps Spencer's greatest influence was on William James, a philosopher and psychologist whom we will discuss later. James's major work, *The Principles of Psychology* (1890), carries the same title as Spencer's work, and James criticized Spencer repeatedly throughout the text. James believed that Spencer had done a bad job of applying evolutionary thought to psychology. As James said:

> He left a Spencer's name to other times, linked with one virtue and a thousand crimes. The one virtue is his belief in the universality of evolution—the 1000 crimes are his 5000 pages of absolute incompetence to work it out in detail. (Boring, 1950, p. 243)

George J. Romanes Romanes was a wealthy Scot whose aims were similar to Spencer's. Romanes's *Mental Evolution in Man: Origin of Human Faculty* (1888) was reported by Joncich (1968) to be the most heavily marked up book in Freud's library, but it is not the book for which Romanes is known. In 1882, he published a popular piece called *Animal Intelligence*, which argued for the existence of human faculties in animals, giving anecdotal accounts of animal mentality.

It seems to us that animals have memories. (In 1871 Darwin claimed that ants' memories spanned at least four months.) It also appears that animals have the faculty of attention (as in the cat waiting by the mousehole). And animals have senses much like ours (at least in the case of higher animals). Might they also have moral qualities, Romanes wondered? There are examples of courageous dogs, thieving crows, and shiftless pigs, are there not?

Romanes made much of the human qualities he saw in animals. His work thus became synonymous with the practice of anthropomorphism, or the ascribing of human characteristics to other things, whether those things be animals or gods. The zoologist Lloyd-Morgan later cautioned against this practice.

Romanes advocated the practice of introspection by analogy as a means of understanding the animal mind. In his view, when we see an animal (or another human) doing something that we have done ourselves and that in our own case was accompanied by conscious experiences, we may assume that the animal also has such conscious experiences. An animal writhing in pain doubtless feels as we do when we writhe similarly. Freud made use of Romanes's reasoning when he argued for the existence of the unconscious (1915). Thus, we may know the unconscious by treating it as another organism and introspecting by analogy.

Conwy Lloyd-Morgan The Welshman Conwy Lloyd-Morgan was a mining engineer who was fascinated with Darwinian principles. At one time, he held the unusual title of Professor of Geology and Zoology. He is best known for his canon, which is often wrongly interpreted as a prohibition of anthropomorphizing. His canon did not forbid the imputing of human faculties to beasts, since he largely agreed with Romanes that animals do possess many human abilities. But there are several ways in which species may differ in the possession and the degree of a mental ability, and he urged that we use the most conservative interpretation.

Species may differ according to the method of levels, such that one species may possess reason, memory, and sensation, for example. A second species may lack reason entirely but possess memory and sensation in the same degree true of the first species. Thus, a dog may possess memory and sensation equal to humans and lack reason entirely. A faculty either is there or is not there, according to this view, which Morgan rejected.

Species may differ according to the method of uniform reduction, so that all have faculties such as reason, memory, and sensation, but lower organisms have less of each. We have the most, dogs have less, rats have still less, and flies have least. But even the flies have some power to reason, remember, and sense. Morgan also rejected this possibility.

According to Lloyd-Morgan, different species may possess more or less of a given faculty, owing to its adaptive advantage, and lower species may have more of some faculties than do higher species. Thus, a dog may have reason, memory, and sensation in different degrees, with less reason and memory than humans but with superior powers of sensation, especially audition and smell. The dog may even have a superior power to form simple associations.

Thus, the cannon states: "In no case may we interpret an action as the outcome of the exercise of a higher psychical faculty, if it can be interpreted as the outcome of the exercise of one which stands lower in the psychological scale." Lloyd-Morgan cautions against attributing the ability to reason to a beast when its actions can be accounted for by a lower faculty, which may be more highly developed than we might think.

The famous case of *Kluger Hans* (Clever Hans) is a good example of what Lloyd-Morgan meant. This horse seemed to be able to solve a variety of arithmetic problems, including the calculation of square roots. He signaled his answers by tapping the ground with a hoof or pointing his head toward an object, and his achievements were declared legitimate by an originally-skeptical panel of distinguished scientists who tested him (Griffin, 1976). It was finally shown by Oskar Pfungst (1965, originally 1908) that Hans *was* amazing, but not because of his mathematical ability. Evidently, the horse was able to notice subtle changes in the facial expression and breathing of his trainer and of other onlookers so that he knew when to stop tapping with his hoof. When his trainer could not inadvertently signal the solution, Hans's mathematical skill vanished. It was assumed that his performance was due to the operation of a higher faculty. Instead, it was a keener-than-suspected faculty of perception that was largely responsible. It was not wholly responsible, since Hans also had to learn to associate cues from the trainer with "that's the answer." His performance was still surprising, but hardly as surprising as the ability to calculate square roots.

TWENTIETH-CENTURY PSYCHOLOGY: THE SCHOOLS

This discussion of the history of psychology will end with a brief description of some major ways of viewing psychology. All of these viewpoints were popular around the turn of the century and therefore formed the setting for the first learning theories. The psychology of Wundt was transplanted to this country and carried on by Edward Titchener, who termed this way of looking at things *structuralism*. A rival group, composed almost wholly of Americans, was impressed with Darwinian evolutionary principles and the adaptive function of behavior and consciousness. This school was named *functionalism* by Titchener. The behaviorists, who were also Americans, and the Gestaltists, who were transplanted Germans, developed their schools of thought in reaction to Titchener and his brand of psychology.

Titchener's Structuralism

Edward B. Titchener was an Englishman who was educated at Oxford and who later obtained a Ph.D. with Wundt at Leipzig (see Figure 1.4). He then joined the faculty of Cornell University, where he remained until his death. His influence on American psychology was immense. Titchener was an extremely capable man who represented

the European (actually, the German) view of the nature of psychology, which made him the target of attacks by critics of such a view. We will briefly describe Titchener's view of psychology here.

What Is Psychology? For Titchener (1910), psychology was the study of the structure of consciousness, the "what" of the matter. He suggested that in any discipline it is possible to approach the subject matter from at least three directions; these are the "what," the "how," and the "why." Before one can even consider the "how" and the "why," one must know something of the "what." That is, before we can understand how our experience is pieced together and why it is that way, we must know what it is that is pieced together. We must use the method of introspection to isolate the elements of consciousness before going further; this is the "what."

The "how" refers to the rules that describe ways in which the elements are joined together. The laws of association by contiguity and by similarity are examples of "how" theories. The "why" approach must rely on the nervous system (or whatever) to explain why we experience the elements as we do and why they are joined together as they are. Titchener insisted that we begin with the "what," of course, and he never progressed far with the "how" and "why" questions.

The Elements of Consciousness Wundt had proposed ideas, affect, and impulse as the basics of conscious experience. Titchener dropped impulse and proposed that sensations (which are strong), images (which are fainter than sensations), and affect are really basic. To Titchener, *affect* included only "pleasant" and "unpleasant." He attributed to bodily tensions the other characteristics of emotion that Wundt described; he did not consider them to be real mental elements. Each sensation and image had its quality (blue, hot, smooth, and so on), its intensity, and its duration, as did affective elements. But sensations and images had two further attributes that

FIGURE 1.4 Edward B. Titchener, 1867–1927. This Cornell psychologist and former student of Wilhelm Wundt headed the structuralist school. *Photo courtesy of the Archives of the History of American Psychology*

were not shared by emotions. Some had the attribute of extension in space. This is the case with visual experiences and touch. Whether auditory sensations were extended in space was a matter of debate, a debate that John B. Watson was later to ridicule.

A last attribute was that of clarity, or attensity; sensations and ideas were ranked in terms of degrees of clearness, which roughly corresponded to their attention-getting power. In fact, this was Titchener's explanation of attention. One may treat attention as a power; we can attend to whatever we choose. Yet, there are some sensations and ideas that a person seems compelled to attend to—for example, when a person hears his or her name called or when the person pricks a finger with a pin. We attend in those cases because of the attention-getting power (that is, the clarity) of the sensations. Why isn't this always the case, even when it seems that we are choosing to attend? Sensations and ideas simply force us to attend to them; the effort of attention may be an illusion.

William James, perhaps the most significant of all American psychologists, made a similar suggestion in 1890. He proposed that when we seem to make an effort to attend to a good thought, we only imagine that we are putting out the effort. For example, when we deny ourselves a piece of pie because of what we will see on our bathroom scale the next day, we imagine that we have made a choice and we congratulate ourselves. What may really happen is a struggle among our ideas for our attention. The idea of eating the pie, if unopposed, would automatically lead us to eat the pie. But those ideas *are* opposed, by the ideas associated with our weight and our appearance. If those ideas dominate, we turn down the pie. When we hesitate, it means that the ideas are more or less evenly balanced; a change in either one of the sets of warring ideas would tip the balance one way or the other.

As long as the ideas are about evenly balanced, we hesitate. Then the scale is tipped; someone asks us if we have been gaining weight, and the anti–pie-eating ideas win. They win because they have become more attention compelling than the pie-eating ideas. Yet, after such an episode, we are apt to feel that we have made a difficult decision. At the time the decision was made, though, it was no contest. We merely recall how tempted we were. If we had made the decision earlier, before the balance was tipped in favor of not eating pie, it would have been a difficult decision, requiring great effort.

Maybe every choice that we make is similarly determined; the balance of attention is shifted in favor of one set of ideas by a thought that we add or that someone else adds, as in the remark above.

This means that we have no free will, in the real sense of the term, a possibility that was repugnant to James. After suggesting that the mechanical battle of ideas could determine what we attend to and therefore determine what we do, James chose as his first act of free will to *believe* in free will. At any rate, this example shows the way in which a structuralist might account for attention.

The Stimulus Error Titchener's subjects, like those of Wundt and other introspectionists, were carefully trained to report conscious experience as it was felt, without interpretation. For example, a subject reporting sensations when hearing a handclap must describe a sharp sound of a particular intensity lasting so long. A subject who says "I heard a handclap" would be describing experience as mediated by past experience; that sound has been heard before and it has occurred when hands were clapped. But we want a description of experience uncolored by past experience or personal theories, at least so far as is possible. The subject reporting the handclap was making the *stimulus error*, describing what was guessed to be the stimulus, or source of the experience, rather than the experience itself.

If one views a round dinner plate from most angles, one will see an ellipse. But we have had so many experiences viewing round objects at such angles that we make what Helmholtz called an unconscious inference and report that the plate is round. This is another case of the stimulus error; our sensation of the plate is elliptical, and that is what is to be reported if we are to describe our experience accurately. One can imagine the tortures undergone by subjects in experiments carried out by Titchener and other introspectionists. Many subjects must have asked themselves the question that Watson and many other theorists asked Titchener: "What is the point? What can such methods hope to accomplish?"

Imageless Elements Introspective analysis was the chief method of Titchener, and one can guess that he was disturbed by the findings of the Würzburg School: If there are imageless elements involved

in the judging of two small weights, then how far can the method of introspection go in dealing with experience? Imageless elements cannot be reported, of course, and they seem to be very common. What did Titchener say to this?

He criticized the Würzburgers as faulty introspectionists, and he denied the existence of imageless elements. He claimed that such elements were sensations and ideas just like other sensations and ideas, but they were so familiar that they dropped from consciousness. We have judged relative weights, colors, distances, and so on many times a day since earliest childhood. In early childhood there are conscious sensations accompanying such acts, but they become unconscious by adulthood. For example, the words *up*, *down*, and *heavy* are apt to make a child look up, look down, or tense muscles—activities that cease as we become adults.

For Titchener, this became an explanation of *meaning* and helps define his version of *context theory*. Every percept consists of sensations and ideas arranged as a core and a context. The word *tree* may call up an image of one tree or many trees, along with other images such as the smell and touch of a tree. This is the core of the percept. The context is all of the half images, images that are dim, sometimes there and sometimes not. Part of the context is also more than what we now think of; it is the sum of all of the sensations and ideas that have ever been associated with trees in our experience. We are not able to report some of these images, since they are now unconscious. But Titchener could say that they still were there, reportable or not. Presumably, some breakthrough in introspective methods would make them conscious; after all, Freud was having success in unearthing unconscious ideas in his patients.

By the first decade of this century, Titchener had identified more than 50,000 mental elements, but his time was running out. The first real critics were the functionalists (as he called them), who were not really opposed to introspection but who were opposed to the sole concentration on the "what." They were interested in the "what for."

American Functionalism

A number of early American psychologists were impressed with the principles of Darwin's theory and thus stressed the adaptive function of behavior and experience. Several of the most influential of these people were James Angell, John Dewey, William James, and Harvey Carr. We will discuss each briefly. It is worth noting that these people were the teachers of the first learning theorists.

James Angell   Angell, the teacher of John B. Watson in Chicago, spelled out the main tenets of functionism in his presidential address of the American Psychological Association, published in 1907 (see Figure 1.5). He said that functionalism was not just concerned with content, as were the structuralists, and he questioned the belief that ideas are stored in our heads and recalled.

> No matter how much we may talk of the preservation of psychical dispositions, nor how many metaphors we may summon to characterize the storage of ideas in some hypothetical deposit chamber of memory, the obstinate fact remains that when we are not experiencing a sensation or an idea it is, strictly speaking, non-existent. . . . [W]e have no guarantee that our second edition is really a replica of the first, we have a good bit of presumptive evidence that from the content point of view the original never is and never can be literally duplicated. (Herrnstein & Boring, 1965, p. 502)

He goes on to say that this makes introspection difficult, if we are trying to report sensations and ideas, since a lot of this is done from memory. (Going back to our earlier example of the handclap, Angell would say that it is our memory of the handclap, rather than the event itself, that we describe.)

Secondly, Angell emphasized that mental content and activity depend on conditions. The content to which Titchener referred depends upon our life experiences, but he was not concerned with how that content changes with changing experiences. Angell believed that it is more interesting to study the origin of our ideas than to dwell on their identity. Consider the origin of the

FIGURE 1.5   James R. Angell, 1829–1916. This functionalist psychologist worked at the University of Chicago at the turn of the century. He is known for presenting the basic tenets of functionalism. *Photo courtesy of the Archives of the History of American Psychology*

differences in abilities in the following example: Most of us can distinguish gross differences in the tastes of teas, whereas a tea taster can make far more subtle distinctions. How are such discriminations learned? What conditions lead to greater memory, power of concentration, and more skillful motor performances? Practical considerations such as these were of no interest to the structuralists, but they were to the functionalists.

The functionalists still were interested in conscious experience, and this was Angell's third point. According to Angell, consciousness must have an adaptive function; presumably, humans have more consciousness than other animals, so this quality must help us in our survival. But consciousness was not to be examined in structural terms as was Titchener's practice. What was of interest to Angell was the function played and the manner in which this function developed from infancy.

In case it seems obvious that consciousness does have an adaptive function, consider two points. First, a simple calculator can do what it does better than most humans. Sometimes it may seem as if we would be better off if we did operate like machines. In fact, many of our most skilled performances are done unconsciously: Try running or ice skating or brushing your teeth while consciously attending to each muscle movement! Secondly, maybe we operate like clockwork mechanisms more than we might think, and perhaps the fact that we are conscious of a lot of what we do is irrelevant. As Freud put it, maybe consciousness is superficial, like the foam on the ocean surface. It is there, but it simply rides on the waves; it does not produce them. We will see that this worried William James, who made a good case for the adaptive function of consciousness.

John Dewey   Dewey, shown in Figure 1.6, was a pragmatist philosopher and educator. In 1896 he published a paper entitled "The Reflex Arc Concept in Psychology." In this paper he attacked psychologists who suggested that humans are mechanisms made up of many discrete parts. He also attacked those who viewed consciousness as the sum of discrete elements such as sensations and ideas. Dewey's chief target was the Meynert scheme, proposed by Theodor Meynert, an Austrian physiologist. Meynert's was a popular model for learning in the late nineteenth century.

According to this theory, a child learns to avoid putting a hand into a flame because of the following sequence of events: The sight of the flame leads to reaching (out of curiosity), the touching produces the sensation of burning, and this sensation produces withdrawal of the hand. When the flame is next encountered, the sight calls up the idea of the burn, and the response is

FIGURE 1.6   John Dewey, 1859–1952. This American philosopher and educator presented a powerful argument against the analysis of behavior and experience into static units. *Photo courtesy of the Archives of the History of American Psychology*

withdrawal rather than reaching. A simple association forms between the sight of the flame and the pain of the burn. This reasonable account is one that James Mill (or Titchener) might give.

Dewey objected to differentiating the events as stimuli (the flame and the burn) and responses (the reaching and the withdrawing). He saw this as another instance of the static subject/object distinction to which we have alluded. The sequence of events may instead be viewed in a dynamic or functional way.

First, the child sees the flame as a shining, dancing, sparkling, curiosity-arousing object. Seeing the flame is not a passive thing; it is a

FIGURE 1.7   William James (right), 1842–1910, with American philosopher and educator Ralph B. Perry (left). James, a Harvard philosopher and psychologist, was a leading functionalist. Perry is best known as James's biographer. *Photo courtesy of Bettman Archive*

"seeing for reaching." After the burn, it is not altogether correct to say that the sight of the flame is associated with the pain of the burn. The experience has literally changed the flame! It is now a shining, dancing, sparkling, painful and hot object. Our interactions with objects give them their meaning; these interactions actually change what the objects are for us. This is compatible with the pragmatic view of meaning. It stresses the importance of interchanges with objects, rather than merely receiving copies of them.

William James   It is sometimes argued that James set up the first psychological laboratory at Harvard in 1875, four years before Wundt's laboratory was founded in Leipzig. The fact is that, although James may have been the best psychologist America has produced, he was no researcher and thus had little use for a laboratory. The few pieces of equipment in his "laboratory" included a device for spinning a frog and a few other items used in classroom demonstrations.

What James *did* do was write the famed pair of volumes, *The Principles of Psychology* (1890), a piece of work widely believed to be unequaled before or since. He was a pragmatist like Dewey, and one sees throughout his work an emphasis on adaptive function. In this work, he emphasized the selective function of consciousness, held that the "stream of consciousness" includes both elements (ideas) as well as relations among them, (relations such as more than, next, for, above), proposed the ideo-motor theory to explain how people act voluntarily, and much more. His chapters on the self, memory, attention, and other topics of psychology are milestones; he has been quoted in countless papers and books (see Figure 1.7).

James defended the adaptive nature of consciousness by proposing what has been called the emergency function of consciousness. According to James, we are conscious of our actions and our sensations when we are acquiring a new habit, such as learning to ride a bicycle. Once the habit is mastered, we no longer attend to the sensations accompanying it; the action is done unconsciously. It seems that conscious attention is thus helpful in the acquisition of new habits. It is also important when an emergency arises. For example, we seldom attend to the sensations of walking, since it is an activity well mastered in early life. Suppose you are walking home one evening, thinking about what you will have for dinner that night or remembering something you should have done yesterday. Suddenly you find yourself alone in an alley, facing a pack of wild dogs. As a result, you become instantly and acutely conscious of your sensations, of the movements of your limbs, particularly your feet. You remain conscious of your movements until the danger is past. In such situations, consciousness arises when habitual action places us in danger. Therefore, it follows that consciousness also functions to aid us when habit fails elsewhere.

James proposed a simple theory of learning, which was simply the association of ideas and movements by contiguity and the strengthening of these associations by frequency. As he stated on the cover page of *Psychology* (1892):

Sow an action and you reap a habit;
sow a habit and you reap a character;
sow a character and you reap a destiny.

James was a mentalist, meaning that he believed that ideas could cause behavior; this was the main feature of his theory of ideo-motor action. It follows that James was *not* a behaviorist, but some of his views must have influenced the behaviorists who came after him. He wrote the following passage concerning consciousness:

The theory of evolution is beginning to do very good service by reduction of all mentality to the type of reflex action. Cognition, in this view, is but a fleeting moment, a cross section at a certain point, of what in its totality is a motor phenomenon. (1879, p. 164)

He even proposed that consciousness may not exist: "Consciousness . . . is the name of a nonentity. . . . It seems to me that the hour is ripe for it to be openly and universally discarded"

(1904, p. 208). Such opinions voiced by the father of American psychology and a respected authority on the mind must have prepared many readers for the behaviorism of Thorndike and Watson.

Behaviorism

The functionalists were never a close-knit group, as were the structuralists and, later, the Gestaltists. They had very different individual interests, not all in psychology, and they agreed only in their emphasis on function rather than structure. Functionalists still were concerned with conscious experience, however, and this led to the appearance of a new group, the behaviorists, led at first by John B. Watson. The behaviorists also stressed function, but they believed that the structuralists' preoccupation with the study of consciousness was not only futile but damaging. In the behaviorists' view consciousness has no special significance. Its study had not produced any useful product and it seemed likely that its future study would be fruitless.

Behaviorists never really denied the existence of what we call private experience, although they have been accused of doing so. What the early behaviorists surely did deny was the virtue of the introspective method, as practiced by Titchener and many functionalists, such as James and Angell. The first major behaviorists were Thorndike (a student of James) and Watson (a student of Angell).

What, exactly, is *behaviorism?* It is a view that holds that the subject matter of psychology may best be viewed as activity rather than as structures. According to behaviorists, we do not have thoughts or images, but we do think and imagine.

The theories presented in this book generally are considered to be behavioral theories, and for many years they have been contrasted with cognitive theories. However, the behavioral/cognitive distinction may no longer be useful. Consider what actually is meant by behavioral and cognitive theories.

The distinction between behavioral and cognitive interpretations was first made more than half a century ago when such a division was more reasonable than it is today. Long ago, *behavior* meant actual muscular activity and movement in space, and *cognitive* referred to representations of things, usually assumed to be done by the brain. Behavioral researchers studied observable activity, and cognitivists used behavior to make inferences about the ways in which their subjects represented reality. For the lay public, it seemed that behavioral psychologists studied what people do and cognitive psychologists studied what people think and feel.

Over the years, *behavior* has come to include activity in general—including activities such as remembering, seeing, planning, concept learning, reading, and other seemingly "cognitive" things. Cognitive psychology has also changed and, although cognitive psychologists still study representations, they are increasingly concerned with activities or behavior (e.g., Neisser, 1967, 1976). Thus the two views are now less distinct.

A second possible distinguishing feature lies in the emphasis placed upon underlying processes, as in the treatment of problem solving as the activity of cognitive processing mechanisms. Although extreme (radical) behavioral views do not refer to underlying processes, most behavioral learning theories do. We will see that Pavlov, Thorndike, Guthrie, Hull, and others constantly stressed underlying mechanisms as explanations for behavior. Sometimes these were assumed brain processes, as was the case for Pavlov, and in other cases the mechanisms were versions of what others call processing mechanisms; this was the case for Hull's theory (cf. Bower & Hilgard, 1981; Malone, 1981, 1990).

If there is a real difference between behavioral and cognitive theories, it lies in the relative emphasis placed on activities versus representations and in the emphasis given to past causes versus present ones. For example, consider how we might explain the occurrence of insightful problem solving. The word *squp* means nothing to us at first, and it might take some time to achieve insight into what it means. A cognitive psychologist points to events in the current situation: The

word *squp* means nothing out of context, but people are likely to understand it if they are standing at the foot of a stairway and someone says *squp* ("let's go up"). A behavioral interpretation, on the other hand, points to causes in the past. If we have never seen the word *squp* in print before, we are unlikely to identify it. That is, our past experience largely controls our current behavior.

Are these really different approaches? Surely the cognitive psychologist knows that stored representations depend upon past experience, and surely the behavioral psychologist realizes that past experience produces changes in us that could be called structures or sets of representations. It is really a matter of relative emphasis. For practical purposes, the behavioral researcher concentrates on those aspects of previous experience that the cognitivist is less concerned with (past causes), while showing less interest in the current product of that experience (present causes) (cf. Branch, 1987; Morris, Higgens, & Bickel, 1982).

As a final note, it should be pointed out that the first behaviorists strenuously opposed introspectionism, as practiced by Titchener and by many other psychologists of the early part of the twentieth century. Modern cognitive psychology is sometimes treated as if it were no more than a current rendition of the old introspectionism, though this certainly is not the case.

There are some similarities between nineteenth-century introspection and recent cognitive psychology (as noted by Neisser, 1976). However, the hallmarks of introspectionism, especially as practiced by Titchener, were the examination of conscious experience and the analysis of it into elements. Current cognitive psychology has become more interested in cognitive activities and is less concerned with conscious content.

SUMMARY

Learning theories are concerned with explaining what is usually called the mind. They attempt to explain what kinds of experiences produce which changes in the way we behave, think, perceive, and feel. Each of the classic learning theories is relevant today. For example, Pavlov's theories have provided methods for the control of the viscera and increased understanding of immunology and drug addiction. In addition, Thorndike, Watson, and Guthrie illustrated the practical usefulness of behavioral methods and provided alternatives to the usual conception of the mind.

Hull was the master of the "engineering" interpretation of learning, reflected in information processing and connectionist theories. Tolman showed that cognition could be objectively treated, and he paved the way for later researchers interested in the animal mind and the human mind. Skinner promoted his views on learning, mental health, society, and philosophy for well over half a century. His fame is well earned, though many who know who he is do not really understand his position.

Topics covered by learning theories range from misbehavior in children to creativity and insight. They include methods for studying and the ways in which our bodies affect our moods. They deal with risk taking, animal communication, machine models of knowledge and purpose, and so on. Many attention-attracting news headlines report ideas that are everyday topics of study by learning theorists.

Science is an enterprise characterized by objectivity (testability or refutability). Scientists seek explanations that express relations between independent and dependent variables. Good explanations are simple, general, and congruent with other knowledge. In addition, good explanations allow what William James called "prediction and control." That is, they are useful.

Behavioral and cognitive theories used to be quite incompatible; *behavior* meant movement in space and *cognition* was often interpreted as mental activity. Differences between the two viewpoints have lessened, but one remains. Both may postulate underlying processes, such as neural networks or cognitive structures, but behavioral theories are more likely to emphasize environmental causes lying in the past. Cognitive theories, by and large, emphasize present causes, such as expectancies and images.

Understanding current research and theory in psychology requires some knowledge of the history of psychology. Since the fourth century B.C. the two major ways of explaining learning (epistemology) have been the rationalist and empiricist viewpoints, which stress the importance of reason and sensation, respectively.

The empiricist philosophers Hobbes, Locke, Hume, and Berkeley developed associationism as a theory of mind, but James Mill proposed a simple version that enjoyed popular appeal. Although Mill's theory was useful, his son, John Stuart Mill, improved upon it. This version was adopted by Helmholtz, who coined the term "unconscious inference" to describe the way in which past sensations influence future ones, acting much like a filter for experience.

Wundt started the first psychology laboratory and used the method of self-observation to analyze conscious experience. His laws of psychic resultants were very different from the simple association-by-contiguity stressed by James Mill. Wundt did not believe that experience could be analyzed into elements, as James Mill did.

Külpe's group reported that mental activity often occurs without images; this meant that introspective reports could not fully describe thought. Their discovery of *Einstellung*, or "set," created great difficulties for Titchener, who carried on a version of Wundt's research in America.

Franz Brentano opposed the analysis of consciousness into ideas, sensations, or any other describable things. He believed that experience is activity, not a sequence of ideas to be reported. Instead, he believed, thought shows intentional inexistence and immanent objectivity.

Titchener's structuralism aimed to analyze consciousness into sensations, images, and affect. He was able to account for a variety of phenomena, including free will, but the reports of imageless thought from Külpe's group proved difficult for him to explain.

Darwinism influenced psychology in many

ways. Researchers such as Spencer, Romanes, and Lloyd-Morgan speculated on the extent or depth of animals' minds. Functionalists such as Angell, James, and Dewey argued against the sole concentration on the content of consciousness. If consciousness is important, they argued, it has functions; it is these functions that should be studied. Dewey criticized the static conception of the reflex arc, Angell specified the main characteristics of functionalism, and James's *Principles of Psychology* remains an inspiration to readers.

Behaviorism arose as an alternative to the structuralism and functionalism of the time. Its chief tenet was that the analysis of consciousness was pointless and that the subject matter of psychology was better treated as behavior. The first advocate of this position was Edward Thorndike, whose theory is discussed in Chapter 2.

GLOSSARY

Act psychology Name given to the view of Franz Brentano, who opposed Wundt's analysis of consciousness. Brentano argued that there is really no static "content" of consciousness; experience is made up of activities, not sensations and ideas.

Assimilation This refers to the influence of a mass of associations on one of its member elements and vice versa. For example, the word "cold" brings to mind snow, quiet, blankets, and so on. This ability of one element (cold) to call up a whole complex is an instance of assimilation. Similarly, presentation of the mass, such as in a picture of a wintry scene, may influence a present thought, by making us shiver. The law of assimilation, a principle of association used by Wundt and may others, is also known as redintegration.

Associationism A view that stresses the analysis of experience into elements (sensations, ideas, and so on) and proposes laws of association to account for the ways in which these elements are joined. In extreme form (e.g., Hume), this view holds that all of our experience and knowledge consists only of associated elements.

Behaviorism A view that holds that the subject matter of psychology may best be viewed as activity (behavior), rather than as "things" or structures. Ac-

cording to behaviorists, we do not have thoughts or images, but we do think and imagine. Further, behavior is considered as significant in itself; a behaviorist does not treat what we do as the result of some underlying mechanism, such as biological centers or repressed wishes.

Beschreibung Name given to the method of studying conscious experience used by Wundt. Carefully trained observers verbally report their "content" of consciousness when presented with simple forms of stimulation. The same method was used by many other early psychologists, although it dropped from favor after Külpe showed its grave limitations.

Complication Term used by many early psychologists to refer to compound associations made of elements from different senses. A cold, wet stone is an instance of complication, including visual, tactile, and thermal elements.

Context theory Explanation of perception and meaning proposed by Berkeley and adopted by others—notably by Titchener, in his core/context theory. Percepts are reducible to a context of elements; distance is a combination of sensations from the eye muscles and the limbs. Meaning is no more than the context of associated ideas connected to a core.

Dynamics Activities and processes (as opposed to statics, which are images, ideas, motives, and so on).

Einstellung The effect of preparation, expectancy, or "set" on the performance of mental and manual activities. *Einstellung* was first stressed by Külpe and the Würzburg School.

Empiricism The doctrine that holds that all knowledge comes from the senses—that we are born with senses but with no innate ideas.

Epistemology The study of the nature and origin of knowledge. The history of psychology is linked with the history of epistemology.

Fusion Wundt's law of association referring to compounds not analyzable to elements.

Functionalism One of the schools of psychology prevalent at the turn of the century. The functionalists stressed adaptive activity rather than the analysis of consciousness into static elements, as practiced by the structuralists.

Introspection Name given to the practice of examining one's consciousness.

Mental chemistry Name given by John Stuart Mill to his theory of association. Mill believed that ideas combine as do chemicals, so that the whole is not simply the sum of the parts. (See *Fusion*.)

Phenomenology What one takes to be the nature of one's own experience. For Titchener this was the sensation, image, and affect; for the Gestaltists it was the structured whole. Phenomenology also has a more technical meaning, referring to philosophies that stress immediate experience and that reject the representative theory of perception.

Psychic resultants One of three main forms of order in mental life proposed by Wundt. Psychic resultants are those forms of association in which the sum of the elements is less than the whole. The laws of fusion, assimilation, and complication are examples.

Rationalism The belief that we are born with innate knowledge or powers of reason that allow us to recognize truth.

Sensation The experience or quality produced by a sensory nerve. Some psychologists, including Titchener, consider the basic irreducible or unanalyzable qualities of sensation to be the basic elements of experience.

Similarity Basic principle of association used by many empiricists. Similarity is often defined in terms of shared elements; thus, an apple is more similar to an orange than to an automobile. In most cases, we are unable to explain perceived similarity.

Statics As used here, the view that psychological phenomena are best cast in terms of things, such as images, ideas, and motives, rather than in terms of activities. (See *Dynamics*.)

Stimulus error Term coined by Titchener to refer to faulty introspection. If a subject describes experience in terms of what he or she believes to be the stimulus for the experience, that person has committed the stimulus error. For example, we may describe a table seen from an angle as rectangular, although the sensation we experience shows it to be trapezoidal.

Structuralism Name given by Titchener to his school of psychology. He believed that the first priority was the analysis of the structure of consciousness through the method of introspection.

Successive associations James Mill's term for sensations and ideas that are connected because they occurred in the past in close temporal order. (Thus, he meant association by contiguity in time.)

Synchronous associations James Mill's term for sensations and ideas that are connected because they occurred previously at the same time. Such things are often objects, since an object provides a set of sensations simultaneously.

Unconscious inference Helmholtz argued that we form expectancies about the commonplace world and that we have no idea this is occurring. We see objects in the distance and it seems that we immediately "see" the distance; actually, we are relying on cues coming from eye muscles and from our past experience of distant objects to guide us. However, such sensations become so habitual that we do not notice them.

RECOMMENDED READINGS

Boring, E. G. (1950). *A history of experimental psychology*. (2nd ed.). New York: Appleton.

    This is an authoritative, though difficult, text. This source is referred to frequently in other history and systems texts.

Herrnstein, R. J., & Boring, E. G. (1973). *A source book in the history of psychology*. Cambridge: Harvard University Press.

    This text provides a set of excerpts from 116 historical sources, ranging from the early Greeks to the early twentieth century.

Robinson, D. N. (1976). *An intellectual history of psychology*. New York: Macmillan.

    This is an interesting and scholarly tracing of the history of psychological thought and of the social conditions throughout that history.

Chapter 2

E. L. THORNDIKE: THE ORIGINAL CONNECTIONISM

BIOGRAPHY

Edward Lee Thorndike was born in Williamsburg, Massachusetts in 1874, the son of a Methodist minister (see Figure 2.1). He attended Wesleyan University as an undergraduate, then studied at Harvard, where he obtained a second bachelor's degree and a master's degree. During this time, he took a course with William James, the most eminent of American psychologists, which led him to concentrate his efforts in psychology rather than English. Before finishing a doctorate, he was attracted to Columbia University, where he obtained his Ph.D. in 1898 under the famous hereditarian and mental tester James M. Cattell. After a year on the faculty at Case Western Reserve, he joined the faculty of Teachers College, associated with Columbia University, where he spent the remainder of his 43-year academic career.

Thorndike's dissertation was published as a monograph, *Animal Intelligence*, in 1898. It included the essential aspects of his connectionism, emphasizing the importance of trial and error (or success and error) in the performing of seemingly insightful acts. Thorndike published more than 450 articles, books, and monographs during his career; the following are some of the more influential pieces:

"Transfer of Training: The Influence of Improvement in One Mental Function upon the Efficiency of Other Functions," 1901 (with R. S. Woodworth)

Educational Psychology, 1903 (first of several editions)

An Introduction to the Theory of Mental and Social Measurements, 1904

The Psychology of Wants, Interests, and Attitudes, 1935

Selected Writings From a Connectionist's Psychology, 1949

Thorndike has had a tremendous influence in psychology and in education, in part because of

FIGURE 2.1   Edward L. Thorndike, 1874–1949.
Photo courtesy of the Archives of the History of American Psychology

his extraordinary productivity. More than any other figure of his time, he argued that psychology could not remain solely concerned with the analysis of consciousness. He claimed that if we treat mind as a part of nature, we find that our thoughts, attitudes, and wants depend upon the same factors that determine behavior in general. His proposal was the first serious alternative to the mentalism of the time.

INTRODUCTION

Section 1 of this chapter discusses the significance of Thorndike's early work for the psychology of

that time. Thorndike was the first to question the view of what has been common sense for thousands of years. His alternative altered the course of education and laid the groundwork for many current ideas.

Section 2 presents his theory of learning, derived from the famous early experiments he carried out with animals. His results were surprising, and, as Tolman said much later, they led to a theory of learning that influenced psychologists for more than a half a century: Later theories could be classified according to whether they agreed or disagreed with Thorndike. This was quite an accomplishment for a 24-year-old psychologist.

Section 3 considers some of the most frequent criticisms of his views, both present and past. If he did truly revolutionize thinking, then one must expect criticisms from those who held to the displaced ways of looking at things as well as from those who questioned the value of his alternative.

In 1923, President Coffman of the University of Minnesota said, "There are only two schools of psychology, one of them is Thorndike's and the other one isn't" (Joncich, 1968). What was it about Thorndike's theories that so strongly (and so rapidly) affected psychology?

1. THE SIGNIFICANCE OF THORNDIKE'S EARLY WORK

Mentalism

Mentalism is the ancient belief that our actions are caused by mental processes; these include our thoughts, hopes, expectations, and so on. Before Thorndike, almost everyone accepted this view; most people still do. We are brought up as mentalists, and it may seem odd that anyone would question such a view.

We all feel that our experience is in large part a private affair. We have ideas, passing thoughts, and daydreams. We feel emotions, urges, pleasures, and pains. This private experience seems totally different from our comings and goings,

TABLE 2.1 Mentalism versus Thorndike's Alternative View

Mentalism

Antecedent Conditions   →   Mental Events
(situation, past history,   (ideas, thoughts,
health, physiological   feelings, and so on)
state, and so on)   ↓

                            Observable Behavior
                            (walking, talking,
                            and so on)

Thorndike's Alternative

Antecedent Conditions   Mental Events

                            Observable Behavior

---

our walking and talking, and the rest of our activity that is open for others to see. It also seems that our outward behavior is often *caused* by private (mental) events. For example, you mentally plan to speak, walk, write, or strike out at someone, and the act follows, unless you mentally decide not to do it. When you find yourself "at a loss for words," you might stop and try to privately recapture your train of thought. Your own experience is yours alone; for the most part, your hopes, dreams, sufferings, and joys can be known to others only if you choose to communicate them. I often find this to be very difficult; private experience is not easily verbalized. One of the marks of great literature, music, and art is its success in communicating such feelings.

The unique nature of private experience is taken for granted by all of us; given our education by society, it is not surprising. This way of looking at things has been common in western society for a great many centuries. The seventeenth-century philosopher Descartes is credited with making the case for the distinction between mind and body, but the belief that our mental and physical aspects are fundamentally different in kind was popular long before. The philosophers of the eighteenth and nineteenth centuries argued that all that we can know are our personal mental activities (see Chapter 1), and it was therefore natural that the earliest psychologists in the late nineteenth century should see their task exclusively as the analysis of consciousness. Given the assumption that our actions depend upon our mental states, it follows that an understanding of these mental states must precede an understanding of our actions.

Mentalism is this doctrine, which holds that the mind is imprisoned in the body and that our actions depend in part upon mental causes. We cry because of (mental) sadness, we solve problems with (mental) reasoning, we attack because of (mental) anger, we recall past experiences because of (mental) memory powers, and so on. All of these causes originate in the mind. The terrible problem with this view is that it leaves sadness, reasoning, anger, and memory unexplained. Instead, we merely begin with some activity, such as recalling the past, and we simply rename it *memory*. In so doing, we neglect the causes of recalling or memory and are no further ahead in an understanding of how we seem to recall the past.

The Alternative to Mentalism

Criticizing mentalism often is seen as suggesting that we have no private experience—no thoughts, dreams, expectations, or memories. This, of course, would be absurd, and, despite rumors to the contrary, no one has ever seriously suggested this. However, some psychologists have denied that the mind is separate from the body and that the mind somehow influences physical processes in the body.

What if we broaden the definition of activity to suggest more than the movement of muscles and the secretion of glands? What if we treat our mental life as part of what we do? As we rise in the morning, work, walk, and talk, we also think, hear, see, and dream. If rising, working, walking, talking, thinking, seeing, hearing, and dreaming are all activities in which we engage, then we can seek out the factors that influence each of these activities. We already know something of the factors that influence overt behavior; could we also train creative thinking, alter moods and attitudes, and improve other mental activities?

Much of western philosophy, as well as common sense, opposes such a possibility; the chasm separating thought and action seems unbreachable. At the turn of the century we seemed limited forever to the analysis of consciousness for its own sake. Indeed this practice had even been extended to the study of consciousness in animals; such "introspection by analogy" had been advocated by both Romanes and Lloyd-Morgan (see Chapter 1). Thorndike believed that mental processes could be treated as part of what we do; thus, he believed that they can be altered just as our outward behavior can be altered. And much of what we do can be explained without the need to refer to mental processes; often, none are present. It was largely Thorndike's influence during half a century that kept this view alive. As he put it, the same general laws of human behavior explain why a student puts his clothes on or takes them off, whether he eats his breakfast, and whether he succeeds or fails in solving a geometry problem (Thorndike, 1917). And awareness is certainly not necessary for learning to occur:

> We should, of course, make the situation identifiable and the response available when it is practicable to do so. Unconscious learning is relatively undependable and slow. But it is not magical or fortuitous. (Thorndike, 1935, p. 70)

2. BASICS OF THORNDIKE'S THEORY

Thorndike's research began with observations of cats learning to escape from 27 problem boxes. He evaluated the results based on his doctrine of the *law of effect*, which held that responses were connected to or disconnected from situations depending on the effect produced by the response. He concluded that the law of effect was sufficient to account for the learning that occurred in the puzzle boxes. That is, some of the cats' behaviors were selected by *satisfiers*, which stamped in connections between situations and behaviors (for example, *sight of string—pull*). Other consequences —*annoyers*—stamped out connections (for example, *sight of wood slats—squeeze through*). Thorndike used the terms *stamping in* and *stamping out* to describe the strengthening or weakening of a stimulus-response (S-R) association.

The question at once arose concerning what makes an event satisfying or annoying. Defining *satisfaction* and *annoyance* is more difficult than one might think, and Thorndike spent a good deal of time wrestling with this problem. He explained some cases of satisfaction and annoyance as due to heredity, such as when an opportunity to rest acts as a satisfier for a weary organism. But what of all the countless cases that cannot possibly be genetically determined? How do praise and money come to act as satisfiers?

This question led Thorndike to a behavioral definition of *satisfaction* and *annoyance* as situations that the organism "does nothing to avoid" or that it does actively avoid. Ultimately, Thorndike relied on the *law of readiness* to explain the action of satisfiers and annoyers and thus to explain the law of effect. By *readiness*, Thorndike meant that the effect of a consequence depends on what an individual is doing when the consequence occurs.

The weakness of the law of effect lies in the difficulty in explaining why (and when) satisfiers and annoyers act as they do. Its strength lies in the fact that it is still immensely useful, even when we are uncertain when and why a given consequence satisfies or annoys. It also forces us to be specific in dealing with problems of education and it gives us a way of avoiding the problems of mentalism.

The Problem Box: Selecting and Connecting

Thorndike's research topic for his thesis at Harvard concerned mind reading in children (Thorndike, 1936). This amounted to a study of the method used by professional mind readers of the day, who were skilled in extracting information from the facial expressions of their subjects as they were asked questions. The topic was unacceptable to the Harvard authorities, who suggested that he do a study of mentality in chickens. (Recall that the analysis of consciousness was extended to animals during the late nineteenth century.) Thorndike obtained the chickens but was unable to progress far in his work because the university had no space suitable for fowls, and, after a series of difficulties, he left Harvard for Columbia. He arrived in New York City in 1897 with a basket containing "the two most educated hens in the world."

Thorndike studied the behavior of chickens in mazes, which he formed using books placed on end. This research as well as research with several other types of animals, particularly cats, led to the 1898 publication of his famous monograph, *Animal Intelligence*, in which he focused on the behavior of cats in *problem boxes*. This work had an immense impact on subsequent psychological views and contained the essence of what would be Thorndike's views for the rest of his long career. Through this work, Thorndike developed his theory of *selecting and connecting*, which describes how satisfiers select a response and connect it to the situation accompanying that response.

Thorndike's subjects were stray cats, which he caught in the alleys near Columbia University. A captured cat soon found itself in the problem box, made of slats of wood, with no exit in sight. The cat typically nosed about exploring the box, reached through the slats with its paws, bit at whatever allowed biting, but remained imprisoned in the box.

Just as it seemed that there was no escape, its paw caught on a loop of string hanging from the ceiling, and the door of the box opened. In other versions of the 27 boxes Thorndike used, the escape trigger may have been a panel on the floor, a lever on the wall, or some aspect of the cat's own behavior (such as scratching its ear with its paw) that led to the opening of the door. Soon after escaping, the cat found itself back in the

box. The question is, did the problem box then pose a problem for the cat to solve? The cat had the solution and now had only to apply it. If, by chance, it did not notice the connection between string pulling and escape during the first trial, surely another trial or two should be enough to make the connection clear to any but the densest cat. Within two or three trials the cat should be escaping at will.

The results were otherwise. A hungry cat placed in the problem box often made its first escape within several minutes, but the second, third, fourth, fifth, sixth, and later escapes showed little evidence that the cat had any insight into the nature of the problem. In a typical sequence of escapes, cat number twelve in box A made its first escape after two minutes and 40 seconds and the second escape after only 30 seconds. But the third escape required a minute and a half and the subsequent escapes took 60, 15, 28, 20, 30, and 22 seconds. After more than twenty trials, the cat was routinely escaping within six to eight seconds, but it was impossible to point to any one instant at which the cat had "gotten the idea." Figure 2.2 plots the escape time per trial for cat number twelve.

Long before these experiments—and today, long after they were done—psychologists had argued about the nature of learning: Does learning occur slowly and mechanically or rapidly, showing insight? Adams (1929) later reported that cats escape from problem boxes far more intelligently and rapidly than Thorndike reported. At least, Adams interpreted his cats' behavior as being more intelligent. He said that his cats attended closely to the important parts of the escape mechanism—a string loop hanging from the ceiling, which lifted a bolt holding the door, which was then pulled open by a rubber band. But, as Woodworth (1938) later noted, some of Adams's cats never escaped and others took far longer to escape than did Thorndike's cats.

The data presented in *Animal Intelligence* (1898), however, portrayed only animal stupidity, rather than insightful, intelligent behavior. It

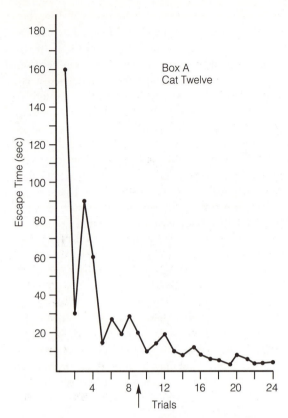

FIGURE 2.2 Results of Thorndike's problem box experiment for one subject, cat number twelve. The cat's escape time diminished over 24 trials, but at no point did the cat seem to gain insight into the problem solution. *From Thorndike, 1898*

seemed to Thorndike that these animals that had every opportunity for intelligent action and insightful solutions showed only the slow improvement that one would expect if the consequences of actions were slowly stamping in some behaviors and stamping out others. In the early trials, the animals reacted with the inherited behaviors that one would expect to be shown by a member of that species suddenly finding itself in confinement. Each response followed by escape and food became somewhat more likely to occur on the next trial, whereas the behaviors accompanied by continued confinement became less likely.

The Law of Effect

The cats' behavior depended on the consequences of past behavior: Responses that led to escape became more likely on the next trial, and those responses that did not lead to escape became progressively less likely. This principle, the law of effect, seems at first sight the most trivial piece of common knowledge imaginable; surely it has been known for many millennia that our acts are affected by their consequences. We humans do not endlessly touch hot stoves, and we do all manner of things for money, praise, and other such consequences.

But what Thorndike pointed out was that the consequences of action account for far more than had been previously suspected; if the law of effect can account for problem solving in cats, why can't it account for problem solving in humans? How much of our behavior and experience depends upon the consequences that have followed them in the past? Can the law of effect account for our comings and goings, our reasonings and imaginings, our attitudes and interests? Thorndike believed that it could, and, in many of the books and articles he published during his career, he tried to show how the law of effect might account for human behavior. Table 2.2 gives some examples.

The law of effect has proved immensely useful during this century, having been successfully applied in teaching, psychotherapy, and even in the training of creativity. But it has its limits as an explanation for all of our behavior and experience. These limits become clear when we consider the nature of satisfiers and annoyers.

If we do not understand how satisfiers and annoyers work, then we cannot predict what will act as a satisfier or as an annoyer. This means that we may have to apply a consequence, note the effect that it has on the frequency of the behavior that preceded it, and then classify it as either a satisfier or an annoyer. Do we really have to do that? Surely we can discover some way to predict whether an event will act as a satisfier or as an annoyer.

TABLE 2.2 Ways in Which the Law of Effect Might Operate in Determining Attitudes, Interests, and Traits

Simple Arithmetic Knowledge

Stimulus:	A teacher asks, "What is eight plus six?"
Response:	A student answers, "Fourteen."
Consequence:	Approval from teacher.
S-R connection:	8 + 6 = 14

Attitudes

Stimulus:	Relatives ask for an opinion on the issue of labor unions.
Response:	"Labor unions damage the economy."
Consequence:	Approval and agreement from listeners.
S-R connection:	Labor unions are bad (example of an antilabor attitude).

Interests

Stimulus:	Someone is presented with paper and pencil.
Response:	The person draws pictures of landscapes.
Consequence:	Approval, admiration from parents and friends.
S-R connection:	The connection is between drawing materials and drawing landscapes (or interest in drawing, desire for drawing materials).

Trait of Perseverance and Effort

Stimulus:	A difficult puzzle or other problem is presented.
Response:	A person displays persistent effort to solve it.
Consequence:	Praise from others.
S-R connection:	The connection is between challenging situations and effort.

Trait of Creativity

Stimulus:	A problem is stated verbally.
Response:	A person gives an unusual answer.
Consequence:	Criticism, repetition of problem.
S-R connection:	A connection forms between verbally stated problems and conventional solutions (or stifled creativity, conformity).

Trait of Aggressiveness

Stimulus:	A schoolmate has an attractive toy.
Response:	A child takes the toy by force.
Consequence:	Possession of the toy.
S-R connection:	A connection forms between others' attractive possessions and taking them (bullying).

Seeing Clearly ("Fidelity of Visual Images")

Stimulus:	A person moving within the immediate environment.
Response:	He or she notices the environment and focuses appropriately.
Consequence:	Moving without bumping into things.
S-R connection:	The connection is between the environment and focusing properly.

Satisfiers and Annoyers: Difficult to Define

In his earliest writings Thorndike used the terms *satisfier* and *annoyer* as if they were synonymous with *pleasure* and *pain*, and many criticisms of the law of effect assume that this is an instance of *hedonism*, the doctrine that all conduct is governed by anticipated pleasures and pains. If one considers the law of effect only in its application to animals' escapes from confinement or their gaining of food, then pleasure and pain seem reasonable attendants.

But when we consider human affairs, such a simple hedonistic interpretation is implausible; after all, the satisfier that Thorndike used most often with people was the word *right*. Thorndike quickly pointed out that the law of effect had no necessary connection with what we usually think of as pleasure and pain. He attempted, with difficulty, to arrive at a proper conception of satisfaction and annoyance.

What do satisfiers have in common? Thorndike began (1913) by suggesting that some states of affairs act as satisfiers owing to heredity. He suggested that for humans such things as being with other humans (especially familiar ones), moving when refreshed, resting when tired, and being partly covered when resting or in bed are innate satisfiers. Innate annoyers include the taste of bitter substances, physical restraint, hunger, being scorned, and the sight of blood and entrails. According to Thorndike, all other desires and aversions grow from these "original" satisfiers and annoyers. (We will return to this topic later in the chapter.)

However, all satisfiers and annoyers are not innately determined; money, praise, and fame have little effect on the behavior of an infant, and Thorndike's list of original satisfiers and annoyers seems to have little bearing on most human behavior. Perhaps satisfiers and annoyers are better defined simply in terms of their effect on behavior; thus:

> By a satisfying state of affairs is meant roughly one which the animal does nothing to avoid, often doing such things as will attain and preserve it. By an annoying state of affairs is meant roughly one which the animal avoids or changes. (1913, p. 2)

But what makes a satisfier a satisfier? What do all of the "states of affairs," which act as satisfiers or as annoyers at a given time, have in common? Thorndike struggled to answer the question by referring to what he called *original behavior series*, a sequence of activities that are determined innately and that constitute satisfaction when completed. When an original behavior series is started and operates successfully, its activities are satisfying, as are the situations they produce.

When he used the term *original*, Thorndike typically meant "hereditary." Thus, he was speaking of sequences of instinctive behaviors, such as pouncing on prey and ingesting food. In an accompanying example, he referred not only to lost food and missed prey, but to a withdrawn toy as examples of interrupted original behavior series. At any rate, the effects of satisfiers and annoyers thus depend on the ongoing behavior series. If the series operates successfully, the results are satisfying. If the series is thwarted, the result is annoyance. The unimpeded completion of an original behavior series is thus referred to as *successful operation*.

The problem remaining is what constitutes successful operation. If we don't know, then we are left with the definition of a satisfier being the successful completion of a behavior series, with *successful operation* meaning "ending with a satisfier"! Thorndike had problems here, as has anyone else who has tried to deal with this problem. Successful operation does not simply mean life furthering and adaptive. (For example, cigarette smoking acts as a satisfier for many people.) Successful operation is finally left as "unimpeded" or "unthwarted" activity. This just means freedom to complete the activities produced by our original nature. Such a conclusion is less than satisfying, however, and the whole matter is translated to the analogy of the neurons; the law of readiness determines when the law of effect works and when it doesn't. Table 2.3 highlights the definition of a satisfier.

TABLE 2.3 What Are Satisfiers and When Do They Work?

Defining Satisfiers

Original Nature (Innate Satisfiers):	Being with familiar humans Moving when refreshed Resting when tired Partial cover when resting And many more
Behavioral Definition:	Things that are not avoided and are often sought and maintained

When Do They Work?

Successful Operation:	A satisfier ends a behavior series "successfully," defined by the law of readiness
Law of Readiness:	Firing of a conduction unit ready to fire, sensitized by units already firing

---

The Law of Readiness

Thorndike's contribution is often summarized as the argument for the widespread application of the law of effect. But his writings usually include two other laws, the law of exercise and the law of readiness. His *law of exercise* refers to his assumption that repetition alone could strengthen a habit. (In 1929 he abandoned this assumption.) His law of readiness was of prime importance to him; it was not, as is often thought, a mere appendage to the law of effect. Readiness specifies the conditions under which effect operates by attempting to define successful operation, those conditions that make a satisfier a satisfier and an annoyer an annoyer.

The law of readiness is cast in terms of the activity of neurons, their readiness to fire and whether they do fire. This readiness is determined by innate factors (original nature). A given situation (for example, the sight of prey or a moving flame) produces firing in some neurons (owing to the seeing) and a readiness to fire in others. The sight of prey thus produces a readiness to chase and seize, and the sight of a flame may produce a readiness to touch. Given a state of readiness, the firing of such a prepared *conduction unit* is satisfying, and the thwarting of it is annoying. A conduction unit that is not ready to fire (unprepared) but that is forced to fire constitutes annoyance (for example, eating your twelfth piece of pizza).

Conduction units aside, we find that Thorndike's law of effect is not the simple formula that critics and some advocates often have supposed it to be. It would be nice if it were possible to choose any behavior or aspect of experience we wish to strengthen and follow its occurrences with food, praise, or another consequence that often acts as a satisfier. But Thorndike, common experience, and a good deal of research tells us that things are just not that simple. The law of readiness says that the effect of a satisfier depends upon preparedness—that is, it depends upon existing, ongoing behavior. Food acts as a satisfier when it is presented in the context of preparatory eating behavior, and praise has an effect only when an individual's behavior is already oriented (prepared) for such a consequence. We now know, for example, that it is immensely difficult to train a pigeon to peck a disk to avoid shock: Pecking is preparatory behavior for eating and not for shock avoidance.

When Is a Satisfier a Satisfier?

It takes little reflection to see that all the things we view as satisfying, as rewards, as payoffs, and as goals have their typical effects only under specific conditions. When we think of them, we usually assume that these conditions prevail, but this often is not the case. For example, food *is* a satisfier, so it can be used to train all sorts of behaviors in all sorts of situations. But the twelfth piece of pizza already referred to has the effect of an annoyer. Ten dollars may be effective as a reward, depending upon whether the customary reward is one or twenty dollars! The effect of praise from a professor may not be the same if it is delivered as you sit in a crowded classroom as opposed to in a personal letter.

In short, the law of effect is not a magic formula, although it may often work so well that it may seem to be. One cannot depend on a given satisfier to increase the frequency of every behavior that it follows under all circumstances. The only safe way to employ the law of effect is to determine what particular consequence acts as a satisfier for the particular behavior of concern to us in particular individuals at the particular time we have in mind.

The Significance of the Law of Effect: Are There General Abilities?

Thorndike's early (and persisting) influence was due to two factors, his amazing rate of publication and the great versatility of his theory of selecting and connecting, especially in comparison with other available theories of the day. The application of the law of effect meant that more attention needed to be paid to the specifics of the teaching and learning process. If learning is the selecting of behaviors and the connecting of them to stimuli or situations, then it is necessary to specify precisely what is to be connected. How does one teach citizenship, mathematics, reading, logic, and so on? Unlike the prevailing mental discipline theories passed on from the nineteenth century, which advocated that mental faculties be exercised as muscles are exercised, Thorndike argued against the possibility of training any such general abilities.

Thorndike argued in his early paper (Thorndike & Woodworth, 1901) that only specifics are selected and connected. The *discipline method* of training memory in general through the forced memorization of poetry was of no help in improving memory in general because there is no memory in general. There are memories for specific classes of things, such as poetry, faces, letters, words, and so on. But practice memorizing per

se does not seem to help us to memorize in general.

Similarly, *attention* is a single word that refers to a host of tendencies. Even attention to words may be restricted to the spelling, length, sounds, or grammatical class (noun, verb, or other) of words. The point is that education should be specific about what is to be learned. For example, educators should consider what is meant by *patriotism*, *understanding of grammar*, and other vague and general goals of education.

All of this argues that many of the terms we use are unsuitable; they either refer to faculties or powers of mind that are, in fact, not single entities (such as memory and attention) or they refer to classes of behavior that also are not unitary things. As Thorndike pointed out in 1913, when we consider ways to deal with anger and aggression, we must distinguish between anger due to restraint, to overcoming an obstacle, to counterattacking, to sudden pain, to combat in rivalry, and to various thwartings, as well as to anger due to other causes. His continual emphasis of specifics, of just what is to be selected and connected, may well be the most important aspect of Thorndike's work.

The specificity of connections established by the law of effect applies to our ideas and experience, as well as to our observable actions. Thorndike illustrated this in a 1933 paper:

> When an animal that runs about seeking food attains it, the strengthening will be more likely to influence the Cs [connections] concerned with its locomotion, its hunger, and its ideas about food and eating than those concerned with contemporaneous casual scratchings of an itching ear, or stray thoughts about Shakespeare's sonnets or Brahms' symphonies. (p. 435)

To complete the picture, the major laws—the laws of readiness, exercise, and effect—must be supplemented by subsidiary laws. These are reasonable principles that were common in nineteenth-century psychology and that appeared in part in Thorndike's early (1900) book, *Human Nature Club*.

Subsidiary Laws

Law of Multiple Response   The first try in learning a new skill or doing a new task is often an inadequate response to a situation and we are forced to keep trying. For example, most of us cannot successfully pronounce the German umlaut sound or do a smooth backstroke or properly swing a baseball bat on the first try. Eventually we do learn and the proper behaviors are selected and connected. But our initial efforts usually are only "the best we can do"; the better of our imperfect efforts are selected either by their natural consequences (for example, we move more smoothly through the water) or by social consequences (for example, we gain approval for our German pronunciation). Our progress in a new situation will therefore depend upon the behaviors we bring with us from the start. This condition describes the law of *multiple response*.

Law of Attitude or Set   Thorndike was well aware of the main findings of the Würzburg School (see Chapter 1) and cited them when he pointed to the importance of set and other terms that refer to the condition of the learner. Selecting and connecting is by no means a simple formula to be carelessly applied to any individual at any time. The effect of a situation depends in great part on the condition of the individual: What instructions has the person been given, and what has his or her experience of the past hour or the past year led the person to expect in a given situation? Is he or she reading for pleasure or because he will be tested in an hour? What effect does twenty years' experience as a poet, a proofreader, a parent, or a minister have on present reactions? Experience acts on individuals prepared in countless ways, and this preparation largely determines the effects of present experience and guides their response in new situations.

Attitudes, *dispositions*, *preadjustments*, and *sets* are synonymous terms that refer to the effects of prior experience and may determine what will act as satisfiers and annoyers. How long has it been since we last ate? Are we throwing a ball for distance or to strike out a batter? Are we running the last mile of a marathon? Consider the following example: A top contender for a boxing title may feel indifferent toward a victory over an opponent which, were we in his place, would be occasion for great rejoicing. In education, the goal is to "set" the student to respond to academic subject matter with enthusiasm, open-mindedness, and a problem-solving attitude. This all reduces to an emphasis of the law of readiness.

Law of Piecemeal Activity   We virtually never respond to all elements of a situation; some aspects act more strongly than others, and we typically react to subtle elements that a dog or cat would never notice. Most elements we ignore.

> [A]ll man's learning and indeed all of his behavior, is *selective*. Man does not, in any useful sense of the words, ever absorb, or represent, or mirror, or copy, a situation uniformly. He never acts like a *tabula rasa*. (Thorndike, 1913, p. 35)

Our responses to words and relations and our insights into new aspects of long familiar situations are constant determinants of what is selected and connected. Our whole past history (and the history of our species) determines which parts of a situation will be connected with some strong response of feeling, thought, or action and which parts will be barely noticed and which will have no effect. The selective nature of perception constitutes the subsidiary law known as *partial or piecemeal activity*.

The selective response in one form is the insight into the essential elements of a situation. For example, attention to the relevant leads the genius to see that electricity, with all of its more conspicuous properties, acts as if it flows. Therefore, it may be treated as a fluid and thus may be stored, channeled, and so on. This belief was held by many scientists, such as Benjamin Franklin. Electricity is not a fluid, nor does it flow. But it appears to, and attention to that aspect of it has proved more useful than the alternative, which is to treat it as magic.

The fact that we do routinely respond to subtle features of situations seems different from the simple conceptions of selecting and connecting. Thus, it seems that selective thinking, responding to abstractions, and attention to relationships is different in kind from the simple formation of habits through selecting and connecting. Thorndike, however, held that this was not the case.

> Man's habits of response to the subtler hidden elements, especially the relations which are embedded or held in solution in gross situations, lead to consequences so different from habits of response to gross total situations or easily abstracted elements of them, that the essential continuity from the latter to the former has been neglected or even denied. Selective thinking, the management of abstractions and responsiveness to relations are thus contrasted too sharply with memory, habit, and association by contiguity. As has been suggested, and as I shall try to prove later, the former also are matters of habit, due to the laws of readiness, exercise and effect, acting under the conditions of human capacity and training, the bonds being in the main with elements or aspects of facts and with symbols therefor. (Thorndike, 1913, pp. 27–28)

Again, Thorndike opposed the belief in *faculties*, or powers of mind, as explanations for our behavior and experience. If selective thinking, the piecemeal response, and insight are treated as part of what we do and as examples of habits no different in kind from our other activities, then we should be able to train selective thinking and insight just as we train other habits. If we propose that such activity depends on some mental power, a faculty of insight, then we gain nothing, having named only what we wish to explain.

Law of Assimilation or Response by Analogy The laws of readiness, exercise, and effect determine what we will do in a given situation; if we find ourselves in a situation that is basically the same as past situations, then we will do what we did in the past. But situations are never precisely repeated. A new situation is simply more or less like previous situations. If we act at all, other than instinctively, we will do what past experience has taught us to do. If a situation is unusual, we will still obey the law of habit and react to it as we did to past novelty.

This is Thorndike's famous principle of transfer by identical elements; he called the principle *response by analogy*. According to Thorndike, we act in a new situation as we did in a past similar situation. In education, this means that the benefits of training may be expected to generalize to similar situations: The more elements shared by the training and the practical situations, the greater the benefit of training. What constitutes similarity is, of course, an immense problem. Very often it is necessary to see how an individual behaves in a new situation before one can say that the person treats it like an old situation.

This further qualifies the apparently simple original notion of selecting and connecting. The laws of readiness, exercise, and effect depend in part on set or attitude, on the fact that only some of the elements in a situation are effective (piecemeal response), and on the similarity of present and past situations, with similarity difficult to define.

Nonetheless, applications of Thorndike's basic principle of selecting and connecting through the action of the law of effect still work quite well. The additional laws do not really muddy things; they simply tell us when and why the law of effect works and when it seems not to work, as well as when learning in one situation will transfer to new situations. The law of effect is not a simple formula that, alone, accounts for all learning.

Law of Associative Shifting *Associative shifting* is a special case of response by analogy, or responding to a new situation as if it were an old one. Associative shifting occurs when the change from the old to the new situation occurs while the old response continues; it thus becomes connected to the newly changed situation. One way in which this occurs takes the form of what was later called classical conditioning. Another way in which it occurs has been called fading.

Let us first look at classical conditioning. Suppose that food in a dog's mouth produces salivation and other food-related behavior. When a new food dish is used, it soon comes to evoke salivation on its own. The dish is presented with the food, which already produces salivation; in Thorndike's view, the response to food and dish generalizes to the dish alone. Just as the dish may come to produce a food-related response, the original responses to worldly goods transfer to the pieces of paper that people use as money. (Thus does the small number of "original" satisfiers grow to the infinite set of adult life.)

In the case of fading, the stimulus complex is gradually changed, slowly enough that the reaction to the original situation is maintained and becomes connected to the new situation. This procedure is now part of the therapy commonly used in the treatment of phobias, or strong fearful reactions to inappropriate stimuli. For example, a patient with a strong spider phobia would be trained to relax in the presence of a therapist, who would then introduce a graded series of spider-like stimuli.

While the patient maintains relaxation behavior, the therapist might present a rubber spider at forty feet, then at twenty feet, then in the patient's lap. The therapist might then progress to presenting real spiders at ever decreasing distances, with successive presentations ordered in such a way that the patient remains relaxed. If properly done, the patient's relaxation (the old response) continues as the situation changes. Through associative shifting, now called systematic desensitization, the behavior of relaxing shifts from spider-absent to spider-present conditions.

Note that the difference between this procedure and the procedure involved in classical conditioning (for example, pairing a dish with food) is only one of degree. In the classical conditioning case, a new stimulus (the dish) is presented in full strength with another stimulus that already produces a given response (food); the situation "food" is changed to the new situation "food plus dish." In the case of fading, the situation is gradually changed.

Thorndike saw associative shifting as the principle that explains how an initially insignificant item, such as a dollar bill or a rejection letter, can become a satisfier or an annoyer. Similarly, other events that may at one time act as satisfiers—such as sports, children's merriment, and daily life— may become annoyers through associative shifting. This could happen if they occur during periods in which we respond to an annoyer, such as continual defeat, the death of a child, or a long illness.

Summary of Subsidiary Laws   The five subsidiary laws make the major laws—readiness, exercise, and effect—reasonable (see Table 2.4). Four of these laws refer to the influence of the individual learner's condition in determining what is learned. The learner comes with a set of behaviors resulting from past training and species membership. The law of multiple response tells us that this repertoire of behaviors is available and that we may expect a varied attack on the problem: When one behavior fails, another from the repertoire will take its place.

Secondly, prior instructions or experience in similar situations which demanded certain behaviors establishes an attitude or set to behave in certain ways. Third, the law of piecemeal response says that only certain aspects of the situation will be attended to, and which aspects these are depends upon the species and the personal history of the learner. If the elements noticed are seen as similar to elements encountered in previous situations, the individual's behavior will tend to be what it was in that earlier situation, according to the law of response by analogy. In addition to the four laws referring to the condition of the subject, conditions outside may cause associative shifting by pairing stimuli that produce weaker and stronger reactions so that the weaker stimulus when later presented alone produces the reaction formerly belonging to the strong stimulus.

Changes in Thorndike's Laws

Experiments done during the early part of the century and some done in the late 1920s with both human and chicken subjects led Thorndike to

TABLE 2.4   Thorndike's Laws

Major Laws (pre-1929)

Law of Readiness:	This law refers to the conditions that determine what will act as satisfiers and annoyers.
Law of Exercise:	Responses are connected to situations simply because they occur frequently in those situations.
Law of Effect:	Responses are selected and connected to situations or are disconnected from situations depending upon the consequences they produce (satisfiers or annoyers).

Subsidiary Laws (referring to the history of the learner)

Law of Multiple Response:	The learner's behavior is not random; rather, he or she comes with a set of responses supplied by heredity or by past experience.
Law of Attitude or Set:	The learner's behavior is influenced by what he or she has been led to expect of a task and its outcome. This may come from instructions or from prior experience.
Law of Piecemeal Activity:	The aspects of a situation that will be noticed depend upon the learner's species membership and past experience.
Law of Response by Analogy:	The learner's behavior will depend in part on the similarity of the present situation to past situations.
Law of Associative Shifting:	A transfer of responses to new stimuli takes place by their pairing with stimuli already connected to those responses.

greatly modify the law of effect and to discard the law of exercise (Thorndike, 1932a).

Exercise or Effect?   Thorndike's long advocacy of the law of exercise was no doubt the product of the strong influence of nineteenth-century psychology, which held that repetition per se was enough to "wear grooves" in the brain and thereby establish habits. Is mere repetition enough, or is the effect accompanying repetition—the consequence produced—also necessary?

Thorndike (1932a) reported the results of a long series of experiments testing the law of exercise, some featuring him as the principal subject. In one experiment a subject (Thorndike) was shown strips of paper, one at a time, and asked to judge the length of each piece as it was shown. The strips varied in length from five inches to eleven inches, with ten instances of each value in quar-

ter-inch steps (5, $5\frac{1}{4}$, $5\frac{1}{2}$, $5\frac{3}{4}$, and so on). The set of 250 strips was shuffled, and the subject made judgments on twenty sittings spanning five days. No feedback concerning the actual length of the strips was ever given.

Thorndike reasoned that frequent judgments of the length of each category of strip should become even more frequent with successive judgments, if the law of exercise is correct. That is, if a strip of whatever length were judged $5\frac{1}{2}$ inches most frequently on the first day, it should be judged to be that length more and more often on the second, third, and subsequent days. What he found, however, was that, although there was some change toward more consistent, stereotyped estimates, it was not clear that those estimates that were frequent during early sessions became the dominant estimates in later sessions.

Another experiment (Experiment 23 of the series) involved the subject hearing a list of 960 words and writing a digit (one to nine) for each word. Subjects were told to try to write the same digit the next time a given word was heard, if they could remember their original response. Some words were repeated 30, 40, 50, or 60 times during the experiment, and Thorndike painstakingly analyzed the responses to determine whether early frequent responses to a word displaced less frequent ones. He concluded that this was not the case.

The best known experiment (Experiment 5) testing the law of exercise was carried out with Thorndike again as the main subject. The task involved drawing lines of specified lengths. Thorndike wrote, "Subject T (the writer), with eyes closed, drew a line to be as nearly as possible 2″ long, then one to be 4″ long, then one to be 6″ long, then one to be 8″ long. This series of four acts he repeated 950 times." Thus, the subject drew 3,800 lines on sheets of paper, twelve lines to a sheet. If the law of exercise were valid, one might expect that the various lines drawn would become more similar in length. Thus, the attempted four-inch lines should not necessarily become any more accurate (closer to four inches long), but those lengths most frequently drawn in the earlier trials should become yet more frequent. Careful analysis convinced Thorndike that this did not occur.

He concluded that the data of the series of experiments "do not give any support to the doctrine that the response which an animal makes oftenest to a maze alley [sic] or puzzle box or a multiple-choice apparatus will thereby gain one iota in the probability of future response." Thus, experiments with human subjects showed that repetition per se cannot explain animal learning! Was Thorndike hasty in abandoning the old law of exercise, the belief that repetition is enough to build habits? Must there always be consequences, whether it be knowledge of results or other satisfiers and annoyers?

We will see that Watson, Guthrie, Tolman, many other psychologists, and the British empirical philosophers (Chapter 1) disagreed with Thorndike's conclusion. A particularly convinc-

ing demonstration of the effect of bare frequency of repetition was provided by Hebb (1961). Hebb's subjects were read nine-digit sequences, presented at a rate of one digit per second. No digit was repeated in a sequence. Subjects were asked to recall the sequence immediately; then the next trial began with a new sequence. Thus, three trials might include sequences like these:

3	9	2	1	7	4	6	5	8
4	9	3	1	8	6	7	5	2
1	6	3	5	2	9	4	8	7

Each subject received 24 trials. One can appreciate the difficulty in recalling the sequences under these conditions. There was no time for rehearsal, and there was maximum interference from preceding sequences since the same digits appeared on each trial but in different order.

In fact, one nine-digit sequence appeared every third trial—a total of eight times. Each other sequence appeared only once. This was largely unnoticed by the subjects, although some reported that there was some repetition in the list; most did not notice even that. Nonetheless, on the last two presentations of the repeated sequence, trials 21 and 24, subjects correctly recalled the sequence more than 60 percent of the time. Other sequences were recalled correctly no more than 20 percent of the time. Melton (1963) confirmed and extended this finding. One must wonder how anything but the law of exercise could explain it.

Estes (1969) carried out simple verbal association experiments, similar to those that Thorndike frequently used, and found that mere contiguous presentation of pairs of items was sufficient to form associations, independent of the law of effect. The law of exercise was sufficient. Table 2.5 provides data from Estes's experiments.

Subjects learned twelve-item lists of letter-digit pairs (for example, LF-26) under two conditions. In one condition, the experimenter presented the stimulus half of the pair (LF) and the subject supplied the response half (26). Then the S-R pair was presented (LS-26). Immediate feedback on the correctness of the response could thus be rea-

TABLE 2.5 Information (Repetition) versus Effect

Group	Mean Trials	Mean Errors
Effect (Feedback)	8.96	45.83
Information (Delay)	7.71	37.79

Estes, 1969

sonably expected to act as a satisfier and to aid the learning of the list. (The group receiving this treatment was known as the effect group.)

A second group (the information group) received quite different treatment. The experimenter presented the stimulus (LF) to the subjects, who made the response (which could have been right or wrong). The subjects in this group received no feedback: There was a pause after the subjects responded and then the next stimulus item appeared; the correct S-R pair was not shown. After going through the whole set of twelve letter-digit pairs, the experimenter presented the set of stimulus and response items while the subject just sat there looking at them. Then another name-the-response-term set of twelve was presented. One would expect that it would take this group far longer to learn the set.

As a matter of fact, all subjects continued until they made one errorless run through the set of twelve letter-digit pairs. When the mean errors were totaled, the information group had made an average of 37.8 errors, and the effect (immediate feedback) group made an average of 45.8 errors! Clearly, the mere presentation of material may be sufficient to learn it, much as Watson, Guthrie, Tolman, and (of course) Estes suggested. This does not mean that the law of effect is invalid; it merely means that it may not be as essential as Thorndike thought it to be.

Does Punishment Work? Thorndike's abandoning of the negative law of effect is similarly open to question. The *negative law of effect* is the portion of Thorndike's classic law that deals with annoyers, or punishers. Until the late 1920s, he had believed the effects of satisfiers and punishers to be about equal but opposite in effect; satisfiers strengthen connections and annoyers weaken them. By 1932 he concluded that annoyers (punishers) do not directly weaken connections. He wrote, "Punishments . . . weaken the connection which produced them, when they do weaken it, by strengthening some competing connection."

Experiment 71 was typical of the research that led to this conclusion and that convinced many educators and psychologists that punishment was not really effective. Thorndike described the experiment, "Nine subjects were given training in choosing the right meaning for a Spanish word from five in a series of two hundred." Responses were rewarded or punished by the experimenter, who announced right or wrong. After twelve or more repetitions of the list, Thorndike analyzed the effects of reward and punishment on the repetition of previous responses. He found that *right* produced a substantial effect on subsequent response choice but that *wrong* did not. In another experiment, subjects learned to match ten behaviors (open mouth wide, pull head back, and so on) with ten patterns drawn on cards. Once again, the effect of being told *right* was substantial, whereas that of *wrong* was "approximately zero."

Experiments with animals seemed to Thorndike to lead to the same conclusion: Punishers do not work in a direction opposite to that of rewards. Thorndike (1932b) reported the most famous of these, in which chicks were given a choice of three paths in a maze. Two led to 30 seconds of confinement, and one led to freedom, food, and company. As was the case in the experiments with human subjects, reward led to increased repetition of the rewarded response, whereas punishment had little effect on subsequent choices.

This conclusion, coming from the inventor and popularizer of the law of effect, was quite a change to propose, especially since they came at a time when Thorndike's views had become almost institutionalized. Yet, he argued that annoyers work only insofar as they produce new responses (or awareness of wrongness) which would then make it possible for satisfiers to act on other behaviors. Thorndike became quite extreme in his opposition to the use of annoyers, charging that the family, the school, and the church had for too long been devising new punishments, even inventing a hell after death to add more.

Thorndike's conclusion was later supported by Skinner (see Chapter 9), whose evidence was similarly meager. Despite the frailty of the evidence, it was widely believed until recently that punishment was ineffective, until overwhelming evidence to the contrary showed that punishers do appear to have a direct weakening effect on behavior. (Chapter 9 discusses these subsequent findings.) This is not to say that punishment does not involve undesirable side effects, nor does it imply that it cannot be misused. It also does not mean that punishers break S-R bonds as Thorndike's early theory had suggested. However, they do seem to work.

3. CRITICISMS OF THORNDIKE'S CONNECTIONISM

When the 24-year-old Thorndike began his professional career in 1898, psychology was almost solely concerned with the analysis of conscious experience. Even John B. Watson, who was soon to do his doctoral thesis on an analysis of conscious processes in the white rat, was not yet an advocate of behaviorism. No one in America had heard of Pavlov, and education consisted largely of the training of mental faculties, such as memory and reasoning.

Thorndike's views were radically different from the prevailing views of the time and from many current views. Over the years his theory has been criticized as too mechanistic, too simple, and/or merely a contemporary version of the ancient doctrine of hedonism, with its emphasis on pleasure and pain as determinants of behavior.

Some of these criticisms apply to any serious attempt to understand the factors that determine our behavior and experience. Some arose because the critics did not fully understand Thorndike's work. Other criticisms arose because of Thorndike's extremely unfortunate choice of the terms *satisfier* and *annoyer*. Although he was not referring to sensory pleasures and pains, it is natural that such terms would be interpreted in that way. Legitimate criticism of Thorndike's position involves his emphasis on S-R connections as the basis for all learning and his emphasis on the law of effect as the key principle in understanding learning.

The Emphasis on Mechanism

It has often been charged that Thorndike's views were too mechanical, that selecting and connecting leaves out the spontaneity we all find in our behavior and experience. The premise of *mechanism* is the assumption that explanations of natural phenomena must not refer to outside agents. This is what is meant by determinism in science. It is absolutely true that Thorndike's was a deterministic view, as was Freud's. But, as a part of nature, human behavior and experience must be as orderly as we find the rest of nature to be. Given that the mind is part of nature, an understanding of what determines its workings is what gives us freedom. As Thorndike said in 1909:

> For, strange as it may sound, man is free only in a world whose every event he can understand and foresee. Only so can he guide it. We are captains of our own souls only so far as they act in perfect law so that we can understand and foresee every response which we will make to every situation. Only so can we control our own selves. (Joncich, 1968)

As discussed in Chapter 1, every scientist must be a mechanist; we have had capricious forces, demons, and magic with us for too long. A controversy about determinism seldom arises except when a particular theorist (such as Watson or Skinner) makes a point of goading the antideterminist forces.

Oversimplifying Behavior and Experience

A related criticism often raised concerns the apparent simplicity of a theory of selecting and connecting, given the great complexity of behavior and experience. William McDougall criticized what he called the "sarbon" theory (S-R bond) in an article published in the 1920s, "The Psychology They Teach in New York" (Joncich, 1968). In his view, connectionism (the sarbon theory) was a "theory of morons, by morons, and for morons." Such critics have persisted over the years and very likely arise because the most basic premise of connectionism can be stated in an overly simple way: Connectionism is the formation of S-R bonds, selecting and connecting by the law of effect.

Any other theory, if stated in terms of its most basic assumptions, also would seem overly simple, whether the theory be Freud's, Piaget's, or anyone's. Over the years, connectionism has been presented in the form of a bare-bones caricature, a never-failing simple formula expressed in terms of stimuli, responses, and consequences. And that is often followed by criticisms of the theory as if the caricature were all that need be mentioned.

But what *is* the "sarbon theory"? Does it require that we be able to take any individual, present what we call a stimulus, reward whatever behavior occurs with food, money, praise, or another arbitrary satisfier, and then rest assured that the behavior and the stimulus have been connected? This is hardly what Thorndike meant. In reality, an individual comes to a situation with a variety of response tendencies (including ideas) as the result of previous experiences: Behavior is in no sense random. The individual brings attitudes, dispositions, and preadjustments depending upon prior instructions, bodily states, and other factors, including prior experience in such situations. All aspects of the situation are not equally effective; prior experience and species membership mean that some clues will be noticed and that others will be ignored (perhaps including what we are calling the stimulus). Finally, the

more a new situation resembles those encountered in the past, the more similar will be the individual's behavior to that shown in the past. In addition to all of this, selecting and connecting will occur only if the intended satisfier is on that occasion a satisfier. Recall the law of readiness: No event is a satisfier or an annoyer for all organisms at all times.

Note that the modifying conditions mentioned in the preceding paragraphs paraphrase Thorndike's subsidiary laws, which were clearly discernible in his earliest writings, such as *Human Nature Club*, 1900. But critics often failed to notice this, preferring to attack the caricature. One of the most famous early critics was Wolfgang Köhler, whose evidence for insight in apes has often been cited as evidence against Thorndike's theories.

Insight versus Trial and Error

The Gestalt psychologist Wolfgang Köhler (see Figure 2.3) spent the years from 1913 to 1920 as director of the German primate research center on the island of Tenerife, in the Canary Islands off the west coast of Africa. He was impressed with what seemed to be insightful problem solving by chimpanzees, and in 1925 his classic observations were published, translated as *The Mentality of Apes*.

In evaluating Köhler's findings, it is important to note that he had little knowledge of the learning theories of the time, including Thorndike's. He interpreted Thorndike's trial and error learning as no more than random and blind fumbling, with consequences mechanically stamping in S-R connections. We have seen that this is not a fair characterization of Thorndike's views, but Köhler was not alone in believing that it was.

Gestaltists, such as Köhler, believe that problem solving, perceiving, learning, and thinking require viewing relevant parts of the environment in a particular way. The Gestaltists stressed insight, rather than trial and error, in learning. *Insight*, as Köhler defined it in 1925, is "the appearance of a complete solution with reference

FIGURE 2.3 Wolfgang Köhler, 1887–1967. Kohler played a key role in the development of Gestalt psychology. Köhler's work stressed the role of insight in learning. *Photo courtesy of Clark University Press*

task," and "the crude stupidities arising from habit." The latter errors were extremely annoying. "It almost makes one angry."

The most famous example of insight was the retrieval of a banana hanging from the ceiling and reachable by stacking boxes underneath and climbing them. Chimpanzees were never very good at stacking two boxes, and, when they managed to do so, it was often without regard for the location of the banana! However, they were able to use a single box as a jumping platform to retrieve the banana, although only one chimpanzee, Sultan, did so without assistance. Others required demonstrations or the placement of the box under the banana before insight occurred.

We all know what it feels like to experience insight, to see things in a new way that changes things and essentially solves a problem. But is the occurrence of such rapid problem solving really damaging to Thorndike's theory? Consider the laws of selective attention, set, and response by analogy in cases of insight. Isn't it true that insight is aided when past experiences have taught us to attend to certain features of situations and to see them in new problem situations? Köhler later essentially agreed with this; he suggested that past experience helps us learn to pay attention to important features of current fields (1959). Harry Harlow showed how this might occur.

Harlow, Learning Set, and Insight

Harlow, Gluck, & Suomi (1972) reported an interesting history of the discovery of the phenomenon of *learning set*, or the "learning to learn" to efficiently solve different problems of the same class. In 1940, Harlow spent a year as a student at Columbia University and attended a seminar held by the great neurologist, Kurt Goldstein. Goldstein is known for his emphasis on the distinction between concrete and abstract thought and for his belief that only humans (with intact frontal lobes) have the capacity for abstract thought.

To demonstrate that one is capable of abstract thought, one must be able to verbalize space, set

to the whole layout of the field." Let us look more closely to see what Köhler meant by this.

Consider a typical problem, in which two sticks may be joined and a piece of fruit may then be retrieved from outside the bars of a cage. In another situation, an obstructing box must be moved before the subject can reach a banana. A typical chimpanzee exhibited plenty of behaviors described as "crude stupidities," but the moment of insight eventually came. In one case, Köhler wrote that "it did not dawn on Tschego for hours to push the obstructing box out of the way."

Köhler believed that his animals' errors could be characterized as "good errors," "errors caused by lack of comprehension of the conditions of the a clock, and perform other tasks. But the most basic test for abstract thought was held to be the ability to solve the Weigl problem. This problem requires a conditional discrimination and may be illustrated with a simple version consisting of two cubes and a sphere. The sphere and one cube are white, the remaining cube is black.

The subject is asked to indicate which two objects are similar, which could be answered in terms of shape or brightness. Once the response is made, the subject is asked to specify another way of grouping them. Soldiers suffering battlefield wounds to the fronts of their heads were not capable of solving the Weigl problem and thus had lost the capacity for abstract thought.

Harlow saw the test as a challenge and set out to train rhesus monkeys and chimpanzees to solve the Weigl problem. He cheerfully conceded that they had a difficult time of it, but eventually, after posing problem after problem in a stepwise fashion, they did solve it, thereby demonstrating "abstract thought." Harlow was shocked and surprised to find that most psychologists did not care. "At least Goldstein cared," he thought. But, Goldstein aside, the discovery of learning sets seemed to solve an old problem.

Rather than interpret learning as a series of insights or as the simplified version of S-R theory that Köhler attacked, Harlow (1949) stressed the importance of learning produced by repeated exposure to problems of the same class. As he wrote:

> Our emotional, personal, and intellectual characteristics are not the mere algebraic summation of a near infinity of stimulus-response bonds. The learning of primary importance to the primates, at least, is the formation of learning sets; it is the learning how to learn efficiently in the situations the animal frequently encounters. This learning to learn transforms the creature from a creature that adapts to a changing environment by trial and error to one that adapts by seeming hypothesis and insight. (Harlow, 1949, p. 52)

The stimulus-response view he criticized was Hull's, which was popular at the time, and the "learning to learn" is the way in which insight is learned. In typical demonstrations of learning set, monkeys were presented with two stimulus objects placed over food wells. Stimulus objects could differ in shape, color, size, and other ways, and the correct stimulus could appear on the right or the left. Suppose that such a problem were presented over 50 trials and then 31 other problems (that is, each with two different stimuli) were presented successively over 50 trials each. Then 200 more problems were presented for six trials each and a final 112 problems were presented for an average of nine trials each. Figure 2.4 shows the percent of correct responses averaged over eight monkeys on the first six trials of each problem, with problems grouped in blocks varying from eight to 100. The lower curve shows the slow improvement in the initial problems; this suggests a slow trial and error process. But the last block of problems shows nearly perfect performance by the second trial. Is this "sudden solution" what is meant by *insight?* Köhler (1959) agreed that learning set may demonstrate the learning of insight. Perhaps close examination will show other cognitive processes to be the products of learning, as Thorndike suggested long ago.

Linking the Law of Effect with Hedonism

Thorndike's choice of the terms *satisfier* and *annoyer* was an extremely unfortunate one. As pointed out earlier in this chapter, he was aware that the action of consequences does not depend upon sensory pleasures and pains. Because of the belief that pleasure and pain are what he meant by satisfaction and annoyance, many critics (Chapter 4) have dismissed what they called the "law of *affect.*" John B. Watson criticized the law of effect because he felt that affect (such as pleasure) was unnecessary for learning to take place. Others criticized it because it is so obvious that the bulk of our activity is not regulated by immediate pleasures and pains.

The point here is that the mistaken belief that Thorndike believed that satisfiers and annoyers must be pleasant and painful led to the perform-

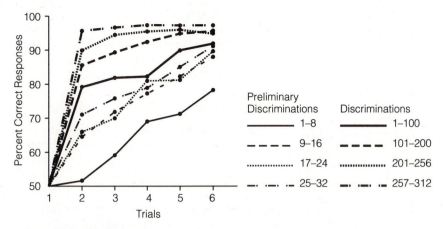

FIGURE 2.4   Data from Harlow's (1949) experiments demonstrating learning set and insight with rhesus monkeys

ing of unnecessary experiments to refute an assumption that was never made. It was inevitable, though, that Thorndike's use of the common terms *satisfier* and *annoyer* would lead to the conclusion that the law of effect was a shallow hedonism.

More Serious Criticisms

More serious are the critics who point to the deficiencies of any S-R psychology in adequately dealing with any behavior, except the most trivial. Is the world really representable in terms of discrete stimuli? Is all of our behavior and experience really represented fully by the letter "R"? Are all of the ways in which the world affects us really captured in Thorndike's laws?

Perhaps the really vulnerable part of Thorndike's theory is the emphasis placed on the law of effect. We will see that Guthrie and Watson disputed the very necessity of the law of effect, and Tolman assigned no great importance to it. And the experiments of Hebb (1961) and Estes (1969), described above, surely show that the law of effect is not necessary for learning.

But we must remember that Thorndike was truly a pioneer who was trying to provide an alternative to the views of the introspectionists in psychology and to the educators who favored the discipline method of training faculties. The law of effect seemed to offer such an alternative. Important as the law may be, it is clear that he overestimated its importance.

Even though he overstated the importance of the law of effect, Thorndike accomplished a great deal. He pointed out that animals are not as complex and mysterious as had been supposed: Much of what people and other animals do is really determined by simple factors. At the time, his news was startling, but we have probably accepted so much of Thorndike's original message into our ways of thinking that we even might wonder why he troubled to bring it to us.

4. OTHER ASPECTS OF THORNDIKE'S WORK

This book is concerned with the psychology of learning and Thorndike is thus of interest because of the impact that his views had on learning theory. But Thorndike applied the same basic point of view to a variety of other areas, from mental testing to the writing of schoolbooks and dictionaries to the testing of aptitudes and the scaling of wants and interests. The remainder of this chapter discusses how Thorndike's views influenced other areas of interest to him.

Books and Other Publications

During his 43-year career and his 10 years of retirement Thorndike published some 450 books, articles, and monographs. His *Arithmetics*, in which he tried to substitute what was known of the psychology of learning for the rote drill of previous books, sold in the neighborhood of five million copies in the 1920s. The *Thorndike Century Junior Dictionary*, published in 1935, sold approximately a million copies by 1940. Needless to say, the royalties from these and other books eased the hardships of the depression for the Thorndikes.

Education: Nature versus Nurture

Thorndike's career was spent at Teachers College of Columbia University, an institution devoted to the training of teachers. Yet, Thorndike's attitudes toward teaching were not what one would expect. He felt that his own education, especially at Wesleyan, would have been improved if unlimited cuts had been allowed; as it was, he spent his time in class at the back of the room doing other things. He was not known as an exceptionally good teacher himself and he often commented that courses were generally a waste of time for all concerned. If this was the case, why the emphasis on proper methods of teaching, on selecting and connecting?

For Thorndike (e.g., 1898), the "most and the best" learning comes from reading books and doing things for oneself, rather than from hearing lectures. This being the case, Thorndike frequently used his lecture notes from a new course as the basis for a textbook, so that future students could rely on his printed words rather than on his less reliable spoken words.

Because of the crudeness of the distinction between environmentalists and hereditarians, Thorndike is often presented as an extreme environmentalist, stressing the importance of experience, rather than heredity, in learning. This seems natural, since his connectionism seems to imply that experience may mold us into infinite forms, depending on what connections are formed. In fact, however, Thorndike viewed the power of education as severely limited by innate endowment; the laws of his connectionism work within the bounds of some 80 percent domination by heredity! This view was apparent early in his career, as it was in the first volume of his *Educational Psychology* (1913), in which he said:

> The physician should know whether original nature lets a child eat too much and chew it not enough; the criminologist should know the relative shares of nature and nurture in the production of assault or theft. (p. 41)

Later, after examining data from 409 pairs of brothers, he said: "The more one looks, the more one is confronted by failures of the environment to do what is expected of it" (Thorndike, 1942, p. 87).

Despite the limits which Thorndike felt were imposed by heredity, society expects its children to be educated, Thorndike noted. The principles of connectionism still provide the best guide for achieving this, although one should not expect too much of any method.

Wants, Interests, and Attitudes

In 1949, the last year of his life, Thorndike wrote that *The Psychology of Wants, Interests, and Attitudes* (1935) was one of his best works. He undoubtedly felt that he had applied the methods of science to a particularly difficult area. Here are some examples of the studies he discussed.

Thorndike showed that interest in learning some facts is greater than that in learning others. For example, subjects learn birth dates of eminent people better than those of nonentities. The truth of a fact makes little difference in whether it is easily learned. Learners remember false birth dates of eminent people, false meanings of rare words, and false biographies of historical figures as well (or better than) they learn the truth, even if they know from the start that what they are learning is untrue.

Other studies (Thorndike, 1949) consisted of questionnaires assessing valuations placed on various activities or events. For example, in one

TABLE 2.6   The following question was asked of 60 employed and 39 unemployed professionals: "For how much money would you suffer each of the following?" Their answers are shown in dollar figures below.

Hardship	Employed	Unemployed
Have one upper front tooth pulled	$ 5,000	$ 4,500
Have all the hair of your eyebrows fall out	100,000	25,000
Become unable to smell	300,000	150,000
Fall into a trance or hibernating state throughout March of every year	400,000	200,000
Be temporarily insane throughout July of every year (would have to be put in an insane asylum)	No Sum	2,500,000
Have nothing to eat but bread, milk, spinach, and yeast cakes for a year	25,000	10,000
Have to live the rest of your life in Boston	100,000	50,000
Spit on a picture of Charles Darwin	20	10
Lose all hope of life after death	6,500	50
Eat a live beetle one inch long	50,000	25,000

Thorndike, 1949, pp. 252–254

study, groups of employed psychologists and unemployed professionals were asked to rate the goodness of various activities for a specified individual. In one example, respondents were asked to rate activities that a forty-year-old chemist might engage in during three hours off on a Thursday afternoon. The activities included studying chemistry, reading literature of the Mormon church, writing unsigned defamatory letters to several men about their wives, and teasing the monkeys in the zoo. His subjects had no trouble ranking such activities.

In a similar study, the same two types of groups were asked to put a dollar value on suffering various hardships, including having the hair in their eyebrows fall out; falling into a hibernating state throughout March of every year; being temporarily insane during July of every year; eating a live beetle; having nothing to eat but bread, milk, spinach, and yeast cakes for a year; and losing all hope of life after death. In general, the unemployed professionals were willing to accept

the hardships for much less money. For example, they were willing to lose all hope of life after death for a mere $50, on average. The employed professionals wanted $6,500 on average for such a hardship! Table 2.6 presents additional data from this study. It may seem that the gain in our knowledge produced by such studies is questionable. However, these were pioneering efforts that helped to convince a great many people that there was no aspect of human behavior or experience that could not be treated scientifically.

SUMMARY

Thorndike saw his contribution largely as having provided an alternative to the mentalism of his (and our) day. He showed that the seemingly complex behavior of cats in the problem box could be simply explained as the stamping in and out of connections between situations and responses through the action of satisfiers and annoyers. Throughout his career he argued that the same principles could account for a great deal of our behavior, including our thoughts and interests.

The law of effect proves to be more complicated than it appears at first sight when one asks why satisfiers and annoyers work as they do. They have no necessary connection with pleasure and pain. Some satisfiers and annoyers are innately determined, but most are not. As a general principle, a state of affairs will act as a satisfier or an annoyer depending on the readiness of the individual for particular consequences. Once a behavior series is begun, satisfaction depends on its successful operation, which is defined in terms of the readiness of conduction units to operate. One may not arbitrarily apply satisfiers and expect them to work invariably.

The law of effect is thus more limited in usefulness than is sometimes believed, but its use by Thorndike called attention to the need to be specific when we seek to alter behavior. Selecting and connecting requires that we specify precisely what behaviors we want to attach to what situations. We must consider, for example, exactly what we mean when we say that we want to teach patriotism or reasoning skills.

The law of effect is further tempered by a set of subsidiary laws. The law of multiple response points out that the learner brings a set of behaviors to new situations, which determine what responses will initially be made. The learner also brings attitudes (also known as dispositions, preadjustments, and sets)—conditions of the learner which determine what will act as a satisfier or an annoyer. The learner will attend to what similar past experience has led him or her to see as salient aspects of a situation (the law of piecemeal activity or selective response), and his or her performance will be greatly affected by the similarity of present and past situations, expressed as the law of response by analogy. A special case of this last principle, associative shifting, refers to what was later called classical conditioning and stimulus fading.

In the early 1930s, Thorndike altered his views somewhat, dropping the law of exercise and the negative law of effect. The opinion that annoyers (punishers) work only indirectly was widely believed for many years, until later evidence clarified the effects of punishment. Critics of Thorndike's connectionism chiefly object to what seems a mechanical conception of humanity, an oversimplification of behavior and experience, and a restatement of the simple hedonistic view of centuries past. Some reflection shows that such criticisms are applicable only to a grossly oversimplified concept of connectionism. Clearly, any model of behavior and experience similarly caricatured would be subject to similar criticisms.

The Gestaltists emphasized the importance of insight but were little concerned with the learning experience that makes insight possible. Harlow demonstrated the phenomenon of learning set, or "learning to learn," thus showing what kind of experience is necessary for sudden solutions to occur.

Thorndike considered himself a basic scientist all his life, though a good deal of his work was aimed at practical application. He was a strong advocate of the influence of heredity, a factor that he felt placed great limits on education, whether carried out using connectionist methods or not. His work in assessing attitudes, wants, and interests seems primitive by modern standards but probably contributed greatly to the belief that such mental entities are subject to precise measurement.

GLOSSARY

Annoyer Thorndike's term for punisher. An annoyer is a state of affairs that stamps out the association between a situation and a response. In Thorndike's pre-1930 theory, a response followed by an annoyer will be less likely to occur in that situation in the future.

Associative shifting One of Thorndike's subsidiary laws corresponding to what was later called classical conditioning.

Attitudes/dispositions/preadjustments/sets Four terms treated as synonymous and referring to the effect of preparation of the learner on the effectiveness of satisfiers and annoyers, as well as on other effects of a new situation on performance.

Conduction unit Used by Thorndike to illustrate the

law of readiness. Depending upon its readiness to fire, the firing or not firing of a conduction unit constitutes satisfaction or annoyance.

Connectionism Thorndike's term for his theory of learning. Learning consists of the connecting of stimuli and responses.

Discipline method Method of education in which drill exercises are used to develop a general mental faculty. For example, the memorizing of poetry was used to develop the general faculty of memory.

Faculties Mental powers that act semiautonomously. Attention, memory, judgment, perception, and imagery are often proposed as faculties.

Hedonism The ancient doctrine popularized in British empiricism, which assumes that pleasure and pain are the essential determinants of conduct.

Insight Term used by Köhler to describe the sudden solutions to problems he observed in his primate subjects (1925). Insight involves the apprehension of relationships in a problem situation, which Köhler contrasted with "blind fumbling" and the action of the law of effect; this was his view of Thorndike's theory. Readers of Köhler's accounts of insight in apes may disagree with his interpretations. Like other Gestalt psychologists, Köhler downplayed the effects of experience in promoting insight. In 1959 he said that, although he had been confused on the issue in the past, he realized that only sudden solutions without prior experience represented true instances of insight. Thus defined, insight may be a relatively rare event.

Law of effect Thorndike's doctrine that held that responses were connected to or disconnected from situations depending upon the effect produced by the response (satisfaction or annoyance).

Law of exercise Thorndike's pre-1929 principle that referred to the connecting of a response and a situation simply because they frequently occurred together.

Law of readiness Also called the law of instinct. Thorndike's law refers to the conditions that determine satisfaction and annoyance. Present stimuli produce a readiness for certain types of consequences.

Mechanism The assumption that explanations must not refer to outside agents, such as demons or life forces.

Mentalism The belief that mental phenomena are different in kind from physical phenomena and that mental events may cause physical events.

Multiple response One of Thorndike's subsidiary laws. This law refers to the behaviors that an individual brings to a learning situation and that determine what behaviors will occur.

Negative law of effect The portion of the pre-1929 law of effect that refers to the effect of annoyers, or punishers.

Original behavior series Thorndike's term for a sequence of activities that are determined innately and that constitute satisfaction when completed.

Partial or piecemeal activity One of Thorndike's subsidiary laws, which referred to the selective nature of perception. We react only to a small subset of the elements of a situation.

Problem box A crude device used by Thorndike and other animal researchers to study problem solving. Typically, a subject placed in such a box could escape by operating a release mechanism, such as a lever or a pull cord.

Response by analogy Thorndike's principle of transfer. We respond to a new situation in the same way that we responded to similar situations in the past.

Satisfier A state of affairs that acts to connect a response with the situation in which it occurred and thus form an S-R bond. Any more precise definition of a satisfier becomes difficult.

Selecting and connecting Term used by Thorndike to describe his theory. Responses are selected by the fact that they produce satisfiers, which also connect them to the situation in which they occurred.

Stamping in or out Term used by Thorndike to describe the connecting or weakening of an S-R association.

Successful operation Term used by Thorndike to specify the conditions for satisfaction. Successful operation refers to the unimpeded completion of an original behavior series.

RECOMMENDED READINGS

Joncich, G. (1968). *The sane positivist*. Middletown, CT: Wesleyan University Press.

This is nominally a biography of Thorndike, but it is much more than that. It is an excellent history of the development of education and psychology in this country, from the nineteenth century onward, with Thorndike's life the thread that runs through it.

Thorndike, E. L. (1949). *Selected writings from a connectionist's psychology*. New York: Appleton.

This is a collection of Thorndike's own papers that he considered most important. Their variety testifies to the considerable range of his interests.

Chapter 3

I. P. PAVLOV: CLASSICAL CONDITIONING

BIOGRAPHY

Ivan P. Pavlov was born in Ryazan, Russia in 1849 (see Figure 3.1). The son of a priest, Pavlov went to school at a theological seminary. He then attended Petersburg University and finally the Imperial Medical-Surgical Academy, where he received an M.D. in 1883. His work on the physiology of the digestive glands led to a Nobel Prize in 1904. Figure 3.2 shows Pavlov and some of his colleagues in his lab.

Pavlov was already well known for his work in physiology when the first translation of his "psychological" work appeared in 1927. Americans earlier had heard news of the conditioned reflex, and some had made use of it in their theoretical writings, but few at the time grasped its real significance. Even today, it is rare that Pavlov is appreciated by American psychologists. The orientation of American psychology has always been very different from Pavlov's. But his way of looking at things may have great virtues: He was not

the "Pavlov" whom you may have come across in a typical psychology textbook.

Some informative publications dealing with Pavlov's theory are listed below. The last three were authored by followers of Pavlov.

Lectures on Conditioned Reflexes, 1928

Conditioned Reflexes, 1927

Selected Works, 1955

Platonov, K. *The Word as a Physiological and Therapeutic Factor*, 1959

Bykov, K.M. *The Cerebral Cortex and the Internal Organs*, 1957

Asratyan, E.A. *Conditioned Reflex and Compensatory Mechanisms*, 1965

Pavlov aimed to work out the principles that govern the workings of the cerebral cortex, the "seat of the mind." In this endeavor he used animal subjects and the conditioned reflex as the main agent of communication with the brain.

FIGURE 3.1 Ivan P. Pavlov, 1849–1936, the year that he won the Nobel Prize (1904). *From Asratyan, 1953*

Twenty years of research produced a model of brain function based on fields of excitation and inhibition. These fields bear a striking resemblance to the neural unit models, for which several researchers working in sensory physiology have won Nobel Prizes.

The influence of Pavlov in America has been restricted to the bare fact of classical conditioning; interest has been restricted largely to parametric work aimed at isolating the necessary conditions for association and the nature of the association formed. Although this has led to some interesting and useful findings, the conditioned response meant a great deal more to Pavlov than that. It was the key to unlock the secrets of the brain; it was not in itself the secret!

INTRODUCTION

Section 1 of this chapter describes Pavlov's influence as a representative of the point of view that has characterized Russian biology and medicine. This point of view has only recently received attention in Western countries. This view sees mind and body as inextricably linked, never to be treated as separate. By and large, American psychologists have not been very interested in this aspect of Pavlov's work. His influence on American psychology lies in the possibility that the conditioned reflex might prove to be the means for an objective, scientific analysis of our behavior and experience.

Although Western psychologists did not appreciate all of Pavlov's work, they were interested in classical conditioning. Section 2 presents the basics of Pavlov's theory and the phenomena of classical conditioning. It includes a brief discussion of theoretical issues that have concerned American psychologists interested in classical conditioning.

Pavlov saw his work as an extension of the work of famed English neurophysiologist Sir Charles Sherrington. A brief summary of Sherrington's analysis of the mechanisms guiding the functioning of the spinal nervous system is provided as a background for Pavlov's theory. The concept of inhibition was central to Sherrington's theory, and Pavlov spent considerable effort showing that inhibition plays a key role in the general functioning of the nervous system. His evidence has been verified largely during the past half century and is discussed in the next section.

Section 2 also describes Pavlov's model of brain function, which posits fields of excitation and inhibition interacting on the surface of the cortex. Although the model is almost certainly wrong in detail, some aspects of the model may well be correct, as suggested by important discoveries made by American researchers in sensory physiology.

Section 3 discusses criticisms of classical conditioning in general, some of which have been directed at overly enthusiastic theorists who were too quick to attempt to use the conditioned response as the explanation for everything. Criticisms of Pavlov's specific model are scarcer, since this model has attracted little notice in this country. However, the notion that fields of excitation and inhibition operate on the surface of the brain has been seriously questioned.

Section 4 considers aspects of classical conditioning that are important in everyday life. The conditioned response is beyond doubt a very important factor in child rearing, education, and advertising in ways that most of us never suspect. The effects of classical conditioning on our internal organs has been shown to be very pervasive and has many implications for what has been called *psychosomatic illness*.

1. PAVLOV'S SIGNIFICANCE IN THE EARLY TWENTIETH CENTURY

The Living Machine

"Pavlov created the body and breathed into it the mind," according to Razran (1965). It will be easier to understand what Razran meant by such praise after reading this chapter. Recall that the thinkers of the past several centuries had passed on the legacy of Descartes, a legacy that lives on in our commonsense views concerning the mind. According to this view, which is really the only one we are taught, it is obvious that we each have (or are) a mind trapped in the physical structure of a body. We view the body as a marvelous machine that carries out all sorts of complicated functions, only some of which we understand. It is indeed marvelous, but it is still a machine. (Science fiction writers have little difficulty convincing us that it is possible that "I"—my mind—could be transferred into a different body, either by a mad genius or as the result of a breakthrough in medical science.)

Pavlov's views, and those of his colleagues, were quite different. For them, the body is also a machine and it is also marvelous, but it is a *living* machine. A body made up of living parts does not require a separate mind to guide it; there is mind, of course, but it is seen as the product of the workings of a living body, not as a separate entity. This is similar to Aristotle's view, and it implies, among other things, that there is no specific ailment that could be called psychosomatic. Psychological and biological factors are inseparable, so any disease is thus psychosomatic. Can any biological malfunction fail to influence the psyche? Can psychic disturbances fail to influence the body?

The relative contribution of psyche and soma to individual ailments may vary, of course, but it is never the case that mind and body act independently so that only *one* is involved. Concerning psychotherapy, Platonov (1959) refers to this difference in Russian and American points of view: "Soviet psychotherapy has developed under conditions entirely different from those in foreign countries and in pre-revolutionary Russia. It is being built on the basis of dialectical materialism, a materialist teaching of the higher nervous activity, the unity of the mind and body, and the determination of consciousness by the conditions of life" (1959, p. 11). Regarding bodily illness, Platonov wrote: " . . . In light of the theory of the unity of mind and body any somatic disease is indissolubly connected with the state of the patient's higher nervous activity" (1959, p. 12).

Given a mechanical (living) body and its product (the mind), how does one understand its workings? Pavlov believed that this was the business of physiology and that the psyche was best studied through the investigation of the physiological activity of the cerebrum. Pavlov's work showed how the adjustments we make as the conditions of the world change around us can be understood as the workings of an integrative mechanism, controlled largely by the cerebral cortex. (This work will be described later in the chapter.) The significance of Pavlov's work was

FIGURE 3.2   Pavlov (left) and colleagues in the laboratory. *From Asratyan, 1953*

seen somewhat differently by early American psychologists.

Shortly after the turn of the century it was widely agreed that psychology must go beyond the sterile analysis of consciousness, which had almost solely concerned the field until that time. The idea as the basic unit of analysis was therefore abandoned, and psychologists began to stress action, as well as function and adaptation. The news of Pavlov's basic discovery seemed to promise a new unit of analysis to replace the idea; this would be the conditioned reflex.

Pavlov had the insight to see the significance of a common and trivial occurrence. As recounted in numerous textbooks, popular articles, and cartoons, Pavlov noticed that his dogs salivated when things that had previously accompanied food were present. Thus, a food dish, the sounds of an attendant's footsteps, or the sight and smell of food produced salivation and general agitation. At this time Pavlov had already won the Nobel Prize for his work in the study of digestion, and so it was natural that he concentrated on the dog's salivary reaction, rather than any other food-anticipating behavior.

Such salivation represented a learned reflex, which Pavlov first called a psychic *reflex*. At birth, or after a period of maturation, we have a set of reflex behaviors that do not depend upon the conditions of our experience; they are *unconditional reflexes*. One such innate response is salivation and other digestive activity produced by food in the stomach or mouth. But such stimulation is usually preceded by a host of cues, including the sight or smell of food, the time of day, the sight of the person who brings the food, and so on. (The term *unconditional* was translated as *unconditioned*. We will use the term in its translated form throughout this chapter.)

As Table 3.1 shows, repeated pairings of food (the unconditioned stimulus) lead such cues to assume some of the response-eliciting power of food in the mouth. Thus, the sight of food becomes a *conditioned stimulus*, producing a *conditioned response* similar to that which only food in the mouth originally produced.

Instead of the sight of food, the sound a bell, the sound of bubbling water, the word *food*, or an electric shock could also become a conditioned stimulus. Thus, we may be able to account for all

TABLE 3.1 Classical Conditioning of Food-Anticipation Behavior

Conditioned Stimuli	Unconditioned Stimuli
Smell of food Taste of food Food dish Attendant	Food in mouth or stomach innate reflex

learned reflex (conditioned response)

Unconditioned Response

Salivation
Agitation
Licking lips
Thoughts of food

of our behavior and experience as the accumulation of conditioned reflexes. If we make such an assumption and leave it at that, however, we part company with Pavlov.

The CR in America

Early American psychologists did propose such a possibility. Given that we are born with a set of reflex behaviors, each elicited by specific (unconditioned) stimuli, is it not reasonable that pairing these behaviors with reliable cues establishes the cues as conditioned stimuli? Then, with new reactions to a host of stimuli, our behavior and experience amount simply to compounds and sequences of reactions to conditioned stimuli. This obviously includes experience, since the conditioned response to food includes the thought of food and of the pleasures of eating!

American researchers and theorists adopted the terms used by Pavlov (these will be discussed below) and concentrated on the specific conditions that produce Pavlovian conditioning, or *classical conditioning*. For example, Pavlov suggested that the conditioned response develops faster if the cue slightly precedes the unconditioned stimulus (by a second or so) but that it still occurs if

far longer delays are used. But what is precisely the best delay between conditioned and unconditioned stimuli? Such information could tell us something about the minimum time required for neural transmission and thus give us clues about the nervous mechanism involved in the formation of a single association. Pavlov showed little concern with such problems, whereas Americans have shown a great deal of concern. This does not necessarily mean that either Pavlov or American researchers were mistaken. It merely emphasizes a basic difference in point of view.

American researchers have concentrated on similar details of the conditioning process, such as the effect of the strength of the conditioned and unconditioned stimuli, the effects of motivation, the effects of drugs, and so on. Such research continues today, in the hope that once we understand the details of the classical conditioning process, we will understand the basic mechanism of association. In fact, this research has led to developments of new theories as well as to some discoveries of practical importance, as we will see in Chapter 9. But such a strategy was not what Pavlov had in mind.

Pavlov's emphasis of the conditioned response as a tool for the study of brain function never caught on in America. Nor did his model of brain function. His irritation with those who failed to appreciate the integrative activity of the organism was plainly evident in his attacks on them (e.g., Pavlov, 1932). Razran (1965) details the objections that Pavlov and his many followers have raised against the American conception of conditioning.

American psychologists saw Pavlov's discovery as fundamentally important. Their reasons were different from those that guided Pavlov. They sought a unit into which to analyze behavior, whereas Pavlov sought a method for studying brain functioning.

Summary

Pavlov viewed humans as living machines, rather than as nonliving robots guided by a separate mind. He used the conditioned response as a means of studying the workings of the brain, not as the unit into which to analyze all behavior. American psychologists welcomed the news of the conditioned response as a candidate for the unit of behavior and experience, replacing the idea. Perhaps we are born with a set of reflex behaviors (UCRs) evoked by a set of unconditioned stimuli (UCSs). With experience, new stimuli are paired with UCSs and thus gain the power to evoke reactions similar to the UCR. Thus, CSs are acquired, and the sum total of them accounts for all of what later determines our behavior and experience. This is how Pavlov's dog came to salivate at the sound of a bell, and it is how we acquire all of the reactions that we now have but that the newborn infant lacks.

2. BASICS OF CLASSICAL CONDITIONING

This section begins with a summary of some of the basic phenomena of classical conditioning and a brief discussion of traditional theoretical issues. Since these phenomena and their interpretations have been emphasized by theorists of various persuasions, it will be useful to treat them here.

We will next consider Pavlov's theory, beginning with a brief discussion of Sir Charles Sherrington's famous work on the mechanisms of the spinal cord, which guided much of Pavlov's work. Sherrington emphasized the importance of excitation and inhibition in the workings of the spinal cord, and Pavlov attempted to show that excitation and inhibition were likewise evident in the workings of the brain. We will consider Pavlov's evidence for inhibition, much of which has been substantiated since his death. Then we will consider his model for brain function in general. This model is similar in some respects to the neural unit models, which have drawn much attention since the 1960s.

Basic Terms and Phenomena

Acquisition and Extinction   The pairing of a signal with an unconditioned stimulus (UCS), such as food in the mouth or an electric shock, transforms the signal into a conditioned stimulus (CS) and it soon comes to evoke a conditioned response (CR). With repeated pairings (CS–UCS, CS–UCS), the CR becomes more reliable and grows in magnitude. The development of an ever-stronger and more reliable CR is often termed *acquisition* of the CR. If, after acquisition, the CS is repeatedly presented without the UCS, it becomes weaker in magnitude and occurs less reliably. This fading of the CR is referred to as the *extinction* of the CR.

Figure 3.3 shows extinction of a salivation CR when the spacing of CS presentations is varied. The CS (sight of meat powder at a distance) was presented for 1-minute periods. Since the dog subject never received the food, no UCS was present, and the CR extinguished. The CR— salivation in cubic centimeters (CCs)—clearly decreased with repetition of the CS, and the forms of the extinction curves are similar for the five cases shown. The interval between CS presentations was increased from 2 minutes to 16 minutes, so the intervals on the X-axis are not constant. For example, the leftmost function spans 15 minutes. The third function from the left, corresponding to the 8-minute interval, spans 54 minutes.

Basic paradigms for the study of acquisition and extinction have varied over the years. Early psychologists used the salivary conditioning paradigm, and a number of devices were constructed to allow the study of such conditioning in humans (e.g., Watson, 1930). Other studies of conditioned responses focused on the flexion of a limb in response to electric shock and the conditioned eyelid response. *Eyelid (or eye-blink) conditioning* results from the pairing of a CS (such as an audible tone) with a puff of air delivered to the cornea. (Currently, this is done less often with human subjects; instead, researchers have studied the

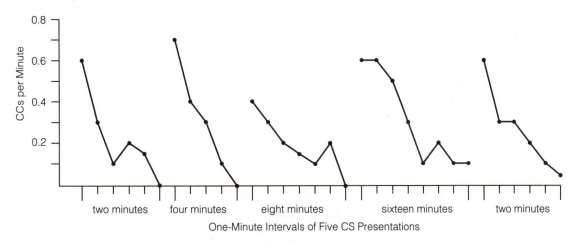

FIGURE 3.3   Extinction with different CS presentation intervals (Pavlov, 1927, p.52).

conditioned eyelid [nictitating membrane] response in rabbits.)

Another popular method for studying classical conditioning is the study of *conditioned suppression*. In this procedure, a CS is paired with an aversive UCS, such as electric shock. Soon a CR appears, which may be indicated by the flinching or the "freezing" of the subject. To more precisely assess the strength of this fear response produced by the CS, it is then presented while the subject is occupied in some other activity, such as pressing a panel for food.

If panel pressing is diminished during the CS, we may conclude that the CS has become aversive and that the decrease in pressing is due to fear-produced suppression. In practice, the degree of suppression is often assessed by calculating a *suppression ratio*, comparing responding just prior to the CS (A) with responding during the CS (B). This ratio, $\dfrac{B}{A + B}$ would be 0.5 if no suppression occurred and would decrease toward zero as the degree of suppression increased (and as responding thus decreased during the CS).

Excitatory and Inhibitory Conditioning   A CS that more or less reliably predicts a UCS is termed an excitatory CS; it is effective in producing a CR. A CS that more or less reliably predicts *no* UCS is termed an inhibitory CS; it does not produce a CR. According to some theories, such as Pavlov's and Konorski's (1948), an inhibitory CS may actually produce a response opposite to the CR (see below). Note that *excitatory* and *inhibitory* refer to the predictive character of the CS, not to whether what is predicted is good or bad. Thus, an excitatory CS may predict food or strong shock.

Generalization and Discrimination   Once a CS has been established, we find that similar stimuli may also produce a CR, with the magnitude of the CR depending upon the similarity of the new stimulus to the CS. This spread of excitation or inhibition is called *irradiation*. Pavlov referred to the irradiation of excitation (and inhibition) from the cortical spot representing the CS to spots representing similar stimuli. We term the effect stimulus generalization. Figure 3.4 shows the results of a dog's responding to tactile stimulation on the skin. Stimulation of the thigh had been paired with food and was thus a positive CS (CS +). The salivation CR decreased as more distant surfaces of the body were stimulated.

If a new stimulus is presented occasionally with no UCS, and our CS is presented at other

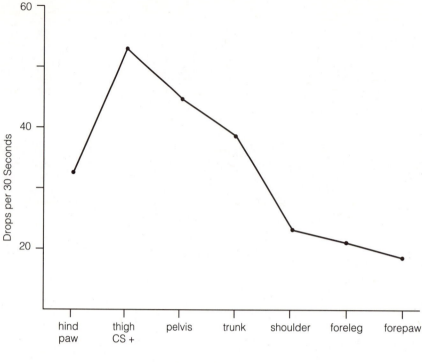

FIGURE 3.4   Irradiation (Pavlov, 1927, p. 185).

times with a UCS, the generalized responding to the new stimulus gradually fades. Pavlov referred to this as the formation of a *differentiation* and we usually term it discrimination learning. The study of the formation of discriminations constitutes a large part of Pavlov's research.

The UCS   An unconditioned stimulus may be food, electric shock, an air puff to the eye, brain stimulation, the sight of a rival, a loud noise, a morphine injection, the caffeine in a cup of coffee, and so on. It is effective if it evokes a reasonably strong bodily response.

Unconditioned stimuli are typically classified as *appetitive* or *aversive*, roughly corresponding to whether we typically view them as pleasant or as unpleasant. We will see later that some powerful UCSs such as stimulation of the stomach or intestines are difficult to classify in this way.

A CR is generally produced more easily when the UCS is more intense. Needless to say, there are limits to this, and it should be remembered that the CR is usually similar to whatever the UCR is. Suppose you are trying to produce an eye blink response and the UCS is intense enough to blow the subject off the chair; such a UCS probably will not lead to a stronger CR.

The CS   Almost everything imaginable has been or could be used as a CS. Pavlov was fond of using spinning disks, the sound of bubbling water, and a metronome as conditioned stimuli. Recently we have found that some stimuli act particularly well as signals for certain UCSs. For

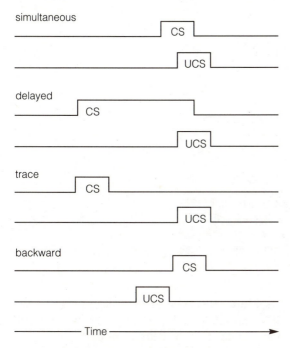

simultaneous

delayed

trace

backward

Time

FIGURE 3.5 Temporal paradigms of conditioning. This figure shows the ways in which a CS and a UCS may be presented in time. For example, delayed conditioning occurs when a CS is presented and remains present over seconds or minutes and the UCS appears at the end of the CS presentation. In trace conditioning, the CS is presented and removed, a period of time passes, and the UCS then appears.

example, tastes are established very quickly as CSs for poison-produced illness (see Chapter 9).

The intensity or general salience of a stimulus is important in establishing it as a CS. Pavlov found that, if two stimuli are presented together, the more salient one could overshadow a less salient stimulus, leaving the latter one ineffective (1927). We will return to this topic in Chapter 9.

The Temporal Paradigms Pavlovian conditioning works best when the CS precedes the UCS by a second or so, which Pavlov called *simultaneous conditioning* (see Figure 3.5). He did not actually present the CS and UCS simultaneously, since he believed that this would render the CS useless as a signal and thus that conditioning would not occur. (In the U.S., the meaning of *simultaneous* is taken literally. To researchers in the U.S., *simultaneous conditioning* means that the CS and the UCS occur at exactly the same time.)

A good deal of research supports Pavlov, but some recent investigators, such as Heth (1976), have found that conditioning may occur when the CS does not precede the UCS. If the stimuli appear simultaneously (and even when the UCS begins shortly before the CS), the CS may become weakly effective. With continued training it may then become inhibitory, as Pavlov found.

If the CS is presented and remains present, with the UCS occurring seconds or minutes later, we have *delayed conditioning*. Pavlov typically began with the CS and UCS closely paired in time and gradually increased the delay between the onset of the CS and that of the UCS. (American researchers typically do not do this.) Thus, a tone would begin to sound and the interval between its onset and the presentation of food might be extended to ten or fifteen minutes or more. Eventually the salivary CR did not begin with the onset of the tone; after one third to one half of the delay period passed, salivation began and continued at an increasing rate until the food was presented. This pattern may appear only after fairly lengthy training, but Pavlov's experiments frequently extended over weeks or months, and he often used the same subjects over years of research.

Pavlov believed that the decrease in responding during the initial part of the delay period was due to the building up of inhibition in the dog's brain. The early part of the period was never paired with the UCS and thus became an inhibitory CS. He further believed that inhibition leads to hypnosis and sleep, and he saw evidence for this in the behavior of many of his dogs. He found that many animals fell asleep, often snoring loudly, during delayed conditioning; even an initially frisky and active dog would quickly doze

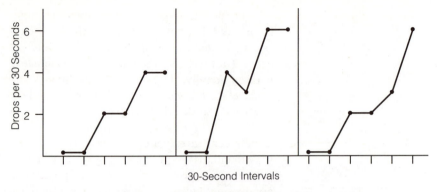

FIGURE 3.6 Results from a delayed conditioning procedure (Pavlov, 1927, p. 90). This figure shows three instances of responding during delayed conditioning. A CS+ (whistle) was presented for three-minute periods, followed by a UCS (weak acid, producing a sour taste). Data points represent salivation during successive 30-second periods within each three-minute presentation of the CS.

off once a session of delayed conditioning began. He referred often to the time and effort he and his assistants spent in rousing the drowsy canines (Pavlov, 1927).

Since conditioning occurs most rapidly when the CS precedes the UCS slightly, it may be of interest to determine the best interval between CS and UCS. It has been pretty well established (e.g., Mackintosh, 1974) that an interval of approximately half a second is best when the UCR is a phasic response, such as the flexing of a limb or the blinking of an eye. If the response is less phasic, such as salivation or a change in the heart rate, a CS–UCS interval of five to ten seconds seems best. (Chapter 9 discusses studies in which the CS–UCS interval spans hours.) Figure 3.6 presents the results from a delayed conditioning experiment.

If a CS is presented, turned off, and later followed by the UCS, the procedure is called *trace conditioning*. Note that it is identical to delayed conditioning, except that the CS ends before the UCS appears. Pavlov called this procedure trace conditioning because he assumed that a CR to the now absent CS was actually connected to a memory trace of the CS. The pattern of responding in trace conditioning is similar to that in delay conditioning; after some training, the CR begins to

occur after one third to one half of the CS–UCS interval has passed and continues increasing in magnitude up to the delivery of the UCS.

Backward conditioning involves the presentation of the UCS before the presentation of a CS signal. It is fairly well established that conditioning does occur under such conditions and that the CS is rendered inhibitory; it signals "no UCS." Researchers Keith-Lucas and Guttman (1975), among others, found that backward conditioning can produce a normal excitatory CS. Other researchers, such as Heth (1976), found that the CS may become mildly excitatory early in training. But typically, given enough training, backward conditioning renders the CS inhibitory. For example, Moscovitch and Lolordo (1968) showed that backward conditioning with an electric shock UCS makes the CS an effective fear reducer.

Controls in Classical Conditioning Control procedures are used to ensure that any CRs that occur are due to the pairing of some CS with some UCS and not to other factors. At least, that used to be the purpose of controls. Things have changed, as we will see. Suppose we begin with a CS that reflexively elicits a UCR. In eye blink conditioning, for example, a bright light CS may produce a blink before an air puff ever occurs. The odor of vinegar produces salivation and thus would be an unwise choice for a CS in salivary conditioning, although it would be fine as a UCS.

Sensitization or pseudoconditioning occur when a CS produces a response that looks like a CR without any pairing with a UCS. For example, if one is using an air puff UCS to produce an eye blink UCR, a bright flash of light or a clap of thunder would be unwise choices for a CS. Either could produce a startle response (eye blinks) that could be mistaken as CRs arising from the CS–UCS pairing. *Pseudoconditioning* occurs when the CS evokes a response because the UCS (such as electric shock) has rendered the subject overly reactive to stimuli in general.

The purpose of control procedures is to ensure that whatever CR occurs is due to the classical conditioning procedure and not to some other factor. In the past, classical conditioning was viewed as the simple pairing of CS and UCS, and the experimenter controlled against the effects of other variables. That changed in 1967 when Rescorla published a paper entitled "Pavlovian Conditioning and Its Proper Control Procedures." He proposed a *truly random control* procedure, in which CSs and UCSs are presented at random times. Although the CS and UCS may occasionally be paired accidentally, no CRs develop. That is because the CS is also likely to be followed by no UCS and thus provides no information about the possible occurrence of a UCS. In order for learning to occur, the CS must reliably signal the UCS. (We will return to this subject in Chapter 9.) In any event, if the CS you use reflexively elicits UCRs, or if the UCS sensitizes the subject so that CRs seem to occur, you will observe what seem to be CRs even using the truly random control procedure. You would thus know that these factors could produce spurious apparent CRs in your experimental groups.

Traditional Theoretical Problems, Briefly

What Is Learned in Classical Conditioning? Pavlov believed that the appearance of a CR meant that the CS had become a substitute for the UCS. For example, when a light is paired with food, a connection forms between the cortical centers representing the light and the food. Once this occurs, the sight of the light activates the CS (light) center, which is now linked with the UCS (food) center and thus a food reaction CR occurs. What has been learned is an association between two stimuli, the light and the food. This is called a stimulus-stimulus, or S-S, association. Pavlov provided evidence for this interpretation: In experiments in which a light was paired with food, Pavlov found that his subjects often licked the light if they could, thus showing that they treated them as they did food.

Sensory preconditioning is a phenomenon that seems to support the notion that classical conditioning is S-S learning, although in fact it simply shows that such associations do occur in common experience (e.g., Razran, 1961). If we present two stimuli, such as a light and a tone, repeatedly (light-tone, light-tone, and so on), there is evidence that an association is formed even though we have applied nothing that could really be called a UCS. This may be shown by later pairing the tone with a real UCS, such as electric shock. This leads to the formation of a CR (the subject's flinch, heart rate change, and so on) to the tone.

If we then present the light, a CR (perhaps a weak one) is also produced, even though the light has never been paired with the shock. This means that the previous pairing of the two stimuli (light and tone) was enough to associate them even in the absence of an obvious response to either of them. Classical conditioning involves the pairing of stimuli and thus probably involves S-S learning.

But there is also evidence that classical conditioning is S-R learning, a view more compatible with American learning theory during this century. Returning to the pairing of a CS and food, it could be that the salivary CR to the CS occurs because that was part of the response last made when the CS was present. Food (the UCS) was also present, and salivation occurred. What was learned was an association between the CS and the last response made to it (R); hence, an S-R association was learned. An early experiment by Harry Harlow, which involved changing the effectiveness of a UCS after pairing it with a CS, provided evidence for an S-R association.

Harlow (1937) used a UCS consisting of the loud noise produced by the popping of a paper bag previously blown up by his graduate student aides. Each bag pop was preceded by a brief buzzer CS, and this CS soon produced CRs of agitation and fear in his chimpanzee subjects. After the CR was established, Harlow repeatedly presented the UCS (bag pop), especially while the chimps were eating. Eventually, the noise lost its earlier effect; the chimps became accustomed to the noise (they habituated) and no startle UCR appeared. How did the habituated chimps respond, then, to the sound of the buzzer? (The buzzer was still a signal for the bag pop, but the pop no longer produced a fear response.) If classical conditioning is, as Pavlov and the previous argument suggests, S-S learning, then the buzzer should have no effect. (It signals a UCS that now has no effect.) But the buzzer did have an effect: The chimpanzees jumped with fright. Why?

Evidently, the buzzer produced fear not because it signaled the impending noise of the bag pop. It produced fear because that was what it produced the last time it was present. The association formed then was between the CS (buzzer) and the UCS (fear). Thus, classical conditioning, as Harlow's experiment shows, is S-R learning.

Is classical conditioning S-S learning? Is it S-R learning? Is it both or neither? Have researchers miscast the problem or the evidence? Are they asking inappropriate questions? We could consider other evidence for both sides and the reader should not be left with the impression that this is an easily resolved issue.

Rescorla (1973) was unable to replicate Harlow's finding, and later research suggested that if it is reasonable to treat classical conditioning as S-S or S-R learning, the ordinary (first-order) conditioning seems largely to be S-S learning. However, second-order conditioning seems largely to be S-R learning (e.g., Konorski, 1948; Rizley & Rescorla, 1972).

Konorski (1948) paired a CS (call it CSa) with food, producing conditioned salivation in his dog subjects. He then paired a second CS (CSb) with CSa. Then CSa was paired with shock, producing a conditioned leg flexion response. But presentation of CSb still produced salivation. Table 3.2 shows this situation.

Holland and Rescorla (1975) sated their rat subjects with food after establishing a light as a first-order CS for food and a tone as a second-order CS. They found that the response to the light was greatly reduced; it was, after all, a signal for food, and food is not an effective CS for a sated subject. The conditioning involved was S-S learning. But when the tone was presented, its effect was not diminished. Although the tone was a signal for the light and the light was a signal for food, the tone was still effective even when the light was not. This must mean that second-order conditioning is not S-S learning; rather, it is S-R learning. (This would explain why the tone was effective even when the light was not.) When the tone was last presented, it produced a response (the CR), and that was what it produced subsequently. If it merely signaled the light (and thus the food), one would expect no response from a sated subject, as was the case with the light.

The picture clouds a bit when we consider several responses. Holland (1977) found, perhaps surprisingly, that different CSs evoke different reactions even when the same US is used. He paired a variety of stimuli with food and then tested the response to each stimulus. The experiment showed that a tone CS elicited strong head jerking and that a light CS did not. But the light elicited rearing, whereas the tone did not. These examples make one suspect that S-R learning is involved; the form of the CR is specific to the type of CS. However, if we look at second-order conditioning, in which other stimuli signal light or tone, no such difference occurs. Is the learning in this case S-S learning?

First- and second-order conditioning may reflect S-S and S-R learning, respectively, if one records standard single CRs, such as suppressed bar pressing, during a CS signaling shock. If one

TABLE 3.2   Three Experiments: S-S Learning or S-R Learning?

Sensory Preconditioning

Procedure	Assumed Process
1. pair light and tone	S_1-S_2 (light-tone) association
2. pair tone and shock	S_1-S_3 (tone-shock) association
3. present light: shock CR	S_1-(S_2)-S_3 association

Changed Effectiveness of the UCS

Procedure	Assumed Process
1. pair buzzer and noise	S-R (buzzer-fear) association
2. habituate noise UCR	noise ineffective UCS
3. present buzzer: fear CR	S-R (buzzer-fear) association intact

Second-Order Conditioning

Procedure	Assumed Process
1. pair CSa and food	S-S association
2. pair CSb and CSa	S-S association
3. pair CSa and shock to leg	S-S association
4. present CSa: leg flexion CR	S-S (CSa-shock) association
present CSb: salivation	S-R (CSb-salivation) association

observes several kinds of responses, first- and second-order conditioning seem to involve S-R and S-S learning, respectively. In short, the results are confusing and inconclusive.

Reinforcement in Classical Conditioning   This problem is actually difficult to separate from the problem of what is learned. The problem concerns the effect of the UCS: Does the UCS act as a reward for whatever CR appears? Or is the UCS strictly an elicitor, which produces a strong CR by producing a strong UCR? This seems at first glance an opaque question, not easily answered. But the evidence clearly shows that the UCS does not work primarily like a reward. If it did, this would mean that the UCS would act like a satisfier, as Thorndike used the term. It would also mean that classical conditioning would simply be a case of *instrumental conditioning*, or learning that depends on the consequences of responses.

Consider some examples: In salivary conditioning, dry food is ordinarily administered to the mouth; Pavlov used dry meat powder. The CR of salivation that occurs surely makes the dry powder more palatable, so the behavior of salivating is thereby rewarded. Not salivating is punished by the discomfort of a mouthful of powder. Similarly, eye blink CRs are rewarded; an anticipatory blink avoids an annoying puff of air to the eye. In normal eyelid conditioning, the consequences of the CR probably maintain the CR. This essentially was Hull's position (see Chapter 6); his theories dominated psychology for many years.

Unlike the problem of "what is learned," the evidence seems to be quite clear in this case. Conditioned responses are not maintained by their consequences. This has been shown in a variety of studies using what Sheffield (1965) calls *omission procedures*. For example, suppose we reward a dog with food for *not* salivating. Given no salivation, we present food. If there is salivation, the food reward is omitted. If the salivation response is maintained by consequences, the omission of food which follows salivation should lead to decreased salivating, and the food presented for not salivating should likewise reduce salivating. But if salivating is determined solely by the UCR produced by the UCS food, it should be impossible for the dog to learn to withhold salivating when the reward is food. And, of course, Sheffield found that it was impossible to train dogs to withhold salivating when the reward was food.

A variety of other data with omission schedules has almost always supported this finding and clearly show that the UCS in classical conditioning does not act like rewards in instrumental learning. Does this mean that classical conditioning and instrumental conditioning are fundamentally different?

Classical and Instrumental Conditioning   The procedures used in classical conditioning and instrumental learning are different; some theorists have suggested that there also is a fundamental difference in the kind of learning that takes place. First, let us consider how similar are the procedures involved.

In classical conditioning, a CS, such as a light, is presented just before a UCS, such as food, which produces a UCR (eating and so on). After the CR to the light is established, the sequence of events is typically as follows:

$$CS \rightarrow CR \rightarrow UCS \rightarrow UCR$$

In instrumental learning, we may reward a response with food in the presence of a (discriminative) stimulus light. Thus, the sequence:

$$light \rightarrow R \rightarrow UCS \rightarrow UCR$$

The only real difference lies in the fact that the CR in the first sequence is elicited by the UCS. In the second sequence the response may be anything we choose (although we will see that a lot of responses that are chosen arbitrarily, such as bar pressing and key pecking, seem to act a lot like CRs). There is still a difference in procedure, of course between classical and instrumental conditioning; this has been emphasized by Catania (1984) and others. In classical conditioning, the UCS occurs independently of the behavior of the subject, whereas in instrumental conditioning the consequences depend on the occurrence of some aspect of behavior.

Earlier psychologists did not distinguish between two kinds of learning. The possibility that Pavlovian and instrumental learning were fundamentally different was suggested by Konorski and Miller (1937), but the real argument for the distinction was made by Skinner in 1938. He suggested that instrumental (or operant) learning is dependent upon the consequences of action (rewards or reinforcers), that it applies only to the skeletal nervous system and the striped muscles which it controls. According to Skinner, classical conditioning (or respondent learning) affects only the autonomic nervous system and the smooth muscles of the viscera and glands controlled by the autonomic nervous system. He also distinguished the two types of learning in other ways, as we will see in Chapter 8.

Some psychologists, such as Mowrer (1947), adopted Skinner's distinction, but many did not. Nonetheless, the distinction between classical and instrumental conditioning has been accepted by a great many psychologists over the past half century. For this reason, there has been a great deal of interest in demonstrations of the instrumental conditioning of autonomic behavior, largely by Neal Miller and his associates (e.g., Miller, 1969). Miller has shown that it is possible to influence heart rate, blood pressure, and other autonomically controlled responses with feedback (that is, providing consequences). Some researchers have questioned Miller's results. In addition, Miller and others have failed to replicate his original findings (e.g., Miller & Dworkin, 1974; Dworkin & Miller, 1986). However, there is little doubt that instrumental conditioning, as a procedure, can influence a variety of bodily activities (cf. Buck, 1988). *How* this occurs, though, is very much a matter of debate.

Researchers also have shown that what was thought to be instrumental behavior, such as the pecking of a plastic disk by pigeons, may be established by what seems to be classical conditioning procedures. For example, Brown and Jenkins (1968) showed that one need only present a lighted key for a few seconds, followed by the automatic delivery of food, to establish key pecking in pigeons. Reliable responding almost always occurs after less than 100 pairings. The lighted key seems to act as a CS, and the birds' pecking, which seems a reasonable CR when the UCR is pecking grain, occurs to the lighted key.

These studies, and other research conducted during the 1970s and 1980s, has blurred the distinction between classical and instrumental learning. If visceral behaviors can be influenced by feedback procedures (instrumental conditioning), and if classical conditioning procedures can influence skeletal behavior, such as key pecking, then the distinction between the two procedures surely does not extend to some basic difference in the two main divisions of the nervous system (autonomic and skeletal) involved. Today, the distinction between classical and instrumental learning is far less popular than it was in the 1960s.

Sherrington's Integrative Action

Pavlov was concerned with the way in which the brain functions, assuming that this was the key to understanding behavior and experience. His work during the beginning of this century, which included the "discovery" of the conditioned reflex, was inspired by the then recent work of the great English physiologist Sir Charles Sherrington. To understand Pavlov's theory, it is necessary to know a little about Sherrington's work.

Sherrington was to win the Nobel Prize in 1932 for his earlier work, published in 1906, concerning the workings of the spinal nervous system. His book, *The Integrative Action of the Nervous*

System, had two major effects. First, it established the reflex as the basic unit of spinal physiology by showing what effects the synapse has on neural activity. (The synapse is the tiny gap between the axon of one neuron and the cell body of another, so named by Sherrington.) Secondly, Sherrington showed how the spinal cord acts as an organ of integration, coordinating the activities of individual organs. This action, which he called *integrative action*, cannot be understood by a concentration on individual reflexes or collections of them. For example, often stimuli are present that would lead to incompatible actions; a touch on the skin may provoke receptors that produce both flexion and extension of a limb. For a while, there is competition between the two antagonistic movements. Unless the limb is to remain stiff, one of the receptor groups temporarily "wins." For example, receptors and their afferent (sensory) arcs, producing flexion of the biceps, also produce flexing of the arm. While the limb is flexed, the muscle producing the antagonistic movement (the triceps muscle) is inhibited. Thus, one effect—the flexing of the arm—involves the contraction of one muscle group and the *reciprocal inhibition* of the antagonist.

This is only a brief sketch of Sherrington's integrative action; it becomes very complex when we consider all of our spinal sensory nerves competing for the limited number of motor nerves (Sherrington's *final common path*) controlling all of our many skeletal muscles. The little processes happen at many levels with every movement that we make, whether it be typing, lifting a coffee cup, swinging a bat, or simply running. According to Sherrington, individual reflexes or their simple sum tell us little.

These mechanical principles of integration apply only to the action of the spinal cord, in Sherrington's opinion. The cerebral hemispheres do not act according to such mechanical principles. Sherrington really was at bottom a mentalist who firmly believed that some sort of spiritual entity—a separate mind, or the like—governed the activity of the brain, as he makes clear in the final chapters of his 1906 book. Nonetheless, it was Pavlov's aim to show that such mechanical principles did apply to the workings of the brain, and he bitterly attacked Sherrington's refusal to consider the possibility (Pavlov, 1955).

Pavlov tried to apply Sherrington's basic approach to the study of the cerebral cortex. And, like Sherrington, he based his conclusions on inferences drawn from behavior, rather than from direct measurements of the activity of the nervous system.

Pavlov's Evidence for Inhibition

Pavlov believed that *inhibition* was as important in the functioning of the cerebrum and thus in the overall function of the individual as Sherrington had shown it to be in the activity of the spinal cord. The usefulness of the concept of inhibition in behavior has been hotly debated during this century, with some theorists accepting it and others (notably B. F. Skinner) arguing strongly against it. The basis for the debate is easy to see if we consider a concrete example in classical conditioning.

Imagine a hungry dog that is occasionally fed a small morsel of food. Just before each piece of food is given, a green light in front of the dog comes on and remains lighted while the food is delivered by an attendant. At other times a tone is briefly sounded and no food is delivered. When neither the light nor the tone is on, no food is presented. Before long, the repeated presentations of the light and the food have their effect; the dog appears to anticipate food when the light comes on, as is evidenced by the dog's salivation and bodily movements. During the tone and during periods with no light or tone, nothing happens; the dog doesn't salivate but appears to be waiting for the light.

During these periods of no response, it seems sufficient to say that there is simply no tendency to respond. The absence of responding does not mean that inhibition is involved. Inhibition would mean that, not only is there no tendency

to salivate (and so on), but that such behavior is actually suppressed.

Then conditions change. When the light comes on, the dog is still given food, but now it is given food on one occasion in which neither the light nor the tone is on. Needless to say, the dog accepts and eats the food. Then the light and food are presented, followed by the tone. This time, however, food is presented during the tone. Does the dog accept and eat the food? Surprisingly, it does not! Instead, it turns away; if the food is forced on the dog, it refuses it! The green light comes on, food is offered, and the dog eats it.

The reason for this seemingly bizarre behavior lies in the conditioned response established in the no light/tone periods and in the tone periods. Just as the light produces an excitatory conditioned response (CR) to the food, the tone becomes inhibitory. As a reliable predictor of "no food," it evokes an "antifood" response—a lack of readiness for food, as defined in terms of Thorndike's conduction units. The no light/no tone periods produce no such effect; due to long experience both with and without food in the no light/tone conditions, such periods predict nothing. The tone, however, has come to mean "no food" and has thus become an inhibitory stimulus for eating.

This observation, reported by Konorski (1967, pp. 325–326), is shown in Table 3.3. It is likely that such effects are common in our experience and behavior, despite the fact that inhibition has often been argued to be unnecessary. After all, the absence of an activity does not have to mean that it is inhibited (that is, that the tendency to do it is less than zero). The tendency, if it exists at all, could simply be too low (near zero) to lead to action. Yet, the tendency to eat during the tone was not simply low, as during the no light/tone periods; during these times, food was refused. It would take more trials than usual to establish a CR to the tone. This deficit in reconditioning shows that the CS was indeed inhibitory.

Pavlov's evidence for inhibition was less startling and was integrated into his presentation of

TABLE 3.3 Konorski's Simple Demonstration of Inhibition

CS+	Intertrial Interval	CS−
Tone paired with food	No food given	No food given
Dog eats free food	Dog eats free food	Dog refuses free food

the basic features of classical conditioning. The following summary presents this evidence, along with a further discussion of some of the basics of conditioning. For simplicity, we will consider the classic case of salivary conditioning, in which a CS tone precedes a UCS of food in the mouth and a CR including salivation appears when the tone is sounded.

As the tone and the food are presented repeatedly, salivation more reliably accompanies the onset of the tone and the rate of salivation increases. Pavlov viewed this as evidence for a connection formed in the brain centers corresponding to the tone and the food in such a way that the tone becomes a substitute for the food. With repeated pairings, the connection becomes stronger, as excitation from the cortical "eating center" drains to the center representing the tone. As conditioning proceeds, the tone becomes a more excitatory CS.

Extinction　If the food UCS is no longer presented and the tone CS appears alone, the reliability and vigor of the salivation CR to the tone decreases until eventually the tone produces no CR; the CR has been extinguished. During this period of extinction, the decrease in the rate of salivation is not smooth but irregular. There may be salivation with one presentation of the tone, none during the next, salivation with the next, and so on. This ragged course of extinction was evidence to Pavlov that conflict was present. The excitatory CS was becoming inhibitory and the irregular rate of decline of the CR was evidence for an excitatory/inhibitory conflict. This is not altogether convincing evidence for the existence of inhibition (cf. Rescorla, 1969), but Pavlov

had other forms of evidence that seem more convincing.

For example, consider the effect of repeated presentations of the tone. Imagine that the subject is a dog (although it need not be) in a standing position in a restraining harness. The tone has been presented a number of times without food, and the dog shows no response to its presentation: No salivation occurs, and the dog does not turn its head toward the source of the tone. The tone continues to be presented again and again at intervals. The dog goes to sleep, often snoring loudly, according to Pavlov's account. The dog occasionally awakens, shows no reaction to the tone, and falls asleep again. The procedure continues and something odd happens.

While awake, the dog beings to act strangely; its muscles relax and it appears to be in a hypnotic state. This is not simply due to boredom, as one might suspect, because, when we look more closely, we see that strange things are happening. If other conditioned stimuli, which earlier had been paired with food, are presented, the dog may not respond to them or to food itself. Oddly, if the dog does react to conditioned stimuli, it responds more strongly to weak stimuli than to strong ones. Pavlov called this the *paradoxical phase* of extinction. In Pavlov's experiments, a weak light CS produced a stronger reaction than a shrill whistle, both of which were paired with food equally in the past.

As the tone continues to be presented in extinction, the *equalization phase* appears. While awake, the dog responds with equal vigor to presentations of weak and strong conditioned stimuli. Finally, this stage gives way to the *ultraparadoxical phase*, in which positive CSs produce no responses but negative CSs produce CRs. In Pavlov's experiments, the dog responded to the tone (the negative CS) but not to the conditioned stimuli that signaled food (the positive CSs).

Pavlov felt that these stages were due to the building up of inhibition produced by presentations of the tone without the food UCS and that this build-up upset the normal balance of excitation and inhibition in the brain. This inhibition also produced sleep, even in rested and alert subjects. Pavlov and his assistants spent a good deal of time keeping the dogs awake. He mentions wearing scary masks and blowing toy trumpets for just this purpose.

The dog's behavior as it passed through these stages often seemed insane and was interpreted as indicating a form of neurosis, called *experimental neurosis*. Interestingly, a fine analysis of the stages through which the dogs passed, as shown in their behavior, corresponds closely to a categorization of stages of mental illness in humans (e.g., Platonov, 1959). For many years the Russians have viewed mental disturbance as the product of excitatory and inhibitory factors, following Pavlov's interpretation. Eysenck (e.g., 1957) favors this general point of view, but other Western psychologists have ignored it, as Razran (1967) noted. Attempts by Americans to duplicate the stages of "sleep" described by Pavlov and by Platonov, and by others (e.g., Frolov, 1937), are rare, if they exist at all.

Pavlov believed that experimental neurosis resulted from a conflict between excitation and inhibition and occurred when an impossible problem is posed. For example, one may pair a circle with food presentations and alternate presentations of an ellipse that appears without food. The discrimination begins with the two stimuli appearing quite different, and the subject quickly comes to salivate only during the presentations of the circle. Gradually, the stimuli are made more similar (the ellipse is made more nearly circular), until the subject no longer can distinguish between the two shapes. This should not cause any

panic in the subject; in fact, a half comatose subject could just let its salivary glands work or not. Food comes with the CS+ no matter what the dog does, and food does not come with the CS− no matter what the dog does.

Although there should be no ill effect, there is one. When the task becomes nearly impossible, the dog becomes agitated, barks, salivates, bites at its harness, and generally goes berserk. To prevent injury, the dog is removed and placed back in the kennel, where it may remain "insane" for months or years. (It is tempting to suppose that similar hazards may conceivably attend familiar methods of education such as a programmed learning task in which steps of successive difficulty are arranged so that a mistake is never made because the successive steps are carefully arranged to prevent it. What if a too large step is inadvertently required?)

Spontaneous Recovery   Let us return to our discussion of the simple extinction of responding to the tone. Suppose that the CS is presented only until responding to it ceases, or perhaps a bit longer. In this case we may avoid the neurotic phases and assume that we have simply done away with the CR to the tone. But that is not the case. Later, whether it be an hour, a day, a week, or much longer, when the tone is presented again, the CR reappears—an effect that Pavlov called *spontaneous recovery*.

In Pavlov's experiments, this proved to him that the connection between the CS tone and the UCS food was not lost during extinction, but was only hidden by the inhibition that had accumulated. Later, when the inhibition dissipated, the excitatory connection was shown to be still there. This occurs because inhibition, for a variety of reasons, was viewed as less enduring than excitation.

Disinhibition   If extinction is carried out to the point at which the CS no longer produces a conditioned response, the introduction of a new stimulus, such as a handclap, often produces the

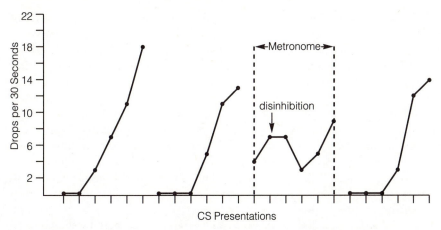

FIGURE 3.7 Pavlov's disinhibition experiment in which he presented a tactile CS with a metronome (Pavlov, 1927, p. 93). The graph shows four presentations of the CS, each three minutes in duration, at intervals of 30 seconds. The metronome was added during the third presentation. Disinhibition appears as increased salivation during the first half of the presentation.

reappearance of the CR. This release from inhibition is called *disinhibition*. Pavlov's explanation for this is too complex to present here; suffice it to say that disinhibition suggests that the strength of the CR has not been decreased to zero during extinction. The excitatory effects of previous conditioning are still there, but the extinction procedure has overlaid the excitatory tendency with inhibition. Figure 3.7 graphs the results of one of Pavlov's experiments with disinhibition.

Extinction Below Zero Recall that Pavlov believed that extinction amounted to the building up of inhibition that acted against the excitation built up during conditioning. Recall also that the repeated presentations of a CS without the UCS (such as food) continued to produce inhibition even after the CR no longer was evident. This was the case in the earlier example of simple experimental neurosis. This means that the tendency to respond not only reduces to zero but goes below zero with continued extinction trials. If this were true, the longer a CS were presented in extinction, the more difficult it would be to

produce responding when the UCS was presented again. Pavlov showed this to be the case, as have other investigators since Pavlov's time (e.g., Konorski, 1948; Reynolds, 1964). This event occurs because the more that inhibition has strengthened, the more excitation produced by the CS–UCS pairings is necessary to counter it. The tendency to respond must be raised from a below-zero level.

Inhibition of Delay When a CS (such as a tone) is followed quickly by a UCS (such as food), we have what Pavlov called simultaneous conditioning. The tone and food are presented almost simultaneously, with the tone slightly preceding the food. After such conditioning, it is possible to introduce a delay between the onset of the tone and the food and still produce a conditioned response. The delay period separating the onset of the tone and the presentation of food may gradually be extended to many minutes. Note that during the procedure, delayed conditioning, the CS (tone) is presented and remains on over the delay period until the food is presented.

Initially, and while the delay period is brief, the conditioned response (salivation, bodily orientation, and so on) may begin with the onset of the tone and continue until the UCS is delivered. But as the training is continued and the delay period is increased, the conditioned response appears only after the tone has been on for a while and increases in strength as the time for food nears. The decrease in responding during the early part of the interval was evidence for Pavlov that inhibition was at work. The beginning of the period was an extinction period, thus rendering it inhibitory. The decrease of responding in this situation is called *inhibition of delay*. Pavlov showed that disinhibition was possible, so that the presentation of a new stimulus (such as a buzzer or a trumpet tone) produced responding during this period.

The effects of inhibition were also indicated in the behavior of Pavlov's dogs. Especially when the delay period had been extended to very long intervals of fifteen minutes or an hour, it became difficult to keep the canines awake. When training with such long delays was carried out for too long, the dogs fell asleep because of the accumulation and spread of inhibition produced by the CS. This occurred even in the case of lively, alert dogs, almost as soon as they were placed in the experimental apparatus. In fact, it was most frequent among these lively, active dogs.

Conditioned Inhibition and Differential Inhibition If the tone is followed by food, and then on other occasions another stimulus (such as a light) is presented with the tone but without food, we find that the CR to the tone/light pair quickly disappears. The tone presented by itself still has its expected effect, and the light presented alone has, of course, no effect. The light has become a conditioned inhibitor, and conditioned inhibition is just a case of the more general principle of differential inhibition, or the inhibition that accompanies the formation of a discrimination (or a differentiation, in Pavlov's terms).

The normal method for the training of a discrimination is to alternate presentations of one CS with food, for example, and presentations of one or more other stimuli without food (that is, in extinction). This is Pavlov's method of contrasts, and it is an excellent way to render a stimulus (the negative CS presented without food) inhibitory. The reasons for this will be clear later, when the operation of Pavlov's fields is briefly discussed. The inhibition produced in this way may be disinhibited; differential inhibition was very important in Pavlov's interpretation of the way in which we learn to discriminate objects in our world.

Algebraic Summation A CS may be shown to be inhibitory by observing its effects when it is presented with an excitatory CS. One of Pavlov's methods for demonstrating inhibitory or excitatory properties of conditioned stimuli is called *algebraic summation*. Suppose that we have a tone that has been paired with food and that regularly produces a strong CR. We may present along with it a second stimulus that may be inhibitory because the CR to it has been extinguished, because it has been present during delayed conditioning, or because it has been presented without food during differential conditioning. If the added stimulus is inhibitory, it will reduce the normal response to the tone, and the amount of reduction will depend upon just how inhibitory is the added CS.

In his demonstrations of algebraic summation, Pavlov was careful to show that the effect was not simply due to the fact that a new stimulus was added, but that it was specific to stimuli that had been rendered inhibitory. For example, if the purpose were to show that a negative conditioned stimulus (CS −) was inhibitory by presenting it along with an established positive conditioned stimulus (CS +), it would not be enough simply to observe a decrease in response to the CS +. Perhaps adding any new stimulus to the CS + would have the same effect. Thus, you would be comparing the effects of a putative CS − with the effects of adding some third stimulus, which had not been rendered a CS − or a CS +. This sort of summation may be shown with excitatory stimuli as well; a CS previously paired with food may increase the reaction to the tone.

Evidence for Inhibition

Subsequent research (e.g., Rescorla, 1969) has largely corroborated Pavlov's findings regarding inhibition. However, such research has not provided evidence that extinction per se is sufficient to render a stimulus inhibitory, which Pavlov contended. It may be that this occurs only in a context in which some other CS is presented with a UCS—that is, in differential conditioning. This conclusion is based upon results from experiments in which currently acceptable tests for inhibition are applied. The tendency for extinction alone to produce sleep and its stages still stands, as far as is known, although Pavlov's interpretation in terms of the accumulation of inhibition has not received notice in the United States.

In addition to reconditioning and algebraic summation, another test for inhibition has become popular (cf. Lolordo & Fairless, 1985). This consists of observing actual movement by the subject. For example, locomotion by a rat or pigeon away from a CS− is now considered good reason to call the CS− inhibitory (Hearst & Franklin, 1977).

The Paradox of Inhibition

Pavlov believed that inhibition accompanies presentations of any CS, and that only excitation produced by a UCS counters it. This is particularly true in delayed conditioning, in which a CS is presented and remains present for seconds or minutes prior to the presentation of the UCS. In one example (1927, lecture 14), a dog received CS–UCS pairings of a metronome and food; the metronome preceded the food by 30 seconds and pairings occurred ten minutes apart. The following day the pairings were applied only 90 seconds apart and the salivation CR steadily diminished, trial by trial. By trial 22, only one drop of salivation appeared, although eleven or twelve drops had been typical.

On subsequent trials, no CR occurred and the dog refused to eat the food presented as the UCS. Was this the simple result of too many food presentations in too short a time? No, that was not the case. When a different CS+ for food was presented, the dog salivated and then ate; when no CS was presented, the dog ate "avidly" when food was offered. Evidently, the metronome CS that signaled food had become an inhibitor of both the CR and the UCR to food!

Kimmel (1966) described demonstrations of this effect. In one case salivation was so inhibited that a dog failed to salivate even during normal feeding. In other cases, human subjects showed inhibition of a variety of CRs, typically when the delayed conditioning method was used. Interestingly, he reported that "organism-wide tranquillity" also often occurred.

For example, in a variety of experiments human subjects were presented tones as CSs preceding electric shock. One aspect of the UCR to shock is perspiration, which can be measured as a change in skin conductance—the galvanic skin response (GSR). In Kimmel's experiments, a tone was sounded and remained on for a few seconds, followed by electric shock; the CR appeared as a GSR reading. As trials continued, typically to a dozen or more, the GSR diminished and in some cases even decreased to less-than-baseline levels. Why did this happen?

It was not because subjects adapted to the shock, making it less noxious—any more than the dog stops salivating and accepting food because it is not hungry. To prove this, all we need to do is present the shock without the CS; a strong response occurs. And if we ask subjects to rate the intensity of the shock, they do not report it as less noxious, even when their GSR to it has decreased greatly.

The subjects reacted as they did because the CS specifically inhibited the CR and the UCR. Kimmel could have extinguished this inhibitory effect by presenting the CS alone, without the UCS, a few times. If he then applied the CS–UCS pair, the UCR would be fine and the CR would appear after a few pairings.

The same effect has been shown in human eye-blink conditioning, in which a CS, such as a tone, is paired with a puff of air to the eye. The CR appears as an eye blink produced by the CS and preceding the air puff UCS. After twenty trials or so the eye-blink CR and the UCR to the puff diminish; but all we need do is present the air puff alone and the eye blink UCR is as strong as ever.

These findings provide strong support for learned inhibition, just as Pavlov described it. They also remind us that classical conditioning is more complicated than it first appears, a fact also well known to Pavlov.

External Inhibition

The inhibitory effects described so far are cases of what Pavlov called internal inhibition, since in his view they depended upon the build-up of inhibition in the cerebral cortex. Another effect, which he termed *external inhibition*, occurs when some new behavior is evoked and interferes with ongoing behavior. For example, during the presentation of a tone CS paired with food, a new stimulus, such as the sounding of a fire gong, may prevent or diminish the CR to the tone. This is due to the orientation of the subject toward the new sound and to other bodily movements that interfere with the reaction to the tone.

Pavlov's Brain: The Fields on the Surface of the Cortex

Pavlov's interests were not concentrated on the analysis of simple conditioned responses, but on the brain mechanisms he believed were responsible for our behavior and experience. Pavlov was trying to discover the principles that governed the action of the cerebrum, much as Sherrington had done with the spinal cord. Following Sherrington, Pavlov felt that the interaction of excitatory and inhibitory influences was basic to the workings of the cortex. Years of experiments led to the following fairly simple conception (Pavlov, 1927).

Presenting specific kinds of stimuli produces activity (excitation) in the brain centers that rep-

resent those stimuli. For example, food in the mouth of a hungry organism produces excitation in the *alimentary* (eating/digestive) *center*. Other stimuli presented along with such stimuli, such as the sight of food, a tone, or whatever, produce milder excitation in their respective brain centers. Since excitation occurs simultaneously in the food (UCS) and the tone (CS) centers, for example, a link forms between them. Excitation from the stronger (food) center flows to the weaker (tone) center and the tone thus becomes an excitatory CS, producing the effect formerly produced only by food.

As the tone and the food are paired repeatedly, strange things happen as the tone becomes more excitatory. Although the excitation is still weak, it irradiates, or spreads across the cortex. During this stage, a variety of tones or other stimuli may produce a CR, since the spreading excitation may include their cortical representations. The response to them will be weak, since the excitation spreading from the CS center is weak. With continued presentations of the tone and food, the tone becomes moderately excitatory and irradiation is replaced by *concentration*. The concentration of excitation at the cortical representation of the tone means that only those stimuli very similar to the tone (such as other tones) will elicit a CR, and the magnitude of the CR will depend upon the degree of similarity to the original tone. Excitation concentrates most strongly at that point and diminishes with distance from it.

Finally, after extremely lengthy training, excitation associated with the tone becomes extremely strong and once again irradiates. This stage, at which responding again occurs to a wide range of stimuli, may never be reached. Figure 3.8 diagrams the stages at which irradiation and concentration take place during discrimination.

At the stage in which irradiation is replaced by concentration, as both excitation and inhibition increase to medium strengths, something new occurs. A presentation of CS+ causes a decrease in the response to the CS− that follows, so responding is lowest immediately after CS+ and increases while CS− is present. A presentation of CS− produces the opposite effect on the succeed-

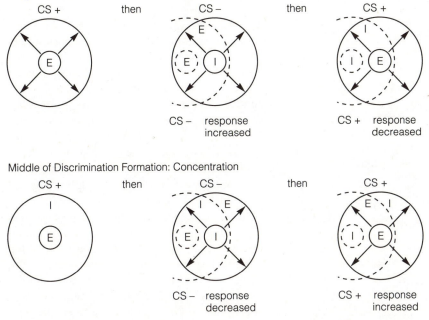

Early and Late in Discrimination Formation: Irradiation

CS +   then   CS –   then   CS +

CS – response increased   CS + response decreased

Middle of Discrimination Formation: Concentration

CS +   then   CS –   then   CS +

CS – response decreased   CS + response increased

FIGURE 3.8 A diagrammatic representation of Pavlovian fields. The upper half of the figure shows postulated processes early and late in the forming of a discrimination. Presentation of a CS+ (upper left) produces irradiation of excitation, represented by the radiating arrows. A subsequent presentation of a CS− (upper center) produces inhibition and its irradiation, but the cortical representation of CS− (the circled *I*) falls on the remnant of the excitatory surround from CS+. This excitation subtracts from the inhibition produced by CS− and tends to increase responding to it. The upper right figure shows a subsequent presentation of CS+; in this case the remaining inhibition from the previous CS− tends to diminish responding to CS+. The lower half of the figure shows the postulated processes midway in discrimination formation, during which concentration replaces irradiation. A presentation of CS+ (lower left) produces excitation at the cortical representation of CS+, as well as an inhibitory surround. A subsequent CS− (lower middle) falls on the remnant of this inhibitory field, which tends to further diminish responding to CS− (negative Pavlovian induction). The inhibitory center at CS− is surrounded by an excitatory field, and the remnant of this sums with the excitation produced when CS+ again appears (lower right). This augments the response to CS+ (positive Pavlovian induction). Sherrington discovered similar effects in spinal cord activity. His *simultaneous induction* was equivalent to irradiation, and *successive induction* was similar to Pavlovian induction.

ing CS+; the response to CS+ is augmented and declines during its presentation. These sequential effects are called *Pavlovian induction*—the former being negative induction and the latter positive induction (see Nevin & Shettleworth, 1966; Malone, 1976). Pavlov attempted to explain these effects in terms of excitatory and inhibitory fields in the cerebral cortex of the brain. Figure 3.9 compares the results of positive and negative induction in an illustrative experiment by Pavlov.

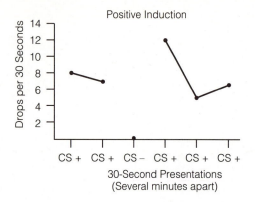

Positive Induction

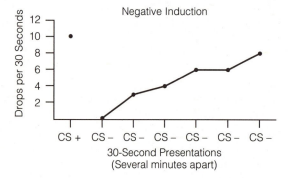

Negative Induction

FIGURE 3.9 Positive and negative induction (Pavlov, 1927, pp. 189, 198). The upper panel of this figure illustrates positive induction. A CS + (tactile stimulation of a dog's forepaw) was repeatedly paired with a food UCS. A CS − (tactile stimulation of a hind paw) was established by presenting it with no UCS. The data show responding when the CS + was presented twice, followed by presentation of the CS − . The salivary CR to the next presentation of the CS + was elevated (twelve drops), compared with previous levels of eight and seven drops.

The lower panel illustrates negative induction. The experiment, performed by Pavlov's assistant, Dr. Krjishkovsky, included an already established CS + and CS − (tone and tone paired with touch on skin). The UCS was a mild solution of acid. A presentation of the CS + alone produced a CR of ten drops. When the CS − was presented, responding was suppressed (negative induction). The CR increased in magnitude during subsequent presentations, showing the gradual fading of negative induction.

The Significance of Pavlovian Fields

Pavlov's model specifies three stages in the formation of discriminations learned by dogs. However, the general principles he described may well be operating in the daily lives of dogs and us, as we learn to sort out the objects of the world around us. We react one way to highly familiar objects: For example, I have seen my old coffee cup so often and in so many contexts that I can make an absolute identification of it. It produces strong excitation, in Pavlov's terms, at its cortical center, and this excitation concentrates, producing the immediate recognition.

There are objects to which we respond less firmly, though, and this becomes evident under unusual conditions. For example, darkness or fog or fatigue may require more care in dealing with objects, even when those objects are familiar ones. If the objects are less familiar, even more care is required. For instance, one must take more care discriminating the pavement from the ditch when driving in a rainstorm at night, when mistakes are more easily made and may be costly.

Between these extreme cases, which represent the third and the first stages of discrimination formation, lie the more common experiences of the intermediate, second stage. This is the stage when discriminations are formed and reliable identifications are made but when comparisons help strengthen the discrimination. For example, the two leading brands of cola do not taste exactly the same, and the difference in their tastes is never more evident than when a sip of one closely follows a taste of the other. In any situation in which we wish to accentuate a difference, we find that alternating the objects involved aids us. Consider for a moment how this represents Pavlov's second stage of discrimination formation, in which induction effects accentuate the reaction to the following stimulus. This may be the case in all of our discriminations where the objects involved are not quite unfamiliar (the first stage) and are not overly familiar (the third stage). Pavlov's fields and their changes as training progresses thus seem compatible with everyday life.

Mach Bands Pavlov's fields consisted of excitatory or inhibitory centers and surrounds of the opposite signs; at least they assumed that form while discriminations were being formed (that is, neither very early nor late in training). Several researchers have noted that such fields bear similarities to the *neural unit model*, first proposed by Ernst Mach during the nineteenth century and recently adapted by workers in sensory physiology, such as Bekesy (1967), Ratliff (1965), and Hubel and Wiesel (1959). Briefly, the neural unit model assumes that any stimulation on a receptor surface (for example, the retina or skin) produces a zone of excitation at the stimulated point and a zone of inhibition surrounding it. Elaborations of such units also form inhibitory centers and excitatory surrounds (Ratliff, 1965).

Before we return to the simple version of Pavlovian conditioning, I should point out that scientists are now quite certain that electrical fields do not operate on the surface of the cortex as Pavlov suggested they might (e.g., Lashley, Chow & Semmes, 1951). But even though Pavlov's model may not be in direct correspondence with brain events, it has some general features in common with later theories of neural networks (Smolensky, 1988).

Summary

This section has included a great deal of seemingly diverse information, all of it comprising the basics of Pavlov's theory. The first subsection introduced the important terms and phenomena of Pavlovian conditioning, presented as they are construed by contemporary psychologists. Pavlov and later researchers studied acquisition and extinction with a variety of specific preparations, with the original salivating dog largely replaced by the blinking human or rabbit. Conditioning can be excitatory or inhibitory, depending upon whether the CS signals a forthcoming UCS or its absence, and the effects of conditioning may spread so that other CSs similar to that used in training produce CRs. The way in which such CSs are discriminated from the original CS as

training progresses is still of great interest, as it was in Pavlov's day.

An effective CS must ordinarily evoke a reasonably strong UCR; this seems not to be the case in sensory preconditioning, although even in that case it is certain that some UCR is evoked. Almost anything, either inside or outside the body, may be used as a CS. A CS and a UCS may be paired almost simultaneously, or there may be a long delay between CS and UCS. If the CS is presented and removed long before the UCS appears, a presumed trace of the CS persists in the nervous system to bridge the gap. Backward conditioning, in which the UCS precedes the CS, eventually renders the CS inhibitory.

Psychologists still are concerned over what is learned in classical conditioning; there is evidence for both S-S connections and S-R connections. There is strong evidence to show that the UCS in classical conditioning does not act in the same way as a reward in instrumental conditioning. Omission procedures provide the most striking evidence that the CR is not simply maintained by the reward of the UCS. Despite the fact that the UCS and rewards in instrumental conditioning do not act in the same way, the old distinction between classical and instrumental conditioning as two fundamentally different forms of learning is not universally accepted.

Pavlov's views on the functioning of organisms were influenced greatly by Sherrington's analysis of the integrative action of the spinal nervous system. Pavlov adopted many of Sherrington's major principles, and we find the emphasis on *simultaneous* and *successive induction* and the importance of excitation and inhibition throughout his writings.

Pavlov presented many lines of evidence for the existence of inhibitory effects in the workings of the brain. Most of this has been substantiated by later researchers. Inhibition may account for spontaneous recovery, for extinction-induced sleep and psychopathology, and for the pattern of responding during delayed conditioning. It appears that extinction may progress "below zero," that disinhibition is possible, and that excitatory and inhibitory CSs may algebraically summate. The best method to render a CS inhibitory is to use it in discrimination training, along with a CS paired with a UCS.

Pavlov's decades of research led him to propose a model of brain function in terms of fields of excitation and inhibition on the surface of the cortex. During discrimination training, excitation and inhibition form at the cortical representations of CS + and CS − . Early and late in training, this excitation and inhibition spreads (irradiates). Otherwise it concentrates, leaving a surround of the opposite sign. This accounts for Pavlovian induction. Pavlov's fields are ever changing, but the general principle suggests that both excitation and inhibition are always present in our reactions to stimuli.

3. CRITICISMS OF PAVLOV'S THEORY

In the final section of this chapter, we will discuss some of the ways in which classical conditioning influences our daily lives. That influence exists whether Pavlov's theory was correct, and it exists whether the theories of American classical conditioning are correct. First, however, we will briefly mention criticisms of Pavlov's views and of the use made of the CR in the theories of early American psychologists.

Criticisms of Pavlov's Specific Model of Brain Physiology

Pavlov's model supposes that fields of excitation and inhibition operate on the surface of the cortex in the ways described earlier. Such a view is seemingly at odds with current notions of neural activity, which emphasize the transmission of neural impulses along neurons and across synapses. This probably would not seem a great problem to Pavlov, who characterized his model as "a schematic" version of the neural processes involved (Pavlov, 1927); in any event, it is not dif-

ficult to make a synaptic network act in the ways in which Pavlov's fields acted (e.g., Thompson, 1965).

Konorski (1948) described a host of data collected since Pavlov's early researchers. The data pretty much support the original model, although Konorski makes some modifications of Pavlov's theory in his translation to a more traditional brain model that does rely on ordinary synaptic transmission instead of fields. Valenstein (1970) provides a good assessment of Pavlov's neurology and its plausibility.

In addition, we have discovered that Pavlovian induction occurs during operant (instrumental) discrimination learning and that its characteristics are as Pavlov described them (e.g., Nevin & Shettleworth, 1966; Malone, 1976). Few researchers, however, have systematically tested Pavlov's theory of how induction takes place (Mackintosh, 1974).

Criticisms of Pavlovian Conditioning as the Basis for All Learning

Pavlov never suggested that all behavior and experience is merely the sum of accumulated conditioned responses (e.g., Pavlov, 1932), although many others *did*. Watson was intrigued with that possibility and mentioned several times in his writings that the CR may be the unit from which all else derives (Chapter 4). Floyd Allport (1924) made bold claims concerning the importance of the CR as such a unit and provoked a torrent of criticism over the years. Hull, a highly influential theorist, also relied on the conditioned response as the ultimate unit of analysis, as we will see in Chapter 6.

It may seem difficult to imagine just how someone could suggest that all behavior and experience is built from CRs, but the argument does have some merit. One must begin with the conviction that we are, after all, biological beings and that we come with a set of inborn reflex reactions. We originally react (with UCRs) only to biologically relevant things, such as food in our mouths, water, warmth, and stroking. These things are

TABLE 3.4 Example of Higher Order Conditioning

CS5: knights, heroes
   CS4: praiseworthy behavior
      CS3: praise   CR: attention, pleasure, and so on
         CS2: attention
           CS1: parent
               UCSs: food, water, warmth, stroking
               UCRs: attention, pleasure, and so on

accompanied by a parent (or other caregiver), who becomes a CS evoking positive CRs. These CRs generalize to other adults, and second-order CRs develop. Table 3.4 provides an example of higher order conditioning and shows how simple UCRs may form the basis for higher motives and behaviors.

Thus, the parent's presence is not sufficient as a CS. The child learns that the parent must be paying attention to him or her. The child receives food (and so on) only then. The child discriminates parent-plus-attention from parent alone, and *attention* becomes a CS for food and cuddling. Then the child finds that an angry parent, while giving attention, less reliably provides UCSs (food and comfort), so *praise* comes to be a third-order CS.

The parent shows the child pictures of shiny buttons (which act as UCSs to capture attention) worn by knights and soldiers, who therefore also (as CSs) capture the child's attention. The knight or soldier appears in a context of praiseworthy endeavors and the shiny button comes to signify (as a CS) praise, honor, and virtue. The child learns to name the knight, because utterances that sound like *knight* are followed by the UCS (parent saying *knight*); and language is built up out of a set of CRs joined together somehow in series.

As a distant precursor of Pavlov put it, this process accounts for "a young girl's tremblings at the first thoughts of love, . . . Newton's creating universal laws, . . . and the behavior of a man with an ideally strong will, acting under some high moral impulse, and perfectly conscious of everything he does" (Sechenov, 1863).

We will see that the CR plays an exceedingly important part in our attitudes, in "psychosomatic" medicine and in the origin of phobias (pathological fears). But as the unit out of which all behavior and experience is constructed, it falls short by quite a bit. The appeal that the CR had for early American psychologists stems from their desires toward reductionism—the analysis of the complex into some sort of units assumed in advance. This was not Pavlov's way, and the pros and cons of reductionism will be clearer in Chapter 6, when we discuss Hull.

4. OTHER ASPECTS OF CLASSICAL CONDITIONING

Classical conditioning affects our reactions to a host of common occurrences of daily life. It explains a number of common likes and aversions that span a lifetime, and it plays a large role in determining our state of health.

Classical Conditioning in Daily Life

Decaffeinated coffee wakes me up, as does regular coffee, as long as I don't drink decaffeinated coffee exclusively. People with oddly bright blue eyes looking straight at me bring to mind a particular brand of cigarettes. Richard Nixon reminds many people in my generation of the presidential seal. For some people, prune juice produces its customary cathartic effect as soon as they taste it. The word *inhale* produces constriction of peripheral blood vessels in the arm. Gloomy gray days make us feel tired and dull. Mealtime produces an upset stomach in some people and a feeling of warmth and security in others.

All of these are instances of classical conditioning, which is so common in our lives that we pay little attention to it. But all of the examples illustrate the central rule that defines classical conditioning: If two elicitors are paired reliably in a certain way, the weaker of the two comes to produce (more or less) the reaction formerly produced only by the stronger elicitor. As the tone produces the salivation appropriate to food in the mouth, the taste, smell, and appearance of coffee come to produce the reaction originally produced only by the caffeine. The blue-eyed people on billboards draw our attention; later, the brand of cigarettes that appear with them in the ads draw our attention (or so the manufacturer hopes). A childhood in which gray days must be spent indoors with nothing to do may lend the feelings of those times to the gray sky (cf. Buck, 1988).

All of these effects occur whether we want them to or not and whether we are aware of it or not. When we inhale, the peripheral blood vessels in our limbs constrict; they also do so when we say or hear the word *inhale*. Classical conditioning is important because it is an automatic process. We may dismiss (as countless people have) the salivation of the dog when the tone is sounded. The tone predicts food and makes the dog anticipate it; he salivates because he expects food— hardly an occurrence of importance. The point is that the dog salivates whether it wants to or not, whether it anticipates or not. In fact, in many cases of classical conditioning, awareness of what is to come plays no conceivable part. Before describing such cases, consider the following example.

Classical Conditioning as an Explanatory Device

A good deal of what seems very complicated human behavior and experience may result from the classical conditioning that affects us every day of our lives. Such examples as the salivating dogs

seem far removed, but the same principle may be operating in our own behavior and experience every day of our lives. Consider the following example of a family in which the parents have chosen breakfast and dinner gatherings as a time for criticism and reproof of a child's current activities. Suppose that this pattern continues for a number of years and produces effects on the child that last for years after. Assuming that criticism of this kind elicits strong bodily visceral/emotional reactions, we have a UCS producing a UCR. Anger, shame, sadness, and discomfort on the child's part is accompanied by stomachaches, perspiration, headaches, and other bodily changes. These reactions are also accompanied by a host of cues that become conditioned stimuli. The sight and sound of the parents, the furniture present, the stimuli accompanying food, the sensations of food passing through the digestive tract, and so on (Buck, 1988).

Suppose, as is likely, that the parents are not criticizing the child during the whole day; their support and encouragement at other times renders them unreliable predictors of impending stomachaches and other aspects of the UCR. Similarly, time is spent in the dining room in the absence of the parents and the cues present there do not act as good predictors. The only fairly reliable predictor of emotional distress and its bodily manifestations is the sight, taste, and smell of food and the stimuli the child carries inside— the sensations of food passing through the digestive tract. Aside from the sensations that go with a very full or a very empty stomach, the child is largely unaware of these sensations, but that is not really important. The body is aware, and such sensations can come to elicit emotional distress.

Imagine the effects in later life, especially since conditioning in which the CS is an event within the body is extremely durable (Razran, 1961). Later aversions to food and eating (and other situations and activities) could later appear and would no doubt be attributed to an endless variety of psychic disturbances. A childhood that includes encouragement and support from the parents during mealtimes could lead to quite different results, of course, but in both cases the simple cause of strange attitudes toward food and eating probably would be neglected. The simple cause is interoceptive classical conditioning.

Interoceptive Conditioning

For our purposes, *interoceptive conditioning* is classical conditioning in which the CS, UCS, or both are applied to a structure within the body. Soviet psychologists break down the definition further, according to the stimulus or stimuli applied internally. Thus, interoceptive/interoceptive conditioning means that both the CS and the UCS are applied internally, as in the example above, in which the CS (movement of food through the digestive tract) and the UCS (internal stimulation producing stomachache, and so on) both occur within us. The sound of a bell paired with shock to the foot represents exteroceptive/exteroceptive conditioning, whereas a bell paired with an injection of insulin constitutes exteroceptive/interoceptive conditioning. The Soviets have studied since 1928 what we will call interoceptive conditioning (see the summary by Bykov, 1957, and the review by Razran, 1961), because they saw very early that it had clear applications in medicine. American researchers also recognized this recently, as we will see in a brief discussion of the exciting work of Ader and Cohen (1982).

Recall that classical conditioning is defined as the outcome of the pairing of two elicitors so that the weaker elicitor (the CS) comes to produce the reaction originally produced only by the stronger elicitor (the UCS). Since the activities of organs, such as the kidneys, lungs, intestines, and so on constitute a set of UCRs, all that we need to do is find a stimulus that acts as a UCS for whatever activity we wish to influence. Having done that, we can pair it with a CS and influence the activity of an organ (or a system of organs) at will. For example, it may be desirable to increase the activity of a sluggish kidney and thus increase its rate of filtration of blood and production of urine. An enema does just that; it acts as a UCS producing an increase in kidney functioning as a UCR.

Bykov's Studies The previous paragraph describes studies summarized by Bykov (1957). According to Bykov, if the sound of a tone, a colored light, or some other stimulus is paired with enemas, a conditioned response to the cue appears after less than twenty trials. Presentation of the CS then causes an increase in the production of urine and continues to do so for some time before extinction occurs. Periodic repairings of the CS and the UCS (enema) may be used to keep the CS effective.

Ventilation of gases by the lungs may be similarly influenced by classical conditioning. For example, Bykov reported an experiment in which human subjects were made to step up on a stool forty times during a two-minute period. This acted as a UCS producing a UCR of increased lung activity, assessed by the experimenters in terms of rate of oxygen consumption. The step-ups were always preceded by the command, "Get ready for the experiment," two minutes before the step-ups began and the command, "Begin work," five seconds before the exercise was to start. Even during the first day or two of conditioning, the first command became a CS. When that command was given two minutes before exercise was to begin, it produced a CR increase of oxygen consumption of more than 250 percent of the level occurring just before the command was given. Such effects are familiar to participants in sports in which strong physical activity begins on signal. We cannot voluntarily alter metabolic activity, such as our consumption of oxygen, although we may augment the CSs that can produce such effects by providing our own CSs. We might imagine the sound of the starter's gun, the way that our muscles will feel in action, and so on.

It should be emphasized that the results in Bykov's study here were not the result of the subject's will. You might imagine that the command that signals the impending work might lead subjects to prepare themselves by breathing more deeply (and so on), and that this preparation could cause the increase in oxygen consumption. However, a series of experiments by the same researchers showed that this was not the case; muscle tensing and hyperventilation (deep breathing) by themselves produced no noticeable increase in oxygen consumption.

Also interesting was their finding that the CS (command) that occurred two minutes before the UCS (exercise) eventually resulted in the CR (oxygen use) appearing only during the minute before exercise. This is the expected result in delayed conditioning, in which the UCS comes some time after the onset of the CS. (A metronome, which also accompanied the exercise, was on during the interval between the CS and the UCS. The metronome acted as a part of the CS, so the procedure was delayed conditioning rather than trace conditioning.) As in other cases of delayed conditioning, it was possible to disinhibit "inhibition of delay" and reinstate a high rate of oxygen consumption during the first minute. This was accomplished by giving the subjects a small drink of coffee or of alcohol in tea, neither of which affected the consumption of oxygen under other circumstances. But the drinks did act as disinhibiting stimuli, and they raised the level of consumption of oxygen during the first minute. Thus, delayed conditioning here was equivalent to delayed conditioning in more familiar procedures, such as when the bell precedes the food to be given to the salivating dog.

In another example described by Bykov, a mild solution of hydrochloric acid (weak enough to just provide a bitter taste) was injected occasionally into the small intestine of a dog through a fine plastic tube. On other occasions, a weak saline solution was injected. The intestine had been surgically connected to the catheter so there was no chance the dog could taste the fluids. Only the small intestine "knew" what was being injected and you must agree that one of the great blessings of life (for us and for dogs) is that we are allowed to ignore our intestines completely! Except in extreme illness, we haven't a clue what they are doing and we leave their daily operation up to them.

It is difficult to believe that the dog was aware of the few drops of fluid placed in its intestine, and it surely could not tell whether the acid or the saline was injected. The contents of the small intestine are not tasted, as far as we know, but they are nevertheless discerned by the body in some way. Paired with the injections of acid was an electric shock to one of the dog's hind feet. The dog was aware of this. Among the components of the UCR to shock is a brief elevation in heart rate. Presentations of the salt solution were not paired with shock. Within sixteen trials the injection of the acid became a CS, producing changes in heart rate, and the salt solution produced no effect. Surely the dog was not aware of the acid injection, but something was telling the foot and the heart that the shock was coming.

A practical application of classical conditioning of an internal organ was reported by Ince, Brucker, and Alba (1978), whose subject was a 40-year-old paraplegic man. He had suffered a complete severing of his spinal cord a year before as the result of an accident and, among other problems, had lost all control over urination. Ince et al. knew that a fairly intense electric shock to the lower abdomen can elicit reflex urination; hence, the shock acts as a UCS. What if the shock were paired with a CS? Could the patient use the CS to control urination?

A mild shock to the inner thigh was used as a CS, paired with the intense shock to the abdomen as a UCS. Conditioning did indeed occur; the CS alone produced a strong urination CR. Thereafter, the patient was able to control urination by applying the CS and eliciting the CR of urination. Interestingly, both thigh and lower abdomen were below the body areas controlled by the patient's functional (upper) spinal cord; this means that conditioning occurred without the brain's involvement.

Occasional sessions in which CS–UCS pairings occurred were necessary to maintain the CS's effectiveness. However, the patient was able to apply the CS hundreds of times (over days and weeks) without extinction occurring. This illustrates the unusual resistance to extinction of visceral conditioning.

Ader and Cohen's Lupus Studies   Another example of the medical applications of interoceptive conditioning was reported by Ader and Cohen (1982), two researchers at the University of Rochester Medical School. They were studying ways of treating the disease systemic lupus erythematosus, which is a malfunction of the body's response to invading microorganisms and other foreign proteins. This illness, usually called lupus, amounts to an exaggerated response of the body's immune system, so that healthy tissues are destroyed and death results.

To study the possible ways of treating this disease, scientists bred a strain of mice that are genetically prone to the disease. These mice usually die within eight to fourteen months of age. If some treatment can be discovered to prevent the death of such mice, we could possibly have the cure that could prevent the death of humans stricken with lupus.

The drug cyclophosphamide can postpone lupus by suppressing the body's autoimmune response. Unfortunately, this is not a practical cure, since the suppression of the autoimmune response leaves us vulnerable to whatever germ may come along and even an ordinarily harmless infection could do us in.

Ader and Cohen treated three groups of these special mice with either cyclophosphamide injections or injections of salt water. The groups were as follows:

C100: The mice in this group received a drink of saccharine water followed by an injection of cyclophosphamide once a week for eight weeks.

C50: The mice in this group received the same treatment as those in the C100 group, except that half of the injections contained salt water rather than cyclophosphamide.

NC50: This group received the same treatment as the C50 group, except that the saccharine water and the injections of salt water or medicine were never paired. The injections were given on different days.

Mice in a control group were given no medicine but received drinks of saccharine and saline injections (unpaired) once a week.

The cyclophosphamide given was not enough to prevent death indefinitely, so all of the mice died, as was fated by their genetic makeup, which brought their unfortunate disease. But which mice died first, which died last, and which died second and third in order? Group C100 subjects lived longest, which is not surprising in view of the large doses of medicine they were given. And the mice in the control group lived the briefest; again, this is not an amazing result, since they received no cyclophosphamide.

What was interesting was the difference in the life spans of the C50 and the NC50 groups, both of which outlived the controls but died sooner than did the C100 group. Both the C50 and the NC50 groups were given the same amount of cyclophosphamide, the same doses of saccharine water, and the same number of injections of salt water. Yet, the C50 group outlived the NC50 group by almost a month and a half (on the average). This amounted to an increase in longevity of about 25 percent. Why should this be?

The secret lies in classical conditioning of the autoimmune response. Group C50 always received saccharine water followed by an injection. Half the time the injection was cyclophosphamide, a UCS that produced a UCR suppression of the autoimmune response. What happened when the saccharine water was added as a CS?

Water taste (CS)
cyclophosphamide (UCS) → suppression of
autoimmune
system (UCR)

The sweet taste soon produced a CR suppression of the immune system whenever it appeared, including when it was presented with saline injections. The mice in the C50 group effectively were getting more medicine than those in the NC50 group. For the animals in the NC50 group, the sweet taste and the cyclophosphamide were never paired and thus no conditioned response appeared.

In their account in *Science* (1982), Ader and Cohen point out the significance of their findings for human sufferers. They suggest that classical conditioning may have many useful applications in the form of such placebo effects. For example, suppose you are dying of a hideous disease, such as some kind of organ cancer and that your life is being prolonged through chemotherapy. The medicine that keeps the cancer in check is very harmful itself; you probably have heard about the horrible side effects of chemotherapy.

What if your dose of medicine could be cut in half, as the dose of cyclophosphamide was cut in half for the mice? Could a distinctive stimulus be paired with the medicine on some occasions and with harmless salt water on other occasions? Would a CR appear, as was the case for the C50 mice? Could the medicine thus have its good effect with half the previous dose, so that unwanted side effects could be reduced?

Of course, the usefulness of the described procedure depends upon what effects of cyclophosphamide or other drugs turn out to be conditionable. Ader and Cohen assumed that the beneficial effects will appear as CRs, sparing the patient the ill effects. But there may be cases in which unwanted effects also appear as CRs, perhaps even more strongly than the beneficial effects. Still, the possible great benefits of such treatments warrant further research.

Countless experiments have been done with both human and animal subjects, showing that bodies are conditionable, even if we have not the slightest awareness of what is going on. Russian researchers, such as Bykov, firmly believe that the cerebral cortex is involved in such conditioning and that sensory information from throughout the body is sent to the cortex, although we are utterly unaware of most of it.

Drug Addiction A good deal of work has been done in the United States investigating the part played by classical conditioning in drug addiction. Horsley Gantt, at the VA hospital in Perry Point, Maryland, did much of this work until his death in 1980. Interestingly, he was the translator of Pavlov's (1928) original lectures. For an example of classical conditioning and drug addiction, consider the demonstration reported by Spragg in 1940, in which chimpanzees were addicted to morphine. After a time without morphine the chimps showed obvious withdrawal symptoms, much like those shown by human addicts. Under these conditions, morphine acts as a UCS producing a UCR (the ending of withdrawal symptoms).

Morphine had been injected using a hypodermic syringe, and it is reasonable to assume that the sight of the syringe and the injection itself had become conditioned stimuli. When Spragg injected salt water, he found that this was the case. The CR brought on by the injection eliminated all signs of withdrawal in the chimpanzees for up to half an hour. Further applications of classical conditioning to drug addiction will be discussed in Chapter 9 when we consider the interesting model of Solomon and Corbit (1974) and the research of Siegel (e.g., 1985).

Semantic Conditioning

One interesting application of classical conditioning, described by Razran (1961), deals with what we usually call meaning in language. Meaning may be defined in a number of ways, such as the associations attached to a word. For example, one definition for the meaning of *tree* is the list of associates commonly produced by the word (for example, green, leaf, wood, shoe). Some theorists, including Collins and Quillian (1969), believe that the order and the speed of production of associates is important in assessing meaning.

Semantic conditioning is a way of assessing the similarity of meaning of words and symbols, as well as what Razran called the "meaning load" carried by parts of a sentence. We will consider three aspects of semantic conditioning: semantic generalization, phonetic generalization, and assessing "meaning load."

Semantic Generalization In semantic generalization procedures, a CR is established to a word, a sentence, or a numerical expression CS, and a second CS typically is made inhibitory (no UCS paired with it). The UCSs include food, a cold disk placed on the skin, and electric shock. Razran presented the data obtained from a thirteen-year-old boy, Yuri, who was conditioned to salivate to sentences and numbers. For example, after the Russian words for *good* and *bad* were established as CS+ and CS−, respectively, a number of sentences were presented. Yuri salivated when a sentence such as "The Russian army was victorious" or "Leningrad is a beautiful city" or "The enemy army was destroyed and annihilated" was presented. But Yuri did not respond much to sentences that referred to "bad" things, such as lazy or disobedient students. The initial training with "good" (CS+) and "bad" (CS−) made it easy to assess what Yuri considered good and bad.

It is not difficult to think of practical uses for this procedure, especially when applied to attitudes that may be unconscious or that the subject does not wish revealed. The CR to the original CS generalizes to other stimuli that are similar in meaning (that is, semantics) for the subject.

Table 3.5 shows semantic conditioning with numerical stimuli. In one case, Yuri was conditioned to respond to the number ten (CS+) and not to the number eight (CS−). Note the difference in response when the expressions presented represented a difference, a sum, a quotient, or a product of ten or eight. The second case shows responding to the items on the left when the CS+ was eighteen and the CS− was fourteen. The latencies given show the pause before salivation began; note how the latency increased with the difficulty of the operation. The final example is especially interesting.

Phonetic Generalization Phonetics refers to the sounds of language, whereas *semantics* refers to meaning. The Russian researchers discussed by Razran (1961) have repeatedly found that younger or retarded children generalize phonetically: After training to respond to the CS+ *tree*, they respond to words such as *bee* and *tea*, rather than to *bush* and *pine*. Older children and adults

TABLE 3.5 Salivation of 13-Year-Old Yuri to Arithmetical Operations

Salivation After Conditioning to 10 (CS+) and 8 (CS−). (Data do not include all that appeared in Razran's [1961] Table 2.)

Stimulus	Drops in 30 seconds
83 − 73	15
20 − 12	2
1000/100	18
48/6	3
4 × 2	2
112 − 102	11
470/47	11
99 − 91	3
88/11	3
35 − 25	25

Salivation After Conditioning to 18 (CS+) and 14 (CS−).

Stimulus	Drops in 30 seconds	Latency (sec)
9 + 9	18	2
90/5	13	6
72/4	9	11
2232/124	2	7.8

Razran, 1961

tend to generalize semantically; that is, from a CS+ to items similar in meaning (for example, *tree–bush*).

The shift from phonetic to semantic generalization also depends on the stage of training. In one experiment adult subjects received CS–UCS pairings in which the CS was a word and the UCS was a cold disk placed on the arm. When test words were presented, the vasoconstriction CR occurred to similar sounding words during early trials (phonetic generalization). But, after 25 trials, the CR occurred to new words similar in meaning (semantic generalization). When the subjects were given tranquilizers, phonetic generalization returned. In the United States, such an effect would be called differences in the level of processing (e.g., Bower & Hilgard, 1981).

Assessing Meaning Load The final type of semantic conditioning research is interesting indeed. The following example involves the use of classical conditioning to estimate the relative contributions of parts of a sentence to the meaning of the whole, but other applications are obvious. For example, Razran (1961) described an experiment in which 30 college students were presented sentences as positive CSs and electric shock to the fingers as a UCS. The finger withdrawal CR was then measured when different parts of the sentences were presented as CSs and no electric shock occurred. The students' CRs were used as an indicant of meaning of parts of the sentences. If a sentence part acts as a strong CS + it is judged to be meaningful.

The results appear in Table 3.6. The slashes indicate which parts of each sentence were presented alone. The percentage of CRs that occurred appears in parentheses. Data is from the first trial for each subject.

Note that in the first example, a CR occurred for both sentence parts; it is reasonable that each part carried the meaning of the whole sentence. In the second example, CRs occurred when the whole sentence was presented, but not when either half appeared, since neither had much meaning alone. In the third example, the second sentence part (the verb *passed*) received the most responses, and the third part also elicited frequent responses. On the other hand, little meaning (or CRs) occurred for the first part of the sentence. The second and third parts make it likely that a student is involved, so it is reasonable that the first part does not evoke much response.

There are many applications of this procedure. Razran suggested that the method be applied to the study of unconscious content, Freudian symbolism, advertising, propaganda, and other areas. You probably can think of other applications.

Summary

Classical conditioning affects us constantly. This is shown in the CR produced by an occasional cup of decaffeinated coffee, typical reactions to

TABLE 3.6 Conditioned Response to Sentence Parts

I am switching on (100%)	/	the shock. (100%)		
The manuscript (0%)	/	was read. (0%)		
The student (10%)	/	passed (87%)	/	the examination. (50%)

Razran, 1961

the figures on billboards, and the life-long eating patterns that grew from listening to parents' criticism during mealtimes. Because classical conditioning affects us daily and can influence our behavior so dramatically, it can actually be applied for this purpose.

Interoceptive conditioning is classical conditioning in which a stimulus is applied to the structure of the body. Soviet psychologists showed that interoceptive conditioning has important medical applications and very recent work in America shows that classical conditioning plays a large part in our reactions to medicines. Any organ or system of organs can be conditioned if a UCS is available. By pairing a convenient CS with an appropriate UCS, we can influence the organ or system involved, whether it be the kidney or the body's metabolic rate. Classical conditioning may also be used to treat drug addiction.

Medicines act as UCSs. Therefore, the sight or taste of medicine or even the label *medicine* can act as a CS. This no doubt accounts for placebo effects, the beneficial effects of sugar pills that a patient believes to be medicine. Placebo effects also occur when the subjects are infant mice and no conception of taking medicine is likely to be in the patient's heads. This points up the fact that classical conditioning need not require awareness that it is occurring. If we assume that the dog salivates because it anticipates food we must also say that the small intestine anticipates shocks!

It should by now be apparent that classical conditioning plays a role in everyday experience; it does not apply only to the case of the tone and the salivating dog. It shows that the entire body is alive and that its organs are affected by our experience, however ignorant of our lives we may believe them to be. Bykov (1957, p. 27) quotes Maupassant in this regard: "Your feet, your muscles, your lungs, all your body has not yet forgotten and keeps saying to the brain, when the brain wishes to lead it along the same hard path: No, I shall not come, I have suffered too much on this path. And the brain accepts the refusal, obeying without arguing the silent language of its comrades." Words, phrases, and sentences act as CSs, as shown in studies of semantic conditioning. Classical conditioning may therefore be used to assess attitudes and meaning and even to explore the unconscious.

GLOSSARY

Acquisition The development of an ever-stronger and more reliable conditioned response (CR) through conditioning. (See *extinction*.)

Algebraic summation Method used by Pavlov to demonstrate the inhibitory and excitatory properties of CSs by pairing them with other CSs. For example, an inhibitory CS introduced along with another CS will cause a decrease in responding to the latter. A positive CS presented with another positive CS should produce a response greater than that to either of the individual stimuli. This method also was used by Rescorla (1969).

Alimentary center Brain center aroused when eating occurs, in Pavlov's theory of conditioning. The alimentary center was strongly activated by food in the mouth (a UCS), and part of this activation spread to the brain centers corresponding to CSs simultaneously present.

Appetitive Category of UCSs. This adjective describes stimuli that we judge to be pleasant, adaptive, or otherwise beneficial for the organism.

Aversive Category of UCSs. This adjective describes stimuli that we judge to be unpleasant, dangerous, or otherwise not beneficial for the organism.

Backward conditioning A conditioning procedure in which the UCS precedes the CS. This was formerly thought to lead to no conditioning, but it has been recognized as the chief means for producing inhibitory conditioning.

Classical conditioning Procedure whereby two elicitors are paired in such a way that the weaker precedes the stronger by a second or more (ideally) and so that the weaker stimulus reliably predicts the stronger. Conditioning is said to occur when the weaker stimulus produces a response similar to that produced by the stronger. For example, the taste of coffee, associated with the effects of caffeine, may actually perk us up. (Most coffee drinkers feel perky long before the caffeine can have a real effect on the body.)

Concentration Process that occurs during classical conditioning, specifically during discrimination learning. Early and late in training, excitation and inhibition associated with CS + and CS − irradiate (spread). Midway in training, excitation and inhibition concentrate, or remain close to their respective brain centers. Concentration is the opposite of irradiation.

Conditioned response (or reflex)/CR Response evoked by a CS after pairing in a specific way with a UCS. The CR resembles the response to the UCS, not the original response to the CS. For example, the sight of a cut onion at a distance may produce a CR secretion of tears.

Conditioned stimulus/CS Weak elicitor that is paired with a stronger elicitor in such a way as to acquire the power to evoke the response originally evoked by the stronger elicitor (UCS).

Conditioned suppression Procedure used to investigate the inhibitory and/or aversive properties of stimuli. For example, a stimulus previously paired with shock may be presented while subjects are bar pressing or proofreading. If the rate of the latter performances is decreased during the presentation, the added stimulus is judged inhibitory.

Delayed conditioning Classical conditioning procedure in which the CS is presented, remains present, and is later followed by the UCS. With training, responding decreases during the early part of the delay interval.

Disinhibition The release from inhibition produced by a new stimulus, such as a handclap or a trumpet blare. This is evidenced by the appearance of responding in the presence of an inhibitory CS.

Differentiation Pavlov's term for discrimination formation. It includes both the discriminating of stimuli and the associating of UCSs with appropriate stimuli.

Equalization phase Stage described by Pavlov that occurs during prolonged extinction training. During this phase, both strong and weak CSs produce the same magnitude CR.

Excitatory conditioning Classical conditioning in which a CS reliably predicts the occurrence of a UCS. This is the opposite of inhibitory conditioning, in which the appearance of the CS means that the UCS is not coming.

Experimental neurosis Bizarre behavior brought on by the presentation of an insoluble problem after experience with similar problems that were soluble. Pavlov believed that a disruption of normal excitation and inhibition in the brain accounted for experimental neurosis.

External inhibition Suppression of a CR produced by the introduction of a stimulus that produces a competing response. For example, conditioned salivation by a dog may be disrupted if the dog's name is suddenly called in a loud voice.

Extinction The decrease and eventual disappearance of a CR, which happens when the CS is repeatedly presented without a UCS. Pavlov believed that extinction brought about the inhibition of the CR.

Eyelid (eye-blink) conditioning Classical conditioning method popular in the United States. A UCS air puff to the cornea produces a UCR eye blink. A CS (such as a tone) preceding the air puff produces a CR eye blink. It is less messy than conditioned salivation, and it has been extended to the blink of the nictitating membrane in rabbits.

Final common path Sherrington's term for the motor path in the spinal reflex system. There are a great many more afferent (sensory) nerves than there are motor outlets, and he described a competition among sensory nerves for the motor outlet, or final common path.

Induction See Pavlovian induction.

Inhibition Basic neural process which Pavlov believed worked with excitation to regulate the workings of the brain. For Pavlov, inhibition meant the suppression of neural activity, directly opposing the activation produced by excitation. It is now known that excitation and inhibition are characteristics of neural activity.

Inhibition of delay A decrease in responding that occurs during the early part of the delay period during delayed conditioning. Pavlov believed that this was due to the fact that time acted as a CS, and, since the time just after the onset of the CS was never accompanied by the UCS, it became inhibitory. A

handclap could restore responding during this period, showing the disinhibition of inhibition of delay.

Inhibitory conditioning Classical conditioning procedure in which a CS reliably signals the absence of a UCS. This is the opposite of excitatory conditioning.

Instrumental conditioning Learning that depends on the consequences of responses. The procedure is similar in some respects to classical conditioning. Instrumental learning is also known as operant learning.

Integrative action Sherrington's term for the coordinated activities of individual organs, with the spinal cord acting as an organ of integration. The integrative action approach studies the workings of the system as a whole and opposes the analysis of discrete units (for example, reflexes).

Interoceptive conditioning Classical conditioning in which the CS, the UCS, or both are applied within the body, to an organ or a system within the body.

Irradiation Spread of excitation and inhibition, which Pavlov supposed to occur on the surface of the cortex. During the formation of a differentiation, irradiation occurs early and late in training.

Neural unit Basic element of sensory experience first proposed by Mach in the last century and adopted by a host of workers in sensory physiology during this century. The neural unit consists of an excitatory center surrounded by a zone of inhibition.

Omission procedures Experimental procedure in which a CS is presented and a UCS thereafter, unless a CR occurred to the CS. Thus, the sight of water might be followed by a drink of water, as long as no salivation occurred when the sight of water appeared. Omission training was first used to determine whether some CRs are affected by their consequences. If a CR occurs whether it prevents a UCS or not then it is a true CR.

Paradoxical phase Stage occurring during prolonged extinction in which weak CSs produce stronger responses than do strong CSs.

Pavlovian induction Effects produced by a CS on responding during a subsequent CS. For example, positive induction occurs when a CS− precedes a CS+ and the response to the CS+ is stronger than when CS− does not precede it. Negative induction occurs when responding to a CS− is suppressed by an immediately preceding CS+. Pavlov believed that induction worked together with irradiation and concentration during discrimination learning.

Pseudoconditioning Apparent CRs produced because the UCS has rendered the subject overly reactive to stimuli in general. This occurs especially with strong, noxious stimuli, such as strong electric shock. Thus, if the CR is a change in heart rate and the UCS is powerful shock, a variety of stimuli other than the CS may produce heart rate change, and responses that occur to the CS therefore cannot be certified as true CRs.

Psychosomatic illness Term referring to bodily illness produced by the mind. Psychosomatic illnesses may be as fatal as other illnesses and are almost surely due to classical conditioning, at least in large part. Because the distinction between mind and body is of questionable worth, the term psychosomatic may be obsolete.

Reciprocal inhibition Term used by Sherrington to refer to the inhibition of an antagonist muscle by a contracting muscle. When the biceps contracts, the triceps is inhibited.

Reflex A reaction produced by specific stimulation. One example of an innate reflex is the constriction of the pupil produced by light in the eye.

Sensitization CRs that depend upon factors other than the specific pairings of CS and UCS. For example, a CS light could evoke eye blink responses independent of the UCS air puff. Additionally, the occasional presentation of air puffs could make such blinks more likely.

Sensory preconditioning Procedure in which two stimuli are presented together and one of them is later paired with a UCS. If the other stimulus also produces a CR, sensory preconditioning has occurred. For example, a light and a tone may be paired a number of times, followed by the pairing of the tone with electric shock. If the presentation of the light produced a shock response, then sensory preconditioning took place.

Sherrington English physiologist who won the Nobel Prize in 1932 for his earlier analysis of the spinal nervous system in 1906. Sherrington is credited with firmly establishing the reflex as the basic unit of physiology, but he chose to emphasize the workings of the nervous system as a whole, calling the reflex "a convenient fiction."

Simultaneous conditioning Classical conditioning procedure in which the CS slightly precedes and overlaps the UCS. They occur almost simultaneously; however, the CS must precede the UCS slightly. (To researchers in the U.S., however, simultaneous conditioning means that the CS and the UCS occur at exactly the same time.)

Simultaneous induction Name given by Sherrington to the fact that the stimulation of a sensory surface may produce a decrease in threshold in adjacent units which would lead to the same response. It was this usage which Skinner later meant when he referred to induction as generalization.

Spontaneous recovery Name given to the reappearance of a CR that had been extinguished earlier. Since the effect occurred only after a period of time had passed since extinction, Pavlov suggested that this was evidence for the accumulation of inhibition during extinction and its dissipation thereafter.

Successive induction Term used by Sherrington to describe the increased responsiveness of a muscle group following release from inhibition. For example, if we flex our biceps strongly for a time and then relax it, we may find our arm straightening more quickly than we expected, due to the strong contraction of the triceps. This is the sense in which Pavlov used "induction," that is, as a successive effect, of "opposite sign." Thus, excitation produces subsequent inhibition and inhibition leads to later excitation.

Trace conditioning Classical conditioning procedure in which a CS is presented, taken away, and later followed by the UCS. CRs that appear are assumed to be caused by a connection between a memory trace of the CS and the UCS.

Truly random control Procedure suggested by Rescorla in 1967 as the only appropriate control procedure for classical conditioning. This procedure also assumes a definition of conditioning as a contingent relation between the CS and the UCS; the CS must act as a reliable predictor. The control procedure defines the absence of classical conditioning by presenting the CS and the UCS randomly, so that occurrence of the CS may mean that the UCS is coming or that it is not; the CS predicts nothing.

Ultraparadoxical phase The stage of prolonged extinction in which positive CSs produce no reactions and negative CSs do produce CRs.

Unconditioned reflex Reflex behaviors that do not depend on the conditions of our experience. Unconditioned reflexes are those reactive behaviors with which we are born.

RECOMMENDED READINGS

Gray, J. A. (1979) *Ivan Pavlov*. New York: Penguin.

    This is an excellent book with an accurate rendition of Pavlov's theory of brain function and related research.

Mackintosh, N. J. (1983) *Conditioning and associative learning*. New York: Oxford University Press.

    This is an authoritative account of contemporary research in classical conditioning by Western researchers. However, it is not a book of light reading for beginners.

Pavlov, I. P. (1955) *Selected works*. Moscow: Foreign Languages Publishing House.

    This is an interesting collection of papers, presentations, and lectures by Pavlov. His opinions on a wide variety of topics are included.

Rescorla, R. A. (1988). Pavlovian conditioning: It's not what you think it is. *American Psychologist, 43*, 151–160.

    A leading authority on classical conditioning shows how recent data have changed our interpretation of conditioning.

Swazey, J. P. (1969) *Reflexes and motor integration: Sherrington's concept of integrative action*. Cambridge: Harvard University Press.

    This biography of Sherrington concentrates on his research that led to his famous Silliman lectures at Yale. The author provides an excellent presentation of the concept of integrative action, as seen by Sherrington.

Turkkan, J. S. (1989). Classical conditioning: The new hegemony. *Behavioral and Brain Sciences, 12*, 121–179.

    This survey of contemporary work in medicine, learning in simple nervous systems, learning in protozoa, physiology, and cognition shows that classical conditioning is more popular than it has been for decades. The author answers her critics, whose commentaries are included.

Chapter 4

J. B. WATSON: THE ORIGINAL BEHAVIORISM

BIOGRAPHY

John Broadus Watson was born on a farm near Greenville, South Carolina in 1878. He received an A.M. at Furman University in Greenville in 1899 and in 1903 was the youngest candidate to have received a Ph.D. at the University of Chicago (see Figures 4.1 and 4.2). After several years as an instructor at Chicago, he was offered a professorship and a department chairmanship at Johns Hopkins, which he accepted in 1908. His academic career was cut short in 1920, due to the conditions surrounding his scandalous divorce, which led to his forced resignation. Abandoned by virtually the entire academic community, he began a second career in advertising, first with the J. Walter Thompson agency and later with William Esty. Watson continued to lecture occasionally during the 1920s and published a good deal, but largely in popular magazines; academic journals were closed to him.

Before 1915 Watson's research was restricted to animal behavior, including several papers on kinesthesia and maze learning in rats, the behavior of noddy and sooty terns, and color vision and imitation in monkeys. From 1915 on, his interest centered on child development, an interest that persisted after he was forced from academics. The following are some of his most representative and influential publications; the last is a collection of popular articles published in *Harper's Magazine*.

"Psychology as the Behaviorist Views It," 1913

Behavior: An Introduction to Comparative Psychology, 1914

Psychology from the Standpoint of a Behaviorist, 1919

Behaviorism, 1930

The Ways of Behaviorism, 1928

FIGURE 4.1 John B. Watson, 1878–1958. This photograph shows Watson as a young man. *Photo courtesy of Clark University Press*

Although Watson often pointed out that he was not the founder of behaviorism, it is certain that he was its most vocal and effective advocate. Watson argued that the emphasis on the analysis of consciousness, which had almost solely occupied psychologists, was misguided and extremely damaging to progress. If humans are treated objectively, we find that we can discover the factors that lead them to act in the ways they do, and, knowing that, we can influence their actions.

A science of behavior can aid us in raising our young and eventually lead to a world fit for human habitation. Watson's views produced strong opposition from his peers, who erroneously characterized behaviorism as a crass mechanical model of humanity, devoid of thoughts, hopes, dreams, and emotions. Attacks on Watson's position were really more successful than was warranted, since there was no way for him to respond to critics after his forced departure from academics.

Tolman, Hull, and Skinner carried on versions of Watson's general point of view, although their theories differed from Watson's in many specifics. However, J. R. Kantor and his followers have espoused a view very similar to Watson's for more than half a century. Watson conscientiously applied his theories in his second career, advertising, and the great success he had there certainly lends support to his cause.

INTRODUCTION

Section 1 of this chapter considers the significance of Watson's radical break with what had been called psychology before 1913. We now pretty much agree that the older psychology was headed nowhere, but it did correspond with our commonsense ways of viewing things, and Watson's attack thus seems as threatening now as it did then! Now, however, psychologists are more interested in practical applications, so Watson's position seems less extreme than it did in his time. His criticisms of reliance on the nervous system and on instinct are as valid now as they were then.

Section 2 examines the specifics of his theory of learning, which arose from countless observations of both animal and human behavior. His study of the behavior of human infants entailed more actual hours than was the case for many later child psychologists, who tended to make only sporadic observations, yielding an odd time-lapse picture of child development.

Watson's basic explanatory terms were *stimuli* and *responses*, but we will see that he did not define them simply and crassly, as did Thorndike and later behaviorists. His treatment of language, memoy, thinking, and consciousness surely raised hackles in his day, but you will see that he was really quite reasonable. Read what he had to say about mental activity and decide for yourself whether he was describing humans as robots, as Hull later did. Watson stressed emotion in all of his writings, and his famous work with "little Albert" was only one instance of his long-standing concern with the harmful effects that certain kinds of parental care can have on the future mental health of children.

In Watson's day most psychologists placed great emphasis on the importance of heredity in determining intelligence and the general features of personality. In England, Sir Francis Galton had argued that superior parents produce superior offspring, with *superior* defined as the characteristics of male leaders in business, science, and the military. In this country James Cattell and others, including Thorndike, held similar views and emphasized the importance of heredity.

Watson fought hard against this view and, almost single-handedly, amassed evidence that showed the strong effects of environment on later performance. His observations of infants were carried out over remarkably long periods, considering that he saw the subjects daily. His conclusion was that the effects of heredity were overrated and that any supposed difference in intelligence or personality that seemed to depend on sex or race was wholly due to the conditions of upbringing. He was thus one of the first leaders in psychology to provide evidence for what could happen if there were true equality of opportunity.

His views of psychopathology also emphasized the effects of personal history; he pointed out that "mental illness" is not an illness, in the sense that a viral infection is an illness. His opinions are shared by many today, and they offer an alternative to the older view that treats psychopathology as illness.

Section 3 considers criticisms of Watson's behaviorism. He has been accused of denying the

FIGURE 4.2   John B. Watson. This photograph of Watson was taken later in his life. *Photo courtesy of Bettmann Archive*

existence of mind and consciousness, which is true. (Consider his reasons and just what it was that he denied!) He called *thinking* "talking to oneself." Consider, though, what he meant by *talking!* Watson has been criticized for being purely descriptive, but we will see that this may be just what is needed if we are to have a practical psychological theory.

Section 4 briefly describes the scandal that forced him to leave academics and to begin a second career in advertising. What happens when one of the best-known psychologists in the world is forced into such a position at the age of 42? His income increased manyfold, and advertising became what we see it to be today.

1. THE SIGNIFICANCE OF WATSON'S THEORIES

Psychology at the Turn of the Century

According to the eminent British philosopher Bertrand Russell, Watson made "the greatest contribution to scientific psychology since Aristotle." This may seem undeserved praise for a man who was made the villain of psychology for over fifty years. Watson is the supposed simpleton or archfiend (depending upon the critic) who denied the very existence of mind and consciousness, reduced us to the status of robots, and urged that we dispense with baby talk and treat our children as little adults. He has been accused of interpreting thinking as nothing more than laryngeal muscle twitches and of denying that we have mental images. How could anyone take such notions seriously? Is it any wonder that he has been so vigorously attacked?

To appreciate Watson's thesis and its significance, one must consider what was called *psychology* at the turn of the century. It was this state of affairs that led Thorndike to formulate his version of *behaviorism* and that produced Watson's even stronger protest.

Thorndike argued that conscious activity is still activity and is therefore subject to learning principles. Watson went further and suggested in 1913 that *mind, consciousness, images,* and *sensations* are really nonsense terms that have no place in psychology. The introspectionists, led by Edward Titchener at Cornell, had long argued that a prerequisite to the understanding of psychological phenomena was an analysis of conscious experience. This view was a continuation of hundreds of years of philosophical and psychological thought, and it was accepted by virtually all influential European and American psychologists. (See Chapter 1.)

The basic elements of consciousness were sensations, images (which were fainter), and affect (emotional elements). Sensations and images had the attributes of quality (for example, blue or cold), duration, clarity, and sometimes extension in space. Emotional elements were characterized only by quality and duration; if you clearly felt an emotion, you were not introspecting properly. One of the most interesting debates during the early part of the century concerned the question of whether auditory sensations had the attribute of extension in space. Does a rich tone from a pipe organ occupy more space than a shrill note from a flute, or is extension in space a characteristic of only visual and tactual sensations?

Difficulties arose concerning the limits of introspective analysis, especially in the reports of Külpe and his followers in Germany, who spoke of imageless elements, illustrated by the following example. Suppose a subject is highly trained to report accurately his conscious experience. An experimenter asks him to describe the feelings that accompany simple judgments of heavier or lighter, but he finds that the experience is indescribable. He feels the weights, but the judgments "same" or "different" seem to come instantaneously. There is no image to report, and the feeling that goes with the judgment itself is therefore an imageless element.

This is an inconvenient finding if one has put all one's stock in such introspective reports. If there is no mental content to be reported in the making of such simple judgments, then what hope is there for such a method when we come to more complex mental activities? For his part, Titchener was content to suggest that the making of such judgments has occurred so frequently in life that the mental content originally accompanying it has become unconscious. Thus, a good part of our experience takes the form of unconscious content.

Watson (e.g., 1930) suggested that anyone critical of his theory first read some of the "pabulum" proposed in the introspective textbooks; and that he or she then will see the virtues of behaviorism. Watson himself was brought up on such pabulum, and his dissertation was concerned with the psychical development of the white rat; introspection by analogy was used even by animal researchers.

The Selling of Behaviorism

Watson was urged by his friends to refrain from his attack on the introspectionists; since he was also a close friend of Titchener, he did refrain for some time. Finally, his restraint ended in 1913, and he attacked vigorously and in language too plain to be misunderstood. He argued that psychology as it was being done was a waste of time and that if it were continued we would still be arguing over whether auditory sensations were extended in space two hundred years hence. According to Watson, one can write a psychology without even using the terms *consciousness*, *mind*, or *images*, since such entities are pure inventions of the introspectionists, having no existence in fact. As he said in 1928, consciousness has never been seen, smelled, nor tasted, nor does it take part in any human reactions! Many were shocked when Watson denied the existence of consciousness. Or did he?

It is important to note that Watson did not deny the existence of seeing, hearing, thinking, hoping, and remembering. But for him, as for Thorndike, these were things that we *do*. Is there really a remainder—consciousness—after we subtract these activities from our experience? Is there really a thing called *mind*, independent of those activities? (Refer to Table 4.1.) Although his suggestion is essentially in agreement with Thorndike, it was Watson who pressed the point and who took the credit or blame for behaviorism in general. And we will see that Watson was far more extreme than Thorndike; it was not only consciousness that Watson questioned.

The goal of psychology was clear to Watson: We want to be able to predict with reasonable certainty what people will do in specific situations. Given a stimulus, defined as an object of outer or inner experience, what response may be expected? A stimulus could be a blow to the knee or an architect's education; a response could be a knee jerk or the building of a bridge. Similarly, we want to know, given a response, what situation produced it. Why do people yawn in crowded auditoriums? What conditions lead to

TABLE 4.1 Two Views of Consciousness

Cognitive Activities		Consciousness
Seeing Hearing Smelling Touching Thinking Remembering Hoping Feeling Attending and so on	AND	Consciousness as a separate entity observing all of this and having contents (ideas, sensations, feelings, memories)
Seeing Hearing Smelling Touching Thinking Remembering Hoping Feeling Attending and so on	IS	Consciousness! There is no special entity that presides over mental activity.

criminal behavior? What leads a person to act and feel depressed?

In all such situations the discovery of the stimuli that call out one or another behavior should allow us to influence the occurrence of behaviors; prediction, which comes from such discoveries, allows control. What does the analysis of conscious experience give us?

Behavior, the Brain, Instinct, and Consciousness

For many summers Watson had studied terns on the island of Tortuga. Having caught some of these birds, he observed their behavior and watched how they mated, raised their young, reacted to predators, and so on. This led to a fair understanding of terns. The same strategy is the only key to understanding more complicated life forms, such as preliterate humans or modern Europeans. There is no shortcut; we must determine what we do, think, and feel under specific circumstances.

Thorndike suggested that our actions depend upon the S-R connections that we are born with and that are modified with experience. For Watson, such dependence upon neural substrata or analogies was unnecessary. In 1919 he pointed out that he presented few pictures of neural structures, since the reader could erroneously conclude that the nervous system was important as a static structure. What is important is the activity of the nervous system as a part of a whole, only *one* part of an acting organism. As he wrote, "one should strive to get the beginner to view the organism as a whole as rapidly as possible and to see in the working of all its acts an integrated personality" (1919, preface). The positing of S-R connections in the brain not only is needless, but fosters the view that the brain is the initiator of action. We act as a whole; we are not controlled by impulses sent from the brain. Rather, we are controlled by external (and bodily) stimuli and situations.

Watson was also extremely opposed to the emphasis of *instinct*, as the term was used by Thorndike and others of the time. Recall that Thorndike was an extreme hereditarian, and in 1913 he included a long list of instincts in his *Educational Psychology*. Are we born with the instincts of rivalry, acquisitiveness, constructiveness, sympathy, and the like? Because of our evolutionary history, is swimming instinctive? Does nature ensure that one of us is marked at birth as a future genius while another is doomed as a dunce? Watson thought it was not the case, and he argued that no one had troubled to observe closely the behavior of infants at birth and to follow the development of later behaviors. If this had been done, we would have found that we all come with a set of instincts, such as grasping and sneezing, and that it is the environment in which we develop that molds the so-called instincts of rivalry and imitation, which Thorndike and James had stressed. The environment also determines subsequent intellectual capabilities. Watson was intensely interested in this developmental process,

evidenced in his research with children, which began in 1915 and continued even after he left academics.

What is psychology without consciousness, S-R connections, instinct, or purpose? It is practical and concrete, and it deals with practical and concrete events: What is that man doing? How may we change it? What is he thinking? What is he feeling? How may we change that? What is he buying? How may we change *that*?

The one cherished possession of the old psychology that Watson did not cast out was emotion, which played a large part in his overall view of psychology. The following section examines the central importance of emotion and Watson's treatment of the traditional areas of psychology. You may then decide whether Watson deserved the censure he has received over the years.

2. BASICS OF WATSON'S THEORY

Learning: Not Thorndike

Watson (1919) said that we are "what we come with and what we have been through," and he believed that what we go through is by far the more important determinant. What we come with is a set of hereditary (reflex) reactions called out by specific stimuli. A touch of the skin produces movement of the infant's limbs, a speck in the eye produces a blink, food in the alimentary canal produces peristaltic movements, a moving object in the visual field may evoke orienting and following with the eyes. While still in the womb we react incessantly, adjusting to the stimulation constantly affecting us. We continue adjusting until death, the final adjustment.

Consider what adjustment means to an infant. The sight of an object such as a bottle produces agitation, movement of arms and legs, cooing and gurgling sounds, internal glandular secretions, eye movements, changes in respiration, and so on. Because of the infant's hereditary equipment and its learning history to date, a variety of stimuli (sights, sounds, touches, smells) produce general reactions; the infant responds with everything it has. How does such generalized reactivity eventually lead to grasping the bottle? It is not easy. If one observes the development of grasping from the 120th to the 200th day of the infant's life, as Watson did, it is clear that manipulation and grasping are not instinctive. The infant "learns to manipulate objects and even its own bodily parts literally by the sweat of its brow" (1919).

The way in which this occurs is Watson's model for all learning and contrasts with the way in which Thorndike would account for the same events (see Table 4.2). For Watson, the bottle produces movement (along with activity of internal organs) that continues as long as it is present as a stimulus. Assuming that the bottle is not being held and withdrawn by a fiend, eventually the infant's arm or hand strikes it. When the infant strikes the bottle with its hand it grasps the bottle, since grasping is an instinctive activity evident at birth. Once the infant successfully grasps the bottle, which may take a great deal of practice, it moves the bottle toward itself or flings the bottle awkwardly away. In either event, the bottle no longer is present as a stimulus, and the generalized agitation or movement ceases. With sufficient repetition, the sight of the bottle may be enough to evoke a smooth and coordinated hand movement and grasping; the infant has learned the requisite habits.

For Thorndike, this episode of learning depends upon the effect of the satisfier involved, the feel of the bottle. Whatever movements produce this outcome are stamped in, and other movements are stamped out—just as the movements of the cat in the problem box are stamped in and out. Watson's view of learning was different and did not require the action of satisfiers, which he likened to the "implanting of habits by kind fairies." If one observes either the cat or the infant, the movements that produce escape from the box or that secure the bottle are the movements that have occurred most frequently, since they must

TABLE 4.2   Two Accounts of How an Infant Learns to Grasp a Bottle

Thorndike's Account
Stimulus (sight of bottle)
Paired with accidental (?) grasping
Consequence: may manipulate, stroke, nurse
Hence: S-R connection "visual bottle" and "grasp" stamped in

Watson's Account
Stimulus (sight of bottle)
Elicits movement of whole body, vocalizations
Hand strikes, grasps bottle
Hence: "sight of bottle" no longer present as a stimulator

occur at least once per trial. Also, since they were the last movements made in the preceding solution of the same problem, they are the most recent actions. What is learned is whatever has occurred most frequently and most recently in that situation or in response to that stimulus. Hence, frequency, recency, and stimulus change are sufficient to account for the formation of habits.

As another example, consider a six-month-old baby, sitting on its mother's lap, learning not to put its hand into a candle flame placed within reach. In Watson's experiment, it took Baby L. two weeks and 150 trials to learn this. (If a severe burn had been allowed it surely would have taken fewer trials, but Watson ensured that a real burn did not occur.) What was learned? Was the behavior of reaching for shining, dancing objects stamped out? Was reaching punished? Watson's interpretation is otherwise. The original stimulus—the bright, shiny, dancing flame—eventually is replaced by a new stimulus—bright, shiny, dancing, painful flame. Our commerce with objects changes them and thus changes our reactions to them. The stimulus is not flame plus punishment; it is literally a different flame, one with the property of producing pain (see Dewey's 1896 very similar interpretation in Chapter 1).

Such is the case with other stimuli. Does food not change as we consume it? Is the eighth piece of pizza the same in kind as the first? Is *wood* the same word or thing to a lumberman, a wood-carver, a beaver, and a musician? Our actions with respect to objects change them and thus change our future reactions to them.

Watson provides charming advice along these lines for anyone who has a problem with egg-sucking dogs or cats. If one injects quinine into the eggs, the animal will soon stop its annoying practice and our eggs will be safe. We have here supplemented nature, which has already arranged that flames burn, by arranging that the insides of eggs taste different. As nature teaches its children to react properly to the objects of the world, we may arrange conditions to produce behaviors we want and eliminate those we do not want.

Watson's View of Classical Conditioning

Most readers will recognize that the above examples of adjustment can easily be interpreted as classical conditioning, and Watson did suggest that himself. To Watson, *classical conditioning* meant no more than the effects of pairing of stimuli—the simple view of classical conditioning discussed in Chapter 3. Pair the pain with the flame or the quinine with the sight of the egg and the conditioned response follows. But Watson was loose and unspecific about the whole process. He did not hesitate to call the picking up of a revolver a conditioned response, clearly a different usage from that of Pavlov.

Motives

Watson also emphasized that a good many of the stimuli to which we adjust are due to visceral needs, such as hunger pangs or sexual urges. Hunger stimuli produce movements that continue until the ingestion of food abolishes the stimuli; in the future, the movements that accompany such an effect will occur again, owing to the principles of frequency and recency. In addition, such successful adjustments may be accompanied by a decrease in emotional tension (as in the ending of great hunger) and perhaps emotional ex-citement. What is absolutely essential for the formation of habits was hazy to Watson in 1919 and even in 1930. Frequency and recency were the most important factors; if something else was necessary, it was not Thorndike's concept of satisfier, which Watson interpreted as a hedonistic theory.

In Watson's opinion, once we have acquired a supply of habits, we can quickly make the adjustments that life requires and we may stop learning anything new. It takes a new situation, requiring adjustment, to produce new learning. For many of us, that may necessitate a fire, a flood, an earthquake, or a stockmarket crash. When new learning is required of an adult, failure to adjust rapidly may lead the person to revert to more primitive habit systems or even to instinctive behavior. Watson gives the example of the 35-year-old man learning to play tennis for the first time. He does not know how to swing the racquet, but he has swung a bat and a golf club and he swings the racquet as he swings them. Repeated failure to efficiently strike the ball using these primitive habit systems may lead to their abandonment and to the appearance of more primitive instinctive reactions that lead to the destruction of the racquet and thus to adjustment, even if not a socially acceptable kind.

Stimuli and Responses

Watson offered further opinions on the nature of learning, most of which are treated in the following sections. One interesting principle suggested in 1919 has to do with the number of habits being learned simultaneously. The larger the number of such habits, the slower the growth in strength of any single habit, as if there exists a finite sum of strength to be shared by these habits. Interestingly, this is the essence of the Rescorla-Wagner theory of conditioning, which has been very popular since 1972 and which is discussed in Chapter 9.

Finally, Watson always spoke of stimuli and responses, S and R, but his usage was unlike that of later writers. *S* was any object shown to be relevant, whether it be hunger pangs, a light flash, one's family, or an education in law. A response could be eating, building a house, swimming, talking, or arguing a case before the supreme court. Watson was interested in accounting for whatever it is that people do that interests us. We cannot expect that the units of description will always be on the same level (see Table 4.3).

Throughout his writings, Watson urged psychologists to make field observations, particularly of children, so they could better understand the learning process. To his credit, he did a good deal of such observation himself, but his post-1920 position made it nearly impossible to continue that work.

Language

The learning discussed in the previous section was concerned with what Watson called *manual habits*, bodily movements produced by the contraction of striped muscles. A second class of habit referred to the learning of words and the use of language; Watson persistently referred to this as *laryngeal habits*, although he pointed out that language was by no means solely dependent upon movements of the larynx. Language depended upon the whole body, and virtually any bodily movement could act as a word.

The simple learning and repeating of words, as done by a parrot or myna, represents only the formation of vocal habits. When words or word substitutes (gestures, shrugs) are used as substitutes for actions and objects, we have evidence of language habits. Sometimes language behavior has nothing to do with words; as Watson (1919) suggested, there are many situations in life for which we have no organized reaction. Curling the lip, shrugging, and uttering *humpf* is all we can do.

Since language habits are defined as substitutes for objects and for actions, Watson opposed free speech:

"[T]he only person who ought to be allowed free speech is the parrot, because the parrot's words are

TABLE 4.3   Watson's Use of *Stimulus* and *Response*

Stimuli	Responses
A puff of air to the eye	An eye blink
A sudden noise	Orienting, startle
A pinprick	Tensing, withdrawing
A red light	Pressing the brake pedal
.	.
.	.
.	.
A medical education	Performing an operation
A general education	Writing a book
Equal distribution of wealth	?
?	A decrease in the crime rate

not tied up with his bodily acts and do not stand as substitutes for his bodily acts. . . . When the agitator raises the roof because he hasn't free speech, he does it because he knows that he will be restrained if he attempts free action. He wants by his free speech to get someone else to do free acting. (Watson, 1930, p. 303)

Memory

Watson did not believe in memory, as the term was used by the introspectionists and by many contemporary psychologists. That is, he was opposed to the notion that what we see, hear, smell, and feel is somehow preserved in little copies in the nervous system and retrieved in the act of remembering. Perhaps you can see the reasons for his objecting to such a conception. If we consider all of the things we do that have any connection with what we mean by *memory*, we find that assuming that experiences are stored and retrieved gains us nothing. It may seem necessary to us that things be stored and retrieved, since we cannot imagine how we can see and hear things that are not now present. But this is not a sufficient reason to concoct such a mechanism; the fact is, we have little understanding of how we see and hear things that *are* present, to say nothing

TABLE 4.4 The Whole Body Remembers

Verbal (Laryngeal)	Visceral	Manual
"That's John Brown."	warm feeling	wave hello
"What's his name?"	visceral arousal	withdraw
"I can't explain how this works."	——	obvious skill in using a device
"I forgive you."	vigorous arousal	smile
"I thought I knew you."	——	uninvited approach

of things that formerly were present but that now are not! Yet, when we glibly speak of the storage and retrieval of memories, we delude ourselves by thinking we have explained something, while in truth we have merely diverted attention away from the real problem. How do we see and hear in the first place?

The study of memory is properly the study of the factors that affect our performance (whether verbal or manual or emotional) after a period of no practice (see Table 4.4). I meet a friend; I nod my recognition, shake his hand, and begin to speak with him of old times. Yet, I cannot for the life of me remember his name! What is it that I do remember? I remember the manual habits appropriate to the situation and I feel glad, angry, or sad that I ran into him. *Memory* is a word for the host of habits developed with respect to him in the past and active at this meeting. A part of the verbal behavior is missing, but after a few minutes, the name comes out. The same thing happens when I run into a piece of equipment that I have not used for a while. Often we are surprised by the memory we have of its workings, shown by our skill in operating it.

Watson felt that those studying memory placed far too much emphasis on verbal memory, our ability to recite words and lists and to produce verbal descriptions of past events. Verbal behavior is not an adequate indicator of what memory should really mean. For example, the two-year-old who says, "Billy ride kiddy car," speaks on a primitive level that certainly cannot be taken as an indicator of his current abilities, which he is capable of coordinating and which constitute his memory.

For adults, verbal habits may become much more important, and a good deal of our memories are cast in almost purely verbal form—"word pictures," as Watson called them. Before we verbalize our experiences we have no way to carry them reliably with us; an unverbalized emotional experience is lost unless translated to words. How many of us are sure to spend some time discussing our triumphs and joys with others immediately after they happen? The retelling of the happy experience and the casting and recasting of the movements and feelings involved in word form puts it in a form we can carry with us.

Before we are capable of verbalization, our moments pass forever away, and early childhood is thus a closed book to us. Watson showed his two-year-old son Billy (of kiddy car fame) the bottle from which he had been weaned as a one-year-old. Billy had no idea what to do with it, nor with his mother's breast! Both had been familiar and important objects to him for half of his life, but that half was preverbal and gone forever. Despite the coaching used to try to evoke some memory of bottle and breast, which Watson (1930) described in detail, Billy seemed genuine in his bewilderment.

Thinking and Consciousness

For Watson, thinking is part of what we do in the business of adjustment. It is talking; recall that language habits were by no means restricted to verbal behavior. We act with the whole body and we think with the whole body. *Consciousness* is a popular or literary term that does not really refer to a thing but only applies a name to our naming activity. We name the universe of objects both inside and outside us; that is what is meant by consciousness. It is all that we have reacted to, labeled, and made a part of what we will respond to in the future.

It is important to note that Watson's critics have greatly misunderstood his position on private experience. It is easy to conclude, as they have, that when Watson denied mind, consciousness, and imagery he was denying experience in general. But Watson was simply denying the existence of mind, thoughts, images, and the like as *things*. In denying images, for example, he was not denying imagination (1919). Imagining is a name for something we do, but is it necessary to say that we imagine images? Do we think or do we think thoughts? Watson believed that imagining and thinking were best treated as activities; enough time had been spent by Titchener and others studying *things* like "images" and "thoughts."

Thinking is a constituent part of every adjustment process; it is also what we do before we take action. It may include verbal elements, false starts, muscular tensions, emotional elements, or more. As a diminished form of action, it follows that thinking can be no better than muscular action. It is not by any means a matter of talking to ourselves, following the rules of syntax and grammar. Watson provided this concrete example:

> A friend comes to you and tells you that he is forming a new business. He asks you to leave your present splendid position and come into the new business as an equal partner. He is a responsible person; he has good financial backing. He makes the offer attractive. He urges the larger ultimate profits you will make. He enlarges upon the fact that you will be your own boss. He has to leave at once to see other people interested in the venture. He asks you to call him up and give him an answer in an hour. Will you think? Yes, you will, and you'll walk the floor too, and you will pull your hair, and you may even sweat and you will smoke. Follow out the process step by step: Your whole body is as busy as though you were cracking rock—but your laryngeal mechanisms are setting the pace—they are dominant. (1930, p. 245)

The fact that much thinking is silent language behavior seemed to be evident to Watson after observing the stages shown by children learning to read. Initially, they read everything aloud, much to the annoyance of whatever representative of organized society is present. Scolding reduces the verbalization to mumbling, further scolding reduces that to whispering, and yet more scolding reduces that to lip movements alone. Finally, "Can't you read without moving your lips?" removes even that vestige of overt activity, and the reader eventually only thinks the written words. The activity still goes on in the form of minute muscular movements, not only of the larynx, but of the whole body. Thinking is doing and there is no difference in kind between the thought and its expression; the difference is in degree only.

Emotion

The third major class of innate reactions (after manual and laryngeal reactions) are those of the viscera, the emotional reactions. The effects, both good and bad, of emotional learning were considered of crucial importance by Watson, who devoted a good deal of research effort to the subject. Watson called these learned behaviors *visceral habits*. When he said that every reaction is a reaction of the whole body, he included the actions of the smooth muscles and glands. Unlike manual and laryngeal responses, which may appear discrete and specific, emotional reactions are always pattern reactions, clearly involving the whole body. A bit of bad news may paralyze the striped muscles, stop digestion, and throw verbal habits into disarray.

For what is usually viewed as a mechanistic psychology, emotion has a special role:

> [E]motions remove the individual from the monotonous level of existence as a highly perfected machine. . . . If all hearts were calm, the great artists would have lived in vain. . . . The world would be a sorry place indeed . . . if the distress of the child, of the weak and the downtrodden moved no eye to tears. (1919, p. 223)

The cold sweat of fear, the head bowed in grief, and the exuberance of youth are not just literary expressions; visceral or emotional reactions are reactions!

Beginning in 1915 and extending into the 1920s, Watson and his students made countless observations of infants at the Phipps Clinic in Baltimore and later at the Manhattan Day Nursery. Out of this came Watson's famous postulation of three basic emotions—the X, Y, and Z reactions, corresponding to fear, rage, and love. An infant shows the innate fear reaction soon after birth, characterized by closed eyes, a catching of breath, spasmodic movements of legs and arms, grasping with the hands, and puckered lips. Such a reaction is reliably produced by a loud noise or loss of support (and by tissue injury producing pain), but by nothing else. Watson exposed six-month-old infants to every sort of zoo animal at close range, to pigeons flapping in a paper bag, to darkness, and to brightness; the infants never showed any sign of fear. Fears of such things appear later in childhood and are instilled by society or by the child's personal experience.

Rage, reaction Y, is produced by anything that impedes movement; holding the infant's limbs is enough to produce the stiffened body, held breath, and thrashing that characterizes rage. Love, the Z reaction, is produced by petting and stroking; the reaction appears as the extending of limbs, smiling, and cooing. Any stimuli that reliably accompany loud noise or loss of support, restraint, or stroking and petting come to evoke fear, rage, or love. Such pairing accounts for the development of phobias (learned fears) and for the neuroses of Freud's patients, who carried with them acquired love reactions toward their parents, who spent much time instilling them.

Watson spent a good deal of time studying acquired emotional reactions, and he observed a great many children. But all of his work seems to have crystallized in the work done with an eleven-month-old infant named Albert, whose case has achieved the status of a myth, appearing in many forms in many textbooks. As Harris (1979) pointed out, many of the details of the case have been related incorrectly in many of the texts, although all that the authors had to do was examine Watson's own account (e.g., 1919, 1930; Watson & Rayner, 1920).

Albert B. was a wonderfully good child of a wet nurse at the Lane Hospital in Baltimore who, at eleven months of age, feared only loud noises and loss of support. When presented with a white rat, he showed only curiosity. As he reached for it, a four-foot-long steel bar, $\frac{3}{4}$ inch in diameter, was struck by a carpenter's hammer nearby but behind him and out of sight. The noise made him jump violently and bury his face in the mattress, but he did not cry. The rat was presented again; as Albert reached for the rat, the bar was again struck. Albert still did not cry, but he appeared so disturbed that no further trials were conducted. After a week, the rat and the loud noise were paired five more times and finally Albert cried. The sight of the rat alone sent him crying and crawling away so rapidly that it was difficult to prevent him from falling off the bed. Albert had acquired a new fear.

After five days Albert was tested with blocks, a white rat, a rabbit, a dog, a sealskin coat, cotton wool, Watson's hair, and a Santa Claus mask with white beard. All of these items except the blocks produced a greater or lesser fear reaction, showing that the acquired fear was not specific to the white rat but occurred to other objects that were white and/or hairy or furry. Watson claimed that Albert was no longer available to the researchers and that it was therefore impossible to investigate methods to remove this acquired fear. Harris (1979) argued that Watson was well aware that Albert was to be adopted and knew well in advance the date of his departure. Why Watson should leave Albert in that state is unclear, since the cure was not hard to find.

Watson (1930) later reported attempts to remove fears in 70 children, age three months to seven years; much of this work was done by Mary Cover Jones, a graduate student at Columbia for whom he was an unofficial sponsor and for whom he had set up the Manhattan Day Nursery. For example, one child, "little Peter," had a host of pre-established fears; he was afraid of rats, rabbits, fish, cotton, frogs, and mechanical toys. How does one remove such fears? Watson described several methods, including disuse (preventing exposure to the feared object); telling the child stories about the feared object, in which the object is portrayed as nondangerous (for example, telling stories about Peter Rabbit to combat fear of rabbits); frequently applying the feared object, now known as *emotional flooding* or implosive therapy; using social methods, such as pointing out that only "fraidy cats" are fearful of rabbits; and, finally, reconditioning. Only the last method proved useful and was successful in curing Peter of his fear of rabbits.

Reconditioning simply attaches a new reaction to the object feared, replacing the existing fear response. This is done by presenting the object in such a way that it produces no fear reaction; for example, the object could be present but at a great distance. Then, while the person is induced to make a response incompatible with fear, the object is brought gradually nearer.

In Peter's case, the rabbit was initially presented at a distance of 40 feet. As Peter ate crackers and milk, the rabbit was gradually brought closer until Peter petted it as he ate. This is, of course, the method of systematic desensitization made popular by Wolpe decades later and already described in Chapters 2 and 3.

Instincts and Innate Traits

Unlike Thorndike, a real hereditarian who pretty much accepted James's long list of instincts, Watson saw no evidence of innate constructiveness, combativeness, rivalry, hunting, and other so-called instincts. Significantly enough, it was Watson and not James or Thorndike who actually *examined* the development of infants over a significant portion of their early lives. Perhaps careful observation of a child's development leads to the conclusion that environment, not instinct, is important. James and Thorndike, who favored instinct, based their judgment only on casual observations.

We may also believe in instinct for the wrong reasons. In Watson's opinion, the belief in instincts and traits (the "gifts" that are passed on from parent to child) reflects only our desire to live forever, in the form of passed on characteristics. "It is hard for most of us to believe that when we are dead we are dead all over, like Rover" (1928a). Is that an important reason for our belief in heredity, or do we have clear evidence that intelligence and other characteristics are passed from generation to generation? Is only body structure inherited?

Based on his observations of the development of many infants, Watson concluded that we do come with many instinctive reactions but that these are more elementary than is commonly supposed (1919). We instinctively have fears (at least of loud noises and loss of support); we sneeze, hiccup, have erections, void, produce tears, raise our heads, kick, and grasp. And we come prepared to react positively to hundreds of objects (such as shiny things or moving things) and to react negatively to a few things (such as loud noises or pain). During development, new stimuli become paired with those producing the original positive or negative reactions, and we live a life of attractions, aversions, and mixtures of attraction and aversion for reasons largely unknown to us. Table 4.5 outlines Watson's findings regarding instinctive and conditioned reactions of human babies.

Two observations struck Watson as significant regarding instinct. First, contrary to some theories of evolutionary recapitulation, swimming is not an instinctive behavior in human children. This was shown by placing a newborn in a tank of water and observing only unmistakable fear reactions. Secondly, contrary to some views concerning the significance of sexuality in infants, there seemed to be no tendency for the infant to touch the sex organs. After 500 periods of

TABLE 4.5 Birth Equipment of the Human Young

Activity	How or When It Occurs
Sneezing	
Hiccupping	
Crying	Soon becomes conditioned.
	Not produced by sounds of others' crying, unless very loud. Any loud sound has the same effect.
Urinating	
Defecating	
Eye movements	Orientation toward faint lights begins soon after birth.
Smiling	Occurs by fourth day; may become conditioned so that smile is returned by 30th day.
Manual responses	
Hand movements	
Arm movements	May be produced by many forms of stimulation.
Leg or foot movements	Kicking is produced by many forms of stimulation.
"Climbing" motions	
Turning over	May occur shortly after birth.
Feeding	Mouth moves toward stimulation as early as five hours after birth; like suckling, mouth movement is easily conditioned.
Crawling	Great variation exists among infants; in some infants it never occurs.
Standing or walking	Begins with the extensor thrust, which may occur after a few months; the first step occurs only after eleven months to a year.
Vocalizing	
Swimming	Does not occur when infants are placed in water; only pronounced fear responses are evident.
Grasping	Newborn can support its full weight with either hand; so can premature infants and those born with no cerebrum.
Blinking	May be produced by air puff or touch at birth; may be produced by a moving shadow at 65 days.
Hand preference	No evidence for hand preference when candy offered at 165 days; there may be no difference in work done with right or left hand at one year.

observation of infants from birth to 300 days, it was clear that the sex organs, like the feet and the rest of the body, are discovered purely by chance at about 150 days.

Watson's argument against heredity, innate "gifts" and the like, is often criticized as an extreme and almost crackpot position. We have so many of the physical attributes of our parents that it seems reasonable that we have inherited more; we may have their intelligence, their morality, their strength of character, their mechanical ability, their athletic prowess, and so on. Such an argument has been made for thousands of years, and there is no doubt that the belief in "good and bad seed" has unjustly kept many a superior person in servitude and many a dunce on the throne. Watson did not deny that heredity was a factor, but he stressed the greater effect of environment. The following famous quote regarding heredity deserves to be presented in a longer version than is customary; the pages preceding this passage are well worth reading but are too much to include:

> Our conclusion, then, is that we have no real evidence of the inheritance of traits. I would feel perfectly confident in the ultimately favorable outcome of careful upbringing of a *healthy, well-formed baby* born of a long line of crooks, murderers and thieves, and prostitutes. Who has any evidence to the contrary? Many, many thousands of children yearly, born from moral households and steadfast parents become wayward, steal, become prostitutes, through one mishap or another of nurture. Many more thousands of sons and daughters of the wicked grow up to be wicked because they couldn't grow up any other way in such surroundings. But let one adopted child who has had a bad ancestry go wrong and it is used as incontestable evidence for the inheritance of moral turpitude and criminal tendencies. As a matter of fact, there has not been a double handful of cases in the whole of our civilization of which records have been carefully enough kept for us to draw any such conclusions. . . . One cannot use statistics gained from observations in charitable institutions or orphan asylums. All one needs to do to discount such statistics is to go there and work for a while, and I say this without trying to belittle the work of such organizations.
>
> I should like to go one step further now and say, "Give me a dozen healthy infants, well-formed, and my own specified world to bring them up in and I'll guarantee to take any one at random and train him to become any type of specialist I might select—doctor, lawyer, artist, merchant-chief, and, yes even beggar-man and thief, regardless of his talents, penchants, tendencies, abilities, vocations, and race of his ancestors." I am going beyond my facts and I admit it, but so have the advocates of the contrary and they have been doing it for many thousands of years. (Watson, 1930, pp. 103–104)

In 1936, after sixteen years out of academics, Watson ended his brief autobiography by expressing his regret that he was never able to set up the three "infant farms" he had earlier planned. Environmental conditions would have been the same on all three and only the inhabitants would have differed. According to Watson's plan, one farm was to be populated with orientals, the second with Negroes, and the third with "pure-blooded" Anglo-Saxons. Watson was certain that the sole effect of racial background would be on physical appearance.

Kuo and the Demise of Instinct

Zing Yang Kuo was an influential figure in biology and psychology during this century, and his views on instinct were obviously the same as Watson's, at least the Watson of 1920 and later. The leading exponent of instinct as a factor in human motivation was William McDougall, a psychologist credited with the founding of social psychology. It is worth examining Kuo's arguments against instinct, since they apply as well today as they did when he published his famous paper, "Giving Up Instincts in Psychology." This was published in 1921 and was written while Kuo was an undergraduate at the University of California.

Kuo denied the existence of instinct not only in humans but in animals as well. How do we explain much of animal behavior if not as the product of instinct? How is it that the chick leaves the egg and immediately starts pecking? Surely it is instinct that guides it. How is it that birds, restrained since birth, fly off unimpaired at the age when unrestrained birds begin to fly? Surely they have a flying instinct! Why do barnyard fowl run off when a cutout resembling a hawk passes overhead? Why do they remain when the cutout comes from the opposite direction, so that it looks like a goose? Surely these are instinctive reactions. Animals must have instincts, even if humans do not.

Yet, Kuo argued that there were no instincts, that their use was no more than a cloak for ignorance, and that the methods used to demonstrate instinct were all faulty. These were his arguments against instinct, and they are as good (or as bad) today as they were in 1921.

The Teleological Emphasis   When we attribute an act to instinct, we are explaining it with respect to its aim or end product. The bird is building a nest, the spider is spinning a web, the birds are migrating to warmer climes, and so on. Once we have classified the activities, we stop, feeling that no further explanation is possible or necessary. But if we closely observe the development of such activities, we find that each is composed of smaller acts; these acts are put together (in part) through learning. Birds do not always build good nests and spiders sometimes botch a web.

Emphasis on Adaptiveness   If we concentrate on instinctive causes for behavior, we are apt to over-emphasize the adaptive nature of the activity of other animals and of ourselves. Instinctive behavior is the product of evolution and therefore should have survival value (be adaptive), but we find that much behavior is not adaptive. A child will eat poison, grasp a flame, and swallow dirt if left to itself. Only the viscera is really acting as a proper adaptive mechanism should, and even it requires some learning. (We do not feed ground beef, spaghetti, or many other things to an infant, because the infant's digestive system needs experience with easier foods before it has learned to digest such things.)

Instinct as a Motive   McDougall and others felt that motivation was entirely dependent on instinct, but Kuo charged that we do not need instinct (or motivation) to explain our activities. We are not mechanical devices that need a motivating engine to make us go. An infant *comes* already active and needs no special source of motivation to account for its actions.

Methods for Demonstrating Instinct   The three main sources of evidence for instinct are all faulty, and we will consider them in turn. The genetic method relies on the existence of a behavior at birth or after a period of maturation as evidence for instinct. Recall that the chick comes out of the egg and spontaneously begins pecking.

Is that not evidence for instinct? Not at all, said Kuo. He showed that the chick is so positioned in the egg that its head rests on its breast. Within its breast is its little heart, beating constantly. As the heart beats, the breast moves up and down and so does the chick's head, which is resting on it. The chick comes out moving its head up and down ("pecking") because that is what it had been doing in the egg! Thus, Kuo regarded this as a clear case of learning. Kuo goes on to argue that other behaviors, such as sexual preferences, are not instinctive either. For example, a pigeon raised with doves will try to mate with doves, spurning pigeons of the opposite sex.

A second form of evidence for instinct relies on the observation that many behaviors are common to all or most members of a species. For example, McDougall describes an ox that became agitated when separated from its herd; evidently it had a herd instinct. We all know many behaviors characteristic of dogs, cats, and other animals; aren't these therefore instinctive? Kuo suggests that we see behaviors common to a species because members are born with the same basic reflex behaviors and they live in similar environments. Cats wash their faces in a certain way because cats are physically constructed in a certain way. Cats raised in very different environments do behave differently; compare a house cat with an alley cat and you will see the truth of this. If the ox that McDougall described had been raised alone, rather than in a herd, it would become agitated when placed in the herd, not when it was removed from it.

Finally, evidence for instinct has come from experiments that have attempted to prevent learning, as was the case with Spalding's birds (1873), which were confined so as to prevent movement of their wings until they reached the age when such birds fly. Despite the confinement, they flew off when released, showing that flying is instinctive. But Kuo pointed out that a simpler alternative is available. If an organism is built like a bird, with a light body and hollow bones, any movement of its wings is likely to lift it off the ground. It may then flap and stay aloft or not flap and fall.

Birds fly because of their bodily construction, not because of a flying instinct.

Kuo's Alternative to Instinct   Kuo believed that we come with no instincts, only a set of basic reflex reactions that occur more or less randomly. These reaction units are selected through trial and error, and the selected acts become habitual. With practice they become integrated, as is the case in eye-hand coordination. The selection of acts may depend upon their natural consequences, as when we learn that a flame burns. It also may depend on their social consequences, as when our early utterances are praised.

If we remain in the same environment, our habits become fixed; if we move to a radically new environment, our set of behaviors changes. Kuo suggests that commonly assumed instincts, such as morality and acquisition, are learned trends, arising from past punishment (in the case of morality) or past encouragement (in the case of acquisition).

In a concrete example, Kuo explains the development of the instinct of construction. See if you can detect a fairly large flaw in his account. First, imagine a child sitting on the floor with a number of blocks before her. She places one block on top of another, stacking them securely. Then she places another on that one and so on. The actions involved are simply selected through trial and error.

But what is a trial? *Trial and error* really means "success and error," but what is a success if we are beginning with essentially random acts? Kuo suggests that the placing of blocks on one another is selected because it produces pleasure. But why does it produce pleasure? Is it because the carrying out of activity motivated by the instinct to construct is pleasant, as McDougall suggested? Kuo really had no answer, although he lamely suggested that the pleasure arises due to certain reflex body effects, to more intense sensory stimulation, or because of approval and encouragement. Since children stack blocks when they are alone, the third explanation is not enough; it also does not explain why they would engage in this

activity for the first time. The other two explanations are obviously meaningless, and Kuo leaves us with the naive hedonism that McDougall tried to replace: The child stacks the blocks because she derives pleasure from doing so, and we do not have a clue as to why that should be.

Child Development

From 1915 to 1920, Watson studied dozens of infants over surprisingly protracted periods (that is, for months), studying the development of simple reactions, such as blinking when an object rapidly approaches, to more complicated coordinations, such as learning to grasp a hanging candy or to avoid grasping a flame. After 1920, he was forced to rely on Mary Jones's observations. When she left for California with her husband in 1926, Watson was left with only the two sons of his second marriage as subjects.

Watson felt strongly that children are greatly damaged by the average upbringing, and he made his views known in 1928 in *Psychological Care of Infant and Child*, a popular book that sold 100,000 copies within a few months. He stressed the ill effects that parents wreak when they stroke and pet their children and thus make their children love them more than they should. Overaffection on the one hand and inculcated fears on the other produce problems for the child that can last a lifetime. Watson believed that parents should not hug or hit a child; rather, he encouraged conditions for the healthy development of the child, including varied experiences, responsibility, and adult treatment as early as possible. This may seem harsh, since it seems unfair to deny children their "childhood." Yet, Watson questioned if a childhood as a pampered pet was really a good preparation for life or a device used by the parent to foster neurotic dependence. Is it better to treat a child as an adult (as far as is possible) or to treat the child as a doll-baby-thing-object-pet until he or she is capable of adult speech? Does the behavior of the child change because of the unfolding of his or her innate dispositions, or is the child simply the product of the environment? According to Watson, there is a good chance that the environment is important; thus more attention must be paid to the specifics of child raising.

Personality and Psychopathology

What is personality? Is personality another name for soul? If it is, then it, like the soul, is beyond our understanding. What of those who have a dominating personality, whose personality seems to fill the room? What about the magnetic personality?

The fact is that *personality* is simply a name given to the sum of our behavioral assets and liabilities, a cross-section of our current manual, laryngeal, and visceral habits. Watson mentions the difference between a Ford and a Rolls Royce and goes on:

> In a similar way this man, this John Doe, who so far as parts are concerned is made up of head, arms, hands, trunk, legs, feet, toes and nervous, muscular, and glandular systems, who has no education and is too old to get it, is good for certain jobs. He is as strong as a mule, can work at manual labor all day long. He is too stupid to lie, too bovine to laugh or play. He will work all right as a "white wing," as a digger of ditches or as a chopper of wood. Individual William Wilkins, having the same bodily parts, but who is good looking, educated, sophisticated, accustomed to good society, travelled, is good for work in many situations—as a diplomat, a politician or a real estate salesman. He, however, was a liar from infancy and could never be trusted in a responsible place. (1930, pp. 269–270.)

We, like John Doe and William Wilkins, start equal with the same body parts and, theoretically, the same chances in life. But our environments are not the same and we soon become unequal.

Is there more to personality than that? What of the individual whose personality seems to fill the room, is magnetic, or dominates? According to Watson, these qualities describe people whose appearance and behavior evoke our infantile reactions to authority; people with those qualities

resemble our fathers and, like one's father, their behavior suggests that swift and certain obedience is expected. We are trained by society, both formally and informally, to recognize cues from those who can demand our obedience and who can punish us when we do not obey quickly enough. Put some of those cues on the face staring at us from the billboard or talking to us from the television screen and you will at least get our attention.

So-called dissociation or splitting of personality makes sense if we accept Watson's interpretation. If personality is a label for the totality of habits characterizing us at a given time, it is reasonable that this totality be subdivided according to the main classes of situations in which we routinely find ourselves. We have a set of manual, verbal, and visceral reactions attached to a situation at work, another for situations with family and friends, another tied to the situations in which we play, and so on. For example, I am a college professor, a husband and father, a bad mechanic, and a former serviceman. Is it not reasonable that different sets of habits have become built up in those different situations? In a very real sense, those different sets define different "personalities," as this term usually is used. The mental patient whose personality is split represents an extreme form of what is true of all of us, and when the subparts are given different names by the patient, it only shows the lack of awareness that this is true.

Mental illness is a normal phenomenon; it is what has become the normal behavior of a specific pathological environment, which produces behavior that society decrees is deviant. Watson put the matter in an amusing but plausible way:

> I know in general what is meant by appendicitis, cancer of the breast, gall stones, typhoid fever, tonsilitis, tuberculosis, paresis, brain tumor, and even cardiac insufficiency. . . . Yet when the psychopathologist tries to tell me about a "schiz" or a "homicidal mania" [sic] or an "hysterical" attack, I have the feeling, which as grown stronger with the years, that he doesn't know what he is talking about. And

I think the reason that he doesn't know what he is talking about is that he has always approached his patients from the point of view of the *mind* rather than from that of the way the whole body behaves and the genetic reasons for that behavior.

To show the needlessness of introducing the "conception of mind" in so-called mental diseases, I offer you a fanciful picture of a psychopathological dog (I use the dog because I am not a physician and have no right to use a human illustration—I hope the veterinarians will pardon me!). Without taking anyone into my counsel suppose I once trained a dog so that he would walk away from nicely-ground, fresh hamburg steak and would eat only decayed fish (true examples of this are now at hand). I trained him (by use of the electric shock) to avoid smelling the female dog in the usual canine way . . . by letting him play with male puppies and dogs and punishing him when he tried to mount a female, I made a homosexual out of him (F. A. Moss has done something closely akin to this in rats). Instead of licking my hands and becoming lively and playful when I go to him in the morning, he hides or cowers, whines and shows his teeth. Instead of going after rats and other small animals in the way of hunting, he runs away from them and shows the most pronounced fears. He sleeps in the ash can, he fouls his own bed, he urinates every half hour and anywhere. Instead of smelling every tree trunk, he growls and fights and paws the earth but will not come within two feet of the tree. . . . He salivates constantly (because I have conditioned him to salivate to hundreds of objects). . . . I then take him to the dog psychopathologist. His physiological reflexes are normal. No organic lesions are to be found anywhere. The dog, so the psychopathologist claims, is mentally sick, actually insane. . . . The psychopathologist says that I must commit the dog to an institution for the care of insane dogs; that if he is not restrained he will jump from a ten-story building, or walk into a fire without hesitation. (1930, pp. 298–300)

Watson goes on to reveal to the psychopathologist what he has done to the dog, and the psychopathologist becomes angry and challenges Watson to cure the dog. He does so, unless the dog is too old or things have gone too far, using the same methods used to create the "mental illness." After arguing thus against psychotherapy as it was (is?) practiced, Watson goes on to suggest that, despite its flaws, the psychopathologist is necessary.

However badly he handles his job at present, we have to go to him when a habit breakdown occurs. If I got to the point where I could not pick up my knife and fork, if one arm became paralyzed or if I couldn't visually react to my wife and children, and a physical examination showed no organic lesion of any kind, I should hasten to my psychoanalytic friends and say: "Please, in spite of all the mean things I've said about you, help me out of this mess." (1930, p. 301)

One may well wonder how a personality constructed as Watson suggests could get in that mess. How does a set of acquired manual, laryngeal, and visceral habits become deranged? It does so because the world changes and the old established habit patterns are no longer appropriate. Watson continues:

Almost any event or happening might start a change; a flood might do it, a death in the family, an earthquake, a conversion to the church, a breakdown in health, a fist fight—anything that would break up your present habit patterns, throw you out of your routine and put you in such a position that you would have to learn to react to objects and situations different from those to which you have had to react in the past—such happenings might start the process of building a new personality for you. (1930, p. 301)

Since it depends on experience, personality can be changed, but it is no easy matter to change the habits of a lifetime. One does not learn chemistry or become a violin virtuoso in a week, and it is unreasonable to expect to change a personality, which is infinitely more complicated, in a short time. But it can be done and Watson predicted that future hospitals would be devoted to doing just that.

One of Watson's manuscripts, never published, dealt with the problem of suicide (Cohen, 1979). During the 1930s, a great many suicides occurred, and for good reason: The great depression made life difficult. Even the relatively well off had little reason to live because of the structure of modern society.

The Native American youth of 200 years ago may have suffered many privations, at least from our point of view, but such youth surely had reason to live. Every day was an opportunity to be a hero. The modern youth graduating from college is hardly in the same position.

Why do people go on living? The question interested Watson, who suffered from depression frequently during his life, and he sent out a letter to 100 people asking the simple question, "Why go on living?" The results were to be presented in an article commissioned by *Cosmopolitan* magazine.

He sent the letters in 1932. The answers he received were depressing indeed. Respondents often said that they feared they would botch a suicide try, that they wouldn't give their enemies the satisfaction, and similar dismal reasons. Only Watson's former friend, Robert Yerkes, replied really positively, saying that life was a contest between himself (the scientist) and the universe and that he enjoyed the game. The general response, however, was so negative that the editor of *Cosmopolitan* refused to publish it; it was too depressing. A few months later, the editor committed suicide himself!

Summary

Watson viewed learning essentially as escape; stimuli call out reactions, which continue until the stimuli are somehow removed. In the case of a noxious stimulus, the removal occurs because we remove ourselves from its presence. Experience with recurring stimuli leads to the formation of habits, made up of those reactions that most frequently and recently occurred in the presence of that stimulus. Watson's descriptions were always cast in terms of stimuli and responses, but these terms did not have the narrow connotations they later acquired in the hands of other psychologists. A stimulus may be a ringing bell or ten years of schooling and a response may be salivation, or the writing of a book. The level of specificity depends on the phenomenon we wish to explain.

Watson interpreted language as a category of behavior similar in kind to manual and visceral behavior. We use words to stand for objects and activities, and this symbolic role may be carried out by bodily activities (gestures and postures) as well as words. Language is important in memory, but much of what we remember has nothing to do with verbal material.

Watson considered thinking to be talking to oneself, but by *talking* he did not mean simply verbal activity. Thinking may involve the whole body, including the viscera. Watson acknowledged conscious activity; we may often note that we are thinking (as well as seeing, hearing, and so on), just as we may note that a fly is in the room. But there is no special entity—consciousness—that is different from the sum of our thinking, seeing, hearing, or other such activity.

We acquire emotional habits through our lifetimes and some of the most important are established in infancy and childhood. Watson believed that parents can do great damage to their children, and he was one of the real pioneers in the treatment of learned fears. He emphasized the importance of the environment in influencing our development, opposing the fashionable emphasis on heredity. His observations of children convinced him that we do come with instinctive behaviors but that such behaviors are certainly not those proposed by the advocates of heredity.

Watson argued that mental illness is not illness at all, but only the result of learning and environment. As we mature, we develop routine reactions to the common situations in which we find ourselves. If something happens to change our world so that routine behaviors are no longer effective, we are apt to suffer a breakdown of our habit systems in general. The problem is a consequence of years of previous learning, and the cure may require years. But the cure, Watson believed, must be directed toward a re-education of the individual, not toward curing a disease.

3. CRITICISMS OF WATSON'S BEHAVIORISM

Many of the criticisms leveled at Thorndike's connectionist behaviorism were applied with even greater fervor to Watson's version, probably since it was Watson who really established behaviorism, even though Thorndike and a number of others are considered the founders. Like Thorndike, Watson was charged with oversimplification and overmechanization of human behavior. Such criticism is as misguided and nonsensical as when applied to Thorndike: The suggestion that something very complex ultimately depends on relatively simple general principles hardly means that the subject matter has been distorted. But Watson was criticized especially for his alleged treatment of thinking and his denial of the existence of mind and consciousness.

Watson's Denial of Mind and Consciousness

Pick up almost any book that devotes a paragraph or more to Watson and you may be certain to read that Watson, denying mind, proposed that humans are mere mechanical contrivances, "penny-in-the-slot" beings, as McDougall charged (Joncich, 1968). Other texts may say that Watson was not really denying the existence of mind and consciousness but just arguing that the mind could not be objectively studied, since we cannot measure experience. Both criticisms are dead wrong, as any author or reader may see by examining any of Watson's substantive works (e.g., 1919).

Defining Mind and Consciousness   Watson did deny the existence of mind and consciousness, as pointed out previously. What he denied, though, was the existence of some magical mental entity— something that might be part of a science fiction plot, in which evil aliens transfer a human mind to another individual. Watson felt that there was no mind as stuff-to-be-transferred; this does not mean that anything familiar and dear to us has been neglected, however. Watson knew that people see, hear, remember, dream, daydream, feel emotion, and so on. These are things that we do, and muscular or glandular activity is important in the doing of it. But, given seeing, thinking, and the rest, what is the mind? To Watson, the mind is a bugaboo that has hampered understanding of human workings for many centuries. Better it be abandoned.

As for studying covert activity, Watson believed strongly that dreams, daydreams, and the like were an important part of what we do (as in seeing and thinking) and surely could be studied (Watson, 1919). Verbal reports were perfectly acceptable to Watson as sources of data, as long as they were properly interpreted. That is, they were part of ongoing behavior and not a reflection of mysterious processes of the mind.

What about mental content? Don't we have thoughts when we think? Don't we see images when we imagine? How did Watson deal with such things?

Mental Imagery   William James (1890) claimed that he was unable to conjure up visual imagery, and he apologized to artist friends that he liked their work but was completely unable to picture it unless the work were present. He referred to a famous survey conducted by Sir Francis Galton that produced results puzzling to Galton but reassuring to James. Galton sent out a questionnaire to prominent Englishmen asking them to what extent they could visualize that morning's breakfast table. Scientists, military leaders, and industrialists claimed that they had no such imagery to describe and some seemed unable even to understand the question! Similar results were obtained when prominent Frenchmen were queried. Believing as he did that imagery plays a large part in thought, Galton was greatly surprised, especially when children answered the same question with detailed accounts of visual imagery.

What did this finding signify? William James suggested that imagery is actually an obstacle to clear and superior thought. As children, we may well have lots of visual imagery, but it later gets in the way. One reason for this is the fact that imagery often produces emotional reactions that are better avoided. If a military commander could clearly imagine the scenes of the next day's battle, it probably would not help him to plan for it. Is it a help to the scientist's rational thought to have constant visual imagery? James believed that imagery and its attendant emotion was damaging to most intellectual activity.

With the advent of Watson's behaviorism, imagery was far less emphasized. It is commonly asserted that Watson denied the existence of imagery, banishing it from psychology. In fact, he did banish the image as it was used by the introspectionists. Of course, he did not banish seeing, hearing, and thinking, and he spoke of reactions to stimuli that were not there; in that sense, he accepted imagery. Suppose, for example, that someone says, "I see a dagger before me," and that you see nothing. That individual's behavior is controlled by what he or she sees. But is that thing a dagger or an image? By arguing against the existence of "pictures in the head," Watson was saying no more than current investigators of imagery would say.

If you, the reader, believe that you have pictures in your head (as I usually believe I do), try this simple test. Picture as clearly as you can a moderately long word, such as *imagination*. Examine the image and read from it to spell the word backwards. You will note that this is much more difficult than spelling it normally. Yet, why should it be if you are just reading the image (cf. Posner & Shulman, 1979)? There is no question that we can, in a sense, see things that are not now present. But current opinion agrees with Watson; there are no pictures in our heads (Neisser, 1976)! Neisser suggests that imagery represents an anticipatory phase of perception, which

blends into subsequent acts of locomotion and perception. This is close to Watson's view.

Criticism of Thinking as Talking to Oneself

Watson viewed thinking as silent speech, or talking to oneself. *Talking* seems to imply that only the activity of the larynx is involved (the making of certain sounds as air passes through the throat), since that is what most of us view as talking. But Watson, who classified thinking as laryngeal habits, often made clear what he meant, although he equally often appeared to enjoy baiting critics with statements such as, "My current laryngeal habits lead me to believe . . . "

Talking, laryngeal habits, and language habits are three ways of referring to symbolic activity, although Watson did not use that term. Words are substitutes for actions and objects. To make the meaning clear here, imagine the origin of the shrug, the wink, obscene gestures, and other bodily word substitutes. These movements are part of thinking; if we suppose that they often may be the larger part, then we have a body talking. Take all of these movements and the speaking in words, which we often do silently, and we have thinking. Yes, thinking is talking to oneself, but talking normally includes much more than words.

Behaviorism as Merely Descriptive

Watson's version of behaviorism as well as other versions have frequently been criticised for being merely descriptive. That is, if we follow Watson's advice and simply seek the situations and stimuli that produce behavior, we will finish with no more than a transient technology. Suppose that we observe and manipulate long enough to discover that the best way to influence people is by directly evoking some emotion, whether it be fear, rage, or love. Or suppose that we find that a man can do 30 percent more heavy labor if we increase the frequency of brief rests that he is allowed. In both cases we now know how to influence behavior, but we don't know why the emotional appeals or the more frequent rests work. We have no explanation, say the critics, if we stick to behavioral explanations. What are the neural processes involved in both cases? What cognitive structures participate? Is the actualizing tendency somehow involved in both cases? Answers to these questions would provide explanations.

The one thing inimical to true behaviorism is the explanation of a phenomenon in terms of some supposed underlying mechanism, whether that mechanism be a model of the nervous system, an imagined actualizing tendency, or whatever. The behaviorist would say that the behavioral account is actually an empirical fact that, when applied to other cases, becomes an empirical generalization. It is useful; it allows us to predict and control. An explanatory account usually does not explain and it is typically not useful.

Edwin Holt (1915) suggested that explanatory accounts, which answer the "why" questions, are popular before a phenomenon is well understood. For example, the rising of the sun was once explained as the work of the sun god Helios, riding his fiery chariot across the sky on his way to pay court to the goddess Ceres. Because the god's action was so charming, the crops watching it were cheered and grew. That is why the sun travels across the sky from east to west, and that is why crops grow.

Holt went on to point out that once we know the "how" of an event, the "why" answers become less interesting. In the case of the sunrise, once we know that the earth turns on its axis and that the sun is more or less stationary with respect to the earth, we still don't know (ultimately) why the earth rotates, why the sun is there, and so on. But the "how" account makes the "why" account seem less important. "How" explanations allow us to predict sunrises and other events in nature. Watson argued that once we can make reliable predictions about human behavior, the gods and ghosts and minds and consciousnesses and other remnants of magic and savagery will be abandoned.

4. WATSON'S WORK AFTER 1920

The 1920 Scandal

Watson's famous divorce and the profound change that it made in his life and his work should be briefly noted. The episode has become part of the folklore of psychology, and it forced Watson into a line of work that he would not have chosen otherwise. It also showed how an academician can apply his or her knowledge to a commercial enterprise that may at first seem far removed from the academic work.

In 1919, Watson was one of the best-known psychologists in the United States. He had spent years in animal research and studied children intensively for four years. He had had many affairs over the years, but, according to a biographer (Cohen, 1979), these were long tolerated by his wife of seventeen years, Mary Ickes Watson. Mary was not disturbed at first when Watson began an affair with Rosalie Rayner, an extraordinarily attractive nineteen-year-old graduate student, Vassar graduate, and daughter of a prominent Baltimore family. But this affair persisted and finally Mary procured more than a dozen love letters written to Rosalie by Watson. She gave them to her brother, who evidently attempted to blackmail Rosalie's father. Watson and Mary were separated in April of 1920, and the letters, delivered either by Mary's brother or by Albert Rayner, fell into the hands of Johns Hopkins president Goodnow in September.

After a faculty meeting in which no support came from Watson's friends, he was called to Goodnow's office and forced to resign. Watson left Baltimore with Rosalie. At the age of 42, Watson—one of the best-known psychologists in the country—was out of work and forever cut off from academics. He moved to New York City, where a friend introduced him to people connected with J. Walter Thompson advertising agency, and Watson got a provisional job with the company. It is likely that he was hired largely because he was "Dr. Watson, the scientist," not because it was seriously believed that he could really contribute to the success of the agency. But Watson did contribute mightily, applying the principles he had advocated for so long.

Advertising Career

Watson's initial assignment was to conduct a survey of the preferences for various types of rubber boots among the inhabitants living along the Mississippi River, from Cairo to New Orleans. After that he was sent to northern Ohio and western Pennsylvania to push Yuban coffee in the groceries of that region. He evidently did well because he was soon made a vice-president of the company, conducting campaigns for Maxwell House coffee, Johnson's baby powder, and Pond's cold cream. Because of his efforts, Johnson's baby powder became synonymous with purity, love, and being a good mother. Pond's became the cold cream of royalty; Watson hired the queens of Spain and of Romania to give testimonials. Advertising before that time was concerned largely with informing the public of the products that were available. With Watson, the scope of advertising expanded to informing the public which products it wanted.

Watson believed that the way to appeal to the consumer was through emotions—the basic fear, rage, and love reactions. Those, together with sex, food, and shelter represented six basic elements that could be combined in 720 ways to sell a product. Johnson's baby powder became a symbol of maternal love; ads showed happy, healthy babies being patted and stroked by a mother applying the powder. How could rage be used to sell a product? Recall that the basic instigator of rage is restraint, interference with movements. What better advertising for a commuter train service than to show the traffic jams that beset motorists, contrasted with the fortunate train traveler, who is free to move about with no worry about weather conditions or snarled traffic. Watson used fear in a campaign for Scott's toilet tissue. Advertisements showed an operating room

with a group of surgeons surrounding an operating table. The operation looked serious and gruesome and the caption read, "And the trouble began with harsh toilet tissue!"

These methods seemed to work well, and Watson was soon living on Fifth Avenue and later on a 40-acre farm in fashionable Westport, Connecticut. During the 1920s, he continued in academics to the limited extent that he was allowed. He supported Mary Cover Jones's work with children and wrote a number of popular articles for *Harper's Magazine*, *Cosmopolitan*, and other magazines. For years he lectured weekly at the New School for Social Research and even invited McDougall to debate him on the virtues of behaviorism in 1928. But his popular articles tapered off after 1930 and with Rosalie's death from dysentary in 1936, his writing ceased. He said many years later that the lack of a laboratory and a ready reference library caused him to "dry up." After so long away from academics he found that he had nothing more to say.

After being shunned by the entire academic community (except for Edward Titchener, who remained a faithful friend until his death in 1927), Watson was belatedly recognized by the American Psychological Association, which awarded him its gold medal in 1957. Watson seemed pleased with this honor, which said that he had "initiated a revolution in psychological thought." At the last moment, though, the award was accepted for him by his son Billy, who had become a psychiatrist. Watson died in 1958 at the age of 80.

SUMMARY

Although Thorndike had opposed mentalism, which stressed the importance of mental states in determining behavior, Watson was widely interpreted as denying the very existence of mental life. He did feel that the introspective psychology of his day was so futile and so harmful to progress that both its method and its language was best abandoned. Hence, he discarded the images, sensations, and thoughts that were the elements of experience assumed by the introspectionists. He did not, of course, deny the existence of seeing, thinking, and imagining.

Watson saw the goal of psychology as the prediction and control of behavior. Given a situation, what behavior may we expect? Given a behavior, what are the factors that produce it? For Watson, behavior included overt muscular activity, thinking, talking, imagining, emoting, buying, and whatever else may be construed as activity. He described activity in terms of stimuli and responses. Depending upon what is to be explained, a stimulus could be a puff of air, a medical education, and so on; a response could be an eye blink, the performance of a surgical operation, and so on.

Watson opposed the explanation of behavioral phenomenon in terms of assumed underlying mechanisms. Thus, he argued against the positing of S-R connections in the nervous system, as was Thorndike's practice. He was opposed to the use of instinct, trait, and purpose, for the same reasons. Watson viewed learning as adjustment; stimuli and situations call out behaviors that persist until the stimulus is removed. He believed the law of effect to be superfluous and whatever it is invoked to explain may be explained in terms of frequency and recency. He adopted Pavlov's conditioned reflex as a provisional model for learning, but his interpretation of what could be called a conditioned response was quite broad.

Watson viewed thinking as "talking to oneself," but talking was by no means restricted to verbal behavior. Thinking is an activity that involves the whole body, including abbreviated verbal behavior, as well as emotional behavior, muscular movements, and tensions. Watson interpreted memory differently from the introspectionists; he did not consider memory to be a storehouse of experiences. Remembering, like thinking, is by no means merely verbal but includes emotional and muscular aspects.

Emotional behavior was very important to Watson. He studied the development and modification of emotional reactions in scores of chil-

dren, in addition to Albert B., even after he was forced from academics. His views on emotion played a large part in his later work in advertising.

Watson stressed the practical goals of psychology. Like Skinner years later, he insisted that behavior was significant in its own right. The answer to the question, "What is that man doing and how may we change it?" was the proper goal of psychology, and any recourse to underlying neural and mental mechanisms could only impede the progress in reaching that goal. This applies as well in industry, in advertising, and in the treatment of psychopathology.

GLOSSARY

Behaviorism The view that the subject matter of psychology is the study of behavior, which usually includes private behavior, such as seeing and dreaming. Behaviorists do not use explanations that refer to hypothetical inner mechanisms, such as mental powers, or supposed neural events.

Emotional flooding Method of psychotherapy in which a feared object is repeatedly presented at close range to the patient, who may react quite violently. Such treatment has been reported to sometimes alleviate unreasonable fears (phobias).

Functionalism Movement in psychology that opposed the emphasis on the analysis of the structure of consciousness. Functionalists stressed the importance of activity, especially adaptive activity. Watson opposed this movement because, despite its emphasis on behavior, it still stressed the importance of consciousness, which he felt was counterproductive.

Instinct Behavior present at birth or after a period of maturation. Older views of instinct treated it as independent of learning, and much research was done to separate instinctive from learned behavior. *Instinct* usually was not applied to obvious reflexive behavior, such as occurs in the process of digestion or in the blinking of the eye when a speck of dust strikes it. Depending upon the theorist, instinct could refer to the nest building of birds and the web spinning of spiders or to the performance of children on so-called intelligence tests and the customs of ethnic groups. Current opinion holds that the crass division of behavior into instinctive and learned is unwise. In Watson's time it was common to invoke instinct as the explanation for differences in the behavior of groups of individuals, whether human or animal.

Kinesthesia Sensory effects produced by muscular movement. When a muscle contracts, muscle spindles produce neural impulses that aid in the coordination of muscular movement. Other feedback occurs when a limb is moved, due to the action of Golgi tendon organs. Without information from muscle spindles and Golgi tendon organs, coordinated movement is difficult.

Laryngeal habits Watson's term for learned behavior that constitutes the use of language. This includes not only spoken words, but any behavior that acts as a substitute for action or as a symbol for an object. Laryngeal habits have a communicative function and include, for example, a shoulder shrug.

Manual habits Watson's term for learned behaviors that involve skeletal muscles and, usually, observable actions. Threading a needle is an example of a manual habit.

Visceral habits Watson's term for learned behaviors involving the viscera, or internal organs. For example, changes in heart rate, perspiration, and gastric activity may occur when we are frightened by a ghost story. This emotional reaction is due to prior learning and thus represents a visceral habit. Our reaction to the pledge of allegiance, the phrases "up against the wall" and "good job" likewise include visceral components. Visceral, or emotional, reactions are part and parcel of most of our reactions, along with the manual and laryngeal components.

RECOMMENDED READINGS

Watson, J. B. (1919). *Psychology from the standpoint of a behaviorist*. Philadelphia: J. B. Lippincott.

    This was Watson's last scholarly effort. Anyone seriously interested in details of Watsonian behaviorism will find this the best source.

Watson, J. B. (1925). *Behaviorism*. New York: Norton.

    This popular presentation of behaviorism appeared in a second edition in 1930, which is still in print.

Chapter 5

E. R. GUTHRIE: PRACTICAL BEHAVIORISM

BIOGRAPHY

Edwin R. Guthrie was born in Lincoln, Nebraska in 1886 and graduated with a degree in mathematics and philosophy from the University of Nebraska (see Figure 5.1). After three years of teaching high school mathematics, he attended graduate school at the University of Pennsylvania, where his doctoral thesis was concerned with philosophical paradoxes. In 1959, the year of his death, he said that his early experience with Bertrand Russell's philosophy and the difficulties encountered by Russell and Whitehead in the *Principia Mathematica* had convinced him that the search for absolutely valid knowledge would be fruitless. As he expressed it, these men had spent 400 pages of tenuous logic in an effort to establish that one plus one equals two, with each step of logic potentially refutable.

Guthrie's first and last job was at the University of Washington, where he was Professor of Psychology and, for a time, Dean of the Graduate School. His theory of learning is the simplest conceivable, consisting of only one main principle. But that principle in his hands was powerful indeed, which you will find if you examine Guthrie's main published works:

General Psychology in Terms of Behavior, 1921 (with S. Smith)

The Psychology of Learning, 1952 (published originally in 1935)

The Psychology of Human Conflict, 1938

Cats in a Puzzle Box, 1946 (with G. P. Horton)

What is most amazing about Guthrie is that he remains current at all. He proposed the ultimately simple theory of learning, which merely holds that we will do in a given situation whatever it is that we did when last in that situation. He conducted virtually no research and his total published work is a small fraction of the output of other major theorists. (Thorndike, for example,

FIGURE 5.1   Edwin R. Guthrie, 1886–1959.
Photo courtesy of Bettman Archive

own behavior incorporates most of the basic methods now used in behavior therapy. Despite such virtues, he never rendered the theory in precise enough form to really make it testable. Depending on one's point of view, Guthrie's theory is either the only one we need or it is no theory at all.

INTRODUCTION

Section 1 considers the two aspects of Guthrie's theory that made it significant at the time. First, he was one of the very few psychologists to propose that learning did not necessarily mean improvement. This led him to oppose the common emphasis on goal-directed behavior and to make some unique predictions about everyday matters, which the other theories neglected. His concern was to make predictions about things that he considered worth knowing, and he criticized the efforts of the other theorists to be as precise as possible: A precise explanation of uninteresting things, Guthrie believed, is not worth much.

Section 2 describes what there is of this theory: In any situation we simply do whatever it was that we did last in that situation! To appreciate his point, we consider eleven examples of applications of the theory to daily life. Then we see how it applies to traditional categories in psychology, such as the effects of practice, reward and punishment, thought, motivation, and so on. We will see that he had some interesting opinions and a real knack for applying his theory to the common problems of life.

How may we change our habits? Guthrie supplied the main methods now in use by behavior therapists, although they seldom give him credit. He tried to show the importance of stereotypy (that is, doing what we last did in the same situation) in a piece of research with cats, published in 1946. The situation was similar to Thorndike's problem boxes, but his interpretation was quite different; unlike Thorndike, Guthrie carefully watched everything done by the cats in their attempts to escape.

published roughly 27 times the number of items that Guthrie published.) He had no real followers, in the sense that other major theorists did, aside from Virginia Voeks and Fred Sheffield, who may not even view themselves as real Guthrians. Yet, he is current and it is an unusual learning textbook that does not devote some space to discussing his views, often more space than is given Thorndike and virtually always more than is allowed Pavlov and Watson.

The reason for Guthrie's continued presence and timeliness lies in the great virtues of his theory, simple though it is, in accounting for a wide variety of behavior. His account of reward and punishment may be more useful than Thorndike's, and his homely advice for changing our

In Section 3 we look at the common criticisms of Guthrie's theory. You might think that there would be many criticisms, given the simplicity of the theory. But the criticisms point more to the incompleteness and vagueness of the theory, rather than to any basic flaws. Section 4 examines this alleged vagueness and incompleteness and finds that Guthrie's view does suffer from these deficiencies. Yet, for practicality, Guthrie's theory cannot be beaten; his basic priniciple comes from the popular psychology of the nineteenth century, and that worked, as does Guthrie's psychology. Whether one likes Guthrie depends upon whether one wants to understand the ultimate nature of our workings in detail or simply to have a practical understanding. Guthrie would disagree with this assessment, but it seems clear that his theory is restricted to practical purposes. Most of us would not consider such practicality a fatal drawback, although we might admit that any theory concerned only with practical matters leaves out a great deal.

1. GUTHRIE'S SIGNIFICANCE DURING HIS OWN TIME

The Basics of Behaviorism: Is All Behavior Goal Directed?

Learning theories were extremely popular in the 1930s and 1940s, signaling, it seemed, the long-awaited independence of psychology from philosophy and the beginning of a real and practical understanding of human behavior and experience. Thorndike and Watson had cast out the methods of the introspectionists, and their essential message had been heard and accepted by a great many psychologists. Their basic views, that the subject matter of psychology was behavior and that behavior was determined by discoverable antecedents, was being shown to be a profitable way of viewing things. There was little concern with either the analysis of consciousness or with the problems of the old philosophies that

had led to the introspectionists' version of psychology. To a great many psychologists the only problem remaining was the working out of the details of the learning process.

Unfortunately, at least in Guthrie's view, most psychologists were making premature simplifying assumptions in their rush to establish a definitive general theory of learning. This was especially true in the common assumption that learning meant improvement. Improvement means that activity is evaluated with respect to some goal and that it consists of errors and successes (trials). This seems a reasonable enough assumption, of course, and it may seem odd to challenge it. Isn't all of our behavior goal directed? If asked what we are trying to do at any time during the day, could we not more or less quickly provide a reasonable answer? All of our activity, it seems, is inherently purposive. This was Thorndike's conclusion, apparently, since his theories stressed the consequences of action. And it is Watson's conclusion, too, since he defined learning as adjustment. It is difficult to cite many psychologists who did not or do not emphasize the essential purposiveness of behavior. Even Pavlov, were he a psychologist, would point out the obviously adaptive function of the conditioned response. Only Edwin Guthrie questioned the virtue of stressing goals, of emphasizing purpose, and of thereby restricting our consideration to goal-directed behavior.

Guthrie felt that the overemphasis on goals left out a lot of what we do. There are meaningless acts, awkwardness, maladaptive and foolish acts, and it is unwise to treat them merely as failures in the course of otherwise reasonable goal-directed activity. In addition, the emphasis on purpose leads to an unwarranted stress on the consequences of action, with the result being the treatment of rewards and punishers as basic determiners of action. A good deal of behavior is goal directed, and there is no question that rewards and punishers are effective in modifying behavior. But stress on purpose and on the importance of rewards and punishers in general will not help us explain all of the behavior of individuals in particular. How does the individual progress or fail to progress toward what the onlooker views as a goal? What determines whether a reward will act as such for individual student X at time Y in place Z? What factors determine when reinforcers and punishers will or will not work?

Back to British Empirism: The Blank Form

Guthrie was not ready for the specific mechanisms proposed by others and sought instead the most general possible principle, the "blank form," which would include all of the specific mechanisms of other theorists as subprinciples. He found his blank form in old *British empiricism*, the school of philosophy represented by Locke and James Mill, both of whom stressed the importance of *contiguity* in space and time as the essential ingredient in the association of ideas. Although the empiricists held that our ideas follow the course they do because they are following the course they did in the past, Guthrie argued that we do what we do because that is what we did in the past. Is this a theory of learning? Guthrie's continued influence suggests that there is something to it.

2. THE BASICS OF GUTHRIE'S THEORY

What Is a Theory of Learning?

In Guthrie's view, learning exemplifies what we mean by *mind*, and the study of learning is therefore the study of mind. An organism that grows, reproduces, and defends itself may thereby show evidence of life, but unless its behavior changes as a function of past behavior it does not show evidence of mind. Having mind, or the ability to learn, means having the ability to respond differently to a situation because of past responses to the situation. But *respond differently* does not mean "improve." We learn bad habits as easily as we learn good ones. Goals and the implied successes and errors are often only in the eye of the onlooker, not the learner.

The goal of a theory of learning is to explain, which is to state the rule of which an event is an instance. For example, an act of aggression by one child toward another may be explained as a manifestation of the working of an aggression center in the brain, as the consequence of frustration, as the effect of previous rewards for aggression, or as the will of God. These and other possible explanations (and there are many) may be more or less successful, but all suffer from a major shortcoming. Each of them refers to the act of an agent—the aggression center, frustration, reward, and God—and this lessens their usefulness as explanations. For Guthrie, an explanation must above all be useful. Explanations that depend upon agents are useful only insofar as we know the ways of the agent. We know little of the workings of an aggression center and less about the ways of God. We do not really understand the factors that produce frustration and under what circumstances frustration produces aggression. Rewards do affect behavior, but often they seem to be ineffective; do we really know the ways of even that agent?

Guthrie's Principle

Explanations that refer to such agents may sometimes be useful, but Guthrie was interested in explanations that are always useful. The one most general rule, which refers to no agent, is "A combination of stimuli which has accompanied a movement will on its recurrence tend to be followed by that movement" (Guthrie, 1952).

"What kind of a theory of learning is that?" you might ask. This is a common reaction by readers and students who first encounter Guthrie's theory. Guthrie appears to be saying that *stereotypy* is the basic feature of learning—that in any situation we do what we did the last time we were in that situation. Not only does that seem untrue, but if it were true it would mean that learning would never take place, since any definition of learning refers to a change in behavior in a given situation! Guthrie's background in philosophy and mathematics seem to have reduced him to a player of verbal tricks, not a person to be taken seriously!

Not only is stereotypy the basic rule of learning, according to Guthrie. But repetition of the combination of stimuli does not increase its tendency to evoke the movement. Practice does not strengthen the connection between situation and behavior. The connection is made in one trial.

How can such a theory explain anything? It appears to say that I will always do what I did last in a situation and that when I am in a new situation whatever I happen to do (reflexively? due to instinct?) will be what I will do in that situation until my dying day. The theory becomes more intelligible once we realize that (of course) we are never in the same situation twice; even if the external setting is largely unchanged, we are not. We are older, our stomachs are more or less full than the last time, and so on. But before going further into this, it is helpful to consider some of Guthrie's examples of applications of his theory. He was a master at application and most of these instances come from his 1952 book.

Guthrie's One-Trial Contiguity Learning

One-trial contiguity learning means that learning consists of associations between stimuli and movements that occur close in time (are contiguous) and that the association is at full strength with the first pairing. (Repetition does not strengthen the connection.) Consider the following examples. You should note that Guthrie's examples assume some things that may not always be the case. Try to identify these assumptions and you will understand his point of view more clearly.

Training a Dog to Come   One way to train a dog to come on signal is to hold a piece of food and call the dog's name. If the dog does not come

when the signal is first given (for example, by calling its name) then giving further calls is unwise; the signal becomes the occasion for not coming. This effect is the reason for the military adage that holds that a commander should never give an order that he does not expect will be obeyed. A skilled animal trainer does not give the cue or call the name until he or she sees that the desired response is about to occur on its own. Wait until the dog happens to move toward you and then call its name, so the name becomes attached to the movement.

A piece of food may prompt the dog to come on signal, but it is not the only way to accomplish this. Anything that makes the dog come will do the trick. Given that the dog is not too large or vicious, a long rope attached to the dog and pulled by you will teach it to come.

Training a Dog to Stop Killing Chickens   Tying a dead chicken around a dog's neck serves as a strong agent for learning. The dog will attempt to get the chicken off, and, if the chicken is skillfully attached, this can require some time and some extreme effort on the dog's part. When the dog has succeeded in getting rid of the chicken, it will have become an educated dog: The last thing the dog did was try to get the chicken away from it and to get itself away from the chicken. The sight of a chicken in future will reinstate the last behavior done in the presence of a chicken: getting away.

Walking on Ice   Situations are always compounds of groups of stimuli encountered in the past. Sometimes the compound is reducible to only two general classes, as is the case when we walk on ice. There are the normal movements involved in walking, called out by the stimuli that regularly accompany such movements. But there is another class of stimuli that has been paired in the past with falling, not walking. This group of stimuli evokes the movements that it accompanied in the past, protective movements, such as holding out the arms to break a fall. This was the last thing we did on a prior occasion when we fell. "Walking on ice" is the compound produced by stimuli attached to walking and those attached to falling.

Overcorrection   The *overcorrection* procedure (Stoltz, Wienkowski, & Brown, 1975) requires no more than forcing the author of a misdeed to atone for it by undoing whatever damage was done (that is, to correct it) and to repeatedly perform the correct behavior (overcorrect). For example, a mental patient who tears up a bed will remake it and make twenty other beds. A child who throws food will clean it up a few times.

Such a practice ensures that the last act performed in a situation is one that is desired by society. How the learner is coerced into doing the overcorrecting is up to whatever agent of society is in control. It is only important that it be done.

Reading in Noise   Guthrie (1952) described the example of a young woman who lived in an apartment near some noisy neighbors who annoyed her with their loud radio. She was unable to study because of the noise, until an acquaintance suggested that she practice reading mystery novels in the noise. The novels held her attention sufficiently so she was able to read despite the noise and was able to study in noise within a week.

Reading While Fatigued   We are always learning, and when we read while very tired or while distracted we learn something new. We learn to read without following, as we will discover when we next try to read while tired or refreshed.

Imitative Laughing   It is difficult to refrain from laughing when in the presence of others who are laughing. The pressure to imitate is strongest when a large number of others around us are laughing. Guthrie felt that this behavior was less the product of an instinct to imitate than it was a case of simple stereotypy. We are in a situation in which we hear loud laughter nearby. In the past, such stimulation occurred when we ourselves were laughing. What were you doing the

last time you heard loud laughter? You were laughing, so that is what you do when you hear others laugh.

Changing Thoughts in Bed   When awakened by a nightmare, we may get up and walk around, turn on the light and read, or simply turn over. But there is one thing that we do not do—we do not remain in the same position and go back to sleep. The stimuli that accompany a body position are a part of the stimulus complex present during the bad dream. If you maintain that posture and go back to sleep, you stand a good chance of doing what you did the last time you were in that situation, which was dreaming the bad dream.

Remembering Names   We do what we did last in a situation and it is helpful if the cues are salient so that more of them are effective. (Guthrie later stressed the importance of stimulus salience and attention in his 1959 final statement of his position.) Thus, if we wish to remember the names of a group of new acquaintances at a party, we may ensure our success by walking up to each of them, asking the name, and shouting it back to the person. In doing this we attach the cues that we want associated with the name (the appearance of the individual) with an exaggerated response on our part. Guthrie doesn't mention it, but this method would guarantee that everyone would remember your name as well.

Negative Practice   Guthrie suggested (after Knight Dunlap) that we may often improve our skills by practicing mistakes, an odd suggestion given his theory. This is called *negative practice*. For example, suppose we make the common error of typing *the* as *hte*. We may rectify this by repeatedly typing *hte* and then practicing *the*. This strategy works because our original error came from a failure to note the cues associated with typing *the* and *hte*. Once we concentrate on the way it feels to type the error we can adjust to a forthcoming error in the future. Such a method may be useful in other areas, such as curing facial tics.

Improvement with Practice: One-Trial Learning?

Daily experience tells us in many ways that Guthrie is wrong; we do improve with practice. (Isn't that the usual definition of learning?) The suggestion that only one trial is necessary could only apply to the exceptional case, and exceptions aren't that interesting.

Guthrie did indeed believe that learning requires only one trial, which sometimes is the case. Voeks (1948), Estes (1964), and others have shown that a change from chance performance to perfect performance can occur on one trial if the task is simple. Learning either occurs gradually, as in the building up of the strength of an S-R bond, or it occurs on one trial. Given that there are instances in which it happens in one trial, can Guthrie's "all or none" theory explain the cases in which improvement is gradual? Similarly, can a theory that holds that learning is gradual explain the cases when it is complete on one trial?

Guthrie's theory works better in accounting for improvement with practice than does the opposing theory in accounting for sudden improvement. The key to understanding Guthrie's position here is the word *improvement*. This word refers to a goal or purpose, more specifically to progress toward that goal. For example, suppose I repeatedly throw a baseball through an old tire hanging from a rope. With time, my aim will improve, and the ball more often will fly through the center as it should.

However, Guthrie did not accept goal direction as the defining characteristic of what is learned. What is learned is what is done, and what is done in this case is a lot of movements. Throwing the ball is an act made up of thousands of individual habits, corresponding to the individual muscle movements required. When I first throw, my movement is awkward; it includes irrelevant responses to irrelevant stimuli. With practice, the irrelevant movements drop out, since the stimuli that produce them are apt to vary from trial to trial, whereas stimuli connected with smooth movement of the arm are there trial after trial and remain connected to individual movements. Other acts, such as smoking and eating, are made up of thousands of habits, which accounts for the difficulty we encounter in breaking such habits. In fact, they are constellations of habits.

Both Voeks (1954) and Estes (1956) have pointed to the misleading nature of learning curves averaged over great numbers of subjects. For example, suppose we plot the percentage of correct answers for students listing the first ten presidents of the United States. We find that with successive trials, performance improves, indicating that the number of presidents correctly named increases gradually with repeated trials. A similar plot could show the increase in correct turns made by a group of rats learning a maze. Such averaged data may give a false impression of the nature of learning. Suppose that on the first trial, one of 30 students can name all ten presidents and the other 29 students can name none. Suppose that on the second trial two of the 29 students can name all ten, leaving 27 who can name none. Suppose that on each succeeding trial, one or two or three or more new subjects go from naming none to naming all ten presidents. With more and more trials the likelihood of perfect performance increases.

The averaged data for the students in this case, or for the rats learning the maze, lead one to believe that improvement was gradual—and it was, for the entire group. But each individual learner could have gone from some correct to all correct on a given trial and remained at that level of perfect performance over the remaining trials.

Guthrie liked to believe that things happened or they didn't; there is simply no need to posit a gradual learning process. "We should probably say, if we are to be exact, not that practice makes perfect but that perfection is seldom approached without practice" (Guthrie, 1952).

One must bear in mind that Guthrie did not mean that every instance of learning occurs in such a fashion; often we are concerned with the learning of what he called acts. These are compound behaviors, such as learning a good backstroke or memorizing a poem. Such things are learned gradually, although each individual element (habit) may be learned on one trial. In a sense, Guthrie's definition of *habit* could be phrased "that which is learned in one trial." This definition includes more than other theorists suspected.

Rewards and Punishers: When Do They Work?

To understand Guthrie's position on the law of effect, you must remember that he was interested in truly general principles, not in special cases. For most other psychologists it was clear that behavior is goal directed and that rewards and punishers are thus basic determinants of action. Guthrie disputed this, of course, pointing out that a lot of what we do is not purposive, but aimless, useless, and even maladaptive.

No one denies that rewards and punishers are obvious determinants of our behavior and the behavior of animals. What Guthrie denied was the assumption that rewards and punishments are basic, primitive, unanalyzable events. Rewards do not always work, and punishers may even actually backfire and increase the frequency of the behavior that produces them. Rewards may decrease the frequency of the behavior that produces them. Why? In what circumstances? How may we know in advance of its application that a putative reward will do what we expect it to do? Since we are not all pleased and pained by the same things, and since the same event may at one time produce pleasure and at another time produce pain, we still have no way of predicting what will act as a reward for a given person at any given time.

Guthrie pointed out that we apply rewards and punishers in very specific ways and that we may understand their workings if we carefully consider the ways in which they are successfully and unsuccessfully applied. For example, when we use food to reward a dog for coming to us when called, we do not throw the food to the side. Doing so would leave us with a dog who approached us and then turned aside. When we reward a rat for turning right in a T-maze, we do not leave the rat in the maze to wander around after it has eaten the food. In both cases, the reward is applied in such a way as to end the sequence of behavior leading up to it and thus leave that behavior as the last thing done in that situation. The rat turns right in the maze and comes in contact with the food. Prior to that, the rat was moving through the maze. That activity stopped when the rat reached the food; the rat forgets the sight and smell of the alley for the moment, and the association between "right turn" and "choice point" remains the last thing done.

Reward may be interpreted as a stimulus change that leaves some behavior as the last thing done in the old situation. For example, the question, "What is the capital of New Jersey?" may be followed by the responses, "Elizabeth," "Rahway," "Camden," "Jersey City," and so on. Each answer is followed by "no," and the original situation remains unchanged—the question is still being asked. At last, the answer "Trenton" is given, followed by "right." The situation is now changed—the question is no longer being posed and the last response in the old situation is attached to the old question.

Motives or Drives

This interpretation of reward as situation change especially applies to situations within us. After going without food for a number of hours, my body tells me that my blood sugar is low; I am hungry. The feeling of hunger (or of thirst, or any other "drive") acts as a disturber, which produces movements. You may verify the movement-producing action of bodily states by holding your breath for several minutes and noting the movements of your body after the first few minutes.

The stimuli of hunger, thirst, and so on produce movement and maintain that movement; this is Guthrie's theory of motivation, and these stimuli are called *maintaining stimuli*. A *motive* is anything that produces activity. As we know, activity means learning. The stimuli of hunger keep me active, with each new behavior becoming associated with the cues present outside of me and the stimuli of hunger within. As a new behavior is attached, the preceding one is displaced. Finally, some behavior ends the series by eliminating the disturber; I find food and consume it, and the behavior that accomplished that is the last thing done. The next time the situation recurs and the hunger stimuli reappear, I will do whatever it was I did last in the former situation. If the situation is precisely as it was last time, so that my feeling of hunger is identical, I am in the same room, wearing the same clothes, and thinking the same thoughts, then I will do precisely what I did on that occasion. If that act doesn't change the situation this time (that is, end the disturber) then I will do something else that does change the situation and that will become the last thing done.

Although it is customary to think of drives as biological things, such as hunger and thirst, Guthrie's view was not that restricted. Biological drives are only instances of the general class of drives, defined as any instigators of action. When we are asked a question or we are bored or startled or bothered by noise or in any situation that makes us act, we are in a drive state.

Tests of Guthrie's Theory of Reinforcement

All possible cases of reward thus become special cases of the general law of stereotypy; we do in a situation what was last done in that situation. When a so-called reward doesn't work, it is because the behavior that we expected to be rewarded was not the last thing done in that situation. Consider the evidence against Guthrie cited by many authors, who allege that Guthrie is proven wrong if it can be shown that not all cases of changing the situation act as a reward.

For example, a rat runs down the alley and falls through a trap door into a black bag; this is an event that surely changes the situation (Seward, 1942). Yet, the rat does not run more rapidly

(if it runs at all) on the next trial. So it appears that Guthrie is wrong! There is no doubt that other changes in the stimulus situation would also prove ineffective. We could pour pancake syrup on the rat, slug it with a ball-peen hammer, pull its whiskers, set fire to the alley, shock it with a cattle prod, scream obscenities at it, put itching powder on its back, pick it up by the tail, and do countless other things that change the situation but that do not act as rewards. But what is it that these events actually do? They change the situation and make the rat do something new. Rather than leave the last movement down the alley as the last thing done, each of these events leaves strong new behaviors that are incompatible with movement toward the goal as the last behaviors done. Itching, flinching, squeaking, struggling, or whatever was the last thing done will be what is done when the situation recurs. Will the rat back in the start box see the cues of the alley and run? Don't be silly. What is learned is what is done and the last thing done was not movement from start box to goal; it was violent and incompatible behavior evoked by our "reward." A stimulus that produces strong new behaviors incompatible with what was last done in that situation is what we mean by a punisher.

Punishment

We sit on tacks that someone has placed on the chair. We train a dog to jump through a hoop using electric shock. A schoolgirl enters her home and throws her coat on the floor; her mother's scolding finally leads her to hang it up. An experimenter is puzzled because he finds it difficult to train a pigeon to peck a plastic disk to avoid electric shock. In all of these cases the effect of an event, whether we call it a punisher or not, lies in what it causes the organism involved to do. *Punishment*, like reward, is a moral term that reflects the intentions of the applier; the effect on behavior depends upon what it leads the recipient to do.

Guthrie noted that when a dog is trained to jump through a hoop using electric shock, it is important at which end of the dog the shock is applied! What is punished or rewarded in such a procedure? One could say that the shock to the dog's derriere punishes standing still, but Guthrie would say that it encourages movement forward. When we sit on tacks, it is not really punishment for sitting; rather the tacks encourage other behavior. Punishers are stimuli that are effective in producing new behaviors. The next time we sit in the chair, we will do what we did the last time in that situation. If the tacks no longer are present, we sit. But the slight recoil, flinch, hesitation, or concerned glance at the seat is part of what we did the last time, when the tacks were there.

Guthrie described the schoolgirl who entered her home and threw her coat on the floor. Each day the girl's mother would tell her to hang it up, but she persisted in the initial throwing to the floor. The problem was that the mother had become a cue for hanging up the coat, since the act had only occurred in her presence. The sequence always ran: cues in the entryway of house, throw the coat on the floor; cues presented by the scolding mother, hang up the coat. Guthrie advised that the girl be forced to go outside and re-enter the house and hang up the coat without the mother's scolding presence. After a few trials of that corrective procedure, the problem would be solved. Of course, the somewhat perceptive reader may note that alternative explanations are possible for this case; the embarrassment of being forced outside may have acted as a punisher for throwing the coat down, so subsequent improved behavior may amount to avoidance of the annoying and embarrassing consequence of not hanging up the coat. Guthrie stressed the effect of any operation on what is done. Initially, the scolding of the mother punished nothing; it simply became a cue for coat hanging. But the coat hanging did not occur in the context required—upon entering the house. Reward and punishment really have nothing to do with this instance: Causing the behavior we want in the context we want is all that is necessary.

Species-Specific Defense Reactions

Perhaps the greatest support for Guthrie's interpretation of punishment comes from research in avoidance learning. For reasons that are at the moment irrelevant, a lot of psychologists have felt that avoidance learning was an area crucially important to our understanding of learning in general. The problem of interest here was the difficulty encountered in training a rat to press a bar or a pigeon to peck a lighted disk to avoid shock. Why should this be difficult to train?

Imagine that you are in a small featureless room and that every ten seconds an extremely powerful and painful shock is administered through your bare feet from the metal grid floor of the room. On the wall near you is a bar, roughly the size of a baseball bat, sticking out. If you push on the bar you receive no shocks for 60 seconds. How long would it take you to learn that the painful shocks you are getting every ten seconds may be completely eliminated if you press on the lever once a minute? Yet, rats and (especially) pigeons were terrible learners in such a situation. It was not their stupidity, since the same animals could quickly learn to press or peck to get food.

Some psychologists felt that the pigeons were not really feeling the shock, since it was administered through the floor and the scaly feet of a bird might act as insulation. Thus, shock harnesses were invented to ensure that they felt the shock; one device amounted to a bathtub stopper chain passed under the bird's "wingpits" to deliver the shock. Despite these efforts, pigeons were still rotten learners.

Finally, Robert Bolles (1970) suggested that the reason for the trouble lay in what the shock led the subjects to do. Rats, pigeons, and other animals are products of evolution, which means they tend to behave in predictable ways, generally, in specific important kinds of situations. For example, in the presence of food, rats manipulate things with their paws and pigeons peck. In the presence of danger, they do other things. Bolles suggested that strong electric shock directly evokes behavior appropriate in life-threatening situations. In the rat, this amounts to running or "freezing." If the animal cannot outrun its predator, it remains still, in the hope that the predator won't see it.

In the typical avoidance learning situation, rats were required to press a bar and pigeons had to peck a key. Both behaviors are more appropriate as food-getting behaviors, and it is not surprising that rats and pigeons rapidly learn such behaviors when they bring food. But what happened in the course of evolution to those rats and pigeons who exhibited food-getting behavior in the presence of life-threatening danger? Did they live to reproduce similar maladaptive organisms? No, the animals that ran, flew, or froze lived to reproduce, and most subjects reflect that selection process. If an experiment requires a rat to run several feet to press a lever to avoid shock, the rat will quickly learn to do it; if you place the rat in front of the bar, it won't learn (Fantino, Sharp, & Cole, 1966).

Bolles called the behaviors elicited by shock or other danger *species-specific defense reactions*, or SSDRs. If we want efficient avoidance learning, the required response should be an SSDR. In Guthrie's terms, the effects of a putative punisher depend upon what it makes the recipient do. Calling it a reward or a punisher tells us only what the administrator of the event has in mind; the effect will depend on the actions it produces.

Intentions

Precurrent responses amount to a readiness for the consequences of past experience; in the past, hunger was the cue for searching, grasping, and eating. Part of that stimulus complex, the hunger feelings, is now present. Hence, part of the behavior that last occurred during hunger appears; I think of food, salivate, lick my chops, and so on.

Such behavior is precisely like Thorndike's readiness; a present cue, such as the sight of prey, attracts my attention and (in Thorndike's terms) sensitizes the conduction units for chasing, seizing, and eating. For Guthrie, conduction units are unnecessary. I see the prey; when I last saw it I was eating it. I cannot actually eat it now, since it is at a distance; but I can begin eating it, so to speak, through my anticipatory behaviors evoked.

Guthrie believed that intentions, readinesses, and expectancies were all fractional parts of complete reactions evoked because part of a stimulus complex was now present. Such readinesses are of great practical importance to us. For example, note the difference in our reading when it is done for pleasure and when it is done in preparation for an examination an hour away. If we are called on to recite, is it not easier when we expect it than when we are taken by surprise? Part of the reason for this difference lies in the fact that in the former case we are already partially reciting, in the form of insignificant body movements, when we are called upon.

Whether a crime is committed intentionally may have great bearing on the sentence meted out, and Guthrie suggests that *intention* may have many meanings. In an often-quoted example, Guthrie cites the case of a man who plans a murder and waits for his victim to come through a door. As the man waits with his finger on the trigger, he thinks over the foul deed he intends and changes his mind. He no longer intends to shoot his adversary. But the door opens unexpectedly, the adversary comes through it and the man pulls the trigger. Was this done unintentionally? Would a judge or jury believe that someone obviously laying in wait with a loaded gun did not intend to shoot the person?

An intention is a readiness to act, and the assailant's verbal change in intention was not effective in altering the bodily readiness, which was, in effect, already committing the crime. Perhaps if more time had been allowed the new intention would have led to new bodily postures and muscular readinesses and the shot would not have been fired.

Guthrie suggested that such readinesses were the basis for the psychological factor in sports. Ideally, the opponent's moves act as maintaining stimuli, keeping us active and producing appropriate readinesses, or partial reactions. Defeatism comes when such cues lose their effect on us and we are controlled by more and more remote cues; our mind is no longer on the match.

Perception and Thought

For Guthrie, percepts are habits. They are always evoked by some present cue and they are specific reactions. Recall the example of "squp" from Chapter 1; the word means little when read, although in spoken form, and in an appropriate context, it is readily recognized. Likewise, "LFMNX" may be meaningful if we hear it said in a restaurant specializing in ham-and-egg breakfasts.

Percepts result from *redintegration*, which is simply Guthrie's word for conditioning by contiguity. Redintegration refers to the ability of a cue that is part of a stimulus complex to call up the rest of that complex. For example, I walk with a friend through a park and then don't see him or the park for several years. One day, while walking through the park, the thought of the friend strikes me; the cues of the park redintegrate the complex present when I was last there, and that complex includes the friend (cf. Chapter 1).

Perception, imagery, memory, fantasy, and dreaming all depend upon present cues and upon redintegration. In thought, we have sequences of redintegrated stimuli. On occasion, competition may arise between sets of stimuli that would lead to different and incompatible actions. Under such conditions we pause . . . cues may lead to furtive movements in one or another direction, until finally the balance is tipped and one action system wins. Such a progression may describe the bulk of our mental life, and movement is an important ingredient.

Is it possible that thinking, perceiving, hearing, and hoping are all reducible to bodily movements? Could Guthrie have believed this? Is thought purely muscle movement and bodily secretions? Guthrie doesn't sound like that is what he means, but it is hard to find an explicit denial of such a view and easy to find an emphasis on the importance of movement in determining mental life.

Guthrie believed that thought usually does involve action: When we picture something, there are detectable eye movements; when we think seriously, there is a lot of verbal (talking) content. But is all of experience reducible to movement? Guthrie did not insist that it was; though much of our thinking does involve action, Guthrie admitted that "The arguments cited are not compelling and involve some speculation" (1952).

Evidence for the importance of bodily activity in determining mental activity is really unnecessary; you may see for yourself just how important the relation is. Find a swift river just wider than you are typically capable of swimming and swim it. (As an alternative, do 500 sit-ups, run a marathon, or fight off a pack of wild dogs.) When you reach the opposite bank of the river and you drop down on it you will note a conspicuous absence of thought. Why should this be? While the muscles are exhausted and relaxed it should be possible to think more clearly, since there is no interference from the body, which is tired. The body may be tired, but should that prevent thought? It does. Think about that.

Changing Habits

Guthrie's theory is most directly concerned with changing behavior, and his methods are used in current *behavior therapy*, although the therapist rarely knows from whence came the methods. The secret to breaking habits is to cause a new behavior in an old situation. If we wish to stop smoking we must substitute some other behavior—even if that other behavior is nothing more than "not smoking" in all the situations in which we habitually smoke. Smoking is thousands of habits, of course, and it is therefore difficult to break all of them. Many a quitter has been surprised to find himself holding a cigarette; a situation previously tied with smoking evokes the old behavior before we know what has happened.

The same account applies to forgetting; this is not the product of memories simply fading away with time; the memories are replaced by new ones. For example, I have a set of movements that allow me to play tennis. If I do not play for a prolonged time I lose my skill; those movements are used in a host of other activities and thus become attached to new cues. I also play chess, but that activity is less easily forgotten. The movements involved there are shared by fewer other activities and thus are less likely to become attached to new cues.

Guthrie's view of forgetting as replacement has received a mass of empirical support (see especially Barnes & Underwood, 1959). Guthrie's replacement theory is the theory of associative interference, the view that forgetting amounts to the interfering influence of new material on that already learned, or vice versa.

Guthrie's Methods for Changing Habits

Sidetracking The method of *sidetracking* consists of identifying the cues for a bad habit (smoking, eating, and so on) and then beginning the movements of the bad habit, followed by emphatic rejection. "Practice the beginning of the act with rejection instead of acceptance," Guthrie suggested in 1952. Hence, I take out a cigarette or a piece of food, bring it near my mouth and then toss it away vigorously while exclaiming "no!" The result of this behavior is the substitution of a new habit for the bad old one in the tempting situation. The disadvantage of this method is that the sidetracked habit still remains as an integrated set of actions and the cues that normally produce smoking or eating still do. A better procedure is to dismantle the habit itself using one of the other methods.

Toleration How may we eliminate a child's fear of the dark or a phobia connected with spiders? We want to change the behavior in the presence of the feared cues, but we are hampered by the

violent reactions of the individual when the cues are present. We change behavior here as we accustom a horse to a saddle—gradually. With the horse, we begin with a saddle blanket on its back and add progressively heavier weights until we approximate the weight of a rider and saddle. We do it in gradual steps, and if the horse reacts strongly, we go back to a lighter weight. So with the child or the phobic; we introduce darkness or spiders gradually, so that their presence is tolerated, and slowly increase the strength of the stimulus. This is the method of graded stimulus presentation later popularized by Wolpe (1958).

Kimble and Kendall (1953) provided an early animal analog of the process. Their rat subjects learned to turn a small wheel to turn off a warning stimulus and avoid an electric shock. After such training, subjects typically continue responding for a very long time after the shock is disconnected; the avoidance response is apparently maintained because it turns off the fear-producing warning stimulus. The fear-producing effect of that stimulus may be comparable to the effect of the spider on the phobic patient and, in both cases, we may ask what is the best method to stop the avoidance behavior (whether wheel turning or phobic reaction).

Kimble and Kendall found that wheel turning diminished faster when the warning light was gradually introduced than when it was presented suddenly at full strength. They interpreted this as evidence that Guthrie's toleration method was more effective than the exhaustion method described next.

Exhaustion The method of *exhaustion* is akin to a different method for training horses—the broncobusting method. In this case, a rider mounts the horse, which bucks for however long it takes to throw the rider or to become exhausted. The exhausted horse no longer bucks; it walks or stands with a rider and has learned a new habit to replace the old habit of bucking when weight is placed on its back.

The application to human behavior is straightforward. Place the child in darkness and the phobic in a spider cage. Eventually the violent reactions will cease and the last thing done will be something other than fearful and agitated behavior. This technique is called *emotional flooding* today. Such treatments have their drawbacks, of course. Overly strong agitation could produce a heart attack or stroke, for example, and it is also possible that the patient may lose a spider phobia only to gain a fear of meeting therapists! In addition, Guthrie would point out that any changes in behavior produced in this way are certain to be situation specific. Thus, the loss of fear when in a room full of spiders may not mean that a single spider encountered in one's kitchen will not produce fear.

Another application of exhaustion is less harsh. Suppose a person wishes to stop smoking very quickly and finds that sidetracking doesn't work. The person could seal him or herself in a small room and chain smoke for a period long enough to exhaust the desire for cigarettes. Part of what would happen is that the person would become nauseated, leading to behavior incompatible with smoking. This brings us to the last of the methods, the method of incompatible stimuli.

Incompatible Stimuli   Suppose I pair the cues of smoking with other stimuli that produce nausea, as above, or I cure my smoking habits by eating constantly, leaving me with a new habit to break. I pet a feared spider while shot full of muscle relaxants. In all three of these cases a reaction is produced by stimuli that we manipulate and that is incompatible with the reaction we want changed. This is the method of *incompatible stimuli*. This, in combination with the fading in of stimuli (the tolerance method) is what is done in systematic desensitization, although Wolpe (1958) attributed his inspiration to a different source.

The Guthrie and Horton Experiment

In the 1930s, Guthrie and a colleague, G. P. Horton, carried out the now-famous observations published in 1946 as *Cats in a Puzzle Box*. Thorndike had used an essentially similar apparatus in his research more than 40 years before, but his aims were very different from those of Guthrie. Thorndike was concerned with showing that ideas are not necessary for the mediation of what appears to be purposeful behavior—escape from a problem box. What Guthrie and Horton wanted to determine was whether the details of such behavior are as predictable as the end result. Their concern was by no means restricted to any improvement in the cat's ability to get out of the box.

The box they used had a large glass front and either a pole mounted vertically on the floor or a tube hanging from the ceiling. The cat was inserted into the rear of the box by means of a smaller box, so that it would not have to be touched by hand. After a wait of from ten seconds to a minute in the entry box, the cat was released into the large box. For the first three trials the glass front door was open and the cat could leave the box and eat from a saucer of salmon. After that it was up to the cat to get out of the box on its own. To open the door, the cat would have to apply pressure to the pole (or the tube). More than 50 cats made over 800 escapes and Guthrie and Horton watched, recording the escapes with movie cameras when they could afford film.

After an average of fifteen minutes of exploration, the cat typically hit the post and the glass door was raised. Usually the post was the last feature of the box to be examined; the cat first spent a lot of time examining the barrier and the periphery of the box. After its escape, the cat was replaced in the box until it escaped again, at which time it was placed back in the box, and so on. With repeated trials the time required for the escape decreased, a finding that would be of no surprise to anyone.

What is surprising (and difficult to convey to the reader, in Guthrie's opinion) was the tremendous amount of stereotypy shown during the entire time that the cat was in the box. Each cat showed a "startling repetition of movements" during its whole stay in the box; stereotypy was not restricted to the movements that operated the escape mechanism. For example, it was common for a cat to repeat a triple tour of the periphery, including numerous stops, in detail from one trial to the next. Further, the unsuccessful movements, those that did not aid in escaping from the box, did not fade. Often, they were as frequent at the end of training as at the beginning!

No one had ever looked very closely at behavior in the puzzle box (or the maze or the Skinner box). And when they did look, they were looking only for improvement, defined as a decrease in wasteful movements that postpone the attaining of whatever we think of as the goal in that situation. What should happen in a reasonable world filled with adapting organisms is what Thorndike seemed to find: Successful behaviors are stamped in and unsuccessful behaviors are stamped out. But did Thorndike ever look that closely, or was he just keeping track of the escape times?

Typically, a cat had several escape routines, of which the final series of movements led to escape. With sufficient training, most cats settled pretty much on one of these, but this outcome was obviously not the product of any gradual "stamping in." And these final movements, which were so predictable for a given cat, were not just the momentary responses that operated the door. There was stereotypy in "the long series of movements which took the cat into a position from which the releasing movement could be made" (Guthrie & Horton, 1946). This sequence of behaviors was as "characteristic as a signature" for a given cat.

Guthrie's findings have been briefly described in most learning texts since 1946, but the real meaning of the data has not gotten through. The reader is usually given the impression that Guthrie and Horton found that a given cat operated the escape pole pretty much the same way trial after trial and that this is the stereotypy that Guthrie showed. This account is usually followed by criticisms concerning the paucity of objects in the box, which means that there is not a lot that the cats could do and so of course their behavior is stereotyped.

These objections are really beside the point. The repetition of behaviors and of sequences of behaviors was not restricted to the final escape series. What Guthrie stressed was not the stereotypy in the final movements, but the repetitiveness seen throughout the cats' stays in the box. How does one communicate such findings? One way would be to publish detailed descriptions of the 800 cases of observed escapes. But Guthrie correctly noted that this would be a waste of time, since no one would read the descriptions. We are left with only Guthrie's word that stereotypy was the striking feature of the cats' behavior during successive episodes in the box.

Actually, it is not necessary that we see the original data for Guthrie's purpose to be served. All we need do is look for the stereotypy that must be daily evidenced in our own behavior as well as in the actions of the beasts and humans around us. If we and the beasts are like his cats, then we should soon be able to do what he could do. Guthrie could not predict the behavior of a given cat on the first trial, but, as he wrote, "after watching the cat through one trial we can bet rather heavy odds that the second trial will repeat most of the routines of the first." If we examine our behavior and that of others can we find as much stereotypy as Guthrie described? I believe that we all would be surprised at the extent to which we did find it!

Support for Guthrie's Theory

The literature reviewed by Morgan (1974) and Mackintosh (1983) provide strong support for Guthrie's theory. These data show that behavior that was originally established and maintained by food or water rewards often persists, even when the reward is no longer of value to the subject. As Guthrie would say, behavior may become stereotyped, or attached to the cues of the training situation. This has important implications for what we call "hunger" and "satiation."

Sated Subjects Work Skinner (1938) gave rats food for lever presses during a first stimulus and not during a second. He then allowed the rats to eat their fill in the presence of the second stimulus; needless to say, pressing did not occur. Yet, when the first stimulus was presented again, they pressed. As Guthrie would point out, satiation is stimulus specific; the rats were not sated when the first stimulus first had been presented and what they did then was to press the lever. That is what they did when the first stimulus returned.

Many others have found similar effects, often classified as the contrafreeloading effect. For example, Davidson (1971) trained four rats to press a lever ten times for each food pellet received. After training, the subjects were given all the food they wanted for eight days and then were placed back in the lever box, with free food present. The free food was ignored and all four subjects pressed the lever and ate the resulting food rewards.

Satiation Cues It is easy for us to believe that we eat until we are satisfied and that the amount eaten may depend upon taste, nutritive value, and so on. But satiation depends on more than that. Kimble (1951) allowed rats to feed on wet mash for twenty minutes a day and found that they normally stopped eating after about fifteen minutes. One might think that fifteen minutes of eating produced satiation, and it did in a sense. But, when a rat was briefly removed from the eating area and then replaced, it began feeding again. As Guthrie believed, hunger and satiation are partly dependent on cues accompanying feeding. "Entering the feeding area" means "hunger," since eating had always occurred immediately after entering. These and other data suggest, as Mackintosh (1983) concluded, that reinforced behavior may become independent (stereotyped) and thus persist even when the reinforcer is no longer relevant. Hunt, Matarazzo, Weiss, & Gentry (1979) described similar effects in human patients and noted the relevance of Guthrie's theory to such data.

3. CRITICISMS OF GUTHRIE'S THEORY

Guthrie's Opposition to the Law of Effect

A frequent misunderstanding of Guthrie's theory lies in the assumption that he was denying the effectiveness of reinforcers and punishers. This mistake is common among undergraduate students first exposed to Guthrie, although it is probably also true of more sophisticated critics. Needless to say, Guthrie did not deny the effectiveness of rewards and punishers; he simply denied that the law of effect was a basic principle. When do the so-called rewards and punishers work? We find that the effect of an event, whether as a reward, a punisher, or neither, depends upon what it makes the subject do. If it makes the subject stop what he or she was doing and effectively changes the situation (as when a question, having been answered, is no longer asked), then it acts as a reward because it stops action and changes the situation. If the event leads to strong new behaviors in the old situation, it is a punisher. What is basic is not the law of effect, but the principle of stereotypy.

Another misunderstanding arises regarding Guthrie's explanation of reward and punishment. Reward works by changing the situation and preserving what was last done. If this is so, why doesn't the rat that has run the alley and received food at the end learn to stand still and make eating movements when next placed in the alley; wasn't that the last thing done? This criticism neglects the fact that the rat will do what it last did in that *specific situation*. If we place the rat at the end of the alley in front of the goal box and food, it will stand still and make eating movements. If we place it at the other end of the alley, it will do what it last did there, which was run.

If we remove food from the goal box, why does the rat stop running, instead of continuing to do what it did in the past? Again, it depends on what is last done in the situation. If we remove the rat from the alley after each run, it may continue running, as we will see later in Chapter 7. But if we leave the rat free to explore, its new movements will become attached to the stimuli of the alley and we will say that running to the goal box was extinguished. As in all cases of extinction, Guthrie believed that the behavior changed because something new replaced it.

Other Theories Can Handle Guthrie's Data

If we recall any of the examples Guthrie loved to cite in support of his theory, we find that it is possible to explain each of them in terms of other theories. For example, the dog who comes because we have pulled him toward us with a rope simply may be showing the effects of negative reinforcement. In the past, when we pulled and he did not come, the rope hurt his neck. To stop or avoid that pain, the creature now moves toward us. Similarly, motivation may be understood in terms of drives, and many rewards seem to work by reducing drives, as when food reduces hunger. Who needs Guthrie when the terms of Thorndike, Skinner, and Hull (as we will see) seem enough?

The fact is that any individual phenomenon may be explained in a variety of ways. We may refer to rewards and punishers, actualizing tendencies, cognitive dissonance, conservation of energy, frustration, self-efficacy, expectancies, fractional antedating goal responses, developmental stages, information-processing mechanisms, and heaven knows what else as explanations for one or another phenomenon. Guthrie accounts for everything that they do, although his generality comes at a price, as we shall see.

All Stimulus Change Does Not Act as Reward

Rewards are effective when they change a situation, leaving the last response to occur in that situation connected to the cues of that situation. This applies even to situations in which we ordinarily do not identify conspicuous rewards. The rat that learns a sequence of eight turns to reach the end of a maze receives the food we identify as the reward, but that is only the last in a series of stimulus changes. The food stops the rat's running and produces eating, leaving running as the last behavior in the maze. But each turn at a choice point also produces stimulus change. The last thing done in the presence of the cues of the choice point was the turn that was made. There is stimulus change throughout the maze, not just at the end. A stimulus change that produces strong new behaviors in the old situation is a punisher. Many demonstrations of the effects of stimulus change per se have amounted to this. Bower and Hilgard are somewhat insincere when they seriously consider this criticism of Guthrie's theory, citing cases in which rats fell through trap doors, are shaken up in black bags, and the like. They conclude that not all changes in stimulation act as rewards, "although psychologists have predicted that they should" (Bower & Hilgard, 1981).

Guthrie's Generality

According to his critics, Guthrie is slippery and vague; the power of his theory is illusory, since in explaining everything, the theory explains nothing specifically. There is a lot of truth in this. Guthrie was interested only in the most general possible principles, and his examples were never predictions, but just "postdictions," made after the fact. The past is much easier to predict than the future. Guthrie's theory does require thought before it can be applied to new problems, which is a great disadvantage compared with the opponent theories, such as Thorndike's, which seem easy to apply. This is the real flaw in Guthrie's account.

One way of appreciating this problem is to consider seriously what is meant by a situation. Guthrie's whole theory depends on situation change or the lack of it. But it is very difficult to identify situation change before the fact. For example, my alarm awakened me this morning and it will do so tomorrow, as long as the two mornings are the same situation in essential respects. How can I tell whether they are? I must see whether I behave the same on successive mornings.

Guthrie was originally a mathematician and philosopher, which may account for his lack of interest in research and in prediction and hypothesis testing. When Estes (e.g., 1950) tried to render Guthrie's theory more precise, Guthrie (1959) reacted skeptically. As was true of James Mill, Guthrie could explain almost anything, although he wasn't likely to provide a precise explanation before the fact.

4. OTHER ASPECTS OF GUTHRIE'S THEORY

Comparison with Watson's Theory

It may seem that what Guthrie was saying was no more than a restatement of Watson's theory. (Watson was out of academics and if not for that no one would have paid any attention to Guthrie!) There is some truth in this suspicion; both were true behaviorists and both opposed the reliance of others on the law of effect. Both were concerned with subjective experience and dealt with it in essentially the same way, as activity largely dependent on bodily muscular and glandular reactions. How was Guthrie's theory an improvement over Watson's? Although they agreed on most points, their positions on goal direction were a bit different, and their views of the effects of practice and of the importance of behavior as movement were dissimilar.

First, although both disputed the basic importance of reinforcers and punishers, Watson nonetheless stressed the basic adaptive nature of behavior. His favorite term for learning was *adjustment*, and we see throughout his writings (e.g., 1919) an emphasis on the importance of adaptation, or successful adjustment. Watson always spoke of maladaptive behavior as maladjustment, whereas Guthrie stressed that learning is always occurring and that goal seeking is usually something inferred by the observer. Watson's functionalist background and his faith in Darwin was always present in his writing. Guthrie's subjects learned maladaptive, stupid behaviors as easily as they learned beneficial ones.

Secondly, Watson stressed the importance of repetition in the formation of habits, from the simplest to the most complex. For Guthrie, practice was often necessary to build up the habits that, taken together, constituted an act such as tying one's shoes, but each of those habits was learned in one trial. Many habits, such as withdrawing one's hands from a painful flame, are learned in one trial, and no amount of practice can strengthen such a habit. The fears that may arise from a single unique experience and that may last a lifetime testify to the fact that one trial learning is common.

Finally, Watson did view behavior as the movement of muscles or the secretion of glands. His psychology was a psychology of the body as a machine. Guthrie largely shared this view and repeatedly pointed out the importance of bodily activity in determining one's mental life. But he was not fixed on the sufficiency of this view, as was Watson. That is, although Guthrie emphasized the importance of bodily activities, he did not insist that all experience depends on bodily movement or glandular secretions. Watson did, and this insistence led to a lot of difficulties for behaviorists, which have persisted to this day.

Emphasis on Practical Matters

The area in which Guthrie and Watson's theories are similar is their emphasis on the solution of problems of practical interest; neither man was concerned with problems that were solely of theoretical interest. Of course, people want to understand humanity's predicament here on earth, and people want to understand why things happen. These are legitimate and important problems, but they are problems mainly for philosophy, which can afford to dally with metaphysics. Metaphysics is the study of the ultimate truths; what is the origin and nature of reality? What is really and verifiably true? Does God exist? These are important but (to say the least) difficult questions, and psychology is helpless in answering them. Leave them to philosophy and religion, where they properly belong, and let psychology do what it can.

What can psychology do? It can predict and influence what we do (including what we think and feel) if it is given the chance and if it concentrates its energies in that direction. Guthrie believed that he was supplying the means to accomplish this goal. His *Psychology of Learning* is a manual filled with examples of what can be done. Whether we are guided by an actualizing tendency or directed by intrapsychic forces is beside the point. It is what is done that is ultimately important, and it is that with which Guthrie dealt. His success in doing so is the reason that his theory is still current.

SUMMARY

Unlike virtually all other psychological theories, Guthrie did not take for granted the purposiveness of behavior. Although much of our activity is goal directed, much of it is not. A theory that deals only with purposive activity leaves out a lot of what we do.

Guthrie sought the most general possible principle to account for activity and found it in the old principle of association by contiguity in time. Actions occurring in specific situations will recur if the specific situations recur. Further, practice is not necessary, since the maximum strength of an association between situation and movement occurs on the first pairing. Learning goes on constantly and does not necessarily constitute improvement. What is learned is what is done and includes awkwardness and errors as well as beneficial actions.

Reward and punishment do not have a special place as first principles; the law of effect just represents a special case of one trial contiguity learning. If an event changes a situation, leaving the last behavior attached to the old situation, we have a reward, and all rewards do their work in this way. If, on the other hand, an event produces strong behaviors that compete with the last behavior produced in a situation, punishment occurs. In both cases, the important factor is not the nature of the putative reward or punisher, but what it makes the recipient do. It follows that virtually any event can thus work as a reward or as a punisher, given the proper conditions.

Guthrie was able to include motivation, intention and purpose, perception, and thinking in his theory: All constitute habit phenomena and all obey the same principles. Despite charges that his theory is too general and vague to be useful, it is likely that his view best characterized many of the procedures currently found useful in behavior therapy. Additional evidence for the usefulness of his theory lies in the fact that he is routinely given detailed treatment in learning textbooks along with Skinner and Thorndike, although, unlike them, he did little research during his life and had few if any real followers.

The one major piece of research he did do showed an amazing degree of stereotypy in the behavior of cats escaping from a puzzle box. Although his choice of escape lever has recently brought the criticism that he was stacking the deck for stereotypy, his data show that one-trial contiguity learning can account for long segments of behavior in cats and probably in humans.

GLOSSARY

Behavior therapy Method of dealing with psychological problems by treating them essentially as behavior problems. For example, anxiety may be a serious problem for an individual. A behavior therapist would seek the conditions that now produce anxiety, such as specific situations or relations with other people. Therapy would aim to eliminate the anxiety reaction to whatever now produces it, perhaps through desensitization. Other therapies, especially the older ones such as psychoanalysis, are less concerned with the current causes of problems and treat afflictions such as anxiety as symptoms of some underlying psychic disturbance. They attempt to treat this "underlying cause," a process that can take years and is often unsuccessful.

British empiricism School of British philosophy represented by Locke, Berkeley, Hume, and later by James Mill and his son John Stuart Mill. Most British empiricists stressed the importance of the association of ideas that occur in close spatial and temporal contiguity (see Chapter 1).

Contiguity Nearness. Spatial and temporal contiguity refer to closeness of events in space and time, respectively. Guthrie's theory emphasizes the importance of temporal contiguity of stimuli and responses.

Exhaustion One of Guthrie's methods for changing habits. The behavior to be eliminated is repeatedly evoked in the presence of the cues that usually accompany it. Eventually, the behavior is "exhausted" and whatever behavior then occurs replaces it. For example, an individual with a strong fear of automobile travel might continuously ride in a car until the fearful reactions subside, or a smoker might smoke cigarette after cigarette until the sight and smell of cigarettes produces a new reaction. *Emotional flooding* is the name currently given to this method. Here, it is ordinarily a phobic stimulus, such as a spider, or the description of other emotion-producing situations that is repeatedly presented until the strong reaction usually produced fades.

Incompatible stimuli Guthrie's method of changing behavior by introducing stimuli that produce a reaction incompatible with the reaction to another set of stimuli. For example, one might treat cigarette smoking by encouraging the patient to eat apples when the urge to smoke arises. It is difficult, though not impossible, to simultaneously eat apples and smoke. In another example, strong anxiety reactions to feared situations could be countered by muscle relaxation training. In both cases, the aim is to somehow produce a desired reaction (nonsmoking or relaxation) in the presence of cues that usually lead to the undesired reaction (smoking or anxiety).

Maintaining stimuli Guthrie's term for stimuli that lead us to action which persists until these disturbers are removed. Others called such stimuli *drives*, referring to hunger, thirst, and so on. But Guthrie included other motivating stimuli, such as those produced when we are asked a question that must be answered.

Motive For Guthrie, an instigator to action. Hunger, a question, a shiny object, and a challenge are all motives. Motives may be viewed as a set of maintaining stimuli, which produce action until removed.

Negative practice Conquering a bad habit by repeatedly performing it in the presence of the cues that normally produce it. For example, we might practice a bad tennis backhand so that we notice the cues that produce it. Then we can practice the correct movements in the presence of those cues.

Overcorrection Changing a bad habit by repeatedly practicing the correct behavior in the situation in which we wish it to occur. For example, when a mistake is made, we stop and repeatedly perform the correct behavior (that is, we overcorrect).

Punishment For Guthrie, a change in behavior produced by stimuli that lead to new behavior in the presence of the old cues. What is learned is what is done, and punishment works when it leads to a new behavior incompatible with previous, recent behavior. For example, electric shock may be used to train a dog to jump through a hoop, providing that the shock is applied to the rear end of the dog.

Redintegration The calling up of a stimulus complex by one or more members of the complex. For example, the smell of roast beef may bring to mind the sight and taste of the roast beef present when last we experienced the smell. The principle of redintegration is really the essence of Guthrie's theory, and he proposed that redintegration was a better term to describe his theory than was conditioning.

Reward For Guthrie, a special case of association by contiguity. A reward is simply a change in stimulus that acts to preserve the association between a set of stimuli and whatever actions last occurred in the presence of those stimuli. If the change produces strong new reactions that are incompatible with the last actions in the presence of the old cues, the effect is punishment.

Sidetracking A method of changing habits, which consists of beginning the movements that constitute the habit, followed by movements incompatible with the habit. One may counter a cookie-eating habit by raising a cookie to the mouth and then throwing it away. This is not a very good method, since the habit to be broken remains intact, with only the initial movements altered. Guthrie stressed his other methods, which amount to dismantling the habit.

Species-specific defense reactions Name given by Robert Bolles (1970) to the reactions naturally called out by danger. Bolles suggested that avoidance learning is aided when the avoidance response is one of the reactions that normally occur when a member of the species in question is threatened. Thus, it is easy to train a rat to avoid shock when the avoidance response is running (an SSDR), but it is difficult when the rat must press a lever to avoid shock. Lever pressing, which involves manipulation with the forelimbs, normally occurs in eating, not in the reaction to danger.

Stereotypy For Guthrie, the repetition of a movement or a series of movements in precisely the form that occurred when the individual was last in the same situation. Much of our comings and goings, our thoughts and our moods, occur in a stereotyped manner. Stereotypy is what Guthrie and Horton found in their famous experiments with cats in the puzzle box and it is the only major principle of Guthrie's theory.

Toleration One of Guthrie's major methods for changing habits. Cues that ordinarily produce unwanted reactions are presented in graded steps while another activity is occurring. If done properly, the unwanted reaction never occurs, since it is replaced by the competing behavior. For example, we may use the method of toleration to train a shy speaker to speak easily before large groups, by first exposing the speaker to an imaginary group, while relaxed, and then introducing an audience one by one. If we maintain the speaker's relaxation through this process, we may finish with him or her facing a large audience with no qualms. Graded presentation of feared stimuli in this fashion is typical of Wolpe's desensitization procedure.

RECOMMENDED READINGS

Guthrie, E. R. (1952). *The psychology of learning* (rev. ed.). New York: Harper & Row.

   Guthrie is known for his charming writing style and commonsense interpretations. This book shows why and provides many examples of applications of his theory to everyday situations.

Guthrie, E. R. (1959). Association by contiguity. In S. Koch (Ed.), *Psychology: A study of a science* (Vol. 5). New York: McGraw-Hill.

   For the more serious student, this final statement by Guthrie includes his opinion of the adaptations of his theory by Estes and his last thoughts on a variety of issues.

Hunt, W. A., Matarazzo, J. D., Weiss, S. M., & Gentry, W. D. (1979). Associative learning, habit, and health behavior. *Journal of Behavioral Medicine*, 2, 111–124.

   These authors are leading authorities in clinical psychology and behavioral medicine. In this paper, they stress the importance of stereotypy of maladaptive behavior, frequently quoting and referring to Guthrie.

Malone, J. C., Jr. (1978). Beyond the operant analysis of behavior. *Behavior Therapy*, 9, 584–591.

   This paper discusses Guthrie's theory and current methods used in behavior therapy. It appears that Guthrie's theory, and not Skinner's, best describes current practices.

Chapter 6

CLARK L. HULL: PHYSICAL BEHAVIORISM

BIOGRAPHY

By his own account (1952a), Clark Leonard Hull was born in a log house on a farm near Akron, New York, in 1884. He graduated from the University of Michigan and taught at a normal school in Richmond, Kentucky, where his load of twenty classes a week did not stop him from beginning the research that would constitute his doctoral thesis. He did his graduate work at the University of Wisconsin, where he subsequently joined the faculty. The most striking aspects of Hull were his ingenuity, his adaptability, and his ambition to become a leader in his field. The latter goal was certainly accomplished; although he died in 1952, his imprint is clear not only in the psychology of learning, but in many other areas where his students and their students carry on work that shows Hull's unmistakable influence.

Hull's ingenuity was demonstrated early, when he first began doing his research at Wiscon-

sin. He was interested in the evolution of concepts and designed and built a device that he called an automatic memory machine. Today, any psychologist interested in such things would be virtually helpless without a computer, and even the poorest researcher would seem better off than Hull, at that time. (Presumably, the facilities at Wisconsin are somewhat better now, despite budget constraints.) Here is Hull's description of his equipment:

I designed and constructed with the few hand tools there available an automatic memory machine which I used throughout most of my dissertation experiment. The drum was made from a tomato can fitted with wooden heads. The automatic stepwise movement of the drum was controlled by a long pendulum; the coarse-toothed escapement wheel controlled by the pendulum was filed from a discarded bucksaw blade. . . . At that time a person with a little initiative could construct a useful behavior laboratory in a wilderness, given a few simple tools and materials; this is true to a considerable

FIGURE 6.1a   Clark L. Hull, 1884–1952. *Photo courtesy of Clark University Press*

extent even now for a wide range of important experiments. (From Hull's autobiography, 1952a, pp. 148–149)

Hull seems to have been marvelously adaptive as well as ingenious. His first teaching at Wisconsin was in aptitude testing, a subject in which he was initially less than expert. But Hull did nothing halfway. He published his course materials in a book entitled *Aptitude Testing* (1928). But this was not to be his life's work:

> The survey leading to the publication of *Aptitude Testing* left me with a fairly pessimistic view as to the future of tests in this field, and I abandoned it permanently. (Hull, 1952a, p. 151)

He was then asked to participate in an introductory course of lectures for medical students. He felt that the general area of hypnosis and suggestibility was useful in medicine and so began studying what was known in the field and teaching it to his students. Over a period of ten years he and twenty students published 32 papers in that area, and in 1933 his book *Hypnosis and Suggestibility* was published.

Other work included a careful study of the effects of pipe smoking on mental and motor efficiency. An antitobacco group requested that he do such a study, and he conducted the experiment superbly. The results were published in 1924, although they were not what the sponsors had wanted.

In 1929, Hull's reputation as a researcher was such that he was invited to Yale to work as a research scientist in the Institute of Psychology, later incorporated into the Institute of Human Relations. As a research scientist, he had no teaching or administrative duties and was left free to devote all of his time to research.

When he arrived at Yale, he planned to carry on his work in hypnosis but was discouraged from doing so by opposition from the medical authorities there. Hull attributed their opposition to a superstitious fear that was not present in the midwest. He was encouraged to contribute toward the grand plan for the institute, which had gathered many psychologists, sociologists, cultural anthropologists, and others in making a unified and integrated contribution to the social-behavioral sciences. Hull (1952a) later wrote that such an enterprise is best carried out with leadership in the form of a scientific führer but that such a system runs counter to our democratic policies and would hamper creativity by the individual members. Evidently, enough of the participating scientists were brought to Hull's general point of view by occasionally attending his seminars that he became de facto director.

Hull was an exceedingly ambitious man (as was Thorndike) who decided as a young man that one must make one's great scientific contribution before the age of 40, since a study of the history of science showed that the greats, such as Berkeley and Newton, performed their major works while young. Unfortunately, Hull was beset with typhoid fever before going to college and crippled

FIGURE 6.1b   A painting of Hull in later life. *Courtesy of the Archives of the History of American Psychology*

with polio at the age of 24. Additionally, his eyes gave him great problems, so his mother had to read to him.

It was while recovering from the polio attack that he decided on experimental psychology as a life's work, and his reasons were these:

> What I really wanted was an occupation in a field related to philosophy in the sense of involving theory: one which was new enough to permit rapid growth so that a young man would not need to wait for his predecessors to die before his work could find recognition, and one which would provide an opportunity to design and work with automatic apparatus. (Hull, 1952a, p. 145)

Hull's conception of psychology and his hypothetico-deductive method seem to have caught on immediately. During the 1930s, Hull was able to attract some of the best students in the world to his laboratory at Yale. Students such as Kenneth Spence, Neal Miller, and O. H. Mowrer carried on what was essentially Hull's project (although each greatly helped shape it) for

years after Hull's death in 1952. Hull was clearly the most influential psychologist of the 1940s and perhaps of the 1950s. His many students and their students are scattered through colleges and universities in the United States, and many of them are keeping Hull's way of looking at things alive (cf. Amsel & Rashotte, 1984). Hull's major publications are:

> *Principles of Behavior*, 1943
>
> *Essentials of Behavior*, 1951
>
> *A Behavior System*, 1952

In addition to these books, Hull and his close collaborators published countless papers from 1920 to 1952. He did not become great by the age of 40—his health problems and other matters delayed the completion of his doctoral dissertation until he was 34. But he did have a research associateship at Yale by the age of 45 and, rereading the history of philosophy and science, he found that greatness was often attained with work done long after the age of 40, as with Locke and Kant.

INTRODUCTION

Section 1 of this chapter examines Hull's significance for psychology, both during the time he worked and during our time. He was influential beyond telling, and his theory set the standard for the psychology of a generation. In 1954 a group of eminent psychologists met at Harvard and evaluated the rival learning theories, as well as Hull's (Estes, Koch, MacCorquodale, Meehl, Mueller, Schoenfeld, & Verplanck, 1954). Significantly, the other theories were praised or condemned to the extent that they resembled Hull's!

Section 2 discusses the basics of the theory itself. Hull believed in the clear expression of the basics of one's theory and in the careful testing of the implications of the theory. We will consider the set of *postulates* presented in 1943, as well as the empirical support for them and the sorts of tests one might subject them to. This *postulate set* is really the core of the theory, and Hull's views on the importance of *drive* are worthy of special consideration.

We will also consider the general *hypothetico-deductive method* which he advocated and which lent great appeal to the theory. It seemed wonderful at the time to have a method that would keep us unerringly on the path toward truth, and this method seemed to do just that.

We will also see how Hull could ingeniously explain complex things as the action of a machine; he insisted that any explanation was complete only if we could build a device that would act as the explanation required. How can a machine show evidence of learning, knowledge, foresight, and anticipation? Hull proposed an answer.

Section 3 presents criticisms of Hull's theory. Critics such as Tolman had difficulty with Hull's view, since the theory seemed to work so well, even when it seemed preposterous on some points. Many critics (even Tolman, half-heartedly) gave up and either joined Hull's cause of threw in the towel. Hull's theory worked surprisingly well, and he was the establishment; it is always difficult to fight the establishment, especially when one loses battle after battle with it.

Nonetheless, Hull's theory includes basic elements, both in its assumptions about psychology and in its views concerning the ways of doing research, that have been vigorously attacked by other psychologists.

Section 4 considers other aspects of Hull's theory. We will briefly discuss applications that he suggested and then consider the work of two notable collaborators. Spence worked with him for many years and made many contributions; we will see that the influence of Hull and Spence is still felt and acknowledged in current research in motivation (see McClelland, 1985). Neal Miller became a prolific researcher, and it is with Miller and Dollard (1941) that social learning theory began. We will point out clear parallels between this early work and the more recent work of Bandura, though the latter is often erroneously viewed as a follower of Skinner!

1. THE SIGNIFICANCE OF HULL'S WORK

In the 1920s psychology was changing; it seemed to many that progress was finally going to be made. The sterile research of the introspectionists, led by Titchener, was losing favor steadily. The functionalists were influential, though disorganized, and Freud's ideas were becoming well known. The Gestaltists had not yet arrived and Thorndike was gaining adherents. At the same time, Watson was loudly calling for a revolution in psychology, and Guthrie, Tolman, Kantor, and others were to join in essentially the same cause. Something was happening; it seemed at last that the scientific study of behavior and experience was to begin, but the movement lacked organization. Everyone opposed the introspectionists, but there was no clear and concrete plan as to how to proceed.

This is where Hull came in. He advocated the organizing of what everyone believed to be true (or roughly true) into a clear form, so that we knew where we were beginning. Then we could derive testable statements from these assumptions and carry out careful experiments to test them. Depending upon the results of the tests, we would modify the assumptions. Thus, our list of "truths" would change constantly and improve gradually. This self-correcting system had great appeal, especially at that time, when we knew that the field was going somewhere but that too many competing theories filled the air. Let us work together under a shared set of assumptions and progress together, rather than continue to compete in a disorganized fashion. Psychology was to be institutionalized and Hull was in a perfect position at Yale to direct such an undertaking.

His initial effort was aimed at accounting for animal behavior, and this was outlined in his *Principles of Behavior*, published in 1943. This was extended nine years later in *A Behavior System* (1952b). A third volume, intended to include human social behavior, was never written, owing to Hull's death. Nonetheless, he felt, as have many others, that the first two works included the essence of all that psychologists need know to study all behavior and experience.

The next section presents the essentials of Hull's theory, and the reader is reminded that his immense influence means that his theory is worthy of careful consideration. Its general assumptions are very much alive today.

2. BASICS OF HULL'S THEORY

Hull assumed three things concerning psychology and the method of doing science. First, he was convinced that an organism must be viewed as a biological machine, or *automaton*. When we get down to it, we are muscle, bone, blood, nerves, and visceral organs, and our explanation of our behavior and experience must not lose sight of that fact. Everything else, our mental life, our purposes, our insights, and so on are ultimately dependent upon the activities of the body. When we explain mental activity, we must do it in terms of bodily actions; as mentioned above, we explain a phenomenon only when we can build a device that operates in the way that we propose we do.

This led Hull to an exclusive emphasis on stimuli and responses. Stimuli are things that produce reactions, things that we can point to in the environment. Responses are the movements of muscles and the secretions of glands; we can also identify these, although in some instances it is difficult. All of our behavior and experience is understandable only when it is translated to stimulus-response terms. This is *S-R psychology* in its pure form; although it may be repugnant to view ourselves as S-R automata, it is difficult to argue that we are not. Biologists have long held this belief, and modern medicine, in large part, assumes that this is the case.

Hull's second assumption was that it is absolutely essential to quantify things, to measure and attach numbers to them. Much of his time was spent in assigning numbers to represent the amount of learning or the degree of motivation present under different conditions. He was a master at this and successfully predicted the results of many experiments, using trains of calculations that aroused the admiration of his followers and that confounded his critics. We will get a flavor of this in the following pages.

Thirdly, Hull emphasized the importance of clearly stating basic assumptions in a way that permitted testing of them. This was essential both to give order to the field and to act as a guide to research. A great many of Hull's followers were attracted because of the appeal of his hypothetico-deductive method. Psychological research often seems to lack direction, but in this case it seemed that a systematic undertaking was under way and that the guidelines were laid out in the *Principles of Behavior* (1943). Turn to any page of Hull's text and find a postulate or corollary, consider its consequences, and there is your experiment.

For example, suppose that one of the postulates says that when we learn something new, such as someone's name, all stimuli present at that time become connected to that name. We test this by putting ourselves in the presence of stimuli that were there at the time the name was learned. We find that some stimuli, such as the sight of the person whose name we have learned, the presence of others who were there at the time, or the room in which the learning took place bring the name to mind more readily than do other stimuli present, such as the clothes we were wearing. We modify the postulate to specify that other people and places are more closely associated with the response than are other stimuli, such as those provided by our clothes. If it is important, we can then continue to refine the class of stimuli that are most effective. We test successive hypotheses until we are satisfied that we know which of them will be effective. This is a difficult task, to be sure, but Hull believed that such an undertaking was the only way to progress toward an eventual understanding of what we do and when we do it. It was certainly slow, but it was certainly sure, and it was about time that psychology got on the sure path!

Hull's Postulates

Hull made every effort to be precise, for this reason:

> It is believed that a clear formulation, even if later found incorrect, will ultimately lead more quickly and easily to a correct formulation than will a pussyfooting statement which might be more difficult to convict of falsity. (1943, p. 398)

Only a clear statement may be tested through experimentation, and only through such tests are we able to determine whether our assumptions are correct. Statements such as the Gestaltists', which spoke of such things as "emergent properties," were too fuzzy to deal with; Hull (1943) referred to their viewpoint as a "doctrine of despair."

The postulates and their derived corollaries were meant to be as clear and testable as possible. The postulates were the principles from which one begins, and Hull's view of doing science em-

phasized the deductive method, widely used in the past by rationalists such as Descartes. According to Spence (1943), Hull adopted the hypothetico-deductive method after reading an impressive paper by Einstein in 1934. This was Hull's version of a theory, stated thus: "A theory is a systematic deductive derivation of the secondary principles of observable phenomena from a relatively small number of primary principles or postulates" (1943, p. 2). The object of theory, of course, is to explain, and this is Hull's opinion of the nature of explanation. An explanation is a "proposition logically derived from a set of definitions and postulates coupled with certain observed conditions antecedent to the event" (ibid., p. 23).

The 1943 postulate set was to serve as the starting point for research, and it proved a very influential guide for the research of the 1940s and 1950s. The set was altered somewhat, though not very drastically, in the 1952 system, and the heart of the system remained what it was in 1943. True followers of Hull ("Hullians," as they are still called) see the changes as much more major than an outsider would. We will concentrate on the 1943 set; for many years, they constituted Hull's theory.

Postulate I: The Stimulus Trace Stimuli acting on us are effective for a time after their removal. We are familiar with visual afterimages, as well as with the aftereffects of pressures on our skin and of loud sounds. Hull believed that the real stimulus was not the light or sound source, but the response of the nerves themselves. He used the lowercase s to refer to the activity of the nerve and capital S to represent the physical stimulus.

Postulate II: Afferent Interaction A gray patch on a blue background looks yellowish, whereas the same patch on a red background looks greenish. Stimulation is affected by other stimulation going on. A newly broken finger makes us forget a small bruise elsewhere that seemed so painful earlier. This postulate was meant to include everything that the Gestaltists were stressing, except for "emergent properties" or anything that Hull felt similarly mystical. Afferent interaction is represented by š.

Postulate III: Reflexes Present at Birth We come with a set of unlearned behaviors, evoked by certain kinds of stimulation. Hull saw these as unlearned S-R connections. These S-R connections are arranged so that a given form of stimulation first produces one innate response, and if that fails to remove the source of stimulation, other innate behaviors appear.

For example, suppose that a speck of dust enters the eye. We reflexively blink and tears flow. If the speck remains, we may blink more vigorously, rub our eyes, and do other things, all occurring automatically. Many reflexive behaviors are controlled by the spinal cord. If the cerebral cortex of an animal is removed, it is still possible to stimulate the animal's skin and to evoke stepping, walking, running, and galloping.

A sequence of stimuli and reflexive reactions occurs when we feed an infant. We may produce turning of the head and opening of the mouth by touching the infant's cheek. The milk entering the mouth produces reflex salivation, and the passage of the milk produces in turn swallowing, peristalsis, secretion of stomach juices, and absorption in the small intestine. The result of these and similar processes is survival.

Reflex behavior is typically produced when a primary need is present. This is a bodily condition that, if left unattended, threatens the life of the individual or the species. The following list was proposed by Hull to include the basic needs. These are the sources of all motivation:

hunger	temperature	sleep
thirst	regulation	activity
air	defecation	sex (nesting,
rest	urination	care of
	tissue injury	young)

These needs produce movement, and movement continues until the need is removed. Hull believed that other motives are derived from biological needs; it may seem to us that most of what

we do is motivated by somewhat more elegant needs. But, in fairness to Hull, we should note that it is such needs that certainly are the prime motives for virtually all animals and for the vast majority of the human population of the earth!

Postulate IV: Primary Reinforcement This is the most important postulate and deserves extended treatment. We do not seem to spend our lives reacting reflexively to a succession of needs; we change our behavior because new S-R connections are formed. Hull called such new connections *habits*, represented in his system by $_sH_R$. Habits are formed through the action of the law of effect. To illustrate the complexity of Hull's postulates, this is how postulate IV reads:

> Whenever an effector activity ($r \rightarrow R$) and a receptor activity ($S \rightarrow s$) occur in close temporal contiguity . . . , and this contiguity is closely associated with the diminution of a need . . . or with a stimulus which has been closely and consistently associated with the diminution of a need . . . , there will result an increment to a tendency (Δ_sH_R) for that afferent impulse on that occasion to evoke that reaction. The increments from successive reactions summate in a manner which yields a combined habit strength ($_sH_R$) which is a simple positive growth function of the number of reinforcements. . . . The upper limit . . . of this curve of learning is the product of (1) a positive growth function of the magnitude of need reduction which is involved in primary, or which is associated with secondary, reinforcement; (2) a negative growth function of the delay . . . in reinforcement; [and so on]. (1943, p. 178)

What the postulate says is simply this: Whenever a response is made in the presence of a stimulus and that stimulus-and-response connection is closely followed by a decrease in a need, there will be an increase in the tendency of that stimulus to produce that response in the future. For example, suppose you are training your dog to come on command. You pair "come!" with the dog's movement toward you when you give it a piece of food, which diminishes a need if the dog is hungry.

How much of an increase in the tendency to come occurs with each piece of food given? It depends upon the amount of hunger and the amount of food given. The greater the need reduction, the greater the effect. The amount of need reduction depends both on the amount of need (hunger) and on the amount of food you give. The effect is greater as the delay between the behavior and the food lessens. Similarly, the effect is greater as the time between the command and the dog's action gets closer. To successfully train a dog to come (or to teach a child to read, or whatever), be certain that a need exists, whether it be hunger or a secondary need for praise, be certain that the consequence of the act reduces the need, ensure that the stimuli you want connected to the deed are present when the deed is done, and do not delay the consequence after the act occurs.

You will notice that Thorndike would not have disagreed with any of these stipulations and you may wonder what it is that Hull has added. Actually, this postulate only adds precision to the law of effect. Hull was dead serious when he proposed the equation below that allows the calculation of habit strength (the strength of the S-R connection), and he was a master at actually calculating habit strengths and showing that his predictions were accurate.

One simple equation for the calculation of habit strength appears in his *Essentials of Behavior* (1951):

$$\Delta_S H_R = F(M - {_S}H_R)$$

This means that the increase in habit strength on a given trial ($\Delta_S H_R$) is the product of a constant (F), which depends upon the situation, and the quantity M minus the current habit strength. M is the maximum habit strength, depending upon the degree of need and the reinforcer used. As training progresses, the quantity ($M - {_S}H_R$) decreases, since ${_S}H_R$ increases on each trial. Thus, the increments added to habit strength become less and less as training progresses. This accounts for the decrease in progress as we proceed. When we begin to learn a passage of poetry, for exam-

ple, the amount we retain on the first reading is greater than that on the second, third, and fourth readings. Part of the reason for this decrease in progress, in Hull's view, was the fact that as we approach M, less is left to be learned and the equation shows that this leads to successively smaller increments in habit strength. This decrease in progress is apparent in Figure 6.2.

Note that postulate IV does not require that reduction of a real (primary) need occur in order for habit strength to increase. Hull (1943) specifies that a "stimulus which has been closely and consistently associated with the diminution of a need" works as well. Let us examine Hull's views of reinforcement in general, because that is what he is talking about in this postulate.

Hull viewed living things, including ourselves, as self-maintaining automatic machines. Our bodies have needs for nutrients, water, constant temperature, waste elimination, activity, sleep, and so on. The parts of our bodies that are not directly concerned with these things have evolved to support the organs so concerned. A muscle mounted on a skeleton is ultimately there to move us and move our limbs so that we can find and eat food, drink water, keep warm, and so on. The same muscle may aid in writing or painting, but that is not the reason for its evolution. We are, figuratively speaking, no more than "traveling stomachs."

We are born with reflexes that can maintain life if food and shelter are no problem. Typically they are not problematic for humans in the United States. But most living things cannot rely on reflexes for long; they have to seek nutrients and shelter and they must be able to learn to do so more efficiently as they grow older. How does such learning occur in a mechanical device? Postulate IV is Hull's answer.

The Importance of Primary Drive

The conception of humans and other animals as drive-animated, satiation-seeking automata is a very common view in psychology; Freud is probably the best-known proponent. To appreciate fully the reasoning upon which the conception is

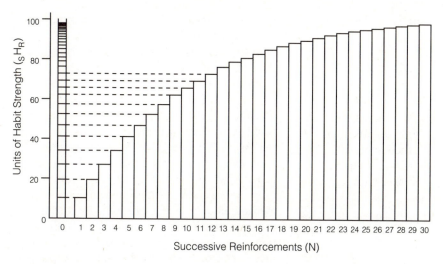

FIGURE 6.2 Growth in habit strength ($_sH_R$) as a function of number of reinforced trials (N). Notice that the increments added are progressively smaller.

based, we will consider some of the traditional evidence for the importance of biological drive in learning and motivation. Later in this chapter we will reconsider the evidence and examine counterevidence.

The General Argument Consider the argument. A cell alone in the wild takes in its nutrients, metabolizes them, excretes waste, and so on. In the course of evolution two cells join forces, with one responsible for locomotion and taking in nutrients and the other for metabolizing them and excreting waste. More cells join (in the course of evolution) and the duties are separated still further. Over the span of time, more and more specialization occurs until an organism develops that seems to bear no resemblance to the original cell. Yet, its functions are basically the same. It must take in food, metabolize it, and excrete wastes; if it fails in any of these functions, it dies. All of the many activities of living things are ultimately done to maintain the life of the individual; if we add sexual behavior, we include the perpetuation of the species as well.

Whatever thoughts and hopes and dreams you may have are possible only if the basic processes

of life continue. You must be fed, watered, kept at a reasonable temperature, and so on. In current American society it is easy to lose sight of this fact, but for 99.9 percent of the living things on earth, motivation lies solely in keeping the basic life functions going. These basic needs are apparent to us when we are aroused; as the electric companies say, "Wait until the lights go out."

A malfunction of basic biological processes often leads to a deficit or an excess of needed materials (such as protein or oxygen) or a departure from some other norm, such as body temperature. Such a departure from normality constitutes a basic need, which usually energizes behavior. In so doing, basic needs act as basic drives. Walter B. Cannon showed in *The Wisdom of The Body* (1932) that the body is in large part a self-regulating system. (Claude Bernard had shown this long before.) Body monitors constantly keep track of levels of nutrients, blood pressure, blood gas levels, temperature, and so on and initiate corrective action if a departure from the homeostatic norm occurs. (Interestingly, this does not occur in the case of oxygen deprivation.) This is what is meant by drive and a large part of the body's work consists of reducing drives. But are drives the real basis for all motivation? Hull thought so. Look at the evidence.

Irrefutable "Evidence" for Drive as the Basis for All Motivation

The Few Motives of Infants Anyone who has had the most casual contact with infants must be struck by the simplicity of their motives. They need warmth, food, comfort, shiny objects, and little else. Henry Murray observed 100 Harvard students in 1938 and proposed the following list of viscerogenic motives, which happen to be the same motives of the infant. These are motives that we carry with us all of our lives. They express the need for:

air	lactation
water	heatavoidance
food	coldavoidance
urination	sentience (sensuous
defecation	needs)
harmavoidance	noxavoidance
sex	(avoidance of
	noxious events)

In addition to these primary needs, Murray and his group listed 28 psychogenic, or secondary, needs. These are the needs of adults and of older children and include needs regarding objects (for example, acquisition), achievement (for example, need for superiority), defence (for example, overcoming defeat), power (for example, need for dominance), affection (for example, need for affiliation), and social affairs (for example, the need to point and lecture).

Where do these secondary needs come from? Murray (1938) and countless others have suggested that they derive from the basic needs. The infant needs milk, which comes from the mother. This association of milk and mother makes the infant need its mother. Mother gives milk and other things when she is attending to the infant, so attention becomes something needed. Attention while praising the infant means that praise becomes a secondary need, and so on. How else could it be explained? The infant's motives are so few and ours are so many; thus, the many motives of the adult must develop from and ultimately depend upon the few motives of infancy. Freud's rendition was different only in particulars.

Specific Hungers A follower of Cannon, Curt Richter, was one of those responsible for the attention paid in the 1930s to the phenomenon of specific hungers. If a rat, child, or other organism is deprived of one of at least eleven nutrients (for example, calcium, milk protein, thiamin) the organism often selects foods rich in the missing nutrient to remedy its deficiency. This seems powerful evidence for the influence of biological drive. The body detects the deficiency and promotes action to remedy it, presumably by sensitizing the taste preferences of the affected organism.

Separation of Drive and Learning Hull believed that learning $(_sH_R)$ and motivation (D) had separable effects. The key evidence for this came from the *Perin/Williams experiments*. If biological drive may be treated as an entity in its own right, having its own independent effects, its status as the possible basis for all motivation is more believable. We will see that McClelland (1985) still sympathizes with this feature of Hull's theory. We will discuss the Perin/Williams experiments in more detail later in the chapter.

Reward as Drive Reduction It is still popular, as it long has been, to argue that all rewards (reinforcers) act as they do because they reduce a primary or a secondary drive. An organism is hungry and this need acts as a drive to energize behavior. Behavior continues, perhaps at an accelerating pace, until food is encountered and the drive is reduced. In the future, when the organism is hungry again, it is apt to repeat behaviors that reduced the drive in the past. Do not all things that act as rewards reduce drives, as Hull believed?

What of the opportunity to explore, which acts as a powerful reward? When a rat presses a lever for the opportunity to explore a maze (see Montgomery, 1953), it may seem a clear case of reward in the form of an increase in stimulation, rather than as a decrease in a drive, unless one proposes an absurd curiosity drive, in which case the whole meaning of drive is lost.

Yet, is it not possible that curiosity, manipulation, and exploration constitute a case of a secondary drive? All that the infant rat or child need do is find that when it examines new objects and explores new surroundings it finds food, water, or another primary reward! Very early in life such behavior may thus become rewarding in itself, through its pairing with real rewards.

Secondary Drive/Reinforcement This whole account of motivation assumes that new objects and activities can evoke secondary drives and act as secondary rewards through past association with primary rewards. Is this not true? Money gains its value through the things that it buys. Solomon, Kamin, and Wynne's account of jumping dogs (described in Chapter 9) shows that a few pairings of a buzzer and shock can render the buzzer a secondary drive producer of great strength and durability. The avoiding or escaping of the buzzer acts as a *secondary* (or acquired) *reinforcer*. In other cases money acts as a secondary reinforcer and its lack acts as a secondary drive.

Drive and Learning Rate It is commonly believed that a motivated child learns more rapidly. Hull long believed that drive acts to speed learning.

Drive and Spontaneous Activity If biological drive is the basis for all motivation, one of its chief functions is its general energizing of behavior; when a strong drive is present, we are driven to action. The general energizing effect of drive may be observed by placing a rat in a closed box mounted on a stabilimeter, which monitors its movements in the box. As the time since the last feeding increases and the rat becomes more and more hungry, its general activity increases. This is the general energizing effect of the hunger drive (e.g., Munn, 1950).

Other Major Postulates

Postulate V: Stimulus Generalization Once we learn to seek food under one oak tree, we may also seek it under other trees. The cries we make when one of our parents comes near may occur as well to other adults. The specific reactions that Hull represented as the formation of a habit ($_sH_R$) generalize to other stimuli; generalized habit strength was represented by $_s\bar{H}_R$. Stimulus *generalization* occurred both with habits and with tendencies not to respond—that is, negative habits. The interaction of gradients of generalized habits to respond and to not respond was the basis for Hull's explanation of discrimination learning. But this explanation was the work of his longtime student and collaborator, Kenneth Spence, and we will leave the discussion of this theory, which is still very influential, until later.

Postulate VI: The Drive Stimulus Hull proposed that biological needs, in their function as instigators of action, may be viewed as stimuli, just as we treat external instigators of action as stimuli. In this way Hull translated motivational influences to S-R terms and subsequently treated motives (drives) as another part of the complex of stimuli influencing behavior from moment to moment. This interpretation is the same as Guthrie's (Chapter 5). Hull used the term *drive stimulus* to refer to those biological drives.

Postulate VII: Reaction Potential Habit strength ($_sH_R$) was postulated as a change in the organism, such that certain reactions were attached to certain stimuli, depending upon the number of times the S-R pairing occurred with reinforcement. But $_sH_R$ strength did not necessarily mean that the presentation of the stimulus would lead to the occurrence of the response. Habits translated to action only when the organism was motivated, which meant that some significant level of drive must be present. Drive was present when the organism was hungry, thirsty, fearful, or in some other way manifesting a need.

We all know what it means to do poorly on an exam when we know the material but cannot get motivated. A football team may have players who have all of the requisite skills (habits) to win, but it may lose because of the players' lack of desire (or motivation). Whether such statements are accurate renditions of the way things are is questionable, but Hull was certain that there is a fundamental difference between learning (habit) and motivation (drive). The more we know and the more motivated we are, the better we do; the greater the habit strength and the more drive, the more vigorous is performance. From the simple lever pressing of the rat to the most complex behavior of humans, performance is the product of habit strength ($_sH_R$) and motivation. Performance was termed *excitatory reaction potential* ($_sE_R$) and Hull believed that it was literally the product of habit strength and motivation (D). That is, $_sE_R = {_sH_R} \times D$! And he had some pretty good evidence that this was the case.

The evidence came from an experiment by Perin (1942), who basically replicated earlier work by Williams (1938). This demonstration is often referred to as the Perin/Williams experiments, and it seems to show clearly that performance is the product (as in multiplication) of learning and motivation.

In these experiments, rats were deprived of food for 23 hours and then trained to press a lever for food. Different groups of rats were trained for different durations of time and thus given different numbers of reinforcers (food pellets). Some rats were given as few as five pellets, while others received as many as 90. In Hull's view, this meant that the degree of learning, in terms of $_sH_R$ strength, differed for the different groups of rats. The rats were later deprived of food for varying lengths of time, from three to 22 hours, in order to establish different levels of drive (motivation).

All of the rats were then tested by placing them one at a time in a box with a lever and seeing how many times they pressed the lever. This estimate of response tendency is known as *resistance to extinction;* pressing the lever produces no food, and eventually the rat will stop pressing. But the more

prior training it has had and the hungrier it is, the more the rat will press before stopping. The rats bore out the truth of this and did even more.

Hull's analysis of the Perin/Williams data showed that both the degree of drive (in terms of hours of food deprivation) and habit strength (in terms of number of pellets previously received for pressing) influenced the number of presses the rats made when no food was produced. The longer they had been without food, the more presses they made; the relationship was approximately linear. Plotting the number of presses as a function of food deprivation yielded a straight line (linear) increasing function. Actually, it was slightly concave upward—showing a positive acceleration—as illustrated in Figure 6.3.

The more pellets the rats received previously, the more they pressed the lever. But the relationship was not linear; rather, it was a negatively accelerated increasing function, leveling off for the groups receiving very large numbers of pellets. This is as Hull would predict, you might recall. He believed that as habit strength increases, the rate of increase becomes less, according to the equation $\Delta {_sH_R} = F(M - {_sH_R})$. Hull's rats performed as they ought.

Most impressive was the joint effect of prior training and the amount of food deprivation. When one examines the performance of the 23-hour food deprivation group that had also received 70 prior pellets and compares it with the 23-hour food deprivation group that had received only 30 prior pellets, one finds that the latter group responded approximately 30 percent fewer times in extinction. Similarly, the 70-pellet group that was then food deprived for only three hours responded only one third as many times in extinction as did the 70-pellet group that was food deprived for 22 hours. The number of presses depended jointly on the number of prior pellets given and the number of hours of recent food deprivation.

Learning and motivation are therefore different because their effects appear as different functions (linear versus negatively accelerated) and because they seem to have a combined effect on

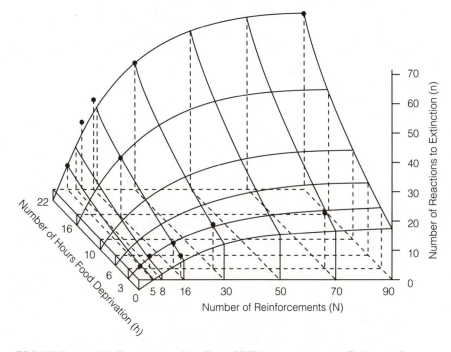

FIGURE 6.3   Hull's analysis of the Perin/Williams experiments. Points on the surface represent the joint effects of hours of food deprivation and number of reinforcements on rats' lever pressing. (Hull, 1943, p. 229)

behavior. But their effects do not simply sum; they actually multiply, claimed Hull. Using special equations beyond the scope of this book, Hull claimed to demonstrate that habit strength and motivation multiply to determine performance ($_sE_R$). It should give one pause to consider what units such a product would come in. If we multiply $_sH_R$ times drive in this experiment, we wind up with $_sE_R$ in "number of prior pellets-hours of food deprivation" units. McClelland (1985) believes that Hull was fundamentally correct, as we will see.

Postulate VIII: Reactive Inhibition   Performance is not determined solely by learning and motivation; there is also inhibition, which accumulates as we move our muscles. Note the way it feels to do 50 push-ups quickly, particularly as you do the last ten. The same effect occurs after addressing

100 envelopes or memorizing a long poem. What we feel is the *reactive inhibition*—an ever-increasing aversive drive—building up and subtracting from our performance. In fact, reactive inhibition (I_R) does literally subtract from our performance.

As we rest and the muscles stop working, or as we pause in our envelope addressing, I_R ceases to accumulate and that which has accumulated dissipates with time. Hull believed that this accounted for the phenomenon of reminiscence in many learning situations. *Reminiscence* refers to improvement in performance, such as in recalling a list of words, after a period of no practice (rest). During this time the reactive inhibition that has accumulated can fade, thereby increasing the available $_sE_R$.

Postulate IX: Conditioned Inhibition   Hull believed that all cases of reinforcement depend upon drive reduction; all reinforcers, such as food, reduce drives, such as hunger. He cleverly argued that this is the way we learn negative habits, or learned tendencies not to do something.

Suppose that we are addressing our envelopes or that the rat is pressing its lever or that the child is memorizing its alphabet letters. The activity continues and, whether it is occasionally reinforced with food, praise, or something else, reactive inhibition keeps building up. Whenever we act, reinforced or not, I_R accumulates. Reactive inhibition is unpleasant, aversive. It hurts to do more push-ups or to address more envelopes; it is a drag to press the bar, and it becomes annoying to continue the alphabet memorizing. Activity becomes unpleasant because I_R acts as an aversive drive, just as hunger does!

What do we do? We stop the push-ups, the envelope addressing, the lever pressing, and the memorizing and it feels good. We have stopped the buildup of I_R and that which has accumulated rapidly begins to dissipate. The aversive drive is reduced, and whenever a drive is reduced, reinforcement occurs. Thus, stopping in that situation has been reinforced, and the next time we are in that situation (doing push-ups, memorizing the alphabet, and so on) there will be a much greater tendency to stop doing it. We refer to this tendency as *conditioned inhibition*. It is represented as $_sI_R$.

The Remaining Postulates   Postulates I through IX are really the heart of Hull's system. Along with a number of corollaries, they served as the guide for the research of countless investigators and as the target for attacks by countless others. The remaining postulates include behavioral oscillation (postulate X), which places limits on the exact prediction of behavior. This oscillation refers to moment-by-moment changes in $_sE_R$ because of all of the inherent variability in living things. All of the variables in the preceding postulates ($_sH_R$, D, $_sI_R$) vary from moment to moment, and, since all contribute to determine the performance at a given time, performance varies somewhat from

moment to moment. Hull treated behavioral oscillation ($_sO_R$) as a form of inhibition, which subtracts from $_sE_R$ as do the other two forms of inhibition.

The eleventh postulate proposes a threshold that must be reached before action occurs. Remember that Hull was thinking in utterly mechanical terms; he felt that he was showing how we, as mechanisms, work and how our behavior can be reduced to the effects of learning (reinforced practice, $_sH_R$) times motivation (drive, D), minus inhibitory factors (I_R, $_sI_R$, and $_sO_R$). But we do not always act, at least in ways that are visible. This is because the resultant of the factors that lead to action or prevent it must be above some minimal value, the threshold, or $_sL_R$. The L comes from *limen*, the Latin word for "threshold," commonly used in the study of sensation to denote the minimal value of stimulation that is detectable.

Postulates XII through XVI deal with measures of $_sE_R$ and with competition among behaviors. Hull proposed that $_sE_R$ will be evidenced to the extent that it exceeds $_sL_R$ (postulate XII) and that it may be assessed in terms of latency or response ($_st_R$), resistance to extinction, and its amplitude (postulates XIII, XIV, and XV). The last of these specifically refers to responses mediated by the autonomic nervous system. The final postulate (XVI) says that when competing response tendencies exist, the one with the higher momentary $_sE_R$ will prevail.

The Significance of Hull's Postulates

Hull meant his postulate system as a starting point; it included much of what was believed be true about the way we work, and it was taken for granted that it would be modified or completely changed as new knowledge was gained. After all, we must begin somewhere, and is it not better to begin with a set of clearly presented statements, rather than a hodgepodge of conflicting and fuzzily put "truths"? Hull wanted to give us a beginning and to do something to end the constant infighting among combatants who had little understanding of what the opponent was saying.

Hull also recognized that there was a lot that was not included in the postulates; for example, there is no explicit mention of anticipation, purpose, cognition, knowledge, emotion, and other things that certainly are part of what all of us think of as psychology. But in fairness to Hull, it must be understood that he planned to include all of these things, and he might have had his life not been cut short. He firmly believed that we must start with simple biological truths (or near truths) and build from there. If we begin with the simple we can progress to the complex, but not vice versa, simply because we will never really understand the complex if that is where we begin.

Hull (1952b) examined experimental evidence confirming and failing to confirm 121 of his set of 178 theoretical propositions (corollaries and theorems related to his postulates). He concluded that 106 were found to be valid, 14 were probably invalid, and only one was definitely invalid.

Hull's Intervening Variables

More than a decade before Hull wrote *Principles of Behavior*, Edward Tolman, Hull's most vocal critic, proposed that we use intervening variables in psychology. Hull agreed fully with Tolman and, when his system was unveiled in 1943, it was composed almost wholly of intervening variables. What is an *intervening variable*? It is really easy to understand, but that question has given more than one graduate student trouble. Let us begin with a list of simple things that make us do simple things and see where an intervening variable might come in handy. Before we begin, remember that Hull was avowedly a behaviorist, as were Watson and Guthrie. Also remember that Watson's main aim was to make psychology practical by concentrating on what we do (including thinking) and what makes us do it. Both what we do and what makes us do it must be identified easily; Watson wanted no fictional things inside

us to explain what we do. Behaviorism speaks only of the world and our activity.

But consider this: Suppose that we simultaneously:

> drink no fluids for two days
>
> lock ourselves in a sauna
>
> tie off our salivary ducts
>
> eat a box of saltines
>
> read *Lawrence of Arabia*

These are *independent variables;* they are things that we can do to produce some change in our behavior or experience. After the application of such measures for a time, we examine our behavior or experience and find that we:

> think of drinking water a lot
>
> are willing to commit crimes for water
>
> would drink water pumped out of a river
>
> would overcome obstacles to get water

These are *dependent variables;* they are indicants of the effects of the independent variables. Water deprivation and other variables lead us to do things to get water, and we are not as particular as we might be otherwise concerning what we have to do to get the water and the quality of the water we get.

Watson's "pure" behaviorism insisted that we explain the effects of these independent variables specifically, to avoid the traps of the old mentalism that he was trying to avoid. We would have to describe this experiment as it happened: When I drink no fluids for two days, lock myself in a sauna, tie off my salivary ducts, eat a box of saltines, and read about deserts, I will think of drinking water a lot, commit crimes for water, consider drinking polluted water, and overcome obstacles to get water! That seems a bit much when we all know that there is a common and familiar factor involved: All of the independent variables listed result in my being *thirsty*. When I am thirsty I will do all of the things listed as dependent variables. Thirst is thus an intervening variable.

It must seem amazing that anyone would object to the use of intervening variables. We drink because we are thirsty, eat because we are hungry, work because we are industrious, study because we are studious, sleep because we are tired, fight when we are angry, weep when we are unhappy, and so on. Everyone knows that this is true, and it is boring and/or insulting to be told by some psychologist that we do such things or that we do not do such things. Intervening variables are the things that we use to tie together lots of causes (in this case, heat, salt, water deprivation) and effects (drinking, thinking about drinking) and they are part and parcel of daily life. As Hull (1943) noted, the electron is an intervening variable!

We will discuss the reasons for the fuss about intervening variables in Chapter 8. Skinner did use some intervening variables in his early theorizing, but later cast them out. In so doing, he seemed to be excluding a lot of what we feel is part of life, but his reasons were compelling and we will consider them in detail.

In Hull's system, the intervening variables were too numerous for us to consider in their entirety; the major ones we have already discussed and a few more are easy to understand:

Independent Variables	Intervening Variables	Dependent Variables
reinforced trials	$_sH_R$	
deprivation of food, water, and so on	D	resistance to extinction
work done	I_R	pause before responding
stopping work	$_sI_R$	frequency of response
amount and quality of reinforcer	K	amplitude of response
similarity of stimuli	$_sH_R$	

with $_sE_R$ bracketing the intervening variables.

Knowledge, Purpose, and Foresight as Habit Mechanisms

In 1930 and 1931, Hull published two important papers that showed the way in which a machine might show evidence for knowledge, purpose, and foresight. The principles he invoked were well-accepted ideas in the psychology of the nineteenth century and it is interesting to see the way in which he used them. This achievement was, in a way, the capstone of the associationist philosophies; it extended their basic views to areas where only philosophers had tentatively ventured and made the associationist-mechanist view seem a natural extension of the known principles of biological functioning. Here is the story.

What sort of behavior and experience would seem to be most difficult for someone like Hull to explain in mechanical terms? How could anyone build a machine (his basic approach) that would show evidence of knowledge, purpose, and foresight? Further, how could this be done in such a way as to roughly follow accepted biological principles? Let us consider two examples, one dull but traditional and another less dull and less traditional. In the first case, consider a rat that is running an alley and receiving food at the end. In the second case, consider yourself on your way to accept an award, to be received in a familiar place. How would Hull account for the behavior shown and for the experience that we (and the rat) have?

Knowledge Hull believed in starting with the most basic determinants of behavior and experience; in so doing he made a number of simplifying assumptions, especially in cases such as the ones we are considering. The first assumption was that the world affecting us may be simply represented. What is the world affecting us? Poets and writers, not to mention philosophers, have anguished over this problem, but for practical purposes, Hull suggested that it be represented as follows:

the world: $S_1 \ S_2 \ S_3 \ S_4 \ S_5 \ S_6 \ S_G$

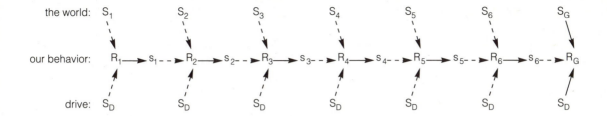

This is surely simple enough; the *S*s stand for stimuli and the sequence from S_1 on represents a "world sequence" of stimuli passing along. The sequence in this case ends with S_G, or a *goal stimulus*. This amounts to food, receiving the award, or some other situation that reduces a biological drive or a secondary drive.

We experience this sequence of stimuli (the "world") either because it is passing as we watch or because we are moving through it. The former case could refer to the watching of a movie or listening to a song, but the latter case is of concern here. We are moving along, and as we move we encounter S_1, S_2, and so on to S_G. The movements of the muscles (including the eyes) provide more stimuli, assuming we are talking about a high-grade organism with proprioceptors. Muscle spindles and Golgi tendon organs let us know the position of our limbs, and they do so by reacting when we move a muscle or a limb. Thus, the feedback from movement becomes an additional source of stimulation, so that our first journey through the sequence of stimuli results in the situation represented above.

The series of *R*s represents our behavior as we progress through the stimulus sequence (that is, the "world series"). Following each R is a lower-case *s* with the same subscript as the preceding R; these are the proprioceptive feedback stimuli produced by each response we make. Each response is different, so each *s* is different. This introduces something interesting and by no means original with Hull. This gives us a basis for knowledge in this organism. Consider what we have so far.

The world sequence is either the sights and smells of the alley, if we consider a rat running

an alley, or the things we see and hear as we are on our way to the award ceremony. The behavior sequence represents movements along the path, and these occur in the presence of the corresponding stimuli; R_1 goes with S_1, R_2 goes with S_2, and so on. Recall that Hull's fourth postulate said that stimuli accompanying responses that were followed by drive reduction become attached to those responses; as long as this series of stimuli and behavior ends with a drive-reducing S_G (food for the rat and the secondary-drive-reducing award for us), those stimuli will become connected with those responses. The next time we or the rat are in the presence of S_1, R_1 will be likely to occur and the succeeding stimuli in the series will be apt to produce the behaviors that last occurred in their presence. Needless to say, the behaviors closest in time to drive reduction, such as R_5 and R_6, will be more closely connected to their stimuli. But unless the delay between S_1 and R_1 is too long, the more remote connections will also be made. The broken lines represent new connections between these stimuli and their responses.

In addition, we also have the proprioceptive consequences of each of these responses and, of course, each of these are different and mirror the responses that produced them. Thus, we have the "world series" of stimuli, each connected to specific responses. Each of these responses produces feedback that we can feel, although we do not ordinarily pay much attention to such feedback. In a real sense, the feedback *s*'s are a copy of the world sequence of stimuli. The sequence of feedback stimuli is within the body and thus acts as a copy of the world sequence of stimuli.

This was Hull's proposed mechanism for the acquiring of knowledge. Is it reasonable?

It certainly is, and put in less gross (S-R) terms, it has a long and distinguished history, especially in American pragmatic philosophy and in functionalist psychology, although Hull cited no sources there. Let us consider a common example. Suppose that you are entering some great hall, such as a huge room in the Versailles palace or a large alien spaceship. Or suppose that you are simply exploring your new home. In all such situations, you may simply stand at the door and see everything within about as well as it can be seen in order for you to get a good impression of what is there. But in all cases, it seems necessary to walk slowly through whatever space is involved and you may walk through it repeatedly. You are getting to know the place, to have knowledge of it which you can carry away with you. And this knowledge comes from what you see, from the effort it almost unconsciously takes to focus on the high ceilings and from the way it feels to walk through it.

Visit someone who lives in a very old fashioned house with a very large living room and very high ceilings. In a 30 ft × 60 ft. living room, one has an irresistible urge to walk around through it to *know* just how big it is! This moving through our surroundings and the way it feels to do so is a large part of the way that we come to know the world. You know that a written description or a picture is no substitute for direct experience. And direct experience must include action on our part. If you want to know what a hammer is as well as I do, hit your thumbs and fingers routinely with a hammer. In large part the world and its objects are our reactions to it and them.

Foresight So the rat running down the alley and our trip to the award ceremony leave connections between the stimuli that pass by and a copy of the trip in the form of movement-produced stimuli. But wait! The movement-produced stimuli *are* stimuli, and therefore they obey Hull's fourth postulate. They are present when a response is made that is followed by drive reduction, and they therefore become connected with the appropriate responses. Thus, s_1 becomes connected with R_2 and s_2 becomes connected with R_3, and so on. This adds quite a bit to the situation.

All that Hull's machine (the rat or us) now needs to get it or us going and continuing to go is S_1. That leads to the first response, R_1, which produces its proprioceptive feedback, s_1, which is connected to R_2; thus, it can produce R_2 even in the absence of S_2. We no longer need the world sequence, because once we have started action, the proprioceptive stimuli can produce the next response, which leads to more proprioceptive stimuli and the next response, and so on. This is a *chain* of behavior. If the initial stimulus is present, the first act leads to the second, and so on, with the intermediation of the response-produced stimulation that goes with each response.

Such chains are common in human life. We go through a sequence of movements in buttoning our blouses, shirts, or sweaters, which is begun and rattled off with no thought on our part. Do you begin buttoning a blouse or shirt at the top or at the bottom? There go your hands, miming the act, right? In such common activities, we rely almost entirely on proprioceptive/kinesthetic stimuli that come from our tendon organs and from our muscle spindles and that lead to the next act. Your fingers know how to strum a guitar or sew a button and your arms "know" how to hit a punching bag or a baseball. If you try to attend to the details of such actions, you will make errors.

What happens then when the rat reaches its goal box and we receive the award? The S_G, or goal stimulus, is a drive-reducing event and produces an R_G, or goal response. The eating of the food reduces the rat's hunger and the receiving of the award reduces secondary drives. Through the whole sequence, the rat is hungry and we have yearnings for the award, which motivate the rat and us as we go through the sequence. Hull viewed all of motivation in terms of drive stimuli, which are like any other stimuli and which become connected to the behaviors that occur as we

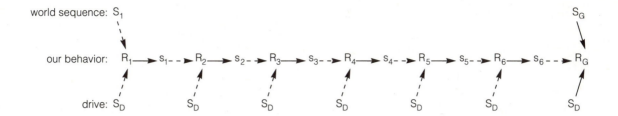

go through the sequence. When we are later in the same drive state (hungry or yearning), we will be more apt to go through the same behaviors that lead to the goal object on this occasion.

Let us now consider foresight. Suppose that the rat is later tracing its familiar route to the food or that we are tracing our familiar route to our award. All of the stimuli of the world sequence are connected to our past behaviors on that route, as are the proprioceptive stimuli (the lowercase s's) that form the chain. And all of these behaviors are also joined to the drive state involved in the past (that is, the S_D). This means that we can carry out the sequence of behaviors leading to the goal stimulus without the specific stimuli of the world sequence. All that is necessary is that the sequence be set off and that it can continue by itself. It happens as shown above.

What has happened is that the stimulus of the world sequence that begins the sequence of behaviors has caused R_1 and that has produced s_1, which produces R_2, which produces s_2, and the rest of the chain (R_3–s_3–R_4 . . .) runs off by itself; we do not need most of the world series. The rat enters the alley and is affected by the sight of the start box and the beginning of the maze; we set out to receive the award and are on our way. In such well-practiced sequences of behavior (or experience) in which the initiating stimuli have had their effect, the rest of the chain goes off automatically, as is common in daily life.

This is a very reasonable explanation for much of what we do. The first time we ride a bicycle, it is necessary to attend to each stimulus coming from our muscles, our organs of balance in the inner ear, and the sight of the ground beneath us. But after we have gone through such painstaking

initial efforts, bicycle riding (or dancing, or driving an automobile) has only to begin, and our past habits carry out all of the specific movements for us. In addition, this chaining of movements and proprioceptive stimuli also accounts for instances of foresight.

Suppose that the sequence we are considering is one that ends with a goal stimulus (S_G) that is something we either value highly, such as high praise, or something we find very aversive, such as being mauled by a pack of wild dogs. We begin a sequence of behavior, with no particular idea in mind as to where we are going. The world sequence sets off the chain of behavior and movement-produced stimuli and we foresee the culmination of our trip. The chain runs off *faster* than the objective world sequence and we reach the S_G long before the sequence of S_1, S_2, and so on leads us to it.

Similarly, such chain-produced foresight keeps us out of the jaws of the pack of wild dogs. As we turn a corner, we recognize that this is the way to the wild dogs' home and the chain of behavior and movement-produced stimuli that have resulted from past excursions in this direction leads us to a mental S_G and allows us to rechart the course and thus avoid the danger to which that course led us in the past.

Purpose "What more do we mean by foresight?" asked Hull. A more potent form of foresight comes from the effect of past goal attainment. Behavior with respect to goals (the rat reaching its food, our reaction to the award) is the goal response (R_G). The goal response is closely related to the particular drive state we are in (the S_D), since that is what makes a goal a goal. Food, water, or activity are S_G's when our S_D (drive state) is hunger, thirst, or need for activity. When such drives are not present, such goals do not act as goals.

After a bit of experience in running through the rat-to-food or the us-to-award sequences, both we and the rat seem to act less mechanically than Hull's basic theory seems to require. The rat runs faster as it progresses down the alley and we may notice drops of saliva on its cheeks. Our path to the award is accompanied by thoughts of it and by anticipation of its presentation. How can mechanical entities, such as the rat and us (in Hull's opinion) seem to show anticipation in this way?

This was explained by Hull (1931) as the effects of the *functional antedating goal response*, sometimes called the anticipatory goal response, and represented by r_G–s_G. This is a totally mechanical addition to Hull's totally mechanical theory, and he used it to account for a variety of things that we and other animals do. Here is how it works.

Why does the rat move in the alley at all, even on the first occasion in which it is placed in it? It has not learned at that time that there is food at the end of the alley, but it is hungry and hunger acts as a drive (an S_D), which produces activity, just as Guthrie's maintaining stimuli produced action. S_D is simply another name for the same thing, although Guthrie meant to include more than biological needs when he referred to such stimuli.

Because of the way the alley is built, the rat will eventually reach the goal box and the food, just as it would probably eventually find food if it were hungry in the wilds. When the rat finds food for the first time, by accident, so to speak, it responds as one does to any goal stimulus (S_G)— with a goal response (R_G). Ingeniously, Hull pointed out that the goal response was a response similar in kind to any other response, and thus subject to postulate IV: It was a response closely preceding the reduction of a drive (obviously) and therefore would become connected to stimuli present at or near the time it occurred. This means that the response will become most strongly connected to the sight of the food, of course, since that is what was present at the time it occurred, but it also will be connected to stimuli present near the time it occurred. Thus, it will be connected to S_6, S_5, and even more remote components of the world sequence, as well as to s_6, s_5, and more remote movement-produced stimuli. With repeated trials, the connections between these stimuli and the goal response (R_G) will become stronger and stronger, and eventually even S_1 and s_1, the first component of the world sequence and the first stimulation produced by movement, will produce a strong (R_G) goal response.

Remember that Hull was trying to build an organism that would act as humans do, and the problem of accounting for anticipation and goal direction was a big problem for such an enterprise. He showed how his model could account for such behavior and, although he has been proved partly wrong in tests that took him literally at his word (see Bolles, 1978), his solution to the problem has had great influence. For example, one process, which will be described briefly below, was adopted by McClelland and his associates (McClelland, Atkinson, Clark, & Lowell, 1953), who used it to justify their method for testing the achievement motive (nAch), and as the basis for a general theory of human motivation, a topic to which we will return.

Getting back to the rat, we now have the goal response (R_G) connected to the stimuli of the world sequence and the movement-produced stimuli that link together the chain of behavior that guides the rat to the food (and us to our award, in exactly the same way, as the reader can imagine). Plus, the goal response is not really *any* response, because the organism involved is in a state of need of one kind or another (for example, the rat needs food), so that the drive state that is current tends to produce the goal response.

Thus, experience going through the sequence and the nature of S_D both lead to the possibility of R_G occurring as soon as the world sequence begins. (Hull (1931) said that this explained premature ejaculation.) The general principle, if true, means that we and the rat would begin showing goal responses as soon as any familiar sequence of behavior begins. And this is not far from the truth.

Suppose the rat begins to think of food, salivate, chew, and make food-grasping movements with its paws as soon as it is placed in the alley. If it continues to do this, what happens? If it stays where it is, or somehow manages to run on two feet while doing this "sham eating," it either never gets to the goal box and the food or it gets there very slowly. This means that when the rat makes the whole goal response when not at the goal, the food and the drive reduction are delayed somewhat or the drive reduction does not occur at all.

Behaviors that require effort but do not lead to drive reduction simply cause a buildup in reactive inhibition (I_R) and no buildup in habit strength ($_sH_R$); thus, the behaviors extinguish (drop out). Thus, the goal response prevents the delivery of food unless it is done when food is present and so it extinguishes at other times. But Hull pointed out that the goal response is a complex set of activities and that not all of them impede the progress of the rat or of us to the goal.

For example, the rat's goal response to food includes its seeing the food, smelling the food, chewing the food, picking up the food, swallowing, and so on. Only the picking up of the food, if done before the rat reaches the food, impedes progress toward the goal. The rat can see (imagine) the food, smell it, chew, salivate, and do other things it does while it eats, and still run. These components of the goal response (R_G), which can go on without slowing or halting the rat's progress toward the goal, are little r_G's, fractional antedating goal responses, and they grow stronger with successive trials.

Those components of the goal response that interfere with the progress toward the goal and drive reduction drop out, since they are not closely followed by drive reduction. These components include things like stopping to seize and eat imaginary food. But the components of R_G that do not interfere have a motivational effect.

The effects of an ever stronger r_G appear in the rat's behavior as visible food-related behavior while running the alley. The rat may salivate, make chewing movements, and do other things that we can see and that suggest to us that the rat is on the way to food, and the rat may be imagining the taste and sight and smell of the food, for all we know. We have all experienced going through sequences that had a predictable ending enough to see the truth of this; how do we act on the way to see a loved one, learn an exam grade, receive a beating, eat breakfast, and a host of other familiar sequences? We "anticipate" the end result of our behavior. We see, hear, and in other ways do what we have done to reach that goal before. We wince or exalt as we have done before when receiving an exam grade, even though the moment of reckoning is yet to come. In a real sense, when we do these things, we are doing what we have done in the past in the presence of goal objects, but the goal object is not yet present and so we do the best we can.

Ralph Barton Perry, biographer of William James, addressed the same matter in a 1918 paper. When a dog is chasing a rabbit, Perry explained, it is actually "eating" the rabbit during the chase. It is making a variety of antedating goal responses, and only the physical grasping of the rabbit is needed to consummate the act.

Besides the anticipatory reactions that occur when we progress toward familiar goals, we also speed our movements toward such goals, the closer we come to them. The rat accelerates as it nears the goal and we speed up as we turn the last corner on the way to receive the award. This cannot simply be due to the fact that our fractional anticipatory goal response is stronger near the goal. Since such responses are closest to the goal and to drive reduction, they *are* stronger, but why should the rat's stronger salivation (and so on) lead it to run more rapidly as it approaches the goal? This does occur, though, because of the stimulus consequences of the anticipatory response.

Just as the movements we make produce sensory consequences (as when R_1 produces s_1), frac-

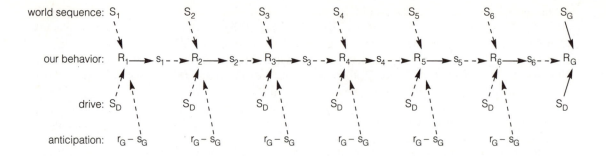

world sequence: S_1 S_2 S_3 S_4 S_5 S_6 S_G

our behavior: $R_1 \rightarrow s_1 \dashrightarrow R_2 \rightarrow s_2 \dashrightarrow R_3 \rightarrow s_3 \dashrightarrow R_4 \rightarrow s_4 \dashrightarrow R_5 \rightarrow s_5 \dashrightarrow R_6 \rightarrow s_6 \dashrightarrow R_G$

drive: S_D S_D S_D S_D S_D S_D S_D

anticipation: $r_G - s_G$ $r_G - s_G$ $r_G - s_G$ $r_G - s_G$ $r_G - s_G$ $r_G - s_G$

tional antedating goal responses produce stimuli, which Hull called s_G. Little s_G is the way it feels to salivate and to prepare in other ways to eat food, and it is the way it feels when we anticipate the receiving of our award. We have already seen how postulate IV specifies that r_G occur in advance of the meeting with the goal object, so there is no difficulty in accounting for why s_G occurs early in the sequence; it is produced by r_G.

However, s_G is a stimulus and it also obeys postulate IV; all stimuli present when responses occur shortly before drive reduction become attached to those responses. So s_G becomes an added determinant of the responses in the sequence, along with the stimuli of the world sequence and the stimuli produced by movement toward the goal object. Little s_G is more strongly attached to those responses that are closest to drive reduction, and this accounts for the acceleration as we approach our goal and the rat's acceleration as it nears its food.

This, then, is Hull's (1930, 1931) explanation for our behavior when we go through a sequence of stimuli that we have gone through often in the past. Knowledge is accounted for as the product of action-produced stimuli, which leave a copy of the world sequence within us, translated into our reactions to that sequence.

To complete Hull's account for knowledge, foresight, and purpose, we have only to add r_G– s_G to the mechanisms described so far. Recall that s_G, being a stimulus, obeys postulate IV and becomes an added evoker of each response, especially those nearest the goal stimulus. This is the

basis for anticipation and the acceleration shown as a goal is approached. The final diagram is above.

Practical Application of Hull's Theory

Hull spent a lot of time applying his theory in animal research, and most of his amazing predictions of experimental results refer to animal research. He was a master at attaching numbers to the habit strengths assumed to be present in a given situation and then going through a complex set of deductions, using equations described in his major works (1943, 1952b) and arriving at results so near those actually obtained that critics blanched. (The reader may wish to consult Hull's 1952 book to see just how good he was at predicting the minutest details of an experimental result.)

But Hull's overall goal was to explain that which is worth explaining; it is clear in his writings that he felt we must first make a convincing case for the possibility of explaining complex behavior. If his death had not cut short his work, he may have gone much further than we might guess in dealing with complicated behavior. His students' work suggests the directions he would have taken, and the transcripts of his "Monday-night group" at Yale outlines the sorts of analyses he planned for a range of complex psychological phenomena.

Hull had no formal duties at Yale from 1929 until his death in 1952, aside from the directing of a mass of research carried out by some of the most capable workers in psychology and biology in the country. He met with collaborators and students on Monday evenings, and the results of the presentations made by Hull and others were recorded. The following applications and interpretations come from a copy of the *Abstract of S-R Sessions of Monday-Night Group*, 1938–1939, of the Institute of Human Relations, Yale University, which was obtained from W. S. Verplanck, a former acquaintance of Hull. The presentations include pieces by Neal Miller, Hull, O. H. Mowrer, Carl Hovland, P. H. French, G. P. Murdock, J.W.M. Whiting, and D. G. Marquis. Hull gave the following homely examples during these sessions to illustrate the strong effects of reinforcement in daily life:

> The principle of reinforcement is operating constantly and we have all been familiar with it since childhood; the only thing strange about it is the name. The meaning of the term will become clear with a few simple examples. . . .
>
> If a nation in need demands a satisfaction of this need from another nation on threat of war, and if the second nation yields, the demanding and threatening by the first nation will be *reinforced* and it will be more likely to repeat the behavior subsequently when a similar situation arises. . . .
>
> If a racketeer attempts any sort of blackmail and the victim yields, the blackmailing behavior will be *reinforced* and therefore strengthened. But if all prospective victims should uniformly refuse to yield, this [blackmailing] behavior will suffer extinction. . . .
>
> If an infant says "da-da" and he is praised and approved, this behavior will thereby be *reinforced* and the child will say it more readily on subsequent similar occasions. . . .
>
> You are painfully ill and you do various things to relieve your illness. Finally you take a certain medicine, whereupon you at once grow better, thus reinforcing the tendency to take that medicine the next time that you are similarly ill. . . .
>
> A child by trial-and-error joins a certain word sequence and escapes punishment—thus *lying* is reinforced.
>
> A person by trial-and-error joins certain words together and his anxieties disappear. Thus *rationalization* is reinforced. . . .
>
> A child speaks certain words to *himself* while in a problem situation and these words evoke a reaction on his part which solves the problem. Thus *reasoning* is reinforced. . . .
>
> Later, special rules are tried out and by trial-and-error those rules which mediate problem solutions successfully are reinforced and the others are extinguished. Those words which survive this trial-and-error procedure become *logic*. . . .
>
> A person with much anxiety, if relieved by psychoanalysis, will have the tendency to go to the analyst and to cooperate with him, reinforced. He will also pay the analyst, reinforcing the analyst's behavior, and thus creating a *reciprocal habit complex*. This circle is said to be broken after a time by a failure of the anxiety to recur. At that time the patient would terminate the analysis. . . .
>
> A person receives a shock in an accident and receives insurance for injury, thus removing the necessity of working, and so reinforces the symptom. Such cases are said to be hard to cure.

Such examples are sufficient to give an idea of the way in which Hull's analysis could apply to international conflicts, blackmail, the learning of words, lying, rationalization, reasoning, logic, the tendency to continue psychoanalysis or other treatment, and injuries that seem to take an overly long time to heal. His analysis actually is no more than an application of the general principle of reinforcement to common behaviors. Thus, it is by no means original with Hull. It is included to show that he was concerned with such problems and that he was confident that S-R associationism and the law of effect was enough to deal with them.

3. CRITICISMS OF HULL

The Stress on Molecular Interpretations

We will see that Tolman (1932) had emphasized the importance of the distinction between molecular and molar treatments of behavior. We will go into the details of this distinction later. Suffice it to say that Hull was a molecular theorist, despite his frequent assertions in 1943 that his was a molar theory.

What was (and is) meant by the molecular/molar distinction is the problem of what constitutes behavior and experience. Suppose I walk to the store to buy milk. How can I describe this act if I am interested in explaining all of what I do? I called the act "walking to the store," but this molar way of describing things may not be appropriate. Such a description defines activity with reference to goals, and Guthrie made a good case for not doing such things. If we see someone walking and it appears to us that she is heading toward a store where milk can be bought, we may guess that this is the goal of the walker. But this may not be the case, and such descriptions are not useful if one wants to do a scientific analysis of behavior. Thus, Hull (despite his denial) was an advocate of molecular analyses of behavior. (Neither he nor Tolman were very interested in experience, but the same point of view would prevail there, whether dealing with behavior or experience.)

Hull was the ultimate molecularist, and this meant that for him any explanation of behavior had to be cast in what Tolman called the ultimate causes of behavior. The walk to the store to buy milk appears so only because we overlook or ignore the real state of affairs. This consists of muscular movements and secretions of glands; although Hull felt himself to be molar because he was not dealing with the contractions of individual muscle fibers, he was in fact concerned with the movement of groups of muscles and the movement of limbs. Although Watson and Guthrie both advocated such a position, they usually dealt with quite large chunks of behavior and they dealt with experience. Hull stayed with the ultimate determinants in theory and in practice.

This is embodied in his emphasis on the importance of being able to test theories by building a machine that functions as the theory predicts. In fact, we are muscles and bone and blood and nerves and glands. And if we are to understand ourselves, we must understand the workings of our bodies.

Hull's mistake, according to critics, was his insistence not only on biological determinants of behavior, but on a molecular view of the workings of the body. Hull was by no means an authority on biological matters, and he accepted the common view that we are a collection of parts and that our behavior is merely the sum of those parts; this was exactly the point of view that James Mill had taken in his account of mental phenomena. In his view, there are numerous separate pieces that, when added up, comprise mental life. For Hull, there are separate muscle movements and secretions of glands, and when you add them up you have behavior.

The general point of view is difficult to criticize. When you hear someone say that an apparent trip to the store to buy milk is really a sequence of muscle movements and glandular secretions, you secretly chuckle. But someone may show you a vial of brown liquid and, after you see, smell, and taste it, you are told that it is really a solution of beef molecules in water. It seemed to be just beef broth. When we get down to it, the world and our behavior and experience are really whatever are the smallest elements into which we can analyze. Isn't everything really made of atoms?

Hull's view was shaped by the status of the sciences in the 1920s and 1930s, which led to his emphasis on molecular analysis. All of the criticisms that the Gestaltists heaped on Titchener count as heavily as criticisms of Hull. We will see in the next chapter that Tolman, who sympathized with the Gestaltists, tried very hard to combat Hull's extension of Titchener's molecularism.

The Hypothetico-Deductive Approach

As mentioned earlier in the chapter, Hull's fascination with the hypothetico-deductive method arose after his reading of a paper by Einstein, which was published in the 1930s. (Kenneth Spence related this information in his introduction to the seventh printing of Hull's *Principles of Behavior*.) Although others dispute Hull's conclusion, Hull was convinced that Einstein had used the method of formal postulates and the deducing and testing of theorems originating with the postulates.

Hull also pointed to Isaac Newton's *Principia* as a model, with its "classical scientific theoretical system of the past," which began with seven definitions (matter, motion, and so on), continued with a set of postulates (his famous three laws of motion), followed by 73 formally proved theorems and many appended corollaries (Hull, 1943, p. 7). Can Newton's method be a bad one?

Given the conditions of the time, Hull's method seemed very attractive, and it is easy to see why it converted so many to his point of view. Instead of the hodgepodge of conflicting theories and the neverending debates among psychologists and philosophers, we would begin together, with a clearly worded set of general principles; together we would make deductions from the postulates and test them. As the tests showed a theorem to be in error, we would modify it. If a number of theorems were so altered, we would change the postulate.

It was taken for granted by Hull that the postulates were no more than reasonable assumptions about the way we work; they obviously were not completely accurate, or we would now understand exactly how we operate. But if we constantly test and modify them, we will slowly but surely improve them and eventually we will have a set of true postulates. Who could argue with such a proposal? What could be wrong with a self-correcting strategy such as this one? Many did not argue and Hull's popularity was undoubtedly in great part due to the promise that this method seemed to hold.

Yet, by the early 1950s, scarcely more than a decade after Hull had unveiled his system, there were few psychologists who still believed that such a method was useful. One reason for the failure of the hypothetico-deductive method was the difficulty encountered by clearly testing theorems. If one could do an experiment that clearly and conclusively shows, for example, that all reinforcers do not involve drive reduction, then one could appropriately modify postulate IV. But there have been countless experiments done with humans and other animals since the 1940s aimed at clarifying the nature of reinforcement. We still do not understand it in the way in which Hull defined *understanding*.

Experiments never come out absolutely, clearly, and unambiguously in favor of or against a hypothesis; such a clear and unambiguous experiment, which shows to everyone's satisfaction that a hypothesis was true or false, is known as a *crucial experiment* and such things are hard to come by.

Hull was in a position to have the best research facilities and the best researchers available, in addition to having tremendous influence with the journals that publish research results. (If the results of an experiment are not published, they do not exist. This means that a research finding must bear the scrutiny of reviewers working for the journals (without pay, of course) before one can be sure that the experiment was properly conducted and therefore that the data are believable.) Opponents of Hull's basic views may have had more than their share of difficulties in getting their work published, and, once it was published, they could expect a counterattack from Hull's group. Many of his assistants and colleagues, such as Spence and Miller, were masters of research and could effectively point out the deficiencies in findings critical of Hull's views and then show experimentally how Hull's position was actually the correct one. Thus, the necessity for crucial experiments and the influential position that Hull enjoyed rendered the self-correcting system more a self-perpetuating system!

Hull's Ignoring of Private Experience

Since Watson's time, critics of behaviorism have charged that behaviorists either deny the existence of conscious experience or claim that it has no place in a scientific psychology. The first charge is absurd, of course, and comes from the insistence of Watson and others that the *terminology* of the introspectionists be abandoned. We found in Chapter 4 that Watson and other behaviorists were interested in experience but that they insisted it be treated as behavior, that is, as activity. This means that we think and imagine but that we do not think thoughts and imagine images. In this way, the early behaviorists, including Thorndike, Watson, and Guthrie, were stressing the importance of action (dynamics), as opposed to statics (images and ideas), which the introspectionists emphasized. The early behaviorists were not denying the existence of subjective experience, nor were they claiming that the study of it was outside psychology.

Hull and his colleagues, on the other hand, did argue that the study of subjective experience was outside scientific psychology. It may be that this was inevitable for Hull, who saw the future in this way:

> Progress in this new era will consist in the laborious writing, one by one, of hundreds of equations; in the experimental determination, one by one, of hundreds of the empirical constants contained in the equations; in the devising of practically usable units in which to measure the quantities expressed by the equations; in the objective definition of hundreds of symbols appearing in the equations; in the rigorous deduction, one by one, of thousands of theorems and corollaries from the primary definitions and equations; in the meticulous performance of thousands of critical quantitative experiments and field investigations designed with imagination, sagacity, and daring. . . . There will be encountered vituperative opposition from those who cannot or will not think in terms of mathematics, from those who prefer to have their scientific pictures artistically out of focus. (1943, p. 401)

If anything characterized Hull, it was objectivity, and subjective experience is not objective. It is a pity that Hull took this position, because his great influence damaged the behaviorist position greatly, to the extent that many believe that all behaviorists fundamentally agreed with Hull and therefore saw themselves building robots and ignoring private experience. Interestingly, Hull's archcritic, Edward Tolman, was in agreement with Hull on this issue, ridiculing any concern with subjective experience shown by those who

were supposed to be engaged in the scientific study of behavior!

Hull's emphasis on objectivity, as embodied in his hypothetico-deductive method, was due to his concern that we be able to tell when we are mistaken. What he opposed was the hiding of a possible mistake "behind weasel words, philosophical fog, and anthropomorphic prejudice" (1943).

The Case Against Drive

Hull, like Freud and many other psychologists, believed that biological drives were the basis for all motivation. This position was especially associated with Hull, and there is no doubt that his authority and data added status to the theory. It may be that drive theory is correct by definition; if we use *drive* to refer to something that energizes our behavior, then we are using the term interchangeably with *motivation*. Motivation is in that case merely a matter of drive arousal and satiation. But drive theories usually mean more than that: A drive is a biological affair. For Freud (1915), the life instinct acted as a drive (*Trieb*) seeking gratification and the whole apparatus of the psyche was built upon this. For Hull and others, all behavior (including thought) ultimately served the basic biological drives, such as hunger and thirst. Many have opposed this view of motivation, and we will illustrate their objections by discussing criticisms of the evidence for the fundamental importance of biological drives covered earlier.

The Few Motives of Infants   Just because we come into the world with few motives and have many in adulthood does not mean that current motivation in any way depends on primary motives. Let us consider this further when we discuss Allport's insightful attack on the instinct and drive positions. We will discuss this in the following subsection.

Specific Hungers   Hunger for specific foods has long been considered one of the wonders of nature. But Rozin (1967) took away much of the wonder when he pointed out that specific hungers may be accounted for largely as an instance of learned taste aversion. For example, the deficiency of a nutrient makes an organism sick and it quickly prefers different food. The deficient organism is not (in most cases) seeking out nutrients to remedy the deficiency. It simply doesn't want to eat its old food, which left the organism sick! We will discuss this explanation of specific hungers further in Chapter 9.

Separation of Learning and Drive It is true that the Perin/Williams experiments showed that it was possible to separate the effects of hunger from those due to amount of previous training, so, in a sense, learning is separable from drive. But even in this case, the division is not so neat as it may seem. The statement that drive and learning are separable and that they multiply (that is, $_sE_R = {_sH_R} \times D$) is true only to the extent that Hull's methods of calculation are accepted; these days they are not (see Seward, 1954). And *learning*, as defined in the Perin/Williams studies, was a function of the number of reinforced lever presses preceding the test in extinction. Since food pellets are drive reducers (in Hull's sense) for hungry rats, was the lever-pressing training really free of the influence of motivational factors?

Reward as Drive Reduction Masses of data collected during the 1940s and 1950s clearly showed that a great many things that do not reduce biological drives act as strong reinforcers. For example, saccharine has no nutritive value and passes unmetabolized through the body. Although it reduces no drive, it acts as a potent reinforcer of the behavior of rats and many other mammals. Other instances, stressed by Harlow and Hebb, show that *increases* in drive may act as reinforcers. A male rat will run increasingly rapidly down a runway for the reward of mounting a female, although he is pulled off before his aims are accomplished (Sheffield, Wulff, & Backer, 1951). It is difficult to interpret such a consequence as a drive reducer!

Secondary Drive/Reinforcement The drive theory of motivation assumes that cues paired with primary (drive reducing) rewards may become rewards in their own right. We may have a secondary drive for attention because attention has been paired with the satisfaction of many primary drives in the past. If we examine surveys of the research showing this process, such as Mackintosh (1974) or Nevin (1973) or Gollub (1977), it becomes clear that the pairing of a cue with a primary reward lends that cue very temporary and fragile reinforcing power (see Chapter 9). On the other hand, cues paired with aversive events, such as electric shock, gain quite considerable power. This has led some drive theorists (e.g., Brown, 1953) to suggest that learned fear is the basis of all motivation. Harlow (1953b) countered that it is the drive theorists who need to be nervous and fearful.

Drive and Learning Rate Common sense tells us that motivation may aid learning but that learning does not improve with increases in the strength of biological drives. Would a food-deprived class of children learn more rapidly than a food-sated class? The research cited to show the beneficial effects of drive on learning involves very simple situations and very simple learned behaviors. Broadhurst (1957) and Spence (1956) are often cited as having provided evidence for the increase in learning rate when drive is increased, but their data probably do not generalize well. Broadhurst observed the effect of air deprivation on the learning of an underwater Y-maze in rats, and Spence's data involve eyelid conditioning in humans. Drive, in Spence's case, was manipulated, for example, by varying the strength of a puff of air directed at the subject's cornea. Increases in hunger, thirst, or other drives may lead to increased speed of running in an alley, but not to improved performance when the learning is even mildly more challenging (cf. Mackintosh, 1974).

Drive and Spontaneous Activity As drive increases, activity does not necessarily increase. Even the rat, left alone in its box on the stabilimeter, does not increase its activity as its hunger increases. Nor would it be adaptive for the rat to become increasingly active; why burn calories moving around, once it is clear that there is no food to be found and that escape is impossible? Campbell and Sheffield (1953) did show that such a rat will respond more and more vigorously when an experimenter comes to look into its box, but that is hardly the blind energizing effect of drive. The rat does become hungrier and hungrier, and when a member of the species that has fed it in the past comes to look in on it the animal reacts more and more vigorously as the time without food increases. If the rat is checked every half hour, with an accompanying burst of activity on its part at those times, it may appear that its general activity increases with time, especially if its activity is plotted in one- and two-hour blocks.

Allport's Functional Autonomy of Motives

In 1937, long before criticisms of drive theory were popular, the personality theorist Gordon Allport (see Figure 6.4) argued convincingly against such theories. He believed that both instinct theories (such as McDougall's) and drive theories (such as Hull's and Freud's) were fundamentally in error. What such theories attempt to do, he claimed, is reduce the seemingly infinite diversity of adult motives to a few instincts or biological drives. For example, if a person is motivated by the desire to keep life as simple as possible, as was Tolstoy after his religious conversion, is that person really manifesting a death wish or the instinct for submission, as Freud and McDougall respectively suggested?

Allport felt that adult motives were far too varied and unique to be reduced to a few basic instincts or drives. (Interestingly, he published a paper listing more than 17,000 trait names corresponding to the same number of motives; see Allport & Odbert, 1935.) How then do we deal with motivation? Do we just conclude that a given individual may be motivated by any of an infinite set of motives and leave it at that?

FIGURE 6.4   Gordon Allport, 1897–1967. Allport, a psychologist and professor at Harvard University, was a noted personality theorist. He was best known for his theory that adult motives may stem from the basic motives of the infant but soon become functionally autonomous. *Courtesy of the Archives of the History of American Psychology*

What we can do is try to understand how this uniqueness comes about. How do the many motives of adulthood gain their power? Allport suggested that they do so because of an earlier connection with the basic motives (instincts and drives) of the infant but that they subsequently become functionally autonomous.

Consider the infant, motivated by hunger, curiosity, and other basic drives. There is a shiny button on a tabletop, out of reach of a crawling child. To get the button, the infant stands (and falls, and stands, and so on). Now it is doing something new, and that something becomes self-motivating. The infant stands whenever it can, until standing is easy and it tries to walk, which itself becomes self-motivating. Once the infant masters walking, it runs; once it can run, it hops; and so on. Watch an infant who has managed to get into an adult's chair for the first time; it is safe to say that the child will repeat the action again and again.

Consider a man who begins work in a furniture factory to earn money to buy food and to satisfy other basic needs. Years pass and his skill in his craft grows, as does his salary. Then times change and the public is not willing to pay the high price charged for finely made furniture. The factory changes to a piecework pay system and the premium is thus placed on quantity, not quality. Yet, the craftsman will not hurry his work; although his income suffers, he still takes the time to do the best job he can. His work, originally done for money, has become functionally autonomous; it is done for its own sake.

In these cases, activity is initially done in the service of a basic motive, such as an instinct or drive, but it becomes autonomous—free of that motive. The connection with the earlier motive is thus historical but not functional. In our lives and in the behavior of animals there are countless instances of similarly autonomous motives, and it is difficult for the drive or instinct theories to account for them.

One example cited by Allport has been rediscovered and termed the contrafreeloading or the Protestant ethic effect. This effect was discussed in Chapter 5. It occurs when we train a pigeon to peck a key or a rat to press a lever and then make free food available. Even though the food is placed in a dish right next to the animal, it will still "do its job," so to speak, and peck or press the lever much as it did before the free food was available. Why is this? Well, it only occurs if the animal has a fairly extended history of pecking or pressing for food. Originally there is no question that the animal works solely for the grain or the food pellet produced, but is it possible that work-

ing becomes functionally autonomous? I have seen cases in which a pigeon pecked normally when its behavior was reinforced with grain according to a fixed-interval schedule. During the early part of each fixed interval, the bird escaped from the box it was in and walked around its end to the food hopper where it ate freely. It then returned to the box and pecked as usual until the end of the interval and the delivery of reinforcement. Had the bird not gained unusual amounts of weight, which led to an investigation, no one would have been the wiser, since the bird's record of pecking was completely normal. Is this analogous to the furniture maker? If not, why did the bird return to "do its work" so regularly?

The best example of functional autonomy is detectable in your own behavior every time you study for an exam or work on a paper while you are tired, hungry, and cold. Why do you do it? Is it because of a secondary reinforcer in the form of a good grade to come? Such a derived motive depends for its power upon attention and praise associated with good grades, which in turn has been paired with mother and father, and ultimately with food, water, and other basic needs.

How could that be true? How could such an acquired motive be stronger than the primary motives that torment you as you work? How can a motive remotely connected with food, sleep, and comfort be so strong that you work on while hungry, sleepy, and uncomfortable? Your motive for working has become free of basic needs, although it may have depended upon them when you first worked.

Allport points out that all of our activities do not become self-perpetuating; the infant does not go on walking endlessly for the rest of its life. Activities that are self-motivating are "habits in the making"; once we perform them reasonably well they occur only in the service of other motives. The infant may walk for the sake of walking, but we walk to get somewhere or to provide exercise and entertainment. The motivating character of nonperfected habits is what marks athletic, scientific, and artistic endeavors. One can never run the perfect mile, swim the perfect backstroke, perform the ultimate experiment, or write a perfect essay or poem, and we may therefore spend a lifetime trying.

Harlow's Case Against Drive

Harry Harlow spent many years running the primate laboratories at the University of Wisconsin and many readers must be aware of his work on "mother love." Some may be aware of his work demonstrating learning set, or "learning to learn." Along with these things, Harlow often and caustically criticized drive theory over the years, arguing for the far greater influence of external stimulation as the determinant of motivation.

Harlow launched strong attacks on drive theory in two papers published in 1953. He criticised the belief that biological needs are significant bases for motivation, and that so-called acquired needs are derived from them. Thus, unlike Allport, Harlow doubted that physiological drives play a major role in motivation, even in infancy. The following list highlights the main points of Harlow's criticism:

1. The human fetus responds to tactual stimulation before it has had any opportunity to experience hunger or thirst. Such biological needs are therefore not the basis for later needs for contact, as shown, for example, by his infant monkeys and the famous "cloth mother."

2. We routinely act *in spite of* hunger, pain, sex, temperature, and other basic needs; it is strange therefore to view our actions as ultimately dependent upon such things.

3. Most of us have never known true hunger or thirst; such drives are therefore largely irrelevant to our experience.

4. Strong drives are inimical to most learning. For example, a food-deprived child will not learn faster; it will close its eyes and cry.

5. Saccharine, a nonnutritive substance, acts

as a marvelous reinforcer, although it obviously reduces no biological drive.

Harlow believed that drive reduction played little role in learning and cited an example as proof. In his years of work with rhesus monkeys, he routinely fed them before the experimental session, even though food was to be used as a reward. During a session, correct choices by the monkey were reinforced with raisins, and errors were not. But rhesus monkeys have cheek pouches in which they typically accumulate a store of raisins, releasing them into their throats whenever they wish. Thus, when an error is made and no raisin received, the monkey just releases a raisin and rewards itself! Drive reduction occurs whenever the animal wishes it to and thus it should never learn. But it does learn, leading Harlow to say that "the Lord was unaware of drive reduction theory when he created or allowed the evolution of the rhesus." (1953a)

As the alternative to the drive theory of motivation, Harlow stressed the importance of external stimulation, leading to curiosity, exploration, and manipulation. Rats learn to press bars to explore a maze and chimps and monkeys eagerly manipulate toys and puzzles. Curiosity and exploration are the important motives, not hunger, thirst, and other so-called primary drives.

But how can Harlow refute the irrefutable argument we noted some time ago? Is it not true that from early in life we and other organisms learn that exploration and manipulation often lead to products that reduce basic drives? The curious animal finds the food and the incurious finds nothing, right? This is a difficult argument to counter, but Harlow felt that he had done so.

He pointed out that this argument, which explains exploration and manipulation as secondary reinforcers, cannot account for the extraordinary persistence of such behaviors. Monkeys have manipulated mechanical puzzles for ten hours straight, with little sign of slowing down. One of Harlow's students, Butler, trained monkeys in a discrimination problem in which the reward was a 30-second view through a window, which allowed the animal to see other monkeys in the animal colony. This experiment was run for four hours per day, included 200 trials per day, five days per week, and ended because Butler could not stand to continue. During all of this time, the monkeys showed no sign of tiring of the task. Harlow suggested that no basic drive is so persistent and that 200 swallows would ban the strongest hunger.

If manipulation and exploration are conditioned reinforcers, then they should extinguish after numerous presentations without food, water, or other primary reinforcers. But they persist and persist, showing no decline in strength. A typical pattern in primates given a new toy or a new area to explore consists of an initial high rate of activity, followed by a decrease, and then a gradual increase up to some stable and amazingly durable final level. This is why he said that it is the drive theorists and not the monkeys who should be anxious!

Many treatments of Harlow's theory of motivation conclude that he was proposing the addition of a set of external drives to the set of internal drives stressed by drive theorists. Thus, we add drives to explore, manipulate, and touch to the standard drives of hunger, thirst, sex, warmth, and so on. This does not seem to be the message in his writings on the subject and, late in life, when he was asked at dinner, he made his opinion clear. According to Harlow (personal communication), he was not proposing to add external drives to the list of basic drives; he was arguing that physiological drives are almost wholly irrelevant and that motivation is dependent upon external drives—period.

4. OTHER ASPECTS OF HULL'S WORK

Aside from the basics of Hull's theory, covered above, the most important aspect of his work was the amazing influence he had on those who became his students and collaborators. Extremely capable people, such as Kenneth Spence, Neal Miller, O. H. Mowrer, Frank Logan, and others spent extremely productive careers in promoting what was essentially Hull's cause. This is not to say that all agreed with Hull; each disagreed on a number of fundamental matters. But all agreed in the general program that Hull proposed; psychology was to be the objective analysis of behavior in S-R terms and investigations were seen as the testing of hypotheses. This way of looking at things is still very popular today, especially since each of Hull's followers produced more students of his own and thus a significant number of current experimental psychologists trace their ancestry to Hull, in a manner of speaking. We will briefly discuss the contributions of Kenneth Spence and Neal Miller, two of Hull's best-known followers. In addition, we will discuss David McClelland's work; he is not widely thought of as a follower of Hull, but his method for assessing needs (for example, for achievement) is based on Hull's theory.

Kenneth W. Spence's Contribution

Spence did his doctoral work at Yale, where his research was directed by Robert Yerkes, not by Hull. But there is no doubt that Hull had an enormous influence on Spence and that Spence contributed greatly to Hull's theory. Spence later worked at the University of Iowa and then at Texas, where he died in 1967. His major contributions were his theory of discrimination learning, which is still current, his interpretation of inhibition, and his emphasis on incentive motivation rather than biological drive.

Discrimination Learning and Transposition Spence proposed his account for discrimination learning in 1937 as a counter to the Gestaltist Köhler (e.g., 1925). Köhler claimed to have shown that discrimination learning consists mainly of learning relationships among stimuli, rather than absolute values. Thus, we learn *darker* or *bigger*, rather than specific values of darkness and size.

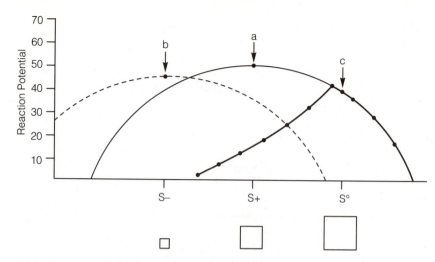

FIGURE 6.5   The Y axis scales tendency to respond and the X axis depicts a continuum of square size. The broken line represents tendency to not respond to S−; its form shows the range of generalization. The solid line centered at S+ (a) shows the tendency to respond to S+ and to other stimuli on the continuum. The diagonal line represents the algebraic sum of the two concave-downward curves. As is apparent, the tendency to respond (Reaction Potential) is greatest at S°.

Consider Figure 6.5. Suppose that a subject were trained to respond to the middle-sized square and not to the smallest square. What would happen if the subject were given a choice between the middle and the largest squares? In such problems, subjects ranging from chickens to children chose relationally. In this case, the subject most likely would choose the larger square; what the subject had learned originally was to choose the larger of the two squares when the choice had been restricted to the two smallest. Given a choice between another two, *transposition* occurs, meaning that the response is based on the relationship of size (larger).

Köhler and others stressed such data as evidence that we do not learn to react to specific stimuli; we always respond to relationships, such as warmer/colder, larger/smaller, and brighter/darker. This exemplified the Gestalt emphasis on innate organizing mechanisms (which we will examine in Chapter 7), and the fact that it occurred in chickens showed that it was a fundamental ability. For Hull (1943), Gestalt theory was a "doctrine of despair" and "philosophical fog."

Spence was to account for transposition in Hull's terms.

Spence's explanation was simple and seemed to remove the need to appeal to mysterious learned relationships. According to Spence, what appears to be transposition can be explained as the simple effects of stimulus generalization. Consider Figure 6.5 again. Suppose that during the initial training the subject learned to respond to the middle square and that the strength of this tendency ($_sH_R$) is indicated by point *a* in the figure. The curve on which that point lies represents the effect of stimulus generalization, spreading with decrement from *a* in both directions along the stimulus dimension of square size. Similarly, suppose that a tendency to not respond ($_sI_R$) develops at $S−$ and that its strength is represented by point *b*. Again, this inhibitory response tendency spreads in both directions.

Since these overlapping gradients represent opposed tendencies—to respond and to not respond—the tendency to respond to any value of the square-size dimension is the algebraic sum of the gradients at that point. Thus, when we pres-

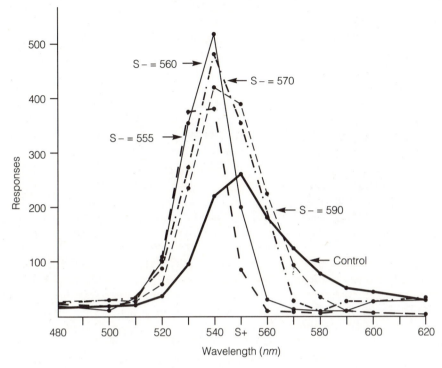

FIGURE 6.6 Results of Hanson's peak-shift study. The figure shows generalization gradients obtained during extinction testing for five groups of subjects. S+ was always 550nm and S− was either 590, 570, 560, or 555nm. The control group was trained only with S+ (550nm).

ent the old *S+* along with a new stimulus, the large square *S*, the net tendency to respond to the new stimulus is greater than that corresponding to *S+*. The subject will respond (or respond more) to the new *S*. What appears to be the learning of relationships, evidenced as transposition when the new large square is presented with *S+*, is merely the result of learning to respond (or not) to specific values and the summing of associated generalization gradients. The "configurationalists," as Spence (1937) called the Gestaltists, were answered!

The Peak Shift and Gradient Summation Other research has lent support to Spence's model, although it does have failings (see Mackintosh, 1974). One conspicuous source of support for the theory in general is the peak shift, a phenomenon

that seems made to order for it. Peak shift was first reported by Hanson (1959), who trained groups of pigeons to peck a disk illuminated with a hue of 550nm (greenish yellow), generated by a monochromenter. Pecks were reinforced occasionally with food, and one group, the control subjects, were then given a generalization test. During the test, the training stimulus was presented for 30-second periods along with twelve test stimuli, ranging from 480nm (blue) to 600nm (red). In Figure 6.6, the gradient labeled *control* shows the rates of response to each of these stimuli, averaged over the test session. It should be noted that this test was carried out in extinction; that is, no food reinforcement was given for responding to any of the stimuli. The logic was that such a test provides a measure of the tendency to respond to each test stimulus, as a result of the previous training to respond to 550nm ($S+$). The control gradient is thus a gradient of stimulus generalization.

Other groups were trained differently before the generalization test was given. Four discrimination groups were presented with a random series of $S+$ (550nm), along with a second stimulus ($S-$). Food was never associated with $S-$ and training was continued until a discrimination criterion was met. This required different amounts of training, since the $S-$ for each group was different; it was either 555, 560, 570, or 590nm. Now, 590nm is yellow enough to be quite easily discriminable from that of 550nm, at least for a human observer. But 555nm is virtually indistinguishable from 550nm. If simultaneously presented, we can distinguish them, but if presented successively in an unpredictable sequence, they are very difficult to distinguish. (Actually, Hanson found that his birds could distinguish differences in wavelength as little as one nm, so the task was evidently not impossible.)

The famous results of Hanson's test appear in Figure 6.6. Note that the gradients for the discrimination groups (555, 560, 570, 590nm) all show peaks at stimulus values different from 550nm, the old $S+$; only the control group showed a peak there. And note also that the degree to which the peak was shifted depended on its distance from $S+$, the degree of shift successively greater in the gradients for the 590, 570, 560, and 555nm groups.

Hanson considered the detailed predictions that Spence's model would make in such a situation and found that all were confirmed by his data, except one that is relatively unimportant. That is to say, the summation of hypothetical gradients of excitation around $S+$ and of inhibition (tendency to not respond) around $S-$ accounted well for the outcomes of the generalization tests.

The salient failure of Spence's model lay in its failure to account for the overall area of the gradients. Thus, if the discrimination gradients represent the algebraic sum of an excitatory gradient around $S+$ and an inhibitory gradient centered at $S-$, why are the postdiscrimination gradients all higher or larger than the control gradient? Can subtraction lead to an increase in something, in this case total responding?

Spence never took into account the effects of training procedure, and he was not aware of what we now know as behavioral contrast. As a matter of fact, Hanson was not aware of it either, since Reynolds's (1961a) report was yet to come. We will discuss behavioral contrast later; for now, note that Hanson's data seemed to lend strong support to Spence's model.

Inhibition and Frustration Spence suggested in his 1937 paper that the inhibition that came from nonrewarded responding and that produced the gradients of inhibition around $S-$ was not due to the accumulation of I_R and the development of conditioned inhibition ($_SI_R$) as responding to $S-$ ceased. Rather, he proposed that inhibition was due to *frustration*, a reaction produced when responding occurs and a reward is anticipated but is not received. Spence carried this idea further in the 1950s and 1960s. Abram Amsel and Allan Wagner continued to argue that the failure to be reinforced for behaving does not work in the passive way that Hull proposed.

Suppose that you are doing something that has led to food or other reinforcement in the past. You are working for wages, dieting to lose weight, or studying to do well on an exam. In the past, these actions enabled you to gain money, lose weight, or get a good grade (respectively). In Hull's terms, you are following the stimuli of the world sequence, in some state of need, and expending energy as you work. If reinforcement occurs, it reduces the (secondary) drives for money, weight loss, and achievement. This leads to an increase in $_SH_R$ (and thus, $_SE_R$), which easily exceeds the I_R that accumulates with effort expended and the $_SI_R$ that increases when you slow down work. We learn to do things that end in the reduction of a primary or a secondary drive because the increase in $_SH_R$ and $_SE_R$ is greater than the inhibitory influences involved ($I_R + {}_SI_R$).

Spence suggested that the failure to be reinforced has a different and a greater effect than Hull believed. In a situation in which we have experienced reinforcement in the past, part of our activity is energized by the fractional anticipatory goal response, r_G–s_G. This is simply a way of saying that previous reinforcements have led to such anticipatory goal responses. We expect a reward, and this is accounted for by the fact that we are accustomed to a reward when the sequence ends, and as we go through the sequence we are already making little r_G's: We are receiving the money, seeing the scale in the morning, and receiving the exam grade. We anticipate the reward just as that rat did; the rat, when following its normal route to food, salivates, licks its chops, and smells what it expects to be at the end of the trip. What happens when the customary reward is not there? Spence, later followed by Amsel and others, suggested that nonreward in the context of reward produces a strong response, termed R_F, or the primary frustration response.

R_F, like R_G, becomes attached to stimuli that precede it, and thus fractional anticipatory frustration responses may begin to occur. These responses, r_F's, produce stimuli just as r_G's do; hence, we have r_F–s_F's occurring during the sequence. Nonreward may at first slow us or the rat down; we cannot be certain that the goal object we are expecting will be there on that trial. But it often is, and the little s_F's act as do any other stimuli; they are present during drive reduction, so they are attached to the responses that occurred prior to drive reduction. They thus add to the total stimuli attached to each response and increase the total $_sH_R$ for each response.

Spence suggested that this means that subjects rewarded 100 percent of the time may not perform as well as subjects that are not given rewards on every trial. This has been shown to be true in a number of experiments, such as that by Goodrich (1959), whose results are displayed in Figure 6.7. Goodrich trained two groups of rats to run down a runway for food placed in the goal box. Rats in the 100-percent group found a food pellet in the goal box on every trial, whereas those in

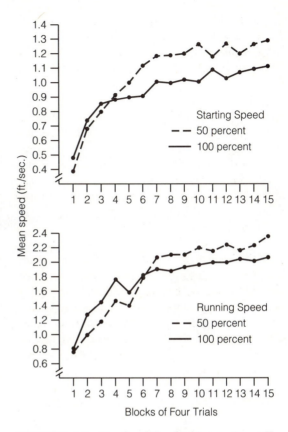

FIGURE 6.7 Results of Goodrich's experiment II. Mean starting and running speeds for groups reinforced on 50 or 100 percent of trials (dashed and solid lines, respectively).

the 50-percent group found a pellet only half the time and there was no telling which times they would be. As training progressed, those in the 100-percent group increased their speed of running the alley faster than did those in the 50-percent group. The latter group was fed only half the time, so $_sH_R$ would increase more slowly and nonreward was producing frustration responses, which would interfere with running. But later in training, the 50-percent group caught up with and surpassed the 100-percent group. Evidently, the fact that the rats continued to run means that s_F became attached to that behavior and gave them the final edge over the 100-percent group.

Amsel (1962) showed how the frustration effect (FE) and r_F-s_F could account for the partial reinforcement effect (PRE), or the fact that subjects that are rewarded on only some trials go on responding longer when no reward is given than do subjects rewarded on every trial. The explanation is essentially that given above. Wagner (1963) similarly emphasized the effects of frustration, suggesting that courage consists of action done in the face of frustration. When we or the rat head for a goal that may or may not be there, and r_F-s_F has not become attached to our responses and it thus just slows us down, we are displaying courage.

Incentive Motivation A number of Hull's critics showed that learning occurred in the absence of reward, a finding clearly in violation of Hull's postulate IV. Spence invented *incentive motivation*, which Hull symbolized as K (for "Kenneth"). We will show how K was used in this regard in the next chapter, where we consider Tolman. For now, we will just look at what it is and what it does. K, or incentive motivation, refers to the motivating effect of the amount and quality of a reward. A dish of bran mash or a thick chocolate milkshake are clearly different from a small, dry pellet and a glass of diet root beer, and in fact, their effects are different.

By the 1950s, Spence also greatly modified Hull's theory by proposing that habit strength ($_sH_R$) does not depend upon reward in the form of drive reduction; rather, $_sH_R$ just increases in strength with repetition, and performance is the energizing of such habits by drive and incentive. This means that learning depends only upon practice; you can see that Spence had come to agree with Watson and Guthrie!

Finally, Spence proposed a biological basis for K, which is quite reasonable. Remember that K represents the motivating influence produced by the amount and quality of the reinforcer. Imagine the milkshake and the diet root beer, which surely differ in quality. They also differ in the reaction they produce. The root beer doesn't produce much, while the thought of the milkshake makes one salivate, swallow, and move the tongue around. These are fractional antedating goal responses. The better the goal object, the bigger the little r_G-s_G, since the bigger was the R_G when such objects were encountered in the past.

Therefore, the amount and quality of the reward produces a bigger physiological response from us (in the form of r_G), and the way it feels to make r_G (that is, s_G) is more noticeable. Since K also depends upon the amount and quality of the reward, why shouldn't K be simply s_G? The sum of the feedback produced by r_G's is what we mean by incentive.

Kenneth W. Spence worked long and hard for Hull and later for his own revised Hullian theory. Hull was mindful of Spence's assistance in preparing the preface to *Principles of Behavior* (1943), although at that time he was not certain of Spence's name. Hull wrote, "To Kenneth L. Spence I owe a debt of gratitude which cannot be adequately indicated in this place." Let us see how the thought of Hull and Spence influenced the study of human motivation, as reflected in the work of McClelland.

Need for Achievement and Other Needs

Recall that Murray compiled an inventory of the needs of Harvard undergraduates in 1938, categorizing them as viscerogenic (primary) or psychogenic (secondary). He also proposed methods for the assessment of degrees of need, such as the *thematic apperception test*, or TAT. Subjects were presented with a variety of pictures—such as two men working on what appears to be a machine, a boy gazing out over an open book, or a father–son conversation—and were asked to write a brief story about each picture. The stories were then analyzed to gauge the kind and degree of motives possessed by the subject. Is this sensible?

This is the rationale for the TAT, which David McClelland and his associates have used extensively (e.g., McClelland, Atkinson, Clark, & Lowell, 1953). They assume that a cue arouses pain, pleasure, or other reactions because it has been paired previously with affect. For example, the pleasures of eating are accompanied by all sorts of cues, such as the sight and smell of food. When one of these cues appears by itself, it produces part of the affect present when eating last took place. McClelland (see Figure 6.8) and others viewed the partial reaction produced by the cue as an instance of Hull's fractional anticipatory goal response. The partial reaction produced by the cue acts as a motive for the full affect, or Hull's goal response (R_G). McClelland, 1985, discusses this interpretation more fully.

Here is where the TAT comes in. Depending upon an individual's motivational state at the time, the content of the picture descriptions will contain fractional goal responses (r_G) produced in the same way that a picture of food produces salivation in a hungry subject! In a 1949 study carried out with sailors deprived of food for one, four, or sixteen hours, McClelland and his associates were able to distinguish the one- and four-hour subjects from the sixteen-hour subjects, based on food-related themes appearing in their TAT responses.

This demonstration was used as evidence that the TAT really *can* assess levels of motivation, and subsequent studies attempted to use it to measure needs for affiliation, power, aggression, and other motives. The real effort has been directed at the assessment of nAch (need for achievement), however, since many view this as an indispensable quality if one is to succeed in life.

McClelland, Clark, Roby, and Atkinson (1949) tried to show that the TAT could accurately measure nAch in an experiment carried out with over 200 male subjects in the Boston area. During a 50-minute class period, subjects were given seven tasks, each taking three to four minutes to complete. The tasks included anagram problems and motor problems requiring that the subjects write backwards as quickly as possible, for example. Some subjects were given relaxed instructions, stating that the tasks were being tried out and their performance on them was nothing to worry about. The other groups were given quite different instructions:

FIGURE 6.8 David McClelland 1917–. Psychologist best known for his work assessing nAch (need for achievement). *Photo courtesy of David McClelland*

The tests which you are taking directly indicate a person's general level of intelligence. These tests have been taken from a group of tests which were used to select people of high administrative capacity for positions in Washington during the past war. Thus in addition to general intelligence, they bring out an individual's capacity to organize material, his ability to evaluate crucial situations quickly and accurately; in short, these tests demonstrate whether or not a person is suited to be a leader.

They went on to say that the Navy was conducting these tests to determine which universities are turning out the best leaders, and scores supposedly obtained by Wesleyan University students were shown to some groups.

One group was then given the tests and shown that they all performed far below the level of their Wesleyan counterparts. This was appropriately called the "failure" group. The other two groups were dropped because of what the experimenters interpreted as odd behavior (!). This was the "success-only" group whose members were told that they had performed above the level of the Wesleyan subjects. The "ego-involved" group consisted of subjects who were not told the scores of the Wesleyan subjects. Finally, one group ("success/failure") was allowed to taste success by being given very low norms (Wesleyan scores) on the first test, only to fail badly on the second, for which they were given very high norms.

All of these subjects were then asked to write stories about four TAT pictures and these were analyzed for nAch. How was that done? The raters counted up the images and themes that referred to achievement in the stories. This included references to needs, impediments, effort, goals, affect, and helps and hindrances. For example, a response might include, "The men in the picture are trying their best to fix the machine and it is a difficult job and time is short, but they will feel proud when they achieve their goal."

As you might expect, the relaxed group scored lowest in nAch, the failure group scored higher, and scores of the success/failure group were the highest. Both of the latter groups had been read the achievement-inducing instructions, and the success/failure group had been allowed that taste of achievement which aroused nAch even more, especially after their subsequent "failure." The success-only group and the ego-involved group were dropped; the former group showed too much nAch, while those in the latter group were so tense that their TAT responses were "uninterpretable."

Since it is possible to assess nAch, it would be nice to know what it is that is being assessed and whether there is any relation between nAch scores and other kinds of performance. Murray initially defined nAch as the motive to "do as well as possible as quickly as possible and to outdo others." One can easily see what is meant by that: *Competitiveness* is a close synonym. But do TAT ratings of nAch correlate with performance in general? McClelland assures us that nAch predicts a variety of forms of achievement, including the achievements of entire nations and the success of businessmen.

Neal Miller's Contribution

Miller obtained his doctorate at Yale as a student of Hull and immediately traveled to the Vienna Psychoanalytic Institute, where he spent several months of 1935. The purpose was to learn as much as possible about Freudian therapy; Hull intended to incorporate whatever he could of psychoanalysis into his theory. Dollard and Miller (1950) published a book that more or less accomplished that aim.

From 1936 to 1966 Miller was a member of the faculty at Yale and thereafter was associated with the Rockefeller University in New York City. Although Miller has not proposed major innovations in theory, he masterfully carried out research and contributed greatly in several areas. We will consider three of his achievements.

The first and most important is his 1941 book with Dollard, *Social Learning and Imitation*. This was not only a simplified version of Hull for the masses but also the beginning of social learning theory, a position now associated with Albert Bandura. Secondly, he showed how Hull's principles could apply to conflict, as stressed by Lewin and other Gestalt-influenced psychologists, who explained such phenomena in terms of fields of attraction and repulsion, a view clearly repulsive to Hull. Thirdly, he performed a classic experiment showing that fear could be viewed as an acquired drive.

Social Learning Theory Miller and Dollard (1941) greatly simplified Hull's mass of postulates and theorems to four basic elements: drive, cue, response, and reward. Drives make us act, the act is a response, the response occurs in the presence of a cue, and rewards that follow the response reduce drives and connect the response to the cue. This is essentially what a barebones caricature of Hull's (or Thorndike's) theory asserts and it has its uses. Miller and Dollard provide many examples of applications. For example, the following amusing passage explains why we like to hear ourselves talk:

> Tom heard himself crying and babbling repeatedly just before major reduction of primary drive occurred. Hearing himself babble, therefore, acquired a secondary rewarding character. Hearing someone else talk is sufficiently like hearing oneself cry or babble to tend to evoke the same relaxation responses. Thus, hearing his own vocalizations came to indicate to the child that the goal was in sight. The same logic also applies, of course, to the mother's footstep, the stimulus pattern of her voice, face, dress, and the like. (Miller & Dollard, 1941, p. 139)

This account of secondary reinforcement is, of course, Hull's account, and it plays a part in the explanation of imitation, which led directly to current views in social learning theory. All of us who have been through the public education system realize the importance of imitation, or the influence of modeling; this determines in large part our values, our heroes, and our clothing and hair styles. Is imitation an instinct, as William James (1890) and McDougall (1908) felt, or is it learned? The matter is by no means settled, but Miller and Dollard proposed a theory that can account for imitation in terms of Hull's principles, and Bandura holds a somewhat similar view, as we will see.

Miller and Dollard provided evidence that imitation is a learned behavior, dependent upon reward (drive reduction), just as other behavior is learned. A simple example involves a child who happens to run to the door to greet Daddy at the same time that an older sibling runs to the door. the older child may have some expectation about what Daddy may have brought, but the younger child just happens to do what the older did on that occasion. The father has candy for both of them and running to Daddy at the door is thus rewarded. As Miller and Dollard put it, this establishes such activity as matched-dependent behavior. The matching, or copying, of the older child's behavior becomes a cue for such behavior, dependent upon the consequences of such imitative behavior. And it is easily interpreted in terms of drive (the younger child's appetite for candy),

cue (the older child's running), response (doing what the older child does), and reward (the candy from Daddy).

Miller and Dollard presented data from a series of experiments, first using rats as subjects, and then showing parallel results with children as subjects. They demonstrated the learning of imitation (or of nonimitation—doing other than the leader does), as well as the generalization of imitating to new similar leaders. They also showed generalization to new situations: A leader imitated in a two-choice problem is imitated in a four-choice problem, whether the subjects are rats or children. Children also quickly learned to discriminate models; "good" models were rewarded and imitated, while "bad" ones were not rewarded and therefore were not imitated. In some cases the good model was a younger child and the bad one was a Yale University graduate student, but fourth-grade children were still quick to learn to imitate the child. Finally, generalization to quite dissimilar situations was shown. Imitative behavior consisting of picking one of two boxes generalized to pulling a ring.

Miller and Dollard noted that good models tend to be older, of higher social status, more intelligent, and technically competent. It is also important that the imitator pay attention to important aspects of the leader's behavior and that the imitator have the cue/response connections available to perform the behavior required. This is what Bandura (1976) calls the capacity for "motoric reproduction." Miller and Dollard also felt it was important that the model be "correct"; as they pointed out, we do not imitate those who make mistakes often. We discriminate leaders worth imitating from those who are not worth it.

Miller and Dollard stressed repeatedly the importance of generalized imitation; what is learned is not the performance of specific behaviors in specific situations with a specific model. In fact, "the wish to match behavior with another can itself become a secondary drive." This point of view was taken up by Baer (e.g., Baer & Sherman, 1964) and it makes a lot of sense. Throughout life, we find that when we do as specific ("good") models do, we benefit. In time, we feel comfortable doing as such models do and uncomfortable when we do otherwise. Needless to say, a good model is "good" only in some situations. We may not imitate the eating habits of our swim coach, but we are apt to attend to and imitate his or her swim strokes.

Bandura and Social Learning Theory   Albert Bandura was educated at the University of Iowa during the period when Kenneth Spence was a faculty member. Although Bandura is often cast otherwise, his thinking has shown Spence's influence; his research is clearly similar to Hull's and this may account for some of the controversies that have arisen between Bandura and followers of Skinner (see Chapter 8).

Bandura's classic research appears in too many other texts to warrant giving it much space here. In 1965 he published the famous Bobo doll study, showing that imitative aggression toward an inflated toy depended upon the consequences received by adult models whom the children watched attacking the doll. Punished models resulted in less aggression on the part of the children, although when queried the children could certainly tell what the model had done. This finding and other aspects of the results of that study were mighty impressive to Bandura, who subsequently proposed a new version of Miller and Dollard's adaptation of Hull, which has become known as social learning theory (Bandura, 1986, renamed his version social cognitive theory).

Incredibly, Bandura (e.g., 1977) attacked the generalized-imitation theory of Miller and Dollard and of Baer and Sherman (1964), claiming that it requires that we should imitate everyone. He also claimed that the theory requires that imitative behavior occur immediately; if imitation occurs an hour later, the theory is wrong! Additionally, the imitative act must be followed immediately by reward, according to that theory. Or so wrote Bandura.

After an unfair critique of Miller and Dollard (via Baer), Bandura proposed his alternative theory. He emphasized the fact that imitation need not occur immediately, and that when it does occur it need not be accompanied by conspicuous reward. Instead of imitation as a generalized tendency to do what certain others do, Bandura stresses the processes that must be responsible. Hence, he proposes attention, memory, motoric reproduction, and reinforcement as basic requirements. Interestingly, reinforcement is viewed in a way similar to that of Hull and Spence, as self-generated anticipatory behavior, basically the same as the fractional anticipatory goal response, although Bandura would not use these words.

What Bandura thinks is important and unique is his emphasis on the role of vicarious experience, symbolic activity, and self-regulation via cognitive activity. We will discuss some of this in Chapter 8, but it should be pointed out here that the gist of Bandura's theory is Hullian, although Bandura uses different terms. Both theorists stressed what was later called molecular treatments of behavior—that is, emphasizing discrete stimuli, responses, rewards, cognitions, and so on, rather than larger, molar, variables (this was pointed out by Malone, 1990).

Conflict   How do we deal with the fields of forces that seem to be operating as we debate whether to go to our room to study or to go with the gang to a movie? It often seems that we are drawn by separate forces in such situations. In other situations, we have other conflicting forces. Suppose, for example, you have a toothache and are told you need a root canalization (root canal). Others have told you the nature of the procedure and it seems very difficult to submit to it, although we know that it is painless and that it may save the tooth. The tendencies to approach and avoid such an operation seem to be in conflict.

Such conflicts may also be cast in terms of Hull's fractional anticipatory goal responses, although Miller did not do this. He did show that such conflicting response tendencies could be measured as behaviors and that we could predict the outcome of such conflicts. Briefly, what Miller did (e.g., 1944) was to train rats to run down an alley for food, and, once he established the tendency to run, he attached a strain gauge to the rat with a harness so that he could measure the force exerted by the rat as it ran. As the rat ran toward the goal of food, its pull on the strain gauge increased and Miller had a measure of the gradient of approach toward the food. The rat's pull on the strain gauge steadily increased as it neared the food.

Next, Miller shocked the rats at the end of the alley, which contained the food, thus making that area aversive. Again, with a harness and strain gauge attached to the rat, he measured the tendency of the animal to move away from that area. In this case, the pull was once again strongest near the end of the alley and became weaker as the rat moved further from the end box. This was the avoidance gradient.

Miller now had a measure of the tendency to approach the end box, because of the food that had been received there, and of the tendency to avoid it, because of the shock that had been given there. The avoidance gradient was steeper, ending closer to the end box, and the approach gradient was relatively shallow, extending farther from the end box and thus closer to the start box. Figure 6.9 presents Miller's results.

Suppose that we take the rats and place them in the start box. In theory, they should wander around until they moved into the approach gradient, at which time they should start for the goal box, accelerating as the gradient rises. They should then hit the avoidance gradient, at which time they should slow down, move about, and eventually move back toward the start. Then, the approach gradient should set them moving back toward the end box, accelerating until they reach the avoidance gradient.

Miller's rats did better than that. At the point where the gradients of approach and avoidance cross, the net tendency to approach or avoid is theoretically zero. Now, few researchers have rats or other subjects that obey theoretical principles, but Miller did. He reported that his rats advanced to the point where the approach and avoidance gradients crossed (and the tendency to move forward or backward was balanced) and

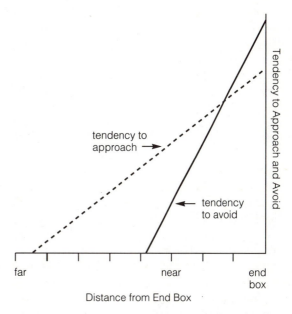

FIGURE 6.9   Miller's hypothetical gradients of tendency to approach and to avoid, plotted according to distance along a straight runway.

then stopped! Here was the vague field theory of Lewin translated into Hull's quantifiable terms and experimentally verified.

Fear as an Acquired Drive   Hull, as well as many other theorists, assumed that money, attention, and all of the other things that act as reinforcers but that do not satisfy biological (primary needs) gain their power simply by their past association with primary reinforcers. Miller's 1948 experiment is often cited as evidence that such is the case. Miller showed that stimuli paired with painful electric shock became secondary aversive reinforcers and that they then acted as other reinforcers.

As an aversive reinforcer, shock may be used to motivate behavior. It then acts as *aversive drive*, meaning that it produces escape and avoidance behavior. It may also be used to reinforce behavior that eliminates or avoids it. Can it be shown clearly that stimuli paired with an aversive reinforcer can also motivate and reinforce behavior?

Miller's rats were placed in a two-compartment box, with one side painted white and the other black. The rats were placed one at a time in the white compartment and given ten trials with electric shock, coming from the grid on the compartment floor. On the first trial, the rat was placed in the white compartment and, after 60 seconds, it was shocked every five seconds for 60 seconds. If it ran into the black compartment, the rat was safe from shock, since there was no shock grid on the floor. On the second trial, the rat was again placed on the white side and shocked, this time after 30 seconds; again, it could escape by running to the black side. On both trials the escape to the black side was blocked by a door until the shock was turned on. During the remaining eight trials, the shock was on at the moment the rat was placed in the white compartment and the door was opened immediately so the rat could run to the black side and escape the shock.

As you might imagine, this experience made the rats less fond of bright white surroundings then they were to begin with (rats typically prefer darker to brighter areas anyway). Miller then placed each of the rats in the white compartment with no shock present to determine whether the white stimuli had gained fear-producing power. Not surprisingly, all of the 25 rats rushed to the black compartment. Thus, the white surroundings had gained the power of a conditioned aversive reinforcer.

Real reinforcers also strengthen the responses that produce them. In the case of aversive reinforcers, they strengthen behaviors that remove them and thus reduce fear. Miller closed the door between the white and black compartments and placed a small wheel on the door. The door could be opened if the rat turned the wheel a fraction of a turn. Would the rat, in its fear of the white compartment, learn to turn the wheel and thus escape to the black side?

In eight trials, in which a rat was placed in the white compartment and a turn of the wheel was required to open the door and escape the fear-producing stimuli, thirteen of 25 animals did turn the wheel and thus show that acquired fear acted as a reinforcer capable of producing the learning of a new response. A small bar was then placed in the box and the thirteen successful rats were given the opportunity to press it in order to open the door and escape to the black side. This they did, showing that a new behavior could be learned to escape the secondary aversive reinforcer.

This often-cited experiment shows that cues accompanying an aversive stimulus can gain fear-producing power, and new behaviors that produce escape from such stimuli will be reinforced. If only such evidence could be provided in the case of appetitive reinforcers, such as food, and the cues accompanying them, life would be much simpler. We will see in Chapter 9 that this has not been the case and that a lot of the support for the position on conditioned reinforcement maintained by Hull and his followers comes from research in which aversive reinforcers, such as electric shock, were used.

SUMMARY

Hull was the great systematizer and organizer who came at a time when the functionalists, the behaviorists, and the Gestaltists had pretty much displaced the old psychology of Titchener and the introspectionists. Perhaps Hull would have done well whenever he had come along, but the time seemed especially ripe for the sort of institutionalizing of psychology that Hull proposed. (Even today, perhaps, many contemporary psychologists would welcome the appearance of someone who could convincingly put order into the chaos of theories and the disputes of opposing groups, as Hull had done in his time.)

Hull proposed that, despite differences in opinion on other points, there was a broad concensus that living things, including ourselves, could be treated as machines and that behavior could best be analyzed in stimulus-response (S-R) terms. He further assumed that it was absolutely necessary to quantify everything and that it was possible to do so. We did not stress this aspect of his theory, but a reading of any of his works shows that he was a master of attaching numbers to habit strength, motivation, and other variables of his theory in a way that allowed him to make surprisingly accurate predictions. This ability was not shared by his followers, and such efforts did not continue long after his death.

Hull and many of his followers have said that the details of his theory were not particularly important; Hull believed that the hypothetico-deductive method was the key to progress. If we begin with a set of clear statements about learning and constantly test and revise them, we will surely improve our understanding of behavior, even if the set of postulates with which we begin is largely erroneous.

Hull's system was composed almost entirely of intervening variables, which were terms used to relate the diverse independent variables that seemed to covary with a set of diverse dependent variables. For example, a host of factors may lead us to eat, and the increase in eating may be assessed in terms of amount of food eaten, rate of eating, money spent for food, and so on. Hull represented the effects of all of the independent variables on all of the related dependent variables with single terms; in this case, the term is *hunger*, and in other cases it is $_sH_R$ or D or any of over a hundred other intervening variables. This aspect of Hull's theory was anathema to Skinner and is one of the many things that make Skinner's theory basically different from Hull's.

We showed how Hull explained complex phenomena, such as knowledge, foresight, and purpose in terms of simple habit mechanisms. Hull's account leaves out the color and zest of our experience (to which literature, poetry, and the rest of the humanities are devoted), but his account was intended to propose the basic mechanisms that underlie our behavior. He felt that movement-produced stimuli were the basis for knowledge and that chaining could account for foresight. He explained purpose and anticipation in terms of fractional anticipatory goal responses, an expla-

nation that had a long history in psychology and that was adopted by many of his prominent followers.

Hull was always concerned with practical application, although he personally was not concerned with dealing immediately with what the public considers to be pressing problems. We must understand the basic determinants of the rat's behavior and our behavior before we can apply anything. But Hull did suggest in outline form ways in which important practical matters could be treated, and his students were more specific in suggesting practical applications. His seminars at Yale in the late 1930s interpreted the conflicts among nations, blackmail, the learning of speech, lying, rationalization, reasoning, logic, psychoanalysis, and malingering, all in terms of habits strengthened by obvious reinforcers.

The research program begun by David McClelland and his associates in the late 1940s and aimed at assessing nAch was a practical expression of Hullian thinking. Even in 1985, McClelland still saw merit in the approach of Hull. The social learning theory of Miller and Dollard showed how practical Hull's theory could be and how it could account for imitation in a plausible way. This account has been criticized by Bandura, although his alternative is also clearly derived from Hullian-like thinking.

The major criticisms of Hull lie in his insistence, despite disclaimers, on molecular (atomistic) analyses of phenomena. Opponents have charged that such a method assumes that there are some units of behavior and experience that are assumed in advance and that the true nature of behavior can be seen only after observation. Most current psychologists are similarly atomistic, however, so this is really not a strong criticism of Hull's theory.

Hull's emphasis on the hypothetico-deductive approach is easier to criticize, especially since such methods are not currently fashionable. The main reason for this comes from the history of work during the 1940s and early 1950s, when it became apparent that the method was unworkable in practice. It is not possible, as Hull tacitly assumed it was, to decisively test a theorem and therefore perform a crucial experiment. The assertion that all reinforcement depends upon the reduction of a drive was debated for 30 years after Hull proposed that it was so and, to an extent, the debate goes on. If one part of one postulate cannot be adequately tested for truth or falsity in almost half a century, one must question the worth of a theory that requires that such tests be made.

A final criticism of Hull may not be fair, given his aims and his desire to make psychology truly scientific. But his refusal to admit our private experience as a legitimate part of psychology was a break from his behaviorist predecessors and served to alienate a great many other psychologists much more than did Watson's insistence that we dispense with the terms of the introspectionists. Watson still left private experience as part of what we must explain, while Hull believed that it was unworthy of study. Since Hull's time, those theorists who called themselves behaviorists are assumed to deny the existence of private experience. We still feel this influence today.

Hull's students contributed greatly to his work, and we briefly considered the work of Spence and Miller. Spence's theory of discrimination learning is still with us and was a godsend to Hull in the 1930s, when the Gestaltists and others who sympathized with their general point of view opposed the analysis of behavior and experience into units of the kind that Hull proposed. His analysis of transposition in terms of the learning of individual habits generalized to stimuli lying on the same continuum was a stroke of genius at the time and has proven a difficult proposition for later workers in generalization and discrimination to disprove.

Spence also proposed that the effect of non-reinforcement was not a passive process, as Hull had proposed, but that it led to a reaction of frustration and that this reaction produced what Hull had called inhibitory effects. This view was elaborated by his students Amsel and Wagner, who were responsible for the great popularity of frustration theory during the 1960s.

Spence also was responsible for the invention of incentive motivation (K), introduced to deal with data produced by Tolman and his aides, which showed that learning occurs in the absence of drive reduction. Spence suggested that goal objects may produce fractional anticipatory goal responses in proportion to the magnitude and the quality of the goal object and that this may act as an added motivating factor, along with drive, to produce rapid learning.

Miller and Dollard attempted to show how Hull's general principles could account for a variety of human social behavior, particularly imitation. Miller also studied conflict situations using animal subjects and showed how one might measure the tendencies to approach and avoid goal objects. His 1948 study of fear as an acquired drive has become a classic.

GLOSSARY

Automaton A machine, or automatic device, built from parts that are known and the actions of which are understood. Hull suggested that we treat ourselves and animals as automata in order to avoid explanations for our behavior that rely on agents whose properties we do not understand. Thus, *purpose* and *knowledge* are understood only when we have built a machine that shows purpose and knowledge.

Aversive drive Stimulation that leads to activity to escape or avoid it. This commonly refers to electric shock and other things that produce pain. Hunger, which may be painful, is referred to as an appetitive drive, since the object that reduces the drive is viewed as pleasure producing, rather than as pain ending. Hull and his followers used the appetitive/aversive distinction, but it is surely vague and has been criticized widely. For example, when we do something to escape the cold, are we driven by the aversive drive of cold, or the appetitive drive for warmth?

Chain A sequence of behavior that is linked together (as a chain) by the consequences of each response. These consequences may be in the form of movement-produced stimuli or stimuli from outside, as when we recite a poem and each word or line acts as a stimulus for the next response.

Conditioned inhibition A negative habit, or tendency not to do whatever response was last done in the presence of the stimuli involved. Like positive habits ($_sH_R$), conditioned inhibition is reinforced by drive reduction. In this case, the drive reduced is reactive inhibition (I_R), which begins to dissipate when action slows or ceases.

Crucial experiment An experiment that yields results that clearly and unambiguously show that a hypothesis is true or false. There are many such experiments in the physical sciences, such as the Michaelson-Morley experiment, which convinced most observers that the theory that held that space is filled with ether was definitely untrue. Hull's hypothetico-deductive approach assumed that such experiments could be done more easily than is the case. Even in the physical sciences, such experiments appear relatively infrequently.

Dependent variable That which we observe or feel as a change in something as the result of some manipulation. The data of most experiments are the dependent variables; they are the effects that we wish to predict. For example, a period without food produces changes in dependent variables such as reported hunger and in the amount of food eaten once it is made available.

Drive Hull's term for all of the factors that motivate behavior. Hull believed that learning per se is not sufficient to produce action; drive is necessary to energize learning.

Drive stimulus Hull's conceptualization of biological drives in stimulus form (stomach contractions, and so on). If drives can be treated as stimuli, then they can enter into connections with responses, as do other stimuli.

Excitatory reaction potential Hull's intervening variable representing the tendency to behave, symbolized by $_sE_R$. It is the product of $_sH_R$ times drive, minus inhibitory factors. Reaction potential may be measured in terms of latency of response, amplitude of response, and resistance to extinction.

Frustration Spence's term for the reaction produced when no reward is received in situations in which it has been anticipated. Spence felt that this was the basis for inhibition. Amsel, Wagner, and others developed a theory in which fractional anticipatory frustration comes to act as an added motivator.

Fractional antedating goal response Also called the fractional anticipatory goal response. This is a partial goal response that may occur well in advance of the meeting with the goal stimulus. When someone is anxious to eat, fight, dance, or whatever, he or she is already making some of the responses that will occur when the goal activity begins. For Hull, the way it feels to make such anticipatory responses is the physical basis for what we call anticipation. Fractional antedating goal response is symbolized as r_G-s_G.

Generalization Stimulus generalization refers to the fact that we respond to a range of stimuli that are similar to stimuli to which we have learned to respond. For example, we may behave in the same way to policemen, even when they are dressed in uniforms unlike those to which we are accustomed. Response generalization refers to a behavior learned in a specific way that may occur in similar, but not identical form. Once we learn to button a sweater, for example, we may do so in somewhat different ways on every occasion that follows. Hull treated this as a case of generalization.

Goal stimulus Hull's term for reinforcers, symbolized by S_G. Such stimuli were assumed to be capable of reducing drives or secondary drives.

Habit Hull's intervening variable representing the effects of learning and symbolized by $_sH_R$. Habit strength depends upon reinforced occurrences of responses in the presence of stimuli. Each reinforcement added an increment of habit strength that was a function of the maximum habit strength possible (M), minus the amount of habit strength already existing.

Hypothetico-deductive method A method for discovering new knowledge, which begins by clearly stating initial assumptions and then deduces reasonable theorems and corollaries that can be tested in some way. Depending upon the outcome of the tests, the derived principles are modified and, if necessary, the postulate is altered. Proponents of this method feel that it provides an organized framework for conducting research. For example, a postulate could state that all stimuli present when a response is made and a drive is then reduced become capable in the future of evoking that response. Derived theorems could say that (1) all stimuli, whether noticed or not, become capable of evoking the response, (2) some response must be made in order for the stimuli to become attached to it, and (3) drive reduction is essential for stimuli to become connected to responses. Hull was the only psychologist to explicitly use this method, although it is implicitly used by many scientists in all fields.

Incentive motivation An intervening variable in the Hull/Spence system that refers to the effects of the amount and quality of the reinforcer. It was symbolized as K, after (Kenneth) Spence.

Independent variable Normally refers to the manipulation done by the experimenter or to some other causal event in a cause-effect sequence. If an experimenter deprives you of food or water, he or she is manipulating independent variables that will produce a change in your eating and drinking behavior. The changes in your behavior are recorded as dependent variables.

Intervening variable Term used to link the effects of several independent variables on several dependent variables. For example, suppose you are deprived of food (independent variable); the more you are deprived of food, the more you eat (dependent variable). You may attribute your behavior to hunger, an intervening variable.

Matched-dependent behavior Miller and Dollard's term for imitation. They emphasized the social importance of imitating models who are older, of higher status, or more technically sophisticated.

Molar Larger, or encompassing more. In psychology, the molar/molecular distinction concerns whether a theory deals with larger or smaller units of stimulation and behavior. A molecular theory may interpret experience in terms of discrete ideas or muscle movements, whereas a molar theory would refer to larger units. For example, molar theorists stress large units of behavior and experience extending over time, but organized according to the relevant goal involved. "Going to the store" is a molar description of behavior, where the individual movements involved would constitute a molecular description.

Molecular See *molar*.

nAch Need for achievement. A motivational construct assessed through analysis of imagery themes in written interpretations of pictures. McClelland is the best known researcher in this area.

Perin/Williams experiments Classic experiments done in the early 1940s that were used by Hull as evidence for the assumption that learning and motivation are two separate things and that learning and motivation multiply to produce performance.

Postulate A clearly stated basic assumption that guides thinking and research. See *hypothetico-deductive method* and *postulate set*.

Postulate set Set of basic assumptions from which are drawn the theorems to be tested empirically. A set of postulates reflects what the author believes to be fairly well accepted principles concerning the phenomena under study. Hull's 1943 list of postulates was as follows:

1. The afferent trace
2. Afferent neural interaction
3. Unlearned S–R connections
4. Learned habits ($_sH_R$)
5. Stimulus generalization ($_s\overline{H}_R$)
6. Drive (D) and drive stimulus S_D
7. Excitatory reaction potential ($_sE_R$)
8. Reactive inhibition (I_R)
9. Conditioned inhibition ($_sI_R$)
10. Behavioral oscillation ($_sO_R$)
11. The reaction threshold ($_sL_R$)
12. Probability of response ($_sE_R - {_sL_R}$)
13. Latency ($_st_R$) of a response as a function of $_sE_R$
14. Resistance to extinction as a function of $_sE_R$
15. Amplitude of response as a function of $_sE_R$
16. Competing responses: the response with the greater $_sE_R$ prevails

Reactive inhibition According to Hull's eighth postulate, muscular or mental activity during learning produces an ever-increasing aversive drive, reactive inhibition (I_R). When activity ceases, this drive is reduced and a tendency to not repeat such activity results. This acts as the reinforcer that produces conditioned inhibition.

Reminiscence Improvement without practice. For Hull, this was the result of the fading of reactive inhibition. For example, when subjects are memorizing long lists of words, periods of no practice often improve performance, compared with the performance of other groups, in which the subjects continued practice without rests.

Resistance to extinction The number of responses made by a subject after reinforcement for responding is discontinued. This was used by Hull and by many other theorists as a measure of the degree of learning produced by a training procedure.

Secondary reinforcement Reinforcement produced by an event that does not reduce a biological drive. Such things as receiving praise or acquiring money are often called secondary reinforcers.

S-R psychology Psychological theories that hold that our

behavior and experience may best be conceptualized as responses attached to stimuli in the world and in us. Such theories often advocate the analysis of behavior and experience into S-R associations. The original S-R theorist was Thorndike, followed by Watson, Guthrie, and many others. The most extreme S-R view was that of Hull and his many followers. Though widely criticized, this view has proven very durable and useful over the years, and a great many current psychologists believe that it is worth retaining.

Transposition Responding to relationships, rather than to absolute values of stimuli. For example, if I learn to choose a larger over a smaller circle and am then presented with the larger circle and one a bit larger than it, I show transposition if I choose the larger of the two. My behavior is controlled by the relationship of size (larger), rather than by the definite size of the specific circle. The Gestaltists stressed transposition, which posed quite a problem for Hull until Spence ingeniously proposed his theory of generalization and discrimination learning.

RECOMMENDED READINGS

Koch, S. (1954). Clark L. Hull. In W. K. Estes, S. Koch, K. MacCorquodale, P. E. Meehl, C. G. Mueller, W. N. Schoenfeld, & W. S. Verplanck, *Modern learning theory*. New York: Appleton-Century-Crofts.

This is an authoritative evaluation of Hull's theory in a volume still frequently cited. At the time it was written, Hull's theory still had great influence.

Amsel, A. & Rashotte, M. (Eds.). (1984). *Mechanisms of adaptive behavior: Clark L. Hull's theoretical papers*. New York: Columbia University Press.

This is a collection of 21 of Hull's major papers. It serves to show the continued timeliness of this influential psychologist.

Chapter 7

EDWARD C. TOLMAN:
COGNITIVE BEHAVIORISM

BIOGRAPHY

Edward C. Tolman was born in Newton, Massachusetts, in 1886, the year in which Guthrie was born and two years after Hull's birth (see Figure 7.1). He was educated at the Massachusetts Institute of Technology, where he received a B.S. in chemistry, and at Harvard, where he earned a doctorate in 1915. His first job was at Northwestern University, where he stayed three years and was dismissed in 1918. He made mention of difficulties he encountered in teaching while at Northwestern, but the university's action against him was publicly attributed to financial constraints.

Tolman went then to the University of California, Berkeley, where he remained for over 40 years and where his fame grew. Unlike Hull, Tolman had few followers and none who were as zealous as Hull's followers. Also unlike Hull, Tolman showered praise on his students, repeatedly pointing out that many accomplishments assumed to be his were actually the result of his students' work.

Tolman opposed the emphasis that Hull and others placed on stimuli and responses, the molecular units of analysis. He was influenced by the Gestaltists and, as a graduate student, had spent some time in Germany with Kurt Koffka, one of the three major Gestalt psychologists. Tolman saw his own theory as an application of Gestalt principles to behavioral psychology. Whether this was true is unimportant; the fact is that Tolman, like the Gestaltists, made life difficult for Hull and other molecularists. Because of Tolman, a number of basic changes were made in the Hull/Spence system, and Tolman's attacks over the years no doubt called attention to the deficiencies of Hull's theory and therefore hastened its demise after Hull's death.

Tolman's theory has been called "molar behaviorism," "purposive behaviorism," "sign learning," and "cognitive behaviorism." The clearest statement of the theory appears in the first work

FIGURE 7.1   Edward C. Tolman, 1886–1959. *Photo courtesy of the Archives of the History of American Psychology*

listed below; the third reference summarizes the major findings reported by Tolman and his students over the years. The second reference illustrates Tolman's concerns over war and his efforts to find ways to avoid it. His pacifist views were well known and probably did not help his career. Tolman's three major works are:

Purposive Behavior in Animals and Men, 1932
Drives Toward War, 1942
"Cognitive Maps in Rats and Men," 1948

This list by no means exhausts Tolman's published work. Tolman and his colleagues wrote many papers during the period from 1932 to 1959, the year of his death.

INTRODUCTION

Tolman believed that his theory was greatly influenced by the Gestaltists (e.g., 1932). For that reason, Section 1 of this chapter provides a brief overview of Gestalt psychology.

In Section 2 we discuss Tolman's significance at the time that his theory was introduced, as well as its importance today. He stressed the purposive aspects of behavior and what he called cognitive aspects. For these reasons, he stressed molar descriptions of behavior and introduced the intervening variable to psychology. Tolman fought Hull's basic premises for many years and was responsible in part for the revisions of that system.

Section 3 covers the basics of Tolman's theory, as presented in his 1932 book and his 1948 paper. How can one be a behaviorist and yet stress purpose and cognition as basic aspects of behavior? Many asked this question at the time, but we will see that there is no basic contradiction; behavioral theories need not ignore or deny cognitive phenomena. We will also consider the classic experiments showing learning without reward, place learning, and other data that gave Hull many sleepless nights.

The fourth section considers criticisms of Tolman's position. Tolman was accused by Guthrie of leaving his subjects "buried in thought," but that was not the most serious criticism of his theory. The fact is that despite his attacks of Hull's views, his theory was similar to Hull's in important respects. He stressed intervening variables, as did Hull, but his definitions of them lacked Hull's precision. Like Hull, he stressed the distinction between learning and performance (Hull's $_sH_R$ and $_sE_R$) and many other aspects of learning were treated much as Hull treated them, although the terms used were different. Even the evidence he amassed against Hull's theory did not prove impossible for Hull's group to counter.

In Section 5, we will note some examples of applications of Tolman's theory, proposed in 1948. Unlike other behavioral views, his does not easily lend itself to application, although he was certainly interested in practical matters and tried hard to offer suggestions for the solution to practical problems.

Tolman's views are experiencing a renaissance of sorts. Journal articles and book chapters published during the late 1970s and through the 1980s show that the problems that Tolman considered important were being considered anew and that much of the research being done to investigate these problems is done with equipment similar to that which he used.

1. GESTALT PSYCHOLOGY

Gestalt is a common German noun meaning "form" or "figure" or "configuration." The three major Gestalt psychologists were Max Wertheimer (1880–1943), Kurt Koffka (1886–1941), and Wolfgang Köhler (1887–1967). A method of psychotherapy called Gestalt therapy, used by Fritz Perls and others, is in no way related to Gestalt psychology, except for the common use of the German noun "gestalt" (see Henle, 1986; Wertheimer, 1979).

The Gestaltists came to America shortly before World War II and they immediately (and vigorously) attacked what they saw as the deficiencies of psychology in this country. Their point of view had its origins with Kant, and it emphasized the importance of innate mechanisms that impart order to the world. The philosopher Kant argued that we come with an innate knowledge of time, space, and reality; likewise the Gestaltists believed that our inborn perceptual mechanisms organize the phenomenal world according to the Gestalt laws.

Relations versus Elements

The Gestaltists' main target was Titchener and the structuralists, who were already largely out of favor by the time the Gestaltists arrived. Experience is not composed of sensations, ideas, and affects that are joined by laws of association. We immediately organize the world into Gestalten, objects that have significance for us. And these objects are not reducible to elements; the whole is more than the sum of its parts. The countless sensations that, together, form the image of a tree do not fully account for our experience of the tree. The tree is more than that; it has "emergent properties" as a Gestalt, properties lacking in the mere sum of supposed sensations that make up the tree.

The Gestaltists were really questioning the identity of the basic units of consciousness. A long history, which we have traced, led to Titchener's assumption that sensations and images were basic. If we truly and objectively could examine our experience, we would see that it is a mass of elementary sensations and their fainter counterparts, the images. The Gestaltists could not have disagreed more violently. In their viewpoint, the basic units of consciousness are things, not sensations. We see trees and horses and houses and rivers and movements because of the innate perceptual equipment we have, not because we construct them from sensations and the laws of association.

Gestalten depend upon relations among things, not upon the things themselves. Thus, the Gestaltists, especially Köhler, emphasized the principle of transposition. When we transpose a melody, we change it from one key to another and in so doing we change the notes involved. But the melody remains; it is determined by the relationships among the notes, not by the specific notes themselves. Similarly, in a learning task, the solution is found when transposition occurs; the learner sees that the important relationships involved in the task are the same as those involved in a different task, successfully dealt with in the past. This realization comes quickly, and this is why insight is important in learning. *Insight* refers to the sudden solution of a problem in the absence of much prior practice with extremely similar problems.

How can we educate children if insight is so crucial? In a posthumously published work, *Productive Thinking* (1945), Wertheimer urged that we do whatever is necessary in order that our children learn to use "A solutions" rather than "B solutions." A "B solution" is one achieved through the use of a learned rule, mindlessly applied. When we teach the method for finding the area of a rectangle by multiplying the base by the height, we are supplying the material for B solutions. If we teach it as more than the learning of a rule, we may allow A solutions, and our pupils will then be able to find the area of a triangle or a trapezoid, because they understand the relations involved and thus have an insight into the general process.

Luchins (1942) provided an example of the influence of B solutions on problem solving in his "water jug" problems. In his study, subjects ranged from elementary school students to college graduates. They were hampered in the solution of easy problems because they persisted in attempting to apply the solution that had worked in a series of previous problems. Table 7.1 displays data from Luchins's study.

For example, subjects were told to measure out a specified amount of water, using three jugs that held specific amounts. Suppose a subject were asked to measure out 100 units and he had three jugs that hold 21, 127, and 3 units respectively. How might the subject accomplish the task? One way would be to fill the second jug (127 units) and empty as much as possible into the first jug (21 units), leaving 106 units in the second jug. Then the person could empty water into the third jug (three units) twice, leaving 100 units in the first jug. The three jugs are labeled A, B, and C, and the solution is B − A − 2C.

Suppose that the next problem is solved in the same way; the subject is asked to measure 99 units, with jugs holding 14, 163, and 25 units. Again the solution is B − A − 2C. After a series of eight or nine such problems, all solved in the same way, the subject no longer is problem solving, but is merely mindlessly applying a B solution.

What happens when the subject is asked to measure twenty units, with jugs of 23, 49, and 3 units? The old method, B − A − 2C, works (49 − 23 − 6), but so does a simpler method; just fill the smallest jug from A, leaving twenty units in the latter jug twice. Luchins found that several

TABLE 7.1   Luchins's Water Jug Problems

	A	Jars B	C	Goal	Solution
1.	21	127	3	100	B − A − 2C
2.	14	163	25	99	B − A − 2C
3.	9	42	6	21	B − A − 2C
4.	20	59	4	31	B − A − 2C
5.	23	49	3	20	B − A − 2C (A − C)
6.	15	39	3	18	B − A − 2C (A + C)
7.	28	76	3	25	*B − A

more problems with similarly simple solutions could be given but that subjects would apply the B solution repeatedly, even when it did not work for several problems in a row. The Gestaltists believed that much education consists of the drill and rote memorization of B solutions and that Luchins's data showed the ill effects that such training can produce.

Laws of Organization

Since we arrive in an organized world, it is necessary to show how that organization occurs; this is the function of the laws of organization, or Prägnanz (see Figure 7.2). They describe the manner in which we tend to structure the world toward "good Gestalten"; many a Gestalt-sympathizing psychologist has difficulty in defining a "good Gestalt." It is simply that toward which organization tends and, since the Gestalt is the basic unit of experience for the Gestaltists, it is difficult to be more precise. We see a row of dots: •••••••••• and call it a line, showing the effects of proximity. We see the same number of dots arranged differently: ••• ••• • •••. We call it four groups of dots, again because of proximity. We tend to see objects as symmetrical, even when they are not; this follows the principle of symmetry. We see a circle with a small gap in it as closed, which follows the law of closure. We see the world as objects on backgrounds, which follows the basic principle of *figure/ground*. We could go on with remaining laws of organization, which

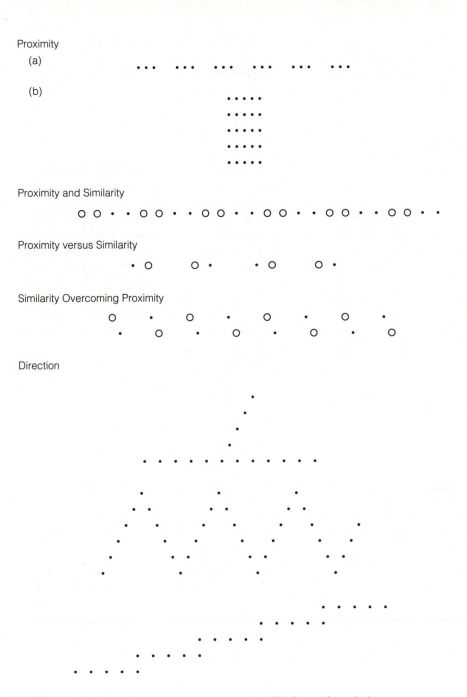

FIGURE 7.2 Some Gestalt laws of organization. The laws of proximity, similarity, and direction determine how and with what we group things. *Max Wertheimer (adapted from Ellis, 1939).*

number over one hundred (similarity, good continuation, sharpening, leveling, and so on), but instead we will consider their relation to other principles, used by the association theories.

The Gestaltists believed that associationists who stressed the importance of contiguity in space and time, along with similarity, were overemphasizing only two of the many laws of organization. The Gestaltists emphasized the importance of similarity themselves, but only as one of many principles, and contiguity is another name for the principle of grouping by proximity. Even the great stress that others placed on the effects of rewards reflected the overemphasis on one Gestalt principle, the law of closure. Closure occurs in both space (as with the ring with a gap) and time. Reward provides closure by ending a sequence of behavior that preceded it, thus making a sort of unit of it. It is by no means the most important principle, any more than are the principles of contiguity or similarity.

2. THE SIGNIFICANCE OF TOLMAN'S THEORY

Molar Behaviorism

Tolman showed the influence of Gestaltist thinking in his distinction between molecular and molar behavior and in his insistence that molar behavior has emergent properties. He noted that earlier behaviorists, such as Watson, were not consistent in the units of behavior referred to from one instance to the next. Watson often referred to movements of small groups of muscles or secretion of glands, as when we flinch or weep. Such behaviors could be traced to simple eliciting stimuli, such as an air puff or the odor of onions. Such simple, discrete, and brief behaviors were termed *molecular behavior* by Tolman.

At other times Watson spoke of behavior in large units; we build a bridge, perform a surgical operation, or make a million dollars a year, for example. In this case, the behavior seems very different from the molecular behaviors above and the stimuli that elicit such behaviors are surely not puffs of air or horseradish in the mouth. In this case, the stimuli may be an education as an architect or a surgeon and a lifetime of hard work and wise choices. These are examples of *molar behaviors* and they seem different indeed from molecular behaviors.

Hull knew this, of course, and, like most other behaviorists, he argued that molecular behaviors only *seem* different in kind from molar behaviors. The fact is that we can understand molar behavior once we analyze it into its molecular S-R units; that is what he was doing in his analysis of the sequence of behavior, which we encountered in Chapter 6. Molar behavior is simply the sum of individual movements and glandular secretions, isn't it? If so, we are best advised to stick with molecular units as the basis for understanding complex behavior.

Tolman disagreed, and herein lies his significance. Just as John Stuart Mill had argued for mental chemistry and as the Gestaltists had argued that the whole is more than the sum of the parts, Tolman argued that molar behavior was not reducible to molecular units. Even if it were possible to analyze building a bridge or writing a book into molecular elements, there is no need to do so. Molar behavior can be understood on its own level.

But what is molar behavior? Is it any activity that is more than a simple reflex movement? What distinguishes molar behavior? How do we know at what level to deal with molar behavior? This is an extremely important and difficult problem, attacked in the 1930s by both Tolman and Skinner.

Tolman's Influence Now

Although every learning textbook published during the twentieth century was sure to discuss Tolman and his work, his theory was not popular for some time. Psychologists of the late 1940s and the 1950s largely concluded that Hull had responded to Tolman's criticisms sufficiently to save Hullian theory, as well as to make Tolman's theory unnecessary.

Beginning in the 1970s, things changed. Even animal researchers are favoring cognitive theories, probably due to the growing popularity of cognitive views in human learning and memory. As a consequence, researchers are conducting experiments that are concerned with the same questions that interested Tolman and that use the same kind of apparatus he used. Tolman probably has become more influential than he ever was during his lifetime.

3. BASICS OF TOLMAN'S PURPOSIVE BEHAVIORISM

Molar Behavior

Tolman (1932) professed a "distaste for most of the terms and neologisms I have introduced" and went on to say that "I especially dislike the terms *purpose* and *cognition* and the title *Purposive Behavior*." Why did he dislike such terms, and, if he disliked them, why did he use them for so many years? The answer seems to be that he wanted to clearly distinguish molar from molecular behavior and needed something to identify molar behavior so that instances of it could be noted.

In a sense, Tolman's problem was like that of the Gestaltists, who were opposed to the analysis of mind into sensations, ideas, or other basic elements. They had to propose an alternative, which was the Gestalt. What is a *Gestalt*? We can define this term but only through appeal to the Gestalt laws of organization.

Tolman's targets were the learning theorists of the day, such as Hull, whose analysis was not in terms of sensations and ideas but in terms of reflexes and habits. Hull's strategy was exactly equivalent to Titchener's in that respect; behavior must be broken down to its basic elements. The problem for Tolman was that the elements of Hull and his fellows had a certain legitimacy, as

did those of Titchener. Because of the way our sensory equipment is constructed, it makes sense to say that the basic unit of experience is the sensation (see Chapter 1). By the same token, Hull could say that because of the way we are built, the S-R habit is the logical unit of behavior. If we agree with Tolman that it is better to deal with larger units of behavior, we are left with the problem of defining *larger*. We cannot observe everything that a simple animal does, to say nothing of a human. What *is* this larger unit of behavior?

Tolman's answer really required him to use terms like *purpose* and *cognition*, as well as other intervening variables, even though he wished to remain a behaviorist. The molar unit of behavior is that behavior which is defined with reference to some goal; it is always characterized by a "getting to or from something, by means of something, with a readiness for shorter routes." If all behavior is so defined, then we are obviously speaking of *purpose*, and there is no getting around it. For Tolman, purpose was not a mysterious mental entity; there was nothing subjective about it, as he says over and over again throughout *Purposive Behavior in Animals and Men* (1932). He was merely saying that we, as psychologists looking at the activities of beasts and humans around us, can take one thing for granted; behavior is always goal directed and thus reeks with purpose.

Recall that purpose was to be inferred from observed behavior. As we watch an organism persisting in some activity which looks to us like trial and error behavior and if we note that the errors decrease with continued activity, we call that behavior purposive; it is *docile* (teachable) and it is trial and error activity.

Similarly, goal-directed behavior is also cognitive. When we train a dog to come to us a thousand times, with the reward of a piece of sirloin on each trial, we may offer a piece of cheese on the next trial. Dogs do eat cheese, but we note in the behavior of the dog that something else was expected; in Tolman's terms, we may say that the dog's cognition was specific to sirloin and not to cheese. Behavior that indicates that a specific goal object is expected is evidence of a *cognition*, though I remind the reader that Tolman meant nothing subjective about this. He was not saying that the dog had a mental representation of sirloin, only that the dog's behavior showed that it acted as though such was the case.

Tolman cites an experiment done by Carr and Watson (1908) that also shows evidence for cognition, as Tolman used the term. Carr and Watson trained rats to run an alley of fixed length for food. After the rats were running reliably for food, the alley was shortened. The authors referred to a "kerplunk" effect, since the rats rammed into the goal box wall, showing that their behavior was sensitive to the distance from the start box to the goal. Why not say that the behavior that shows evidence of control by the type of goal and its distance is influenced by cognition?

Tolman distinguished his position from that of Hull and his followers by reference to molar, rather than molecular analyses, and immanent, rather than ultimate determinants. *Immanent determinants* are the unique characteristics of molar (goal-directed) behavior.

Molecular Behavior	Molar Behavior
movements of muscles and secretion of glands associated with discrete stimuli, such as light flashes and tones all interpreted as reflexes and habits; these are the ultimate determinants of behavior	goal-directed acts, characterized by: purpose (trial and error, docility) cognition (control by the nature and location of goal objects) purpose and cognition are two of the immanent determinants of behavior

Demands and Means-Ends Readinesses

Given that behavior is goal directed, what do we then do? Do we merely walk around pointing out all of the marvelous instances of purpose that we

see? Not at all; learning still occurs and there is a unit of learned behavior. It is certainly not the S-R habit; it is the *means-ends readiness*, or MER. Some kinds of MER are the *expectancy*, the hypothesis, and the sign-Gestalt expectancy. An MER is a tendency to act in specific ways in given situations and is thus the analog of the reflex (for innate MERs) and the habit. *Signs* are analogous to stimuli that elicit reflexes and habits.

With the MER as the unit of behavior, we need a unit of motivation; for Tolman, that was the *demand*. A demand refers to the motivating power of a goal object, because it is food and we are hungry, it is water and we are thirsty, or it is effective for other reasons. A demand can turn a common MER into a *signified sign-Gestalt expectation*, which seems a bit much to infer into the behavior of a rat, Tolman's perennial experimental subject. But what Tolman meant is actually simple and can be explained with the following example.

Suppose I spend enough time in a specific situation that I can find the bathroom, sleeping areas, kitchen, eating areas, and so on. I have MERs including each of these areas simply because I have wandered around each of them while feeling fine; I have not had to use the bathroom, nor was I sleepy, hungry, or otherwise goal oriented. I have formed what Tolman called a *cognitive map* of the area. This does not mean that I am walking around with some sort of mental picture of anything; Tolman had no concern with such things. It simply means that I know the routes; I am ready to go from the kitchen to the sleeping area or from the dining room to the bathroom if a demand arises. A demand was Tolman's way of speaking of motives and a demand charges a goal object, or gives it motivating power.

Consider another example. I have often been to restaurants where the sauce advertised as "hot" or "spicy" was indeed hot or spicy. The eating of a bit of such sauce would create a strong and insistent demand, which (in Tolman's terms) activates my MERs. Typically, one of them is appropriate to lead to lots of cold water or milk.

The demand activates the MER; if you are not paying close attention, this seems to be exactly what Hull was saying! The sauce produces an aversive drive, leading to activities (old habits) that persist until the drive is reduced. But there is a very great difference in Hull's and Tolman's views. For Hull, knowledge (in the form of habits) exists only because past action has led to reward, in the form of drive reduction. Thus, my familiarity with my surroundings would be of no use to me in finding water to counter the action of the sauces unless I had previously been in need of water and had found it. For Tolman, my unrewarded wanderings around the house were enough to establish the MERs necessary to find water. All that is needed is a demand for water to set them into action; reward is not necessary for learning to occur. Tolman and his students showed that learning is possible (and common) in the absence of reinforcement; we will briefly describe this research later and will note Hull's response to this challenge to one of his most basic premises.

A means-ends readiness is an association between significant parts of the world, such as an association between a particular location, the path to that location, and important things, such as food or pain, that are found at that location. If the association is weak, the MER may only have the status of a *hypothesis*, a provisional expectancy; if it is strong, it is a full-fledged sign-Gestalt expectation. A sign-Gestalt expectation is a signified means-ends readiness; it means that a clear MER exists and that there is a demand for whatever the goal object is. The demand *signifies* the MER.

All of this seems an overabundance of terms all referring to the same thing, and Tolman felt bad for using so many terms to refer to the same things. But it seemed necessary to distinguish gradations of expectancy. If I know that this path leads to food, I have an expectancy. If I am not entirely sure that the path leads where I think it does, the expectancy is a hypothesis. If I am certain, then the expectancy is a bona fide means-ends readiness. Finally, if I am sure of the path

and if a demand for the goal exists, I have a signified sign-Gestalt expectation. In many ways it may appear that Tolman is not so very different from other learning theorists, who rely on classical and instrumental conditioning as explanations of behavior. But he was different.

Every behaviorist before Tolman insisted that learning takes place only as the result of relevant action; for Guthrie and Watson, we learn what we do and for Hull we learn what has been reinforced. For Tolman, learning does not occur if no action is taken, but we do not simply learn what we do; passing through new surroundings leads to knowledge of those surroundings in the form of MERs, and these do not amount to the learning of movements but to the noticing of objects and routes to those objects. Such learning is also not dependent upon the rewards or punishments encountered on the way. Although Tolman was a behaviorist, he disagreed with most other behaviorists of his time concerning the importance of actual movements in the production of learning. He also steadfastly denied the necessity of reinforcement in producing learning.

Moods of the Sign-Gestalt Expectation Tolman made much of the ability of both simple and complex organisms to judge spatial directions and to tolerate delays in the getting of goal objects, since both of these seem at first sight to be beyond the capacity of simple S-R mechanisms. The fact that simple animal subjects can show an appreciation of spatial and temporal relationships was often cited by Tolman as evidence for cognitive capacities. Such abilities were the reason for his distinction between the three moods of the sign-Gestalt expectation.

The first mood, which he termed *perception*, refers to a sign-Gestalt expectation arising at a time when the sign, the significate (goal) and the signified means-ends readiness are all present. For example, I may be thirsty, see a distant water fountain, and note that the hall leading to the fountain is clear. My thirst makes the water a signified object, the sight of the fountain is a sign for water, and my past experience has taught me that clear hallways may be traversed; this last item is the MER.

Sometimes only the sign is present, and the signified goal object and a specific route to it are absent; Tolman called this type of sign-gestalt expectation a *mnemonization*, after the Greek term that means "pertaining to memory." This type of expectation would occur if I were again thirsty, and the sign were a gas station, school, or other building in which I had found water in the past.

The third mood of the sign-gestalt expectation, the *inference*, also occurs when only the sign is present but in situations in which I have had no direct experience. Tolman's favorite example for this form of expectation lies in *place learning*. I may have wandered the corridors of a completely unfamiliar building, when I again become thirsty. I saw a water fountain some time ago and I have an idea that it is in a particular and distant part of the building. Rather than literally trace the steps I have taken since I saw it, I infer that if I cut across this corridor and go to the right I will arrive at the fountain. The fact that rats learning a maze more often enter blind alleys that point toward the goal (Tolman, 1932) suggests that rats also make such inferences.

Means-Ends Capacities   Hull's subjects had little in the way of capacities. A rat can move; its movements are energized by drives; it is responsive to stimuli; and its learning is no more than the establishment of connections between stimuli and responses that are followed by drive reduction. Perhaps the greatest difference between Hull and Tolman was Tolman's emphasis on the differing capacities of different species and of different individuals within a species. Some of the basic *means-ends capacities* that Tolman (1932) assumed organisms possess (or lack) are the following.

sequence: the ability to perceive a series of events

differentiation: the capacity to distinguish one event from another

distance: the capacity to perceive distance

direction: the capacity to perceive direction

similarity: (self-explanatory)

multiple trackness: the capacity to see that several routes lead to the same end

This list is by no means exhaustive and the examples above are provided only to give the reader an idea of the sorts of things that Tolman took for granted to be basic capacities of organisms.

Motivation   Tolman believed that we should be concerned with molar, rather than with molecular behavior; thus, most of his 1932 book consists of evidence for the importance of cognitive maps, expectancies, and capacities in rats and humans. Consequently, he did not treat the topic of learning per se until page 319, and the topic of motivation does not appear until page 270. His concern was to present the molar viewpoint, rather than to specifically treat the standard areas of learning and motivation, as was done by the molecular theorists.

Like Hull and others, Tolman suggested that curiosity, gregariousness, self-assertion, and other drives may be learned, based upon primary drives. They are thus *secondary drives*. However, unlike most others, Tolman suggested that secondary drives may become independent of the primary drives that first produced them. A craftsman placed on a piecework pay schedule may continue his slow and careful methods of production, even though this reduces his rate of output and thus his pay. This means that a higher order need for craftsmanship may be stronger than the need for food and shelter, as represented in wages received. Tolman did not make much of this, but he was one of the very few to recognize the possibility (cf. Allport in Chapter 6).

Tolman's Laws of Learning

The laws of learning were of basic importance for Hull and other behaviorists, but the issue for Tolman was the treatment of behavior as molar, rather than molecular. We have already seen that his unit of behavior was the expectation, the

MER that is activated as a sign-Gestalt expectation. How are such things learned? Do we need Hull or Guthrie or Thorndike to provide a law of learning so that Tolman's rats can acquire their cognitive maps? Why do his rats move?

Tolman was quite cavalier concerning the ways in which cognitive maps and MERs are translated into movement. When Guthrie (1952; originally 1935) criticized him for "leaving the rat buried in thought," Tolman (1949) simply added Guthrie's whole theory of S-R contiguity learning to his molar theory! Guthrie's theory thus became a necessary but insufficient feature of purposive behaviorism. As Tolman wrote in 1949, referring to what he called motor patterns:

> It will be noted that this category has to be included by me because I do not hold, as do most behaviorists, that all learning is, as such, the attachment of responses to stimuli. Cathexes, equivalence beliefs, field expectancies, field cognition modes, and drive discriminations are not, as I define them, stimulus-response connections. They are central phenomena, each of which may be expressed by a variety of responses. The actual nature of these final responses is, however, also determined by the character of the motor patterns at the organism's command. . . . Finally, as to the laws for the acquisition of motor patterns *per se*, I suggested that Guthrie's principle of simple conditioning may perhaps be correct (p. 155).

We will briefly discuss the other five types of learning that Tolman mentions in the passage and then summarize his opinion of classical conditioning, instrumental conditioning, and purposive behaviorism.

Six Types of Learning Tolman called the first type of learning the learning of *cathexes*, a Freudian term used in essentially the way that Freudians used it. This refers to the association of certain objects (such as food, water, sex partners, and dangerous objects) with basic drives (such as hunger, thirst, sexual arousal, and fear). This only acknowledges that we come into the world with drives and that experience is required if we are to learn that a given drive, such as hunger, may be

quieted if we have commerce with certain kinds of (food) goal objects. The internal disturbances we feel thus lead to positive dispositions for some objects and negative dispositions against other types of objects.

The second type of learning was the acquiring of *equivalence beliefs*. This was Tolman's version of secondary reinforcement and simply amounts to the connecting of subgoals and goals. We treat a sign for food or other goal as equivalent in many ways to the goal object itself and we have a chain built up; basic drives are attached to goal objects through cathexis and signs or subgoals come to be treated as equivalent to these goals.

The third category is that of field expectancies, the term used in 1949 as a replacement for *sign-Gestalt expectations*. No one had used his latter term, which was routinely shortened to *expectancies*, so Tolman compromised with field expectancies. This refers to the tendency of a rat or a human to acquire knowledge of the layout of a familiar situation. This includes more than a simple string of S-R associations, however. It includes apprehension of "interconnections or field relationships" among groups of stimuli. The best evidence for the existence of field expectancies is the taking of shortcuts or roundabout routes, rather than the tried-and-true path to the goal.

Field Cognition Modes Learning consists of the acquiring of MERs, for which the general term is *field expectancies*. But during an episode of learning, the field expectancies formed depend not only on practice, but on the way the situation is perceived, what is remembered, and what inferences are made. Thus, *field cognition modes* is a new term for what was earlier referred to as the moods of the sign-Gestalt expectation. New expectancies are constantly formed and new ways of perceiving, remembering, and inferring are formed. These new ways of perceiving, and so on, may then be used in other situations. As a simple example, we may learn that, when the top light on a traffic signal is lighted, we must stop. Later, after experience with nonstandard arrangements of traffic lights, it is the color and not the position of the light that is important. We change our perception of a traffic signal from that of a vertical column of lights to that of three colors of light. If we drive for the first time in Boston, we use a field cognition mode when we infer that a green flashing light means something different from simply proceed.

Drive Discriminations This refers to the connecting of specific drives with specific behaviors. Suppose that when I am hungry I learn a specific path to food and that when I am thirsty I learn to take a different path to water. This would suggest that I am able to discriminate thirst and hunger and to take the appropriate path when I am either hungry or thirsty. Could anyone doubt that I can do this, or that a rat can do this? Surprisingly, there were psychologists who believed that *drive* is a general thing; lack of food, water, or warmth contributes to a central stockpile of drive, as does pain or the threat of pain. Once behavior is energized by drive, the last reinforced behavior that led to the reduction of any drive would be the behavior carried out!

In fact, Spence produced evidence (Spence & Lippett, 1946) that seemed to show that drive was general and that individual drives could not be discriminated. For example, thirsty rats ran down one arm of a Y-maze and found water, but a run down the other arm led to food. The rats were not hungry, so they did not eat, but surely they still learned which arm had the water and which had the food! Nonetheless, when the rats were deprived of food and thus made hungry, they continued to go to the water side of the maze. One must conclude that the deprivation of food produced a drive state, but not specifically a hunger drive state. When the drive made them run, they ran to the side that had previously reduced their drive, even though the drive in force on those previous occasions was thirst.

Despite such evidence, Tolman cited evidence from early studies by Hull (1943) and by Leeper (1935) that showed the opposite results. In both experiments, rats were sometimes hungry and sometimes thirsty and when the two arms of a maze led to water and food respectively, they learned to turn to the food side when hungry and the water side when thirsty.

One gets the impression from Tolman's discussion of this type of learning that he was by no means prepared to accept the evidence for the then-popular notion of generalized drive. Our common drives are surely discriminable and thus become features of our cognitive maps, lending significance to different types of goal objects, which are also features of the maps. The alternative, that drive is a unitary thing, puts the organism into action but does not give it any direction; it will do whatever has been most often reinforced in similar surroundings. This was a view that Tolman could not accept and that Hull did not hold during most of his career.

Motor Patterns We have already spoken of this last form of learning, which was largely a concession to Guthrie and others who asked how Tolman's subjects ever get moving. We all have cognitive maps and means-ends readinesses, but how do we learn the actions that carry us along the parts of the world corresponding to the map? The answer for Tolman was Guthrie's theory of one-trial contiguity learning, and that, together with Tolman's maps, gives us a cognitive behaviorism that includes cognition and action. This principle of learning is called *motor patterns*.

Classical and Instrumental Conditioning versus Purposive Behaviorism

Tolman (1932) divided theories of learning into three categories: conditioned reflex theories, trial and error theories, and Gestalt theories. He saw his theory as a form of the last category. We will say a few words about his views on each of these forms of theory.

Classical Conditioning American psychologists of the 1920s and 1930s saw the conditioned response as a possible building block for all of behavior. But these and other psychologists really believed that the key principle in classical conditioning and in conditioning in general was the pairing of stimuli or of stimuli and responses. The more frequent and recent the pairings, the stronger the tendency of a CS to produce its response.

Tolman (1932) argued that a CS must be a sign, that it must be believed, and thereby form a part of a sign-Gestalt expectation. This is actually the view that is current in classical conditioning theory, in which more and more researchers are speaking of expectancies as a way of saying that a CS is effective only if it is a reliable and unique predictor; mere pairing is not enough, as we will see in Chapter 9. Such an assumption was always part of Tolman's thinking.

Yet, Tolman seemed ignorant of the means by which a CS becomes a sign. Concerning the factors that make a stimulus a sign in classical conditioning, he refers only to frequency, recency, and primacy of pairings with a UCS. *Recency* is the influence on behavior produced by the most recent experience in a situation. By *primacy*, Tolman meant that a CS may gain power partly because it was the first cue paired with a UCS; thus, spontaneous recovery occurs because time has passed since extinction and the newly presented CS produces the expectancy (and the CR) that it produced earlier, when it was first paired with the UCS. This primacy effect may outweigh the subsequent presentations of the CS in the absence of the UCS, which led to the expectancy "no UCS," as a recency effect.

Finally, despite his emphasis on molar behavior, Tolman still allowed the possibility that molar behavior may well be constructed of CRs! Despite the fact that his plea for the importance of molar behavior was opposed for decades, he was willing to give his opponents their chance. Perhaps that is why his popularity came only a half-century after his major book was published. Hull was not nearly so chivalrous with his opponents.

Trial and Error Learning Instrumental conditioning, or trial and error learning, has almost always been interpreted in the same way, though there have been variations on this common theme. The theme is essentially that of Thorndike: Actions followed by rewards are stamped in and those followed by punishment are stamped out. "Trial and error" is not merely a name for an observed set of phenomena, it is a theory proposed to explain such phenomena. Actions become more or less likely in the future insofar as they are trials (which bring rewards) or errors (which do not).

Reward, reinforcement, satisfaction, or whatever one wishes to call it is the defining attribute of trial and error learning and Tolman's most notable assertion was his denial of the need for reward in order for learning to occur. Expectancies (MERs, sign-Gestalts, field expectancies) are established merely through our daily experience in the world. The building of cognitive maps, which is another way of saying organized expectancies, consists of the grouping together of signs following the laws of frequency, recency, and primacy. For example, I enter a room and smell garlic. In the corner I see a can of insect repellent, a sandwich, and a box of Band-aids. I am not in a special state of need for any of these things and I pass on. Weeks later I am bothered by insects and I know that I am in the vicinity of that room; I rapidly go to it, imagine that I smell garlic, and spray myself with insect repellent.

Evidently, I learned something about the room and its contents on my last visit and, when a state of need arose, my knowledge was energized and I went to the room. The more frequently I had gone to the room in the meantime and the more recent was my last visit, the more likely I would be to go there when the state of need arose. My first visit to the room was accompanied by the smell of garlic, and so, through a primacy effect, my later experiences of the room are apt to be accompanied by the same aroma. Frequency and recency act as the other two principles that establish cognitive maps. They hook together the sight of the room, the smell, the sight of the objects resting there and whatever else I may notice. This knowledge of the room is translated to performance when a need lends a valence to one of the objects. (Valence refers to the motivating powers of goal objects.) In Tolman's terms, a sign-Gestalt expectation then exists; the MER established by my visits becomes a signified MER which is a sign-Gestalt expectation.

One wonders that anyone could doubt that the above example could occur or that it in fact does occur countless times in our daily lives. Who could possibly believe that rewards were necessary for any learning to occur? Hull and his followers did, of course, and so do many other psychologists. Do they deny that episodes like this one occur?

They surely do not deny that episodes such as this one occur, but they feel strongly that this is by no means evidence for learning without reward, or *latent learning*, as Tolman called it. What such an episode shows is only the fact that an adult human with education (including language), placed in a situation very much like those encountered repeatedly in the past, is a poor subject to use to show that learning has occurred without reward! Possible secondary reinforcers, already established during experience long past, abound in such situations; the real evidence for learning without reward must come from careful experiments with naive subjects in unfamiliar surroundings. This is where Tolman's evidence came from, as we will see. For now, suffice it to say that he did not believe that reward is necessary for the formation of expectancies and the establishment of cognitive maps. Primacy, frequency, and recency of groupings of objects are all that is required for learning to occur, and learning is energized, or shown in performance, when a drive (or, demand, in Tolman's words) is introduced.

Purposive Behaviorism The laws of learning for Tolman's purposive behaviorism were qualifiers added to classical conditioning and trial and error learning, along with an added category, which he termed inventive learning. This last category refers to creative actions that do not seem clear instances of classical or instrumental conditioning.

All three categories depend upon capacity laws which refer to the abilities of specific species or of individuals within a species. The capacity to discriminate stimuli and to predict that one stimulus is the signal for another is important in all three types of learning, and "consciousness-ability" is important in trial and error and inventive learning. This presumably concedes that classical conditioning may occur without awareness, whereas trial and error and inventive learning seem often to require it. Inventive learning requires a special capacity, which he called creative instability, referring to the ability to produce new behaviors that are not necessarily the direct product of past learning experience.

In addition to capacity laws, Tolman's three paradigms are influenced by stimulus laws, which apply to all three cases. These consist of the Gestalt laws of organization, the laws of frequency, recency, and primacy; motivation; and what he called emphasis. This last item refers to the salience of different stimuli depending upon species membership; we find, for example, that a smell that is very noticeable to a dog may not be noticed at all by a human.

These, then, are the laws of learning insofar as Tolman specified them. They boil down to the ancient laws of association (primacy, frequency, and recency), the argument against the law of effect and for the learning/performance distinction, and the stressing of capacity and stimulus laws. As pointed out earlier, specifics of the learning process were less important to Tolman than was the emphasis on molar behavior as the starting point for psychology. We will now see how Tolman treated some common phenomena of interest to all psychologists and then consider the major forms of evidence that Tolman proposed in support of his position. Finally, we will briefly note how Hull and his followers could (and did) counter this evidence.

Purposive Behaviorism: Applications to "Mind"

Tolman was certainly a behaviorist, but he was not an S-R behaviorist, as were Thorndike, Watson, Guthrie, and Hull. Also unlike these theorists, he spoke constantly of *purpose, cognition*, and *expectancy* as basic terms, not phenomena to be analyzed into the S-R units of others. How did he treat mental phenomena, such as consciousness, language, sensation and perception, and feeling and emotion?

Conscious Awareness and Ideas   Recall the way that other behaviorists treated such things as consciousness. Thorndike simply held that mental activity was also activity and that it, like overt behavior, was subject to the law of effect and was therefore trainable; we will see that this is essentially Skinner's view. Pavlov was not especially concerned with mental activity, although, like Thorndike, he was certain that it obeyed the same laws that governed other activity. Watson saw mental behavior as largely a product of muscular, laryngeal, and visceral activity; this view essentially was shared by Guthrie, although Guthrie did not insist that all cerebration be accompanied by bodily action, as was sometimes assumed by Watson. Tolman was a behaviorist who stressed the basic importance of cognition and purpose and who regularly referred to such things as expectancies and cognitive maps. One wonders how his (1932) chapter on conscious awareness differs from the views of these predecessors; in particular, how does it differ from the views of Hull, his contemporary, who virtually ignored consciousness?

Tolman begins his chapter with an apology for the "shameful necessity of raising the question" of the place of consciousness and ideas! His definition of consciousness holds that it is "running back and forth behavior"; it "accomplishes nothing new." He also said that behavior is no different, whether conscious or unconscious! The experience itself, the "raw feels," as he called it, is outside science. Yet, cognition is one of the basic "immanent determinants" of behavior in purposive behaviorism. Doesn't cognition imply conscious awareness?

Although he does not want to dwell on the subject, Tolman clearly viewed consciousness and ideation as activity, behavior similar in kind to overt behavior. We will see later that this is Skinner's view, and we saw that it is what ... rie, Watson, and Thorndike believed. But To... man added a bit more; thinking, ideation, and other aspects of consciousness may best be viewed as "surrogate behaviors," "implicit behaviours," or "feints." Citing Watson, Tolman suggested that ideation is actually performing a behavior (such as running a maze, or making a jump) without moving; there need not be any muscular tensions or movements, as he assumed that Watson's theory required. He usually referred to these activities as *behavior adjustments*. Nonetheless, his view of consciousness is not so different from Watson's, although no one ever was tempted to treat Watson as a cognitive behaviorist!

Finally, borrowing a page from William James (1890), Tolman suggested that we are conscious (have ideas, and so on) to the degree that our overt behavior is blocked. When our actions flow smoothly, there is no need to bother with ideation. Activity continues in a Hullian chain or involves steps so carefully and skillfully graded that blocks to action do not occur. When a block occurs, I engage in Tolman's surrogate behavior and ideas are thus prominent. My favorite example concerns the behavior of individuals who became aware suddenly that they are in a restroom intended for the opposite sex. That is enough to produce some conscious experience, if anything can.

Language   For many contemporary cognitive psychologists, language is a peculiarly human phenomenon. What is the position of Tolman, who was concerned with cognition in rats? It is actually difficult to see how he would fit into today's controversy. On the one hand, he believed that "ideation or creative thinking precedes speech"; thus, like Titchener (Chapter 1), he would agree that animals do not speak because they "have nothing to say." On the other hand, he argued that verbalization does not convey information about internal processes (the insides); it is simply one more tool that some organisms have. Animal cries may be divided into "procla-

nands," and thereby act as behav-
n progress toward some goal. The
guage is thus left hanging, aside from
onviction that speech does not reveal
rocesses; it is something that we (and
) *do.*

Feeling and Emotion   Tolman essentially accepted
the theory of emotion proposed by William James
(1890) and Danish physiologist Karl Lange.
According to this theory, the experience of fear,
rage, love, or other emotions is largely the
product of our bodily reactions: "I see a bear, I
run, and I am afraid," as James put it. Tolman
adopted this general point of view, translating it
into the language of sign-Gestalt expectations.
Before we consider what that might mean, we
should think about what *is* emotion; how does
one explain, describe, or otherwise deal with
emotion?

For much of British empirical philosophy and
for most psychologists, whether behaviorists,
cognitivists, or others, there is little problem here:
There are two emotions, pleasure and pain. For
some psychologists, such as Watson, there are
several basic emotions, and these are treated as
basic bodily responses to specific kinds of stimuli;
recall Watson's X, Y, and Z reactions. Other
emotions, such as pride, are combinations of
these basic reactions, along with learned postures, facial expressions, and other behaviors of
the skeletal muscles. But for most psychologists,
from Freud to Skinner or McClelland, pleasure
and pain are the emotions of interest, and pride,
sadness, gloom, and diffidence are given little
attention.

For Tolman, pleasure and pain were the para-
mount emotions, produced by stimuli that produce sign-Gestalt expectations, including the
promise of physiological quiescence or the opposite. In other words, pleasure is a part of a sign-
Gestalt expectation that includes the reduction of
a biological need. This sounds a lot like Hull,
since drive reduction is the major factor, and one
might think that in equating drive reduction with
pleasure, Tolman was simply equating reinforce-

ment with pleasure and then downplaying
reinforcement!

Tolman felt that this was not actually the case.
In stressing the importance of drive reduction as
the basis for reinforcement, Hull was talking
about the aftereffect of behavior, acting to connect S-R connections in a mechanical being. Tolman viewed the promise of drive reduction as a
part of an expectancy, exerting its effect before
behavior occurs. Stimuli that signal the pleasure
of impending drive reduction or the pain of impending injury or restraint become part of the
sign-Gestalt expectation and thus lend valence to
the sign. This emphasis on the importance of
signs as motivational-emotional determinants is
very much like the two-factor theories of later
psychologists.

Evidence for Tolman's Theory

The evidence that Tolman and his students and
sympathizers published was meant to support the
view that learning is best viewed as the formation
of cognitive maps and expectancies. This was
proposed as an alternative to what Tolman
viewed as the dominant behaviorist position, exemplified in Hull's theory. Is our behavior simply
the establishment of S-R connections produced
by drive-reducing rewards or is it the formation
of cognitive maps? The research described here
argued in favor of the cognitive map interpretation and forced Hull and his followers to modify
greatly their position. After we discuss this evidence, we will see how Hull was able (sometimes
weakly) to counter it. This will give us a better
idea of the ways in which cognitive and S-R behaviorists differ.

Latent Learning   By far the most potent evidence
against S-R associationist theory such as Hull's,
which depended entirely on the action of rewards
and punishments, was the demonstration of latent learning, or learning without reward. The
original experiment was done by Blodgett (1929)
and was repeated by Tolman and Honzik in 1930.
Details of the experiments were different, but the

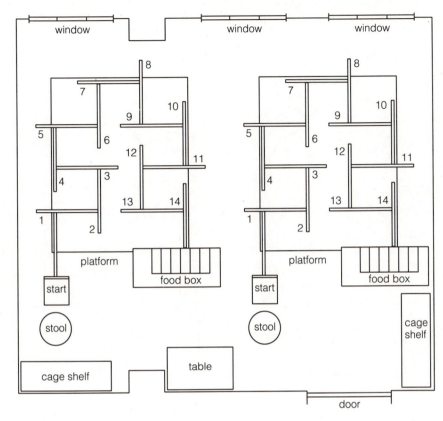

FIGURE 7.3 Fourteen-unit T-mazes used in Tolman and Honzik's latent learning experiments with rats (after Honzik, 1936).

results were the same; we will consider the second of the two studies.

Tolman and Honzik trained three groups of rats in a fourteen-unit T-maze, illustrated in Figure 7.3. The rats had to progress from a start box to a goal box through a maze that included fourteen choice points; a straight section of alley (like a miniature runway) led to a choice point, where the rat could go either left or right. In each case, one choice led to a blind alley, and the other led to another choice point. Such a maze is difficult for rats, and you might find more difficulty than you imagine if you found yourself in a human-scaled equivalent!

One group of rats received food in the goal box, but two other groups found nothing; they reached the goal box and were removed from the

maze and placed in their home cages, where they were fed hours later. The three groups were run for one trial a day for ten days and the experimenters recorded the errors each rat made (that is, entrances into blind alleys). Figure 7.4 shows a graph of the experimenters' data.

By the tenth day, the rats that received food in the goal box had decreased their errors from almost ten per day to about three; it seemed that the food reward was strengthening the appropriate correct-turning habits just as Hull would have predicted. The two groups that received nothing in the goal box also decreased their average number of errors, from about ten per day to about seven per day; this is really not a significant improvement, especially compared with the food-rewarded group.

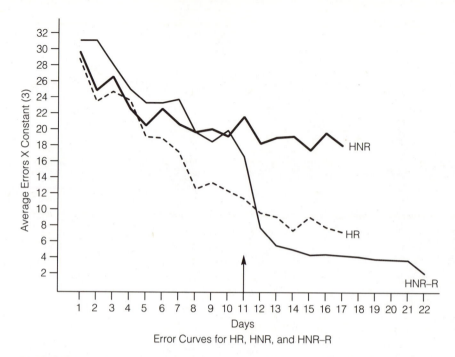

FIGURE 7.4   Decrease in daily errors made by Tolman & Honzik's three groups. Note the rapid improvement by Group HNR-R on Day 11, the first day after food was added.

On the eleventh day one of the nonrewarded groups suddenly found food in the goal box and food was found there from then on. How should this affect the rats' behavior? Now that group, which presumably had just been wandering through the maze for no particular reason, could start to learn the maze; there was reward now at the end and thus learning could proceed. In time, this group should slowly catch up with the group that had always received reward. The other nonrewarded group continued to run with no food in the goal box.

True enough, the group that started finding food in the goal box on the eleventh day did eventually catch up with the group that had always found food. "Eventually" amounted to only one day! On the twelfth day, that group averaged only about two errors and its performance remained better than the always-rewarded group over a subsequent week of training. How could this be?

Tolman believed that the answer lay in the fact that the nonrewarded group had learned something about the maze during the first ten sessions and the adding of the food on the eleventh day simply gave the rats a reason to show what they had learned. The cognitive map corresponding to the maze was established in the daily trips through it, and the presence of food on subsequent days transformed the rats' means-ends readiness into a sign-Gestalt expectation, with the food signifying it and thus turning knowledge into performance. But why were the newly rewarded rats almost immediately performing better than the always-rewarded rats?

One possibility lies in the fact that the rats that always found food in the goal box had the food "in mind" during their trips through the maze; thus, they were apt to hurry and to notice fewer of the features of the maze. The group that was not rewarded until the eleventh day had no such distraction; successfully completing the maze just meant that they went back to their cages. In that case, why hurry? Why not stop to smell the flowers, so to speak, and see what there was to see in the maze? Such behavior probably will lead to a better map of the maze than would be true for the "hurry-to-food" group, and, when food was in the goal box and there was a reason to get there as quickly as possible, the group that had run for ten days with no food would make fewer errors, since their map was better than that of the other group.

Learning is thus possible in the absence of clear reward and a number of subsequent experiments led to the same conclusion. One of Tolman's favorites was done by his opponents, Spence and Lippitt (1940). In this case, rats were run in a Y-maze, with food in the goal box of one arm and water in the goal box at the end of the other arm. During training, the rats were not hungry or thirsty; presumably the reason that they ran at all was because they were removed after the run and replaced in their home cages. When half of the rats were then deprived of food and the other half deprived of water, they again ran the maze. The hungry rats ran to the food side and the thirsty rats tended to turn to the water side; they knew where food and water were, although their previous runs had never been reinforced with food or water. An experiment done to refute Tolman's views produced results that supported them. Learning does not require reward, at least not reward in the form of an explicit drive reducer such as food or water, acting in its capacity and reducing a drive.

Vicarious Trial and Error A second variety of evidence for Tolman's position was termed vicarious trial and error, or VTE, by Muenzinger (1938). This refers to the "hesitating, looking-back-and-forth" behavior that is often observed when a rat or other subject reaches a choice point in a maze. To an observer, it seems that the animal is mentally making the choice; in a manner of speaking it is running its cognitive map and thus vicariously running the maze into which it has been placed. Tolman viewed this activity as incompatible with simple S-R explanations of maze learning, which seemed to treat the subject as a passive machine making this or that choice because of the mechanical effects of present stimuli and the consequences of previous choices.

A favorite device for producing VTE behavior was the Lashley jumping stand (1930). In a maze, the subject can take its time; it may speed through some choice points and dawdle through others, but Lashley invented the jumping stand to allow the experimenter to force a choice between alternatives when he or she—not the subject— wants the choice to be made. The stand consists of an elevated platform, just big enough for a rat to perch on and a vertical panel just within jumping distance. Mounted on the panel are two or more doors, which may be marked with different stimulus patterns or shades of gray. The rat's task is to jump to the correct door; when it hits the door, the door opens and the rat finds itself on a ledge behind the door with a food reward available. If the rat jumps toward the wrong door, it finds it locked and, in most cases, it falls into a net hung at some distance below the doors. (In Tolman's experiments, this was not the case; instead, Tolman placed a small ledge in front of the doors so that if the rat made an error it would not have to fall.)

If the rat's task is to learn to jump to a door marked with a cross and not jump to a door marked with a circle, a number of errors are bound to be made before the solution is routinely applied. The problem seems simple to us, because, as Tolman put it, we already have our instructions; the rat has to learn them. All that it can know initially is that it is on a high platform and that it cannot stay there indefinitely: An electric shock or swat on the tail eventually forces the rat to jump.

Suppose the rat jumps to the door on the right, which is marked with a cross. The door opens and the rat is fed. On the next trial it jumps to the left door, marked with a circle. The door is locked and the rat falls into the net. On the third trial the rat has a problem. On the right is a door marked with a circle, and the door on the left is marked with a cross; which way should it jump? Should it go for the door on the right? That door opened when it was last struck, but on that trial it was marked with a cross! The last time the rat jumped toward the cross it wound up in the net. Whether it is the position of the door (left or right) or the pattern on the door (cross versus circle) that identifies right and wrong depends on the instructions, which is to say that it depends on the purposes of the experimenter. Only after more jumping can the instructions be known to the rat.

In cases such as this, Tolman and his followers claimed to see a good deal of VTE behavior, in the form of furtive movements toward one or the other door before the jump was actually made. Such behavior peaked just as the rat seemed to be catching on and it vanished once the rat routinely made the correct choice. If the problem were altered in a way that made it more difficult, VTEing returned. How else may such behavior be explained other than as surrogate behaving? Is it not obvious that the rat was "jumping" in its cognitive representation of the situation?

The Search for the Stimulus   This finding was first reported by Hudson (1948) and was later replicated and extended by Keith-Lucas and Guttman (1975). Tolman cited it since it seemed to show that rats seek out significant features of their environments and incorporate them in their cognitive maps, rather than reacting in a mechanical way, which Hull's S-R theory seemed to require.

Hudson's experiment was done with juvenile rats, each living in its own cage, where it received its food and water. The experiment itself was conducted in one trial, which was carried out as follows. On a day that must have seemed to the young rat like any other day, a distinctive stimulus card appeared above the food dish and, when the rat approached the food dish, it received an electric shock. Hudson noted that the rat seemed to pay attention to the card after the shock, as if it were "looking for what hit it." Subsequently, the experiment was repeated in such a way that the delivery of shock was accompanied by a blackout; in the darkness, the stimulus card was automatically and quickly removed from the box. When the lights came back on, the card was gone. Later, when the card was replaced over the food dish, the rats showed no unusual interest in it; it was as though the card attracted attention only when it was present immediately after the shock, not when it was present immediately before the shock.

In their replication and extension, Keith-Lucas and Guttman paired different stimuli (call them S_1 and S_2) with the period just before shock and just after shock, and the shock was applied through the metal spout of the rats' water bottles. S_1 was present, the rat went for a drink, it was shocked, and everything went black. When the lights came back on, S_2 was there in place of S_1.

What happened later when water was available from two spouts, one paired with S_1 and the other presented with S_2? Hull, as well as anyone familiar with classical conditioning, would predict that the rats would avoid S_1; that stimulus was present immediately before the shock was delivered and could well have become an aversive CS or, in Hull's terms, an aversive conditioned reinforcer. The second stimulus, S_2, was present only after the shock and, if anything, should have become a signal for safety.

The rats clearly showed that it was S_2 and not S_1 that was aversive. They drank from the S_1 spout and they not only failed to drink from the S_2 spout but also removed it insofar as they could, by piling up shavings from the floor of the cage in an effort to bury S_2! Keith-Lucas and Guttman further showed that if only S_2 was present and thus that spout had to be used eventually, the rats kept their distance from it by "elongating" and keeping their rear paws as far from the spout as they could.

If S_2 is treated as a CS paired with the shock UCS, this finding must be interpreted as an instance of backward conditioning, as we saw in Chapter 3. We also saw that it has long been believed that backward conditioning does not occur, or at least that it is extremely unreliable. What happened in this case, in which such conditioning appeared to occur in one trial?

If one accepts the reality of the effect (and many did not), it appears that only Tolman's explanation applies. We and rats search out the significant aspects of our surroundings and construct our cognitive maps to include them. S_1 was just a new stimulus card placed on the old familiar water spout and thus was not the subject of much concern. Then the shock was delivered and the lights went out. "What hit me?" thought the rat; when it looked up at the source of the shock, it saw S_2. The shock lent significance to the water spout and to its identifying features, which were the same as always, except for the presence of S_2.

Hypotheses in Rats The demonstration of so-called hypotheses in rats derived from the observations of Ira Krechevsky (1932), who was later known as David Krech. A rat is said to be using a hypothesis when it shows a systematic series of behavior that, to a human observer, suggests that a hypothesis is being tested. For example, in a complex maze with a dozen or more choice points, we may note that a rat initially chooses only paths that lead to the right. When this fails, it may choose only left turns and later it may alternate right and left paths. Series of choices that show such regularities seemed evidence to Tolman that the rat was testing successive versions of its cognitive map, continuing until the proper map was constructed and no further hypotheses need be tested.

Spatial Orientation A rat with an accurate cognitive map of a maze is not restricted to following the same route that previously led to the goal box if a new route is made available. Similarly, if the starting point of the maze is changed, such a rat need not go through the old set of movements that previously led to food but that now do not. Such behavior was taken by Tolman as evidence for place learning, or learning that shows evidence for an application of spatial relationships. Tolman called this *spatial orientation*. Such learning was contrasted with Hull's theory, which proposed the learning of specific S-R connections, which Tolman referred to as response learning.

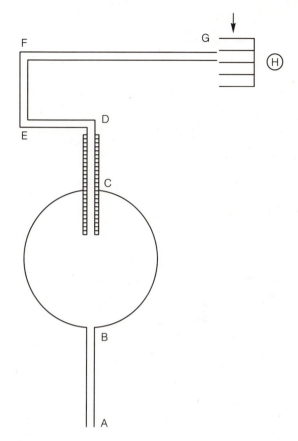

FIGURE 7.5   Elevated maze used by Tolman, Richie, & Kalish during the first twelve trials of training. A–B is the initial runway, and D, E, & F indicate the turns required to reach the goal (G). The alley was shielded by walls near C.

In 1946, Tolman, Richie, and Kalish trained rats to run a roundabout route to food on an elevated maze (see Figure 7.5). Beginning on a round tabletop, the rats ran a short distance down a runway and followed the runway as it turned left, then right, and finally right again. A run straight down the last piece of runway led to food. After twelve trials run over four nights, the maze was changed.

Now the alley that they had entered first during those four nights was blocked and twelve new paths radiated out from the table like a sunburst (see Figure 7.6). After nosing a few inches into

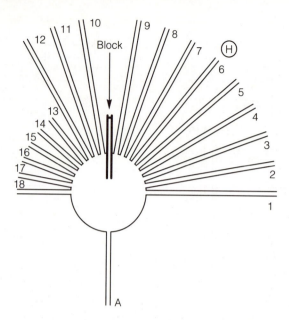

FIGURE 7.6 Sunburst maze used by Tolman, Richie, & Kalish during test trials. The alley used on earlier trials was blocked and the rats were given a choice of 18 runways (numbered 1 to 18). The circled H shows where food was gotten on earlier trials.

several of the new paths, the rats chose one and ran. The majority of them chose a path that led to or near the spot where food formerly had been found; 36 percent of the rats actually chose path number six, which ended at a point about four inches from where the food had been found! This seems remarkable, since the earlier experience of these rats had required a circuitous route to food; nonetheless, they seemed to know where it was. They had learned the location of significant objects in space (that is, a cognitive map was constructed), rather than a set of very specific movements (S-R connections) as Hull's theory seemed to demand.

Response Equivalence Tolman believed that learning consists of the building of cognitive maps and the establishment of means-ends readinesses. If I learn that my position is X and that food is found at Z and that I will pass Y (or A, B, C . . .) on the way, I may manifest such learning in many

varieties of performances. Thus, if I learn a maze by being pulled through it on a small trolley, I may then successfully run it under my own power. I likewise may learn to run a maze that is then flooded with water so that I must swim it. Rats have been shown to do so successfully. The successful performing of learned behavior, even when the specific actions required to carry out the act have been altered, is called *response equivalence.*

Perhaps the most impressive evidence for the fact that learning is not simply the learning of specific movements, as Hull had suggested (recall the diagram on page 162), lies in some of the evidence reported long ago by Lashley (1929, 1950). He trained rats to run mazes differing in difficulty and then operated on their brains in a variety of ways, hoping to discover what brain structures are necessary for learning. In one case, he destroyed the cerebellums of trained rats, an operation that seriously interferes with the control of motor behavior, both in rats and humans. After the animals had recovered from the operation, they were placed in the maze they had learned earlier. The rats had difficulty walking, and they were thus reduced to crawling, squirming, and rolling through the maze. But when they came to a choice point, they crawled and rolled down the correct alley! What better proof could one find in the support of Tolman's position? What is learned are MERs, and this knowledge may be manifest through a variety of movements, not just by the movements present during the original learning.

Reward Expectancy In a classic experiment by Tinklepaugh (1928), apes watched someone place a banana under an inverted flowerpot and then showed great annoyance when they later found a piece of lettuce under the same pot. Other studies have shown that rats seem similarly vexed when their customary reward of wet bran mash is replaced by dry food pellets. In such cases, behavior is not simply stamped in by anything that may be construed by the experimenter as a reward; Tolman believed that the MERs that are established include specific expectancies concerning the nature of the reward objects. This brings to mind Thorndike's efforts to specify what acts as a satisfier and his conclusion that the effectiveness of rewards depends upon the ongoing behavior preceding their receipt.

Hull's Response to Tolman

Some of the evidence for Tolman's view was obviously very damaging to Hull's position and, in fact, Hull and his followers spent a good deal of time dealing with it. Some of Hull's responses amounted to fairly fundamental changes in his theory, while others were more or less convincing reinterpretations of Tolman's data in ways that preserved Hull's basic position. His success in dealing with Tolman is reflected in Tolman's admission (1948) that he often had been impressed with the fact that Hull's theory could explain anything and that he therefore was tempted to abandon his own theory and to accept Hull's theory and its equations after all.

Here, we will very briefly mention ways in which Hullian theory could deal with Tolman's evidence. In some cases, there is not much that we can say. In other cases, Hull's proposal is apt to produce reflex lip curling.

Latent Learning How on earth could Hull account for findings such as those of Tolman and Honzik (1930)? Rats that had run a complex maze for ten days with no food reward almost immediately caught up with and surpassed the performance of rats that had received food from the first day. This is obviously evidence of learning without reward, which was seen as soon as the unrewarded rats had a reason to quickly get to the goal box! There seems no way that Hull could explain this.

This is the main reason that Spence proposed and Hull adopted the variable K, or incentive motivation. Recall that this is an intervening variable that depends upon the amount and the quality of reward and that Spence suggested refers to the aggregate of little s_G, or stimulation produced by fractional antedating goal responses. How can K explain latent learning?

Pretend that we are Hull viewing Tolman and Honzik's data and that we are trying to account for the extremely rapid improvement in performance of the group of rats that has only recently found reward in the goal box. We believe that all learning depends upon the reduction of drives, but this seems to apply only to the group that regularly received food in the goal box. However, we are now prepared to believe that habit strength ($_sH_R$) is energized not only by drive (D), but by incentive motivation (K). For the group that was regularly reinforced, we may postulate so much $_sH_R$ because of drive reduction, energized by so much drive and so much incentive motivation.

The group running the maze for ten days without food cannot be said to have accumulated no $_sH_R$, even though there was no obvious drive-reduction reinforcement. We noted that this group reduced its errors from an average of ten to seven per day over the first ten days; perhaps reaching the goal box and being removed reduced fear that the rats may have had while running the maze. Without some reinforcement, how may we account for their improvement? How would Tolman account for it?

When food was available on the eleventh day, a clear drive-reducing reinforcer was present and more rapid learning could proceed. In fact, learning can actually occur at a greatly accelerated rate, because the appearance of food after ten days of having no food effectively increases the incentive value of food! This means that the incentive value of the "new food" is not just whatever value of K it may have been for the always-rewarded group; it is effectively "super K." The rats thus may only begin to really learn the maze on the eleventh day, but the greater K produced by food-when-food-has-been-absent produces super performance. That is why the latent learning group caught up with and surpassed the always-rewarded group.

Years after Hull offered this explanation, new data showed that rats' tendency to explore new environments may have accounted for some of what appeared to be latent learning. Mac-Corquodale and Meehl (1954) trained rats to run in a complex maze, with food reward and with the blind alleys blocked off. Thus, only the correct path would be followed. When the blocks were later removed, *every* rat entered every blind alley! Such exploratory behavior could well account for the relatively slow reduction in errors shown by Tolman and Honzik's rewarded group. The nonrewarded, latent learning group would have completed its exploring by the tenth day, accounting for its rapid reduction in errors once food was placed in the goal box.

As further evidence for this possibility, the same authors allowed rats to explore a complex maze for 30 minutes before training began. Subjects given this advance opportunity to explore subsequently made only 20 percent of the number of errors made by a group given no advance opportunity to explore. Hence, Tolman and Honzik's case for latent learning was not as strong as it first appeared; Hull need not have worried over it as much as he had.

Vicarious Trial and Error This was not a serious problem for Hull, since it could be reasonably well accounted for with a simple mechanism that Hull had included in his earliest papers. When Tolman's rats were furtively moving first one way and then another before making the move that committed them, they could be viewed as a Hullian rat doing one of two things, neither of which had much to do with vicariously running through cognitive maps.

First, they could merely be showing conflict between two habits, neither of which was strong enough to dominate, as proposed by Hull in his (1943) postulate XVI. As different components of the stimulus complexes corresponding to the two choices become effective, one habit becomes dominant and leads to action. Secondly, cases of VTE simply reflect fractional antedating goal responses, activities that Hull had included in his theory from the very beginning. One can almost see the rat furtively moving toward the door that had just led to a fall and withdrawing with a pained expression on its face. Repeated furtive movements toward one and then the other alternative show that the complex of stimuli comprising the two alternatives has not been sufficiently tied to the outcomes of jumping, so that neither approach nor avoidance is unequivocally tied to either alternative. This seems as reasonable an explanation as Tolman's for such behavior.

The Search for the Stimulus It is really difficult to see how Hull could account for Hudson's findings, and he made little effort to do so. Until much later (e.g., Keith-Lucas & Guttman, 1975), cases of backward conditioning were deemed so rare as to not deserve attention.

Hypotheses in Rats The problem with evidence such as this is that it is very much in the eye of the beholder, more so than is the case with other forms of data. If one does a series of studies with groups of rats, cats, fish, or humans, using a task that requires the learning of a series of responses, one will find evidence for systematic strings of behaviors, such as Krech reported. However, one may also find seemingly random "trial and error" behavior, and preferences for manipulanda, sides of the experimental chamber, and so on. Subjects do not universally show predictable sequences of responding, such as a series of left turns at successive choice points, and when such behavior does occur it is difficult to show unequivocally that it amounts to the testing of a hypothesis.

Spatial Orientation Tolman's evidence for place learning was a good deal more substantial than his evidence for hypotheses, and a great many experiments were done during the 1940s and 1950s to determine when and if it occurred. In experiments done by Tolman and his followers, evidence for place learning was found, as in the Tolman, Richie, and Kalish (1946) experiment. In other experiments, done chiefly by Spence and his colleagues, place learning was not found; their rats made whatever responses they had learned and seemed to fail to know the spatial location of the goal box.

To make a very long story short, it appears that under some conditions place learning does occur and that under other conditions, response learning is predominant. (After all, Guthrie amassed quite a collection of evidence for response learning, so it must occur occasionally!) Tolman tended to run his rats on elevated mazes, so, as the rat ran down an alleyway, it could not see the goal box but it could see the clock on the wall, windows and lights in the room, and other cues outside the maze. There is no question that this helped the rat gauge the spatial location of the goal box and of itself in various parts of the maze. The Hull-Spence rats tended to run in covered mazes resembling tunnels, in which the influence of extramaze cues would be far less.

Also, the Hull-Spence rats tended to run more trials before a test for spatial learning was conducted. It is amazing to learn that Tolman ran his subjects one or two trials per day for only a few days before testing. It seems obvious that if I am tracing the same path for the 200th time I will tend to make the same responses I made in a test for spatial learning in which the maze is altered. And this is what the Hull-Spence rats did.

So place learning does occur, especially if my route has not been overpracticed and if I can have extramaze cues to guide me. On the other hand, if I have worn grooves in the floor of the maze in trial after trial of training and if I cannot see anything outside of the piece of alley I am now in, I probably will show response learning and not place learning when the maze is altered. The question here is simply more complex than Tolman had estimated it.

Response Equivalence This is a tough one for Hull and there is no very compelling argument he can make. Let us consider only the rat that is towed through the maze on a trolley and subsequently learns the maze faster than does the rat that has never seen the maze. And there are Lashley's rats, which could still run their mazes after an operation that disrupted their normal motor behavior.

For Hull, learning is the formation of specific S-R connections, and none of his postulates (stim-

ulus generalization, inhibition, and so on) will help much here in countering Tolman's theory regarding response equivalence. All that Hull could suggest is that movements were involved in both examples of learning and that they mediate behavior in the second instances. Did the rat on the trolley make small movements of its limbs and its head—movements that became attached to the stimuli of the maze and that subsequently helped it run the maze? Before the operation, Lashley's rats may have built up all kinds of S-R connections in the maze. After the operation, they may have seemed utterly uncoordinated, but enough S-R connections evidently remained under their control to allow successful negotiation of the maze. These are not wholly convincing arguments, but they have been raised and their proponents have felt that their weakness is still preferable to the alternative that Tolman raised: Learning cannot be merely the formation of cognitive maps.

Reward Expectancy To deal with this item requires both Hull's concept of the fractional antedating goal response and the fractional antedating frustration response, first suggested by Spence and greatly elaborated upon by Amsel and others, such as Wagner (see Chapter 6). The frustration effect was emphasized by later Hullians precisely because it dealt with such expectancies and therefore Tolman was again effective in forcing major alterations in the Hull-Spence system. The apes and rats that reacted violently to the lettuce under the flowerpot and the dry food pellets were showing a frustration response that occurred because a fractional antedating goal response was already present when the substitute goal object was discovered.

4. CRITICISMS OF TOLMAN

Overemphasis of Goal-Directed Behavior

Tolman's virtue lies in his directing attention toward molar behavior, larger and more reasonable units of behavior than the S-R connections of

Hull, Thorndike, and Guthrie. But just as Hull could defend the S-R unit as a natural unit of behavior, as we discussed earlier, Tolman felt that some criteria were necessary to define molar behavior. It seemed appropriate to define molar behavior at the level of goal-directed behavior; defined at this level, one sees the purpose and cognition that Tolman felt were the "warp and the woof" of behavior.

But there are at least two reasons for questioning the wisdom of this choice and the usefulness of such a conception for psychology. In the first place, if attention is restricted to goal-directed behavior, we may leave out a great many interesting phenomena. Is the seemingly random play of the infant or the playing with a puzzle by the chimp really goal directed? If not, are we willing to ignore it and to study only behavior that is obviously directed toward or away from some goal object?

A second objection lies in the danger of bias that could arise from the too casual use of the term *purpose*. If all behavior worth noting is purposeful, then we are apt to impute purpose where there is none, such as in the building of a spider's web, the migration of salmon in order to spawn, and the slow zebra sacrificing itself to the lion to allow the rest of the herd to escape! Skinner noted that all of the experimental equipment that Tolman used took the form of mazes and the like, which were concrete embodiments of cognitive maps! Purpose and cognition were always found because the tasks posed for his subjects allowed no other finding.

Intervening Variables

Tolman (1932) really introduced intervening variables to psychology and made the argument for their usefulness, which was adopted by Hull and many others since. We discussed Hull's use of intervening variables in Chapter 6 and Tolman's earlier in this chapter, so there is no need to rehash the definition of an intervening variable nor to give reasons for using them (see Chapter 6 if

you are in doubt about this issue). Why may it be a criticism of Tolman to point out that he was responsible for the first serious use of intervening variables? How is that a flaw?

In Chapter 8, we will see how Tolman could be *blamed* for popularizing intervening variables; here, we will mention only briefly why their use may be objectionable. The theories of Thorndike, Watson, and Guthrie, and the early theories of Freud were different from the "old psychologies" of the past. These newer theories treated what people do as important in its own right. Where the older psychologies wondered how we "see images" and "think thoughts," the newer psychologies asked more direct questions: How do we see things and what factors influence thinking? Walking, talking, seeing, thinking, and so on were not treated as manifestations of some hidden processes; in the terms of Chapter 1, psychology was finally progressing from the statics of the nineteenth century to the dynamics of the twentieth century.

What Tolman did was return to the emphasis of statics, in the form of his intervening variables, such as the means-ends readiness and the cognitive map. Add to those *memory, attention, learning versus performance,* and a few other similar terms and it seems that we are suddenly back in the nineteenth century! One reason we know that we have regressed is that, with Tolman, we have a behaviorist theory that has little practical application.

The Problem of Action

We noted earlier that Tolman's theory lacked an important feature that all of the S-R learning theories possessed: It did not seem to account for action. For an S-R theory, this was no problem, of course; what is learned are connections between stimuli (or situations) and specific responses. When those stimuli are present, the attached responses occur. On the other hand, Tolman's subjects learned cognitive maps and means-ends readinesses, which could be evidenced in the occurrence of a variety of activities. But once a rat has acquired a stable and accurate map, what leads it to act? Why does it not, as Guthrie asked, simply stay buried in thought? It may be hungry and possess the necessary cognitions concerning the location of food, but what determines its going to get the food? Such a question was the central concern of other major theories of learning.

In fact, Tolman was not terribly concerned with the answer to this question. One just assumes that a hungry animal (that is, an animal with a demand for food) that has accurate cognitions concerning the location of food will go to the food, taking the shortest path it knows or the path it has most recently or most frequently used. In Tolman's (1949) list of the basic kinds of learning, the sixth and last kind, motor learning, was evidently added to answer Guthrie's question, although it appears as almost an afterthought. Motor learning is Tolman's tentative explanation for the occurrence of specific activities and this is no more than Guthrie's one-trial contiguity learning, which was added as the means to translate the cognitive maps and the expectancies to action.

5. OTHER ASPECTS OF TOLMAN'S THEORY

Clinical Applications

Although we noted that Tolman's was the first behavioral theory that was not useful in practical affairs, he did make a number of reasonable suggestions for applications that he saw as derived from his theory. These are at best rough applications to mental illness and social problems; in his words, these suggestions should be taken as "a *rat* psychologist's *rat*iocinations offered free" (1948).

Regression A traumatic event or less obvious causes may lead to a person's behavior changing to that of a less mature person. The loss of a loved

one may lead a person to begin dressing in the clothing worn by much younger people and to attempt to behave as such people behave. In extreme cases, this *regression* may lead to infantile behavior, so that the individual must be cared for as a child. Why should such a thing occur?

In Tolman's opinion, our view of the world is represented in our current cognitive map, including all of our knowledge of places, people, and so on. Trauma or other emotional pressure may cause us to abandon our complex current map and go back to an earlier and simpler map; this is what happens in regression. We go back to the map of early adulthood or childhood, since this was the map we used the last time we were under emotional stress; childhood and early adulthood are stressful periods.

Whether this is a reasonable or a helpful way of viewing regression is a matter of taste, but it is interesting to note that when Tolman attempted to be practical, it was Guthrie's rule that he followed! Regression, according to this view, is no more than doing what one did when last in the same situation. When under current stress, regression amounts to doing what one did when last under comparable stress earlier in life.

Fixations A *fixation* is a rigid connection between a sign and a goal object. Often, stress may lead to extremely persistent forms of behaving, even though the fixated behavior is ineffective in attaining our goals. Behavior that inevitably leads to family squabbles may occur over and over again for no other reason than that it has occurred so many times before (as Guthrie would say). For Tolman, this consists of the undue persistence of maps that should have been replaced long ago. This behavior preserves the old maps of childhood and early adulthood so that when regression occurs these earlier fixated maps are again adopted.

Tolman points out that overmotivated rats tend to fixate a specific map (for example, a particular route followed in a maze) so that when the customary route is blocked the rats have great difficulty learning a new route. In the following paragraphs we will consider Tolman's advice for avoiding such an occurrence.

Displacement of Aggression onto Outgroups We, like other primates, tend to live in groups and to share the interests and goals of the other members of the group. Because of our common interests with members of our group, factors that produce aggression, such as frustration, lead to a displacing of the aggression to those outside our group. This phenomenon may be viewed as a narrowing of the map to our group and an expressing of aggression to extramap individuals or groups. Tolman proposed that we lessen the displaced aggression between America and Russia, for example, through preaching the virtues of reason, which is another way of saying through the broadening of cognitive maps.

Education and Motivation Tolman and Honzik's latent learning experiment showed that the group of rats that received no reward during the first days in the maze may have learned more about the maze than did the rats that were hurrying through with the food in the goal box on their minds. Overmotivation may be the cause of narrow maps in children, as well as rats.

> [C]hild trainers and world-planners of the future can only, if at all, bring about the presence of the required rationality (i.e., comprehensive maps) if they see to it that nobody's children are too over-motivated or too frustrated. Only then can these children learn to look before and after, learn to see that there are often round-about and safer paths to their quite proper goals—learn, that is, to realize that the well-beings of White and of Negro, of Catholic and of Protestant, of Christian and of Jew, of American and of Russian (and even of males and females) are mutually interdependent.
>
> We dare not let ourselves or others become so over-emotional, so hungry, so ill-clad, so over-motivated that only narrow strip maps will be developed.

Like his rats, Tolman saw all of us in a maze, "that great God-given maze which is our human world" (1948, p. 155).

Tolman's Influence Today: Animal Cognition

Unlike other behaviorists, Tolman was greatly interested in the capacities of his subjects: How well could they discriminate sounds, what could they remember, and what problems could they solve? There is a similar interest shown today by many researchers in human and animal learning and we will discuss a few examples of their work in animal cognition. The examples are taken from the contributing authors' chapters in Hulse, Fowler, and Honig (1978). A greatly expanded volume on the same subject appeared as *Animal Cognition* (Roitblat, Bever, & Terrace, 1984).

Concept Learning David Premack investigated the possibility of language use in chimpanzees and other aspects of animal cognition. In the Hulse, et al. volume, he tells why he believes that pigeons are not as bright as chimpanzees and why a talking pigeon would be an uninteresting conversationalist. His argument rests with the pigeon's alleged inability to learn abstractions and particularly its failure to learn the concepts *same* and *different*. We will see that pigeons can readily learn what seem to be quite abstract concepts, such as *people*, *good capsule*, *water surface*, and others (see Chapter 8). And there is evidence that pigeons are passable at generalized delayed matching to sample (DMTS). That is, a pigeon may learn to choose red after it is shown as a sample and it is given a choice between red and green. But can it *generalize* the concept involved to new problems?

Premack believes that pigeons form absolute concepts, while we and chimpanzees tend to form relational concepts. Premack showed that a chimp can learn to use the relational operator "color of," applying it to red/apple, purple/grape, and so on—a feat duplicated by no pigeon (and by few chimps!). Further, some abstract concepts, such as *giving*, are beyond the pigeon's understanding. Indeed, the only giving in pigeon daily life is the giving of food to a fledgling by an adult.

But the real problem with pigeons is their failure to make spontaneous judgments of same/different, which we and chimpanzees do all the time. The pigeon's tendency to categorize things along a continuum of similarity, rather than in a categorical (same/different) manner limits the ability of the bird to form abstract concepts. This accounts for Premack's view that "it would be difficult to talk to a pigeon."

Animal Memory David Olton has studied memory in rats, essentially in the same way that researchers studied memory in humans not too many years ago. His typical apparatus for this is a radial-arm maze with a central platform and eight arms radiating from it, each 86 centimeters (about 32 inches) long. The experimenter places food at the end of each arm, and a rat is allowed to go where it wants in the maze. The rat will want to go where the food is, and the question is whether it can retrieve the food from the ends of all eight arms without entering the same arm twice. Can the rat remember where it has been?

Olton found that it can and that the rat does not simply rattle off a set chain of behaviors, nor does it follow a fixed strategy, such as proceeding in a clockwise direction from alley to alley. It does not leave a trail (scent-marking or other trail). The rat remembers where it has been.

Olton showed that proactive interference occurs, as is true of human memory. That is, the rat is more apt to make an error on the seventh or eighth entry than on the second or third. But, unlike humans, rats show no serial order effect, so the rat is not more likely to re-enter the first arm chosen nor is it more likely to choose an arm recently entered. Further, there is little effect of intertest interval, although it would be reasonable if there were. Would it not be confusing to face a new problem soon after you had finished the previous trial? Yet, the rats performed almost as well when trials were one minute apart as they did when they were a day apart.

Olton concluded that rats do possess a working memory, or a short-term memory lasting long enough to handle at least seventeen and perhaps as many as 25 items. Olton's data seem sufficient to convince any doubters that rats do have memories of greater capacity that we may have thought.

Spatial Memory Perhaps the research most closely related to Tolman's cognitive maps has been done by Emil Menzel. He has studied chimpanzees and other primates for many years. Menzel believes that animals' memory may be better than ours under some conditions. Menzel's aim, however, was not to show us how smart chimps really are or to demonstrate the wonders of insight in animals. In fact, he feels that the use of tools by animals, made much of by Köhler as evidence for insight, appears only after extensive social experience (see Chapter 2).

Years ago, Menzel participated in a study at the Yerkes Institute that attempted to assess the importance of early experience on later behavior of the chimpanzee. Sixteen chimps were raised in isolation during the first two years of life and then were observed and tested frequently over the next twelve years. Immediately after the isolation the chimps were horribly deficient in many ways; for example, they showed fear of most novel objects and walked off the surface of tables. With time, their behavior improved, although they remained impaired by comparison with their normally reared peers.

More recently, Menzel has examined the chimpanzee's ability to remember the location of objects in its daily surroundings. In his "traveling salesman" study, a young (five- to seven-year-old) chimp was carried through its yard, watching as an experimenter hid eighteen pieces of fruit in various locations. When that chimp and several others were released, the animal that had watched the food being hidden found an average of 12.5 of the 18 pieces, while the other animals found an average of 0.21 each per trial. In retrieving the hidden fruit, the chimp almost never rechecked hiding places from which it had already taken the fruit and it searched the area in an efficient manner, traveling the least distance between hiding places in many cases.

SUMMARY

Tolman opposed mentalism, as did other behaviorists, but, unlike most of them, he emphasized the study of molar behavior, which he felt to be characterized by cognition, purpose, and behavior adjustments. These sound like mentalist terms, but they refer only to descriptive features of behaviors defined with respect to goals, which was what he meant by molar behavior.

Tolman was the first psychologist to make much use of intervening variables, although others, such as Hull, were to use them to a far greater extent. His chief intervening variables were purpose, cognition, behavior adjustments, and expectancies, each of which was inferred from the observable behavior of his rat subjects. Tolman also was the most vocal at arguing that reinforcement (reward) was not necessary for learning to occur; experience leads to the formation of expectancies, or means-ends readinesses, which show themselves in performance when motivation (that is, demand for a goal object) is present. Learning consists of a set of cognitions arranged on a cognitive map and the means-ends readinesses representing the expectancies associated with the individual features of the map. An activated means-ends readiness was termed a sign-gestalt expectation, which appeared in three forms, or moods—perception, mnemonization, and inference.

Tolman stressed the capacities of organisms more than did other behaviorists. These include abilities to discriminate, remember, make inferences, learn cathexes, form equivalence beliefs, use different field cognition modes, discriminate drives, and learn motor patterns. He emphasized the function of the Pavlovian CS as a sign, much as is currently done, and he treated classical, instrumental, and purposive learning as ways in which elements of cognitive maps become organized—through frequency, recency, and primacy.

Although Tolman stressed the importance of cognition, he was by no means willing to accept private experience as a legitimate part of a science of behavior; most other behaviorists were willing to do so. He viewed thinking and consciousness as surrogate behavior, although *behavior* did not mean that muscular movement or tensions need be present.

Over the years, he provided evidence for the usefulness of his theory, attempting to show that experience leads to the formation of cognitive maps and means-ends readinesses and that reinforcement is not necessary for such learning to occur. This is shown in his work, which demonstrates latent learning, vicarious trial and error (VTE), the search for the stimulus, hypotheses in rats, learning of spatial orientation (place learning), response equivalence, and reward expectancy. Hull was able to deal in a more or less successful way with most of these evidences for Tolman's (and against his own) theory, partly because pressure from Tolman's work forced modification of his own theory.

Tolman may be criticized for overemphasizing the goal-directed nature of behavior and for overusing intervening variables. Additionally, his emphasis on cognition, rather than action, led to the charge that his subjects were left "buried in thought."

Tolman's theory is not well suited for application, although he tried to show applications to the phenomena of regression, fixation, displacement of aggression, and education. These suggestions refer only to the factors that lead to wide versus narrow cognitive maps and do not really differ from what most other theories suggest. Although he clearly was eclipsed by Hull during the period from 1930 through the 1950s, Tolman's orientation is staging a comeback in the form of renewed interest in cognition in general, both human and animal.

GLOSSARY

Tolman, unlike most theorists, included a glossary at the end of *Purposive Behavior in Animals and Men* (1932, pp. 437–454). When his definitions, which must be considered authoritative, appear with the terms below, they are set off in quotation marks.

Behavior adjustment "The non-overtly observable surrogate for an actual running-back-and-forth. . . . The important thing about them is that, whatever they are, sub-vocal speech, minimal gestures or what not, they achieve the same 'sampling' of alternatives or succedents which actual runnings-back-and-forth in front of such alternatives or succedents would have achieved." Thus, behavior adjustments occur when a choice is to be made. For example, vicarious trial and error occurs preceding the actual overt choice. The subject is running its cognitive map.

Cathexes A cathexis is the learned association of a demand (drive) with an external object. We learn that external objects such as food items or aspirin reduce demands produced by hunger or pain.

Cognition We say that cognition is present in behavior when the effect of a specific means-ends readiness is evident. Thus, a rat may repeatedly run to a specific goal box in which it finds food. If the environment is altered so that food is no longer present, the behavior will be disrupted and learning will occur. In general, cognition refers to the appreciation of the location of significant objects and the reflection of this in behavior.

Cognitive map An individual's surroundings, including features both near and distant, as represented within him or her (that is, centrally). The ability to take a shortcut is often cited as evidence for cognitive maps in animals.

Consciousness For Tolman, the "process of running-back-and-forth in front of environmental objects, placed as alternatives or succedents." Thus, consciousness is essentially a form of behavior adjustment.

Demand "An innate or acquired urge to get to or from some given instance or type of environmental presence or of physiological quiescence or disturbance." Tolman treats demand as synonymous with purpose.

Docile The characteristic of molar behavior that is better termed "modifiability" or "teachability." If a given behavior does not get the organism to a demanded goal object or if it involves a long route, the behavior will change in such a way as to get to the goal object or to use a shorter route to get there.

Drive "A demand for or against a given type of goal object or situation" plus a vague readiness as to the proper way to get to that goal object.

Equivalence beliefs Learning to treat a subgoal as equivalent to a goal object. This is Tolman's term for secondary reinforcement; thus, I may treat a restaurant sign as equivalent (in a sense) to the food that I have found inside it.

Expectancy The cognition that, given a present sign, a second event will follow or that, given a present sign, if I do such and such a second event will follow. A means-ends readiness is an expectancy, as is a hypothesis and a sign-Gestalt expectation.

Field cognition modes Another term for the moods of the sign-Gestalt expectation—that is perception, mnemonization, and inference.

Figure/ground Basic Gestalt principle that says that the elementary unit of experience is in the form of figures (objects) on backgrounds. This is also the way that the Gestaltists treated attention.

Fixation A rigid (nondocile) connection between a sign and a goal object. A rat may persist in a position habit, such as always choosing the left alley in a maze, even though it is never the correct choice. Similarly, human sexual perversions may be viewed as the attachment of the sex drive to inappropriate signs.

Gestalt psychology Twentieth-century school of psychology that stresses innate organizing powers in perception, learning, and memory. It should not be confused with Gestalt therapy.

Gestalt(en) Literally means form or configuration in German. The Gestalt psychologists believe that innate laws of Prägnanz organize the world into Gestalten.

Higher order drive "Certain secondary demands and sign-Gestalt readinesses" (e.g., gregariousness, curiosity, imitation, self-assertion, self-abasement, etc.). Such drives were presumed to be largely learned and dependent upon primary drives.

Hypothesis A provisional expectancy, which may become a sign-Gestalt expectation if it regularly produces goal objects.

Immanent determinants "A functionally defined variable (purposive or cognitive) which is inferred as immanent or 'lying' in a behavior-act." What Tolman refers to here are the unique characteristics of molar (goal-directed) behavior. The chief examples are purposes and cognitions.

Inference One of the moods of the sign-Gestalt expectation. "In inference commerce with the sign object only has ever occurred before." For example, after experience in a complex maze, a rat may be able to circumvent a block placed in its customary path by using a roundabout path. A familiar sign, such as the sight of the entrance to the blocked path, has previously been the signal to enter the path. In this case, it acts as a signal for a new behavior, the taking of the roundabout path. The shortcuts taken as evidence for place learning were used by Tolman as evidence for inferential behavior.

Insight The sudden solution of a problem in the apparent absence of much prior practice with very similar problems.

Latent learning Learning without reward. Rats wandering through a maze still learn something about it, even when there is no reward in the goal box. When the goal box is then baited, the learning previously gained is shown in more rapid learning to reach the goal box than is true for inexperienced rats.

Means-ends capacities "The innate (and acquired) capacities whereby a given organism or species is capable of having commerce-with and expecting means-end-relations." The latter refers to the sensitivity of the organism to direction, distance, similarity, multiple trackness, and so on.

Means-ends readiness Abbreviated to MER. "It is equivalent to a judgement that commerce-with such and such a type of means object should lead on by such and such direction-distance relations to some instance of the given demanded type of goal-object."

Mnemonization One of the three moods of the sign-Gestalt expectation. In this case, a sign is present, but the goal object is not.

Molar behavior "Any organic activity the occurrence of which can be characterized as docile relative to its consequences." To be docile, a behavior must be teachable, or improvable as a function of its consequences. This amounts to goal-directed behavior.

Molecular behavior "A conception of behavior which stresses its underlying physical and physiological character." Molecular views tend to emphasize natural elementary units of behavior, such as the reflex, conditioned reflex, or habit.

Motor patterns A principle of learning added to Tolman's theory in 1949. This consists of Guthrie's theory of contiguity learning as an account for the way in which cognitions are translated to action.

Perception One of the three moods of the sign-Gestalt expectation. In this case, all relevant stimuli (sign, goal object, and so on) are present.

Place learning The learning of the location of objects in space. This is the chief form of learning in a theory that posits cognitive maps.

Primacy A perhaps enduring effect produced by the first exposure to a new situation. For example, one's first experiences with a maze (or a bicycle or a spider) may have lasting effects even though more recent experiences were quite different.

Purpose "A demand to get to or from a given type of goal-object." Such behavior shows persistence, as in continued trial and error, and docility, or improvement with practice.

Recency The influence on behavior produced by the most recent experience in a situation. For example, the repetition of an error made on the preceding trial could be viewed as a recency effect.

Regression The often pathological return to earlier modes of behavior. A middle-aged person may begin to think and act as he or she did as an adolescent or even as an infant.

Response equivalence The successful performing of learned behavior even when the specific actions required to carry out the act are greatly altered. A rat which had learned to run a maze may as skillfully swim to the goal box when the maze is flooded.

Sign One of the three parts of the sign-gestalt, along with the means-ends readiness and the signified (goal) object. A colored panel that signals impending food is a sign.

Signified sign-Gestalt expectation A sign-Gestalt expectation that consists of sign, means-end readiness, and goal object, when a demand for the goal object is present and the goal object is thus signified.

Spatial orientation Another term for place learning.

RECOMMENDED READINGS

MacCorquodale, K., & Meehl, P. E. (1954). Edward C. Tolman. In W. K. Estes, *et al.* (Eds.), *Modern learning theory*, 177–266.

This is a classic analysis of Tolman's theory, from the point of view of writers more sympathetic to Hull's theory.

Tolman, E. C. (1948). Cognitive maps in rats and men. *Psychological Review, 56*, 144–155.

This is the best single source if you are interested in the general principles of Tolman's theory and in the research that he presented in support of it.

Chapter 8

BURRHUS F. SKINNER: RADICAL BEHAVIORISM

BIOGRAPHY

Burrhus F. (Fred) Skinner was born in Susque-hanna, Pennsylvania, in 1904 and received his undergraduate degree in English from Hamilton College (see Figures 8.1 and 8.2). His early am-bition was to be a writer, and he spent some time after graduation in a workshop in his parents' home, attempting to write the "great American novel." He finally realized that an author needs more than a knowledge of grammar and a good writing style; an author must also have something to say! Since he had nothing to say, he considered writing to be a waste of time. To remedy this situation, he applied to graduate school at Har-vard, where he received a doctorate in psychology in 1931. During the years at Harvard he found something to say and he has been saying it in various ways during the past half century. After graduation, he remained for several years as a research fellow at Harvard and then joined the faculty at Minnesota, where he remained until 1945. He was then chairman at Indiana for three years, after which he returned to Harvard, where he remained until his death in August 1990.

Skinner was never an S-R theorist, as were Thorndike, Guthrie, and Hull, although he is often portrayed as one. The only other major theorist with whom he felt any kinship was Tol-man, since he shared Tolman's concern for molar, rather than molecular, behavior. His best work was probably the strategy he proposed in the 1930s for the discovery of order in behavior. This was an insightful solution of the problem of the appropriate units into which behavior should be divided and thus provided an alternative to the molecular/molar controversy represented in the views of Hull and Tolman.

Skinner's view of operant conditioning and its application, presented in popular books, has made him familiar to the general public. *Operant conditioning* is the process whereby a particular class of response is shown to be more frequent as a function of the consequences it produces. In

221

addition, the *Journal of the Experimental Analysis of Behavior* was founded in 1958 as an outlet for operant research. With the loss in popularity of Hull's theory, Skinner became the representative of behaviorism, in the opinions of both academicians and laypersons. His views are often confused with those of Hull. However, these two theorists are as different as night and day, as a reading of Skinner's major publications will show. His most influential publications include:

The Behavior of Organisms, 1938
Science and Human Behavior, 1953
Schedules of Reinforcement, 1957 (with Ferster)
"Behaviorism at Fifty," 1963

The following are two of his best-known popular books:

Walden Two, 1948
Beyond Freedom and Dignity, 1971

INTRODUCTION

Section 1 examines Skinner's significance at the time his theory was introduced, as well as his significance today. Unlike most psychologists, he believed that *theory*, in the usual sense, is not only unnecessary, but harmful. His analysis of the reflex led to a conception of the behavioral unit that was far more useful and sophisticated than was the S-R habit of Hull and Guthrie and the molar definition of behavior proposed by Tolman. His emphasis on contingencies promised a fruitful alternative to the intervening variables used by Hull and Tolman, and it was clear very early that his views were far more useful in application than were the views of most of his rivals and critics. Unlike Hull and Tolman, Skinner held (since 1945) that private experience is an important part of the phenomena our theories must explain.

Section 2 presents the basics of Skinner's theory, beginning with his arguments *against* the usefulness of theories! We will then discuss his early analysis of the reflex and his strategy for discovering order in behavior and experience. This will

FIGURE 8.1 Burrhus F. Skinner, 1904–1990.
Photo courtesy of Random House

be followed by a discussion of his rationale for the operant/respondent distinction, or the basic distinction between classical conditioning and instrumental learning. This leads to a consideration of the empirical law of effect, which we will see differs greatly from the conceptions of Thorndike and Hull. We will then discuss Skinner's views on stimulus control, secondary reinforcement, punishment, drive, and emotion. Next, we will examine schedules of reinforcement, considering their applications and reasons for studying them. Finally, we will examine Skinner's views on the relation between heredity and environment and his treatment of private experience.

In Section 3, we will consider criticisms of Skinner's position. The most important issues (and the most relevant to his theory) are the role

FIGURE 8.2 Skinner in the laboratory at Harvard, 1930. *Photo courtesy of Bettman Archive*

of species-specific behavior (instinct) and the place of cognition, particularly in behavior therapy. Section 4 deals with other aspects of Skinner's theory. In this section we will consider behavior therapy, performing animals, and pigeon simulations of cognitive activity.

1. THE SIGNIFICANCE OF SKINNER'S WORK

When John B. Watson "founded" behaviorism in 1913, he stressed that activity is the basic subject matter of psychology and that our goal should be to discover the factors that influence that activity. As we saw in Chapter 4, Watson's "theory" was almost incidental; what was important was the answer to the question: Given a stimulus, what may we expect as a response; given a response, what may we discover to be the stimulus (Watson, 1930)? Recall that by *stimulus* Watson sometimes meant such things as a flash of light and at other times such things as an education to become an architect. By *response* he meant anything from an eyeblink to the building of a bridge.

But as behaviorism grew more popular, attention turned from the observation of the world and its effects on us to the postulating of internal mechanisms causing our behavior. The dozens of intervening variables proposed by Hull and the cognitive maps and expectancies of Tolman were substitutes for the world and for behavior. Skinner advocated a return to the basic strategy of Watson, which meant abandoning intervening variables and the theories that proposed them.

Instead, he proposed the intensive study of behavior itself. If we can discover the principles that influence the occurrence of a simple behavior, such as bar pressing by a rat, we may find that we can apply them to behavior in general, including human behavior and experience.

We find that simple behaviors are influenced by their consequences and that a schedule of reinforcement that keeps a rat steadily pressing a bar will also keep a gambler operating a slot machine. In the 1950s it seemed that the study of reinforcement schedules would answer many important questions concerning human behavior, and the success of Skinner's methods in commercial animal training, education, and mental health seemed to lend strong support for this possibility.

Skinner felt that an analysis of *contingencies*, or the relations between stimuli, behaviors, and consequences, would eventually account for attending, remembering, learning, perception, dispositions, traits, and any other activity we might consider. To date, some progress has been made and many hold Skinner wholly responsible for advances in programmed instruction and behavior therapy. Although this is an exaggeration, his influence in these areas is undeniable. Let us examine the basics of Skinner's "theory" and discover just what he means by contingencies and see what their study can do for us.

2. BASICS OF SKINNER'S THEORY

Why Theories Are Unnecessary

When Skinner argued against the use of theories (1950), he puzzled a great many of his colleagues and students, and this puzzlement has continued. In the view of many people, science *is* the development of theories; do we not praise Newton's, Einstein's, and Darwin's theories? What can we do if we abandon theories? Even if we simply make observations and classify organisms we seem to require a theory that specifies what goes in what class!

But Skinner was really arguing against a specific definition of *theory*, which was cast in terms other than those referring to the phenomena the theory was intended to explain. For example, when we train a child to say "bunny" when we present a rabbit, we might interpret the learning involved as the formation of an association between the sight of the animal and the sound of the word. We might represent the association as a habit ($_sH_R$) and conclude that the connection between sight and naming is strengthened by our praise when the behavior occurs. The child remembers the word and the rabbit, and expects to be praised for properly associating the two. Perhaps the new knowledge is represented as a change in the child's cognitive structure, and the child processes the image of the rabbit, retrieves a memory copy, compares the image and the copy, retrieves the corresponding name, and so on.

One could go on endlessly explaining this simple behavior, attributing it to actualizing tendencies, need for achievement, an innate tendency to imitate or to name everything. But what we actually see is quite simple: In the presence of a specific stimulus (the rabbit), a specific behavior (saying "bunny") is followed by a reinforcer (our praise). Thus, it is an example of a simple and familiar rule popularized by Thorndike and used by Hull. That rule explains the behavior and no further theory is necessary or helpful.

Consider some other so-called explanations that Skinner criticized.

Behavior	Explanation
argumentativeness, testiness	aggressiveness, frustration
recalling a list of names	memory
not eating a candy bar	willpower
scoring well on tests	intelligence
working hard for long hours	industriousness, achievement need
salivating to the sound of a bell	associating bell and food
having a cup of coffee	thirst

Such explanatory terms not only are used in theories, they are used by all of us every day—and for good reason. Why would Skinner or anyone else object to their use? The reason is simple; although we often treat such terms as explanations, they are more often only names for the behavior in question. Further, in treating them as explanations, we are creating what Skinner called *unfinished causal sequences* (1963). This is naming-as-explaining; a few examples will illustrate the point.

When someone behaves rudely or testily toward you, you may seek the cause for such behavior by asking someone who knows the person better than you do. You may be told that he or she is a nasty, aggressive person and that is why he or she acted in that way. For practical purposes, that may be all you want to know—that the person typically behaves in this way and that you can take care in the future to avoid the person. But all you learned is that the names you already gave to the behavior—rudeness and aggressiveness—are appropriate names for the person's behavior much of the time. You by no means have an explanation for that behavior.

The real explanation for that behavior lies in the history of the individual. Perhaps the manner in which he or she was raised, a history of failure, recent disappointments, a chronic toothache, or a thousand other factors are responsible. It may be the case that aggressive behavior in the past has been rewarded in the form of deference or attention from others. You may not care what the real cause of the rudeness is, but merely naming it as aggressiveness or nastiness is no explanation.

Similarly, when we see someone scan a list of 30 words and recite it back in perfect order, we attribute it to a good memory. Is that an explanation, or is it another case of mere naming? Is memory the cause or do we have another unfinished causal sequence? We call such behavior a feat of memory; but how do we explain memory? Is it possible that it is caused by past practice with such lists? Was the individual using a special mnemonic device?

We call someone who works long and hard industrious; what past influences have led to hard work or industriousness? What past training led to the high test scores that determine what we call intelligence? What past experiences put a person in a position where he or she can turn down a candy bar? Does willpower add anything but a name for such behavior? When I drink a cup of coffee, do I do so because I am thirsty? Do I want to wake up? Or do I drink it because the president has invited me to coffee at the White House? Motives are never explanations; at best, they are labels.

By now, you should get the point; explanations should refer to the activity we wish to explain and to the factors that influence the activity. As Skinner put it, when we talk about "increasing the self esteem of the poor and reducing their frustration," we are saying nothing about how we will do it and how this will change their behavior (1953). On the other hand, suppose we say that we will improve their living conditions, get them jobs that have high social status and promise for advancement, and ensure their safety and health. If we do these things for the poor and they tell us

they are happier, then we are going in the right direction.

To sum up, if we discover that practice learning lists of words leads to improvement in the ability to read and then recite lists, do we aid matters to attribute the change to an improved memory? Skinner felt that our knowledge of the conditions that produced the improvement is the only explanation necessary. Is it helpful to say that practice influences memory, which is then responsible for improved performance? By the same token, the many intervening variables of Hull and Tolman are really not necessary.

The Behavioral Unit

Skinner published two papers (1931, 1935) outlining his strategy for the discovery of order in behavior. Together, they constitute a brilliant piece of work. They show that the unit of behavior need not be molecular, as Hull proposed, and it need not be molar, as Tolman proposed. Skinner's rejection of the traditional molecular and molar alternatives and his proposal of a different kind of molar unit has often been misunderstood. In fact, half a century after they were written, Skinner himself seemed to misunderstand them! Malone (1987) and Staddon (1967) pointed out that he tended to emphasize molecular interpretations, despite his earlier arguments against them. His inconsistency concerns his followers and provides fuel for his critics. The essential points of these early and classic papers by Skinner are presented here.

The Concept of the Reflex Skinner's 1931 paper, "The Concept of the Reflex in the Description of Behavior," traces the history of the *reflex* from Descartes's time to the present, showing that some superfluous properties associated with the reflex have been dropped over the centuries. For example, in his original treatment of the reflex, Descartes proposed that animal spirits were responsible for reflex action. The spirits filled muscles, causing them to swell and thus decrease their length. This, in turn, produced the movement of a limb.

Once it was discovered that muscles do not "expand when they contract," theorists dispensed with the concept of animal spirits, but other superfluous properties were left. Even as late as the nineteenth century, there was talk of a vis nervosa, or "life force of the nerves." And the great physiologist Friedrich Goltz spoke of a "soul of the spinal cord" that governed reflex action! During this century, the acceptance of the neuron theory and evidence for the synapse left the reflex arc of neurons as the only essential basis for reflex action. And this seems as it should be; is it not true that the reflex arc *is* the reflex?

Skinner argued that even the arc itself was superfluous. It is not an essential part of the definition of the reflex and, after all, reflexes had been discovered many years before the first reflex arc was traced. When we get down to it, the reflex is really a conceptual expression, referring to a certain correlation between stimuli and responses. There are rules for the discovery of reflexes that tell us when we have isolated one and the discovery of a reflex is an explanation for part of our behavior.

For example, light causes the pupils of the eyes to constrict; when this (pupillary) reflex was discovered, that small part of behavior was explained. It was not explained because a reflex arc of specific neurons was shown to be responsible and Skinner never suggested that behavior was a collection of simple reflexes. Consideration of simple physiological reflexes is simply the starting point for the discovery of higher forms of order.

Discovering Reflexes   How do we isolate even a simple physiological reflex? Ordinarily, the procedure is to stimulate organisms in various ways and to look for effects on behavior. I tickle a dog on its side and it scratches with a hind foot. Have I discovered the scratch reflex or is the behavior a combination of reflexes? I know that it is a true reflex if it obeys the laws that govern reflex be-

havior in general; these laws may be arranged in two groups, which Skinner called the *static laws* and the *dynamic laws* of the reflex. For example:

Static Laws	Dynamic Laws
threshold	fatigue
afterdischarge	summation of subliminals
magnitude	refractory phase

Thus, if I find that a certain magnitude of stimulation is required before scratching occurs, the behavior obeys the law of the threshold. If scratching continues for a while after stimulation ends, and if stronger stimulation produces more vigorous scratching, the behavior follows the laws of afterdischarge and the relation of magnitude of response to magnitude of stimulation. I probably have found a reflex.

If I stimulate repeatedly, I find evidence for behavior conforming to the dynamic laws. Repeated stimulation leads to decreased responding (that is, fatigue) and, if I softly but repeatedly tickle the dog, the individual weak stimulations seem to add up and finally produce a response (summation of subliminals). Finally, a refractory phase is evidenced in the fact that after I elicit a response, I will be unable to evoke another for a brief time thereafter. My reflex *is* a reflex, since it obeys both the static and the dynamic laws governing reflexes. If I add up all of the reflexes that I can evoke from a dog or from a human, I find that I can account for some of its behavior. I can explain the action of the digestive system and the rest of the viscera, as well as the parts of behavior that contribute to walking and maintaining balance. But I am really interested in other things; how do I deal with more interesting behavior?

Larger Units   I continue the same strategy for larger units but change the overall level of my analysis. Reflexes are correlations between stimulation and responding that obey static and dynamic laws, and I can apply the same method to the discovery of Pavlovian conditioned reflexes. I will find the same static and dynamic laws that I found to be true of the real reflex, and I can add two important dynamic laws—the law of conditioning and the law of extinction of Type S (Skinner's term for classical conditioning). That is, when I have found a behavior that I believe to be controlled by a CS, I can strengthen the reaction by pairing the CS with a UCS, and I can weaken the reaction by repeatedly presenting the CS alone (extinguishing the CR).

This allows me to explain much more of the behavior of my subject; I can list the reflexes that appear at birth or shortly thereafter and then add the acquired reflexes that are elicited by one or another CS. For example, if I am attempting to account for an infant's crying, I may search for stimuli that I have discovered elicit reflexive crying. Is the infant reacting to pain produced by a diaper pin? Is the infant cold or wet? If I can find no stimulus that might elicit reflexive crying, I seek a CS that may be eliciting conditioned reflex crying. Perhaps a dog's bark has evoked reflexive crying in the past and the sight of a dog has thereby become a CS, producing conditioned reflex crying.

Earlier theorists, such as Watson, had left matters there. The analysis of all behavior is restricted to the discovery of stimuli that elicit reflexes and those that have become CSs. (Skinner called behaviors that are elicited by specific stimuli *respondents*. Classical conditioning is therefore respondent conditioning.) But Skinner felt that such a strategy was hopeless; even if there are stimuli responsible for every aspect of behavior and experience, they are too numerous and too difficult to discover to make such a strategy plausible. What we should do is use the same method we used to discover reflexes and conditioned reflexes and move our level of analysis higher, to the behavior that seems to occur spontaneously and for which no obvious eliciting stimuli can be found. If we can show that such behavior, properly defined, is also reflex (in the sense of being orderly), then we will have taken a great stride forward.

However, if the reflex is defined in terms of obeying static and dynamic laws, we have an immediate problem. Static laws are those characteristics of the reflex that are observable with single elicitations of the reflex (for example, the threshold), and dynamic laws refer to characteristics of the reflex when it is elicited repeatedly (for example, fatigue). Spontaneous behavior, by definition, is not elicited; it appears in the absence of any eliciting stimulus, as far as we can tell. Of what use are the static and dynamic laws in identifying the reflex in this case?

As a matter of fact, the static laws *are* useless here; we cannot elicit spontaneous behavior, so there is no way to examine it when it is elicited once. But we may yet appeal to the dynamic laws of the reflex, since such behavior occurs repeatedly on its own, even though we cannot identify an eliciting stimulus. To make a long story short, we find that such behavior is influenced by the consequences it produces; we can influence the rate of occurrence of such behavior by manipulating such consequences.

Thus, the law of conditioning of Type R (that is, operant behavior and the law of effect) and the law of extinction of Type R may be used as dynamic laws to help us identify the unit of spontaneous behavior, or the operant. As long as orderly changes occur as we vary the consequences of such behavior (including the use of various schedules of reinforcement), we may be certain that we have extended the concept of the reflex to the level of freely occurring behavior.

Let us return to our example of the crying infant. It may well be that we can find no eliciting stimulus; we must then assume that the crying is neither reflex nor conditioned reflex. But, when we vary the consequences produced by crying, the frequency of crying changes. Perhaps it is our concern and attention that acts as a reinforcer for operant crying. If we ignore bouts of crying and find that it decreases in frequency, then we know that it is operant crying.

Practical Application The same strategy may be applied to the analysis of any behavior, whether it be aggression, crying, reading, anxiety attacks,

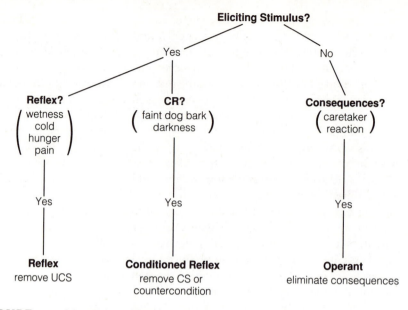

FIGURE 8.3   Identifying behavioral units: causes for an infant's crying.

hard work, and so on. We identify reflexes (show order) in the following manner:

1. We look for an eliciting stimulus. If it is a stimulus that elicits traditional reflex behavior (for example, painful withdrawal of a limb), we influence the behavior by removing or altering the eliciting stimulus. If it is a CR, we find the CS and extinguish responding to it or use counterconditioning.

2. If we can find no eliciting stimulus, we look for consequences that may be maintaining the behavior. If we find them, and if we alter the behavior when we alter the consequences, then we know that we are dealing with an operant (or operants).

Figure 8.3 presents a diagram of this method of identifying units of behavior.

For example, if we wish to alter the speed of handwriting in a slow writer, we find no eliciting stimulus. We may ask the writer to copy written prose and find that altering the consequences of such behavior alters its rate. But we find that when we reinforce this behavior according to different schedules of reinforcement, its rate does not change as does the rate of operants thus reinforced. Either handwriting is not a true operant or our definition of handwriting is inappropriate; we have not defined it in the proper units. Suppose that we reinforced the handwriting of so many pages per day of original, good-quality prose, as occurs in many business situations. Perhaps then we will find that writing speed behaves as do other operants when we reinforce it according to different schedules.

The discovery of a reflex, conditioned reflex, or operant does not guarantee that what we are specifying as the stimulus (in the first two cases) or the response is appropriate. Showing that a behavior is elicited by stimuli or influenced by consequences is only the beginning.

The Generic Nature of Stimulus and Response

The discovery of a reflex is not complete with the isolation of a unit that obeys the static and dynamic laws of the reflex. Whether we speak of a flexion reflex, as did Skinner (1935), or a more complex phenomenon, such as aggression, it is necessary to refine our definition of stimulus and response if we are to have a useful unit of behavior. The unit that we discover initially almost certainly includes irrelevant aspects of stimulation and responding. It also probably fails to emphasize aspects that are essential.

Let us consider an example. Rather than the flexion reflex, which Skinner used (1935), we will use aggression in our example. Skinner would not have approved of such an example in 1935, since aggressive acts must include instances of all three varieties of reflex behavior—the biological reflex, the conditioned reflex, and the operant. But the use of such an example will make it easier to illustrate Skinner's strategy for discovering useful behavioral units and will serve as an example of the way in which the strategy may be extended. Let us begin as the popular press often does and treat all behavior that could be viewed as aggression as a single entity. Thus, we must include aggressive play by children, the killing of prey by predators, angry words produced by a headache sufferer, random killings done by a murderer, the aggressiveness of a businessman or a football player, international conflict, sibling rivalry, and whatever else could be called aggression.

In searching out eliciting stimuli, we find that some of these forms of aggression are produced by obvious stimuli, as in the cases of the headache and predation. In other cases, we find that the consequences of the aggressive activity influence it, as in the case of children's aggressive play and in the aggressiveness of the businessman and football player, as well as in international conflict and sibling rivalry. Random killings could fall into either case.

We find that, although we have applied a common class name—aggression—to all of these cases, we really have a number of fundamentally different cases, which is why I chose the example. Let us narrow down our definition of aggression so that we can be more certain that one case of aggression is equivalent to another case. For example, we might consider the aggressiveness of the football player, the businessman, and the children. We soon find that all of them are dependent upon the consequences they produce and therefore qualify as operants. Our only problem is to identify instances of what we are calling aggression in the three cases. We could begin by including all actions in which damage or the threat of damage to people or property is present and note the effect of the consequences produced; this is what Skinner called the extreme generic position.

But we find that this doesn't serve us very well. Some aggressive acts, defined in this way, are clearly atypical: The businessman inadvertently ruins a friend, the football player breaks a teammate's leg, and the child accidentally pushes a playmate into a lake. These consequences do not increase the occurrence of aggression in general. Our definition, then, is too general. Let us go to the other extreme and call each individual act that involves damage to others the unit of aggression. The child pushing an individual playmate is a different form of aggression from the kicking of the playmate; the football player aggressively tackling a particular opponent is fundamentally different from the same player blocking an opponent. But clearly this is not a useful strategy to take; it limits us to predicting and influencing only specifically defined instances, even though we feel that many instances have something in common. So how do we find what it is they have in common?

The answer lies somewhere between the first and the second alternative, of course. What we must do is observe instances of aggression and refine our definition, beginning with the extreme generic case. We will find that at some point order will appear, as the frequency of the behavior we are counting changes in a lawful way with changes in the consequences it produces. What will this definition include? It depends upon the behavior we are concerned with.

No one can safely predict in advance exactly what behaviors will hang together to form our definition of one or another kind of aggressive behavior. We may find commonalities among some behaviors of the child, the businessman, and the football player, but we may not. If we were to find that the three kinds of aggressive behavior, when defined in a certain way (for example, producing injury to other people belonging to the same social group and not resulting in retaliation) vary in frequency as we vary the consequences (in money, praise, and so on), then we could say that we are dealing with essentially the same unit of behavior.

More likely, we will be unable to do this and we will have to be satisfied with concentrating on one of them. For example, we observe aggression among children, specifying as clearly as we can what we mean by aggression and noting the effects of praise and other payoffs for such behavior. At some point our definition will be refined so that we can predict quite precisely what will happen to the whole class of behaviors when we vary their consequences. When this occurs, we may be sure that we have adequately described what we mean by aggression of this sort; we have discovered a reflex, in Skinner's sense of the term. We have a unit of behavior that varies in an orderly way as we vary its consequences or when other variables (for example, lack of sleep) produce changes in the overall level of behavior.

Our unit, therefore, is not determined in advance. We do not treat behavior and experience as a set of habits, or as goal-directed behavior in general, as was done by Hull and Tolman, respectively. We seek out eliciting stimuli or consequences that influence the behavior in question and then narrow our definition of that behavior until we discover the class of behaviors that vary together in an orderly way.

In practice, the discovery of an operant class may reveal some behaviors as members we could not have foreseen. Suppose we alter the consequences of specific aggressive behaviors on the playground by removing the consequences that normally maintain such behavior. We pay no attention to the aggressive behaviors and we arrange that other children do likewise. As the pushes and hitting that we have identified as ag-

gression on the playground decrease in frequency, we may find that other behaviors decrease in frequency as well, such as surliness toward adults and giggling in class. The class of behaviors we termed *aggression* may belong to a larger class, including disruptive behavior in class; whether it does or not depends upon what behaviors covary, since that is the definition of the operant class and the criterion for the demonstration of order in behavior.

The Stimulus and Response Classes

In defining the reflex, the conditioned reflex, and the operant, we always refer to correlations between aspects of the world and behavior and to the things that are correlated as classes. The reflex and the conditioned reflex are correlated classes of stimuli and responses, whereas the *operant* is a class of behaviors that depends upon similar consequences. As we saw earlier, the membership of all of these classes may not be obvious; we discover those behaviors that constitute the class.

In the simplest case, the membership of the *response class* may be more or less obvious. We may train a rat to press a bar, with reinforcement presented occasionally in the form of a food pellet. Once the rat is reliably pressing, we find (as Skinner did in 1938) that the operant class we have strengthened is defined as any behavior that depresses the bar enough for us to count it as a press. It matters not whether the rat used its left or right paw, a hind foot, or even its snout. Any act that depresses the bar counts and, should we increase or decrease the frequency of reinforcement, we find that this whole class of behaviors changes in frequency.

We may refine the operant class if we wish by altering the requirements for reinforcement. If we require that the bar be pressed only with the right forepaw, we may find that the other members of the operant class decrease in frequency and that the new class consists of the various ways in which the bar may be pressed with the right forepaw. We have created a new operant class, using a method often used by animal trainers, as we will see later.

The concept of stimulus and response classes was always central in Skinner's thinking, and we should note that this is very different from the ordinary S-R association theories of others, most notably Hull. For such theories, reinforcement involves the strengthening of specific responses, and if the strengthening appears to affect other behaviors it must be due to the generalization of the specific reinforcing effect. Such response generalization is not the same as the concept of a response class, where the response is the class of behaviors that covary.

The confusion between Skinner's definition of the response class and traditional S-R interpretations may be evidenced often in attacks on Skinner, considered to be the foremost behaviorist and often assumed to hold the same S-R position as Hull. Critics such as Noam Chomsky (1959) argue that the learning of language is not the learning of specific associations between objects and words; rather, it involves an innate knowledge of the deep structure of a language. But consider the way in which Skinner's notion of classes applies to the learning of language.

A child learns that the sight of his or her mother is an appropriate time to say "mommy," because when the child says this there is general rejoicing among other family members, who pay loving attention to the child. Saying "mommy" does not happen all at once, of course; we may assume that it is the product of refinement, similar to the rat's pressing of the bar with its right forepaw. Even Chomsky would not question the fact that words are learned, so there is no need to belabor this process. What is it that the child has learned? Has the child learned to say "mommy" in a very specific situation (at home, in its room, with mother present) in a specific tone and volume?

If we watch the child we find that what has been learned is a correlation between a class of stimuli and a class of behaviors. In a variety of

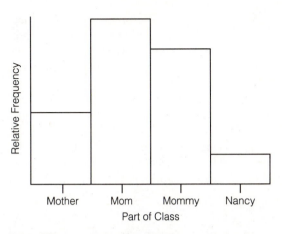

FIGURE 8.4 Stimulus and response classes. The names the child uses to refer to his or her mother form the response class. The names the child hears his or her mother called form the stimulus class.

situations (but not all) we find that the child says "mommy" in a variety of tones and volumes. This set of situations is the *stimulus class* and the child's names for his mother form the response class. Other women may initially be called mommy, and other terms may be added to the class of inflections and volumes in which *mommy* is uttered. With time, the child learns that *mother*, *mom*, and other words produce the same effects that *mommy* produces, so these words become part of the same class.

When the child is older, he or she learns that mommy is called another name, such as *Nancy*, by other people, and this name may become a less frequently used member of the "mommy" class (see Figure 8.4). In a recent newspaper story, a child trying to attract his mother's attention ran through stronger members of the "mommy" class, such as *mother*, *mom*, and so on, but these words produced no effect. At last, the child called *Nancy* and finally caught the mother's attention. In the future, one might expect that this will occur more frequently, especially if it continues to produce effects that *mommy* and *mom* fail to produce.

Since we do not learn specific responses, there is no reason why we cannot learn rules, such as those referring to noun-verb order and other rules of grammar. We will see later that animals can easily learn far more abstract concepts, so that there is no reason to doubt that children can learn more than discrete reactions to concrete and specific stimuli. We will discuss this later; suffice it to say that arguments such as Chomsky's are valid only insofar as they criticize simple S-R associationism, a view that never characterized Skinner.

Summary

In summary, the reflex, conditioned reflex, and operant are all defined in terms of classes of stimuli and responses or responses and consequences. Only through observation may we know the membership of these classes, and we may often be surprised at the identity of some of the members. This interpretation, which is unique to Skinner, is far different from the old associationist behaviorisms, which assumed that a stimulus was a stimulus and a response was a response. It is toward such views that many current criticisms of Skinner are properly directed.

We may note that Skinner's definition of the reflex and identification of stimulus and response classes are actually a refinement of Watson's cruder treatment of stimuli and responses. For Watson, *stimulus* and *response* are molar terms if the phenomena of interest are molar things, such as the kind of education (stimulus) that produces efficient reading (response). In other cases, *S* and *R* refer to molecular things, as when one discovers a cue that produces a facial tic.

The Empirical Law of Effect

A great many psychologists have concerned themselves with the problem of reinforcement: How is it that reinforcers work as they do? We have seen that Thorndike struggled with this and concluded that satisfiers have their effect (or lack of it) depending on the activity of the organism prior to the receipt of a satisfier. Thus, he appealed to a law of readiness.

It is often difficult to determine for what consequences an organism is ready until after the fact, so Hull proposed a more specific (and popular) explanation: All reinforcers work as they do because they either reduce a drive (such as hunger) or they are stimuli that have been paired with the reduction of a drive (such as the sight of food). Both of these explanations are attempts to specify the *theoretical law of effect*, which means they attempt to explain why reinforcers work as they do. Other possible explanations hold that reinforcers work because they provide pleasure, activate reward centers in the brain, increase general sensory stimulation, act to further life, or provide information. We are still far from a clear understanding of why all reinforcers work under all of the conditions they do. Is it really important that we know?

Skinner long argued that it is not important and that efforts to explain the action of all reinforcers are misdirected. For him, the law of effect is an empirical fact; we find that many events under many conditions act to increase the frequencies of many operants, and that is enough. Food, water, attention, and praise reliably reinforce many behaviors. Depending on circumstances and our purposes it is no great difficulty to discover an effective reinforcer and, once we have done that, we may discover what operants are influenced by it. According to this *empirical law of effect*, a reinforcer is defined as that which influences the strength of an operant, and that is the end of it (see Table 8.1). The law of effect is thus a useful rule that allows us to show order in behavior and experience. This, in turn, allows us to predict and control behavior and experience, which is our main aim.

Treated in this way, the law of effect is circular, a fact that has concerned and dismayed many supporters and critics of Skinner. An operant is a class of behaviors that is affected by reinforcers. Reinforcers are things that affect operants. We are left with the operant as a class of behaviors affected by things that affect such classes of behavior! A reinforcer is an event that affects behaviors affected by reinforcers! The law of effect is

TABLE 8.1   Law of Effect

Theoretical law: Specifies an independent criterion that tells us when a consequence will
act as a reinforcer.

For example: readiness (Thorndike)
drive reduction (Hull)
brain centers (James Olds)

Empirical law: Defines reinforcers by their effects.

| operants (behaviors that are sensitive to their consequences) | followed by | reinforcers (consequences that affect behaviors sensitive to such consequences) |

Note the circularity in the definition of operants and reinforcers. In
physics, terms such as *force* are difficult to define independently.

circular because we cannot define a reinforcer or an operant independent of one another. Can this be true? And if it is true, can we leave it at that?

It is true and we can leave it at that, as far as Skinner is concerned. It is enough to say that we find specific kinds of correlations between classes of behavior (lever pressing by rats, crying by infants, working by factory workers) and specific consequences (food, attention, money). We seek out such correlations and, having found one, show that much more order in the world. The empirical law of effect may be circular, but we find that there are many other circular laws and that these laws are useful. For example, we may use the equation force (F) = mass (M) × acceleration (A) without being able to define independently *mass, force,* or *acceleration*. If F = MA, then M = F ÷ A, right? It is true that we can independently define *acceleration* (as change in velocity per unit time), but *mass* and *force* are still as difficult to define as they were for Newton. The great physicist was apologetic about the use of such terms at the beginning of his *Principia* but urged the reader to bear with him, since the use of such terms as *force* would be seen to be justified by its usefulness in his overall system. This is essentially Skinner's position concerning the law of effect.

Positive and Negative Reinforcers   We normally think of a reinforcer as increasing the frequency of a behavior because the behavior produces the reinforcer; the receipt of food for bar pressing increases the frequency of pressing, and praise or a high test score increases the studying behavior that produced such consequences. Reinforcers that produce an increase in the frequency of the behavior class that produce them are termed *positive reinforcers*. Other consequences may act as reinforcers because an operant removes or ends them. For example, our withdrawal from a hot stove top is reinforced by the cessation of the discomfort the stove produces, just as a rat's bar press may be reinforced because such action turns off a powerful electric shock. Reinforcers that strengthen the behavior that removes them are termed *negative reinforcers*.

Note that all reinforcers, by definition, produce an increase in the frequency of a behavior class. The distinction between positive and negative reinforcers refers to whether the reinforcer is produced or removed by the behavior in question (see Figure 8.5). There has been confusion over the years about the distinction between negative reinforcement and punishment, although the difference is simple enough. A punisher is a consequence that decreases the frequency of the

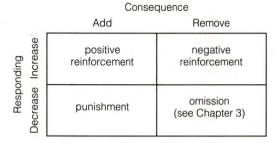

	Consequence	
	Add	**Remove**
Responding Increase	positive reinforcement	negative reinforcement
Decrease	punishment	omission (see Chapter 3)

FIGURE 8.5 Classification of effects of consequences. Note that reinforcers always increase the frequency of behavior. Omission could also be called negative punishment; in this case the occurrence of a behavior prevents a consequence.

behavior that produces it; thus, an angry word from a parent or the delivery of electric shock may decrease the frequency of the misbehavior or the bar press that produced it.

The problem is that negative reinforcement seems to imply the involvement of an aversive event (which is true), and we think of aversive events as punishers. To remember the proper usage of negative reinforcement and punishment, remember that all reinforcers increase the frequency of a behavior class, either because they are produced or terminated by members of that class.

Punishment   The decrease in frequency of an operant behavior as a function of the consequences it produces. Because of the results of a few informal experiments, Skinner (e.g., 1938) felt that punishers do not directly affect behavior in the way that reinforcers do. For example, when a rat's bar pressing, which previously had been reinforced with food, produced only a slap on the paws by the lever, bar pressing was temporarily suppressed. However, when the slaps were discontinued and food was again provided for pressing, the rate of bar pressing quickly increased and even exceeded the level present before punishment was begun. This led Skinner to conclude that the effects of punishment were temporary and that any behavior that was suppressed during punishment was "saved up," only to reappear

once punishment ended. The suppression of responding during punishment was due, in his opinion, to emotional side effects, rather than to a real decrease in the strength of the punished behavior. In Chapter 9, we will discuss Skinner's evidence for this view, along with later and more convincing evidence provided by Estes (1944). Azrin and his colleagues have shown that punishment does work; Skinner's and Estes's results were not representative.

The Operant/Respondent Distinction

In his early work, Skinner argued that elicited behavior and operant behavior form two fundamental classes and that the processes involved are different in a number of ways. In 1938, Skinner proposed the following classification:

Type S (respondent conditioning)	*Type R (operant conditioning)*
Involves stimuli (CS and UCS)	Involves responses and stimuli (R and reinforcers)
Stimuli elicit responses	Stimuli set the occasion for responding
May begin at zero strength	Must occur with some frequency
Involves a new reflex	Involves intensifying an existing behavior
May have a negative reserve	Never has a negative reserve
Involves the autonomic nervous system	Involves the skeletal nervous system
Deals with involuntary behavior	Deals with voluntary behavior

The first of these distinctions is valid, since it refers to the methods used in classical (respondent) and operant conditioning. In the first case, stimuli (CS and UCS) are presented independent of the behavior of the subject, whereas in the second case reinforcers are presented dependent on the occurrence of a behavior. The remaining distinctions are less certain. We will discuss them in a later section.

Is Conditioning Gradual or Rapid?

Operant conditioning is usually thought to occur gradually, as is the case in respondent conditioning. Each successive reinforcement adds an increment to the strength of the operant, and it may take many reinforcements before maximum strength is reached. Even Guthrie, who emphasized one-trial learning, felt that operant strength increases gradually, since an operant is an act; it is each specific response that contributes to the act that is attached on one trial.

Yet, Skinner (1938) devoted several pages to presenting evidence showing one-trial learning of operants (1938, pp. 69–73). He suggested that a single reinforcement may suffice to raise an operant to its maximum strength and that such an instantaneous change is common, if not actually typical. Skinner suggested that, when maximum effects do not occur on one trial, it may depend on a number of interfering factors. Thus, a sluggish feeder may actually be interposing a delay between response and reinforcer, the form of the response required may be unusual and thus difficult for the subject, other behavior may be reinforced and competing with the behavior in question, the subject may be in an emotional state, and so on.

Generalization and Discrimination

As noted above, operants commonly are influenced by environmental stimuli, which set the occasion for responding. Such stimuli are termed *discriminative stimuli*, or S^D; an operant under such *stimulus control* is a discriminated operant. Thus, a rat may press a lever only when a tone signals that reinforcement is available, and we learn as children to react to discriminative stimuli such as the sight of a policeman or the verbal signals "Watch out" or "Look what I have for you." In

all cases, the S^D tells the rat and us that some operant behavior (pressing, watching out, or coming to see what is there for us) will be reinforced.

We generalize to other stimuli, an effect that Skinner always called *induction*, after Sherrington's simultaneous induction. After the rat learns to press when the tone is on, it will press when other tones are on. Similarly, we learn to react to uniformed elevator operators and to boy scouts and girl scouts as we react to policemen. Early in life we may react also to a loud shout "You are correct," as we react to a loud shout that warns us of danger.

Following Thorndike and Hull, Skinner suggested that generalization occurs to the extent that other stimuli are similar to the S^Ds that have signaled consequences for operant behavior. But, unlike Thorndike, who defined similarity as "common elements," and unlike Hull, who defined it in terms of discriminability, Skinner treats similarity as a relation defined by responding.

When we speak of a black square and a gray square being more similar than a black square and a white square, we may refer to the possession of shared elements or differences in discriminability. In other cases, it is harder to specify what we mean by similarity. Is a horse more similar to a cow or to a camel? Is an X more similar to a Y or a V? In such cases, shared elements and discriminability lead to less clear-cut conclusions, so we base our assessment of similarity on the behavior of our subject. If we are dealing with a child, we may tell him or her to say "horse" when we show a picture of a horse, but not otherwise. If the child then says "horse" more often when shown a picture of a cow than when shown a picture of a camel, we may conclude that the cow is judged to be more similar to the horse than is the camel. On the other hand, we may note the similarity of functions of the three animals and judge the camel to be more similar to the horse.

According to Skinner, the reinforcing of an operant in the presence of an S^D leads to generalized or induced responding to similar stimuli and it is only through *differential reinforcement* that discrimination occurs and responding is restricted to the S^D. This simply means that the rat receives food only for presses in the presence of the S^D tone and that we receive verbal confirmation when we say "policeman" only when a policeman is present. When a different tone is on or when we call an elevator operator a policeman, food and verbal confirmation are not forthcoming and the behavior is extinguished in the presence of such stimuli. These stimuli, for which responding is not reinforced, are termed S$^\Delta$s. Hence, we learn to respond when an S^D is present and not when an S$^\Delta$ is present.

That is as far as Skinner goes in explaining generalization and discrimination. Operant conditioning leads to induced responding to stimuli similar to the S^D, and differential reinforcement (reinforcement when S^D is present and not when S$^\Delta$ is present) leads to the extinction of responding to S$^\Delta$. Since the response that is extinguished is an operant, its strength may approach zero but does not go below it, as Pavlov and Hull claimed it could.

Shaping and Chaining

Skinner always viewed operant behavior as a constantly changing thing; we act and the consequences of our action modify our behavior. The child who mumbles requests will find them often unanswered and the scholar whose study habits do not produce the desired consequences will alter them if possible. Since our environment shapes our behavior, the complexity and originality of our actions, both overt and private, depend in large part on the complexity of the environment with which we interact. Our behavior is constantly being shaped, much as a sculptor shapes a piece of clay.

Shaping by Successive Approximations When we purposely shape an operant class, we call the technique used the method of successive approximations or *shaping*. This technique enables us to

modify greatly an existing behavior class or create an entirely new behavior. We may apply this method to teach a dog to stand up, to teach a new word to a child, or to teach pigeons to play Ping-Pong, one of the first uses of the method. If we have higher aspirations, we may shape creative behavior in human or beast and even shape patriotic American prisoners of war to readily and frequently inform on their buddies!

The method used in all of these cases is the same. We begin by monitoring the behavior we are interested in (the dog's posture, the child's utterances, the pigeon's behavior toward a Ping-Pong ball) and find something we can use as a reinforcer, be it food, praise, or whatever. In the case of the dog, we may give it a bit of food with our arm raised in front of us and reinforce the dog's moving upward for the food until the sight of us makes the dog raise its head upward. If we do not want the dog following us around with upward-gazing eyes, we may reinforce head raising only when we give the command "stand up." In this way we place the behavior under the control of a discriminative stimulus (S^D).

Once the dog is reliably raising its head, we narrow the range of head raises that we reinforce, thus extinguishing lesser head raisings. The process of extinction typically leads to increased variability in behavior and we find new and higher head raisings occurring, with the dog's forepaws leaving the ground. We now have a new class of behaviors, with the average head raise far higher than was the case a few minutes ago and we again restrict the range that we reinforce. This leads to extinction of the lower raises in this behavior class, which leads to increased variability of behavior and new and higher leaps that we can selectively reinforce.

What we could have in the end (if we are tall enough or the dog is small enough) is a dog that leaps high in the air on command. This may be a behavior never before shown by the dog; we have created it through the method of successive approximations. The same method will work with the child, the pigeon, or whomever. In the case of creativity, we need only specify what we mean by *creative* and shape behavior in that direction. In the famous case of the creative porpoise (Pryor, Haag, & O'Reilly, 1969), two porpoises' novel behaviors were reinforced. This was an unusual demonstration, since it was not specific responses that were shaped, but the class of behavior that could best be called doing something new. (That *is* what we mean by creativity, is it not?) After a period in which only new behaviors were reinforced, the porpoises exhausted the behaviors commonly shown by their species (for example, porpoising, inverted swimming, and tail slap) and even behaviors infrequently seen (for example, beaching, back porpoise, spitting, and tail walk). Then they began showing heretofore unheard of behaviors (for example, back flip, spinning, inverted leap, and tail wave). As the members of the class of common behaviors were extinguished, overall behavior became more variable and new behaviors occurred that could then be reinforced. If the shaping of creative behavior is possible in such animals, should we be surprised when we find that we can do the same with children?

In the last example, psychiatrists who interviewed American POWs after the Korean War found that the Chinese had used ingenious shaping methods in their prison camps, which probably contributed to the large number of our soldiers who remained in China after the war. Their simple method consisted of reinforcing soldiers' "confessing" to minor misdeeds of their fellows, with the assurance that no punishment would follow. For example, if a soldier told the guards that his buddy took more than his share of potatoes at dinner, then both the soldier and his buddy would be rewarded with cigarettes and privileges. Prisoners soon arranged to regularly inform on one another, thinking the whole thing a joke and evidence of the stupidity of their captors, at least at first. As informing became a way of life, the possibility of escape decreased immensely. Who would confide his plans to his fellows, whose help he would need, after he had informed on them and they on he dozens and dozens of times (Whaley & Malott, 1971)?

Establishing a Chain   Once a behavior is shaped, it may be made a member of a chain of behaviors, as is the case with many of the behaviors shown by trained animals at amusement parks and in circuses. This procedure is called *chaining*. For example, suppose we wish to duplicate Skinner's "tour de force," as he called it (1937), and train a rat to pull a string that releases a marble from a rack. The rat then picks up the marble with its forepaws and carries it to a tube that sticks up two inches from the floor. The rat raises the marble to the top of the tube and drops it in, whereupon the rat receives a food pellet. How would you go about training a rat to do such a thing? A rat's normal lifetime would probably be too short a time for you to accomplish such a feat, unless you know what you are doing.

Before considering how we would do it, consider a simpler task. Suppose we wish to train a rat to press a bar four times when a green light goes on, which turns the light to red, and four further presses to turn the light to blue. After the light turns to blue, four more presses are followed by receipt of a food pellet. How would we train a rat to do this?

The trick is to begin with the final member of the chain, which is more obvious here; the first thing to do is to train the rat to press the bar while the blue light is on. We would first shape this behavior, reinforcing movements of the rat as it orients toward the bar, and then only when it is progressively closer to the bar. If we can keep it close enough to the bar by skillfully delivering pellets, the rat is bound to touch the bar sooner or later and we can require touches and then presses before food is delivered. Without too much difficulty we can thus train the rat to bar press.

Once we have established pressing, it is easy to increase to four the number of presses that bring food; we now have a rat busily pressing four times (or many more if we wish) for each pellet of food. Note that the rat is pressing while the blue light is on. What if we replace the blue light with red? Chances are the rat will still press, and, if it does not, we may shape its pressing as we did before; but this time we find that if we momentarily change the light from red to blue, the shaping effect is similar to that produced by food! The blue light, which was on in the past when pressing brought food, now acts as a reinforcer itself; it has become an S^D, signaling food, and a *conditioned reinforcer*.

When the rat presses the bar and the light is red, we change the light to blue and the rat goes through its four presses, which bring it food. Then we require two, three, and finally four responses when the light is red to change it to blue. Each time we allow the rat to go through its four-press sequence, which ends in food. Now we have a rat that presses four times in red, followed by four presses in blue, which brings food.

Finally, we begin with a green light, and when the rat presses, as it surely will, we change the light to red; after four presses, we change it to blue and deliver food for four presses in blue. We raise the response requirement to four presses in green and our chain is established. We have a rat that presses four times in green for the (conditioned) reinforcement provided by the change to red. Four presses in red are reinforced by the change to blue and the presses in blue are reinforced with food.

A *homogeneous chain* such as this, in which the same response is required in each member of the chain, is vastly easier to establish than is the *heterogeneous chain* described earlier, in which different responses are required in each member of the chain. But the principles involved are the same in the two cases. We begin with the final member of the chain, reinforcing the behavior required there with food, or some other potent reinforcer. Then we go to the penultimate member of the chain, shaping that behavior with reinforcement in the form of the opportunity to perform the final behavior of the chain. In the case above, changing the light from red to blue meant that the rat could then perform the behavior required in the final member of the chain. Then we work backwards, shaping each subsequent behavior with the conditioned reinforcement provided by access to the next member of the chain.

Training Pliny In the case of Skinner's demonstration (1937), the performance seems far more difficult to train, which is why the original account appeared in *Life* magazine. What was the final behavior in that chain? A large part of the skill required in establishing such a chain lies in the identification of the successive behaviors that we define as the chain of behaviors. What we want is a rat that walks over to a string, pulls it, picks up a marble, carries it to the tube, lifts the marble, and drops it in the tube. What is the last member of the chain? Is it dropping the raised marble into the tube? How would we establish such a behavior?

The method described in the following paragraphs is probably the best strategy for establishing a chain, but it is not clear that this is the method that young Skinner followed with his famous rat, Pliny. The *Life* account is merely a picture story, and Skinner does not spell out the method he used in his 1938 reference to Pliny. He did view it as quite a feat, however, and it appears to have taken him a long time, so he may have used a less enlightened method.

If we were to place a rat next to the tube and give it a marble at a height sufficient to allow the rat to drop the marble into the tube, we probably would not be wise. True, we might be able to place it in the rat's paws and the rat would surely drop it. But I think you will agree that the likelihood is not very high that the marble would enter the tube, and both we and the rat would tire of the handing-dropping sequence long before we and the rat were successful. How else could we do it?

Suppose we simply place the marble at the edge of a hole, flush with the floor. When the rat in its travels happens to push the marble into the hole, we immediately give the rat a food pellet.

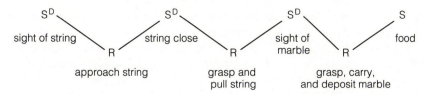

FIGURE 8.6 Establishing a chain of behavior with Pliny, Skinner's famous rat. This diagram shows one way of dividing the sequence of steps involved.

Soon, this simple behavior will be established and the rat will routinely walk over to the marble and push it into the hole. Then we place the marble an inch away from the hole and feed the rat when it pushes the marble over to the hole and drops it in.

Then what? Suppose that we then insert the tube in the hole so that the marble could not just roll in and the rat has to lift it a bit to push it in the hole. We progressively raise the tube, say a quarter of an inch at a time, until the opening is a full two inches above the floor. If we are patient and careful, it should be no great trick to shape this final behavior in the chain. The rat will lift the marble to the top of the tube; the dropping of the marble will be anticlimactic. One could define the dropping in as the final member of the chain; the lifting up of the marble is reinforced by the opportunity to drop it.

Next, we move the marble farther and farther away from the opening, requiring the rat to retrieve it, carry it to the tube, and drop it in. That becomes a third and easily established member of the chain. Our setup here will likely do much of the shaping for us; the sight of the marble should be enough to set the occasion for carrying it to the tube, as long as we do not position it too far away at the outset. Now we are ready for the final (actually, the initial) member of the chain—pulling the string to release the marble. How do we establish this step?

We could place marbles in a rack so they are visible to the rat but out of its reach and held in place by a gate that is opened when a string is pulled. We place the rat in the box, with the tube and the rack of marbles visible. Both are paired with the receipt of food and we may therefore expect our rat to be active. As it moves around the area of the marble rack, we shape its approach to the string by releasing marbles one at a time, each time allowing the rat to go through the rest of the chain, thus more securely establishing the final members. In time, we require touching the string and finally pulling the string before a marble is released. In the end, we have a rat that readily pulls the string, takes the released marble to the tube, raises it, and drops it in the hole. We have established a sequence of behaviors, each of which occurs in the presence of specific stimuli, and each of which is reinforced with the stimuli that allow the next step of the chain to be entered. The string pulling occurs in the presence of the string and the rack of marbles and is reinforced by the release of the marble. Carrying the marble occurs in the presence of the marble (as an S^D) and is reinforced by the stimuli of the marble over the tube opening. The dropping of the marble occurs in the presence of the marble over the opening and is reinforced with the delivery of food. Figure 8.6 illustrates this sequence.

The Significance of Shaping, Chaining, and Conditioned Reinforcement

These principles account for a great deal of our behavior and experience. They are effective whether they are used intentionally, as in the examples above, or as used by society or nature, where the intention is less clear or absent. Let us consider some examples.

Obviously, we learn to pronounce words when our attempts are shaped by the listeners in our family. Are the sentences we learn simply chains of such words that are joined together? Think of the way in which we establish behavioral chains and you will conclude that this is not the way in which we learn sentences! Shaping is important in the learning of words, in acquiring manual skills, and in every activity in which we engage. If we work for a supervisor who compliments us for suggesting new ways of doing things, then our behavior is shaped toward making suggestions; we become more creative.

Might we view the sequences of activities in which we engage on a daily basis as a chain or even as a series of chains of behaviors? Early behaviorists suggested that we could, but they were certainly mistaken. Let us consider why.

To remain simple and concrete, consider the words in a sentence such as "I plan to go to the beach." If we naively think of this as a chained sequence of spoken or read words, we miss an important point concerning the proper identification of behavior classes. What sort of education is required to enable us to use such sentences? Is it practice in the linking together of words, or is it practice in the rules of sentence construction, that leads to the ability to use and respond to such sentences? We learn that sentences must have at least a subject and a verb and that modifiers, objects, and subordinate clauses may be used only in prescribed ways. What is shaped is the proper use of syntax, not a chain of spoken words.

In other cases chaining seems more probable. In a boxing match a fighter's behavior is shaped and maintained by the reactions of his opponent, and signs of fatigue or damage to the opponent may act as signals that the desired outcome is approaching; this reinforces the behavior that produced these signals and sets the occasion for new behavior that has been useful in the past, when other opponents have shown similar signs. But even here, we are not talking about a rigid chain of behaviors "rattled off" in a simple and fixed way. The class of behaviors comprising each member of the chain is far more complex and seems clearly lawful only to a boxing expert or to someone who is familiar with the techniques of the fighter involved.

The point is that shaping, chaining, and conditioned reinforcement are surely important in regulating our daily activities, but we must remember that the behaviors and conditioned reinforcers involved are not as easily analyzed as is the case with the trained rat.

In addition, we may return to Skinner's early definition of the reflex and ask whether an established chain may act as a unit of behavior in its own right, rather than as a sequence of activities. Is the very experienced rat progressing through a series of string pulling, marble lifting, carrying, and dropping, or can the whole series be viewed as a single behavior? In the example of the boxer, thousands of hours of training may establish a chain consisting of a left jab followed by an overhand right, but does this remain a two-element chain in the champion?

According to Skinner's criteria for the identification of behavioral units, we may vary factors such as food deprivation, sleep, amount of reinforcement, and other things and note whether orderly changes occur in the behavior under consideration. If we find that the rat goes through its chain more or less quickly or that the boxer uses his jab–overhand-right combination more or less frequently, we are justified in referring to these chains as unitary behaviors. But Skinner continued to treat chains largely as sequences of individual behaviors, although he occasionally refers to a chain as a response.

How may chaining apply to language? In considering language, it is apparent that, although sentences may in some cases amount to the chaining together of words, typical language is surely more than that. We learn classes of behavior that are more accurately called *using sentences that conform to the rules of syntax*, and the individual word is no more an elementary unit than is a particular muscle contraction that occurs in pressing a bar or throwing a ball. Skinner's critics, such as Chomsky (1959) should not be overly criticized for assuming that he, like some earlier psychologists, viewed language as no more than the chaining of words. We will see later that this was by no means the case.

Schedules of Reinforcement

Until the 1950s, psychologists were very unsuccessful in accounting for behaviors that occur over any appreciable span of time; it was risky enough to predict the choice a rat might make in a maze or the amount of forgetting a human subject would show after practicing a list of words. Ferster and Skinner (1957) were the first to show that the scheduling of reinforcers could produce extremely reliable patterns of behavior that could be maintained as long as was desired, often extending over a considerable fraction of the life of an experimental subject such as the rat. The rule by which reinforcers are delivered is called a *schedule of reinforcement*.

Skinner (e.g., 1974) identified parallels to simple reinforcement schedules in the everyday life of humans and, in a number of cases, explained some puzzling aspects of human behavior. If we show that compulsive gambling is maintained because the schedule of reinforcement involved is one that has been shown to maintain persistent behavior in rats or pigeons, we have explained gambling in a real sense. Unfortunately, the number of such examples has remained small and in most cases there is no obvious counterpart in our lives for the great number of reinforcement schedules that have been studied. Nonetheless, the study of schedules of reinforcement has told us some extremely interesting things, many of which have not yet had a real impact on our views of the control of behavior and experience. Before we consider these recent findings, we will discuss the more common reinforcement schedules and describe the patterns of behavior they produce.

Fixed-Interval Schedules   The simplest schedules provide reinforcement based either on the passage of time or on the completion of a response requirement. A *fixed-interval* (FI) *schedule* reinforces the first response that occurs after a set period of time has passed. Thus, a fixed-interval one-minute schedule provides reinforcement for the first response that occurs after one minute has elapsed since the last reinforcement was delivered. A reasonable organism on such a schedule would wait for a minute or more, respond, wait for a minute or more, respond, and so on; only one response is required for each reinforcer delivered.

Such is not the case, however. Pigeons, rats, and other animals (including humans under many conditions) respond many times more than is necessary, even after months and months of daily experience with the same FI schedule. The typical pattern of responding appears as a scallop, which consists of a pause at the onset of the interval, responding beginning after a third to a half of the interval has elapsed, and an increase in the rate of responding up to the time that food is delivered. This pattern is illustrated in Figure 8.7. One might think that subjects behave in such a way because they simply fail to time properly; they underestimate the time remaining until reinforcement is available and thus begin responding too early. But this does not appear to be the case. One would think that some improvement in time estimation would occur after weeks or months of experience with the same schedule value, but this does not occur. Instead, the scallop simply becomes smoother, with little change in the number of responses involved. In addition, the one-third to one-half interval pause occurs over a fairly wide range of schedule values. If time estimation were involved, there would be some intervals (for example, ten seconds) that a reasonable subject could accurately estimate.

Note that the scallop pattern of responding is exactly what occurs in Pavlovian delayed conditioning, where a CS is presented and a UCS appears after a delay period. The Pavlovian procedure does not require a response, of course; the UCS comes no matter what the subject does. The analogous schedule of reinforcement is a *fixed-time schedule*, which is a fixed-interval schedule without the response requirement. Many

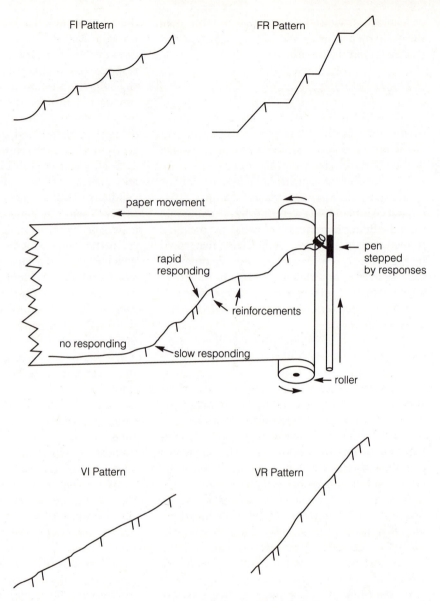

FIGURE 8.7   Patterns for basic schedules of reinforcement. *After Mazur, 1986*

popular examples of FI schedules in daily life actually refer to fixed-time (FT) schedules, as we will see later.

Fixed-Interval Schedules in Daily Life   We may train a rat, a pigeon, or a child on a fixed-interval schedule and be assured that the appropriate pat-

tern of responding will endure day after day for as long as we want to keep the schedule in effect. Are such schedules in effect in daily life? If we could show that they were and that the appropriate pattern of behavior were maintained, we could thereby explain such behavior. Suppose we find that students study little immediately after an examination and that they increase their rate of studying as the next scheduled exam approaches. Similarly, we may find that workers slack off just after payday and increase their rate of working as the next payday approaches. Is this an instance of the influence of FI schedules in daily life?

This may seem to be the case until one considers what behaviors are occurring and what behaviors are being reinforced. In the case of students' studying, the behavior of writing the examination answers and turning them in is actually what is reinforced. True, studying may be a prerequisite for writing proper answers, but it is not the studying itself that is reinforced with a good grade, in the sense that the first key peck after a fixed interval has elapsed is reinforced with food. Unlike the studying that precedes the exam, the key pecks preceding the reinforced one are not in any sense required. The same holds with the relation between rate of working and time since payday. Pay is actually given according to a fixed-time schedule, with the proviso that the worker be an employee. To be an employee usually requires that work be done between paydays, but the schedule clearly is not a simple FI arrangement.

Examples of fixed-interval reinforcement in daily life must refer to simple cases. Although a watched pot never boils, we may repeatedly check it to see if it has; eventually, one of these checks will be reinforced. If we live in an area where buses run on reliable schedules, we may see fixed-interval behavior in the form of looking down the street in the direction from which the bus will come; as the scheduled time nears, the frequency of looking may be seen to increase.

Variable-Interval Schedules A *variable-interval* (VI) *schedule* provides reinforcement for the first response occurring after some average period of time. Thus, on a VI one-minute schedule, reinforcement may come for the first response after ten seconds has passed, then after five minutes, and then after thirty seconds. But the average value of the interval is one minute. Subjects on such schedules respond at moderate and fairly constant rates, even when the frequency of reinforcement varies quite widely. For this reason, VI schedules have been used often as a baseline against which to assess the effects of other factors, such as punishers or drugs.

Variable-Interval Schedules in Daily Life In daily life we have to look long and hard for simple examples of VI schedules. In fact, it is so difficult to find examples that we will suggest one that is only close to a valid example (Schwartz, 1978). If we are trying to call New York on Christmas Day, we will frequently get busy signals or recorded messages telling us that all lines are busy. At some time, we know not when, the lines will be free and our dialing will be reinforced; our call will get through. This is a variable-interval schedule even if we try our call only until the effort pays off; whether we continue dialing after that time, lines are free after variable periods of time pass and those times indeed do have some average value. But on a true VI schedule, once an interval has elapsed and a reinforcer is made available, it remains available, unlike that in our example. A line may be free for only a matter of seconds, and if we do not call quickly enough it will no longer be free. This is thus a VI schedule with a *limited hold*, which in this case is also of variable duration. This means that after the interval elapses, reinforcement is available for only a fixed time and if a response is not made within that time the reinforcer is lost and we must wait for the next interval to pass. If you live in an area where the time of mail delivery is variable, checking your mailbox may provide an example of behavior maintained by a VI schedule.

Fixed-Ratio Schedules A *fixed-ratio* (or FR) *schedule* requires that a given number of responses be made before reinforcement is delivered. For example, an FR 20 schedule requires twenty responses for each reinforcement. Animals on FR schedules behave similarly—each reinforcement is followed by a pause that is then followed by a high steady rate of responding. These high response rates remain more or less the same when the ratio requirement is changed; it is the pause after reinforcement that increases when the ratio requirement is increased and that decreases when fewer responses are required.

Fixed-Ratio Schedules in Daily Life   We can easily recognize instances of FR schedules in daily life. One common example is paying workers on a piecework basis; fixed amounts of pay are given for so many units of work performed. It may seem, as we watch a subject on an FR schedule responding at a high rate, that he, she, or it must like responding under such conditions. But this apparently is not the case. When we ask workers, they often express dissatisfaction with piecework pay. When we ask the pigeon on an FR schedule, we get the same answer. How do we "ask" the pigeon? Needless to say, we cannot ask it directly, but we can do so indirectly, as was shown by Azrin (1961).

If a pigeon is pecking a lighted key and an FR schedule with a large response requirement is in effect, we may add a second key that has no effect other than to turn off the FR key and stop the FR schedule. Azrin found that pigeons occasionally pecked such a key, typically during the pause after FR reinforcement. This is an interesting finding, since no one is forcing the bird to peck the FR key in the first place. If it wants a respite from pecking, it need only stop, ignore the key, and rest! Why not simply do that, rather than pecking a second key to turn off the FR key?

Perhaps this is why workers complain about piecework pay, and perhaps it tells us something important about reinforcement schedules. An FR schedule prescribes what behavior is required for reinforcement and any organism under the control of an FR schedule behaves in the same way; it pauses after reinforcement and responds at constant high rates. Whether it likes the schedule is not relevant.

Variable-Ratio Schedules   On a *variable-ratio* (VR) *schedule*, reinforcement is delivered after a varying number of responses, depending upon the average requirement of the schedule. That is, a VR

25 schedule requires an average of 25 responses per reinforcement, although some reinforcements may be produced by two responses and others by a hundred; the average number is 25. Animals on VR schedules respond at fairly high constant rates, even through periods in which the response requirement is in the hundreds. Once such a large requirement is met, the next reinforcement may come after a requirement of only two or three responses; these easily obtained reinforcers more than make up for the sections of the schedule that require hundreds of responses.

This conclusion is indicated by the finding that animals choose a VR schedule over an FR schedule of the same value; that is, given a choice, a rat or pigeon will spend its time on a VR 25, rather than an FR 25 schedule, even though the average number of responses required for each reinforcer is the same on both schedules (Fantino, 1967; Herrnstein, 1964). Evidently, the animals weight the easily gotten reinforcers more than those less easily obtained.

Variable-Ratio Schedules in Daily Life   Here we have no trouble finding parallels in the daily life of many humans. Slot machines pay off according to VR schedules, and it is a well-known fact that a brief "lucky streak," which occurs when in a part of the schedule requiring a few low response requirements, is enough to keep the gambler responding through the large response requirement portions of the schedule. This is when the house wins, having found long ago that humans, like rats and pigeons, are more affected by the low ratios than by the high ones. Perhaps pigeons and rats believe in lucky streaks, though they probably deserve more credit than that.

Another common instance of VR-like scheduling appears in the video arcades, which have replaced the pinball machines and the pool halls of the past. The parallel is not exact: A video game does not require so many repetitions of the same response for payoff, but if we consider such behavior as a class of responses, the parallel is close. Thus, a class of responses all have the common effect of destroying an invader from space, or saving a small bulemic person from ghosts. Some skill may be involved, but a pigeon's skill in pecking at high rates and in hitting the key also is required on a simple VR schedule. And, unlike the video-game "addict," the pigeon at least receives food for its labors. Those who feel that an unfathomable gulf exists between human and beast are well advised to watch a pigeon pecking for food delivered according to a VR schedule and then go to a video arcade.

Other Schedules of Reinforcement   The number of ways of scheduling reinforcements is infinite, of course, and researchers have studied a large variety of schedules, both with animal and human subjects. Time is a defining property of FI and VI schedules, as well as of DRL and DRH schedules. Differential reinforcement of low rates of response schedules, or *DRL schedules*, require that responses be spaced. For example, a DRL ten-second schedule requires that a response occur and that the next response occur no sooner than ten seconds later. If a response occurs earlier (for example, at seven or nine seconds), a timer resets and no response must occur for ten seconds from that time. A response that occurs once every nine seconds would therefore never be reinforced.

A schedule such as this is rare in daily life, although it may be imposed to alter certain kinds of behavior. For example, an obese patient may receive pieces of food for pressing a button, with the food delivered according to a DRL schedule. This would produce low rates of responding if food were to be obtained regularly. Such a method has proven effective in changing the eating habits of obese patients.

One may well ask how this could be; how can such training change eating habits? It happens that there is evidence that the obese do eat more rapidly than do nonobese people (Schachter, 1971), independent of their state of "hunger" (time since last feeding). In addition, they eat fewer meals, so it follows that they eat more per meal. Unless a person is eating alone, the duration of a meal is more or less fixed by the person's eating mates. So if one could induce an obese

patient to eat more slowly, he or she would eat less overall.

Differential reinforcement of high rates of response schedules, or *DRH schedules*, provide reinforcement only if a specified number of responses occur within a set time. This resembles the procedure on some TV game shows, in which answers must be given within a set time. Whether we are talking about a pigeon pecking twenty times in five seconds or a person naming all of the states beginning with the letter *N*, the result is the same: The procedure produces high rates of response.

Some other schedules combine time and response requirements in other ways. A *conjunctive schedule* requires that both a response requirement and a temporal requirement be met: One might have to respond at least twenty times over 30 seconds for reinforcement. On an *alternative schedule*, the meeting of one requirement is enough; the subject may respond either twenty times *or* once after 30 seconds. An *adjusting schedule* may change the response requirement as time passes. For example, a response requirement of twenty may change to 25 after ten seconds if the required twenty responses do not occur. At ten seconds the requirement could jump to 30, and so on. Or the change could go in the opposite direction; an initial requirement of 100 responses could decrease to 80 after ten seconds, to 60 after twenty seconds, and so on. A lazy subject could just wait for a minute and respond once for reinforcement.

Schedules may be combined in many ways. A *concurrent schedule* provides two or more available schedules of reinforcement simultaneously; a subject may respond to the lever or key of only one of these schedules at a time, but he, she, or it may switch among schedules as often as desired. Such schedules are widely used in the study of the *matching law*, which holds that relative response rates match relative reinforcement frequencies. The matching law will be discussed in greater detail in Chapter 9.

Tandem schedules, like tandem tractor-trailers, are linked together in sequence. A TAND FI 2 FR 10 DRL 2 requires that two minutes pass, whereupon a response changes the schedule to FR 10. After ten responses, the schedule becomes DRL 2 (usually seconds), so that one response, followed by at least a two-second pause, is reinforced. All three schedule requirements must be met, and the fulfilling of one schedule requirement puts the next schedule in effect. In a tandem schedule, no stimuli signal which schedule is in effect. When there *is* a signal, we have a *chained schedule*. Hence, a red light may mean that FI 2 is in effect; when a response occurs after two minutes, the light may change to green, signaling the FR 10 member, followed by orange, signaling DRL 2.

Schedules may also be presented successively, independent of the subject's behavior. A *mixed schedule* provides fixed periods of different schedules in succession with no distinctive S^D signaling each. Thus, a MIX FR 20 VI 5 may provide a two-minute period during which FR 20 is in effect, followed by two minutes of VI 5, followed by two minutes of FR 20, and so on. If a distinctive stimulus signals the schedule in effect, thus identifying the *component* of the schedule in effect, we have a *multiple schedule*. Multiple schedules typically are used in studies of discrimination learning, as discussed earlier. We might alternate periods of red and green accompanied by VI reinforcement and extinction (EXT) respectively, to assess the ability of our subject to distinguish colors.

Human Performance on Reinforcement Schedules

You may wonder if people really show these patterns of responding when they are used as subjects in laboratory experiments studying reinforcement schedules. It seems clear that piecework and gambling do influence human behavior just as fixed- and variable-ratio schedules influence animal responding. But would a normal human on a fixed-interval schedule show "scallop-patterned" responding, and, if the schedule were changed to fixed-ratio, for example, would the pattern of responding change appropriately? The

answer to this question depends on whether the human subjects receive the same "instructions" as animal subjects. That is, if human subjects are told to press a button to make a counter count, they press and their pattern of pressing does not change much as the reinforcement schedule changes.

This illustrates the powerful effect of rules on human behavior, a topic to which we will return. Subjects who follow the verbal rule "press the button" do just that; if the counter occasionally counts, that maintains their pressing, but the patterning of counts does not strongly influence the patterning of their responses.

To avoid such effects, Matthews, Shimoff, Catania, and Sagvolden (1977) ingeniously shaped humans to press a lever, using a counter and a light and a button corresponding to "food magazine operated" and "eat," respectively. Such labels were not actually used, but readers familiar with the shaping of a pigeon's response to a key would view the procedure as identical. The experimenters were not visible to the subjects and shaped the subjects' pressing and eating without the use of verbal instructions. After this was done, the human subjects' responding was appropriate for the different reinforcement schedules that were used.

The Significance of Schedules of Reinforcement

It is difficult to imagine the excitement of researchers of the 1950s, when the study of reinforcement schedules was probably at its peak. For the first time, we could completely control the behavior of a vast number of living things. Not only could we precisely predict the behavior of an individual over days, weeks, or months, but we could also predict that one individual rat would behave like another rat, or like a pigeon, or like a cat, dog, rabbit, child, or Nobel prize winner. Surely, we were on to something!

In addition, if we look to the world around us, we can identify schedules operating in daily life;

after all, we have the pieceworkers and the gamblers responding on FR and VR schedules. To change behavior in these and other cases, we need only change the schedule in force.

Besides controlling behavior and identifying schedules already in force in the world around us, many researchers felt that the study of schedule behavior was important in another way. Through their study, we can find out more about the mechanisms underlying behavior. Performance on interval and DRL schedules can tell us something about a subject's ability to estimate time, for example. FR performance may provide clues regarding the ability to count. Through the analysis of schedules we can assess the importance of conditioned reinforcement, chaining, temporal discrimination, and even of such faculties as attention and short-term memory.

Such hopes were dashed during the 1960s and 1970s. As Jenkins (1970) and Mackintosh (1974) concluded, on the basis of masses of evidence, schedule behavior is not explainable in terms of any simpler, more complex, or more vague principles, such as conditioned reinforcement, expectancies, or memory. Subjects that can easily time a twenty-second interval nonetheless waste thousands of responses on a fixed-interval schedule, even after months of daily sessions.

Reinforcement schedules are just *there;* they are basic laws governing behavior, as Morse and Kelleher (1977) and others have argued. They have made a good case for this, showing that the effect of a schedule per se is enough to keep a cat, rat, or monkey responding for weeks when the only reinforcer is electric shock. These data have implications for human masochism. The study of schedules is justified when it leads to important discoveries such as this.

Treatment of Human Psychotics

Many patients in mental hospitals spend decades as so-called hopeless cases, unresponsive to psychotherapy or to drugs. Such patients often refuse to eat, to dress themselves, and to practice the most basic personal hygiene. Ayllon and Haughton (1962) proposed to apply Skinner's principles to treat a population of such patients, diagnosed as chronic schizophrenics.

But how may that be done? What could act as a reinforcer to alter the behavior of patients who appear to want nothing and whose files show them to be "out of reality contact," subject to psychotic intrusions," and suffering from faulty "ego identification" (Ayllon & Haughton, 1962)? Using food as a reinforcer seemed out of the question, since half of the 45 patients refused to eat, even after tube and intravenous feeding and electroshock treatment. When they ate, they were spoon-fed. How does one induce such patients to eat without assistance?

In a situation such as this, the therapist considers the reinforcement contingencies that currently maintain the patients' behavior and those that might alter the behavior. These patients had refused to eat unless spoon-fed; in one case, this had gone on for seventeen years. Could it be that the attention accompanying spoon-feeding acted as a reinforcer, maintaining the refusing-to-eat behavior? How could that situation be changed so that the health of the patients would not be endangered?

Ayllon and Haughton began a simple and effective procedure involving 32 patients. Each meal was available at a fixed time and access to the dining room was available for 30 minutes; then the door was locked and those patients who did not come to the dining room on their own missed the meal. Meals were missed at first, but patients who had not done so in years soon entered the dining room and ate without coaxing. Two patients refused to cooperate and went hungry for seven and fifteen days, during which time their health was closely monitored by the staff. But, eventually, they came to the dining room as well. The 30-minute access was reduced to twenty minutes, then to fifteen minutes, and finally to five minutes. The change in the patients' behavior was a "revelation to the nurses" (Ayllon & Haughton, 1962), who had spoon-fed the patients for years, but it should not have occasioned surprise. Food acts as a reinforcer under many circumstances, but so does spoon-feeding, which provides personal attention, as well as food.

The therapists later required that a penny be dropped in a collection can for access to the dining room and they even established some social cooperation behavior, by requiring that two buttons be pressed for access to the room. The buttons were far enough apart that two patients had to press simultaneously. All but one of 43 patients learned to do this. All of this is not much improvement, you might say. But imagine what the staff charged with the care of these patients thought of it! It was only weeks before that many of these patients had to be fed, clothed, and groomed by others.

In a later study, Ayllon and Azrin (1964) used a simple strategy to alter the eating behavior of eighteen patients who refused to pick up their cutlery and consequently did much of their eating with their hands. It took three months to achieve almost 100 percent success, but all it took was the addition of contingencies for a specific behavior. Patients who picked up all three pieces of cutlery immediately went to the serving line, while those who did not were sent to the end of the line awaiting trays and cutlery. This meant a delay of only five minutes or so, but it acted as a sufficient consequence to establish the new behavior.

The most elaborate treatment using Skinner's principles is the famous token economy established by Ayllon and Azrin in the early 1960s. This was described in 1965 and presented in more detail in 1968. A *token economy* arranges reinforcement for socially-desirable behaviors. The patients in their study were female psychotics, many of whom had spent twenty to 30 years in the chronic schizophrenic ward. Instead of using food as the sole reinforcer, the therapists chose things that seemed valued by specific patients. Some of these were:

Choice of one of five sleeping rooms	A twenty-minute walk
Use of a personal chair	A trip to town
Choice of eating group	A room divider
A personal coat rack	Candy, books, and other goods

All of these things were purchased with metal tokens that were contingent on work done by the patients. A choice of room cost from one to 30 tokens per day, depending on the room, a trip to town cost 100 tokens, a twenty-minute walk required two tokens, and so on. The television set was coin operated (fifteen minutes per token) and access to the dining room was through a token-operated turnstile.

In one situation, eight psychotic subjects worked outside the ward; they served food, typed and answered the phone, cleaned the laboratory, or worked in the laundry. Each job paid 70 tokens per day. Patients volunteered for the jobs and shifted to nonpreferred jobs when payment was no longer given for preferred work. When tokens were given free, work ceased, so their behavior was not solely dependent on the opportunity to leave the ward or to do work that was intrinsically satisfying.

The program was expanded to include 44 patients, most of whom were diagnosed as chronic schizophrenic and who had been hospitalized for an average of sixteen years. All suffered from "severe psychosis" (Ayllon & Azrin, 1968), many had extremely low IQ test scores, and some were very deficient in verbal abilities. Yet all were affected by the token system; when appropriate behavior produces tokens exchangeable for little things that are valued by patients, patients respond. Aside from eight patients who did little but sleep and eat, all worked steadily as waitresses, clerks, janitors, and launderers. The least responsive still showed improvement in grooming and other self-care behaviors.

Bear in mind that these patients had been diagnosed as hopeless, had been hospitalized for many years, and initially were incapable of even the most rudimentary self-care. Yet, the alteration of consequences for their behavior transformed them. Where passivity had been reinforced with attention (for example, in spoon-feeding), work that could become satisfying in itself was reinforced with tokens, a currency that could purchase things of value to the patient. And it seemed at the outset that there were no things of value to them.

Concept Formation

The class of stimuli controlling an operant class need not be composed of simple and concrete elements. Often the effective stimulus class takes the form of a concept; rather than being controlled by lights, sounds, and tastes, behavior is controlled by concepts such as truth, beauty, people, water surface, edible object, and noun-verb order. There is nothing mysterious about such concepts and their influence has even been studied with animal subjects. Simply put, a concept refers to the fact that groups of particulars are treated as a class; they are exemplars of that concept. For example, the concept of truth includes all that I count as an aspect of my experience that has not been negated by other experience. My concept of people is the set of common characteristics according to which I identify individuals as people. This includes bodily characteristics such as arms and legs, as well as behavioral characteristics, such as the ability to use language. How did I come to have such a concept? Following Plato, we could assume that I was born with a concept of people; when I encounter an instance of this concept it awakens whatever innate archetype I possess and I recognize an individual as a person. On the other hand, my concept could arise from my training and education. Since I was an infant, I have been taught that such and such a being was a person and that other beings, though they have arms and legs, were not. Which alternative is more likely correct?

During the Second World War Skinner and his colleagues, in their attempt to aid the war effort, showed that pigeons were capable of learning fairly abstract concepts. The military had developed missiles for use against the Japanese, but a reliable guidance system was lacking. The missile was in the form of a glider that could be launched from a large bomber, but where it went then was very uncertain. The Japanese had solved the problem with a living guidance system and the kamikaze was essentially a missile directed by its human occupant. Skinner proposed a living guidance system in the form of pigeons.

In the laboratories of General Mills in Minnesota, pigeons were trained to peck a semiconductor screen, through which was visible a target projected on the wall. A target could be a film of a Japanese ship, although a photo of an intersection in northern New Jersey was also a frequently used target. The pigeon was strapped in a harness and its beak tipped with gold; pecks on the screen controlled the direction of movement of a "missile," consisting of a table on wheels driven by small motors. As the pigeon pecked the screen for occasional food, the mock missile moved across the room to the target.

Eventually, several pigeons were incorporated into the system to increase reliability. Suppose that two Japanese ships appeared on the screen and that the pigeon pecked alternately at both; the missile's course could be disrupted so that both were missed. This possibility was avoided through the use of a panel of three pigeons, which "voted" on the target of choice. As many as eight pigeons were sometimes placed on such panels (personal communication from Norman Guttman, a worker on the project).

The device worked beautifully. The pigeons acquired the concept of "Japanese ship" of such and such class and developed a peculiar interest in an aerial view of a location in New Jersey. (The system was demonstrated to the military in Washington, which saw its potential usefulness, but which declined to fund its further development. Work going on at the time in New Mexico was receiving higher priority, and it promised to eliminate the need for precise bombing!) See Skinner (1983b) for further details concerning the project.

Another example of *concept learning* in pigeons was reported by Thom Verhave (1966), then a scientist working for Lilly pharmaceutical company. In the manufacture of capsules for their drugs, Lilly relied on skillful women, who sorted capsules as they passed along a conveyor belt. They picked out faulty capsules and their pay was docked if later inspection revealed that they had made many mistakes. This was not an enviable job! Yet, it had its glamour; accurately spotting faulty capsules required a lot of experience and could not be done by novices. The concepts "good capsule" and "bad capsule" took time to learn.

Verhave quickly trained pigeons to do the job as well as and even better than the human sorters. By placing a pigeon in a box by the conveyor, the pigeon could see the capsules as they came and it was occasionally fed for picking a clear key (or window) when a good capsule went by. One could also train it to peck a second key when a bad capsule was present. After food reinforcement for identifying clearly good and faulty capsules, samples more difficult to classify were used until the pigeons were correctly sorting capsules that previously required a skilled human inspector to classify. The birds had learned the concept of "good capsule."

Like Skinner's Project Pigeon, this method remained an example of the learning of concepts by pigeons; it was never used by Lilly. Apparently, their public relations people advised against pigeon pill inspectors, since undesirable images were bound to be conjured up by the public. Nonetheless, Verhave, supported by Lilly, applied for a patent, which was ultimately denied. A suit was filed against the Federal Patent Office, challenging the denial; Verhave believed that the denial could not have been due to the fact that living things were involved, since many other devices (such as horsecollars and typewriters) require living things for their operation.

The answer finally came and revealed the government position on animal mentality. The patent was denied because "one cannot patent a mental process," thereby indicating that the simple performances of these birds was evidence for mental activity. There is little doubt that the women capsule inspectors were relieved that the project was not used by Lilly; many workers have been replaced by machines, but being replaced

TABLE 8.2 Concept Learning by Pigeons. General method used by Verhave (1966), Herrnstein and Loveland (1966), Herrnstein, Loveland, & Cable (1976), and Skinner (1983b).

Training

1. Samples of clear "positive instances" (of ships, pill capsules, trees, people) —mixed with—	Pecking produces occasional food
2. Samples of clear "negative instances" (of friendly ships, bad capsules, scenes with no trees, people) —followed by—	Pecking produces no food
3. Samples of less clearly different positive and negative instances —followed by—	Pecking positive produces occasional food

Testing

4. Presentations of positive and negative instances not included in the training sets	Pecking has no consequence

by an animal, especially a pigeon, would be especially unpleasant.

In a similar study, Herrnstein and Loveland (1966) showed that pigeons readily learn the concept of *people*. They trained pigeons to peck a key when a slide included people or parts of people and not to peck when people were absent. Then they showed the subjects some new slides. The pigeons were amazingly good at distinguishing new slides based on the presence or absence of people. If pigeons can easily learn such a concept, it is likely that humans learn such concepts as well, which is contrary to Plato's theory. See Table 8.2.

However, a few years later the same authors reached different conclusions. Herrnstein, Loveland, and Cable (1976) showed that pigeons could learn the concepts of *trees*, *water surface*, and a *particular young woman* extremely quickly, too quickly in the authors' opinion. They suggested that pigeons must be born with knowledge of

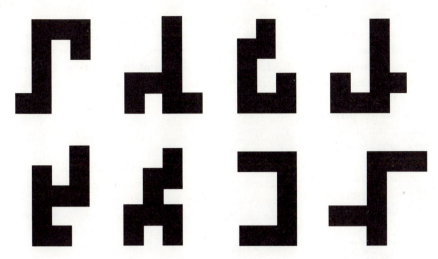

FIGURE 8.8   Some of the forms presented to the subjects (pigeons and humans) in Hollard and Delius's mental rotation experiments.

many things, in the form of templates or schemata that assist them in rapidly learning concepts that correspond to common features of the world. Since there could be no precise schema for the young woman the pigeons came to know, their foreknowledge must be in the form of a readiness of some sort to learn particular concepts.

The authors referred to these concepts that the pigeons seemingly came prepared to learn as "natural concepts." Later, Herrnstein's group showed that pigeons also seem prepared to learn the concept of *fish* extremely quickly (Herrnstein & deVilliers, 1980). Why pigeons should come prepared to learn such a concept is anyone's guess; perhaps such a finding suggests that Herrnstein and Loveland's earlier explanation was accurate after all.

Mental Rotation

In Skinner's opinion, mental activity is actually no different in kind from other behavior (e.g., 1963). Further, if conditions have been arranged to demonstrate an aspect of mental activity in humans, they may be arranged similarly to demonstrate the same activity in animals. This was demonstrated in the case of mental rotation.

One of the most publicized pieces of research during the 1970s was the demonstration of mental rotation by Shepard and his colleagues. For example, Cooper and Shepard (1973) presented human subjects with letters or digits as they normally appear or as mirror images. Then they presented these numbers and digits rotated to various extents and asked the subjects to identify them as normal or mirror image. An interesting effect appeared. Subjects' reaction time (RT) depended upon the degree of rotation; it increased linearly as a function of angular rotation. Thus, it seemed that subjects were "mentally rotating" the display in order to determine whether it was normal or mirror image, and the farther it had to be rotated, the longer it took. Is the ability to manipulate images mentally an example of the higher mental functioning of which we humans are capable? Or can pigeons duplicate the feat?

Hollard and Delius (1982) cleverly investigated the capacity for mental rotation in pigeons (see Figure 8.8). Pigeons were trained in a matching to sample (MTS) task in which one of the forms was presented on a response key. After fifteen pecks to that key, a display appeared on each of two keys on the left and right of the center key. On one comparison key was the form presented on the center sample key; on the other comparison key was the mirror image of the sample form. For half of the birds, pecks to the matching key were reinforced with food; for the others, pecks to the mirror image key led to food.

After training on a variety of forms, tests were conducted with various of the forms presented with comparison forms (normal and mirror image) rotated in one of five steps, ranging from zero degrees (normal) to 180 degrees. The reaction times of the birds, which were performing essentially the task required of Cooper and Shepard's subjects, was recorded, as were the errors made with various degrees of rotation.

After the data were collected, the pigeon chamber was disassembled, except for the end of the box holding the three keys and the feeder. Twenty-two college students were brought in and trained to perform the pigeons' task; correct responses were reinforced with the equivalent of half a cent each (pigeons had been reinforced with grain). The students were tested much as the pigeons were, and the results were analyzed and compared with the pigeon data.

The human subjects performed much as did Cooper and Shepard's subjects. Their reaction time and accuracy depended on the degree of rotation of the forms, with the greatest accuracy and fastest RT when the comparison forms were not rotated. Accuracy decreased and RT increased as the degree of rotation increased up to 180 degrees. How did the pigeons compare?

Amazingly (perhaps), the authors found that the birds were "more efficient than humans"! Human RT varied from about 1.5 to 2.75 seconds as the degree of rotation increased; the pigeons' RT was always less than a second. And the degree of rotation had no effect on the pigeons' RT. The percentage of errors was approximately the same for the birds and the humans, with the salient difference being that the birds made more errors at rotations of 90 degrees, while the human errors were greatest at rotations of 180 degrees.

The authors suggested that the superior performance of the pigeons may be due to the fact that human estimates of orientation are made with reference to gravity, what we perceive as "down." Birds, on the other hand, use no such reference; for them, orientation is arbitrary and relative to the position of the observer. No one teaches them the artificial coordinates in which we frame the world.

Problem Solving

Skinner's specific views on problem solving appeared in 1966 and are generally consonant with the views of other learning theorists on the topic. He believes, as did they, that there is nothing special about problems set for solution. As Skinner wrote:

> [T]here is probably no behavioral process which is not relevant to the solving of some problem. . . . [A]n exhaustive analysis of techniques would coincide with an analysis of behavior as a whole. (1966a, pp. 225–226)

Unlike his predecessors, Skinner emphasizes the distinction between contingency-shaped and rule-following behaviors. An outfielder's response to the problem of the approaching fly ball has been shaped by past contingencies; what has been the consequence of various responses in the past? Like the wisdom of the old country doctor and the answers that intuition provides, the contingencies involved have not been formulated in verbal rules. (In what situation does a given behavior produce such and such a consequence?)

Contrast that with the commander in charge of the retrieval of an incoming satellite. His behavior has been shaped by an education in the rules of ballistics and the calculating of trajectories. So-called rational, or rule-governed, behavior is shaped without need for exposure to the actual contingencies involved. Such rules are passed on by cultures in the form of maxims and proverbs and in all of the verbal education we receive.

But thinking and problem solving are by no means purely verbal; Skinner believes that operant behavior in all its forms is involved. The contingencies involved may be subtle, and they may

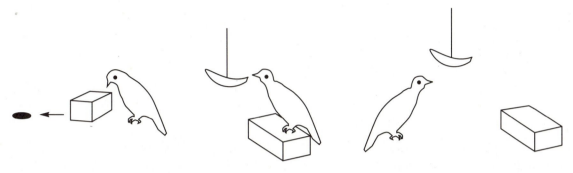

1. The pigeon is trained to move a box to a specific spot.

2. The pigeon is trained to climb onto a box and peck a banana.

3. Test: A banana is suspended out of reach and the box is positioned away from the banana.

FIGURE 8.9   Simulation of insight in problem-solving experiments by Epstein, Kirshnit, Lanza, and Rubin (1984).

shape behavior even though they are experienced only in the form of learned rules. Needless to say, Skinner opposes models such as those of information processing. The fundamental error committed is the assumption that we are input/output mechanisms; such an assumption then requires cognitive processes to relate input and output and research done only for the purpose of testing predictions of specific cognitive models. Are we interested in how we solve problems or in how contrived cognitive processes may work?

As an illustration of a possible Skinnerian approach to problem solving, consider Epstein, Kirshnit, Lanza, and Rubin's study of insight in pigeons (1984). They proposed that the insight shown by Köhler's chimpanzees, evidenced in the subjects' use of a box as a jumping stand to retrieve a suspended banana, was possible only because of specific past learning experiences. Köhler's subjects must have learned to push objects toward targets and to climb on objects to reach other objects. Köhler's chimps were adults and had had plenty of time to acquire such learning.

The two learned skills are irrelevant to the lives of most pigeons. But could pigeons that were trained to push and to climb then insightfully put the objects together to retrieve an object hanging out of reach? Epstein, et al. trained pigeons to push a small cardboard box toward a green spot located at various positions over a period of one to eight weeks. The pigeons also were shaped to climb onto a box placed under a suspended facsimile of a banana. They were then tested with the banana suspended out of reach and the box positioned away from it (see Figure 8.9).

Like Köhler's chimps, the birds first appeared "confused" (Epstein, et al., 1984) and looked back and forth from the banana to the box. Then "suddenly" they pushed the box to a position under the banana, "sighting" the banana as they did so. They placed the box appropriately, stepped onto it, and pecked the banana. Is that insight, in the sense that Köhler defined it? The birds never were trained to push the box toward the banana, but their experience in pushing and climbing allowed their insight. Birds that were trained to peck the banana but not to climb, or to climb and peck but not to push, or to climb and peck and push randomly showed no insight when tested.

This is one way to study problem solving. It is of little help to argue that the occurrence of insight requires past learning experience unless the nature of that experience is specified. Similarly, it is of little help when Köhler (1925) suggested that insight is not "blind trial and error" but requires that attention be paid to "structural properties" of the situation. In the box-and-banana problem, insight depends on having learned to push objects toward targets and to climb on objects to reach other objects. Needless to say, other cases of insight require other previously learned skills.

Skinner and Language

Skinner was always interested in literature, as any reader of his popular works can see. After decades of work, Skinner published *Verbal Behavior* (1957), which presents his views on language. In this book, he attempted to provide a *behavioral* account of language; it consisted of only an outline of an operant analysis of language use. No data were included and no great interest was shown initially by Skinner's followers. *Verbal Behavior* did not seem to be a barn burner.

Noam Chomsky, the noted linguist, noticed the book and evidently felt that, as a behavioral treatment of language, it epitomized what he disliked in older linguistic theories. In 1959, Chomsky published a scathing review of it, which was far more widely read than Skinner's book. No one responded to Chomsky until 1970, when MacCorquodale reviewed Chomsky's article. The reason for the long delay was that Chomsky's attack was so unrelated to Skinner's views that no one felt the appropriate object of the attack.

Chomsky's criticism was directed toward the behaviorisms of the 1940s and 1950s that derived from Hull's theory. It attacked the theory of reinforcement based on drive reduction and the extreme molecular view that might explain language as the stringing together of letters and words. In fact, Skinner held no such views. Skinner's view of language stresses its function, and letters, words, sentences, paragraphs, or *whatever* may be appropriate units (1957).

Skinner's point, which is not original, is simply that verbal behavior *is* behavior and, as such, it is learned as is other behavior. Does this mean that language derives from the deliberate rein-forcing of spoken words that are then hooked together in chains? Since other behavior is not so characterized by Skinner, there is no reason that language should be.

The functional unit of any behavior is that class of behaviors that covaries as a function of consequences (that is, as a class). Reinforcers are consequences that increase the frequency of occurrence of a class of behavior. Behavior also comes under the influence of a stimulus class that includes whatever stimuli or situations set the occasion for the behavior. Does all of this hold for verbal behavior?

The unit of verbal behavior is not a letter, word, or phoneme (basic sound); as is the case with other behavior, there is no fixed unit. As we learn to speak, our verbalizations are shaped by the reactions of those around us. The function of speech is to influence the behavior of others, and, therefore, the form of our speech is molded so it is effective in doing that. I speak loudly and clearly because that has been effective in the community in which I live. The unit of speech is sometimes a word, and at other times a phrase, idiom, or passage (Skinner, 1953, 1957). I use proper grammar because I am more readily understood when I do so. All of this should be no revelation; speaking is behaving and it is shaped by consequences as are other behaviors.

Not everyone shares such a functional view of language. For example, the philosopher Bertrand Russell marveled that the whole of human knowledge and thought was the consequence of 26 shapes! Letters and their combinations were all that seemed essential in Russell's view of language. Skinner (1957) criticized him, suggesting that one could use Morse code and marvel that all knowledge and thought is expressable with *two* symbols. In fact, of course, the bare symbols we use are a small part of language in general; meaning comes not from combinations of symbols, but from our experience behaving in a complex environment. There is no context-independent pure language. This functional view of language is similar to the pragmatic view of James and Dewey (Chapter 1).

Whether we speak and what we say at a given time is influenced by a host of factors, including the current situation, what we have just said, and so on; verbal behavior typically is controlled by multiple factors. Our current repertoire of verbal behavior depends upon the past consequences of various kinds of verbalization; some reinforcers of verbal behavior are attention, approval, affection, and submission (Skinner, 1953). Skinner (1936) invented an "auditory Rorschach" in the form of the verbal summator as a means of examining a person's current verbal stock.

The summator was a recording that was played in a nearby room; it was designed to resemble difficult-to-understand speech. Subjects that were told to interpret the conversation in the next room actually heard sounds like "eye-uh-ah-uh" and "oo-ee-uh-uh," presented either faintly or against a noisy background. Their reports, like responses to the ink blots of the Rorschach, reflected their current repertoire of verbal behavior.

Private Experience

Recall that early behaviorists, such as Thorndike and Watson, believed that thinking, remembering, seeing, and other mental activities could be studied as other behavior is studied. But Hull and his associates cared little about private events, and Tolman was clear in throwing "raw feels" out of science. Due to their great influence, behaviorism came to be seen as a mindless position and, to this day, a good many behaviorists and critics of behaviorism feel that behaviorism and mental activity are incompatible.

Radical Behaviorism

Skinner's first statement on private experience and behaviorism appeared in a 1945 paper: "The Operational Analysis of Psychological Terms." In it he criticized contemporary operational analyses, citing what he called "*methodological behaviorism.*" This is the view that there is a distinction between public and private events and that psychology (to remain scientific) can deal only with

public events. Skinner noted that this is the position that accepts the arid philosophy of truth by agreement; something is real if at least two observers agree. Methodological behaviorism leaves the mind to philosophers.

In the same paper, Skinner referred to his own view, which he called *radical behaviorism*, and which does not distinguish between private and public events. It treats a toothache as a stimulus as physical as a typewriter and "seeing" as an activity no different in kind from walking. This view follows Watson in denying the "mental" as different in kind from the physical. It does not mean that all is physical, but that all is of a kind.

Skinner certainly does not deny the existence of private experience, nor does he feel that its study is beyond us. What he does deny (as did Thorndike and Watson) is the mind-body dualism of the mentalists and the methodological behaviorists. There is no separate realm of nonphysical images, thoughts, and feelings: private and public, inner and outer are the same in kind. Thinking is something that we do, just as walking is something that we do. And we think mental thoughts no more than we walk mental steps. Our names for feelings are words that refer to real stimuli just as words refer to objects we see. To feel pain is a reaction to pain-producing stimulation, just as recognizing a friend is a reaction to other stimulation. It is important, however, to realize that feelings do not make us act. When we touch a hot stove it hurts and it makes us pull the hand away. However, withdrawing the hand is a reflex response that would occur whether we felt pain or not. We do not withdraw because it hurts (Skinner, 1974).

Awareness Our families and educational systems obviously teach us to name the objects of the world we seem to share. Society allows the very young child to refer to all four-footed animals as "bow-wows," but it later expects that proper names be used corresponding to different species and later requires that names for subspecies be used correctly. We learn to name things because society (the verbal community) reinforces correct naming. "That's right; she *is* a cocker spaniel," or "That *is* a fir tree." The learning of language is in large part the learning of the verbal community's names for things.

The verbal community also teaches us to name aspects of private experience. "That is a bad bruise; it must hurt." "You have eaten too much, you must have a stomachache." "After all of that work, you must feel tired." "You tried so hard, but failed; you must be disappointed." "After what he did, you must be angry." Based on what circumstances it finds us in and what it can see us doing, the verbal community teaches us the labels for our private experiences. We learn the names for pain, fatigue, disappointment, anger, impatience, sadness, and the other aspects of our experience.

But Skinner suggests that we ultimately know our subjective experience less well than we know the public world around us. This is because of the limitations faced by society as it teaches us to name the varieties of our private experience. Those around us can often tell when we are in pain or tired or disappointed or angry by seeing what has happened to us and/or what we are doing. But in many cases they cannot.

Society may or may not be able to tell when we are diffident, embarrassed, hungry, determined, or in pain. On occasions when it cannot tell, it cannot teach us to label our experience appropriately. Much of the function of great literature, art, and music is to produce private experiences and, in some cases, to provide labels for them. A literary piece that evokes wonder or sadness in the reader helps to teach us to properly label such private experiences when they occur in the future. Great literature is highly valued, in part because it is so scarce; it is no mean feat to evoke strong private reactions in readers.

Once society has taught us to name whatever private experiences it can, it urges us to report such experiences later. "Are you hungry?" "What do you see?" "How does your stomach feel?" We are repeatedly drilled in the reporting of internal events and we become more or less adept at doing

it. But reporting that we see a car coming is no different in kind from reporting a stomachache; the main difference is that we can lie more easily about the stomachache, since the questioner cannot see this experience, as he or she can see the oncoming car. There is no reason why a behaviorist cannot study the factors that determine that we see cars or that we feel stomachaches.

However, since society finds it harder to train us to label private experience, we will always be less able to know our private experience. One way in which we do discern such experience uses the same method that society uses to infer it in us so that the proper labels can be taught. That is, just as the verbal community judges our private experience in part by observing our actions, we often judge our own experience by observing our actions.

What does it mean to say that I was "hungrier than I thought?" Such a statement might be made by someone who had ordered food, eaten it, and still wanted more. The individual had estimated his or her feelings of hunger and ordered food that was judged sufficient to quell that hunger. The food is now gone but the hunger remains; the earlier estimate of hunger was mistaken, as is revealed by the fact that the individual still feels like eating.

In another common circumstance, we may believe that we have forgiven someone for a wrong done to us; yet, when we next meet the person we find that we scowl and clench our fists. We didn't realize that we were still angry, but our reaction shows that we are. Similarly, tears and a feeling of sadness when we hear the name of a lost loved one tells us that we still grieve, although we were certain that our grief was past.

Such cases are common and show that we are often poor judges of our feelings. In a great many cases we judge our private experience on the basis of what we know to be our actions, just as society does when it teaches us to name those experiences. What are our feelings toward brown bread, nuclear war, the plight of the poor, or the existence of God? When we consider our opinions on

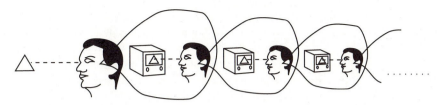

FIGURE 8.10   The copy theory of perception and thought.

such matters, we often think of our behavior with respect to the issues. If an acquaintance eats nothing but brown bread, writes pamphlets opposing nuclear war, and gives freely to the poor, we assess his opinions on such matters accordingly. The next time that you are asked for an opinion on some matter and you must consider it, see whether part of what you consider is what you have recently done with respect to the matter at hand. If it is, then you are judging yourself in the same way that you judge others, based on your own past actions (cf. Bern, 1967).

Conscious Content   The British philosophers of the eighteenth and nineteenth centuries believed that the real world was within us, and early psychologists saw their task as the analysis of this "content of consciousness." We do have dreams and reveries, imagine distant places, and recall events from the far distant past. Wilder Penfield (1958) reported that electrical stimulation of the brain apparently produced detailed memories in his patients, evidently roused from their storage chambers in the cortex. How does radical behaviorism deal with such conscious contents?

Skinner illustrates the ancient point of view regarding the content of consciousness by referring to a popular film sponsored by Bell Telephone, called *The Gateways to the Mind*. According to this film, the nervous system resembles (not surprisingly) a telephone system. Stimulation of the body surface produces messages, resembling little lightning flashes, that travel to the brain. In the brain is a television screen that shows a display, which is seen by a "little man" in our heads. Depending on the message, the little man presses various buttons and pulls levers that lead to an outgoing series of little lightning flashes, producing appropriate movement of our body. Thus is explained sensation and perception, thinking and judgment, and action: The little man does it all. What we see, hear, and feel is represented by copies produced on the TV screen and (presumably) by the audio equipment available to the little man.

Needless to say, the little man is intended to represent the wonders of the functioning of the brain and the explanation is fine unless one wonders how the little man operates. Does he have a little TV screen in his head and a yet smaller little man to see it? Such explanations provide only an infinite regress; we never get to any more than copies within us and copies of *us* within us. What have we gained?

It is true that copies of stimulating objects do exist in the nervous system. Visual stimulation is copied on the retina, in the optic nerve, in the lateral geniculate of the thalamus, and in the cortex. But do such copies tell us anything about seeing? A Leica camera makes far better copies than does the retina, but does it see?

The copy theory (Figure 8.10) was invented and remains popular because it seemed to explain how experience changes us; we react to the world by copying it, as a camera or a computer copies and saves things. Skinner (1987) proposed a far more apt metaphor for the way in which experience changes us. He suggests that, instead of being like a computer saving its input, we are more like storage batteries. We put electricity in the battery and we take electricity out of the battery. But there is never any electricity *in* the battery.

When we put it in and take it out, we are changing the battery, much as experience changes us. In both cases nothing is copied.

Mental Way Stations   In Skinner's view, the "little man," or "inner man," as he calls it, has been pressed into service to do much more than just our perceiving and reacting. He is actually a summary term for all of the unfinished causal sequences that abound in explanations of our behavior. It is he who has memory, ambition, aggressiveness, self-control, and all of the other mental way stations that have been proposed. He has moods, personality disorders, cognitions, and expectancies; in short, he is the embodiment of all of the intervening variables that Skinner believes act to obstruct a real understanding of our workings.

Skinner (1980; 1989) examined the etymology of some common English words that refer to inner states, or mental way stations. Interestingly, their original referent was to external things; they were descriptors of activity. Presumably, their meanings changed over time in such a way that they came to refer to internal states. Here are some examples:

Term	Original Meaning
wish	to strive for
yearn	to ask for
envy	to emulate
scorn	to humiliate (as by removing horns)
sad	to be sated

Other examples are easy to find. To the Greeks, *idea* meant "an image or likeness," and *glad* originally meant "shiny or bright." How many other terms originated as referents to observable situations, objects, or actions and eventually came to refer to inner states?

Skinner believes such mental way stations to be harmful, not because the things to which they refer do not exist, but because they represent unfinished causal accounts. When we describe someone's actions as due to a bad mood, we have only applied a name to certain kinds of behavior that we classify as representative of a bad mood. Why the behavior occurs is left unexplained. Similarly, when we recall or fail to recall a name, referring to a good or bad memory adds nothing to the observation. As discussed earlier, such naming is often treated as explaining, yet the observed behavior has merely been referred to something imagined to be inside the individual. The factors leading to our ability to recall or not (that is, to have a good or bad memory) lie in the past experience of the individual, as well as in aspects of the present situation.

Secondly, assuming such way stations often requires that people can accurately report subjective experience and that they be aware of factors influencing them. Masses of research, as well as daily experience, shows that this is not true, as we have noted already. "Inner man" remains a mystery to most of us, as well "he" should.

Phylogeny and Ontogeny

Skinner presents his position on the influences of heredity and environment in "The Phylogeny and Ontogeny of Behavior" (1966b), which begins with a quote from Blaise Pascal:

> "Habit is a second nature that destroys the first. But what is the nature? Why is habit not natural? I am very much afraid that nature is itself only first habit as habit is second nature."

The French physicist was suggesting that the distinction between effects of environmental experience (habit) and heredity (nature) is misplaced. Rather than assume that habit replaces instinct, it seems more natural to view learning and heredity as depending on similar processes; that is, habit is natural and nature is first habit.

Skinner agrees with this interpretation. He points out that behaviorists realize that much of our behavior is inherited; for example, we do not have to learn to pump our blood or digest our food. If internal behavior is thus genetically determined, so might be much of our other behavior. But what does it mean to say that behavior is inherited?

Inherited behavior is commonly believed to have been selected in the course of evolution. It is chosen for its survival value from some pool of behaviors and it is defined in terms of some sort of unit, like the fixed action pattern. It may take intermediate forms in successive generations, as different gradations prove more useful in promoting survival. We should expect variation in behaviors (and structures) as the selection pressures change.

All these characteristics of genetically selected behaviors apply as well to operant behaviors "selected" during an individual's lifetime (that is, in ontogeny). One need only substitute the phrase *contingencies of reinforcement* for *natural selection*! Thus, operants are chosen either by nature or human design. They are defined as a unit by the class of responses producing a common consequence and they come under the control of discriminative stimuli. And when reinforcement contingencies are altered, we find increased variation in operant behavior until the new contingencies select the final form of behavior.

Along these lines, recent critics of behaviorism have pointed to exceptions to the laws of learning. Among these exceptions is the discovery by the Brelands that the performances of animals trained for commercial purposes (for example, television and movies) were often disrupted by the intrusion of species-specific behaviors. The influence of phylogenic behavior on learned behavior is by no means exceptional, and there are cases in which the reverse occurs. Skinner (1977) noted that one bird in Project Pigeon came to peck at targets on the screen very rapidly and it also came to peck too rapidly at its food to allow it to eat. If this had not been noticed the bird could have starved. In this case, the so-called misbehavior involves the influence of learning on innate behavior.

In these and other cases there is no point in attempting to clearly separate learned and innate behavior. In many cases, such as aggression, territoriality, and courtship, there are varying contributions by innate and learned factors. In the case of aggression it is obvious that selection pressures in phylogeny could favor aggressive in-

dividuals, and it is obvious that aggressive behavior is often reinforced as an operant. A single case of aggression could depend on either or both factors.

3. CRITICISMS OF SKINNER

Skinner is extremely well known, largely because of his popular writings and autobiography. He has come to represent behaviorism in the minds of many, and thus be has been criticized as if he held the views of all other behaviorists, both living and dead. Most frequently, he is charged with holding the mechanistic S-R position of Hull. This is not to say that Skinner is not criticizable—far from it. Let us consider briefly the criticisms that are not legitimate, followed by those that are.

A critic who argues against the following is not criticizing Skinner; the real target is Hull and simple-minded S-R associationism:

1. Learning involves the establishment of specific S-R associations. Our goal is to analyze behavior into such units.

2. Reinforcers reduce biological drives.

3. Private experience is irrelevant.

This is *not* Skinner's view; *learning* for him is a poor term that refers to the formation of correlations between classes of behaviors and classes of stimuli. These are in no sense S-R associations; orderly relations between behavior and the world are something to be discovered. By the same token, reinforcers do not share any fundamental property aside from the fact that they may be observed to act as reinforcers under given conditions. Private experience is important and may be dealt with in the same manner as other behavior; experiencing *is* behaving (see Morris, 1988).

The following criticisms of Skinner are more legitimate. The first criticism is the assumed lack of concern for cognitive processes, especially in behavior therapy. The second is his relative neglect of instinctive behavior.

Cognitive Behavior Therapy

Skinner's critics have included behavior therapists; this may seem paradoxical, since the methods used by behavior therapists derive in large part from Skinner's writings. Behavior therapy is a general label that applies to a number of methods for changing behavior. An early example of behavior therapy is Watson and Raynor's (and Mary Jones's) demonstration that phobic reactions could be both instilled and removed (Chapter 4). Behavior therapy was not really popular until the 1960s, following the success of systematic desensitization (e.g., Wolpe, 1958), the application of operant methods to children's problem behavior (e.g., Bijou & Baer, 1961), and the treatment of mental patients (e.g., Ayllon & Azrin, 1968).

The procedures used in behavior therapy derive in large part from the basic methods used in classical and operant conditioning. Over the past few years therapists have found that reinforcement, extinction, shaping, conditioned reinforcement, and other so-called behavioral methods long used in animal research are very effective means for treating human problem behaviors (e.g., Martin & Pear, 1983). Judicious use of reinforcement and basic learning principles have been used to alter behavior in problem children, to foster beneficial new behaviors in mental patients, to help the obese lose weight, and to deal with a host of other problems. Behavior therapy works because the major principles of the classic learning theories are sound.

The majority of behavior therapists were trained at universities that stressed what Seligman (1970) called General Process Learning Theory (GPLT), an extreme and simplified view of conditioning and learning theory, because it served as a clear alternative to the more traditional therapies, which rely on explaining psychopathology through reference to intrapsychic forces and similar mechanisms. So, many behavior therapists learned their trade in such university training programs, which Mahoney (1977) called "behavioral boot camp." *Behavioral* here refers to this simple view, and in the institutions that make

up that "boot camp" it is evidently taught that behavior therapists deal only with behavior and that behavior is movement in space. Good behaviorists do not take note of or deal with patients' private experience, imaginings, or thoughts! We have already discussed this view; it is what Skinner (1945) called methodological behaviorism.

What a state of affairs, given the position on private experience held by Skinner, as well as by Thorndike, Guthrie, and (even) Watson! But much of psychology had become GPLT by 1960 and it is not surprising that behavior therapists should accept it wholeheartedly. Part of the reason for this acceptance was that even GPLT worked better in the treatment of problem behavior than did competing therapies. But GPLT has its drawbacks, and these have not gone unnoticed by behavior therapists.

Many therapists became dissatisfied with the strictures of GPLT, which seemed to require that human patients be treated essentially as are the animals in Skinner boxes (a term actually coined by Clark Hull). But humans can do a bit more than other animals. Humans can be taught to monitor their own behavior, to imagine various things, to set goals, to think positively, to notice what they are thinking when a headache comes on, and so on. The precepts of GPLT taught in the training centers of only a few years ago did not allow therapists to take advantage of such capabilities, and thus a rebellion of sorts occurred.

One result of this rebellion was the founding in 1977 of the journal *Cognitive Behavior Therapy*, edited by Michael Mahoney. The title is somewhat misleading, since it does not mean "cognitive" in the sense that this term is normally used (see Chapter 1). Instead, cognitive behavior therapy simply allows mental activity back into conditioning and learning, as it was before the coming of GPLT.

If one views mental activity as behavior, as did Thorndike, Guthrie, and Watson, and as did Skinner, this new journal contains nothing that is radically new. For example, would earlier learning theorists object to a therapist teaching patients to dispel disturbing thoughts by saying "stop!" to themselves when the thoughts arise? Would they object to advising patients to note the thoughts they experience when a severe headache occurs so that such thoughts can be avoided? Is it not acceptable to imagine oneself as very obese when tempted by a sweet and then to picture oneself as slim after refusing it? Why shouldn't patients be taught to monitor their own behaviors and to set goals for changing it? Only a very restricted view of conditioning and learning would deny the possible usefulness of such methods. Yet, that is what learning theory had become. "Behavioral boot camp" accepted GPLT, just as many research-minded psychologists did since the 1950s.

Bandura has attacked GPLT, and his alternative, unlike most others of the cognitive behavior therapy movement, *is* radical (1977; 1986). During the 1960s, he and his colleagues demonstrated the importance of imitation in human affairs by showing the effects of modeling, or observational learning (e.g., Bandura, 1965). Children especially are apt to imitate models, particularly those who are older and of higher status in other ways (cf. Chapter 6, discussion of Miller & Dollard's earlier work). It seemed to Bandura that GPLT (which he called "connectionist S-R psychology" in 1977, 1986) could not account for imitation; he proposed that such behavior requires central cognitive processes to code experience and to retain it as symbols so that it can later guide behavior ("Am I imitating accurately?").

Bandura was also aware of some of the data described in Chapter 9, and he cited it as further evidence that central cognitive processes are necessary to explain even simple classical and operant conditioning. For example, Bandura often mentions Rescorla's (1967) demonstration of the importance of contingency in classical conditioning and Herrnstein's (e.g., 1970) evidence for the matching law. These findings tell us that organisms are sensitive to relations among events occurring over time; this is true and interesting. But Bandura argues that central processing mechanisms must be invoked to explain such things,

and he believes they are necessary to explain modeling.

This is a classic case of using the complex and vague (central cognitive processors) to explain the simple and clear (operant and classical conditioning). Beidel and Turner (1986) criticized Bandura and cognitive behavior therapy in general for this mistake. They charge that cognitive behavior therapists reject a simple and outdated S-R theory in favor of a so-called cognitive model. They then propose that cognitions be changed so that behavior will be changed.

Beidel and Turner examined the methods used by a variety of cognitive behavior therapists, including Bandura, and concluded that there is really nothing new or nonbehavioral in any of them. And, when methods are successful, it is always the case that the change in observable behavior is responsible. If anything, the change in cognitive activity accompanies or is produced by the behavior change, rather than the other way around.

Neglect of Species-Specific Behavior: Misbehavior?

Keller Breland worked with Skinner at General Mills during the 1940s; Marion, who was to become his wife, was a research technician. They established Animal Behavior Enterprises in Hot Springs, Arkansas, and successfully trained animals for commercial purposes. By 1961 they had trained more than 6,000 animals belonging to 38 different species to perform a variety of tricks; in 1951 they published a paper describing their methods and applications.

But the Brelands are known today largely for a paper published in 1961, in which they describe difficulties they encountered over the years. Oddly enough, they strongly criticized the sufficiency of the theory that had guided them over the years, arguing that the instinctive behaviors of the animals they worked with caused problems for them. Such instinctive behaviors were paid little attention in the theory of conditioning and learning which Skinner had taught them, and they felt that this was a serious failing of behavioral theories in general.

Although Skinner's *Behavior of Organisms* (1938) included the major methods that the Brelands had employed successfully, it neglected the instinctive behavior of animals, which often appeared to provide difficulties. This amounted to "misbehavior" in their view, and their 1961 report was thus entitled "The Misbehavior of Organisms." Here are some of their examples of misbehavior.

The "dancing chicken" involved a hen that walked three feet to a loop of string, which she pulled, thereby starting a four-note tune playing. She then stepped onto an eighteen-inch disk, which rotated as she stood on it. As the disk turned, she vigorously scratched and after fifteen seconds she was fed. As you may imagine, observers might be led to believe that the hen was turning on the juke box and then dancing, a cute trick.

It is a cute trick, but it is not what the Brelands originally had in mind. Their initial purpose was to train the chicken simply to stand still on the disk for fifteen seconds, followed by food reinforcement at the end of that period. But the chicken developed the annoying habit of scratching with her feet on the disk, just as a chicken scratching for grain or grubs might do. The behavior that normally precedes eating intruded on the behavior the Brelands were trying to establish. To salvage the situation, they took advantage of the intruding instinctive scratching and came up with the "dancing" chicken.

In a related case, a chicken was to pull a loop that released a plastic capsule containing a toy or charm, which slid down a chute. The bird was then to peck out the toy or charm through an opening for a human observer who (presumably) had deposited money in the slot. (Such devices, using mechanical rather than real chickens, used to be fairly common in the entranceways of discount stores.) As training progressed, the Brelands encountered problems that they could not overcome and that may account for the mechanical chickens. Their real chickens frequently grasped the capsule in their beaks, shook it, and banged it on the floor, much as a chicken does when trying to break open a seed pod or kill a grub or larva! Here again, instinctive feeding behavior intruded, disrupting the behavior that the trainers were trying to establish.

Other forms of instinctive behavior were evident in the case of a raccoon. The animal was trained to deposit a wooden coin in a small box; although it became difficult to get the raccoon to drop the coin, it eventually learned to do so. The trouble really began when the raccoon was required to drop two coins in the box. It then did what raccoons do with food: It rubbed the coins together for minutes at a time and dipped them into the box, just as it would dip food into water to soften it. The coins, which had become associated with food, came to be treated as food and the project was scrapped.

A pig showed similar "misbehavior," despite the fact that the Brelands had long found pigs to be excellent and rapid learners. This pig was to deposit a large wooden coin in a piggy bank, a task it learned quickly; soon it was carrying four and five coins to the bank for each food reinforcement. Then, after weeks or months of training (depending on the specific pig), the pig began to slow down and, finally, to drop the coins and root at them. With time, this misbehavior became worse and worse. Instinctive eating behavior disrupted the performance which the Brelands were trying to establish.

Similar cases of misbehavior occurred when the Brelands tried to train cows to kick, cats to move away from the feeder, and whales to refrain from swallowing inner tubes that they were supposed to manipulate for food reinforcers. It was clear that animals come with species-specific behaviors and that these place limits on what animals may be easily trained to do.

The Significance of Instinctive Drift   The Brelands (1961) wrote that these things were a shock to them and that they represented a "clear and utter failure of conditioning theory." Why should animals conditioned to perform a specific learned

TABLE 8.3 Instinctive Drift among the Brelands's Animals

Training	Outcome	Reason
chicken fed after fifteen seconds on rotating disk	scratched disk vigorously	food-getting (scratching) behavior intruded
chicken fed after pecking capsule through opening	grasped and shook capsule	eating behavior intruded
raccoon fed after depositing two coins in a box	rubbed coins together and "dipped" them	food-softening behavior intruded
pig fed after depositing coins in a bank	dropped and rooted at coins	food-getting (rooting) behavior intruded

response show a gradual *instinctive drift* to natural food-getting behaviors (see Table 8.3)? The misbehaviors delayed or prevented the delivery of food and required a lot of energy, thus violating the "law of least effort" (a seldom-mentioned law, which was really stressed only by Tolman). Misbehavior showed that species differences are not insignificant and that all responses are not equally conditionable to all stimuli. Instinctive behaviors do exist and one must be at least somewhat mindful of them.

But didn't everyone already know this? Was there a learning theorist who actually believed that we may take any organism, place it in any situation, and reinforce any behavior, without considering the species with which we are dealing? Thorndike surely would not believe that, nor would Watson, Guthrie, or Tolman. It is hard to believe that even Hull and his followers would be so obtuse!

Yet, by the 1950s and 1960s the majority of experimental psychologists did believe that one could ignore species differences. For years the favored subjects of psychological research had been rats and pigeons and whatever laws applied to the pressing of levers and the pecking of keys were assumed to be generalizable to all behaviors of all organisms at all times. The Brelands were the first animal psychologists to point out that

this was not the case, and the revolution they initiated continues to the present.

Remember, however, that the Brelands were terribly successful in training animals, even though they had firmly believed the simple view of conditioning which they attacked in their paper until the cases of instinctive drift mounted to such a level that they could not be ignored. They admitted that they did not mean to "disparage the use of conditioning techniques," since these methods had served them well for many years. But one must take species-specific behaviors into account. Just after the paper was accepted for publication, Keller Breland wrote the following in a letter to Skinner:

"We have been concerned here for a number of years with the area of observations commonly called instinct (a rosebush by any other name is just as thorny) and an article discussing the type of problem one encounters in this area will soon appear in the *American Psychologist*. That is the occasion for this letter since, after looking at the galley proofs, it occurred to us that it might convey impressions not intended. Perhaps we did not state strongly enough our feeling as to the efficacy of operant conditioning in the control of organisms. This conviction is so 'old hat' with us that I am afraid that we sometimes forget that it is not shared by all American psychologists." (Skinner, 1977, pp. 1006–1007)

Skinner added the following remark:

His letter concluded: "Viva la operant! (Such a pregnant notion as the operant must be female.)" It was, of course, necessary for the Brelands to use the phylogenic repertoires of the various species with which they worked (and they did so in a most ingenious way), but they continued to be dependent upon the shaping technique we discovered in Project Pigeon in developing that behavior for commercial purposes. (p. 1007)

In the same article, Skinner noted that misbehavior may occur in the reverse fashion; learned behavior may intrude upon and disrupt instinctive behavior. This occurred during the ORCON project, in which pigeons were trained to peck at targets visible on a large screen in front of them, thus guiding a missile. One bird pecked at the targets extremely rapidly and this high rate of pecking occurred whenever it pecked. This made it difficult for the bird to eat, and it lost weight. It had to be trained to peck more slowly, so that its learned high rates of pecking would not disrupt its instinctive eating behavior! Despite the discovery of misbehavior, the Brelands found Skinner's methods generally sound, as we will see below.

4. OTHER ASPECTS OF SKINNER'S THEORY

Examples of Skinner's theory in operation usually refer to instances of behavior therapy, since that work is best known to the public. Yet, behavior therapy really illustrates the influence of behavioral methods in general, not just Skinner's version of behaviorism. More appropriate examples lie in the training of animals for commercial purposes and in Skinnerian interpretations of self-control, avoidance learning, the effect of contingencies per se, and the Columban simulations.

Performing Animals

While a graduate student of Skinner's, the same Keller Breland now known for his contribution to the misbehavior paper saw the possibilities of using operant conditioning methods in the commercial training of animals. He and his wife Marion had many clients; for example, Quaker Oats, General Mills, the U.S. Army and Navy, the Veterans Administration, the Department of the Interior, Marriott's Great America Parks, Six Flags Over Mid-America, and Opryland. Part of their advertising reads as follows:

Want a show or exhibit featuring trained common domestic animals? Since 1947, ABE has produced shows featuring barnyard animals.
Want a dolphin or sea lion to perform in the open ocean? Since 1963, ABE has pioneered in open ocean training of marine mammals.
Want a seagull, raven, pigeon or other bird to fly free and perform at your command? Since 1965, ABE has freeflown birds over distances of several miles.
Want long-range invisible control of dogs, cats, or other species of land animals? ABE has developed and tested techniques for controlling certain land animals at distances of several hundred yards.

Want to know how they do this? Breland and Breland (1951) reveal the basics.

Animal Behavior Enterprises will send you an animal version of a video game for a price. Their exhibits include Skyline Hen (the tightrope walking chicken), the fortune-telling chicken, the capsule vending chicken, the baseball-playing chicken, the piano- or drum-playing chicken (or duck), the kissing bunny, the gambling rabbit, the tic-tac-toe chicken, the basketball-playing chicken, and much more. The Brelands are now better known for their 1961 paper emphasizing "misbehavior." But their commercial success testifies to the effectiveness of Skinner's training methods.

The Columban Simulations

Through the years, Skinner had argued that anything that we may think important in psychology may be explained in terms of contingencies. In works such as *Science and Human Behavior* (1953) and *Beyond Freedom and Dignity* (1971), the term *contingencies* is used almost as a literary device to refer to the fact that something is learned. Hence, he attributes thinking, selective perception, the concept of self, beliefs, and many other things to the effects of contingencies, without going very deeply into how these contingencies operate and how they produce these products. But how could he illustrate how such things happen? The so-called Columban simulations are one way of doing this. (The term *Columban* refers to the order *Columbae*, the group of birds that includes pigeons and doves.) The Columban simulations are attempts to show how contingencies can shape behavior indicative of higher mental processes. Two simulations show how the behavior of pigeons may seem to suggest that they have a genuine concept of self and that they are capable of symbolic communication. They even leave themselves notes, seemingly foreseeing that their memory may fail.

The nature of self-concept was examined by Epstein, Lanza, and Skinner (1981), using a method devised by Gallup (1970) for assessing the existence of a self-concept in monkeys. Gallup found that chimpanzees, marked with red dye on an eyebrow, showed that their mirrored image was recognized as an image of themselves. The chimps examined the red area on their own bodies, while seeing it only in the reflection from the mirror. Monkeys were unable to use the mirror image in this way; in one case, a rhesus failed to show any recognition that the monkey in the mirror was itself after as long as 2,400 hours of opportunity to do so! Gallup concluded that only humans and the very highest subhuman primates are capable of recognizing a mirror image of themselves, which means that only they have (or are capable of having) a self-concept. This was a rash conclusion.

Epstein, et al. felt that the ability to respond to a mirrored image of oneself could be demonstrated in organisms far lower than chimpanzees. To show this, they trained pigeons to peck at a blue spot placed in various locations in their box, with pecks reinforced with access to grain. They went on to present the blue spot on the end of a clear Plexiglas rod, so that the birds would be used to pecking at it in various locations in space. Finally, they placed press-on blue spots on the birds' bodies, in places where the animals could see them. The birds soon reliably pecked at blue spots, whether on the wall, in space, or on their legs.

Then came the interesting part: Would a pigeon recognize a mirrored image of itself and thus show evidence for a self-concept, according to Gallup's definition? The blue spot was placed on the pigeon's breast and a bib was placed around the bird's neck. Mirrors were set up outside the Plexiglas box in which the birds worked. The bird could see the blue spot reflected in the mirror image, but if it bent to look at its breast, the bib covered the spot. Thus, when the bird stood upright, the blue spot was visible in the mirror's reflection. If the bird looked down, the bib covered the spot. The only way in which the bird could see the spot was in the mirror's reflection (see Figure 8.11).

The photographs in Epstein, et al. clearly show the birds pecking downward at the bib, over the point at which the spot was hidden. When the mirror was covered, the birds did not peck at this spot, showing that the bird was not simply pecking where it felt the spot to be. Do pigeons recognize themselves in mirrored images? Yes! Do they therefore have a self-concept, as we think of it? Don't be silly! And neither did Gallup's chimps. The ability to recognize oneself in a mirror image is not a good criterion for a concept of self, unless we extend the ability to have a self-concept to pigeons. At least, this was the conclusion of Epstein, et al.

A second experiment was done in response to demonstrations of animal communication through symbols, which have appeared in the popular press. Several projects have claimed to show human-like use of language by chimps and gorillas, such as Washoe, Koko, and Sarah. The animals do not actually speak, of course; they communicate through the symbolic gestures of American Sign Language (ASL) or manipulate plastic symbols mounted on a magnetic board. In other cases

1. The pigeon pecks a blue spot at various locations in the chamber.

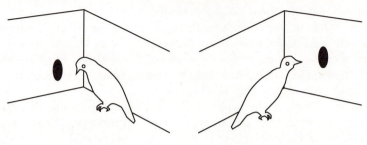

2. The pigeon pecks a spot on a Plexiglas rod.

3. The pigeon pecks a spot on its own body.

4. A blue spot is placed on the pigeon's breast (a), hidden by a bib (b), and visible only in a miror (c). The bird pecks at the bib (d).

a.   b.   c.   d.

FIGURE 8.11   Self-concept experiment by Epstein, Lanza, and Skinner (1981) using pigeons.

the animals use symbols mounted on a computer keyboard. According to the investigators involved, these animals actually have a rudimentary use of language. They do communicate, just as we do. (Interestingly, they often seem to adopt other human behaviors, such as sleeping in beds, rather than in trees, and eating with plates and silverware.)

Savage-Rumbaugh, Rumbaugh, and Boysen (1978) published an account of chimpanzee communication, in which one animal asked another where food was hidden and the other answered the question. This was described as a marvel in primate intelligence. What other animal had the innate capacity for language to allow it to accomplish such a feat? Chimpanzees do resemble humans to a degree, and most people are therefore willing to share such an intrinsically human faculty as language use with them.

But these chimps did not spontaneously begin to converse with symbols; they were taught to do so. Given that training is necessary, is it still the case that only the highest primates may benefit from training? Could the same sort of training lead to communication in pigeons? If such lowly animals could be trained to duplicate the chimps' behavior, we might then conclude that all of us learn to communicate in such a way but that no one bothers to teach animals, so most of them do not talk. Or we might conclude that the special training given the chimps produced only the appearance of true language use, since few would grant the lowly pigeon the ability to use language.

Savage-Rumbaugh, et al., had taught chimpanzees to name foods by pressing buttons marked with symbols corresponding to various foods. They then were taught to request foods. Finally, one chimpanzee watched as food was hidden; the experimenter then asked it to name the hidden food by pressing the appropriate button when another chimp was present. If the second chimp then correctly asked for that food, both were fed. Later, both chimpanzees were observed to spontaneously "ask" each other for food. Remember that in all of these cases the naming and asking was done by pressing buttons. None-

theless, here was an example of language use in higher primates.

Epstein, Lanza, & Skinner (1981) showed that such behavior was not unique to chimpanzees. In a charming piece, which described pigeons' behavior in the same warm terms that the chimpanzee behavior was described by the Rumbaughs and others, Epstein's group showed that pigeons were capable of symbolic communication. Two pigeons named Jack and Jill worked in a chamber divided down the middle by a clear Plexiglas barrier. Jack began by pecking a key with *WHAT COLOR?* written on it. Jill then looked at a panel of three lights recessed in the upper right corner of her side of the box and covered by a curtain. She had to stick her head behind the curtain to see which of the three lights—red, green, or yellow—was lighted (see Figure 8.12). Jack could not see this three-key display from his side of the chamber.

Jill then moved to a vertical column of three keys on the left half of her chamber, which Jack could see. These were marked *R*, *G*, and *Y*, and Jill pecked the one corresponding to the hidden color that was lighted. When the key was pecked, it was illuminated and stayed illuminated. Jack looked at it and pecked a key on his side marked *THANK YOU*, at which time Jill was automatically fed. Jack then pecked the appropriately colored key on a horizontal display on his side, after which he was fed. Jack then requested another color name by pecking the *WHAT COLOR?* key and the cycle began again.

The final performance was remarkably like those reported by the Rumbaughs and other primate researchers. One animal "asked," another "answered," the first "thanked," and both were fed. After a description of the experiment, which was cast in the somewhat nonobjective terms used by the primate researchers, Epstein, et al., ended with:

> We have thus demonstrated that pigeons can learn to engage in a sustained and natural conversation without human intervention and that one pigeon can reliably transmit information to another entirely through the use of symbols. (p. 696)

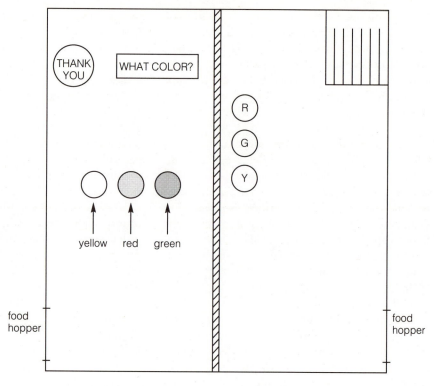

FIGURE 8.12 Panel of chamber for Jack and Jill, the pigeons in Epstein, Lanza, and Skinner's symbolic communication experiments.

They continued with the following:

> It has not escaped our notice that an alternative account of this exchange may be given in terms of the prevailing contingencies of reinforcement. (p. 696)

They go on to point out that they did *train* the birds to do this, using standard fading, shaping, chaining, and discrimination procedures. "A similar account may be given of the Rumbaugh procedure, as well as of comparable human language," they added.

After this experiment, Jack and Jill were given experience in both roles. Each learned to "ask," choose the communicated color, and "thank," as well as to look and communicate. The birds were then placed, one at a time, in the chamber, without the partition. To be fed, all the bird had to do was look at the hidden color (as Jill had done)

and go to Jack's side and peck the same color. No one had to ask "what color?" or say "thank you," or peck the *R*, *G*, or *Y* keys.

But an odd thing happened. Jack, in going from the hidden colors recessed in the upper right wall of the chamber and covered by the curtain, sometimes forgot the color that was lighted. By the time he reached the left side of the chamber, he didn't know where he was to peck the color on the keys mounted there. How do humans solve such a problem? How do we guard against such a lapse in memory? We leave notes for ourselves!

Epstein and Skinner (1981) showed photographs of Jack "leaving a note," by pecking the *R*, *G*, or *Y* keys on the right half of the box, on his way to the keys on the left. The bird then went to the row of color keys on the left and clearly looked over his shoulder to see which of the labeled keys was lighted (that is, he looked at his "note"). He then pecked the appropriate color key. Jill did the same thing, though less frequently; in both cases, the birds apparently were leaving a memorandum to which they referred when reaching the color keys on the left side of the chamber.

And they were doing just that, although they had not been trained to do so! When the color keys on the left were lighted only after a delay, which strained the birds' memories, both animals reliably pecked the "reminder keys" so that they could look back at them. When a disruptor, such as a loud buzzer, went off between the time that the hidden color was seen and the color keys were lighted, both birds more often "left a note."

Does this mean that pigeons, which have no neocortex and only a shred of cerebral cortex, are as intelligent as chimpanzees and humans? No, it only means that when animals are placed in situations in which human-like contingencies are in effect we may expect human-appearing behavior, insofar as the animals are capable of it. The same occurs when humans are placed in human and nonhuman situations. Thus, we need not be surprised to find contingencies (in the concentration camp or in the ghetto) producing behavior that we are reluctant to accept as human.

SUMMARY

Skinner carried on the spirit of Watson's rendition of behaviorism, although he disagreed with what Watson felt to be the fundamental principles of conditioning. Like Watson, he felt that theories were not only unnecessary, but were an impediment to progress. For Skinner, a theory was a way of explaining behavior and experience that translated what we wish to explain to other terms, such as the language of neurons and of mechanical devices, such as information processors. Most damaging were those theories that referred to the common explanations of popular psychology, such as the thoughts, traits, and faculties we all refer to when we speak of people with a good memory or an aggressive nature. Such so-called

explanations, like references to higher cognitive processes, do no more than name what we wish to explain. They are better dispensed with, so that we can get to the real explanations, which lie in the past history of the individual (or the species).

Skinner's papers during the 1930s brilliantly outlined a strategy for the discovery of behavioral units. The unit is the reflex, although his definition of the reflex is not what most of us think of when we hear the term. *Reflex* means "order," and the discovery of the physiological reflex was possible long before it was possible to trace the anatomical path involved. Skinner proposed that the static and dynamic laws of the reflex are a more reliable means for identifying reflexes than is the anatomical path, and that the same strategy that allows us to identify reflexes may be applied to the identification of conditioned reflexes and operants, although the latter occur in the absence of any obvious stimulation.

Reflexes, conditioned reflexes, and operants are always defined as correlations between stimulation and responding (or responding and stimulation, in the case of the operant) defined at that level of specificity at which orderly changes occur as the result of manipulations of third variables, such as hunger, emotion, and fatigue. Stimuli and responses are never spoken of as such; we always speak of classes of stimuli and responses. This makes Skinner's behaviorism far different from the S-R associationism of Hull and his associates. The result of the reinforcement of an operant may lead to changes in behaviors that seem very unlike the behaviors that were reinforced explicitly; the identity of the response class need not be intuitively obvious before conditioning occurs. Similarly, the stimulus class need not include only obvious and specific stimuli; there is no reason why abstract concepts may not be learned, just as reactions to more concrete stimuli are learned.

The law of effect is an empirical law; there is no property that all reinforcers have in common, such as the ability to produce pleasure or to reduce biological drives. The law of effect is a useful tool, and its usefulness is extended whenever we show yet another behavior that is influenced by its consequences. There are so many things that may act as reinforcers under one or another condition that the attempt to find a single basis for their effect (such as the activation of reward centers in the brain) is doomed to failure.

All reinforcers increase the frequency of behaviors that produce them. Positive reinforcers do so because they are produced by those behaviors, and negative reinforcers do so because a behavior removes them. Punishers decrease the frequency of behaviors that produce them. Although Skinner (1938), following Thorndike and Watson, downplayed the effectiveness of punishers, work by Azrin clearly shows that punishers are effective, although their application may be tricky.

Skinner is largely responsible for the distinction between operant and respondent learning; although there is a difference between the procedures used in the two types of conditioning, he is responsible for the belief that two different learning processes underlie the two methods. This belief, which is inconsistent with his position on theories of learning, has recently been decisively refuted.

Operants come under the control of discriminative stimuli, and the effects of reinforcement generalize to other stimuli, a process Skinner called induction. Differential reinforcement leads to extinguishing of responding to nonreinforced stimuli, which is the basis for discrimination learning. Operant behavior may be shaped, using the method of successive approximations, and a sequence of shaped behaviors may be joined to form a chain. In the course of shaping, we restrict reinforcement to only certain members of an operant response class, such as bar presses of a given force or greater. The other members of the class extinguish and behavior becomes more variable, increasing the number of instances that can be reinforced. In time, we may have a distribution of responses totally different from that with which we began. Once a behavior has been shaped, we may reinforce its occurrence only in the presence of a given S^D; we may then use that

S^D as a conditioned reinforcer for a second behavior. When we pair a second S^D with that behavior, we have a two-member chain. In theory, we may extend the chain indefinitely, although in practice there are real limits, especially with animal subjects.

Schedules of reinforcement specify the rule by which reinforcement is delivered. The basic schedules specify that either a fixed or a variable number of responses occur or that a fixed or variable time period pass, after which responding is reinforced. In addition to the basic FR, VR, FI, and VI schedules, there are many variations specifying time and/or response requirements, including discriminative stimuli, and sometimes comprising a combination of simpler schedules.

Examples of reinforcement schedules in daily life are few, but obvious daily life applications are not important. Rather, the schedules tell us important things about the relations between behavior and its consequences. Perhaps the most important thing that psychologists have learned is that orderly relations between the world and behavior appear more frequently when we consider behavior over extended periods of time. The matching law and the work of Neuringer and Chung, which are described in Chapter 9, represent two salient examples of this.

Skinner's treatment of motivation, emotion, and other such terms follows from his opposition to the use of intervening variables. If we think of all of the things we mean when we describe ourselves or others as "hungry," or as "angry," we can appreciate his reasons for stressing the use of independent and dependent variables, rather than intervening variables.

Skinner's methods have been applied to the study of concept formation, beginning in his wartime efforts to build a pigeon-piloted missile. Further work with pigeons, porpoises, and humans has shown that our concepts are probably all learned rather than present at birth, as Plato had suggested. However, there is growing attention paid to the rapidity with which animals learn concepts, suggesting that they may come prepared to acquire some concepts.

Unlike Hull and Tolman, but like Thorndike and Watson, Skinner considers private experience to be part of what a behavioral science must explain. According to his radical behaviorism, mental activity may be treated in the same manner as other activity, and private stimuli, such as those that produce pain, may be treated as other stimuli. Skinner believes that society teaches us to identify items of personal experience, just as it teaches us to identify objects in the world. It is harder for our teachers to identify our private experiences, since they must rely on our behavior to do so; consequently, we can never know our own experience as well as we can know the objects of the world.

In 1966, Skinner set forth his views on innate behavior. He suggested that the factors that change behavior during the course of an individual's lifetime are similar to those that change the bodily and behavioral characteristics of a species during the course of evolution. Variation, selection, and heredity act in essentially the same way in both cases, and it is a mistake to try to separate the influence of nature and nurture in dealing with specific cases. Had Skinner published such a paper twenty years before he did, we might have seen less interest in the exceptions to the laws of learning. But he did not.

Criticism of Skinner is often misplaced. Frequently he is criticized as though he were the distillation of all views of all people who have called themselves behaviorists. Most often, though, he is criticized as though he were Hull, because Hull's influence was so great and because so many of his students have kept his basic ideas alive. There *are* serious criticisms that do apply to Skinner, however. The most serious is his failure to appreciate the significance of his early thoughts regarding the unit of behavior. Too often he reverts to molecular analyses that convince critics that his views really are the same as those of Hull.

The power of his approach is well illustrated in the success of professional animal trainers, such as the Brelands, and in the series of papers describing the Columban simulations. In the latter series, pigeons have been trained to show behaviors that indicate self-concept, communication, and note leaving. Other researchers have shown that pigeons can show self-control and that rats can react to fairly subtle differences in sequences of events acting over prolonged periods of time; these topics will be covered in Chapter 9. These are the sorts of demonstrations that show the applications of Skinner's theory, and we could have benefited from them long ago.

GLOSSARY

Adjusting schedule Schedule of reinforcement in which the value of the interreinforcement interval or the response requirement changes as time passes since the last reinforcement. For example, an adjusting schedule could begin with a value of FR 10 and increase that value by ten every twenty seconds. This should lead to high response rates, since, in effect, the schedule penalizes low response rates.

Alternative schedule Schedule of reinforcement in which reinforcement depends on the passage of time *or* the fulfilling of a response requirement.

Chaining (Chained schedule) The joining together of a sequence of behaviors by a series of discriminative stimuli that also act as conditioned reinforcers. The occurrence of the first behavior produces the S^D for the second member of the chain, and so on. The appearance of the S^D acts to reinforce the first behavior and set the occasion for the second member, which leads to the appearance of the next S^D.

Component Basic unit of a multiple schedule, consisting of a specific S^D, schedule of reinforcement, and duration. Components are presented successively. One example of a component would be a two-minute period in which a green light was lighted and in which a VR 25 schedule was in effect.

Concept learning Discrimination learning in which the class of stimuli involved do not consist of specific concrete things like lights and tones. The concept may be "all four-legged creatures" or all true statements. We train concepts by presenting numerous examples of instances of the concept and reinforcing responses by our subject and by presenting noninstances without reinforcement.

Concurrent schedule Schedule of reinforcement in which two or more independent schedules are simultaneously in effect, with a lever or key corresponding to each. For example, two different VI schedules may be available, with two response keys present, one for each schedule. A subject may get into the habit of switching keys, since the longer the time spent on one key, the more likely reinforcement becomes for responses on the second key. Switches between keys therefore may be reinforced. To prevent this, a changeover delay (COD) is usually used with concurrent schedules. A COD prevents the receipt of reinforcement for responding on a key for some fixed time (a few seconds) after a switch from the other key to that key.

Conditioned reinforcer According to some usages, such as that of Hull, all reinforcers that do not reduce drives arising from bodily needs are assumed to be conditioned reinforcers; their power derives from an association with primary reinforcers. Skinner's view defines conditioned reinforcers as things that act as reinforcers because of some pairing with already-effective reinforcers. The latter may act as such for a variety of reasons, and the difference between conditioned and other reinforcers lies only in the fact that conditioned reinforcers act as such only after association with effective reinforcers.

Conjunctive schedule Reinforcement schedule in which reinforcement is delivered only after the passage of time and the completion of a response requirement. For example, 47 responses may be followed by reinforcement if two minutes have passed since the last reinforcement.

Contingencies Another word for *schedule*. When Skinner speaks of the contingencies responsible for the development or maintenance of a behavior, he refers to the requirements that govern the delivery of reinforcement. These may depend upon the passage of time, the occurrence of specific responses, the presence of specific stimuli, or a combination of these things.

Differential reinforcement Another way of describing the selecting of behaviors, depending upon reinforcement of some responses in the presence of some stimuli and the nonreinforcement of other responses in the presence of other stimuli. Shaping, discrimination learning, and all of our learned behavior may be viewed as the result of differential reinforcement.

Discriminative stimulus Operants usually are reinforced only in the presence of some class of stimuli, the S^D. Skinner believes that such stimuli come to "set the occasion" for reinforcement, thus acting as discriminative stimuli. He also believes that stimuli that elicit reflex behavior or conditioned reflex behavior operate differently, by eliciting the responses which they control.

DRH schedule Schedule of reinforcement that reinforces high rates of responding. A differential reinforcement of high rates schedule requires that some number of responses occur within a fixed time period if reinforcement is to be received.

DRL schedule Schedule of reinforcement that reinforces low rates of responding. A differential reinforcement of low rates schedule requires that no responses occur during some fixed period since the last response if reinforcement is to be received.

Dynamic laws Factors that influence the strength of a reflex, conditioned reflex, or operant response, which show their influence as the behavior repeatedly occurs. For example, the law of fatigue and the laws of conditioning and extinction are such laws.

Empirical law of effect Skinner's version of the law of effect, which holds that reinforcers need not share any properties except their ability to act as reinforcers. We discover that something acts as a reinforcer under given conditions; we do not concern ourselves over why it does so. (For example, we do not ask whether it reduces drives or if it is pleasure producing.) The law of effect is thus an empirical generalization. It is a useful rule that we have found to apply in a large number of cases, and its value and usefulness depend upon how far we may extend its application. Why reinforcers act as they do is an unanswerable question.

Fixed-interval schedule Schedule of reinforcement that requires that a set period of time pass, after which the first response produces reinforcement. Fixed interval is symbolized as FI.

Fixed-ratio schedule Schedule of reinforcement that requires that a set number of responses occur to produce each reinforcement. Fixed ratio is symbolized as FR.

Fixed-time schedule Schedule of reinforcement that provides reinforcement after fixed periods of time since the last reinforcement, independent of the subject's behavior. This schedule is indistinguishable from classical delayed conditioning. Fixed time is symbolized as FT.

Heterogeneous chain Chain of behaviors that are not of the same topography. For example, the rat Pliny performed a chain consisting of pulling a string, carrying a marble, and dropping it. (See *homogeneous chain*.)

Homogeneous chain Schedule of reinforcement composed of a chain of behaviors in which the behaviors in each member of the chain are topographically similar. For example, a chain FR 2 VR 8 schedule requires that two lever presses occur in the presence of one stimulus, which leads to a change in the S^D, and the pressing an average of eight times then leads to reinforcement. The response required in both members (for example, lever pressing) is the same, unlike in a heterogeneous chain.

Induction Actually means "generalization." Skinner used this term, after Sherrington, to refer to induced changes in responding to one stimulus, as the result of reinforcement for responding to a similar stimulus.

Instinctive drift Name given by the Brelands (1961) to the disruptive effect of species-specific (instinctive) consummatory behavior on the learned (operant) performances of their animal subjects.

Limited hold A requirement that may be added to a VI or FI schedule, such that a response must occur within some set period of time (the LH value) after the schedule has made reinforcement available. For example, on a FI one-minute LH two-second schedule, reinforcement is available for two seconds after the passage of a minute. If a response does not occur, that reinforcement is lost.

Matching law Also called the molar law of effect. The matching law holds that relative response rates match relative reinforcement frequencies. For an explanation of what this means and what it signifies, see Chapter 9.

Methodological behaviorism Name given by Skinner (1945) to the view that holds that we can deal objectively only with observable behavior and that mind exists, but cannot be meaningfully studied. Skinner opposed this view and labeled his contrary position radical behaviorism.

Mixed schedule Schedule of reinforcement in which two or more different schedules are in effect for set periods of time, these periods appearing in sequence. For example, a mixed FI 2 VI 3 schedule might alternate two-minute periods, in which FI 2 and then VI 3 schedules were in force. If these periods are signaled by discriminative stimuli, we have a multiple schedule.

Multiple schedule A mixed schedule in which different S^Ds signal the schedules that are in effect.

Negative punishment This occurs when a response decreases in frequency when its occurrence is followed by the offset of something. For example, a bit of misbehavior may be followed by the turning off of a television set. Like negative reinforcement, the behavior removes some stimulus. Like other cases of punishment, this produces a decrease in the frequency of the behavior which causes this consequence.

Negative reinforcement An increase in the frequency of a response that produces the offset of something. Like negative punishment, negative reinforcement involves the termination of something; like positive reinforcement, it leads to an increase in responding. When we pull a window shade to stop the sun from shining in our eyes, the negative reinforcement that results makes it more probable that we repeat that act the next time the sunlight annoys us.

Operant Class of responses that vary together in strength as a function of the consequences produced by members of the class. Pressing a lever acts as an operant, as does creative behavior, going to the store, and a myriad of other behaviors. We can identify an operant class only after we have observed that a given behavior is influenced by its consequences. It may take some time to identify most or all of the responses that make up an operant.

Operant conditioning The process whereby an operant class is shown to become more frequent (that is, to increase in strength) as a function of the consequences it produces. Thus, a rat may more frequently press a lever when presses are reinforced with food, and an infant may increase its emission of vocalizations when vocalizations are followed by praise and attention.

Positive reinforcer A consequence of behavior that produces an increase in the frequency of that class of behavior.

Punishment The decrease in frequency of an operant behavior as a function of the consequences it produces. Skinner argued that punishment is not a basic effect and that effects attributed to it depend upon side effects of the aversive events used as punishers. We now know that he was mistaken and that punishers seem to work in a way opposite to the effects of reinforcers.

Radical behaviorism Position described by Skinner in 1945 and 1963, which proposes a philosophy for a science of psychology, independent of specific theories of learning, whether Skinner's or anyone else's. According to this view, the entire subject matter of psychology may be treated as activity (behavior) and therefore mental activity is essentially the same in kind as physical activity; we may speak of thinking and seeing as behaviors, just as we do when we speak of walking and talking. Radical behaviorism argues against the usefulness and the existence of intervening variables and especially of internal copies of the world. Some writers have pointed out the similarities between this point of view and that of modern European phenomenologists, such as Merleau-Ponty and Sartre. There is little doubt that Skinner named this view after the radical empiricism of William James.

Reflex For Skinner, refers to order. The discovery of a reflex is the discovery of an orderly relationship between the world and behavior. Skinner extended a masterly analysis of the concept of the reflex to conditioned reflexes and operants in the 1930s.

Respondent Skinner's term for reflex and conditioned reflex behavior, which is elicited by an identifiable stimulus. *Respondent conditioning* is his term for Pavlovian conditioning, or conditioning of Type S.

Response class The set of behaviors that change in frequency together. This applies to reflex, conditioned reflex, and operant behavior. The response class may be composed of members that do not intuitively seem to go together. For example, aggression is no doubt a number of response classes, some controlled by external stimuli, and others by consequences. Each class may contain members discoverable only after long observation of behavior under a variety of conditions.

Schedule of reinforcement Rule by which reinforcers are delivered. The rule may include response requirements (as in ratio schedules), temporal requirements (as in interval schedules), or both. The first major analysis of reinforcement schedules and their effects was published by Ferster and Skinner in 1957.

Shaping Commonly used term for the method of successive approximations. This method involves the selective reinforcement of some subset of a class of operant responses. This leads to extinction of the

nonreinforced members and a consequent increase in the variations of behaviors emitted. The requirement for reinforcement may be progressively restricted until the final product is a set of behaviors very different from the original behavior class.

Static laws In Skinner's early papers on the identification of reflexes, static laws referred to changes in responsiveness visible with single elicitations of the reflex. For example, we may see an increase in the magnitude of the response as we apply stronger eliciting stimuli. On a given occasion, a stronger stimulus produces a stronger response, irrespective of when the last stimulation was given.

Stimulus class The set of stimuli that may be shown to control a reflex, conditioned reflex, or operant class of responses. Like the response class, the stimulus class may be composed of elements that may not seem intuitively obvious. What we call "concepts" are names for stimulus classes.

Stimulus control The effect of external stimuli on behavior. The study of stimulus generalization and discrimination learning is now called the study of "stimulus control."

Tandem schedule Two or more schedules of reinforcement arranged in sequence, so that the requirement of one schedule must be met before the next schedule begins. Food or other reinforcement is delivered only after all schedules in the sequence have run. If different stimuli signal the successive schedules, it is a chained schedule.

Theoretical law of effect Attempts to explain the fact that reinforcers work as they do by postulating some underlying process. For example, Hull's suggestion that reinforcers work by reducing biological drives was a theoretical law of effect. One could suggest that all reinforcers promote survival, produce pleasure, or share some other characteristic. All such attempts have failed, and Skinner believed that we only waste time and effort by trying to work out a theoretical law of effect. His reasons are the same as those he uses to argue against theories of any kind.

Theory For Skinner, a translation of terms. For example, if we attribute intelligence to properties of the brain, information processing mechanisms, a "smarts" center (to use Stephen Gould's term), or the like, we are proposing a theory. More generally, theories involve the use of intervening variables, rather than the independent and dependent variables we should be interested in. Acceptable explanations refer only to the phenomena to be explained and the concrete conditions that influence them. The translation of these basic terms into hypothetical entities (habits, motives, and so on) should be avoided.

Token economy Method of psychotherapy originated by Ayllon and Azrin in the early 1960s. Patients, for whom other methods of therapy had failed, were reinforced for grooming, working, eating in an acceptable manner, and other activities.

Type R Skinner's term for behavior that is sensitive to its consequences—that is, operant behavior. Type R conditioning is therefore operant conditioning.

Type S Skinner's term for classical conditioning, in which the emphasis is placed on the eliciting CS rather than upon the consequences of the elicited behavior. Classical conditioning is conditioning of Type S.

Unfinished causal sequences Skinner's term for the common practice of explaining behavior and experience by reference to some hypothetical inner state or process. Hence, we may explain unruly behavior as the product of aggressiveness and the ability to recite well as the result of a good memory. In both cases, we have done no more than name the behavior involved and, unless we explain aggressiveness and memory, we are left with unfinished causal sequences, not real explanations.

Variable-interval schedule Schedule of reinforcement, symbolized as VI. This schedule provides reinforcement for the first response that occurs after some mean interval of time has passed since the last reinforcement. For example, a VI six-minute schedule would reinforce the first response occurring after an average of six minutes. Some interreinforcement intervals could be as short as a few seconds and others could be ten minutes long or longer.

Variable-ratio schedule Schedule of reinforcement, symbolized as VR. This schedule provides reinforcement after the completion of some number of responses. The number varies from reinforcement to reinforcement, and the value of the schedule is the mean number of responses required. Thus, a VR 25 schedule provides reinforcement after a varying number of responses, the average requirement being 25.

RECOMMENDED READINGS

Verplanck, W. S. (1954). Burrhus F. Skinner. In Estes, et al. (Eds.), *Modern learning theory*. New York: Appleton-Century-Crofts.

  This is still considered the most perceptive evaluation of Skinner's theory. It was written by a former colleague.

Skinner, B. F. (1972). *Cumulative record* (3rd ed.). New York: Appleton-Century-Crofts.

  This is a collection of Skinner's papers selected from publications since 1930. The reader will find many topics covered, dealing with theory, application, and others of personal interest to Skinner.

Skinner, B. F. (1974). *About behaviorism*. New York: Knopf.

  Skinner explains what is meant by radical behaviorism in this clear and entertaining little book.

Skinner, B. F. (1983). *A matter of consequences*. New York: Knopf.

  This is the third and last volume of Skinner's autobiography, covering the period beginning with his return to Harvard in the late 1940s to the 1980s. It is more a professional than a personal autobiography and provides many insights into Skinner's treatment of psychology.

Skinner, B. F. (1984). Canonical papers of B. F. Skinner. *Behavioral and Brain Sciences*, 7, whole number 4.

  This special issue of this journal is composed of six statements by Skinner dealing with basic issues, each followed by commentators' statements. Skinner replies to approximately 150 such commentators.

Chapter 9

ADVANCES IN RESEARCH

There have been many advances in conditioning and learning research during the past decades and many of them are discussed in the preceding chapters. Others have not been included, either because they were not uniquely relevant to a particular theorist's ideas, or because they would have required an unreasonable lengthening of a chapter. This would have been the case for the Pavlov and Skinner chapters in particular.

This chapter provides a selection of important research related to operant and classical conditioning. It includes only research that has important practical applications or that has real significance in furthering our understanding of ourselves. I have purposely left out two kinds of research: that which already appears in textbooks so frequently that most students cannot help but be exposed to it and that which has no obvious practical relevance, though it may nevertheless be important. An example of the first category is the work of Piaget, and an example of the second is modern connectionist (neural network) theory.

I have been at pains to include findings that are of great importance and that are not widely known, though they already may be appreciated by specialists. Examples are found in the novel interpretation of conditioned reinforcement by Neuringer and Chung, in reinterpretations of what were formerly called "pleasure centers," and in research on behavioral contrast.

1. INSTRUMENTAL CONDITIONING AND THE LAW OF EFFECT

The Law of Effect and Hedonism

We have seen that Thorndike (e.g., 1913), Skinner (e.g., 1938, 1953) and other advocates of the law of effect repeatedly emphasized that satisfiers and annoyers, as well as reinforcers and punishers, had nothing necessarily to do with sensory pleasures and pains. Yet, there seems little doubt that the law of effect will continue to be viewed as a hedonistic principle, both by its critics and by some of it adherents. Needless to say, the same interpretation appears in less authoritative sources, and things would no doubt be clearer were it not for Thorndike's sad choice of terms, which invite such interpretations, as well as Skinner's common remark to the effect that we find this or that "reinforcing" (e.g., 1953, 1983b). The virtue of the law of effect, as demonstrated by Thorndike, Skinner, and many others, lies in its application as an empirical generalization referring to the important effects that consequences have on our behavior and our experience. Naturally, some of these consequences are accompanied by pleasures and pains, but often they are not. Being told that one's answer was "right" acts as a reinforcer for the answer that produced it, but is such a consequence really that pleasant? Is it pleasant to touch a wound to see if it still hurts? Yet, the slight pain that ensues acts as a strong reinforcer for touching. If we treat such mild pain as pleasant, we lose whatever meaning pleasure and pain have. They are important in our lives but utterly irrelevant to the law of effect.

The reason that *hedonism* is brought up in a chapter devoted to research developments is that we now have abundant evidence that almost anything can act as a reinforcer or as a punisher under the proper conditions. To understand some of the following developments, we must realize that reinforcement and punishment are not synonyms for pleasure and pain.

With this view, it will be instructive to examine recent research concerned with so-called reward and punishment centers in the brain. This topic has received a lot of popular attention, and the belief in the existence of such centers reflects the influence of the old hedonistic view. If such centers exist, it must be that pleasures and pains are fundamental causes of thought and action. But are things that simple? Could stimulating electrodes provide us with pleasure whenever we wished? The press suggests that this is the case, but consider the data.

Pleasure Centers in the Brain

A well-publicized discovery was made through experimental error. James Olds, a postdoctoral student of Donald Hebb at McGill University in Montreal, was learning to perform electrode implants in the brains of rats. His purpose was to insert a stimulating electrode in the reticular formation and determine whether stimulation led to faster maze learning. Hebb believed that this area of the upper spinal cord and medulla was responsible for arousal of the entire forebrain and that stimulation there might speed up learning. Moruzzi and Magoun (1949) had named the area the Ascending Reticular Activating System, or ARAS.

As it happened, the electrode bent on the way to the ARAS and lodged far forward, in the medial forebrain bundle. Both Olds and Peter Milner, who was working with him, noted the odd effects of stimulation produced by this implant. When stimulated, the rat returned to the place where it was standing when the stimulation was delivered; when a lever was added and pressing produced bursts of stimulation, the rat pressed!

Is this a significant finding? According to Hebb (1976), who wrote a eulogy after Olds's death, little attention was paid to it at the time. But a newspaper reporter for the *Montreal Star* came around to see what was new around McGill University and took some notes on Olds's and Milner's finding. As Hebb put it, the reporter "laid his story away in a drawer until one day when he was short of copy and turned it in as current news on the university scene." A higher-up in the newspaper was anxious for local news for the front page and ran a headline something like, "McGill Scientists Open Great New Field of Research," along with a lengthy story. This sensationalism embarrassed the university in general and Hebb in particular.

Whether Olds had actually discovered pleasure centers in the brain is another matter, which we will discuss later. But, given the publicity, it was difficult for him to believe that he had not done so, and he spent years defending the fact that he had (e.g., Olds, 1956). It is true that some placements of electrodes in the brains of rats (and humans) *appear* to produce pleasure and there is no question that such stimulation can act as a potent reinforcer.

The limbic system, where brain stimulation is effective, was named by the neuroanatomist James Papez in 1936. It is located deep in the center of the brain. Rats will press a lever over long periods of time when the only payoff is brain stimulation; Valenstein (1973) reported a rat pressing a lever 850,000 times over 21 days for such a reward. Others have reported that a rat may starve in the presence of food because it is "chained" to the lever that provides electrical stimulation of the brain (ESB), or intracranial stimulation (ICS), as it is also called. During the 1960s, science fiction writers used ICS as a theme in a number of pieces, in which evil "electro-garths" enslaved populations with stimulating electrodes implanted in their brains.

Olds did show that ICS may act much as other reinforcers, such as food. A rat will press a lever for it and will cross a shock grid to get it. Additionally, the discovery of Olds's so-called reward center was only a reasonable extension of what José Delgado had found a few years earlier; he had reported the existence of so-called punishment centers in the brain.

What Delgado found at that time (published years later) was that cats and other animals appear to dislike stimulation in some parts of the limbic system (1955). Not only will they learn to press a bar to avoid or escape it, but such stimulation seemed to punish other behaviors. In an obviously theatrical demonstration, Delgado (1969) showed that ICS can stop the charge of a "brave bull." The demonstration occurred in a rented bull ring in California, where Delgado stopped the bull as it was about to trample him! He also showed that ICS could punish eating, as well as interrupt the care of infant rhesus monkeys by the normally attentive mother. Little doubt remained in the minds of many that Delgado had demonstrated the existence of punishment centers in the brain. Olds's discovery just supplied the other side of the coin.

We have noticed that the theory of hedonism seems inadequate to explain the behavior of ourselves or of animals. Nonetheless, this theory has such a long history and is so ingrained in the minds of both laypersons and brain researchers that we all are prepared to believe that there might be brain centers specifically devoted to the experiences of pleasure and pain. Larry Stein, a prominent researcher, even suggested that reward and punishment circuits are permanently wired in the brain and that they are served by two different neurotransmitters. He suggested that punishment circuits pass through the midline of the limbic system, just adjacent to the cerebral ventricles (Stein, 1964). This periventricular system is supposed to be a cholinergic network; the neurotransmitter involved is acetylcholine. The lateral portions of the limbic system are assumed to be adrenergic; the neurotransmitter is norepinephrine and this network mediates reward—the pleasure center.

Olds tried very hard to show that ICS did indeed tap the biological bases activated by normal rewards and punishments. Olds and Milner (1954) showed that rats would press bars for ICS, would cross charged grids for it, and that its effects increased when animals were hungry. Similarly, Neal Miller (1958) argued that such stimulation produced actual hunger and thirst. ICS makes sated animals eat food as well as inedible objects! Isn't that real hunger?

A Reappraisal Since the early work of Delgado and of Olds and Milner, countless studies have been conducted to investigate the nature of rewarding and punishing ICS, as well as merely to use it in the course of other investigations. At the same time, it has become increasingly evident that we may have been hasty in describing the effects of ICS as the activation of reward/pleasure and punishment/pain centers.

ICS and Hedonism   We now have clear evidence that the rewarding effects of ICS have nothing to do with pleasure and pain. Even before the accident that led Olds to the discovery of the effects of ICS in rats, a surgeon at Columbia University named Robert Heath had stimulated the limbic system in humans. His purpose was to provoke some sort of effect in schizophrenic patients, who are often characterized by the lack of emotional expression. Heath knew that the limbic system had been linked with the experience and expression of emotion since the 1930s and he decided to try electrical stimulation of limbic structures in patients for whom nothing else seemed to work.

This work was begun as early as 1950 (Valenstein, 1973), and continued through the 1960s. No patient reported feelings of great pleasure, even though the sites stimulated were in structures that were later defined as part of the reward system (for example, the septum, medial forebrain bundle, and lateral hypothalamus). According to Valenstein, Heath and other researchers found that some patients reported some pleasure, especially if they had been in pain; others reported pleasure and they continued to report it long after the stimulating equipment was turned off! Remember, the subjects were not average persons; they were people in such condition that they had submitted to an operation involving the implanting of an electrode in the middle of their brains!

In addition to a conspicuous lack of pleasure when the so-called pleasure center was stimulated, there were no reports of hunger, thirst, and so on when various parts of the hypothalamus were stimulated. The typical effect of hypothalamic stimulation was "abdominal discomfort, a feeling of warmth and a feeling of fullness of the head, and a pounding heart" (Valenstein, 1973).

Delgado and Punishment   Valenstein (1973) was very critical of Delgado as the most casual reader of his book must perceive. In Valenstein's view, Delgado has sometimes promoted his views by using somewhat deceptive evidence. Take the case of the brave bull, which appears in many introductory textbooks. As mentioned earlier, Delgado rented a bull ring in southern California, called the press, and demonstrated that ICS of a punishment center could cause the inhibition of aggression in the animal. Delgado had implanted a stimulating electrode, which could be remotely activated and which would stop the bull's charge. When the big moment came and the cameras were rolling, the bull charged Delgado, who stopped it in its tracks just before the beast reached him. The punishing stimulation was so effective that Delgado could walk up to the bull and pet it!

But Delgado was stimulating the caudate nucleus, an area with motor functions in humans and other animals (excluding birds). If the caudate nucleus on one side is stimulated in a human, perhaps in an attempt to treat Parkinsonism, the effect is paralysis, turning of the head in the direction away from the side stimulated. How does this relate to the bull? Films of the charge show clearly why the bull stopped before reaching Delgado; it was too busy turning and, presumably, becoming momentarily paralyzed. Delgado may have stopped the bull, but describing the effect as activation of a punishment center was clearly misleading.

ICS, Reward, and Punishment   The findings reported by investigators using ICS have indeed been very informative. The assumptions of the original researchers have proven false; there are not necessarily reward and punishment centers as such in the brain, and reinforcement and punishment surely are not synonyms for pleasure and pain. What does happen when a rat presses a lever 850,000 times in 21 days for the ICS that each lever press produces? By most definitions, such stimulation is a reinforcer, but our ignorance about the nature of reinforcement means that we do not really understand why such stimulation is reinforcing.

One finding that gives clues in this regard concerns a difference between ICS rewards and conventional reinforcers. Apparently, rats and other subjects that respond to produce ICS often seem to forget how pleasant the stimulation is and therefore must be primed, or given a few free stimulations before they return to the lever that produces it. This might seem odd; equally odd, if we believe that the rat that presses hour after hour enjoys it, is the finding that cats and rats also press a lever to turn off ICS. An experiment by Phillips, Cox, Kakolewski, and Valenstein (1969) illustrates what happens and how these data might be interpreted if one is looking for specific centers in the brain.

Rat subjects were given electrode implants in the so-called lateral hypothalamic reward system. They were then placed in a box containing two photocell assemblies, one at each end of the box. When the rats interrupted one photo beam they received brain stimulation, which continued until the beam at the other end of the box was broken. What did the rats do under such circumstances? They ran back and forth, turning on the stimulation, turning it off, turning it on, and so on.

Then food pellets were placed on the side of the box, where stimulation was turned on. The animals picked up a food pellet, carried it to the opposite end of the box, and dropped it when the stimulation ended. Thus, the stimulation seemed to be eliciting a common rat behavior, hoarding: the reward center also acted as a "food-hoarding" center! But that is not the whole story.

When other objects, such as rubber erasers, were placed at one end of the box, these were also carried and deposited at the other end of the box. Does this mean that the stimulation was activating a "hoarding of office supplies" center? Next, a rat pup was placed at the "stimulation on" end of the box and it was carried across the box and deposited. Since this resembled the retrieval of pups that occurs as a part of rat parental behavior, one could imagine that a "parental behavior" center had been activated.

But the stimulating electrode was always in the same site; only the material available to be carried was varied. After this training the rats' tendency to carry objects across the box was so strong that when there was nothing to carry, the animal occasionally picked up its tail or one of its forelegs, struggled across the box, and "deposited" it. If some specific center were being activated, it is clearly difficult to assign it a name. Also, though all of the subjects were nominally stimulated in the same hypothalamic region, the individual placements varied quite a bit. What was going on?

The effect occurred only when the on and off beams were at opposite ends of the chamber; if the same pattern of stimulation was given independently of the animals' position, no carrying occurred. One can only conclude that when rats are motivated to move back and forth and when this is accompanied by a parallel arousal and calming, they are apt to carry things. Our old conception of specific centers does not seem to help us here. We need a better conception of reward and punishment than that provided by the "brain centers" view, and from the old theory of hedonism. Let us consider some more promising alternatives.

Premack's Principle: The Relativity of Reinforcement

How does the law of effect work? Why is it that some things fairly regularly act as reinforcers and others as punishers? We saw that Thorndike had difficulties with this problem and concluded only that the effects of satisfiers depend on readiness, or the ongoing preparatory behavior that precedes them. Many reinforcers, such as food and water, obviously act to reduce biological *drives*, as Hull emphasized. But many other reinforcers seem to increase drive levels, as is the case when an organism learns to press a bar for the opportunity to explore or when we travel across the city to watch a horror movie.

By the late 1950s it seemed that we would never explain the law of effect, as Hull had tried to do. Yet, it seemed unsatisfying to be left with no more than Skinner's empirical law of effect, which defines a reinforcer as anything that acts to strengthen a behavior. This leaves the law of effect as a circular law: We don't know what behaviors are reinforceable until we apply what we hope is a reinforcer. And we know that it is a reinforcer only when we see its effect. Meehl (1950) attempted to deal with the problem by suggesting that reinforcers are *transsituational;* we may have to try out our reinforcers initially, but once we have found one, we can use it to strengthen any behavior. But what this provides is a list of reinforcers, which is little more than we began with, and we quickly find so many exceptions to transsituationality that we throw out our list.

David Premack, in a number of insightful papers (e.g., 1959, 1965) seemed to solve this problem; the *Premack Principle* could tell us in advance what would act as a reinforcer or punisher. To use it required a change in our basic views of stimuli, behaviors, and consequences.

First, it has been common to treat the world, our behavior, and its consequences as separate things; hence, the distinction between stimuli, responses, and reinforcers seems natural. Premack suggested that a better way of casting things is in *response language*. Our behavior is a set of actual and possible activities that range along a continuum of *value*. Rather than speak of a response (of no intrinsic value) reinforced by food (of high intrinsic value), we constantly experience transitions among activities, each of some value. The value of an activity, such as eating, resting, or watching television, may change from time to time, of course, but that is not a major problem. At any given time we may assess the value of various activities by observing how much time we (or our subject) spend engaged in them.

The essence of the Premack Principle lies in the suggestion that engaging in an activity (such as bar pressing) will be reinforced if it provides access to a higher-valued activity. At first sight this may seem to be merely restating the obvious: food reinforces bar pressing because eating is of higher value than pressing: hardly a startling revelation. Premack's Principle accounts for familiar cases of reinforcement but seems to add little to our understanding of what is going on. But that is not the case. The Premack Principle also accounts for a variety of instances of reinforcement that have escaped our notice because of our preconceptions about pleasure and drive reduction.

For example, a rat will run for the opportunity to eat under some circumstances, which have often been taken for granted. Does this mean that running is just a no-value behavior and that eating is always a reinforcer? What if we feed the rat to bursting while confining it in a little cage? Food will no longer reinforce anything, and running may become a very highly valued activity. It is then possible to train the rat to eat for the opportunity to run. The opportunity to engage in a higher-valued behavior always reinforces a lower-valued behavior, even when the latter appears to be a *real* reinforcer.

The same event may even act as a positive and a negative reinforcer at almost the same time. (Recall that a negative reinforcer strengthens a behavior that removes it; a burn negatively reinforces the removing of our hand from the hot stove.) Consider the following conditions for a rat: In its cage, there is a running wheel with a bar to press and a water tube to lick mounted on the inside axle, so that pressing and licking can occur while the rat is running. Pressing the bar (a low-valued activity) allows the occurrence of a higher-valued activity; the wheel unlocks and is turned by a small motor, allowing easy running. The problem is that the motor continues turning and running becomes less appealing as time goes on. Of course, one need not run, but the alternative is tumbling, as the clothes in a dryer do.

Premack (1965) showed that rats would press a lever, which started the wheel, and would lick a water spout, which then stopped the wheel. Forced running thus acted as a positive reinforcer for lever pressing and shortly after as a negative reinforcer for spout licking. That's not very surprising? Once shown that the same activity may act as a reinforcer under some conditions and as a punisher or a negative reinforcer under others, it is easy to believe that we always knew it. But we actually did not; when we think of food, praise, money, and so on as reinforcers we do not typically bear in mind that such things act as reinforcers only under specific conditions. Virtually anything we do will act as a reinforcer for something else we do if the conditions are right. And what are the right conditions? All that is required is that the value of the two activities differ and that the lower-valued activity produce access to the higher-valued activity.

The only problem with this is the difficulty encountered when we try to assign values. Time spent in different activities may work in some cases, as when we assess the value of a child's playing with different toys, or the value of a rat's running, pressing, or gnawing wood. But what of activities such as eating, watching television, reading, and sleeping? Is thirty minutes spent eating equivalent to the same amount of time watching TV or sleeping? If a person spends an hour a day running and eight hours sleeping, is the value of sleeping eight times that of running? This problem of *commensurability of units* of activities gave Premack a good deal of trouble, and he never really resolved it. Nor did he resolve the problem of changes in the value of activities with time. For example, as a rat is eating for the opportunity to run, the value of running surely decreases with repeated opportunities. Do we reach a point at which the value of running is lower than that of eating and acts only to punish eating? *Value* is nebulous and always changing; it is not as easy to scale as Premack assumed.

Response Deprivation

The problem of dealing with activities differing in value was pointed out first by Eisenberger, Karpman, and Trattner (1967) and later was elaborated upon by Timberlake and Allison (1974). What is really important in Premack's Principle is not differences in the values of activities but the restriction of access to activities used to demonstrate the reinforcement of lower- by higher-valued activities. For example, consider two activities, eating and running, in humans or rats. Assume that running currently is the higher-valued activity. This means that our subject will eat if such activity produces access to running, but it will not run for the opportunity to eat; our subject

will simply continue running if given the chance, and any eating will have to be forced. But if we look closely at our demonstration of this fact we find something very interesting.

To demonstrate that our subject will eat for the opportunity to run, we have to restrict its running, allowing only a limited amount of it to occur after so much eating. Could it be that this restriction is the really important factor, whatever the values of the activities? We decided that running was of higher value than eating, since we saw that our subject spent more time running than eating just before our experiment. We then restricted its access to running to a level less than it wanted by requiring so much eating for opportunities to run. But what if we reversed the contingencies here and restricted the opportunity to engage in the lower-valued activity so that eating could not occur even at its low-value level? Suppose we then require an increase in time spent running for opportunities to eat and find that the amount of running increases. The lower-valued activity (eating) acts as a reinforcer for the higher-valued activity (running). Timberlake and Allison report numerous instances of this kind (though not this one), all showing the importance of what they called *response deprivation*. For example, if given a choice between licking drinking spouts that provide three-percent or four-percent sucrose, rats spend more time licking the four-percent solution; in Premack's terms, it is the higher-valued activity. Suppose now that access to the less preferred three-percent solution tube is blocked and an increase in licking the four-percent solution tube provides brief access to the three-percent tube. Licking the four-percent tube increases, reinforced by access to the less favored solution, which remains acting as a reinforcer as long as access is restricted.

Thus, one need only have a measure of the baseline (unrestricted) levels of occurrence of whatever activities are of interest in whatever units seem appropriate. The units could be time spent in one activity and frequency of occurrence of another; the units need not be commensurate. If access to one activity is then restricted so that it cannot occur at its baseline level and a second, unrestricted, activity produces access to it, the latter will increase above its baseline level; it will be reinforced.

Practical implications of this extension of the Premack Principle are easy to imagine. For example, to influence the behavior of school-children, one needs no tokens or other externally imposed reward system. All that is necessary is to monitor current levels of several behaviors, such as sitting quietly, reading, playing, fighting, or whatever else occurs with some frequency. If a restriction is then imposed, so that one (or more) behavior(s) cannot occur at baseline levels and an increase in another behavior allows access to the first, the latter will increase in frequency. Access to the restricted behavior acts to reinforce the behavior that produces access and will continue to do so as long as the restricted behavior is not allowed to occur at its baseline level. This means that any behavior may be used to reinforce any other behavior, given that both originally occur at some baseline level. The opportunity to read may reinforce sitting quietly, just as fighting may be reinforced by the opportunity to read.

Consider a hypothetical example illustrated in Figure 9.1. The left column represents observed levels of four behaviors shown by a child over a seven-day period. Note that talking with friends and solitary play are scaled in average time in minutes per day, while reading and running are recorded as average number of bouts greater than five minutes duration occurring per day. The units in which activities are scaled need not be the same.

Suppose, for illustration's sake, that one wishes to increase the time that such a child spent reading. According to the response deprivation principle, restriction of access to a second activity renders the opportunity to engage in that activity a reinforcer for other behavior that produces access to the restricted behavior. Naturally, the level of restricted behavior must be kept below its unrestricted baseline throughout.

We might easily restrict the opportunity to talk with friends (assuming the presence of other chil-

dren, as is the case while the child is in school). We then could require that the time spent reading increase from its average of five minutes per hour to fifteen minutes per hour; when such a longer bout occurs we allow a ten-minute break to talk with friends. We continue this procedure, being certain that the time allowed talking with friends remains below the baseline level of 100 minutes per day. Alternatively, what would happen if we decided to reinforce time spent in solitary play with opportunity to read? Could it be done?

This view of reinforcement (and punishment) seems so obvious that one wonders why it was not proposed earlier. In fact, Premack (1971) seemed to show some irritation in his last general attempt to get the point across; it is frustrating to speak to deaf ears. As simple as Premack's principle and Timberlake and Allison's extensions are, they have not been universally received. A reasoned criticism of Premack's Principle appears in Smith (1974); unless you understand the principle well, Smith's criticisms are difficult to counter.

Conservation Theory

A recent derivative of Premack's view appears in the simple conservation theory of Allison, Miller, and Wozny (1979). By the way of background, they cited a number of studies that used both animal and human subjects and showed odd relationships between work requirements and payoffs (Collier, 1972).

1. As work required increases, work output increases, but total payoff decreases. This occurs well before a "ceiling effect" on work output is reached. Subjects will simply work so much, even though this means that payoff decreases.

2. As magnitude of payoff increases, total payoff received increases, but work output decreases.

3. If one behavior is required for access to a second behavior, increases in the former are accompanied by decreases in the latter.

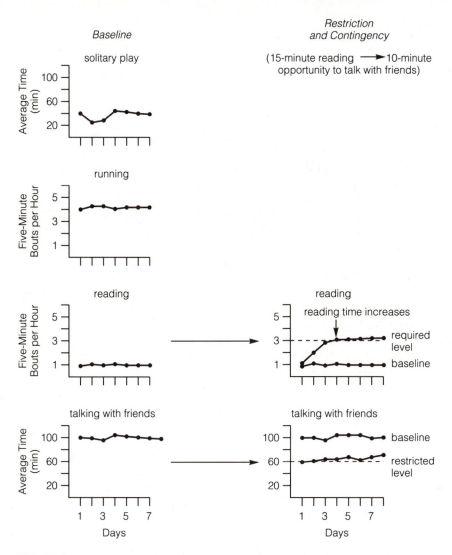

FIGURE 9.1   Results of response deprivation for a child's activities.

These effects suggest a *conservation process*, whereby total behavior (e.g., working and eating) remains constant as work requirements and payoffs change. Allison, et al. cite to "the total amount of a dimension" that is conserved. To illustrate, they describe a hypothetical experiment, beginning with a baseline session in which a rat is free to press a lever or drink from a water spout. They assume, for purposes of illustration, that each lever press requires twice as much work as does a one-second drink. Suppose that during the base-line session the rat drinks for 1,194 seconds and presses three times. In their terms, this reflects the operant level of pressing and drinking, or Oi and Oc, where "i" refers to pressing (an instrumental behavior) and "c" refers to drinking (a consummatory behavior).

Total work (in drinking units) is $kOi + Oc$. The constant "k" is used to express pressing in drink-sec units; in this case, $k = 2$. Thus, the work done during baseline is $kOi + Oc = 2(3) + 1{,}194 = 1{,}200$ drink-sec units. This is the quantity that is conserved when conditions are changed and the change amounts to a reciprocal schedule. Such a schedule requires so much of one activity for access to so much of another activity, for access to so much of the first activity, and so on. This will be clear below.

What happens when this rat is required to press once for a ten-second opportunity to drink, which is required for a second opportunity to press, which is required for a second ten-second drink, and so on? How many times will the rat go through this cycle? If 1,200 units occurred in baseline, that is what will occur under this contingency. One press for ten seconds of drinking translates to $2(1) + 10 = 12$ units; the rat will therefore go through the press/drink sequence $1,200/12 = 100$ times if conservation holds.

In general, $N(kI + C) = kOi + Oc$, which means that the subject will perform the two responses $(kI + C)$ required by the reciprocal schedule N times. N is the number of times necessary to equal the total amount of behavior during baseline $(kOi + Oc)$. Thus, $N = kOi + Oc/kI + C$. Such conservation holds, the authors tell us, in studies using rats drinking saccharine solutions, as well as when humans study Russian for the opportunity to sew or knit!

As an example of their evidence, the first experiment reported baseline levels of drinking and pressing for rats. Then, in different conditions, they required either twenty, 30, or 40 seconds of drinking for ten, twenty, or 30 seconds of pressing (for twenty, 30, or 40 seconds of drinking, and so on). As the requirements for the two behaviors were varied, conservation obtained; the obtained and predicted time spent pressing and drinking corresponded closely. And, as the required pressing increased, total pressing increased but total drinking decreased. As the drinking required increased, total drinking increased but pressing decreased.

Other experiments corroborated the conservation theory, which is presented here only to give a flavor of the type of research that has evolved from the Premack Principle. You may

see that there are some problems with the conservation model and with similar models, by examining the original article in *Journal of Experimental Psychology: General* (Allison, Miller, Wozny, 1979). That particular issue of the journal is devoted wholly to such models, and a survey of the various viewpoints presented shows that matters are not as simple as Allison, et al. considered them (see Staddon, 1979). Premack's Principle and derivatives certainly depart from older conceptions of the law of effect. They emphasize the relativity of reinforcement as a relation among activities, blur the distinction between behaviors and reinforcers, and surely advance our understanding beyond a simple hedonism.

The Matching Law: The Molar Law of Effect

A great deal of interest has focused on what Herrnstein calls the matching law (e.g., 1958, 1970). Simply put, an organism obeying the *matching law* distributes responses so as to match the relative frequencies of reinforcement associated with a set of alternative behaviors.

For example, suppose that a child, a rat, or a pigeon spends an hour a day in front of a panel of buttons—one red, one white, and one green. Suppose also that button presses are reinforced occasionally by candy, food pellets, or grain. Finally, suppose that responding to green is reinforced ten times per hour, whereas responses to white and red are reinforced five times per hour, respectively. What will our subject spend its time doing? It could find that green pays off a lot more often than does white or red and simply spend all of the time pressing or pecking green. In the same way, an animal that forages in several areas could well spend all of its time in that area most abundant in food. Herrnstein (and many others since) have shown that the child, rat, or pigeon tends to match relative responding to the three alternatives to the relative frequencies of reinforcement associated with each. In our example, the relative frequencies of reinforcement for red, white, and green are 0.25, 0.25, and 0.50. Hence, our subject will make half of the responses to green and a quarter of the responses to each of the other buttons.

Why is this noteworthy? Assuming that the matching law is a basic fact of life (some dispute this), it tells us something interesting about the operation of the law of effect. That is, the effect of reinforcement of a given behavior is really predictable only if the effect of other behaviors and their reinforcement frequencies is taken into account. This is contrary to the common notion that we may select a target behavior and affect it independently of other behaviors; this view stresses the interdependence of behaviors.

This interdependence of behaviors and the relativity of the law of effect makes some sense of failures to find effects produced by many variations in reinforcement contingencies. For example, we believe that big reinforcers are more effective than little ones and that delay of reward is harmful. Yet, if you examine all of the studies seeking to show that this is the case, it becomes clear that the effects of magnitude and delay of reward are very unclear (e.g., Mackintosh, 1974). The rats running for the big pellet do not necessarily run faster than those getting the small one.

However, give the rodent exposure to both big and small pellets and it will quickly know about relative size. For example, the effect of a large reward is dependent upon the size of reward gotten a few minutes ago or concurrently available for other behaviors.

If the matching law still seems unrelated to things that happen in the real world, consider Baum's (1974) experiment. Oddly enough, Baum built the largest Skinner box in history by attaching a feeder and two response keys to the outside of his house. One perch was placed under the keys so that vagabond pigeons from the area could land, peck the keys, and be fed for it. Reinforcements were scheduled independently for pecking each key, and a group of twenty to thirty pigeons eventually came to congregate there. Now, the perch could accommodate only one bird at a time,

so it is easy to imagine the flock of birds hovering around the feeder, successively displacing one another, with the key clicking, the feeder clanking, and the pigeons (clucking?) cooing. In spite of the bizarre conditions, the flock may as well have been one bird, because the relative frequency of pecking on the two keys closely matched the relative frequency of reinforcement for pecking them. This is therefore a powerful law, applying to the behavior of groups as well as individuals.

Self-Control

Rachlin and Green (1972) and Ainslee (1974) showed that one version of the matching law can account for self-control and went on to demonstrate this with pigeons. Their simplified version of the matching law was as follows:

$$\frac{V_1}{V_2} = \frac{A_1}{A_2} \cdot \frac{T_2}{T_1}$$

V_1 and V_2 refer to the relative values of two alternatives, A_1 and A_2 represent the amount of payoff for each, and T_1 and T_2 refer to the delays in obtaining the payoffs. Note that value is reasonably assumed to be proportional to the amount of payoff, and it is inversely proportional to the delay in receiving it. Thus, our valuation of an alternative depends on what we get and how long we have to wait. Since value depends on both of these factors, self-control occurs when we choose a larger payoff even though we have to wait for it. We save our money because of the large payoff we will receive in the future.

Time affects the relative values of alternatives so that it is easier to make a wise choice that commits us in advance of the actual choice between alternatives. If I find it difficult to save money, it is because the present value of spending it is greater than the value of accumulating it far in the future. Thus, given the choice, I spend it now. I may control myself by eliminating my choice: I sign up for the payroll savings plan and thus agree in advance to choose the wise alternative. This may be expressed as follows:

$$\frac{V_1 \text{ (spending)}}{V_2 \text{ (saving)}}$$

$$= \frac{A_1 \text{ (use of small amount of money)}}{A_2 \text{ (use of large amount of money)}}$$

$$\cdot \frac{T_2 \text{ (months)}}{T_1 \text{ (minimal)}}$$

With money in hand, V_1 is larger than V_2 and I spend my money. If I agree to begin the payroll savings plan in a month or two, I add that time period to both T_1 and T_2, thus neutralizing the discrepancy between them.

In illustrating this form of self-control in pigeons, Rachlin and Green (1972) presented the birds with two white keys. Pecking the right key changed the colors of the keys to red and green. Further pecks on the red key led to access to food for two seconds, and pecking the green key led to four seconds of food after a four-second delay. A wise bird would always peck the green key, wait for four seconds, and get twice as much access to food. But no bird did this. Given the choice between red (a small immediate reward) and green (a large delayed reward), every bird always pecked red, thus showing no self-control. Refer to Table 9.1.

If, when the keys were white, the left key was pecked, one key changed to green and the other went off. Only green could then be pecked, producing the large delayed reward. But no bird pecked the left key, though earlier forced trials ensured that the animals were familiar with the results of pecking either key. They always pecked the right key, giving them the choice of red or green, and then they always pecked red, giving them the small immediate payoff.

When the "payroll savings plan" was introduced, all of the birds eventually signed up. This amounted to interposing a delay before the keys turned to red and green. When the delay was greater than four seconds, the birds began showing self-control by pecking the left (commitment) key, which then (after four seconds) gave them only the option of pecking green (the wise choice). When the delay was as great as ten seconds, the

TABLE 9.1   Two Examples of Self-Control and the Matching Law

1. $A_1 = 2s$ No self-control
$T_1 = 1s$
$A_2 = 4s$ $\dfrac{V_1}{V_2} = \dfrac{A_1}{A_2} \cdot \dfrac{T_2}{T_1}$
$T_2 = 5s$

$$= \frac{2s}{4s} \cdot \frac{5s}{1s} = \frac{10}{4}$$

2. $A_1 = 2s$ Self-control with 10s Delay
$T_1 = 11s$
$A_2 = 4s$ $\dfrac{V_1}{V_2} = \dfrac{A_1}{A_2} \cdot \dfrac{T_2}{T_1}$
$T_2 = 15s$

$$= \frac{2s}{4s} \cdot \frac{15s}{11s} = \frac{30}{44}$$

left key was chosen much more often; the birds showed self-control.

For people and pigeons this suggests that we always choose the higher-valued alternative and that value depends on both time and amount of payoff. I sign up for payroll savings in advance of receiving my pay, when the value of saving is greater than the value of spending, just as the pigeon "signs up" for the green key in advance. When I receive my pay, the value of spending is greater than the value of saving, just as the immediate small reward is of high value for the pigeon when it is faced with the red/green choice.

In both the human and the animal case, there is no real self-control; in both cases the choice is made for the higher-valued alternative *at the time*. Similarly, we place an alarm clock at a distance from the bed before going to sleep, when the value of getting up is high and the value of staying in bed is low. We do so because we know that the values may be reversed in the morning and that the value of staying in bed will likely be greater than the value of getting up. Are all instances of self-control reducible to such a principle?

Autoshaping: Relevant to the Operant/Respondent Distinction?

Many researchers have studied the behavior of pigeons pecking a lighted plastic response key. According to popular belief, one trains a pigeon to peck a key through shaping its behavior, using the method of successive approximations (see Skinner, 1953). This amounts to shaping behavior arbitrarily, "as a sculptor shapes a piece of clay." Not only key pecking may be shaped, of course, since we can easily shape all manner of behaviors. But most basic researchers in operant conditioning hand-shaped their birds to peck the key, often spending hours doing it with a difficult bird. Some birds just could not be hand-shaped, regardless of the skill of the shaper; these birds were kept in the uppermost cages in the bird room and were taken down only if one wanted to try (once again) to shape them.

Then Brown and Jenkins (1968) showed that the art of shaping was not necessary, at least in the case of key pecking by pigeons. They showed that all we need do is take any pigeon (even from the top row of cages) and induce it to eat from a grain hopper. In their experiment, they set up equipment to pair the lighting of the key with operation of the food magazine. The light came on for eight seconds, followed by the operation of the food magazine. The key light was then off for a variable period (such as a minute) and then was lighted again, followed by the delivery of food. Brown and Jenkins found that their 36 subjects all began pecking the key within 119 trials, with the average bird pecking on the 45th pairing of light and food.

If the birds pecked the lighted key, it immediately turned off and the food hopper operated. But pecking did not have to produce any effect. When the light stayed on for eight seconds even when the bird pecked it, eleven of twelve birds still began pecking, with the average bird beginning to peck on the 54th trial.

Brown and Jenkins noted that the procedure they used was essentially a classical conditioning procedure, with the key light acting as a CS and the food as the UCS. The reason that the birds pecked at the key was presumably the same reason that Pavlov's dogs licked a CS light if they could, though Brown and Jenkins suggested that it was due to a species-specific tendency for pigeons to peck what they look at. Finally, they suggested that this autoshaping could somehow depend on superstitious operant conditioning.

Williams and Williams (1969), however, showed that autoshaping was not due to superstitious reinforcement, and they did so in a simple and persuasive way. They used essentially the same procedure that Brown and Jenkins used, but with a single and important difference. If the pigeon pecked the lighted key, it prevented the operation of the food magazine on that trial. Thus, the key light was illuminated and food was delivered, unless the lighted key was pecked. In that case, no food came. Whether the birds involved had been previously hand-shaped, autoshaped, or were naive, they pecked! The key light went off and no food was delivered. Hence, the key peck in autoshaping is not maintained because of a superstitious connection with food; it persists even though it prevents food. Not surprisingly, it takes a number of light-food pairings, as is the case in autoshaping, before pecking begins; once it does begin and food is never received, it is apt to stop. This means that food will once more be delivered, which means that pecking will begin again, which will prevent the delivery of food, and so on.

Maybe pigeons just have to peck something when food is on the way, and if some alternative to the food-preventing key were available, the bird could peck harmlessly and still get food. The Williamses introduced a second key, which came on when the old key did but had no consequence when pecked. Reasonably enough, the birds quickly learned to peck this "irrelevant" key, thus having their pecking and their food too. But just any irrelevant key would not do; it had to signal food as did the other key. If an irrelevant key was left on all the time, except when the food was being delivered, it was seldom pecked; the birds went back to the old key and to their lost reinforcements. When they did peck this irrelevant key, it was always when the "relevant" key was on.

What do we make of this? The method of successive approximations still works, of course, even though it may be unnecessary if we wish to train a pigeon to peck a key for grain. But this case is clearly out of the reach of a standard operant analysis, meaning that there is something special about pigeons pecking for a food reinforcer. Is the key peck a CR, since autoshaping and automaintenance (shown by the Williamses) amount to classical conditioning and omission training, respectively? Recall from Chapter 3 that Sheffield (1965) used omission training to see whether CRs such as salivating were sensitive to their consequences. He found that dogs could not learn to withhold salivation when rewarded with food, showing that salivation was a true CR. Food is a UCS that elicits salivation, and salivation occurs even when it prevents the delivery of food. Since pecking occurs even when it prevents the delivery of food, is it a CR?

It seems that it clearly is, although debate raged on what seems to be such a simple matter. Pigeons eat by pecking at grain and other food items, followed by the ingesting and swallowing of the food. Just as salivation is a CR because it is a fractional component of the UCR, pecking is a CR because it is a fractional component of the pigeon's UCR to food.

Why is this finding damaging to traditional conceptions of learning? Well, if one takes Skinner's distinction between operant and respondent conditioning seriously (1938), and notes that key pecking has long been studied as a typical operant, the discovery of autoshaping is noteworthy. Thousands of studies have shown that key pecking is an operant, because it has been shown to be sensitive to its consequences more times than one can count. But autoshaping shows that key pecking acts as a CR, or respondent, as well. Many studies (e.g., Gamzu & Williams, 1971, 1973) have shown that autoshaped pecking occurs only under conditions in which Pavlovian CRs occur—that is, where there is a *contingency* between the CS and the UCS. Just pairing the key light and food is insufficient; the key light must predict the delivery of food, much as the CS must predict the UCS if classical conditioning is to occur.

Another reason for believing that the auto-shaped key peck is a CR lies in the evidence that the form of the peck depends on the UCS, or reinforcer, involved. When the reinforcer is food, the autoshaped peck is made with beak open. When the reinforcer (or UCS) is water, the peck occurs with beak closed (e.g., Moore, 1973). It happens that pigeons peck at grain with an open beak and at water, if it could be called a peck, with beak closed. Thus, when autoshaped with food, the beak is open, as it is when the bird eats grain and when autoshaped with a water reinforcer, the (CR) peck is made with closed beak. The autoshaped response is thus a CR, since other CRs are fractional parts of the UCR to whatever UCS is coming.

Other evidence, cited in the scholarly review by Schwartz and Gamzu (1977), shows that when other organisms and reinforcers are used, the autoshaped response also resembles the normal response to the reinforcer. Thus, when access to a sexual partner is the UCS, the autoshaped response is similar to the sexual response, and when opportunity for aggression is the reinforcer, the autoshaped response is aggression. It has even been shown that pigeons may react to a stimulus preceding electric shock by striking at it with their wings (Rachlin, 1969).

Contrast and the Interdependence of Behaviors

Those favoring the operant model, both in behavior therapy and in basic research, have usually assumed that behavior is divisible into independent units. Hence, changes in the frequency of a target behavior may occur in the absence of changes in other behaviors, especially when the other behaviors seem quite different from the target behavior. In the same way, basic researchers have often confined their attention to whatever behavior operates the lever or key, assuming that other behaviors remain essentially unchanged (cf. Staddon & Simmelhag, 1971). If other behaviors do change when the target behavior does, the effect is usually attributed to generalization.

Recall that Skinner's early definition of the operant by no means restricted that unit to behaviors that appear similar in form or that conform to our notions of what a "behavior" should be (Skinner, 1931, 1935). An operant class may be composed of a number of behaviors that at first sight seem very dissimilar.

Wahler (1975) described data gathered from observation of children over several years and reported that changes in the frequency of a given behavior were often accompanied by changes in other behaviors that did not seem obviously related to the first. He referred to this as evidence for clusters of behaviors, which is another way of saying that the response class may be composed of quite different behaviors. They form a class because they tend to covary.

Another form of behavioral interdependence is quite different, appearing as a divergence or contrast among behaviors. Reynolds (1961a) showed that the frequency of one behavior may be greatly influenced by a change in the consequences produced by a second behavior. This effect, *behavioral contrast*, has been found to be quite pervasive in animal learning and has clear parallels in human behavior, as Reynolds (1975) pointed out.

We will begin with an illustration with pigeons pecking a clear plastic response key. Initially, pecking is occasionally reinforced with food equally frequently when the key is lighted with either a red or green light. Some time later, reinforcement is discontinued when the key is green but continues at the same rate when the key is red. Responding in green decreases, of course, and it increases greatly in red, even though the reinforcement conditions in red are the same as always. Those conditions are better, however, relative to green, and the increase in responding in red is aptly called contrast.

Consider Figure 9.2. The left panel of the top figure shows responding to two stimuli, $S+$ and $S-$, when the frequency of reinforcement in each is equal. The right panel shows what typically occurs when the frequency of reinforcement in one stimulus is decreased, making $S-$ a real $S-$. Response rate in $S-$ decreases, of course, but the rate of response also increases in $S+$; why should this be? It would seem that only a very odd sort of person would find this occurrence strange. After all, is it not plausible to assume that the value of $S+$ increases because it is now associated with more frequent reinforcement relative to $S-$? Aren't our evaluations of things always relative? Is five dollars the same thing to me as to a Vanderbilt? Why should it be different for pigeons, rats, monkeys, children, and all of the other animals in which behavioral contrast has been observed?

This was essentially Reynolds's explanation, and it is essentially correct. He showed (1961b) that contrast occurs when a stimulus presented with VI reinforcement is alternated with timeout periods (no stimulus on the key and no reinforcement available for responding), or with extinction. But contrast does not occur when a VI schedule is alternated with a DRO schedule. A DRO (differential reinforcement of other behavior) schedule provides reinforcement for not responding. Such a schedule may provide as frequent reinforcement as a VI schedule, but rates of responding are near zero. This showed that a decrease in reinforcement frequency in $S-$ was necessary for contrast; just a reduction in response rate is insufficient.

Local Contrast If you recall Pavlovian induction (Chapter 3), you will immediately recognize *local contrast* as the same phenomenon. Nevin and Shettleworth (1966) showed that during the formation of a discrimination responding in $S+$ and $S-$ is influenced by the immediately preceding stimulus. The effects they found (and called transient contrast) are illustrated in the lower part of the figure.

The lower half of the figure illustrates local contrast occurring between presentations of two stimuli, $S+$ and $S-$. However, the data here

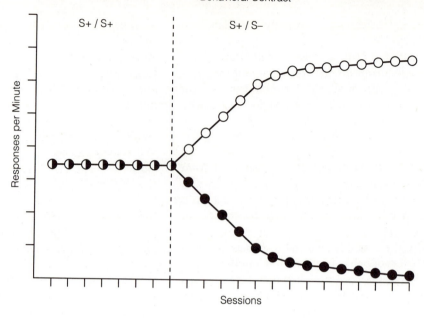

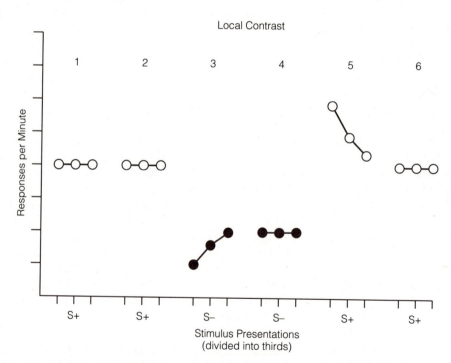

FIGURE 9.2 The upper panel shows behavioral contrast, a change in response rate appearing over sessions. An increase in responding in S+ occurs when reinforcement is discontinued in one stimulus, which becomes S−. This is positive behavioral contrast. Under other conditions, negative behavioral contrast occurs. The lower panel shows positive and negative local contrast. This effect appears among individual stimulus presentations. See text for details.

represent responding in stimuli as a function of the immediately preceding stimulus; typically, data show responding during successive segments of a stimulus presentation (that is first third, second third, third third). For example 1 to 2 in the figure show responding in S+ (2) when preceded by itself (1) averaged over one or more sessions. Responding in the two S+ presentations is similar.

On the other hand, 2 to 3 represents the presentation of S− (3) on those occasions when it was preceded by S+; note that responding is initially depressed and increases during the presentation. This is negative local contrast. Instances 4 to 5 show the effect of an S− (4) preceding an S+ (5); note that responding is initially elevated and decreases during the presentation. This is positive local contrast. These effects may last only a few sessions (e.g., Malone, 1976; Nevin & Shettleworth, 1966), as Pavlov (1927) often found to be true of Pavlovian induction. But if many stimiuli are used and/or they are very similar and therefore difficult to discriminate, local contrast may persist over months (Malone & Staddon, 1973). As far as is known, local contrast and Pavlovian induction share all important characteristics (Malone & Rowe, 1981).

Contrast and Behavior Therapy In the human case, contrast occurs, for example, when unruly behavior is maintained, if unintentionally, by consequences it produces on the playground and at home. In both cases, attention (at the very least) reinforces such behavior, just as the pigeon's pecks were reinforced in both red and green. Suppose that a teacher or behavior therapist manages to eliminate those consequences on the playground and that this leads to a decrease in unruly behavior there. Like the pigeon's pecks, which are still reinforced in red, unruly behavior will likely produce its customary consequences at home and one should therefore expect an increase in unruly behavior at home (Reynolds, 1975).

Reynolds's suggested parallel between pigeon and child is by no means farfetched, although at first sight it may appear to be. Wahler at the University of Tennessee Child Behavior Institute, has been interested in this parallel. He has noted (personal communication, 1989) that reports from parents of increased troublesome behavior in the home often accompany successful treatment of such behavior in the school. If we wish to decrease or eliminate the pigeon's pecking in red, we stop providing reinforcement in red. So too with the unruly child. Wahler, Winkel, Peterson, & Morrison (1965) found that the real method for dealing with unruly behavior is through training of parents as "therapists" so that the inadvertent reinforcement of such behavior in the home is ended.

This contrast among behaviors is not always the rule, of course, and behavior therapy is largely predicated on the assumption that treatment effects generalize to a greater or lesser degree across situations. But when might one expect such generalization and when might contrast be expected? There are cases in which treatment of troublesome behavior at school generalizes to behavior at home. Yet, there are cases when behavioral contrast seems to occur. The answer to this question is unknown at present. All we can turn to are the animal studies that have been done to date, and there have been many; but they have been unable to determine the conditions that lead to generalization or contrast. It is probably safe to say that if the behaviors in question (key pecks or troublesome behaviors) belong to the same response class, they are apt to covary in quite similar situations. (That is actually the definition of a response class.) Also, the more similar the situation (red/green, school/home), the more we may expect generalization of treatment effects from one situation to the other. The increase in the child's misbehavior at home depends in part on the dissimilarity of the school and home situations as well as the altered consequences for unruly behavior at school. This is not terribly helpful, but it is helpful to know that there is considerable evidence for contrast effects in animal learning and thus we should not be overly surprised when we find similar effects in analogous situations involving human behavior.

We might also know more about the causes of contrast if it were not for the great reluctance of basic researchers to accept such interactions among behaviors. It is more convenient to treat them as independent. One researcher (Bloomfield, 1969) went so far as to suggest that behavioral contrast shown by pigeons represented the avian analog of human psychopathology! That is, our pigeon pecking along in red had no right to peck faster in red when reinforcement was eliminated in green. Reinforcement conditions were unchanged in red and response rate should have not changed; hence, the bird was insane.

Neuringer and Chung: Conditioned Reinforcement

It has long been believed that any event that acts as a reinforcer of the behavior of a given species does so for one of two reasons. First, it may act as a reinforcer because of the nature of the organism, in which case its power would be evident at birth or shortly after. Warmth, food, water, and other *primary reinforcers* have obvious biological utility and their deprivation quite rightly gives them reinforcing power.

But few of us spend our lives as do most animals, constantly governed by needs for food, water, and other primary reinforcers. In fact, much of our behavior goes on in spite of such needs, especially when we are concerned with goals such as great achievement, riches, or fame. How do such "higher goals" gain their reinforcing power? We do not all wish fame or riches or great achievement. Often it is solitude and peace that seem the more powerful reinforcing agents. Yet, we do all like the attention of others; being ignored by all would be unpleasant indeed. How does attention from others gain their reinforcing power?

The argument can be made that all events that act as reinforcers but do not act as such at birth (or shortly after) derive their power through association with primary reinforcers. This is a very popular view and, logically, is very hard to fault. We saw in Chapter 6 that this view was strongly

criticized by both Allport and Harlow. Nonetheless, it has remained the leading interpretation of acquired reinforcement. For example, consider the infant whose motives are restricted to hunger, thirst, warmth, contact, and other primary reinforcers. At present our infant is hungry, thirsty, cold, and bored. An adult human appears and provides food, warmth, and entertainment, all of which act as reinforcers for the cry or whatever other behavior brought the adult. This scene happens over and over in the infant's early life and it is no surprise when someone suggests that the infant comes to associate the adult with satisfaction of basic needs. The adult acquires reinforcing power and thus the tale begins.

The adult indeed signals impending food, warmth, comfort, and entertainment, but only under certain conditions. An adult sitting quietly reading or knitting provides no such comforts; it is only when the adult's attention is directed toward the infant and the adult notes the infant that primary reinforcers are forthcoming. Thus, attention itself becomes associated with adults and primary reinforcers and gains reinforcing power that lasts throughout our lifetime. Later, it becomes clear that attention alone is often not enough to guarantee primary payoffs; approving, praiseful attention predicts food and the like more reliably. So we add approval and praise to the list of secondary reinforcers, the power of which still depends on the linkage with food, water, warmth, and so on.

Even curiosity and manipulation may be added to the list, thus dealing with Harlow's critique. When a cat or rat or monkey presses a lever for the opportunity to explore a maze or manipulate a puzzle, we are still dealing with acquired reinforcers ultimately dependent on associations with primary reinforcers. Is it not true that in the early life of any organism exploration of new surroundings is often rewarded with the discovery of food, water, and shelter? Although Harlow (1953 a, b) and others make a good case against such an account, the fact is that it makes a lot of sense. We are biological entities and life is basically the fulfilling of basic needs.

This general interpretation has appeared in so many texts, in so many forms, and has such a surface plausibility that it seems foolish to question it. Nevertheless, there is considerable evidence against it, derived both from daily life and from experience.

In brief, there is remarkably fragile evidence for the establishment of new reinforcers through association of some sort with already potent reinforcers. Gollub, who has spent many years concentrating on the nature of acquired reinforcers, comments on the irony of the situation at the conclusion of a very comprehensive review of basic research in the area (1977). The fact is that the aggregate of laboratory research shows that the pairing of new stimuli with current reinforcers lends only the feeblest reinforcing power to those stimuli. Yet, we see daily how powerfully tokens (including money) control behavior. How does that come to be?

What is bizarre here is not that tokens work but the belief that their power must somehow be based on real reinforcers and that acquired reinforcers are by their very nature of no value. Every time a child is reluctant to turn in tokens for candy, and every time we work on a term paper while tired and hungry, the plausibility of the traditional account is called to question. Isn't it odd that the acquired reinforcers, or *conditioned reinforcers*, in these cases seem more powerful than the primary reinforcers upon which their power is supposed to rest?

The truth is that new reinforcers are acquired and that they may have something to do with current reinforcers. But it is not the case that an acquired reinforcer acts as such simply because it has become a predictor of food, water, warmth, or other real and biologically reasonable events. The following is a very speculative outline of an alternative interpretation of acquired reinforcement. It is not without its problems, but see if it is not more reasonable than the classic explanation (or no explanation at all).

Neuringer and Chung (1967) found that new stimuli, such as brief darkness or tones, could act as potent reinforcers when presented in a specific way. In the simplest case, they reinforced pigeons' key pecks according to a variable-interval (VI) schedule of reinforcement. On the average of once a minute a key peck was followed by the delivery of food.

After baseline levels of responding were established, conditions were changed so that each eleventh response produced some consequence. In some conditions the consequence was a brief tone, in others the chamber was briefly darkened, and in others the key light was briefly turned off. The exact nature of the consequence did not matter; each eleventh key peck produced something. So the birds were getting food on the average of once a minute, and every eleventh peck produced some other brief consequence. What did the addition of such consequences do to the rate of pecking for food? Nothing, of course. Why should a food-deprived pigeon, pecking a key for occasional food, be at all mindful of occasional and meaningless added stimuli?

But a slight alteration in conditions did produce impressive results. Food delivery was scheduled by a timer that determined which pecks would be followed with food. Suppose that food was delivered only after a series of eleven pecks. That is, the bird would peck along, receiving a brief tone after every eleven pecks; there would be eleven pecks then a tone, eleven pecks then a tone, and then after two or three or six pecks, the timer would schedule a reinforcement. But the bird would have to complete its eleven-peck sequence before the food was delivered. In this way, something always happened eleven pecks from the last tone or food and never after more or less than eleven pecks. Eighty-five percent of the time eleven pecks produced only a tone, but fifteen percent of the time, they ended in food. Response rates almost immediately doubled. Why should the addition of a seemingly irrelevant consequence produce such an effect?

Here is a hint. In control procedures, birds receiving the same pattern of food and other consequences showed no change in response rates. For example, subjects receiving brief blackouts or tones after every eleventh response but receiving food for the first response after the timer scheduled reinforcement showed no change in response rates. Thus, an added irrelevant stimulus produced large changes in responding when it was produced in exactly the same way that food was produced—namely, by eleven responses. The same effect appeared when a fixed-interval-like requirement producing food or other consequences was added to the variable-interval schedule of food delivery.

Here is an intuitively plausible explanation of acquired reinforcement that does not depend upon the role of neutral events as predictors of events that already act as reinforcers. The brief consequences here really predict no food, at least for the short run, but they did confirm the effectiveness of responding in a certain way; something always happened after eleven responses and sometimes that something was food delivery.

Could it be that tokens, money, praise, and perhaps scolding and pain may come to act as acquired reinforcers if they are produced by the same behaviors that have in the past produced already effective reinforcers? When an infant is good, he or she is petted and stroked; later, the same behavior produces attention and praise, and later it produces a quarter. If hard work, formerly reinforced by money and praise, were to begin to be followed by hallucination of a green mist, wouldn't the significance of such experiences soon change for us? Needless to say, hard work must on other occasions be followed by more customary consequences, but doesn't the hallucination correspond closely to the feeling of a job well done? This explanation, speculative as it may be, attempts to account for the heretofore mysterious durability of conditioned reinforcers and their seemingly infinite variety without requiring that their power ultimately reduce to the prediction of food!

For practical purposes, the implications are obvious. Almost anything, be it a word, a token, or the opportunity to do something, may become an acquired reinforcer if it is made available according to the same contingencies that produce already effective reinforcers. Serious studying by

a high school student may be reinforced both by good grades on an examination or by parental praise. Given such a history of payoff, other consequences may be substituted. "You've done such a good job with your homework that I'm going to let you rake the leaves for a while tomorrow." Imagine such a reward given seriously by a parent who normally gives only praise for such behavior and who has not used the opportunity to rake leaves as a form of punishment in the past. Would such an opportunity act as a reinforcer for doing homework?

Avoidance Learning

Suppose that a rat or pigeon or human subject were placed in a situation in which shocks occur every ten seconds. In the chamber is a lever (or button or key) that, when pressed, postpones the next shock—say, for a minute. Suppose also that a light comes on a few seconds before an impending shock. Most subjects, whether rodent, avian, or human, learn to press (or push or peck) when the light comes on and thus avoid the shock.

This is called signaled avoidance conditioning. A signal (CS or S^D) precedes shock, and a response turns off the signal and postpones the shock. If a subject responds at least once per minute (in our example), then it is never shocked. Rat and pigeon subjects do so, and the question arises: What reinforces the pressing or pecking response?

Early explanations (e.g., Mowrer, 1947; Miller, 1948) suggested that the signal preceding the shock became a conditioned aversive stimulus (CAS). Through classical conditioning, the signal became a CS, producing fear; the avoidance response, which turned off the signal and avoided the shock, was reinforced by the ending of the signal.

However, avoidance responses are learned even when there is no signal preceding shock. Sidman (e.g., 1953) showed that when shock is delivered at regular intervals, rat and pigeon subjects will press or peck to avoid them, even when there is no explicit signal preceding the shock. He suggested (after Schoenfeld, 1950) that this occurs because all other behaviors are eventually paired with shock and the only nonpunished behavior is pressing or pecking, which avoids shock! Surely, this explanation is one of the curiosities of psychology.

Still, why *is* the avoidance response made? Imagine yourself in a room with no features, but a large red button mounted on a wall. Every ten seconds you receive shocks that leave you trembling. Before long you would hit the red button and find that you weren't shocked for a while. Soon, you would be pressing at least once a minute and would never receive any shocks. Would you continue pressing for hours, days, and weeks after the last shock? Probably not. You would occasionally slack off for a minute, which would be long enough to remind you that shock comes when the button is not pressed for a minute.

But theorists wondered what reinforced the avoidance response. You press the button and nothing happens. (You or I might say that it is not *nothing*—a nonevent—per se; it is nothing in the context of *something*—a shock when no press is made.) This thinking, which requires that every discrete response is reinforced by a discrete event, is typical of much psychological thought. Freud's intrapsychic forces were invented to provide present causes for effects where the real causes happened years ago.

At any rate, Anger (1963) provided a present cause for avoidance responding. He suggested that, as time passed since the last shock or response, the subject "timed" the interval. As time passed, temporal stimuli became more aversive, since time elements that were more and more distant from a response or shock were more closely paired with shock. Thus, the passage of time includes temporal stimuli, which become increasingly aversive as the time for shock approaches. These conditioned aversive temporal stimuli (CATS) act as a drive to produce a response that "resets the clock" and reduces the drive. This theory, proposed by a follower of Skinner who thought in the discrete response/consequence terms of Hull, thus explains avoid-

ance learning. The subject continues to make avoidance responses to escape the CATS occurring with the passage of time.

This two-factor theory, like the earlier view of Mowrer, explains unsignaled avoidance as it explains signaled avoidance. One just has to look harder for the signal. The subject responds, the signal is turned off (or reset, in the case of CATS), and the reduction in conditioned fear thus produced reinforces the avoidance response.

This theory, which was popular for many years and which required something to reinforce the avoidance response, underestimates the importance of contingencies acting over time, which is the emphasis of good Skinnerian theory. This was pointed out in an excellent experiment done by Herrnstein and Hineline (1966).

In their experiment, rats received shock according to a variable-time (VT) schedule with an average value of 6.7 seconds. That is, shock was delivered to the floor (and walls) of their chamber every 6.7 seconds, independent of their behavior. Or almost independent of their behavior. If they pressed a lever in the box, a different VT schedule was in effect, which produced shocks less frequently (every twenty seconds). When the shock came, and it did, the schedule was changed back to every 6.7 seconds.

Whatever the rats did, they were shocked. If they did not press, it came every 6.7 seconds (on the average), and if they did press it came on the average of every twenty seconds. Imagine yourself in their position, in a small room with a lever on one wall and intense shock delivered on the average of every few seconds. You press the lever and the schedule changes from shock every 6.7 seconds to shock every twenty seconds. But, depending on the tape programming the VT 20-second shocks, you could press the bar and immediately get a shock. How long would it take you, given no instructions, to learn to press the lever? You still get shocked, but *in the long run* you get shocked less if you frequently press the lever.

Rachlin (1976) compared the subject's dilemma to that of a New Hampshire resident who moves to Florida. If it's snowing on the day the person leaves and if the person arrives in Florida during a freak snowstorm, there is apparently nothing to distinguish the weather in the two states. Prior knowledge or time spent living in the two states would be required for the person to know that weather in the two states is different in the long run.

But seventeen of eighteen of Herrnstein and Hineline's rats showed stable lever pressing on the first day. Later, when the frequency of shock was made equal on the two tapes, responding eventually ceased. Thus, pressing was not merely shock-elicited flailing at the lever; it was maintained only when overall shock frequency was reduced by pressing. Lambert, Bersh, Hineline & Smith (1973) later showed that rats also learned to respond for reduction in overall shock frequency, even when each response produced an immediate shock.

What reinforced each press? Is that a reasonable question to ask? The fact is that the rats' behavior was best described as *lever pressing*, not as *lever presses*. That is, pressing was an activity that occurred over time and that was not best described as a set of discrete instances (that is, as presses). Pressing was reinforced by reduction in overall shock frequency; a behavior occurring over time depended on consequences occurring over time.

Azrin and the Effects of Punishment

It requires little reflection to see that punishment and the threat of punishment is the main instrument whereby society controls us. The law is a set of rules specifying which acts are punishable, not what will be rewarded. Can you imagine being stopped by the police and congratulated for driving safely? Parents spank their children and send them to bed, and teachers keep misbehaving students after school or force them to miss recess. The church tells us of heaven, but many denominations prefer to emphasize the horrors of hell. We are especially influenced by the punishments of the natural world around us, by the pain that punishes fire touching and the bruise that punishes slipping and falling.

We cannot deny that the schools, our families, the church, and nature itself do not reward us, but punishment also is used at least as often (especially by government) and has been for a very long time. With this in view, it may be surprising to learn that expert opinion has denied the effectiveness of punishment and opposed its use for many years.

You will recall that Thorndike decided, over the period from 1929 to 1932, that annoyers did not work to stamp out S-R connections, as proposed in his original rendition of the law of effect. Punishment, when it works at all, does so simply because it evokes a new behavior that can then be rewarded. Otherwise, "it tends to work best where it is least needed," leaving the "callous and base" unaffected, and it simply adds "fear and shame" to continued sinning. If punishment is to be used, Thorndike urged, we must at least avoid "doctrinaire, haphazard, fantastic, and perverted" punishments (1935).

Skinner (1938) made the same argument a few years later, pronouncing that punishment was generally ineffective, its influence on behavior was transient, and it produced unwanted byproducts. This was substantiated in an experiment in which rats were first trained to press a bar, with occasional presses reinforced by the delivery of a food pellet. Such training was followed by periods of extinction, in which food delivery was discontinued until responding ceased. After a number of changes from reinforcement to extinction, Skinner assessed the effect of punishment on the rate of decline of responding during extinction.

After a period of food-reinforced pressing, extinction began and each press was punished in an interesting way: A device was connected to the mechanism controlling the pivoting of the bar in such a way that when the bar was pressed it pressed back, giving the rat a sharp slap to its paws. The slaps were discontinued after the first ten minutes of extinction. Skinner found that such punishment did indeed reduce the rate of bar pressing, but once it was discontinued pressing recovered, increasing to levels higher than those that occurred in the absence of punishment. It was as if the presses suppressed during punishment were "stored up" and appeared as soon as punishment ended. Other and less formal experiments used other punishers, such as throwing the rat into the air, pricking its tail with needles, and shining bright lights into its sensitive eyes. Again, the effect of punishment was only temporary, and suppressed responses seemed to be stored, augmenting response rate once punishment ceased. Additionally, the rats' behavior suggested that the punishers had emotional effects, and Skinner maintained that this could be sufficient to disrupt pressing enough to account for the decrease in response rate. (The rats were also less kindly disposed toward Skinner himself, who had become a conditioned aversive stimulus because of his association with aversive events!)

Sturdier support for these conclusions was provided by the data of Estes (1944), who followed Skinner's general procedure but used shock as a punisher. Estes found that mild shock produced the same effects reported by Skinner, a temporary suppression of responding followed by an increase after the termination of shock. If the shock were intense, responding was greatly suppressed over several postshock sessions. Even then the rat eventually recovered to the pre-punishment level. Are the effects of punishment only temporary, as Skinner suggested?

Perhaps the most interesting aspect of Estes's data was the finding that the suppressing effects of shock were the same whether it was response dependent or not! *Punishment* means response dependent, of course. If shock presented independently of responding also suppresses behavior, we can hardly call it the effect of punishment. It amounts only to the general disruption in behavior, which could be produced by strong emotion, such as fear of shock. Thus, the decrease in responding was merely a by-product of emotional

disruption produced by aversive stimulation (shock), exactly as Skinner had argued.

These data have had great influence for decades: I frequently have been asked for a good source that cites the best evidence showing that punishment doesn't work! Indeed, a special term was even invented for cases in which punishment did seem to work. Think about the possible meaning of *passive avoidance!* Active avoidance refers to behavior that is maintained because it prevents or postpones the occurrence of a noxious event. *Active* means that something is done; an act is performed. So what is passive avoidance? Is it the prevention or postponement of a noxious event by remaining passive? For example, when I placed my hand in a fire in the past (as a much younger person), it burned me. I now passively avoid such noxious events by keeping my flesh out of the fire. Put in a slightly different way, pain has punished the act of reaching into fires; I therefore no longer reach for such things. When punishment was banished, passive avoidance became its surrogate (Catania, 1984).

Happily, later data have come to the rescue of common sense; punishment is back. The credit for this belongs to Nathan Azrin and his coworkers, whose data led an authority on learning processes to conclude that the effectiveness of punishment now "admits of little doubt" (Mackintosh, 1974). Given the prevailing expert opinion at the time he was working (circa 1960), Azrin had to prove his point convincingly.

Basically, Azrin questioned the methods used by Skinner and Estes. When Skinner and Estes introduced punishment, it was done in extinction. Thus, the first shock told Estes's rats that further presses would be shocked and that there was no reason to press anyway, since food was no longer forthcoming. This surely is not the case in daily life. When a child is punished for bullying others, the punished behavior is maintained by the reinforcements it produces, such as the goods and services and fear and deference that come from those who are bullied. Occasional punishment is simply added to the consequences that already occur. When speeding is punished by a costly ticket, the reinforcers that maintain speeding are still available; speeding may be fun and it does get you where you are going in less time.

A more realistic test of the effects of punishment would apply it to behavior that is simultaneously maintained by reinforcement. Using pigeons as subjects, Azrin (1956) found that electric shock produced by key pecking suppressed pecking maintained by a schedule of food reinforcement. When shock was applied independently of responding, he found, unlike Estes, that responding was reduced relatively little; response-produced shock (that is, punishment) had a far greater effect.

In 1960 Azrin showed that the degree of response suppression depended upon the intensity of shock and that with fairly intense shock the suppression was long-lasting. In addition, the pattern of responding maintained by the schedule of food reinforcement was not disrupted. Thus, the decrease in response rate was not due simply to the generally disruptive emotional effects posited by Skinner and Estes. For example, Azrin (1959) showed that shock produced for every response maintained by a fixed-ratio schedule of food reinforcement left the fixed-ratio run (see Chapter 8) intact but produced an increase in the pause after reinforcement. This is exactly what happens when the ratio requirement is increased and the frequency of reinforcement therefore is decreased. Punishment thus seems to act in the same manner as a decrease in reinforcement frequency.

All of this shows that punishment does work directly; it is not effective only through emotional by-products. But Skinner and Estes also had charged that the effects of punishment were only temporary; in their view, when you stop the punishment the punished behavior returns stronger than ever. This is in fact the case, but it is hardly an argument against the effectiveness of punishment. Aren't the effects of reinforcement temporary? If my behaviors that are currently maintained by money, praise, feelings of health,

and not falling down are no longer followed by such reinforcers, will I indefinitely continue to show such behaviors?

The one argument against the use of punishment that remains does warrant consideration. That is, punishers are often things that cause pain or physical injury, and thus their misuse is more serious than is the case with reinforcers. Also, as is the case with reinforcers, punishers work if applied immediately and appropriately (remember Thorndike's term *readiness*). The warning given a misbehaving child that he will "get it when his father comes home" is poor practice indeed. When his father comes and the misbehavior is long forgotten, a spanking may punish something but it will likely be the behavior of running up to and greeting his father! Further, as Guthrie made clear, punishment works best when it leads to a new behavior that can then be reinforced. We cannot quite follow Guthrie's advice when he points out that in training a dog to jump through a hoop using electric shock, "it is important at which end of the dog the shock is applied," but we can encourage acceptable, reinforceable behaviors when we punish the ones we want eliminated (e.g., Whiting & Mowrer, 1943; Herman & Azrin, 1964).

2. CLASSICAL CONDITIONING

Contiguity and Contingency: The Rescorla-Wagner Model

Since the 1920s, when classical conditioning was first introduced in America, American researchers and theorists have viewed it as a mechanical stamping-in process. A stimulus, such as a tone, becomes associated with another stimulus, such as food, because the two occur together. That is all there is to it. Pavlov often referred to the conditioned stimulus as a *signal* for the UCS, and the fact that it must act as such, rather than be merely paired with a UCS, was appreciated a half century after Pavlov's work became known. To be a signal, a stimulus must provide information, so to speak. There must be a contingent (if/then) relation between conditioned and unconditioned stimuli.

The truth of this was established by Rescorla (1967, 1988) who showed that the mere pairing of CS and UCS did not guarantee that classical conditioning would occur. For example, let us suppose that a brief tone is paired with the delivery of shock to your ankle. After a few pairings, the tone will take on a new meaning for you and, should the new meaning escape you, it will not escape the notice of your viscera! The tone will make you wince, move your ankle, increase your heart rate (and later, decrease your heart rate), and perhaps cry out. The pairing of tone and shock has produced a CR of fear, along with autonomic arousal and other anticipatory reactions. Suppose that you are left on a schedule of tone/shock pairings for some time and that CRs reliably occur, which would be the case. Further, suppose that extra tones that are not accompanied by shock are added to that schedule. You will still react to the tone, but less vigorously and reliably; the tone is no longer an absolutely reliable predictor of shock. Suppose next that extra shocks are added to your schedule, occurring in the absence of a warning tone. Your *Nos* and *pleases* may still occur but no longer in reaction to the tone, only to the shock. Your conditioned winces, heart palpitations, and so on will also fail to occur when the tone comes on, because the tone is no longer a CS. It tells you nothing about the occurrence of shock, and both you and your viscera see this. The original set of pairings of tone and shock remains as before, but the added tones and shocks have taken away the once predictive relationship. Classical conditioning requires a contingent relationship between CS and UCS; mere pairing is not enough.

A second, and related, effect has been studied by Kamin (1968) and a number of others. Kamin drew attention to what is known as *blocking*, which is related to the phenomenon of *overshadowing*, originally described by Pavlov. If in the situation above we maintain the tone/shock contingency so that the tone always precedes shock and also reliably produces unpleasant CRs, what will happen if we add a flashing light, so that light and tone always precede shock? You will continue to react as you did and, if we present the tone alone, we will find that it still has its power. But if we present the light alone there is no reaction! How can this be? The light has been paired with shock, as was the tone; should it not also produce fear and trembling? The answer is no and the reason is that the tone already tells us all there is to tell about the shock; the added light adds nothing. But why should this be? Why should the tone alone be an effective CS while the light, which also predicts shock, fails to become one? We shall see.

Overshadowing may provide a clue. If, strapped in your chair with the shock-giving electrode on your ankle, your initial experience involves the onset of a flashing light and the onset of a tone followed by shock, will both stimuli become capable of evoking equally strong CRs? Chances are that they will not. One of the stimuli will overshadow the other. One way of putting this is to say that one will be more salient. That stimulus, be it light or tone, may gain most or all of the CR-evoking power. This need not be, of course, since the tone and light could be more or less equally salient and thus share the CS power, but in many cases one or the other stimulus overshadows the other.

All of this caused a good deal of unrest during the late sixties; it appeared that classical conditioning was a complicated and less predictable process than had been believed. If it depends upon contingency rather than simple pairing by *contiguity*, and if a stimulus becomes a CS only if it provides information (is nonredundant), then classically conditioned organisms become contingency-evaluating, information-processing entities—a horrible prospect, since it means that what was simple and lawful is now vague and unpredictable!

Luckily, this problem was averted by Rescorla and Wagner (1972), who proposed a model for classical conditioning that has become extremely popular. We refer to it as the *Rescorla-Wagner model*. Taking their cue from a little-known paper of Hull's, published in 1947, Rescorla and Wagner showed how what seems to be contingency and informativeness can be reduced to simple pairing by contiguity. Their model is simple and reasonable, and it works.

They begin with the often-made observation that learning acquisition curves are negatively accelerated. That is, with practice we learn most on the early trials and progressively smaller increments are added as practice continues. In classical conditioning, the increase in magnitude and reliability of the CR increases rapidly at first and more slowly thereafter until asymptote is reached—until no further increase is possible unless conditions are changed (for example, by increasing the intensity of the UCS). Hull called this maximum M; Rescorla and Wagner call it λ (*lambda*).

On each reinforced trial improvement occurs in ever-decreasing increments. Hull suggested that the amount of increase (in habit strength, or $_sH_R$) is a constant fraction of the difference between current habit strength and M, or maximum habit strength. An early estimate of this fraction was $\frac{1}{25}$. Thus, on a given trial, the increment added to what is learned is $\frac{1}{25}(M - {_sH_R})$. As $_sH_R$ increases and M remains fixed, the quantity (M $- {_sH_R}$) decreases and the added increments decrease in magnitude. This may not seem fascinating, but it is a reasonable way to account for the progress of learning as long as one doesn't worry excessively about the problems involved in calculating initial values of $_sH_R$ and the value of M.

Rescorla and Wagner adopted this model with a change in terms, as follows:

$$\Delta V_{n + 1} = K (\lambda - V_n)$$

Thus, the increment (ΔV) added to associative strength (V; habit strength is out) on the next trial (n + 1) is a fraction (K) of the difference between asymptotic associative strength (λ) and current associative strength (V_n). K represents the salience of the CS and falls between zero and one, and lambda depends upon the intensity of the UCS. To see how this accounts for the negative acceleration in the slope of the acquisition curve, consider the following series of three trials, letting V be set initially at 10, λ at 100, and K at 0.5:

1. $V_1 = 0.5(100 - 10) = 45$;
   V_2 is then $V_1 + V_1 = 55$
2. $V_2 = 0.5(100 - 55) = 22.5$;
   V_3 is then 77.5
3. $V_3 = 0.5(100 - 77.5) = 11.25$;
   V_4 is then 88.75

As is clear, the increments added to V become progressively smaller (45, 22.5, 11.25) as V increases (10, 55, 77.5).

There is nothing new here, but the next step is what counts and is what derives from Hull's 1947 paper. Rescorla and Wagner propose that all conditioning is actually compound conditioning; that is to say, associative strength develops not only to the CS but to the other stimuli in the background. This contributes to a total V and thus influences the rate of conditioning to a given CS. Given two explicit stimuli, the effects are more obvious.

First, take our light and tone paired with shock and suppose the light to be blindingly bright, near, and salient as can be, while the tone is faint, far, and less salient, though clearly noticeable. To examine the way in which conditioning affects them, it is necessary to consider them separately, using the equation above. Although they are considered separately, the fact is that they do appear together as a compound and it is their joint associative strength that is then important. This is the real point of the model and it is the joint associative strength (V_{ax}) that allows it to work its wonders. Remember that the light was more salient than the tone, so its K fraction will be greater. Let the initial associative strengths of the light and tone (L and T) be 10 each and let their saliences be 0.8 and 0.1. Lambda is still 100, and the joint associative strength of the two stimuli is represented by V_{LT}. Here is what happens in a few trials:

$$\text{Light: } V_L = L(\lambda - V_{LT})$$
$$V_L = 0.8(100 - 20) = 64$$
$$\text{Tone: } V_T = T(\lambda - V_{LT})$$
$$V_T = 0.1(100 - 20) = 8$$

After one trial, V_L is 74, V_T is 18, and V_{LT} is 92 (almost asymptote).

$$V_L = 0.8(100 - 92) = 6.4$$
$$V_T = 0.1(100 - 92) = 0.8$$

After two trials, V_L is 80.4, V_T is only 18.8, and V_{LT} is 99.2.

It can be seen here that the bulk of the associative strength goes to the light, and simple changes in parameters (such as setting V_L and V_T at initial values of 1 or 2, rather than 10) would result in V_L totally swamping V_T. This is the way in which the model accounts for overshadowing, and it is easy to see that it accounts for blocking as well. Pretraining with the tone alone, for example, would produce a high value of V_T, so that later introduction of the light (salient though it may be) would be to no avail; the tone could have already grabbed all of the V to be had.

The model also accounts for the effects of contingency noted above. It simply depends upon where the associative strength goes, to the CS or to the background stimuli. For example, if you introduce extra shocks, you introduce new conditioning to these background stimuli. Since there is a maximum of associative strength for any reinforcer (that is, any given frequency or intensity of shock in this case), the background stimuli compete with the tone. If the background stimuli acquire enough associative strength, the tone may have no more strength than the background stimuli have. In this way, it loses its function as an effective CS. This accounts for the effects of contingency, leaving the important factor as the simple contiguity of stimuli and UCS.

Solomon and Corbit: The Opponent-Process Model

The opponent-process model tells us something important about classical conditioning and about a variety of familiar phenomena, from risk taking to drug addiction to the basic categories of emotional experience. The major paper describing the model was published in 1974, but the real story began 30 years earlier, in the strange findings of Solomon, Kamin, and Wynne (1953), who were investigating methods for the curing of *phobias*.

These authors acted on the belief that unnatural fears of spiders, darkness, and so on, which greatly trouble many people, are simply CRs established earlier in life. For example, a spider present during the experience of great pain or fear produced by some other cause may become a CS producing fear. Their strategy was to establish a conditioned fear in dogs and then to investigate various methods of abolishing ("curing") it. Unlike a phobic reaction, the dog's fear was based on very reasonable grounds.

The dogs were placed (one at a time) in a shuttle box, a very popular device at the University of Pennsylvania. Such a box is made up of two compartments with a barrier in the middle. The barrier is about shoulder-high (on the dog) and may, with a bit of difficulty, be jumped over. The training began with the dog on one side of the box and with the route to the other compartment blocked by a gate, which the experimenters could raise. A buzzer sounded for ten seconds and the gate was raised. To the dog's surprise and dismay, this was followed by an extremely intense electric shock delivered through the floor to the footpads of the animal. As the authors described it, the shock level was "just subtetanizing," which means that it was just short of paralyzing the creature. Within a few trials, the dog learned to head for the barrier and leap it when the buzzer sounded and the gate was raised. If the dog did not "shuttle" to the other "safe" side, it received three seconds of the shock.

When the dog reached the other compartment, the gate was lowered and all was well—for a while. But soon (can it be?), the buzzer sounded, the gate was raised, and shock was forthcoming, so the dog jumped again. Then the buzzer sounded again, the gate was raised, and so on. Very quickly all dogs were shuttling back and forth, never getting shocked, and probably the exercise was doing them good. Here was a conditioned fear. The buzzer had become a CS producing fear, analogous to the phobic stimulus plaguing a human sufferer. How may such fear be eliminated, the dog's jumping be stopped, and the human's phobia be cured?

The simplest method is extinction, in which the CS (or phobic stimulus) is presented over and over until the reaction to it ceases. This was not at all successful in treating the dogs' fear of the buzzer, though. After the shock generator was turned off, two dogs continued jumping for 190 and 490 trials, respectively. The dogs showed no sign of stopping and their latencies actually showed a decrease with trials! They may have stopped after a few hundred (or a few thousand) further trials, but the authors wearied of going to work day after day watching the dogs endlessly jump. Clearly, extinction was not an efficient method for eliminating conditioned fears.

How about punishment? Although this would not increase the popularity of a therapist, it is possible that punishing phobic reactions with a strong shock or a slap in the face could work. Thus, conditions were changed in a novel way. As before, the buzzer sounded, the gate was raised, and the dog jumped—but not to safety. The gate was closed after the jump, and the dog found itself part of an electrical circuit; it had jumped into three seconds of intense and inescapable shock! Surely, this would give it pause. But it didn't; for 100 trials the animal jumped as quickly as it had before, and it knew what it was jumping into. As the experimenters reported, the dog's trip through the air was often accompanied by "an anticipatory 'yip' which changed to a 'yelp'" when the grid on the other side was reached.

Maybe the punishment wasn't strong enough, thought the experimenters, so the duration of shock was increased to ten seconds! Imagine, if you can, some time in your life when you received a strong and painful shock. Now imagine that shock (or a stronger one) lasting for ten seconds. In fact, try timing ten seconds to get a feel for the dog's plight. Yet, as you might have guessed, the dog continued jumping as rapidly as before!

This is indeed odd. One of the dogs initially had received only eleven pairings of buzzer and shock, and some of those shocks were experienced only briefly since the dog was jumping before the three-second shock period was over. Fear of the buzzer had lasted through 490 no-shock extinction trials, 100 trials punished by three seconds of inescapable shock, and 50 trials punished with ten seconds of inescapable shock. Was the dog's fear of the buzzer greater than its fear of the shock itself? (Is it true that we have nothing to fear but fear itself?)

Finally, the experimenters resorted to what they called "reality testing" to stop the jumping. As you probably have surmised, the dogs continued jumping because, although Solomon knew that the shock following the buzzer was discontinued, the dogs did not. How can we show the dog that it is safe to stay? (He knows that it is dangerous to jump.) The next day, the dog jumped for the 53rd, 54th, and 56th time into ten seconds of inescapable shock. But on the next four trials that day it didn't jump. This was because the experimenters installed a heavy glass plate over the barrier. The dog jumped, smashed into the glass, and landed in the same compartment from whence it had jumped. On subsequent trials it did not jump. What it did was stay on the same side barking, panting, and drooling. It was cured! After only 647 extinction trials, including over 150 with inescapable punishment, the fear produced by the pairing of eleven shocks with the buzzer was conquered. On the next day the buzzer sounded and the dog jumped, but only three times. It was indeed "cured." But why was the cure so difficult? Solomon must have wondered why, off and on for 30 years, until the answer dawned. The answer came during research in which dogs' heart rates were monitored during the administration of electric shock (Solomon & Corbit, 1974).

This time the dog being shocked was not in a shuttle box. It was simply resting in what is called a Pavlov sling, which is a canvas suspended from overheard with openings to accommodate the dog's four legs; in effect, the dog is hanging from the ceiling. As the ten-second shocks were applied to the dog's foot, its behavior was noted and its heart rate was monitored. The dog appeared terrified. It screeched, it thrashed, its pupils dilated, its eyes bulged, its hair stood on end, its ears were back, its tail was curled, it defecated and urinated, and its heart rate rose from 100 to 250 beats per minute. Fortunately, there is a happier ending coming. (In any event, this is not even a real dog. What is described is a composite of canine experiences in the laboratories of Solomon, his students, and collaborators.)

After a few shocks the dog was released from the sling and showed clear signs that it would now be a poor pet. It acted suspicious, unfriendly (wouldn't fetch), and stealthy—hardly surprising, given its recent treatment. The daily sessions of shock continued and, after a while, the dog's behavior changed. During the shock, it no longer appeared terrified but only anxious and annoyed. This was reflected in its heart rate, which scarcely increased at all and sometimes actually decreased during the shock periods. This reaction was not really surprising; we (and dogs) show *habituation* to prolonged stimulation, even when it is quite painful.

What was surprising was the behavior of the dog after these later shock sessions. Earlier, the dog seemed justifiably suspicious, but now it seemed perky, joyful, happy to the point of euphoria. In addition, its heart rate decreased as much as 50 to 60 beats per minute below baseline levels. This was a happy dog.

Why should painful electric shock have such an effect? Could it be that the dog was simply glad that it was over? Of course not. If that were

the case, one would expect a euphoric dog after the earlier sessions, where the shock produced real terror, with its bodily accompaniments. Why should the dog be euphoric after shock sessions in which there is no sign of terror, no increase in heart rate, no bulging eyes? What is interesting here is that the sequence of states occurred as it did; terror was followed by stealthiness, and slight annoyance was followed by gaiety.

Noting this, as well as a number of similar cases, Solomon and Corbit proposed that a specific opponent process physiological/affective reaction was responsible. That is, any strong affect (pleasure, pain, terror, grief, and so on) may be accompanied by an affective reaction in the opposite direction. To keep things clear, we will stay with the shocked dog for a moment. The first few shocks produced strong negative affect (terror and sympathetic arousal), which was followed by a return to relative normalcy (stealth). The initial reaction (terror) is termed the *A state* and the opponent reaction the *B state*. Both occur at the same time and sum algebraically; hence, the shock produces sympathetic arousal and terror (A state) and a decrease in arousal (B state) simultaneously. The A state is much the stronger of the two, and evidence for the B state appears at first only after the offset of the shock and the end of the A state.

With repetition, the B state increases in strength and continues to outlast the A state. Since the reactions are literal opposites, the increase in magnitude of the B state subtracts progressively more from the A state until the A state virtually disappears. Thus, after a number of sessions the dog ceases to show terror during the shocks and its heart rate no longer increases (and may even decrease below baseline). After the shock, the now mighty B state shows itself in euphoric behavior and decreases in heart rate to a level far below baseline. Since the A and B states no longer resemble their original forms, the terms A' and B' are applied to these, the opponent reactions as they appear after long training.

The *opponent-process model* thus posits opponent reactions, A and B, where B is produced by (and simultaneously with) the A reaction. With repetition, the B reaction increases in strength and subtracts from the A reaction. After the stimulating event ends, the B reaction persists. In the case of the shocked dog, the persisting B (actually B') reaction may last an hour or more; in other cases, the B' state may endure for twenty years!

Human risk taking may provide an analog to the shocked dog. Humans who skydive for recreation must make that first jump, and for most people it is a terrifying experience. Behavior during the first few jumps closely approximates the signs of terror shown by the shocked dog, and the aftereffect is a feeling of quiet dullness. When we are momentarily filled with terror upon seeing someone backing down an exit ramp toward us we feel a sort of numbness thereafter, before the anger comes. Why would anyone continue skydiving if the effects were always terror and later numbness? The fact is that the skydiver, like the dog, later shows no sign of terror before and during the jump; what appears instead is a tenseness and eagerness. After the jump, the numbness is replaced by an exhilaration, which is accompanied by a lowered heart rate and which may last for hours. The parallel to the A and B states of the shocked dog giving way to the A' and B' states is obvious.

Where else may such a mechanism be operating? Solomon and Corbit suggest a number of other cases. For example, puppy love is characterized by an A state of excited happiness when the loved one is near and a B state of loneliness in his or her absence. After much experience, the loved one evokes an A' state of normalcy, commonly reported by old married couples. But what is the B' state, which is shown when the loved one is removed? It is the deep grief and depression that has come to be called the separation syndrome. The principle here is the same as that governing the shocked dog and the skydiver. Solomon applies the principle to a host of phenomena, including feeding in infants, imprinting in ducklings, and the behavior of humans struck by lightning (Solomon, 1980).

One significant aspect of this model is the evidence showing that the unconditioned response (UCR) is biphasic (Has A and B states). In addition, the fact that these reactions are unconditioned responses means that each can be evoked by conditioned stimuli (CSs). This has clear application to the problem of opiate addiction and was of central concern in Solomon and Corbit's argument for the model.

Users of opiates such as morphine and heroin typically report a pleasurable rush with each administration, followed by a later feeling of normalcy and perhaps a brief craving. This is true of new users. Users who have long experience have different reports, however. For them, the rush is minimal or completely gone and the drug is taken to eliminate a very strong craving which, according to many accounts, is agony itself. It thus appears that such addiction follows the opponent-process model and its sequence of stages. An initially pleasurable A state (the rush) is followed by a B state (normalcy or mild craving). With continued use of the opiate, the A state diminishes to an A' state (normalcy) followed by a progressively stronger B state, the B' state of craving (withdrawal). We simply have the mirror image of the shocked dog or skydiver and an exaggeration of the love/grief example.

If this is the case, how may drug addicts be treated? There is some evidence that the B state dissipates with time; the euphoria of the dog and the skydiver do not last forever, and even the separation syndrome eventually passes. But the B' state appearing as withdrawal from heroin may last decades! Further, since the A and B states involved are really unconditioned responses to heroin, it is certain that a variety of conditioned stimuli are established that can make the addict's prognosis grim indeed.

Suppose that the cues present during the administration of heroin can become CSs for the A (and A') reactions. The heroin itself, friends present, the hypodermic syringe, and even money (which becomes closely linked to the obtaining of a "fix") may become CSa's, which evoke a CRa, a fractional component of the A or A' reactions. The evoking of the A reaction produces the B reaction, which thus strengthens the B state and increases the craving. Hence, it is best to stay away from such cues while trying to break the addiction.

But the B reaction is also a UCR and conditioned stimuli may as easily be associated with it! Thus, police stations, hospitals, non-drug-using friends, and other cues present during the B' (craving) state may become CSb's and directly evoke the B state. When the B state is evoked, it gains in strength. Whichever way the addict turns there is no escape; the craving increases!

Solomon and Corbit provide convincing evidence that conditioned stimuli may become associated with A and B states in such a way and leave us wondering how any heroin addict is ever cured if such a process is going on. In fact, a lot of addicts don't get cured, and those who do overcome the addiction do so by biting the bullet, tolerating the agonies of withdrawal, and showing that the B process does eventually dissipate and that this dissipation slowly overcomes the augmenting that owes to the CSs that constantly add to the B state.

Other data, including some anomalies, may depend upon the same opponent-process mechanism. For example, Siegel (1978) has shown that the CR produced by a CS paired with morphine injection is opposite in direction to the effect of the UCS (morphine) itself. Morphine produces UCRs that include a decreased sensitivity to pain and increased body temperature. A CS paired with morphine produces a CR of increased sensitivity to pain and decreased body temperature. Similarly, glucose injections lead to hyperglycemia (elevated blood sugar), whereas a CS paired with glucose produces a CR of hypoglycemia. In addition, it has often been reported that the CR to a CS predicting shock is a decrease in heart rate, whereas the UCR for shock is, of course, increased heart rate. (Eikelboom and Stewart, 1982, dispute Siegel's interpretation. For example, they argue that glucose injection and hypo-

glycemia are not viewed properly as UCS and UCR. They are actually a single event, the UCS. The actual UCR is the release of insulin by the pancreas that causes a decrease in blood sugar level. Thus, the CR and UCR are not opposite in direction in this case.)

An opponent-process mechanism could well account for such instances of what seem to be homeostatic compensations. Very likely such opponent CRs represent the evoking of a B' state, thus occurring after some minimal number of CS–UCS pairings. If this were the case, earlier presentations of the CS should produce CRs in the same direction as the UCRs. The data that could substantiate such a possibility are not available, but it is an interesting possibility.

In summary, the Solomon and Corbit model tells us some interesting things. The unconditioned response is not a unitary thing and the basic nature of its two states may change drastically with continued evocation. Terror/numbness may become annoyance/euphoria, and ecstasy/loneliness may turn to normalcy/grief. Also, the existence of opponent pairs of emotions may be more reasonable than has been supposed (cf. Wundt, 1896). But instead of happy/sad and fear/relaxation we may have happy/fear and love/sadness if Solomon and Corbit's opponents are what they seem to be.

Finally, and anticlimactically, we know why Solomon, Kamin, and Wynne's dogs continued jumping day after day and why such extraordinary means were required to stop them. Those first few shocks produced an A state of pain and fear, followed by a B state of relief as the dog jumped. Even after the shocks no longer were received, the buzzer and the raised gate acted as CSs for the A state, which produced a CRa and a CRb. Every jump by the dog was accompanied by CSs for the B (relief) state, and that state consequently was strengthened on every trial. Throughout their long training, the dogs were jumping into a huge B (actually B') state, which was evidently more powerful than the effects of the punishments used to stop the jumping.

Learned Taste Aversions

John Garcia demonstrated a phenomenon that many viewed as very damaging to traditional learning theory and it was difficult for him to publish at first. What Garcia showed was the apparent uniqueness and specificity of a particular kind of learning, that of the association of taste and illness. He showed that taste, and not other cues, was specifically tied to subsequent illness and that the interval between the taste and the illness could be very long.

For example, in one of his best-known studies, Garcia and Koelling (1966) fed rats "bright-noisy-tasty" water, paired with electric shock or illness. The brightness came from flashing lights, the noise came from a clicking relay, and the taste came from saccharine or salt added to the water (see Figure 9.3). The electric shock came from a 0.5-second, 0.08–0.20-milliamp shock source and the illness was produced by a dose of metal poisoning (lithium chloride, or LiCl) mixed with drinking water, or by 54r (roentgens) of 250-kv (kilovolts) X rays delivered in twenty minutes. Both the LiCl and the X-irradiation has been shown to produce severe gastro-intestinal illness some time (many minutes or hours) after ingestion. What should happen in such a situation? Suppose I drink sweet water and become sick, or I drink salty water and become sick; suppose I drink sweet or salty water and receive shock. Would I avoid that water in the future?

Some of Garcia and Koelling's rats, which were poisoned, either with X-irradiation or lithium chloride, later avoided the sweet and the salty tastes, which had been paired with poisoning. But these rats showed no aversion to the flashing lights or the clicking relay, which also had been present when they were poisoned. On the other hand, the rats that were shocked while drinking sweet or salty water showed no later aversion to sweet or salty fluids; they avoided the flashing lights and the clicking relay.

What does this mean? What it surely suggests is that rats are more apt to associate tastes (sweet or salty) with subsequent illness than they are to associate lights and sounds with illness. By the same token, they associate lights and sounds with other unpleasant stimulation, such as the pain produced by shock. And this occurs for obvious adaptive reasons.

Assuming that we give some credence to the doctrine of evolution by natural selection (which has been ignored by some learning theories), we may expect that an omnivorous animal like the rat would be likely to pay attention to the tastes of the foods it eats and to the accompanying gastric effects. If a rat becomes violently ill, it consequently avoids any novel tasting foods it may have had during the recent past. This helps rats survive. And thus it is difficult to rid an area of rats by using poison.

But the rats did not avoid tastes that were accompanied by shock; they avoided the lights and clicks that were present with shock. And that also makes sense. They avoided those cues that accompany externally produced pain; those cues are usually externally sensed cues. When pain is internal, as in the case of nausea, an animal might "think" of what it ate and avoid eating it again. As evolution proceeded, rats that followed this rule survived to produce rats that behave similarly, and those rats that did not follow the rule did not survive to produce similar rats.

This was a striking finding and it has been repeated so many times that its truth is beyond question. Mammals associate the tastes of recent foods with subsequent illness. They do not easily associate the place where the food was gotten with illness, nor do they associate other sights or sounds with illness. The external sights and sounds are associated with pain produced by shock, and tastes are not so associated.

Equally startling was the finding that the CS-UCS interval could be measured in hours, rather than in minutes or seconds. Garcia, Ervin, and Koelling (1966) showed that a learned aversion to apomorphine poisoning (which causes regurgitation) occurred even when the saccharine taste that preceded the poisoning occurred more than 75 minutes before. In other cases, such as that reported by Smith and Roll (1967), an aversion was

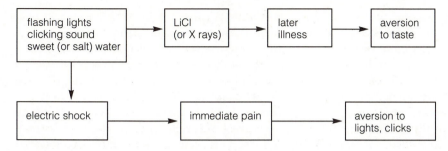

FIGURE 9.3   Learned taste aversions. *Garcia and Koelling, 1966.*

learned to saccharine-flavored water and irradiation after a CS-UCS interval of as long as twelve hours! In the Garcia, et al. study, rats experiencing electric shock showed no aversion to saccharine, as in the Garcia and Koelling study.

What does this mean? A rat, tasting saccharine or salt in the presence of flashing lights and clickers, is later (hours later) offered saccharine or salt or flashing lights or clickers. The rat will not drink fluids that taste like those it tasted before being poisoned an hour ago, or twelve hours ago. (The maximum duration is uncertain, but let us accept the twelve-hour figure for now.) But the poisoned rat will drink fluid that was presented hours ago with flashing lights and clicking sounds. What is this?

Garcia and others have reasoned that rats, being omnivorous "eaters of opportunity" are apt in their foraging to eat a number of toxic things. Those rats that have survived the process of natural selection and thus exist at present are those that have learned to react to nausea in the same way. When seriously ill, as is the case when Garcia exposed them to X-irradiation or lithium chloride poisoning, such rats looked back to what they last ate. They did not look back to where they last were, since they (and past rats) often ate different things in the same place. When sick, think of what you have eaten, not where you have been. On the other hand, when you have been injured from outside your body, by predator or otherwise, you are better off remembering the place where it occurred than what you had been eating.

Is Taste Aversion Learning Just Classical Conditioning?   First, is it a mystery that taste, rather than lights and clicks, is aversive? Recall from Chapter 1 that one of the oldest of associationist principles is the law of association by similarity. Now consider the stimuli present when you drink sweet, bright, noisy water. As Garcia and Koelling suggested, it is possible that tastes become connected with nausea because of the similarity in the stimuli involved. That is, when a light flashes or a clicker clicks, it is a discrete, phasic stimulus; it has a clear beginning and an end. But when you become nauseated, it usually occurs more gradually. Unlike a light flash or a click, a taste also has a gradual onset, much like the stimulus pattern in nausea. Thus, we and the rat associate taste and nausea because of their similar patterns of gradual onset and offset, but we associate physical pain, such as that produced by shock, with abrupt signals from our surroundings, since such signals more often predict pain of that sort than they do illness. Testa (1975) illustrated that this might be the case by showing that rats are particularly apt to show fear when a light pulses at the frequency at which shock has been delivered in the past. Thus, it could be that the specificity of the taste-illness connection is no more than an instance of the old GPLT principle of association by contiguity.

But what of the long CS–UCS delay, perhaps extending over twelve hours? Imagine yourself made sick. You drink some sweet-tasting solution and thereafter are subjected to a dose of radiation or of lithium chloride poisoning. Hours later you are sick—very sick! When we are very sick in this way, we exhibit emesis—which is to say that the reflex mechanisms in the gastrointestinal tract begin reverse peristalsis to bring up the offending substance. We regurgitate. While we are sick, we are apt to partially regurgitate a number of times, and the food that we recently ate is thus apt to be retasted. Thus, there is really no hours-long delay between taste and illness; when we retaste the food while sick, we pair the taste and illness. This could be the explanation for the long delay between CS (taste) and UCS (feelings of illness) in taste aversion learning.

Tempting and reasonable as that may sound, it is not the answer. The reason we know this is simple: rats do not regurgitate, as humans do. When rats become ill, the contents of their stomachs are prevented from returning up the esophagus by the cardiac sphincter. And even if some aftertaste from the stomach does find its way up, the learned aversion still is demonstrably not due to the association of present illness with a present aftertaste.

Revusky and Bedarf (1967) showed that novel tastes are more apt to produce learned aversions than are familiar tastes, even while the latter were more recently experienced (and thus more likely to produce aftertastes during subsequent illness). In two experiments, they familiarized different groups of rats with either milk or sucrose or with sucrose and grape juice. Then each group was given a taste of both the familiar and the unfamiliar flavor (for example, first sucrose, then grape juice) in both orders. A rat familiar with sucrose might get a taste of sucrose followed by a taste of grape juice, while another rat also familiar with sucrose might taste the grape juice and then the sucrose. The rats were then exposed to X-irradiation, which made them ill later (see Figure 9.4).

During subsequent choice tests, the rats avoided the unfamiliar flavor that had preceded poisoning, for obvious reasons. It was as if they retrospected and behaved as we would, blaming their illness on something recently tasted and also

unfamiliar. Taste aversions to novel tastes are learned far more readily than to familiar ones. Since these results applied to novel tastes presented both after and before the familiar ones, it seems obvious that an aftertaste produced by the illness could not be the cause of the aversion. (Rozin, 1969, showed that aversions may quickly be learned to specific concentrations of taste solutions. This occurs even when poisoning occurs a half hour later, when differences in aftertastes should be negligible.)

Specific Hungers Rozin (1967) suggested that learned taste aversions provide a simple explanation for an intriguing set of phenomena investigated since the 1920s and 1930s by Curt Richter and others. This is the effect appearing as specific hungers, and it is one of the most impressive instances of an "isn't nature wonderful?" phenomenon (cf. Chapter 6).

Suppose that we deprive a rat of thiamine (vitamin B_1) by feeding it commercially available rat food that lacks thiamine. Then, when we give the rat a choice of foods, it selects thiamine-rich food, which will remedy its deficiency. By 1930, researchers demonstrated that a variety of animals deprived of sodium, vitamins, proteins, sugars, fats, and minerals would select those foods that supplied whatever was missing. This is really an amazing finding.

The reason that it is amazing lies in the mechanisms that must be necessary to allow self-selection of needed nutrients. Since there are at least a dozen specific hungers that have been demonstrated, it follows that there must be at least a dozen specific sensors in the body that monitor the levels of those nutrients in the blood. When the level of one of them is down, the sensor (presumably in the hypothalamus) must detect it and somehow induce the organism to eat foods that contain that nutrient. The "somehow" is the real trick! If I am low on fats or vitamins, for example, does my body tell me to eat peanut butter? If I am low on calcium, how does my body tell me to drink milk?

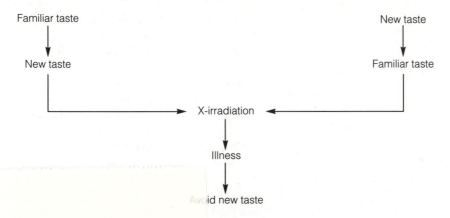

FIGURE 9.4 Familiar versus novel tastes in learned taste aversions. *Revusky and Bedarf, 1967.*

is a change in [...] I am low on [...] self, "I really [...] calcium defi-[...] would love a [...] glass of milk—not Coke or orange juice, but milk!" The whole thing [...] we are talking about us and our long history [...] perience with a large variety of foods. If I feel sluggish, a dough-nut seems appealing, because in the past when I ate a doughnut I was temporarily pepped up. Maybe the other tastes I have from time to time—for pizza, Coke, or coffee—come from the fact that in the past my feelings of disquiet have been quieted when I ate specific foods. I have learned what to eat to feel better.

Why must we assume that animals [...] eaten only laboratory food pellets during their entire lives? If they know to eat that which contains the nu-trients they need, then the whole matter is basic biology: Nature is wonderful! The sensors in the body detect a deficiency in some vital nutrient and then they somehow make foods that contain such nutrients taste better! Can we really assume that there are twelve or thirteen special sensors to influence preferences for a dozen different tastes? Probably not.

Rozin (1967) suggested an alternative that can explain specific hungers far more simply (see Fig-

ure 9.5). Instead of an organism sensing a defi-ciency in one of a dozen nutrients and seeking out foods that contain the needed nutrient, as sug-gested by the "isn't nature wonderful?" account, Rozin suggested that all the creature needs to know is that it is now sick and to remember what it has eaten recently. Specific hungers could be merely an instance of taste aversion learning.

That is, when an organism has been eating a diet deficient in thiamine, it associates the taste of that diet with feelings of illness, just as does the rat poisoned with lithium chloride. And, just as is the case with the poisoned rat, the thiamine-deficient rat avoids food recently eaten (and thus develops paleophobia); if given a choice, the rat eats unfamiliar foods or old foods that were not associated with illness. So the occurrence of spe-cific hungers is not really evidence that creatures seek out foods containing specific nutrients. In fact, sick animals avoid familiar foods because they may have caused the sickness and settle for novel foods, whether those foods contain the missing nutrient or not (that is, show neophilia). Of course, if they eat the new food and remain sick, the new food becomes old and is apt to be avoided as is the original old food (cf. Rozin & Kalat, 1972).

Rozin suggested that this analysis may account for many cases of diet selection but not all cases.

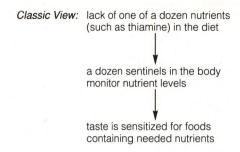

Classic View: lack of one of a dozen nutrients (such as thiamine) in the diet

a dozen sentinels in the body monitor nutrient levels

taste is sensitized for foods containing needed nutrients

Rozin's Suggestion: lack of one of a dozen nutrients in diet

the organism feels sick

the organism avoids recently eaten food (paleophobia) and chooses new tastes (neophilia)

FIGURE 9.5 Classic view versus Rozin's view of specific hungers.

For example, there apparently is a real specific hunger for sodium, and there are cases in which rats and humans select a balanced diet from a set of foods presented them. There are many animals running around in the wilds right now that manage to eat a more or less balanced diet. Such wise food selection cannot be explained entirely in terms of learned taste aversions, can it?

The Significance of Taste Aversion Learning Since the first reports of learned taste aversions by Garcia and his colleagues, there have been countless studies replicating and extending the effect. Why has such attention been paid to such a simple effect? How could such a finding play a large part in changing the direction of experimental psychology?

The answer is simple, though hard to believe. It lies in the fact that taste aversion learning seems obviously to fit the simple paradigm of classical conditioning but has characteristics not shared by other forms of classical conditioning. In classical conditioning, common belief had it that all stimuli could be as effective as CSs, regardless of the UCS used. We may use a tone, bubbling water, a light, a word, or anything as a CS, and it should work about as well as any other CS, as long as the intensities are not wildly different. And classical conditioning occurs only if the interval between CS and UCS is relatively brief; it may be a matter of seconds or of minutes, but not much longer.

Then we discover taste aversion learning, half a century after Pavlov introduced classical conditioning to us. We find here that just any stimulus is not effective; rats are affected by taste and birds by color. Evidently, whatever cues are used in normal feeding are effective in the learning of taste aversions. We also find that the interval between the CS (taste) and the UCS (illness) may be very long, perhaps several hours.

All of this tells us that nature has made taste aversion learning special. Those organisms that learned to avoid tastes that made them sick lived to bear offspring with the same talent. Perhaps taste aversion learning is not an odd case of classical conditioning; maybe it is a species-specific form of learning. And that means there must be other species-specific forms of learning. Don't most humans learn language remarkably quickly? Don't birds fly and don't fish swim? How about the migration of the salmon up the streams of their youth at spawning time? How about the migration of the arctic tern? Surely we knew that there were many species-specific behavior tendencies.

The discovery of taste aversion learning and the realization that it involved hereditary dispositions came as a shock to many who had placed too much faith in the simplified versions of conditioning and learning theories that appeared in the textbooks of the 1950s and 1960s. These books emphasized primarily the views of Hull and his followers; when other theorists, such as Tolman or Skinner, were covered, their views were presented as variations of Hull's theory.

Thus, by the 1960s psychologists had favored a simple S-R associationism, and that view did not have a place for instinct.

Some denied that learned taste aversions were special or that they really violated the laws of learning. For example, Revusky (1971) suggested that such learning was an instance of classical conditioning, differing only in the fact that it is taste (in the case of mammals) that is associated with illness. This "belongingness" of taste and illness is what makes the phenomenon unique, not the fact that the CS–UCS interval may span hours. Revusky suggested that in ordinary classical conditioning, such delays prevent learning because of interference produced by stimuli during the delay.

For example, if we present a brief tone CS and follow it reliably by an electric shock an hour later, we are not likely to see a CR produced by the tone. This is because of the interfering effect of all of the sights and sounds that are sure to occur during a one-hour CS–UCS interval. But in the case of taste aversions, the only stimuli capable of interfering are other tastes, and it is likely that none (or few) will occur during the hour interval between taste and illness.

Revusky considers taste aversion learning semi-special, therefore. The possible long CS–UCS interval is not special; it is simply made possible by the "belongingness" principle, which does make the learning special. Revusky and others have pointed out that taste aversions resemble normal classical conditioning in most respects. That is, learning is better when the CS and UCS are moderately intense, when the CS–UCS interval is brief, and when other stimuli do not block, overshadow, or appear during the CS–UCS interval.

It could be that Revusky did not go far enough. Maybe taste aversion learning is really just classical conditioning, and maybe "belongingness" can be explained in terms other than those of hereditary dispositions. In fact, Mazur (1986) suggested that taste aversion learning has become accepted as a case of classical conditioning and

pointed out that the taste-poison paradigm has become one of the favorites for studying classical conditioning!

SUMMARY

Instrumental Conditioning

Although the law of effect has little to do with hedonism, reinforcers and punishers often have been treated as equivalent to pleasures and pains. This is unfortunate, since hedonism is a very vulnerable point of view. Much of the recent research in instrumental conditioning shows, among other things, that it is long past time to bury hedonism once and for all.

It was the implicit belief in hedonism that led to a misinterpretation of Olds's discovery; what were formerly called "pleasure centers in the brain" are now better understood. Something that acts as a powerful reinforcer need by no means be "pleasant." Similarly, so-called punishment centers were mislabeled. Like the effects of stimulation elsewhere in the limbic system (for example, evoking feeding, fasting, or aggression), the effects are far more general than had been believed. Olds's discovery did not advance our understanding of the law of effect.

Premack showed that reinforcers and punishers are not fixed classes; they are better treated as activities, and, under the right circumstances, any activity can act as a reinforcer or punisher of any other activity. The flaw in Premack's theory was the necessity to scale activities on a continuum of value. This was not practical and turned out to be unnecessary in any event. The theory of response deprivation requires only that one activity be available less than is preferred by a subject; access to it may then be used as a reinforcer for another activity. Allison suggested that a sort of conservation applies here, such that the amount of reinforced and reinforcing behavior remains constant as access to each is altered.

All of the research stemming from Premack's theory treats the law of effect as a molar entity, defined as changes in relative amounts of behaviors over time. This is true also of the matching law, first proposed by Herrnstein. Masses of data show that animal and human subjects distribute their responses to a number of alternatives so as to match the relative payoff provided by each alternative. Like the Premack Principle, the matching law shows that reinforcement is a relative thing; the effect of a given frequency or magnitude of payoff depends upon the payoffs available for other available alternatives. The matching law may even explain cases of self-control, if we consider time as well as magnitude of payoff.

Autoshaping was originally believed to be damaging to extant theories of learning, since it showed that much of what was assumed to be operant behavior was actually classically conditioned. This is really only of great interest if one believes that the operant/respondent distinction is very important and that responses have to be emitted *or* elicited and kept separate! Although autoshaped behaviors may be elicited, we find that this has little effect on our understanding of behavior in general.

Researchers over the years assumed that behaviors could be treated as independent and that manipulation of one could be carried out without affecting others. Behavioral contrast and local contrast have now been documented often enough to show that they are reliable and that (once again) effects are always relative. Responding to one stimulus depends in part on the rate of reinforcement in other, successively presented components.

Understanding conditioned reinforcement has been a problem for many years. Although it seems that tokens and other acquired reinforcers gain their power from pairing with already effective reinforcers, research has not clearly supported the pairing theory. An alternative interpretation is that things become acquired reinforcers when they are produced in the same way as are already effective reinforcers. This ex-plains why simply pairing *may* be effective and it explains why many consequences of our daily behavior come to act as reinforcers.

Avoidance learning is obviously important to many species. Yet, it has proven difficult to explain how such learning takes place. The main difficulty has been in understanding how an avoidance response is maintained when it is never reinforced, except by the nonoccurrence of the harmful event. Two-factor theory assumed that some signal always accompanied harmful events and that responses that removed such warning stimuli were reinforced by the reduction of fear. More recent research has shown that organisms respond to decrease the overall level of the stimulus (such as shock), even when each response is followed by the stimulus. Such findings invalidate two-factor theory and show that a molar viewpoint removes the mystery that comes with molecular viewpoints, as was the case with the matching law and conditioned reinforcement.

After 1930, Thorndike argued that annoyers work indirectly, by encouraging new behavior. This position was similar to that of Skinner, who believed punishment to be a by-product of emotion produced by the aversive event. This view was supported by evidence, such as Estes's, suggesting that punishment had temporary effects no stronger than those produced by randomly administered aversive events. However, Azrin and his colleagues demonstrated in the 1960s that punishment does work as directly as does reinforcement, though with opposite effect.

Classical Conditioning

Rescorla showed in the 1960s that classical conditioning occurs only when the CS predicts the UCS; it is not enough that it is paired frequently with it if it also frequently appears independently of it. Shortly thereafter, Rescorla and Wagner proposed a variant of a very old model to explain how Rescorla's evidence for the importance of contingency could be explained as contiguity (pairing) of CS and UCS. The model also explains overshadowing and blocking and has been applied to stimulus generalization phenomena.

Solomon and Corbit proposed the opponent-process model to account for a number of motivational and emotional phenomena, as well as for drug addiction. Their evidence shows that many UCRs are biphasic; a strong response during earlier conditioning trials diminishes over sessions, due to the development of an opponent response. Thus, the effect of a UCS depends upon frequency and spacing of application. Their model may account for seemingly paradoxical effects, such as those reported by Siegel.

John Garcia showed that many organisms are predisposed to associate taste with subsequent gastrointestinal illness. Aversions following illness are specific to tastes accompanying poisoning, even when taste and illness are separated by many hours. Taste aversion learning initially was believed to be damaging to current learning theories, but subsequent research has not supported this view. In fact, the taste aversion paradigm is now a popular procedure for those studying classical conditioning. Learned taste aversions may well explain many instances of what have been called specific hungers.

GLOSSARY

A state Solomon and Corbit's term for the initial reaction to an affect-producing UCS, such as electric shock. With repetition, the A state diminishes in strength. This occurs because the opponent B state increases in strength over trials. (See *opponent-process model*.)

B state Solomon and Corbit's term for the opponent reaction produced when the A state is produced. If the A reaction appears as an increase in heart rate when shock is applied, the B reaction is a decrease in heart rate. The B reaction is assumed to increase in strength with repetition and to thus eventually reduce the A state to the diminished A′ state. (See *opponent-process model*.)

Behavioral contrast An increase or decrease in response rate to a stimulus when a change in conditions occurs during a second stimulus. When reinforcement rate is decreased for responses to a red light, response rate may increase greatly during green, even though there is no increase in reinforcement frequency in green.

Blocking Term used by Kamin to refer to the effect of pretraining with one CS on subsequent failure to establish a CR to a second stimulus presented along with the original CS. In terms of the Rescorla-Wagner model, the first CS gains the majority of the associative strength available, preventing additional conditioning to the added CS.

Commensurability of units The major problem with Premack's Principle, as originally proposed, in which widely different activities are scaled on a common continuum of value. It becomes difficult to assume that one unit of an activity is commensurate, or translatable, into one unit of another activity. For example, is one minute spent eating commensurate with one minute reading?

Conditioned reinforcer An acquired reinforcer; one that gains its reinforcing power during an individual's lifetime.

Conservation Principle applied to allocation of activities under schedule constraints. Allison and his colleagues have shown that total behavior per session remains constant under many conditions. Thus, more of one activity means less of some others.

Contiguity Closeness in space and/or time. Pavlovian conditioning was formerly thought to depend only on the simple contiguity of CS and UCS in time.

Contingency Contingent events have an if/then relationship. As an example, a CS which unequivocally predicts a UCS has a clear contingent relationship with the UCS. A CS which is always followed by a UCS does not have such a contingent relationship if the UCS also appears at other times.

Drive The chief way of treating motivation in many psychological theories, especially Hull's. Biological imbalances, or needs, lead to behavior aimed at reducing the need. A need acting to produce behavior is termed a drive.

Habituation A decrease in response with repeated stimulation. For example, the startle response to a gunshot diminishes with repetition.

Hedonism The doctrine that our conduct is regulated largely by pleasure and pain.

Local contrast A sequential effect that occurs during discrimination learning. (See Pavlovian induction, Chapter 3.)

Matching law Also called the molar law of effect. Herrnstein demonstrated that relative response rate is equal to (or matches) relative reinforcement frequency.

Opponent-process model Solomon and Corbit's theory of acquired motivation. According to this model, strong stimulation produces either positive or negative reactions (the A state) as well as a compensating reaction in the opposite direction. With repeated stimulation, the opposing reaction (the B state) increases in strength and subtracts from the A reaction. The model provides a plausible account of the mechanisms involved in risk taking, drug addiction, and other phenomena.

Overshadowing Effect first reported by Pavlov, who found that when more than one CS is presented at the same time, the more salient one may "overshadow" the less salient one, leaving the latter ineffective.

Passive avoidance Avoidance of noxious stimulation achieved by not responding. We passively avoid burns by not placing our hands in fires. The term was often used in place of the term punishment during the several decades when it was believed that punishment was ineffective.

Phobia An unnatural and usually unreasonable fear of common stimuli. Agoraphobia, for example, refers to a fear of open spaces; siderophobia is a fear of railroad trains.

Premack Principle Revision of the law of effect first proposed by David Premack in 1959. According to this view, activities in which we engage may be ranked along a continuum of value. Reinforcement occurs when lower-valued activities provide access to higher-valued activities. When a higher-valued activity produces access to lower-valued activities, the former decrease in frequency (are punished).

Primary reinforcer A reinforcer that acts as such in the absence of prior experience with it; its power does not depend upon learning. Food and water are usually viewed as primary reinforcers.

Punishment A decrease in the probability of a behavior owing to the consequences it produces. Electric shock produced by a response is a commonly used punisher.

Rescorla-Wagner model Theory of classical conditioning published by Rescorla and Wagner in 1972. According to this theory, conditioning always involves a compound CS and a limited amount of available associative strength, determined by the nature of the UCS. Associative strength gained by one element of the compound CS detracts from that available to other elements. Increments in associative strength on successive trials depend upon the maximum (asymptotic) level possible and the amount of associative strength already gained. The model accounts for overshadowing and blocking, for which it was formulated, as well as for other phenomena.

Response deprivation Name given by Timberlake and Allison to their revision of the Premack Principle. According to this theory, reinforcement occurs when a behavior is restricted so that it can occur only at less-than-baseline level and when a second behavior is required for access to the restricted behavior. The second behavior will increase in frequency (be reinforced) as long as the restricted behavior remains available at less than its baseline (unrestricted) level.

Response language Name given by Premack to his way of viewing the law of effect. Instead of speaking of behaviors producing reinforcing stimuli, such as food, Premack spoke of behaviors producing access to other behaviors, such as eating.

Transituational Term used by Meehl in 1950 to refer to the power of a reinforcer of one behavior (such as bar pressing) to act the same in different situations and with different behaviors (such as key pecking).

Value Intervening variable used as a basic term in Premack's theory. Value refers to the attractiveness of activities and may be assessed in terms of time spent in one or another activity.

RECOMMENDED READINGS

Brain Stimulation (or So-Called Pleasure Centers in the Brain)

Valenstein, E. S. (1973). *Brain control.* New York: Wiley.

Valenstein is a well-known researcher in this field and presents an entertaining and authoritative summary of research on brain stimulation and psychosurgery.

Pribram, K. (1971). *Languages of the brain: Experimental paradoxes and principles in neuropsychology.* Englewood Cliffs, NJ: Prentice-Hall.

This book provides the advanced student with a scholarly review of findings in neuropsychology as well as a speculative model for memory.

Instrumental Conditioning

Honig, W. K., & Staddon, J.E.R. (Eds.), (1977). *Handbook of operant behavior*. Englewood Cliffs, NJ: Prentice-Hall.

This handbook contains chapters written by authorities in fields ranging from the control of feeding to language. More recent research may be found in the *Journal of the Experimental Analysis of Behavior*.

Mackintosh, N. J. (1974). *The psychology of animal learning*. London: Academic Press.

This is a difficult, scholarly compendium of research and theory in the associationist tradition. A shorter but equally difficult treatment of more recent work appears in Mackintosh (1983). See also the *Journal of Experimental Psychology: Animal Behavior Processes*.

Classical Conditioning

See recommended readings following Chapter 3.

REFERENCES

Adams, D. K. (1929). Experimental studies of adaptive behavior in cats. *Comparative Psychology Monographs, 27*.

Ader, R. & Cohen, H. (1982). Behaviorally conditioned immunosuppression and murine systemic lupus erythematosis. *Science, 215*, 1534–1536.

Ainslee, G. W. (1974). Impulse control in pigeons. *Journal of the Experimental Analysis of Behavior, 21*, 485–489.

Allison, J., Miller, M., & Wozny, M. (1979). Conservation in behavior. *Journal of Experimental Psychology: General, 108*, 4–34.

Allport, F. H. (1924). *Social psychology*. Boston: Houghton Mifflin.

Allport, G. W. (1937). *Personality: A psychological interpretation*. New York: Holt.

Allport, G. W., & Odbert, H. S. (1935). Trait-names, a psycho-lexical study. *Psychological Review Monographs, 47* (No. 1).

Amsel A. (1962). Frustrative nonreward in partial reinforcement and discrimination learning. *Psychological Review, 69*, 306–328.

Amsel, A., & Rashotte, M. (Eds.). (1984). *Mechanisms of adaptive behavior: Clark L. Hull's theoretical papers*. New York: Columbia University Press.

Angell, J. R. (1907). The province of functional psychology. *Psychological Review, 14*, 61–91.

Anger, D. (1963). The role of temporal discrimination in the reinforcement of Sidman avoidance behavior. *Journal of the Experimental Analysis of Behavior, 6*, 477–506.

Asratyan, E. A. (1953). *I. P. Pavlov*. Moscow: Foreign Languages Publishing House.

Asratyan, E. A. (1965). *Conditioned reflex and compensatory mechanisms*. Oxford: Pergamon Press.

Ayllon, T., & Azrin, N. H. (1964). Reinforcement and instructions with mental patients. *Journal of the Experimental Analysis of Behavior, 7*, 327–331.

Ayllon, T., & Azrin, N. H. (1965). The measurement and reinforcement of behavior of psychotics. *Journal of the Experimental Analysis of Behavior, 8*, 357–384.

Ayllon, T., & Azrin, N. H. (1968). *The token economy:*

A motivational system for therapy and rehabilitation. New York: Appleton-Century-Crofts.

Ayllon, T., & Haughton, E. (1962). Control of the behavior of schizophrenic patients by food. *Journal of the Experimental Analysis of Behavior, 5,* 343–352.

Azrin, N. H. (1956). Some effects of two intermittant schedules of immediate and nonimmediate punishment. *Journal of Psychology, 42,* 3–21.

Azrin, N. H. (1959). Punishment and recovery during fixed-ratio performance. *Journal of the Experimental Analysis of Behavior, 2,* 301–305.

Azrin, N. H. (1960). Effects of punishment intensity during variable-interval reinforcement. *Journal of the Experimental Analysis of Behavior, 3,* 123–142.

Azrin, N. H. (1961). Time-out from positive reinforcement. *Science, 133,* 382–383.

Azrin, N. H., & Holtz, W. C. (1966). Punishment. In W. K. Honig (Ed.), *Operant behavior: Areas of research and application.* New York: Appleton-Century-Crofts.

Baer, D. M., & Sherman, J. A. (1964). Reinforcement control of generalized imitation in young children. *Journal of Experimental Child Psychology, 1,* 37–49.

Bandura, A. (1965). Behavioral modifications through modeling procedures. In L. Krasner & L. P. Ullman (Eds.), *Research in behavior modification.* New York: Holt, Rinehart, & Winston.

Bandura, A. (1977). Self-efficacy: Toward a unifying theory of behavioral change. *Psychological Review, 84,* 191–215.

Bandura, A. (1986). *Social foundations of thought and action.* Englewood Cliffs, NJ: Prentice-Hall.

Barnes, J. M., & Underwood, B. J. (1959). Fate of first list associations in transfer theory. *Journal of Experimental Psychology, 58,* 97–105.

Baum, W. M. (1974). Choice in free ranging wild pigeons. *Science, 185,* 78–79.

Beidel, D. C., & Turner, S. M. (1986). A critique of the theoretical bases of cognitive-behavioral theories and therapy. *Clinical Psychology Review, 6,* 177–197.

Bekesy, G. (1967). *Sensory inhibition.* Princeton, NJ: Princeton University Press.

Bem, D. J. (1967). Self-perception: An alternative interpretation of cognitive dissonance phenomena. *Psychological Review, 74,* 183–198.

Bijou, S. W., & Baer, D. M. (1961). *Child development: A systematic and empirical theory* (Vol. 1). New York: Appleton-Century-Crofts.

Blodgett, H. C. (1929). The effect of the introduction of reward upon the maze performance of rats. *University of California Publications in Psychology, 4,* 113–134.

Bloomfield, T. M. (1969). Behavioral contrast and the peak shift. In R. M. Gilbert & N. S. Sutherland (Eds.), *Animal discrimination learning.* London: Academic Press.

Bolles, R. C. (1970). Species-specific defense reactions and avoidance learning. *Psychological Review, 77,* 32–48.

Bolles, R. C. (1978). The role of stimulus learning in defensive behavior. In S. H. Hulse, H. Fowler, and W. K. Honig (Eds.), *Cognitive processes in animal behavior.* Hillsdale, NJ: Erlbaum.

Boring, E. G. (1950). *A history of experimental psychology* (2nd ed.). New York: Appleton-Century-Crofts.

Bower, G. H. & Hilgard, E. R. (1981). *Theories of Learning* (5th ed.). Englewood Cliffs, NJ: Prentice-Hall.

Branch, M. N. (1987). Behavior analysis: A conceptual and empirical base for behavior therapy. *The Behavior Therapist, 10,* 79–84.

Breland, K. & Breland, M. (1951). A field of applied animal psychology. *American Psychologist, 6,* 202–204.

Breland, K. & Breland, M. (1961). The misbehavior of organisms. *American Psychologist, 16,* 681–684.

Broadhurst, P. L. (1957). Emotionality and the Yerkes-Dodson law. *Journal of Experimental Psychology, 54,* 345–352.

Brown, J. S. (1953). Problems presented by the concept of acquired drives. In *Current Theory and Research in Motivation.* Lincoln, NE: University of Nebraska Press.

Brown, P. L., & Jenkins, H. M. (1968). Auto-shaping the pigeons' key peck. *Journal of the Experimental Analysis of Behavior, 11,* 1–8.

Buck, R. (1988). *Human motivation and emotion.* New York: Wiley.

Bykov, K. M. (1957). *The cerebral cortex and the internal organs.* New York: Chemical Publishing.

Campbell, B. A., & Sheffield, F. D. (1953). Relation of random activity to food deprivation. *Journal of Comparative and Physiological Psychology, 46,* 320–322.

Cannon, W. B. (1932). *The wisdom of the body.* New York: Norton.

Carr, H., & Watson, J. B. (1908). Orientation in the white rat. *Journal of Comparative Neurological Psychology, 18,* 27–44.

Catania, A. C. (1979). Operant theory: Skinner. In G. M. Gazda & R. J. Corsini (Eds.), *Theories of Learning*. Itasca, IL: Peacock.

Catania, A. C. (1984). *Learning* (2nd ed.). Englewood Cliffs, NJ: Prentice-Hall.

Chomsky, N. (1959). Review of B. F. Skinner's *Verbal behavior*. *Language, 35,* 26–58.

Cohen, D. (1979). *J. B. Watson: The founder of behaviorism*. London: Routledge & Kegan Paul.

Collier, G. (1972). *Reinforcement magnitude in free feeding*. Paper presented at the annual meeting of the Psychonomic Society, St. Louis, MO.

Collins, A. M., & Quillian, M. R. (1969). Retrieval time from semantic memory. *Journal of Verbal Learning and Verbal Behavior, 8,* 240–247.

Cooper, L. A. & Shepard, R. N. (1973). Chronometric studies of the rotation of mental images. In W. G. Chase (Ed.), *Visual information processing*. New York: Academic Press.

Darwin, C. (1859). *On the origin of species by means of natural selection, or the preservation of the favored races in the struggle for life*. London: Murray.

Darwin, C. R. (1871). *The descent of man, and selection in relation to sex*. London: Murray.

Darwin, C. (1872). *The expression of the emotions in man and animals*. London: Murray. (Republished in 1965, Chicago: University of Chicago Press.)

Davidson, A. B. (1971). Factors affecting keypress responding by rats in the presence of free food. *Psychonomic Science, 24,* 135–137.

Delgado, J.M.R. (1955). Evaluation of permanent implantation of electrodes within the brain. *Electroencephalography and Clinical Neurophysiology, 7,* 637–644.

Delgado, J.M.R. (1969). *Physical control of the mind*. New York: Harper & Row.

Dewey, J. (1896). The reflex arc concept in psychology. *Psychological Review, 3,* 357–370.

Dollard, J., & Miller, N. E. (1950). *Personality and psychotherapy*. New York: McGraw-Hill.

Dworkin, B. R., & Miller, N. E. (1986). Failure to replicate visceral conditioning in the acute curarized rat preparation. *Behavioral Neuroscience, 100,* 299–314.

Eikelboom, R. & Stewart, J. (1982). Conditioning of drug-induced physiological responses. *Psychological Review, 89,* 507–528.

Eisenberger, R., Karpman, M., & Trattner, J. (1967). What is the necessary and sufficient condition in the contingency situation? *Journal of Experimental Psychology, 74,* 342–350.

Ellis, W. D. (1939). *A source book of gestalt psychology*. New York: Harcourt Brace.

Epstein, R., Kirshnit, C. E., Lanza, R. P., & Rubin, L. C. (1984). "Insight" in the pigeon: antecedents and determinants of an intelligent performance. *Nature, 308,* 61–62.

Epstein, R., Lanza, R. P., and Skinner, B. F. (1980). Symbolic communication between two pigeons (*Columbia livia domestica*). *Science, 207,* 543–545.

Epstein, R., Lanza, R. P., and Skinner, B. F. (1981). "Self-awareness" in the pigeon. *Science, 212,* 695–696.

Epstein, R., & Skinner, B. F. (1981). The spontaneous use of memoranda by pigeons. *Behaviour Analysis Letters, 1,* 241–246.

Estes, W. K. (1944). An experimental study of punishment. *Psychological Monographs, 57* (3, Whole No. 263).

Estes, W. K. (1950). Toward a statistical theory of learning. *Psychological Review, 57,* 94–107.

Estes, W. K. (1956). The problem of inference from curves based on group data. *Psychological Bulletin, 53,* 134–140.

Estes, W. K. (1964). All-or-none processes in learning and retention. *American Psychologist, 19,* 16–25.

Estes, W. K. (1969). Reinforcement in human learning. In J. Tapp (Ed.), *Reinforcement and behavior*. New York: Academic Press.

Estes, W. K., Koch, S., MacCorquodale, K., Meehl, P. E., Mueller, C. G., Jr., Schoenfeld, W. N., & Verplanck, W. S. (1954). *Modern learning theory*. New York: Appleton-Century-Crofts.

Eysenck, H. J. (1957). *The dynamics of anxiety and hysteria*. New York: Praeger.

Fantino, E. (1967). Preference for mixed- versus fixed-ratio schedules. *Journal of the Experimental Analysis of Behavior, 10,* 35–43.

Fantino, E. J., Sharp, D., & Cole, M. (1966). Factors facilitating lever-press avoidance. *Journal of Comparative and Physiological Psychology, 62,* 214–217.

Ferster, C. B., & Skinner, B. F. (1957). *Schedules of reinforcement*. New York: Appleton-Century-Crofts.

Freud, S. (1970). The unconscious. In W. Russell (Ed.), *Milestones in motivation*. New York: Appleton-Century-Crofts. (Original work published 1915).

Frolov, Y. P. (1937). *Pavlov and his school*. New York: Oxford University Press.

Gallup, G. (1970). Chimpanzees: Self-recognition. *Science, 167,* 86–87.

Gamzu, E. R., & Williams, D. R. (1971). Classical conditioning of a complex skeletal response. *Science, 171*, 923–925.

Gamzu, E. R. & Williams, D. R. (1973). Associative factors underlying the pigeon's key-pecking in autoshaping procedures. *Journal of the Experimental Analysis of Behavior, 19*, 225–232.

Garcia, J., Ervin, F. R., & Koelling, R. A. (1966). Learning with prolonged delay of reinforcement. *Psychonomic Science, 5*, 121–122.

Garcia, J., & Koelling, R. (1966). Relation of cue to consequence in avoidance learning. *Psychonomic Science, 4*, 123–124.

Gardner, R. A., & Gardner, B. T. (1988). Feedforward versus feedbackward: An ethological alternative to the law of effect. *Behavioral and Brain Sciences, 11*, 429–493.

Gollub, L. R. (1977). Conditioned reinforcement: Schedule effects. In W. K. Honig & J.E.R. Staddon (Eds.), *Handbook of operant behavior*. Englewood Cliffs, NJ: Prentice-Hall.

Goodrich, K. P. (1959). Performance in different segments of an instrumental response chain as a function of reinforcement schedule. *Journal of Experimental Psychology, 57*, 57–63.

Gray, J. A. (1979). *Ivan Pavlov*. New York: Penguin.

Griffin, D. R. (1976). *The question of animal awareness*. New York: Rockefeller University Press.

Guthrie, E. R. (1938). *The psychology of human conflict*. New York: Harper & Row.

Guthrie, E. R. (1952). *The psychology of learning* (rev. ed.) New York: Harper & Row. (Original work published 1935).

Guthrie, E. R. (1959). Association by contiguity. In S. Koch (Ed.), *Psychology: A study of a science* (Vol. 2). New York: McGraw-Hill.

Guthrie, E. R. and Horton, G. P. (1946). *Cats in a puzzle box*. New York: Rinehart.

Hanson, H. M. (1959). Effects of discrimination training on stimulus generalization. *Journal of Experimental Psychology, 58*, 321–334.

Harlow, H. F. (1937). Experimental analysis of the role of the original stimulus in conditioned responses in monkeys. *Psychological Record, 1*, 62–68.

Harlow, H. F. (1949). The formation of learning sets. *Psychological Review, 56*, 51–65.

Harlow, H. F. (1953a). Mice, monkeys, men, and motives. *Psychological Review, 60*, 23–32.

Harlow, H. F. (1953b). Motivation as a factor in the acquisition of new responses. In *Current Theory and Research in Motivation*. Lincoln, NE: University of Nebraska Press.

Harlow, H. F., Gluck, J. P. and Suomi, S. J. (1972). Generalization of behavioral data between nonhuman and human animals. *American Psychologist, 27*, 709–716.

Harris, B. (1979). Whatever happened to little Albert? *American Psychologist, 34*, 151–160.

Hearst, E., & Franklin, S. R. (1977). Positive and negative relations between a signal and food: Approach-withdrawal behavior to the signal. *Journal of Experimental Psychology: Animal Behavior Processes, 3*, 37–52.

Hebb, D. O. (1961). Distinctive features of learning in the higher animal. In J. F. Delafresnaye (Ed.), *Brain mechanisms and learning*. Oxford: Blackwell.

Hebb, D. O. (1976). James Olds remembered. *APA Monitor, 7*, 5.

Helmholtz, H. V. (1866). *Handbook of physiological optics*. (J.P.C. Southall, Trans.). Rochester, NY: Optical Society of America.

Henle, M. (1986). *1879 and all that*. New York: Columbia University Press.

Herman, R. L., & Azrin, N. H. (1964). Punishment by noise in an alternative response situation. *Journal of the Experimental Analysis of Behavior, 7*, 185–188.

Herrnstein, R. J. (1958). Some factors influencing behavior in a two-response situation. *Transactions of the New York Academy of Sciences, 21*, 35–45.

Herrnstein, R. J. (1964). Aperiodicity as a factor in choice. *Journal of the Experimental Analysis of Behavior, 7*, 179–182.

Herrnstein, R. J. (1970). On the law of effect. *Journal of the Experimental Analysis of Behavior, 13*, 243–266.

Herrnstein, R. J., & Boring, E. G. (1973). *A source book in the history of psychology*. Cambridge, MA: Harvard University Press.

Herrnstein, R. J., & deVilliers, P. A. (1980). Fish as a natural category for people and pigeons. In G. H. Bower (Ed.), *The psychology of learning and motivation* (Vol 14). New York: Academic Press.

Herrnstein, R. J. and Hineline, P. N. (1966). Negative reinforcement as shock frequency reduction. *Journal of the Experimental Analysis of Behavior, 9*, 421–430.

Herrnstein, R. J. and Loveland, D. H. (1966). Complex visual concepts in the pigeon. *Science, 146*, 549–551.

Herrnstein, R. J., Loveland, D. H., & Cable, C. (1976). Natural concepts in pigeons. *Journal of Experimental Psychology: Animal Behavior Processes, 2*, 285–301.

Heth, C. D. (1976). Simultaneous and backward fear conditioning as a function of number of CS–US pairings. *Journal of Experimental Psychology: Animal Behavior Processes, 2,* 117–129.

Hineline, P. N., & Wanchisen, B. A. (1990). Correlated hypothesizing and the distinction between contingency-shaped and rule-governed behavior. In S. C. Hayes (Ed.), *Rule-governed behavior: Cognition, contingencies, and instructional control.* New York: Plenum.

Holland, P. C. (1977). Conditioned stimulus as a determinant of the form of the Pavlovian conditioned response. *Journal of Experimental Psychology: Animal Behavior Processes, 3,* 77–104.

Holland, P. C., & Rescorla, R. A. (1975). Second-order conditioning with food unconditioned stimulus. *Journal of Comparative and Physiological Psychology, 88,* 459–67.

Hollard, V. D., & Delius, J. D. (1982). Rotational invariance in visual pattern recognition by pigeons and humans. *Science, 218,* 804–806.

Holt, E. B. (1915). *The Freudian wish and its place in ethics.* New York: Holt.

Honig, W. K., & Staddon, J.E.R. (1977). *Handbook of operant behavior.* Englewood Cliffs, NJ: Prentice-Hall.

Honzik, C. H. (1936). The sensory basis of maze learning in rats. *Comparative Psychology Monographs, 13* (Whole No. 64).

Hothersall, D. (1990). *History of psychology* (2nd ed.). New York: McGraw-Hill.

Hubel, D. H., & Wiesel, T. N. (1959). Receptive fields of single neurons in the cat's striate cortex. *Journal of Physiology, 140,* 574–591.

Hudson, B. (1948). One trial learning: A study of the avoidance behavior of the rat. On deposit in the Library of the University of California, Berkeley (from Tolman [1948]).

Hull, C. L. (1924). The influence of tobacco smoking on mental and motor efficiency. *Psychological Monographs, 33* (No. 150).

Hull, C. L. (1928). *Aptitude testing.* Yonkers-on-Hudson, NY: World Book.

Hull, C. L. (1930). Knowledge and purpose as habit mechanisms. *Psychological Review, 37,* 511–525.

Hull, C. L. (1931). Goal attraction and directing ideas conceived as habit phenomena. *Psychological Review, 38,* 487–506.

Hull, C. L. (1933). *Hypnosis and suggestibility: An experimental approach.* New York: Appleton-Century-Crofts.

Hull, C. L. (1943). *Principles of behavior.* New York: Appleton-Century-Crofts.

Hull, C. L. (1947). Reactively heterogeneous compound trial-and-error learning with distributed trials and terminal reinforcement. *Journal of Experimental Psychology, 37,* 118–135.

Hull, C. L. (1951). *Essentials of behavior.* New Haven, CT: Yale University Press.

Hull, C. L. (1952a). [Autobiography]. In E. G. Boring, H. S. Langfeld, H. Werner, & R. M. Yerkes (Eds.), *A history of psychology in autobiography* (Vol. IV). Worcester, MA: Clark University Press.

Hull, C. L. (1952b). *A behavior system.* New Haven, CT: Yale University Press.

Hulse, S. H., Fowler, H., & Honig, W. K. (Eds.). (1978). *Cognitive processes in animal behavior.* Hillsdale, NJ: Erlbaum.

Hunt, W. A., Matarazzo, J. D., Weiss, S. M., & Gentry, W. D. (1979). Associative learning, habit, and health behavior. *Journal of Behavioral Medicine, 2,* 111–124.

Ince, L. P., Brucker, B. S., & Alba, Augusta (1978). Reflex conditioning in spinal man. *Journal of Comparative and Physiological Psychology, 92.* 796–802.

James, W. (1890). *The principles of psychology.* New York: Holt.

James, W. (1892). *Psychology.* New York: Holt.

James, W. (1904). Does consciousness exist? *Journal of Philosophy, 1,* 477–491.

James, W. (1962). The sentiment of rationality. In W. Barrett & H. D. Aiken (Eds.), *Philosophy in the twentieth century* (Vol. 1). New York: Random House. (Original work published 1879).

Jenkins, H. M. (1970). Sequential organization in schedules of reinforcement. In W. N. Schoenfeld (Ed.), *The theory of reinforcement schedules.* New York: Appleton-Century-Crofts.

Joncich, G. (1968). *The sane positivist.* Middletwon, CT: Wesleyan University Press.

Kamin, L. J. (1968). Attention-like processes in classical conditioning. In M. R. Jones (Ed.), *Miami symposium on the prediction of behavior: Aversive stimulation.* Miami: University of Miami Press.

Keith-Lucas, T., & Guttman, N. (1975). Robust single trial delayed backward conditioning. *Journal of Comparative and Physiological Psychology, 88,* 468–476.

Kimble, G. A. (1951). Behavior strength as a function of the hunger drive. *Journal of Experimental Psychology, 41,* 341–348.

Kimble, G. A., & Kendall, J. W., Jr. (1953). A comparison of two methods of producing experimental extinction. *Journal of Experimental Psychology, 45*, 87–90.

Kimmel, H. D. (1966). Inhibition of the conditioned response in classical conditioning. *Psychological Review, 73*, 232–240.

Kling, J. W. and Riggs, L. A. (1971). *Experimental psychology*. New York: Holt, Rinehart & Winston.

Köhler, W. (1925). *The mentality of apes*. (E. Wister, Trans.). New York: Harcourt, Brace & World.

Köhler, W. (1959). Gestalt psychology today. *American Psychologist, 14*, 727–734.

Konorski, J. (1948). *Conditioned reflexes and neuron organization*. Cambridge, UK: Cambridge University Press.

Konorski, J. (1967). *Integrative activity of the brain*. Chicago: University of Chicago Press.

Konorski, J., & Miller S. (1937). On two types of conditioned reflex. *Journal of General Psychology, 16*, 265–272.

Krechevsky, I. (1932). "Hypotheses" versus "chance" on the pre-solution period in sensory discrimination learning. *University of California Publications in Psychology, 6*, 27–44.

Kuo, Z. Y. (1921). Giving up instincts in psychology. *Journal of Philosophy, 17*, 645–664.

Lambert, J. V., Bersh, P. J., Hineline, P. N., & Smith, G. D. (1973). Avoidance conditioning with shock contingent on the avoidance response. *Journal of the Experimental Analysis of Behavior, 19*, 361–367.

Langer, E. J. (1989). *Mindfulness*. Reading, MA: Addison-Wesley.

Lashley, K. S. (1929). *Brain mechanisms and intelligence*. Chicago: University of Chicago Press.

Lashley, K. S. (1930). The mechanism of vision. I. A method for rapid analysis of pattern vision in the rat. *Journal of Genetic Psychology, 37*, 453–460.

Lashley, K. S. (1950). In search of the engram. *Society of Experimental Biology*, Symposium 4, 454–482.

Lashley, K. S., Chow, K. L., & Semmes, J. (1951). An examination of the electrical field theory of cerebral integration. *Psychological Review, 58*, 123–136.

Leeper, R. (1935). The role of motivation on learning: A study of the phenomenon of differential motivation control of the utilization of habits. *Journal of Genetic Psychology, 46*, 3–40.

Lolordo, V. M., & Fairless, J. L. (1985). Pavlovian conditioned inhibition: The literature since 1969. In Miller, R. R., & Spear, N. E. (Eds.), *Information processing in animals: Conditioned inhibition*. Hillsdale, NJ: Erlbaum.

Luchins, A. S. (1942). Mechanization in problem solving: The effect of *Einstellung*. *Psychological Monographs, 54* (Whole No. 248).

McClelland, D. C. (1985). How motives, skills, and values determine what people do. *American Psychologist, 40*, 812–825.

McClelland, D. C., Atkinson, J., Clark, R., & Lowell, E. (1953). *The achievement motive*. New York: Appleton-Century-Crofts.

McClelland, D. C., Clark, R. A., Roby, T. B., & Atkinson, J. W. (1949). The projective expression of needs: IV. The effect of the need for achievement on thematic apperception. *Journal of Experimental Psychology, 39*, 242–255.

MacCorquodale, K. (1970). On Chomsky's review of Skinner's *Verbal Behavior*. *Journal of the Experimental Analysis of Behavior, 13*, 83–100.

MacCorquodale, K., & Meehl, P. E. (1954). Edward C. Tolman. In W. K. Estes, S. Koch, K. MacCorquodale, P. E. Meehl, C. G. Mueller, W. N. Schoenfeld, & W. S. Verplanck, *Modern Learning Theory*. New York: Appleton-Century-Crofts.

McDougall, W. (1908). *An introduction to social psychology*. London: Methuen.

Mackintosh, N. J. (1974). *The psychology of animal learning*. London: Academic Press.

Mackintosh, N. J. (1983). *Conditioning and associative learning*. New York: Oxford University Press.

Mahoney, M. J. (1977). Cognitive therapy and research: A question of questions. *Cognitive Therapy and Research, 1*, 5–16.

Malone, J. C., Jr. (1976). Local contrast and Pavlovian induction. *Journal of the Experimental Analysis of Behavior, 26*, 425–440.

Malone, J. C., Jr. (1978). Beyond the operant analysis of behavior. *Behavior Therapy, 9*, 584–591.

Malone, J. C., Jr. (1981). A fourth approach to the study of learning: Are "processes" really necessary? *Behavioral and Brain Sciences, 4*, 151–152.

Malone, J. C., Jr. (1987). Skinner, the behavioral unit, and current psychology. In Modgill, S. M., & Modgill, C. M. (Eds.), *Consensus and controversy: B. F. Skinner*. London: Falmer Press.

Malone, J. C., Jr. (1990). William James and habit: A century later. In Johnson, M., & Henley, T. (Eds.), *The principles of psychology at 100: William James after a century*. Hillsdale, NJ: Erlbaum.

Malone, J. C., Jr., & Rowe, D. W. (1981). Local contrast, local dimensional effects, and dimensional contrast. In M. L. Commons & J. A. Nevin (Eds.), *Quantitative studies of operant behavior: Discriminative properties of reinforcement schedules*. Cambridge, MA: Ballinger.

Malone, J. C., Jr., & Staddon, J.E.R. (1973). Contrast effects in maintained generalization gradients. *Journal of the Experimental Analysis of Behavior, 19*, 167–179.

Martin, G., & Pear, J. (1983). *Behavior Modification*. Englewood Cliffs, NJ: Prentice-Hall.

Matthews, B. A., Shimoff, E., Catania, A. C., & Sagvolden, T. (1977). Uninstructed human responding: Sensitivity to ratio and interval contingencies. *Journal of the Experimental Analysis of Behavior, 27*, 453–467.

Mazur, J. E. (1986). *Learning and behavior*. Englewood Cliffs, NJ: Prentice-Hall.

Meehl, P. E. (1950). On the circularity of the law of effect. *Psychological Bulletin, 47*, 52–75.

Melton, A. W. (1963). Implication of short-term memory for a general theory of memory. *Journal of Verbal Learning and Verbal Behavior, 2*, 1–21.

Menzel, E. M. (1978). Cognitive mapping in chimpanzees. In S. H. Hulse, H. Fowler, and W. K. Honig (Eds.), *Cognitive processes in animal behavior*. Hillsdale, NJ: Erlbaum.

Mill, J. (1967). *Analysis of the phenomena of the human mind* (2nd ed.). New York: Augustus Kelley Publishers. (Original work published 1829).

Miller, N. E. (1944). Experimental studies in conflict. In J. M. Hunt (Ed.), *Personality and the behavior disorders*. New York: Ronald Press.

Miller, N. E. (1948). Studies of fear as an acquirable drive: 1. Fear as motivation and fear reduction as reinforcement in the learning of new responses. *Journal of Experimental Psychology, 38*, 89–101.

Miller, N. E. (1958). Central stimulation and other new approaches to motivation and reward. *American Psychologist, 13*, 100–108.

Miller, N. E. (1969). Learning of visceral and glandular responses. *Science, 163*, 434–445.

Miller, N. E., & Dollard, J. (1941). *Social learning and imitation*. New Haven, CT: Yale University Press.

Miller, N. E., & Dworkin, B. (1974). Visceral learning: Recent difficulties with curarized rats and significant problems for human research. In P. A. Obrist, A. H. Black, J. Brener, & L. V. DiCara (Eds.), *Cardiovascular Psychophysiology*. Chicago: Aldine.

Montgomery, K. C. (1953). The effect of activity deprivation upon exploratory behavior. *Journal of Comparative and Physiological Psychology, 46*, 438–441.

Moore, B. R. (1973). The role of directed Pavlovian reactions on simple instrumental learning on the pigeon. In R. A. Hinde & J. Stevenson-Hinde (Eds.), *Constraints on learning*. London: Academic Press.

Moore, B. R., & Stuttard, S. (1979). Dr. Guthrie and *Felis domesticus*, or, tripping over the cat. *Science, 205*, 1031–1033.

Morgan, M. J. (1974). Resistance to satiation. *Animal Behavior, 22*, 449–466.

Morris, E. K. (1988). Contextualism: The world view of behavior analysis. *Journal of Experimental Child Psychology, 46*, 289–323.

Morris, E. K., Higgens, S. T., & Bickel, W. K. (1982). Comments on cognitive science in the experimental analysis of behavior. *The Behavior Analyst, 5*, 109–125.

Morse, W. H., & Kelleher, R. T. (1977). Determinants of reinforcement and punishment. In W. K. Honig & J.E.R. Staddon (Eds.), *Handbook of operant behavior*. Englewood Cliffs, NJ: Prentice-Hall.

Moruzzi, G., & Magoun, H. W. (1949). Brain stem reticular formation and activation of the EEG. *Electroencephalography and Clinical Neurophysiology, 1*, 455–473.

Moscovitch, A., & Lolordo, V. M. (1968). Role of safety on the Pavlovian backward fear conditioning procedure. *Journal of Comparative and Physiological Psychology, 66*, 673–678.

Mowrer, O. H. (1947). On the dual nature of learning: A reinterpretation of "conditioning" and "problem solving." *Harvard Educational Review, 17*, 102–150.

Muenzinger, K. F. (1938). Vicarious trial and error at a point of choice, I. A general survey of its relation to learning efficiency. *Journal of Genetic Psychology, 53*, 75–86.

Munn, N. L. (1950) *Handbook of psychological research on the rat: An introduction to animal psychology*. Boston: Houghton Mifflin.

Murray, H. A. (1938). *Explorations in personality*. New York: Oxford University Press.

Neisser, U. (1967). *Cognitive psychology*. New York: Appleton-Century-Crofts.

Neisser, U. (1976). *Cognition and reality*. San Francisco: Freeman.

Neuringer, A. J., & Chung, S. (1967). Quasi-reinforcement: Control of responding by a percentage reinforcement schedule. *Journal of the Experimental Analysis of Behavior, 10*, 45–54.

Nevin, J. A. (1973). Conditioned reinforcement. In J.

A. Nevin & G. S. Reynolds (Eds.), *The study of behavior*. Glenview, IL: Scott, Foresman.

Nevin, J. A., & Shettleworth, S. J. (1966). An analysis of contrast effects in multiple schedules. *Journal of the Experimental Analysis of Behavior, 9*, 305–315.

Nisbett, R. E., & Wilson, T. D. (1977). Telling more than we can know: Verbal reports on mental processes. *Psychological Review, 84*, 231–259.

Olds, J. (1956). Runway and maze behavior controlled by basomedial forebrain stimulation in the rat. *Journal of Comparative and Physiological Psychology, 49*, 507–512.

Olds. J., & Milner, P. (1954). Positive reinforcement produced by electrical stimulation of septal area and other regions of rat brain. *Journal of Comparative and Physiological Psychology, 47*, 419–427.

Olton, D. S. (1978). Characteristics of spatial memory. In S. H. Hulse, H. F. Fowler, & W. K. Honig (Eds.), *Cognitive processes in animal behavior*. Hillsdale, NJ: Erlbaum.

Papez, J. W. (1936). A proposed mechanism of emotion. *Archives of neurology and psychiatry, 38*, 725–743.

Pavlov, I. P. (1927). *Conditioned reflexes*. New York: Oxford University Press.

Pavlov, I. P. (1928). *Lectures on conditioned reflexes*. (W. H. Gantt, Trans.). New York: International Publishers.

Pavlov, I. P. (1932). The reply of a physiologist to psychologists. *Psychological Review, 39*, 91–127.

Pavlov, I. P. (1955). *Selected works*. Moscow: Foreign Languages Publishing House.

Penfield, W. (1958). *The excitable cortex of conscious man*. Liverpool: Liverpool University Press.

Perin, C. T. (1942). Behavior potentiality as a joint function of the amount of training and degree of hunger at the time of extinction. *Journal of Experimental Psychology, 30*, 93–113.

Perry, R. B. (1918). Docility and purposiveness. *Psychological Review, 25*, 1–20.

Pfungst, O. (1965). *Clever Hans: The horse of Mr. von Osten*. New York: Holt, Rinehart & Winston. (Original work published 1908).

Phillips, A. G., Cox, V. C., Kakolewski, J. W., & Valenstein, E. S. (1969). Object-carrying by rats: An approach to the behavior produced by brain stimulation. *Science, 166*, 903–905.

Platonov, K. (1959). *The word as a physiological and therapeutic factor*. Moscow: Foreign Languages Publishing House.

Popper, K. (1968). *The logic of scientific discovery*. New York: Harper & Row.

Posner, M. I., & Shulman, G. L. (1979). Cognitive science. In E. Hearst (Ed.), *The first century of experimental psychology*. Hillsdale, NJ: Erlbaum.

Premack, D. (1959). Toward empirical behavior laws: I. Positive reinforcement. *Psychological Review, 66*, 219–233.

Premack, D. (1965). Reinforcement theory. In D. Levine (Ed.), *Nebraska symposium on motivation*. (Vol. 13). Lincoln, NE: University of Nebraska Press.

Premack, D. (1971). Catching up with common sense or two sides of a generalization: Reinforcement and punishment. In R. Glaser (Ed.), *The nature of reinforcement*. New York: Academic Press.

Premack, D. (1978). On the abstractness of human concepts: Why it would be difficult to talk to a pigeon. In S. H. Hulse, H. Fowler, & W. K. Honig (Eds.), *Cognitive processes in animal behavior*. Hillsdale, NJ: Erlbaum.

Pribram, K. (1971). *Languages of the brain: Experimental paradoxes and principles of neuropsychology*. Englewood Cliffs, NJ: Prentice-Hall.

Pryor, K. W., Haag, R., & O'Reilly, J. (1969). The creative porpoise: Training for novel behavior. *Journal of the Experimental Analysis of Behavior, 12*, 653–661.

Rachlin, H. (1969). Autoshaping of key pecking in pigeons with negative reinforcement. *Journal of the Experimental Analysis of Behavior, 12*, 521–531.

Rachlin, H. (1976). *Behavior and learning*. San Francisco: W. H. Freeman.

Rachlin, H., & Green, L. (1972). Commitment, choice, and self control. *Journal of the Experimental Analysis of Behavior, 17*, 15–22.

Ratliff, F. (1965). Mach bands: Quantitative studies of neural networks in the retina. San Francisco: Holden-Day.

Razran, G. (1961). The observable unconscious and the inferable conscious in current Soviet psychophysiology: Interoceptive conditioning, semantic conditioning, and the orienting reflex. *Psychological Review, 68*, 81–147.

Razran, G. (1965). Russian physiologists' psychology and American experimental psychology. *Psychological Bulletin, 63*, 42–64.

Rescorla, R. A. (1967). Pavlovian conditioning and its proper control procedures. *Psychological Review, 74*, 71–80.

Rescorla, R. A. (1969). Pavlovian conditioned inhibition. *Psychological Bulletin, 72,* 77–94.

Rescorla, R. A. (1973). Effect of US habituation following conditioning. *Journal of Comparative and Physiological Psychology, 82,* 137–143.

Rescorla, R. A. (1988). Pavlovian conditioning: It's not what you think it is. *American Psychologist, 43,* 151–160.

Rescorla, R. A., & Wagner, A. R. (1972). A theory of Pavlovian conditioning: Variations in the effectiveness of reinforcement and nonreinforcement. In A. H. Black & W. F. Prokasy (Eds.), *Classical conditioning II: Current research and theory.* New York: Appleton-Century-Crofts.

Revusky, S. (1971). The role of interference on association over a delay. In W. K. Honig & P.H.R. James (Eds.), *Animal memory.* New York: Academic Press.

Revusky, S. H., & Bedarf, E. W. (1967). Association of illness with prior ingestion of novel foods. *Science, 155,* 219–220.

Reynolds, G. S. (1961a). Behavioral contrast. *Journal of the Experimental Analysis of Behavior, 4,* 57–71.

Reynolds, G. S. (1961b). An analysis of interactions in a multiple schedule. *Journal of the Experimental Analysis of Behavior, 4,* 107–117.

Reynolds, G. S. (1961c). Relativity of response rate and reinforcement frequency in a multiple schedule. *Journal of the Experimental Analysis of Behavior, 4,* 179–184.

Reynolds, G. S. (1964). Operant extinction near zero. *Journal of the Experimental Analysis of Behavior, 7,* 173–176.

Reynolds, G. S. (1975). *A primer of operant conditioning* (rev. ed.). Glenview, IL: Scott, Foresman.

Rizley, R. C., & Rescorla, R. A. (1972). Associations in second-order conditioning and sensory preconditioning. *Journal of Comparative and Physiological Psychology, 81,* 1–11.

Robinson, D. N. (1976). *An intellectual history of psychology.* New York: Macmillan.

Roitblat, H. L., Bever, T. G., & Terrace, H. S. (1984). *Animal cognition.* Hillsdale, NJ: Erlbaum.

Romanes, G. J. (1912). *Animal intelligence.* New York: Appleton. (Originally published 1882.)

Romanes, G. J. (1888). *Mental evolution in man: Origins of human faculty.* London: Kegan Paul, Trench & Co.

Rozin, P. (1967). Specific aversions as a component of specific hungers. *Journal of Comparative and Physiological Psychology, 64,* 237–242.

Rozin, P. (1969). Central or peripheral mediation of learning with long CS-UCS intervals in the feeding system. *Journal of Comparative and Physiological Psychology, 67,* 421–429.

Rozin, P., & Kalat, J. W. (1972). Learning as a situation-specific adaptation. In M.E.P. Seligman & J. L. Hager (Eds.), *Biological boundaries of learning.* New York: Appleton-Century-Crofts.

Rumelhart, D. E., & McClelland, J. L. (1986). *Parallel distributed processing: Explorations in the microstructure of cognition. Vol. 1: Foundations.* Cambridge, MA: MIT Press/Bradford Books.

Savage-Rumbaugh, E. S., Rumbaugh, D. M., & Boysen, S. (1978). Symbolic communication between two chimpanzees (*Pan troglodyles*). *Science, 201,* 641–644.

Schachter, S. (1971). Some extraordinary facts about obese humans and rats. *American Psychologist, 26,* 129–144.

Schoenfeld, W. N. (1950). An experimental approach to anxiety, avoidance, and escape behavior. In P. H. Hock & J. Zubin (Eds.), *Anxiety.* New York: Grune & Stratton.

Schwartz, B. (1978). *Psychology of learning and behavior.* New York: Norton.

Schwartz, B., & Gamzu, E. (1977). Pavlovian control of operant behavior. In W. K. Honig & J.E.R. Staddon (Eds.), *Handbook of operant behavior.* Englewood Cliffs, NJ: Prentice-Hall.

Sechenov, I. M. (1863). *Reflexes of the brain.* Cambridge, MA: MIT Press.

Seligman, M.E.P. (1970). On the generality of the laws of learning. *Psychological Review, 77,* 406–418.

Seward, J. P. (1942). An experimental study of Guthrie's theory of reinforcement. *Journal of Experimental Psychology, 30,* 247–256.

Seward, J. P. (1954). Hull's system of behavior: An evaluation. *Psychological Review, 61,* 145–159.

Sheffield, F. D. (1965). Relation between classical conditioning and instrumental learning. In W. F. Prokasy (Ed.), *Classical conditioning: A symposium.* New York: Appleton-Century-Crofts.

Sheffield, F. D., Wulff, J. J., & Backer, R. (1951). Reward value of copulation without sex drive reduction. *Journal of Comparative and Physiological Psychology, 44,* 3–8

Sherrington, C. S. (1906). *The integrative action of the nervous system.* New Haven, CT: Yale University.

Sidman, M. (1953). Avoidance conditioning with brief shock and no exteroceptive warning signal. *Science, 118*, 157–158.

Siegel, S. (1978). Tolerance to the hyperthermic effect of morphine in the rat is a learned response. *Journal of Comparative and Physiological Psychology, 92*, 1137–1149.

Siegel, S. (1985). Drug-anticipatory responses in animals. In L. White, B. Tursky, & G. E. Schwartz (Eds.), *Placebo: Theory, research, and mechanisms*. New York: Guilford Press.

Skinner, B. F. (1931). The concept of the reflex in the description of behavior. *Journal of General Psychology, 5*, 427–458.

Skinner, B. F. (1935). The generic nature of the concepts of stimulus and response. *Journal of General Psychology, 12*, 40–65.

Skinner, B. F. (1936). The verbal summator and a method for the study of latent speech. *Journal of Psychology, 2*, 71–107.

Skinner, B. F. (1937, May 31). Smart University of Minnesota rat works a slot machine for a living. *Life*.

Skinner, B. F. (1938). *The behavior of organisms*. New York: Appleton-Century-Crofts.

Skinner, B. F. (1945). The operational analysis of psychological terms. *Psychological Review, 52*, 270–277.

Skinner, B. F. (1948). *Walden II*. New York: Crowell-Collier-Macmillian.

Skinner, B. F. (1950). Are theories of learning really necessary? *Psychological Review, 57*, 193–216.

Skinner, B. F. (1953). *Science and human behavior*. New York: Crowell-Collier-Macmillan.

Skinner, B. F. (1957). *Verbal behavior*. Englewood Cliffs, NJ: Prentice-Hall.

Skinner, B. F. (1963). Behaviorism at fifty. *Science, 140*, 951–958.

Skinner, B. F. (1966a). The phylogeny and ontogeny of behavior. *Science, 153*, 1205–1213.

Skinner, B. F. (1966b). An operant analysis of problem solving. In B. Kleinmuntz (Ed.), *Problem solving*. New York: Wiley.

Skinner, B. F. (1969). *Contingencies of reinforcement: A theoretical analysis*. Englewood Cliffs, NJ: Prentice-Hall.

Skinner, B. F. (1971). *Beyond freedom and dignity*. New York: Knopf.

Skinner, B. F. (1972). *Cumulative record*. (3rd ed.). New York: Appleton-Century-Crofts.

Skinner, B. F. (1974). *About behaviorism*. New York: Knopf.

Skinner, B. F. (1977). Herrnstein and the evolution of behaviorism. *American Psychologist, 32*, 1006–1012.

Skinner, B. F. (1980). *Notebooks*. Englewood Cliffs, NJ: Prentice-Hall.

Skinner, B. F. (1983a). Can the experimental analysis of behavior rescue psychology? *The Behavior Analyst, 6*, 9–17.

Skinner, B. F. (1983b). *A matter of consequences*. New York: Knopf.

Skinner, B. F. (1984). Canonical papers of B. F. Skinner. *Behavioral and Brain Sciences, 7*, (Whole No. 4).

Skinner, B. F. (1987). *Upon further reflection*. Englewood Cliffs, NJ: Prentice-Hall.

Skinner, B. F. (1989). The origins of cognitive thought. *American Psychologist, 44*, 13–18.

Smith, K. (1974). The continuum of reinforcement and attenuation. *Behaviorism, 2*, 124–145.

Smith, S., & Guthrie, E. R. (1921). *General psychology in terms of behavior*. New York: Appleton.

Smith, J. C., & Roll, D. L. (1967). Trace conditioning with X-rays as an aversive stimulus. *Psychonomic Science, 9*, 11–12.

Smolensky, P. (1988). On the proper treatment of connectionism. *Behavioral and Brain Sciences, 11*, 1–74.

Solomon, R. L. (1980). The opponent-process theory of acquired motivation: The costs of pleasure and the benefits of pain. *American Psychologist, 35*, 691–712.

Solomon, R. L., & Corbit, J. D. (1974). An opponent-process theory of motivation: I. The temporal dynamics of affect. *Psychological Review, 81*, 119–145.

Solomon, R. L., Kamin, L. J., & Wynne, L. C. (1953). Traumatic avoidance learning: The outcomes of several extinction procedures with dogs. *Journal of Abnormal and Social Psychology, 48*, 291–302.

Spalding, D. A. (1873). Instinct, with original observations on young animals. *Macmillan's Magazine, 27*, 282–293.

Spence, K. W. (1937). The differential response in animals to stimuli varying within a single dimension. *Psychological Review, 44*, 430–444.

Spence, K. W. (1956). *Behavior theory and conditioning*. New Haven, CT: Yale University Press.

Spence, K. W., & Lippitt, R. (1940). "Latent" learning of a simple maze problem with relevant needs satiated. *Psychological Bulletin, 37*, 429 (Abstract).

Spence, K. W., & Lippitt, R. (1946). An experimental test of the sign-gestalt theory of trial-and-error learning. *Journal of Experimental Psychology, 36*, 491–502.

Spencer, H. (1855). *The principles of psychology*. London: Longman.

Spencer, H. (1904). *Autobiography. Vol. II*. New York: Appleton.

Spragg, S.D.S. (1940). Morphine addiction in chimpanzees. *Comparative Psychology Monographs, 15* (7, Serial No. 79).

Staddon, J.E.R. (1967). Asymptotic behavior: The concept of the operant. *Psychological Review, 74*, 377–391.

Staddon, J.E.R. (1979). Operant behavior as adaptation to constraint. *Journal of Experimental Psychology: General, 108*, 48–67.

Staddon, J.E.R., & Simmelhag, V. L. (1971). The "superstition" experiment: A reexamination of its implications for the principles of adaptive behavior. *Psychological Review, 78*, 3–43.

Stein, L. (1964). Reciprocal action of reward and punishment mechanisms. In R. G. Heath (Ed.), *The role of pleasure in behavior*. New York: Hoeber.

Stoltz, S. B., Wienkowski, L. A., & Brown, B. S. (1975). Behavior modification: A perspective on critical issues. *American Psychologist, 30*, 1027–1048.

Swazey, J. P. (1969). *Reflexes and motor integration: Sherrington's concept of integrative action*. Cambridge, MA: Harvard University Press.

Testa, T. J. (1975). Effects of similarity of location and temporal intensity pattern of conditioned and unconditioned stimuli on the acquisition of conditioned suppression in rats. *Journal of Experimental Psychology: Animal Behavior Processes, 1*, 114–121.

Thompson, R. F. (1965). The neural basis of stimulus generalization. In D. I. Mostofsky (Ed.), *Stimulus generalization*. Stanford, CA: Stanford University Press.

Thorndike, E. L. (1898). Animal intelligence: An experimental study of the associative processes in animals. *Psychological Review Monograph, 2* (Suppl. 8).

Thorndike, E. L. (1900). *Human Nature Club*. New York: Chautauqua Press.

Thorndike, E. L. (1903). *Educational Psychology*. New York: Lemcke & Buechner.

Thorndike, E. L. (1904). *An introduction to the theory of mental and social measurements*. New York: Science Press.

Thorndike, E. L. (1913). *Educational Psychology* (Vol. 1–3). New York: Teachers College.

Thorndike, E. L. (1917). The psychology of thinking in the case of reading. *Psychological Review, 24*, 220–234.

Thorndike, E. L. (1932a). *The fundamentals of learning*. New York: Teachers College.

Thorndike, E. L. (1932b). Reward and punishment in animal learning. *Comparative Psychology Monographs, 8* (Whole 39).

Thorndike, E. L. (1933). A proof of the law of effect. *Science, 77*, 173–175.

Thorndike, E. L. (1935). *The psychology of wants, interests, and attitudes*. New York: Appleton-Century-Crofts.

Thorndike, E. L. (1936). The value of reported likes and dislikes for various experiences and activities as indications of personal traits. *Journal of Applied Psychology, 19*, 285–313.

Thorndike, E. L. (1937). Valuations of certain pains, deprivations, and frustrations. *Journal of Genetic Psychology, 51*, 227–239.

Thorndike, E. L. (1942). Heredity and environment. *British Journal of Educational Psychology, 12*, 85–87.

Thorndike, E. L. (1949). *Selected writings from a connectionist's psychology*. New York: Appleton-Century-Crofts.

Thorndike, E. L., & Woodworth, R. S. (1901). Transfer of training: The influence of improvement in one mental function upon the efficiency of other functions. *Psychological Review, 8*, 247–261, 384–395, 553–564.

Timberlake, W., & Allison, J. (1974). Response deprivation: An empirical approach to instrumental performance. *Psychological Review, 81*, 146–164.

Tinklepaugh, O. L. (1928). An experimental study of representative factors in monkeys. *Journal of Comparative Psychology, 8*, 197–236.

Titchener, E. B. (1910). *A textbook of psychology*. New York: MacMillian.

Tolman, E. C. (1932). *Purposive behavior in animals and men*. New York: Appleton-Century-Crofts.

Tolman, E. C. (1938). The determiners of behavior at a choice point. *Psychological Review, 45*, 1–41.

Tolman, E. C. (1942). *Drives toward war*. New York: Appleton-Century-Crofts.

Tolman, E. C. (1948). Cognitive maps in rats and men. *Psychological Review*, *55*, 189–208.

Tolman, E. C. (1949). There is more than one kind of learning. *Psychological Review*, *56*, 144–155.

Tolman, E. C., & Honzik, C. H. (1930). Degrees of hunger, reward and nonreward, and maze learning in rats. *University of California Publications in Psychology*, *4*, 241–275.

Tolman, E. C., Richie, B. F., & Kalish, D. (1946). Studies in spatial learning: 1. Orientation and the shortcut. *Journal of Experimental Psychology*, *36*, 13–24.

Turkkan, J. S. (1989). Classical conditioning: The new hegemony. *Behavioral and Brain Sciences*, *12*, 121–179.

Valenstein, E. S. (1970). Pavlovian typology: Comparative comments on the development of a scientific theme. In L. R. Aronson, E. Tobach, D. S. Lehrman, & J. S. Rosenblatt (Eds.), *Development and evolution of behavior*. San Francisco: Freeman.

Valenstein, E. S. (1973). *Brain control*. New York: Wiley.

Verhave, T. (1966). The pigeon as a quality control inspector. In R. Ulrich, T. Stachnik, & J. Mabry (Eds.), *Control of human behavior*. Glenview, IL: Scott, Foresman.

Verplanck, W. S. (1954). Burrhus F. Skinner. In Estes, W. K., Koch, S., MacCorquodale, K., Meehl, P. E., Mueller, C. G. Jr., Schoenfeld, W. N., & Verplanck, W. S. (Eds.), *Modern learning theory*. New York: Appleton-Century-Crofts.

Verplanck, W. S. (1962). Unaware of where's awareness: Some verbal operants-notates, monents, and notants. In C. W. Ericksen (Ed.), *Behavior and awareness*. Durham, NC: Duke University Press.

Voeks, V. W. (1948). Postremity, recency, and frequency as bases for prediction in the maze situation. *Journal of Experimental Psychology*, *38*, 495–510.

Voeks, V. W. (1954). Acquisition of S-R connections: A test of Hull's and Guthrie's theories. *Journal of Experimental Psychology*, *47*, 137–147.

Wagner, A. R. (1963). Conditioned frustration as a learned drive. *Journal of Experimental Psychology*, *66*, 142–148.

Wahler, R. G. (1975). Some structural aspects of deviant child behavior. *Journal of Applied Behavior Analysis*, *8*, 27–42.

Wahler, R. G., Winkel, G. H., Peterson, R. F., & Morrison, D. C. (1965). Mothers as behavior therapists for their own children. *Behavior Research and Therapy*, *3*, 113–124.

Watson, J. B. (1913). Psychology as the behaviorist views it. *Psychological Review*, *20*, 158–177.

Watson, J. B. (1914). *Behavior: An introduction to comparative psychology*. New York: Henry Holt.

Watson, J. B. (1919). *Psychology from the standpoint of a behaviorist*. Philadelphia: Lippincott.

Watson, J. B. (1928a). *The ways of behaviorism*. New York: Harper & Brothers.

Watson, J. B. (1928b). *Psychological care of the infant and child*. New York: Norton.

Watson, J. B. (1929). Behaviorism. Chicago: Encyclopaedia Britannica.

Watson, J. B. (1930). *Behaviorism* (3rd ed.). New York: Norton.

Watson, J. B. (1936). John B. Watson. In C. Murchison (Ed.), *A history of psychology in autobiography*. Worcester, MA: Clark University Press.

Watson, J. B., & Rayner, R. (1920). Conditioned emotional reactions. *Journal of Experimental Psychology*, *3*, 1–14.

Wertheimer, M. (1945). *Productive thinking*. New York: Harper & Row.

Wertheimer, M. (1979). Gestalt theory of learning. In G. M. Gazda & R. J. Corsini (Eds.), *Theories of learning*. Itasca, IL: Peacock.

Whaley, D. L., & Malott, R. W. (1971). *Elementary principles of behavior*. New York: Meredith.

Whiting. J.W.M., & Mowrer, O. H. (1943). Habit progression and regression: A study of some factors relevant to human socialization. *Journal of Comparative Psychology*, *36*, 229–253.

Williams, D. R., & Williams, H. (1969). Auto-maintenance in the pigeon: Sustained pecking despite contingent non-reinforcement. *Journal of the Experimental Analysis of Behavior*, *12*, 511–520.

Williams, S. B. (1938). Resistance to extinction as a function of the number of reinforcements. *Journal of Experimental Psychology*, *23*, 506–521.

Wolpe, J. (1958). *Psychotherapy by reciprocal inhibition*. Stanford, CA: Stanford University Press.

Woodworth, R. S. (1938). *Experimental Psychology*. New York: Holt, Rinehart & Winston.

Wundt, W. (1896). *Grundriss der Psychologie*. Leipzig: W. Engleman.

Wundt, W. (1907). *Lectures on human and animal psychol-*

ogy. (J. E. Creighton & E. B. Titchener, Trans.). New York: Macmillan.

Zeamon, D., & House, B. J. (1963). The role of attention in retardate discrimination learning. In N. R. Ellis (Ed.), *Handbook of mental deficiency: Psychological theory and research*. New York: McGraw-Hill.

NAME INDEX

Spencer, H., 16, 27
Spragg, S.D.S., 86
Staddon, J.E.R., 225, 286, 290, 293, 316
Stein, L., 279
Stewart, J., 307
Stoltz, S. B., 124
Stumpf, C., 14
Suomi, S. J., 47
Swazey, J. P., 92

Terrace, H. S., 216
Testa, T. J., 309
Thorndike, E. L., 24–27, 29–53, 98, 99, 113, 119–121, 129, 132, 133, 135, 143, 144, 146, 178, 187, 199, 201, 202, 211, 214, 221, 223, 224, 232, 235, 255, 260, 263, 277, 278, 281, 298, 300
Timberlake, W., 283, 284, 316
Tinklepaugh, O. L., 210
Titchener, E. B., 11–14, 18–20, 22, 24–26, 96, 97, 116, 144, 148, 164, 191, 195, 203

Tolman, E. C., 30, 43, 49, 94, 144, 155, 163, 164, 166, 176, 189–223, 225, 230, 255, 263, 312
Trattner, J., 283
Turkkan, J. S , 2, 3, 92
Turner, S. M., 261

Underwood, B. J., 131

Valenstein, E., 80, 279–281, 317
Verhave, T., 249, 250
Verplanck, W. S., 144, 163, 187, 275
Voeks, V. W., 120, 125

Wagner, A., 174, 176, 185, 213, 300–303, 316
Wahler, R. G., 291, 293
Watson, J. B., 19–21, 24, 26, 43, 45, 48, 49, 60, 80, 93–118, 120, 121, 136, 137, 144, 155, 165, 166, 176, 187, 194, 196, 197, 202, 203, 204, 214, 223, 227, 232, 255, 260, 263

Watson, Mary I., 115
Watt, H. J., 13, 14
Weiss, S. M., 134, 139
Wertheimer, M., 191, 193
Whaley, D. L., 237
Whitehead, A. N., 119
Whiting, J.W.M., 163, 300
Wienkowski, L. A., 124
Wiesel, T. N., 79
Williams, D. R., 289, 290
Williams, H., 289
Williams, S. B., 152
Wilson, T. D., 6
Winkel, G. H., 293
Wolpe, J., 131, 132, 139, 260
Woodworth, R. S., 29, 33, 38
Wozny, M., 284, 286
Wulff, J. J., 167
Wundt, W., 10–14, 18, 23, 26, 307
Wynne, L. C., 151, 303, 307

Yerkes, R. M., 112, 171

SUBJECT INDEX